The Greenwood Encyclopedia of Multiethnic American Literature

The Greenwood Encyclopedia of

MULTIETHNIC AMERICAN LITERATURE

Volume III

I – M

Edited by Emmanuel S. Nelson

GREENWOOD PRESS
Westport, Connecticut • London

Library of Congress Cataloging-in-Publication Data

The Greenwood encyclopedia of multiethnic American literature / edited by Emmanuel S. Nelson.
   p. cm.
   Includes bibliographical references and index.
   ISBN 0–313–33059–X (set : alk. paper) — ISBN 0–313–33060–3 (v. 1 : alk. paper) — ISBN 0–313–33061–1 (v. 2 : alk. paper) — ISBN 0–313–33062–X (v. 3 : alk. paper) — ISBN 0–313–33063–8 (v. 4 : alk. paper) — ISBN 0–313–33064–6 (v. 5 : alk. paper)
   1. American literature—Minority authors—Encyclopedias. 2. Minorities—United States—Intellectual life—Encyclopedias. 3. Pluralism (Social sciences) in literature—Encyclopedias. 4. United States—Literatures—Encyclopedias. 5. Ethnic groups in literature—Encyclopedias. 6. Minorities in literature—Encyclopedias. 7. Ethnicity in literature—Encyclopedias. I. Nelson, Emmanuel S. (Emmanuel Sampath), 1954–
   PS153.M56G74 2005
   810.9'920693—dc22   2005018960

British Library Cataloguing in Publication Data is available.

This book is included in the *African American Experience* database from Greenwood Electronic Media. For more information, visit www.africanamericanexperience.com.

Library of Congress Catalog Card Number: 2005018960
ISBN: 0–313–33059–X (set)
    0–313–33060–3 (vol. I)
    0–313–33061–1 (vol. II)
    0–313–33062–X (vol. III)
    0–313–33063–8 (vol. IV)
    0–313–33064–6 (vol. V)

First published in 2005

Greenwood Press, 88 Post Road West, Westport, CT 06881
An imprint of Greenwood Publishing Group, Inc.
www.greenwood.com

Printed in the United States of America

The paper used in this book complies with the Permanent Paper Standard issued by the National Information Standards Organization (Z39.48–1984).

10 9 8 7 6 5 4 3 2 1

For Trevor again, with love

Set Contents

List of Entries

Guide to Related Topics

Okita, Dwight
Sone, Monica
Uchida, Yoshiko
Uyemoto, Holly
Yamada, Mitsuye
Yamamoto, Hisaye
Yamashita, Karen Tei
Yamauchi, Wakako

Jewish American Literature

Abish, Walter
Acker, Kathy
Agosín, Marjorie
Algren Nelson
Alkalay-Gut, Karen
Allen, Woody
Antin, Mary
Apple, Max
Asimov, Isaac
Auster, Paul
Behrman, S. N.
Bell, Marvin
Bellow, Saul
Bernstein, Charles
Berryman, John
Bessie, Alvah
Bloom, Harold Irving
Bodenheim, Maxwell
Broner, E(sther) M(asserman)
Brown, Rosellen
Budy, Andrea Hollander
Bukiet, Melvin Jules
Burnshaw, Stanley
Cahan, Abraham
Calisher, Hortense
Calof, Rachel Bella Kahn
Chabon, Michael
Chernin, Kim
Cohen, Sarah Blacher
Comden and Green
Dahlberg, Edward
Dame, Enid
Doctorow, E. L.
Elkin, Stanley
Elman, Richard M.

Endore, Guy
Englander, Nathan
Epstein, Joseph
Epstein, Leslie
Espinosa, María
Falk, Marcia
Fast, Howard
Faust, Irvin
Fearing, Kenneth
Federman, Raymond
Feinberg, David B.
Feldman, Irving
Ferber, Edna
Fiedler, Leslie
Field, Edward
Fierstein, Harvey Forbes
Finkelstein, Norman
Frank, Waldo
Freeman, Joseph
Fried, Emanuel
Friedman, Bruce Jay
Friedman, Stanford
Fries, Kenny
Fuchs, Daniel
Funaroff, Sol
Gelbart, Larry
Gerber, Merrill Joan
Ginsberg, Allen
Glickman, Gary
Glück, Louise
Glück, Robert
Gold, Herbert
Gold, Michael
Goldreich, Gloria
Goldstein, Rebecca
Goodman, Allegra
Graham, Jorie
Green, Gerald
Greenberg, Joanne [Goldenberg]
Grossman, Allen
Halper, Albert
Hart, Moss
Helprin, Mark
Hecht, Anthony
Hecht, Ben

Mexican American Literature
Acosta, Oscar Zeta
Alarcón, Francisco X.
Alfaro, Luis
Anaya, Rudolfo
Anzaldúa, Gloria E.
Arte Público Press
Baca, Jimmy Santiago
Bless Me, Ultima
Border Narratives
Born in East L.A.
Bruce-Novoa, Juan
Burk, Ronnie
Candelaria, Cordelia Chávez
Cano, Daniel
Cantú, Norma Elia
Castedo, Elena
Castillo, Ana
Castillo, Rafael C.
Catacalos, Rosemary
Cervantes, Lorna Dee
Chavez, Denise
Cisneros, Sandra
Culture Clash
Cumpian, Carlos
Curiel, Barbara Brinson
De Casas, Celso A.
Del Castillo, Ramón
Fernández, Roberta
Flores-Williams, Jason
Fontes, Montserrat
Galarza, Ernesto
Garcia, Richard
Garcia-Camarillo, Cecillio
Gómez-Peña, Guillermo
Gonzáles, Jovita
Gonzales-Berry, Erlinda
Hinojosa-Smith, Rolando
House on Mango Street, The
Hunger of Memory
Islas, Arturo, Jr.
Jimenez, Francisco
Limón, Graciela
López, Josefina
Martínez, Demetria

Mena, María Cristina
Mexican American Autobiography
Mexican American Children's Literature
Mexican American Drama
Mexican American Gay Literature
Mexican American Lesbian Literature
Mexican American Poetry
Mexican American Stereotypes
Montalvo, José
Mora, Pat
Moraga, Cherríe
Nava, Michael
Navarro, Joe
Niggli, Josephina Maria
Niño, Raúl
Ortiz Taylor, Sheila
Paredes, Américo
De la Peña, Terri
Pineda, Cecile
Ponce, Mary Helen
Preciado Martin, Patricia
Quiñonez, Naomi Helena
Ramos, Luis Arturo
Ramos, Manuel
Rechy, John
Rivera, Tomás
Rodrígues, Joe D.
Rodriguez, Richard
Rodríguez-Matos, Carlos A.
Ruiz, Ronald
Ruiz de Burton, Maria Amparo
Sáenz, Benjamin Alire
Salinas, Luis Omar
Santiago, Danny [Daniel James]
Seguín, Juan N.
Soto, Gary
Suárez, Mario
Tafolla, Carmen
Tenorio, Arthur
Urrea, Luis Amberto
Valdés, Gina
Valdez, Luis
Vallejo, Mariano Guadalupe

I

I KNOW WHY THE CAGED BIRD SINGS **Maya Angelou**'s *I Know Why the Caged Bird Sings* is her first and most celebrated autobiographical narrative, and its publication in 1970 amounted to an urgent demand for black nationalists and white feminists alike to recognize the singular over-coming of adversity that marks the experiential "lifework" of black womanhood.

Taking its cue from the last stanza of **Paul Laurence Dunbar**'s poem "Sympathy" (1899), Angelou's title refers to the narrator's achievement of empowering self-awareness in the face of personal injury. With the dissolution of their parents' marriage, three-year-old Marguerite Johnson (Angelou's name by birth) and her four-year-old brother, Bailey Jr., are sent from Long Beach, California, to Stamps, Arkansas, to live with their paternal grandmother, Mrs. Annie Henderson, or "Momma." In time Marguerite learns the racist social codes that separate black from white by observing those who patronize or pass by Momma's general store. Tempering the ever-present threat of a Klan lynching is Angelou's account of certain hilarious episodes of overzealous, even violent, worship by the church faithful.

When she is eight, Marguerite and Bailey are taken by their father, Bailey Sr., to stay with "Mother," Vivian Baxter, in St. Louis. Here Marguerite is molested and eventually raped by Mother's live-in boyfriend, Mr. Freeman. Soon after being found guilty of these crimes in court, Freeman is murdered, presumably by Baxter men out for revenge. Traumatized by this series of events, Marguerite returns to Stamps a morose, introverted child. It is Mrs. Bertha Flowers, Momma's educated neighbor and friend, who patiently relieves Marguerite of her silent mourning of innocence lost by encouraging the fragile but motivated girl to read books from her personal library.

Marguerite and Bailey move away from Stamps when they are teenagers to live with Mother in San Francisco. A turning point in Marguerite's life is the harrowing summer she spends with her father in his mobile home in Los Angeles: After being knifed by his live-in girlfriend during a heated argument, Marguerite settles among other abandoned and drifting youth in a junkyard for a month. Her return to San Francisco sees Bailey falling out with Mother, leaving home for good, and Marguerite fighting discriminatory hiring practices to become the first African American to work on the city's streetcars. The narrative ends with Marguerite, pregnant after having consensual sex for the first time, giving birth to her son as a sixteen-year-old single mother.

Despite offering imaginative and critical insight into black female **identity** formation and American social history more generally, Angelou's autobiography has been the target of censorship in intermediate and secondary schools across the nation. In particular, parents and administrators have objected to its "pornographic" representation of child sexual abuse in the form of Marguerite's rape. What goes unnoticed in such reproof is the main reason why schools took up the book in the first place: Angelou's coming-of-age narrative confronts the often harsh realities of her past as a means of inspiring readers to locate hope, determination, and self-assurance in their own lives. (*See also* African American Autobiography)

Further Reading

Braxton, Joanne M., ed. *Maya Angelou's "I Know Why the Caged Bird Sings": A Casebook.* New York: Oxford UP, 1999.

Jaquin, Eileen O. "Maya Angelou." *African American Autobiographers: A Sourcebook.* Ed. Emmanuel S. Nelson. Westport, CT: Greenwood Press, 2002. 10–28.

Megna-Wallace, Joanne. *Understanding "I Know Why the Caged Bird Sings": A Student Casebook to Issues, Sources, and Historical Documents.* Westport, CT: Greenwood Press, 1998.

Smith, Sidonie Ann. "The Song of a Caged Bird: Maya Angelou's Quest after Self-Acceptance." *Southern Humanities Review* 7.4 (1973): 365–75.

Kinohi Nishikawa

IDENTITY   Identity, in general terms, relates to the specifics of who, what, and where about the person(s) and includes a series of markers that identify that person in terms of **race**, class, culture, gender, religion, **ethnicity**, and/or nationality. One's identity is an important aspect of self, but its varied representations in all forms of literature, in different genres as well as different time periods ranging from ancient to contemporary settings, delineate how identity reflects and marks up one's culture. The theme of identity or identity-in-the-being is thus a predominant one in literature. Countless examples of thematic exploration of identity can be found in ancient, medieval, modern and postmodern literature. In the contemporary context of **multiculturalism** and transnational globalization, identity assumes even more significant relevance in cultural and sociological as well as economic terms.

Although each individual may be unique, social distinctions based on one's color, class, shared views, and lifestyle delegate people into distinguishing groups. Those sharing similar traits in a group become identified with that group—sometimes leading to a hierarchy among the groups. Historically, those identified with Euro-western norms, and racially visible as white, have been ascribed as the standard example of the preferred group in the social hierarchy. All others have been given the label of an "ethnic" group. With the turn-of-the-century globalization, a need for comprehension of ethnicity has increased in life as well as in art.

Ethnic Identity in America

The contemporary multicultural scenario in what was earlier seen to be a world defined by Eurocentric norms now demands that attention is given to non-European interests. As a result, the term "ethnic identity" has come to the forefront in contemporary ethnic literature worldwide. In the U.S. multicultural context, ethnic identity has posited different ways of perceiving ethnicity according to different perceptions about American identity itself. A predominant question about identity in ethnic American literature is whether it is changeable or fixed. For instance, can a non-American become American by just crossing the border or is there more to acquiring an American identity? In terms of literary representation such questions point to the so-called politics of identity. Can a specific ethnicity be represented in only one way or are there other possible ways of representing that ethnic group? When some ethnic writers represent ethnic concerns differently they are seen as attempting to claim Americanism or catering to Western ideology. Likewise if some ethnic writers represent their ethnic group as "too ethnic" they are not fully accepted by "American"/Western readers.

Comprising a history of colonization, enslavement, racial discrimination, and immigration, the United States now epitomizes a conglomeration of diverse cultures and ethnicities amidst a rich mixture of languages, norms, religions, and values and offers the world a "crossroad culture," so to speak. Ethnic identity—the sense of sharing an ethnic heritage comprising common ancestry, shared beliefs, and lifestyles—is valued by many as the core of their sense of belonging. At the same time, living in America, the land of immigrants, and becoming American demands that ethnic identity not be merely exclusionary. It should rather enhance one's cultural heritage than exclude one from other coexisting groups and ethnicities. Thus important questions arise pertaining to how much of one's ethnic background should be abandoned for full acceptance or to become truly American. It becomes equally important to create an identity that is both ethnic and American simultaneously.

Discussions regarding ethnic identity in a North American context center on two existing characteristic models. The first model is commonly identified as the "melting pot" metaphor of **assimilation** that primarily caters to the Eurocentric notion of race mixing. Derived from Israel Zangwill's 1922 play "The Melting Pot," the term refers to assimilationist urgency wherein old ethnicities are surrendered in favor of a new Anglophone American identity. In this case, the original ethnic identities "melt" and give way to an Americanized identity. The assimilationists thus believe that the minorities in America must discard their inferior racial/ethnic traits in order to be accepted in the American mainstream. A growing awareness of American multiculturalism has caused some Americans to challenge the earlier notions of the nation as a "melting pot" and to reconsider other models of identity that would strive to maintain a balance between one's ethnic identity and one's interaction within the American setting. Consequently, the second model of multiculturalism is based on cultural pluralism and strives to maintain diversity by preserving ethnic affiliations and differences. Commonly identified with the "salad bowl" metaphor, the second model, by preserving differences, hinders complete acceptance in the American culture. The multicultural world of America that tends to portray a melting-pot ideology or a pluralist national identity marks ethnic identity in hegemonic terms of difference and marginality. Thus ethnic identity always remains ethnic in a minimalist way and is different from the normative, mainstream American identity. This has become a kind of struggle for many contemporary writers. For instance, the reason why writers such as **Bharati Mukherjee** and **Richard Rodriguez** protest against their ethnic or hyphenated labeling and instead present themselves as exemplary American writers is that ethnicity (for them) works as a minimalist experience. Such impositions of an ethnic identity become defining terms of subjectivity against which these writers constantly struggle.

Writers of ethnic literature narratively perform, negotiate, resist, and even transgress identities within specific historical contexts. In doing so, these writers pursue the reexamination of available models and methods that shape our understanding of categories like "American," "ethnic," "multiculturalism," and "immigrant sensibility." In one way or another, ethnic literature, especially that written in the contemporary era, thus challenges a unitary concept of identity that defines one essentially as "Self" or as the "Other." Writers define identity in ethnic literature in terms of shared spaces that deal with history, memory, violence, home, and other concepts linked to ethnic discourse. At the same time, such representations also point to our assumptions about ethnic identity as being a prefixed notion and raises questions about ethnic labeling and assimilation in America. The idea that ethnic identity can be a constantly, dynamically changing concept and ultimately no longer exclusively "ethnic," calls our attention to our perception of ethnic identity only in terms of marginality or as a "minority" identity. When some ethnic writers represent such a concept of "Americanization," in which ethnic identity assimilates or acculturates, they are challenged for occluding ethnic origins and even encrypting ethnic identity.

Representations of ethnic identities in American literature are chiefly drawn from historical references and portray a diverse methodology of approaching cultural differences. Literary representations of ethnic identity are thus manifested through historical and sociological factors of the times influencing the experience of people identifying with a particular ethnic or group affiliation. For example, identity in African American literature of the nineteenth and twentieth centuries is portrayed in relation to socially oppressive systems, such as slavery, and racial as well as gender discrimination. Likewise ethnic identity in Asian American literature of the nineteenth and twentieth centuries draws upon the experience of discrimination faced through exclusionary, prohibitive immigration laws, as well as racial and gender discrimination.

Identity in the Context of Diaspora, Exile, and Migration

An understanding of certain key terms such as "**diaspora**," "exile," and "immigrant" is helpful in understanding the dynamic of the way a particular ethnic identity is represented in ethnic American literature. The word "diaspora" was originally used to refer to the dispersion of Jews outside of Israel when they were exiled to Babylonia. On a broader level, the term now refers to the dispersion of a community of people outside their homeland. The experience of diaspora thus entails a condition of "living" in two spaces at the same time. Expatriate communities who share a common diaspora share similar traits including a collective memory or vision of their ancestral homeland. They feel a sense of alienation and prejudice caused by their view that they will never be fully accepted by the host country where they now live. Their emotional bonds are more with the original homeland as they hope and believe that they will return there eventually. Because of these bonds, they strongly believe in collective commitment to maintenance and prosperity of the original homeland. The condition of "exile" is a more painful and traumatic emotional one when a sense of danger in the original homeland is involved, as it suggests punishment or banishment from one's homeland (although leaving can be voluntary or involuntary). Exile can be a solitary experience compared to diaspora, which is always collective. Thus an exile feels an even more extreme sense of alienation in the host country than a diasporic community does. Such a person feels nostalgic desire and pines for return to the homeland. Although in diasporic communities, the loss of homeland is replaced by collective efforts to maintain a "home outside home" as in ethnic enclaves like Chinatowns and Greek towns, the exiled individual feels a painful sense of homelessness. Such pulls and tugs of cultural as well as geographic dislocations have a considerable impact on one's identity.

The immigrant deals with similar concerns of displacement and cultural dislocation yet has a different outlook on the whole situation. The immigrant does not feel a state of perpetual exile, homelessness, or lifelong commitment to an ethnic affiliation. The term "immigrant" has been used in different ways in third world and minority people's struggles against invasion, colonialism, and political oppression. It seems now that in a rapidly globalizing world, the immigrants themselves conceptualize and express their identities in terms of individuality and choice rather than those of sociology as in the case of exile or diaspora. The immigrants thus learn to see and interact with the world and interpret it rather than relinquish it for the sake of their original homeland. However, the host country sometimes looks at the immigrant with suspicious eyes due to the perpetuation of certain ethnic stereotypes.

Thematically speaking, identity in ethnic American literature is thus represented as an experience of diaspora, exile, or migration. Ethnic American literature deals with issues of identity in flux or movement in relation to an American mainstream. The people in such literature are represented to be desperately seeking meaning as minorities, struggling with their circumstances of cultural displacement, or learning to maintain a balance between an ethnic heritage of the past and their identities adapting to the mainstream culture around them. Whereas ethnic heritage is represented through the shared historical past as in the circulation of myths, folk-tales, or legends, and the passing on of different familial and cultural values than the mainstream world, the adaptation of identities to mainstream culture is expressed through a multicultural approach that accepts the American ideals also.

Ethnic American writing is commonly categorized based on ethnic identity as in Asian American, African American, Jewish American, Native American, and Hispanic literatures. Respectively these branches of ethnic literature depict struggles and challenges faced by those of a particular ethnic identity. For example, in African American literature the vast range of experiences are drawn from slavery in the slave narratives, the oral transmission of folklore and myths, and the aesthetic of rebellion and protest. African American writing of the **Harlem Renaissance**, the **Civil Rights Movement,** and the modern day call for acknowledgement of a strong African American identity in multicultural America. Works of **Frederick Douglass**, **Charles W. Chesnutt**, **W. E. B. Du Bois**, **Ralph Ellison**, **Harriet Jacobs**, **Toni Morrison**, **Zora Neale Hurston**, and **Toni Cade Bambara** are notable for their contribution to American literature.

Contemporary ethnic writing in America has greatly contributed to the way we understand ethnicity and multiculturalism. Writers such as **Carlos Bulosan, Bharati Mukherjee, Maxine Hong Kingston, David Henry Hwang, Gloria Anzaldúa, Cherríe Moraga, N. Scott Momaday, Amy Tan,**

Leslie Marmon Silko and many others have enriched the American literary scene.

Further Reading

Knippling, Alpana Sharma. *New Immigrant Literatures in the United States.* Westport, CT: Greenwood Press, 1996.

Sollors, Werner. *Theories of Ethnicity: A Classical Reader.* New York: New York UP, 1996.

Parvinder Mehta

IGNATOW, DAVID (1914–1997) Jewish-American poet. David Ignatow, one of America's foremost poets of the working-class "second generation"—born after the great **immigration** of the turn of the twentieth century—was born in Brooklyn, New York, on February 7, 1914, to immigrants Max Ignatowsky and Yetta Reinach. He graduated from New Utrecht High School in 1932. After a series of sales jobs, young David started work at his father's bindery in Manhattan. "I Can't Stop It," his first published story, appeared in the New Talent section of O'Brien's *Best American Short Stories* in 1933. Ignatow worked as a Works Progress Administration (WPA) researcher and reporter and wrote for a series of literary magazines. He married the artist Rose Graubart in 1937, and they had a son, David, at the end of the year; in 1956 a daughter, Yaedi, was born.

After a long series of service and industrial jobs and a return to management of his father's bindery, Ignatow turned to academe in the 1960s. He held visiting professorships at the universities of Kentucky and Kansas and, from 1969 to 1983, a full-time teaching position at York College of City University of New York. Until the 1990s he taught part-time at Columbia University's School of the Arts. In 1981–82 Ignatow was Poetry Society of America president. He received numerous awards, including Guggenheim and Rockefeller Fellowships, a National Institute of Arts and Letters Award, the Shelley Award, and the Robert Frost Medal. David Ignatow died on November 17, 1997.

Ignatow's poetry is far less distinguished by its style than by its fierce and passionate devotion to its vision: a prophetic pageant of the daily suffering and redemption of ordinary Americans, especially working people. His themes include the conflict of fathers and sons and the consequent reinvention of the world by each generation; the creation, or rather the calling forth, of "god" by human beings thrown together in collective action; the role of nature in providing a mythos for death and rebirth; the horrors of war; and the respite created by human love—of all kinds—in the midst of chaos and despair. In one of his most famous poems, "Sunday at the State Hospital," he manages to represent a father's visit to his schizophrenic son, whose sandwich, uneaten, freezes in the air like an unconsumed sacrament, as a version of the failure of all love to change the course of nature.

Although Ignatow's work is recognizably "Jewish" in that it locates itself firmly in the biblical traditions and the particular suffering of modern Jews, these are mere launching pads for the poet's exploration of universal themes. Ignatow himself was opposed to **racism** of all kinds, including that practiced by Jews against others. Near the end of his life, he used the assassination of Israeli Prime Minister Rabin by a fanatic nationalist as an occasion for speaking out against the abuse of traditions. Instead of the experience of a **race**, Ignatow's poetry locates itself in the experience of men and women, their growth and death, their reproduction and their production. It is no accident that he was a leader of the movement of creative artists, not only against the Vietnam War in the 1960s, but also against nuclear proliferation in the 1980s and the Gulf War in 1990–91. The poet who could write of people murdering for trivial reasons was also the man who could speak out against the abuse of poetry to support power.

David Ignatow was the author of twenty-four books of poetry and hundreds of poems in journals and magazines. The recipient of a number of prestigious awards, he never stopped teaching and mentoring younger poets and encouraging editors of small press publications. More than a year before his death, he called in to a radio show to say, like an urban Mark Twain, that premature reports of his demise were "greatly exaggerated." (*See also* Jewish American Poetry)

Further Reading

Mills, Ralph J., Jr. "Earth Hard: David Ignatow's Poetry." *Cry of the Human: Essays on Contemporary American Poetry.* Ed. Ralph J. Mills Jr. Urbana: U of Illinois P, 1975. 67–133.

Pacernick, Gary. "David Ignatow: Prophet of Darkness and Nothingness." *Memory and Fire: The American Jewish Poets.* New York: Peter Lang, 1989. 143–63.

Stocking, David M., ed. *A Chapbook for David Ignatow.* [Special issue.] *Beloit Poetry Journal* 26.1 (Fall 1975): 1–7.

Terris, Virginia R., ed. *Meaningful Differences: The Poetry and Prose of David Ignatow.* Tuscaloosa: U of Alabama P, 1994.

Barry Fruchter

IMMIGRATION One of the great claims of American mythology is that America is a nation of immigrants. "We all came from somewhere else," the celebratory saying goes, and whether the nation's diverse communities are represented through "melting pot," "salad," or other liberal pluralist metaphors, the myth presumes that the United States grants all people—regardless of creed and color—the rights of life, liberty, and the pursuit of happiness. This celebrated plural "we," though, is paradoxically quite exclusive: it excludes the indigenous Native American population, whose presence on the continent posed a fundamental challenge to the founding of the country, and all of whom were either killed or removed from their territories and placed on reservations; likewise, it obscures the forced migration of millions of Africans during the transatlantic slave trade. Finally, the myth erases an intricate history of the nation's "natives"—composed primarily of Anglo-Saxon Protestants—shaping immigration law in order to control the make up of the nation. Thus, discussing U.S. ethnic literatures requires understanding the ways in which U.S. legal discourse articulates specific notions of American **identity** by defining who is allowed in and who should stay out. Understanding immigration requires attending to the many different ways the experiences of displacement, loss, and refashioned notions of belonging are represented through cultural production. Lisa Lowe has powerfully formulated this double-edged analytical value seen in the term "immigration": It is "[both] the locus of legal and political restriction . . . [as well as] the site for the emergence of critical negations of the nation-state for which those legislations are the expression."

Scholars of American literature, history, and the law have, since at least the mid-1990s, unpacked legal discourse to trace how immigration constructs understandings of **race**, class, and national belonging. The starting point for this discourse is America's first naturalization statute, codified in 1790, which made available the rights of national citizenship to all "free white persons." Although the statute was altered in 1870 to include those of "African nativity and persons of African descent" to ensure that the recently liberated slave populations and their families could be legally—if often not in practice—part of the nation, it was not until 1952 that naturalization was offered regardless of racial distinction. A tenuous term, the "**whiteness**" codified in 1790 was flexibly interpreted by the courts to sometimes include—and sometimes exclude—immigrants from a wide range of European, Middle Eastern, and Central Asian countries.

But naturalization presupposes that individuals have been allowed to enter the country in the first place. There has been a long history of legislation greatly curtailing or excluding immigration by certain populations altogether, and this legislation often expressed the fear of racialized foreign others taking American jobs. The first major immigration law was the **Chinese Exclusion Act** of 1882, which, as the title makes clear, denied immigration to a certain segment of Chinese nationals. Under pressure from Anglo laborers working primarily in the newly settled frontiers of the American West, the law was passed to suspend the immigration of Chinese workers, a class of people who previously had provided inexpensive labor during the development of Western cities and the transcontinental railroad. The Act's protectionist tenor was made clear in that it permitted the entry of Chinese students, teachers, merchants, and those merely interested in tourism, all populations that posed no economic threat to American citizens. Nevertheless, the Act explicitly refused all Chinese nationals naturalization. It was not until December 1943 that the Act was formally repealed.

The Chinese Exclusion Act set the tone for a nation whose interest in immigration became concerned with "gatekeeping." As Erika Lee makes clear, the Act established Chinese immigrants as the "models by which to measure the desirability (and 'whiteness') of other immigrant groups" (38). When there were increases in immigration from other regions of the world, including elsewhere in Asia, southern and Eastern Europe, and Mexico, "nativist" calls to close the gates to certain immigrants inevitably compared these populations to the Chinese. Although the immigrants from Europe were often deemed "white enough" to be permitted naturalization, their high rate of migration put pressure on employment. Mexicans, many of whom were attempting to return to lands from which they had been displaced in the wake of the Mexican-American War (1846–48), were both a cheap labor force and a population deemed "racially inferior," a notion produced primarily during the U.S. conquest of Mexican territory.

This gatekeeping ideology continued to structure immigration policy through much of the twentieth century. Controlling immigration was seen as a way of controlling the meaning of a racialized American national identity; thus, while Western European nationals were in many instances given an open door, immigration of nonwhite and so-called "undesirable" peoples slowed to a trickle. For example, the Immigration Act of 1917 required that prospective immigrants pass a literacy test and go through a screening process in order to weed out those with "radical" political views. 1917 also saw the suspension of entry from a broader array of Asian countries. The Immigration Act of 1924 set the first permanent restrictions on immigration based on a national origins quota system. This system was in effect until 1952, and set the annual limit of immigration at 150,000, doling out caps to specific countries based on proportional representation already present in the U.S. population. Quotas were not filled on a first-come first-served basis; rather, a series of preferences was devised, privileging mostly children, parents, and spouses of U.S. citizens, as well as those workers who were skilled in agriculture (of which there was a dearth in the United States at the time). The law also institutionalized the use of documentation, registration, and the granting of visas by U.S. consular offices abroad. It also, notably, barred all Japanese immigration. A 1934 law expanded that ban to immigration from the Philippines, a territory that at the time was being formally governed by the United States.

The McCarran-Walter Act of 1952 brought the broad array of immigration-related legislation under one statute, and updated much of it for the contemporary concerns of the cold war. Although the Act formally eliminated racial distinction as a potential bar to naturalization, it reaffirmed and refashioned the importance of racial difference inherent in the quota system by, among other things, putting a very low cap on immigration from what had come to be termed the "Asia-Pacific triangle." Also, the preference system was expanded to include not only skilled agricultural laborers, but also those workers whose skills were "urgently needed" by U.S. industries. With the fear of communism brewing, the Act broadened the amount of information immigrants had to provide upon entry into the country, and eased deportation restrictions so that any foreign national who engaged in activities "prejudicial to the public interest" or "subversive to national security" could be promptly expelled from the country.

The early 1960s was a time in which a liberal multiculturalist ideal of American freedom dominated the national myth. With the sweep of decolonization throughout much of Africa and Southeast Asia, the United States pitted itself against the Soviet Union to create alliances with the many newly formed nation-states; American freedom was imagined as accessible to all who sought it. The gates that had been closing since 1882 were opening again. This sentiment was expressed in the 1965 overhaul of immigration law. The Immigration and Nationality Act Amendments of that year eliminated the national origins quota system, and thereby removed race, along with national origin and ancestry, as bars for immigration. However, quotas were still maintained; instead of basing them on the previous categories (which the **Civil Rights Movement** and anti-colonial resistance had permanently tarnished), quotas were defined by hemisphere. Annual immigration from the Eastern Hemisphere was capped at 20,000 immigrants per country, totaling up to 170,000. Western Hemisphere immigration was limited to 120,000 annually, but there was no cap placed on the number originating from a particular country.

After 1990, although the rhetoric of "gatekeeping" still structured much of the legal discourse around immigration policy, the restrictive logics in place since the Chinese Exclusion Act were thought of as an antiquated remnant of the past. A major result of the post–cold war reworking of immigration policy was a considerable increase in the numbers of people immigrating to the United States from around the world. Simultaneously, though, the policing of the country's entry points became much more rigorous. In particular, the border with Mexico became a site of significant tension, primarily because Latino so-called "illegal aliens" were thought to be unfairly taking jobs away from American citizens. Here one can witness the return of the racialization of labor interests first glimpsed in 1882. After the attacks on the World Trade Center and the Pentagon in 2001, the McCarran-Walter era concern for national security reemerged, this time with the creation of the Department of Homeland Security, which, among its many other duties, strictly monitors immigration, especially from countries considered a threat to national security.

The other side to this history of an immigration policy used to express notions of national identity is the flourishing archive of novels, poetry, songs, essays, and other cultural productions written by immigrants. Some texts are critical of the contradictory and paradoxical expressions described above, while others affirm and celebrate acts of migration and settlement in the United States, and see immigration as an exquisite act of personal reinvention.

C. L. R. James's *Mariners, Renegades, and Castaways: The Story of Herman Melville and the World We Live In* (1952) is overly critical of the paradox at the heart of the American myth. Written primarily while detained by the Immigration and Naturalization Service (INS) on **Ellis Island**, James simultaneously makes his own case for staying in the country, and retells one of

America's **canon**ical narratives in a new and challenging way. The Trinidad-born James had moved to the United States in 1938 and was an anticolonial literary critic concerned with resisting the growth of American imperialist ideology. Detained and later deported for what the INS called "subversive activities," James masterfully reinterpreted one of the central novels of American literature, Melville's *Moby-Dick*. Although most scholars had read *Moby-Dick* as an allegory of Ishmael's essential goodness challenging evil Ahab's totalitarian monomania—an interpretation fostered by the U.S. confrontation with the Nazis in World War II and the Soviet Union at the dawn of the cold war—James deftly describes how Ahab and Ishmael were in fact two sides of the same coin, the latter merely an intellectual expression of the former. For James, *Moby-Dick* instead offered an entry point into describing the scene of contemporary American resistance, with the whaling ship's polyglot multicultural crew, a community of "mariners, renegades, and castaways," standing in for James himself—and the country's many other immigrants—who had been targeted by the national security state for their so-called un-American behavior. The result is a powerfully argued text that reimagines national belonging by resituating immigration and cultural difference at the core of U.S. culture.

A more affirmative take on the transformative possibilities of immigration can be seen in novels like **Bharati Mukherjee**'s *Jasmine* (1989). Hers is a story of the title character's journey from being a young despairing widow in India to an assimilated and successful American in the United States. The protagonist becomes a common-law wife of a banker from the American heartland, becomes Jane Ripplemeyer, and adopts a Vietnamese refugee. While reinscribing many of the disabling notions of American success—Jasmine's success requires a transformative **assimilation** divorcing her from tradition, community, and heritage—the novel also emphasizes the complex hybridity that poses challenges to any homogenous construction of national identity.

Further Reading

Jacobson, Matthew Frye. *Whiteness of a Different Color: European Immigrants and the Alchemy of Race.* Cambridge, MA: Harvard UP, 1998.

Lee, Erika. "The Chinese Exclusion Example: Race, Immigration, and American Gatekeeping, 1882–1924." *Journal of American Ethnic History* 21.3 (Spring 2002): 36–62.

Ngai, Mae M. "The Architecture of Race in American Immigration Law: A Reexamination of the Immigration Act of 1924." *Journal of American History* 86.1 (1999): 67–92.

Keith Feldman

INADA, LAWSON FUSAO (1938–) Japanese American poet and scholar. Lawson Fusao Inada is regarded as the "father of Asian American literature" by some, and he has earned this appellation as his work occupies a central place in the history of Asian American poetry. His collection

Before the War: Poems as They Happened (1971) was the first book of poetry written by an Asian American to be published by a major New York publisher. He also participated in editing *Aiiieeeee! An Anthology of Asian-American Writers* (1983). In addition, Inada recovers and edits the works of earlier Asian American writers, like **Toshio Mori**, and conducts workshops to encourage new poets.

Recently Inada edited *Only What We Could Carry: The Japanese American Internment Experience* (2000), which juxtaposes written and visual texts such as letters, propaganda, and memoirs, requiring readers to engage in multiple literacy practices to read into the trauma and violence of the **internment**. The anthology's title refers first to a stipulation in Executive Order 9066 (1942–45), which ordered the incarceration of all Americans of Japanese descent during World War II, and that permitted internees to take only what they could carry to the internment camps. As the collection's multiethnic writings and illustrations clearly indicate, however, Executive Order 9066 inflicted a national wound and sense of loss that many Americans carried. Japanese Americans survived this injustice and heroically carried their families through to postwar lives. Yet the internment continues to haunt Americans as this history challenges national values of liberty, equality, and justice.

Inada's poetry is a powerful voice in speaking out about the internment of Japanese Americans as he writes from his memories of his family's incarceration. The voices within his poems range from those of a young boy and his grandfather as they recall their release from the camps in "Denver Union Station," to the no-no boys who refused conscription for military service while their families were unjustly incarcerated in "Drawing the Line," to a representative individual recounting the suffering caused by legalized **racism** in "Concentration Constellation."

Inada's calls to poetry come from both his cultural heritage as well as his passion for **jazz**. His poetry consistently honors the strength of Japanese American immigrants and their communities and contributions, and the audience can hear this in his grandfather's accented call of "Lawson" in "Denver Union Station." The other call is vocalized by Billie Holiday in "Jazz" as she gently sings his name while she signs an autograph. Inada identifies this moment as the genesis of his poetry writing, and his writings often celebrate the great jazz musicians. Inada's poetics articulate these two different callings of "Lawson," one Japanese American and the other African American, as they contribute to his poet-musician voice which ably explores such themes as relocation, loss, survival, home, and cultural identity in written, oral, and performance media.

In addition to the voices of his family and jazz icons, Inada also acknowledges another call in poems such as "Kicking the Habit." Here, he questions the boundaries of standard languages and their limited capacity for expression. His poetic persona renounces the use of English and converses in the language of nature or whatever it is he hears as he steps away from his ordinary life momentarily. This openness to listening and trying out other vocalizations brings rewards of new rhythms, vocabularies, signifi-ers, and even modes of expression, enabling the persona not only to hear but also see in new ways.

The questioning of the limits of English and an openness to new voices are essential to hearing the poetics of internment. Inada's performance piece titled "Children of Camp" recognizes the nontraditional poetics of internment whose language is that of harsh landscapes, prison barriers, family bonds, and communal strength. As a voice speaking out against a silence that wishes to erase this part of American history, Inada pays tribute to and continues the art, music, and poetry whose creative roots were planted behind barbed wire.

Further Reading

Chang, Juliana. "Time, Jazz, and the Racial Subject: Lawson Inada's Jazz Poetics." *Racing and (E)Racing Language: Living with the Color of Our Words.* Ed. Ellen J. Goldner and Safiya Henderson-Holmes. Syracuse, NY: Syracuse UP, 2001. 134–54.

Sato, Gayle K. "Lawson Inada's Poetics of Relocation: Weathering, Nesting, Leaving the Bough." *Amerasia Journal* 26.3 (2000–2001): 139–60.

Yogi, Stan. "Yearning for the Past: The Dynamics of Memory in Sansei Internment Poetry." *Memory and Cultural Politics: New Approaches to American Ethnic Literatures.* Ed. Amritjit Singh, et al. Boston: Northeastern UP, 1996.

Karen Li Miller

INDIAN AMERICAN FILM. *See* South Asian American Film

INDIAN AMERICAN LITERATURE. *See* South Asian American Literature

INTERNMENT In 1942, under Executive Order 9066 issued by Presi-dent Franklin D. Roosevelt, about 120,000 Japanese immigrants and Ameri-can-born Japanese were uprooted from their West Coast homes and interned in inland camps.

The internment of Japanese Americans during World War II has been identified as one of the most regrettable events in American history. Offi-cially declared to be a "military necessity," the relocation and incarceration of the West Coast Japanese Americans were really measures based on racial profile. Although the United States was also fighting Germany and Italy, German Americans and Italian Americans did not face the same mass internment as Japanese Americans. Also, although Hawai'i was in close proximity to Japan and the site of the Pearl Harbor bombing, Hawaiian Jap-anese Americans were spared the mass relocation. As Japanese Americans composed a significant portion of the Hawaiian population and were an indispensable workforce on the islands, they were not interned like their continental counterparts. Thus, the ground to intern Japanese Americans on the West Coast proves to be, not a "military necessity," but **racism**.

Internment of Japanese Americans, 1942. *AP/Wide World Photos.*

In fact the internment symbolizes the climactic point of half a century of anti-Japanese (and anti-Asian in general) sentiment on the Pacific Coast. Long before World War II, many **immigration** laws were enacted to bar the flow of Japanese (and Asian) immigrants and restrict them from becoming naturalized citizens. The passage of a series of alien land laws, which prohibited "aliens ineligible for citizenship" from buying and owning any real properties, created tremendous difficulties for them to gain a livelihood in America. However, the harsh laws and legislation did not repel Japanese Americans. On the contrary, the hardship compelled them to form strong ethnic communities. Although Japanese American communities were strengthened and indeed prevailed, the hostility and resentment of white farmers and workers were also aggravated. The Pearl Harbor incident turned racial prejudice and hatred into hysteria and paranoia.

Of the 120,000 internees, there were about 7,000 American citizens. Many of them were school-age children and elderly people. They were first taken to sixteen temporary assembly centers and then further transported to ten relocation camps in desolate places, including Tule Lake and Manzanar in

California, Minidoka in Idaho, Heart Mountain in Wyoming, Topaz of Utah, Postona, and Gila River in Arizona, Amache in Colorado, and Rohwer and Jerome in Arkansas. Both assembly centers and relocation camps were hastily installed buildings that resembled army barracks. An average apartment, measuring twenty feet by twenty-five feet, accommodated a family of four to six persons. It was also insufficiently and crudely equipped with a stove, army cots, and straw mattresses. Internees had to use communal bathrooms and waited in long lines to have their three meals in mess halls. Apart from the poor condition of housing and repressive daily routine, internees were also struggling with tough weather and environs on a daily basis.

The detrimental effects of the internment, which were not only financial and physical, but also profoundly psychological, are reflected in Japanese American writings. Japanese American writers grappled with questions of loyalty, home, and **identity**, in works published in camp magazines such as *Tulean Dispatch* (Tule Lake, California), *The Pen* (Rowher, Arkansas), and *Trek* (Topaz, Utah). In the immediate postwar decade, Mine Okubo's *Citizen 13660* (1946), Yamamoto's "The Legend of Miss Sasagawara" (1951), and **Monica Sone**'s *Nisei Daughter* (1953) focus on Japanese American identity and on internment life and its effect on the characters. Later, the ethnic movement and the redress movement encouraged more writers to reexamine the history and recuperate personal memories. For example, **Jeanne Wakatsuki Houston** and James Houston's *Farewell to Manzanar* (1973), an autobiographical text, depicts camp life and difficulty with reintegration into American society. **Mitsuye Yamada**'s collection of poems titled *Camp Notes* (1976) also centers on the internment experience and postwar resettlement. In 1982 **Yoshiko Uchida**, a well-known author of children's literature, published *Desert Exile*, an autobiography chronicling her family's displacement and internment during World War II. (*See also* Japanese American Autobiography)

Further Reading

Chan, Sucheng. *Asian Americans: An Interpretive History*. New York: Twayne, 1991.

Simpson, Caroline Chung. *An Absent Presence: Japanese Americans in Postwar American Culture, 1945–1960*. Durham, NC: Duke UP, 2001.

Takaki, Ronald. *Strangers from a Different Shore: A History of Asian Americans*. Boston: Little, Brown and Company, 1989.

Yogi, Stan. "Japanese American Literature." *An Interethnic Companion to Asian American Literature*. Ed. King-Kok Cheung. New York: Cambridge UP, 1997. 125–55.

Shuchen Susan Huang

INVISIBLE MAN   Published in 1952 and recipient of the National Book Award in 1953, **Ralph Ellison**'s *Invisible Man* has been hailed as a masterpiece of African American, American, and world literature. Informed by the epic scope of Herman Melville, the existential vision of Fyodor Dosto-evsky, and the **blues** ethos of black cultural expression, the only novel Ellison completed before his death in 1994 is an allegory of the alienated continuity of the black experience in the United States.

The book begins with a confession: "I am an invisible man." Thus are readers introduced to the unnamed black protagonist who says that his narrative will explain why he has been in "hibernation" for so long and why the present is the time for "action." His story is initially set in the Deep South, where he participates in a "Battle Royal" that has black boys fighting each other for the entertainment of whites. The narrator is also subjected to deliberate sexual prohibition when a voluptuous white stripper dances in front of the boys and white men. Left in an abject state of guilt and disgust, he ironically receives a scholarship to attend a college not unlike Tuskegee Institute.

Though his first years at school are promising, the narrator makes an unforgivable faux pas when he takes Mr. Norton, the white benefactor whose philanthropy is more a function of liberal condescension than genuine concern, to see the destitute and incestuous Trueblood family. Norton's exposure to the family rekindles sexual longing for his dead daughter, and condemnation of the narrator is a way to lash out against his own perversion. Dr. A. Herbert Bledsoe, the president of the college, is an ingratiating public figure who caters to white demands in order to secure power and prestige over other blacks; he expels the narrator after the Trueblood episode.

The narrator moves to New York City and there finds a job in the Liberty Paints factory making the aptly named "Optic White." When that predictably suffocating position terminates in a machinery explosion, he returns to Harlem and is quickly enlisted in the Brotherhood, a quasi-communist revolutionary group led by the white, one-eyed Brother Jack. Jack's counterpart is Ras the Destroyer, a militant **Garvey**ite who criticizes the Brotherhood for its patronizing stance toward blacks. The narrator thus finds himself caught between a white socialist and a black nationalist, neither of whom "sees" him for who he is. Tod Clifton, a black activist formerly linked to the Brotherhood, is similarly disillusioned with Harlem politics and resorts to selling Sambo dolls on the street. In search of a scapegoat, the Brotherhood blames the narrator for Clifton's disappearance from its ranks; he responds by going undercover and impersonating a man-about-town. But when Clifton is killed by a white police officer, a full-blown riot erupts in Harlem, and the resulting fracas sees the narrator literally go undercover. In a manhole he suffers a castration fantasy that paradoxically frees him of all "illusion," thereby granting him the resolve to commit his story to paper.

Ellison's is the most compelling novel about psychic estrangement from a sense of social and cultural belonging in postwar American letters. Moreover because it signaled upon publication a definitive break from the African American literary protest tradition, it has enabled countless black authors since to write not necessarily "for" or in the name of their **race** but on terms of their own artistic choosing. (*See also* African American Novel)

Further Reading

Baker, Houston A., Jr. "To Move without Moving: An Analysis of Creativity and Commerce in Ralph Ellison's Trueblood Episode." *PMLA* 98.5 (1983): 828–45.

Callahan, John F., ed. *Ralph Ellison's* Invisible Man: *A Casebook*. New York: Oxford UP, 2004.

Nadel, Alan. *Invisible Criticism: Ralph Ellison and the American Canon.* Iowa City: U of Iowa P, 1988.

Warren, Kenneth W. *So Black and Blue: Ralph Ellison and the Occasion of Criticism.* Chicago: U of Chicago P, 2003.

Kinohi Nishikawa

IRANIAN AMERICAN LITERATURE   Although many Iranians came to the United States prior to the Iranian Revolution of 1979 (ostensibly for higher education and training during the period of close U.S.-Iran relations with the former Shah), the largest number arrived here after the popular uprising that led to the overthrow of Mohammad Reza Shah and the establishment of the Islamic Republic and clerical rule. Approximately three million Iranians left Iran between 1979 and 1985; the largest number of these exiles, refugees, and immigrants settled in the United States and a smaller number settled in Western Europe. Many Iranians temporarily settled in major urban centers such as Los Angeles, Houston, Chicago, and New York, hoping to return eventually to their homeland, but with the outbreak of the Iran-Iraq War, which lasted for nearly a decade, many Iranians made the United States their permanent home.

Expatriate Writing Prior to 1979

Although prior to 1979, Iranians living in the United States did not suffer from the dramatic stereotypes and stigmas associated with the revolution and the taking of U.S. hostages at the American embassy in Tehran, writers of Iranian origin still had to contend with the difficulties of trying to convey their culture to an American audience largely unfamiliar with their background. These writers contributed to a body of work that introduced American readers to ideas about Iranian culture and history, and embodied an expatriate sensibility—that is, they wrote about their individual sojourns as immigrants or rendered in English their memories and experiences of Iran. Early Iranian American writers include novelists Taghi Modaressi (*The Book of Absent People* [1986] and *The Pilgrim's Rules of Etiquette* [1989]), **Nahid Rachlin** (*Foreigner* [1978], *Married to a Stranger* [1983], and *Veils* [1992]), Manoucher Parvin (*Cry for My Revolution: Iran* [1987]), and Donné Raffat (*The Caspian Circle* [1978]). **Ali Zarrin** and **Bahman Sholevar** are among the first published Iranian American poets to write in English. The impetus of these writers is in part to maintain a connection with their homeland and to make sense of the expatriate experience; the novels suggest a kind of "outsiderness" in the United States as well as in their native Iran. Each of these authors had been living outside of Iran for a considerable time before writing their respective novel(s).

Modaressi, Parvin, and Raffat, the three male novelists, have a preoccupation with politics, history, and the social struggles within Iran. Readers are guided through a labyrinth of political and sociological shifts taking place in Iran before and after the revolution: Raffat's *The Caspian Circle* is foregrounded by events surrounding the overthrow of Mohammad Mossadeq; Modaressi's novels deal with the political repression of the Shah and its impact on one family, as well as the tumultuous events of the revolution and its impact on the intellectual elite; and in Parvin's novel, an Iranian student living in the United States has aspirations to overthrow the Shah. These authors articulate a concern with the male discursive realms of politics, history, and social discourses.

Rachlin, on the other hand, who herself immigrated to the United States as a student and married an American, is preoccupied with her status as an Iranian woman trying to negotiate her Iranian upbringing with some of her newfound liberties as a woman in the United States. Rachlin's first novel, *Foreigner,* was, to a great extent, a pathbreaker since it was the first time American audiences had heard directly from an Iranian woman.

Exile, Memory, and Translation—Post-1979 Writing

The revolution and its aftermath made exiles of writers and intellectuals, many of whom experienced their exile as what Hamid Naficy has called a "profound dystopia"—a sense of paralyzing crisis and a nostalgia for home (Naficy 10–15). For postrevolutionary writers, loss of their physical home, their language, culture, and even the audiences with which they communicated became even more remote with the establishment of the Islamic Republic and the backlash against intellectuals and writers who were perceived as too Western. Being part of the intellectual elite that faced certain censorship or persecution in Iran after the establishment of the Islamic Republic, many disaffected writers and artists settled in the United States after 1979.

For those who did survive the move west and transformed their exile into a literary creation, memoirs and autobiographies were the genre of preference. First generation Iranian writers often wrote from the perspective of their exile and alienation as individuals, but also presented narratives of collective dissolution. Living outside Iran had both its positive and negative aspects; for women, particularly, exile presented opportunities to refashion themselves against the strict edicts of the new Islamic government preoccupied with dictating women's behavior, dress, and position as part of its attempt to define a new national, Islamic **identity**. But exile also conjures fundamental losses that, despite living in the more liberal West, cannot be healed.

Autobiography, Ethnography, and Exilic Memoirs

Memoir, whether political or literary, represents the most successful example of this emergent literature engaging mainstream interest and acceptance. The memoir form lends itself perfectly to a concern with the past and with personal memory, particularly the period before the Iranian Revolution. A number of political and literary memoirs have also been marketed as "personal accounts" of the "Islamic revolution" or have been cast as counter-narratives to the often simplistic and stereotyped image of Iran and Islamic people that was often portrayed in the U.S. media. These memoirs have presented an opportunity for individual Iranians to speak for themselves and to step outside the rhetoric of politics, particularly the radical poles of Iranian and American official government rhetoric, and to voice an individual subjectivity. Among those memoirs written in the late 1980s and early 1990s are Shusha Guppy's *Blindfold Horse: Memories of a Persian Childhood* (1988) and *Daughter of Persia: A Woman's Journey from Her Father's Harem Through the Islamic Revolution* (1992) by Sattareh Farman Farmaian (coauthored with American writer Dona Munker). Both of these memoirs feature childhood memories of growing up in prominent, aristocratic families and portray a nostalgic and somewhat exoticized image of Iran. These works belong to a category we might loosely label the "exilic memoir"; an autobiographical narrative with an exilic sensibility and a social, political, and cultural relationship to Iran informed by his or her family's political and economic prominence. These "exilic memoirs" are driven less by an interest in literary expression and more urgently on a narrative of past events and ethnographic details that are under threat or lost in the upheaval of the revolution.

Blood and Oil: Memoirs of a Persian Prince (1997), an autobiographical text by another member of the Farman Farmaian family (half-brother of Sattareh), Manouchehr Farman Farmaian, coauthored with his daughter Roxanne Farman Farmaian. *Blood and Oil* can be read as a political memoir since it documents Manouchehr's involvement with the oil ministry of Iran under the Shah's government and his subsequent exile to Venezuela after the revolution.

From Memoir to Iranian American Literature

The memoir form has been central to the development of Iranian American literature in English largely because it has the capacity to encompass both personal and national history—something with which Iranian Americans continue to be very preoccupied as they struggle with their place as outsiders in Iranian culture and in U.S. society. In addition to the three previously mentioned memoirs, two writers of a younger generation offer their perspective of the Iranian Revolution and the forced migration of their families. Both Tara Bahrampour's *To See and See Again: A Life in Iran and America* (Farrar, Strauss, and Giroux, 1999) and Gelareh Asayesh's *Saffron Sky: A Life Between Iran and America* (1999) chronicle a return to Iran after a period of absence from the country of their childhood and documents the dissonance between the Iran they grew up in and the Iran that they revisit as grown women long after the revolution. The theme of the return to Iran after a long separation surfaces again and again in much of the recent literature of the Iranian **diaspora** because it reflects the growing interest of young people, whose life circumstances were affected by the revolution, to travel to Iran but who, because of the nature of U.S.-Iran political relations or Iran's internal difficulties, were unable to visit Iran during the previous twenty years. This geographic, historical, and cultural rupture serves as the backdrop to these more recent memoirs that chronicle the shifting loyalties between Iran and the United States, and document the ongoing attempt to negotiate those divides as both a personal and literary "journey."

These texts describe the return journey to Iran after a period of separation following the revolution—a central theme in the narratives of their divided/bicultural identity. A further difference distinguishing these texts from narratives by exiles is their departure from Iran during childhood; and although the politics of the revolution affected them directly, they were less conscious of how it would shape them. They rely less on nostalgic memories, and instead attempt to negotiate past and present, thus recognizing that their childhood memories, although strong, have been clouded by the experience of having lived a life in America—a life between cultures. Bahrampour's book received considerable attention because her biography reflects a relatively common experience; she is the product of a mixed marriage between an Iranian father and an American mother. *To See and See Again* moves from the nostalgic recollections of her childhood in Iran to her present-day adult perspective when she returns to a pay a visit to her family as a thirty-year old woman.

The Emergence of a Distinct Iranian American Voice

The most recent memoir published to date, *Funny in Farsi: A Memoir of Growing Up Iranian* (2003), inaugurates a different sensibility. Rather than taking life in Iran as the primary focus (as in the previously mentioned memoirs), Firouzeh Dumas writes about her experiences of childhood and some of the cultural dissonance of growing up Iranian in the United States. Her memoir begins with her family's arrival in 1972 (a time when many young Iranian students and professionals were coming to the United States to study or work). Dumas had a comfortable few years in America afforded by her father's professional life. All that changed, however, when the revolution took place and her father lost his position in the

National Iranian Oil Company. Like many of her generation, Dumas documents the painful memories of growing up in the United States during the period of the hostage crisis when many Iranians concealed their national identity by declaring themselves Turkish, Russian, or French. This memoir points to one of the themes shared in recent writing by second generation Iranian Americans—the hostage crisis and its coverage in the U.S. media as the galvanizing moment for Iranian American identity. Although it had the effect of shaming and silence many young children, it also became the impetus for writing.

Many of the pieces in the first anthology of Iranian American writing, *A World Between: Poems, Short Stories, and Essays by Iranian-Americans* (1999), helped to articulate and solidify the literary and cultural concerns of second generation Iranian Americans. The short stories and personal essays in the collection, like much of the recent fictional work by Iranian American writers, suggest that the preoccupation with a dual perspective—Iran and America, past and present, Iranian and American—are themes that all ethnic groups work through in their literature. Perhaps this duality or in between-ness has been made more pronounced due to the depiction of Iran in the U.S. media and the difficulties of having access to Iran and Iranian culture after the revolution. Because whole families were scattered across the globe and because of the political situation, the war, and the difficulties of acquiring visas to the United States, Iranians have not felt quite settled in their new environment. Writing by this second generation—those who have spent a majority of their life in the United States and who have been cut off from the staples of everyday Iranian culture and customs—articulate the Iranian American identity beyond the memoir form.

A number of novels have also been recently published by Iranian American authors. These include Susanne Pari's *The Fortune Catcher* (1997), **Gina Nahai**'s *Moonlight on the Avenue of Faith* (2001) and *Cry of the Peacock* (2000), and Farnoosh Moshiri's *At the Wall of the Almighty* (1999) and *The Bathouse* (2003). Nahai and Pari both deal with the fallout of the Iranian Revolution and its impact on their respective protagonists. Pari's novel chronicles the return of her hero and heroine, Dariush and Layla, from the United States to a turbulent, postrevolutionary Iran where they secretly marry in 1981 against the wishes of Dariush's fundamentalist grandmother, Maman Bozorg. Nahai's most recent novel weaves a tale of political turmoil but this time from the perspective of Iran's Jewish community. The novel is narrated from the perspective of five female voices and uses magical realism to weave a tale of two places: Tehran and Los Angeles.

Farnoosh Moshiri, who comes from a prominent literary family, fled Iran in 1983 and has been writing in English for a number of years. *At the Wall of the Almighty* addresses the experience of imprisonment in Iran under the Islamic Republic. Unlike the two previously mentioned novels, *At the Wall* is concerned with the brutality of the prison experience after the establishment of the Islamic Republic and the suppression of political dissent.

Moshiri's narrative suggests that although migration may be a large part of the Iranian diaspora experience, the untold stories of the revolution, of brutality, torture, and the struggle to reconcile those stories with the experience of having left that world behind are equally important.

Whence This Emergent Literature?

Iranian American literature, like all literatures of diaspora, is in the process of establishing and articulating a new face and vocabulary on American soil. The fact that this literature has begun to find an audience and is expressing the common sentiments associated with exile, adjustment, **assimilation**, and cultural pride nearly twenty-five years after the largest population of Iranians arrived North America is not surprising. Iranian Americans as a group, like many ethnic groups of the United States, initially find their voice in the midst of historical events, stereotypes, and the resurgence of cultural pride after a period of self-concealment and shame.

Further Reading

Davaran, Ardavan, ed. "Exiles and Explorers: Iranian Diaspora Literature Since 1980." *The Literary Review* 40.1 (Fall 1996): 5–13.

Karim, Persis, and Mohammad Mehdi Khorrami, eds. *A World Between: Poems, Short Stories, and Essays by Iranian-Americans.* New York: George Braziller, 1999. 21–27.

Karimi-Hakak, Ahmad. "The Literary Response to the Iranian Revolution." *World Literature Today* 60.2 (Spring 1986): 251–56.

Naficy, Hamid. *The Making of Exile Cultures.* Minneapolis: U of Minnesota P, 1993.

Rahimieh, Nasrin. "The Quince-Orange Tree, or Iranian Writers in Exile." *World Literature Today* 66.1 (Winter 1992): 39–42.

Sullivan, Zohreh T. *Exiled Memories: Stories of Iranian Diaspora.* Philadelphia: Temple UP, 2001.

Persis Karim

IRISH AMERICAN AUTOBIOGRAPHY   The evolution of Irish American autobiographical writing is intricately connected to the shift in the social status of the Irish immigrant population in the United States from a poor, unskilled labor class during the industrial revolution to predominantly middle-class by the 1920s and, ultimately, to an economically powerful and politically influential class by the time John F. Kennedy was elected to the office of president in 1960. The current image of the Irish in America as upwardly mobile (especially the predominantly university-educated population that left Ireland to escape the collapsing Irish economy in the 1980s) is both affirmed and contested in autobiographical writing of the past two decades. Furthermore, class division among Irish Americans—between the so-called shanty and lace curtain Irish—has been the source of much contemporary autobiographical writing.

Between 1815 and 1920, over five million Irish immigrated to the United States, with the largest number leaving during and after the potato famine of 1845–49. In the United States, the Catholic Irish were often discriminated against by Anglo American Protestants who classified them as lazy, savage, and slovenly. As a result of this discrimination, Irish immigrants—who in Ireland saw the plight of their bondage by the British as comparable to the plight of slaves in the United States—found themselves competing with (and often opposed to the political and social equality of) black Americans. Many "autobiographical" Irish American narratives written during this period, such as *The Life and Travels of Father Quipes, Otherwise Dominick O'Blarney, Written by Himself* (1820), are satirical and ridicule Irish stereotypes by exaggerating them. In *The Life and Travels of Father Quipes,* the anonymous author parodies the form of the campaign biography and writes about emigration from the west of Ireland to Pennsylvania.

With very few exceptions, nonsatirical Irish American autobiographical writing did not become a prominent or even recognizably distinct literary genre until the 1930s and 1940s. One notable exception is *Some Account of the Fore Part of the Life of Elizabeth Ashbridge, Who Died in Truth's Service at the House of Robert Lecky at Kilnock in the County of Carlow Ireland; the 16th of 5th mo. 1755. Written by Her Own Hand Many Years Ago* (1755). In this brief autobiography, Ashbridge chronicles her journey from Ireland to the United States at the age of nineteen and tells a story of religious conversion from Anglican to Quaker, as a result of her frustration with the exclusion of women from the Anglican ministry. Ashbridge's narrative illustrates the importance of autobiographical writing as a tool for social resistance and self-affirmation within a potentially oppressive political and religious climate. In many ways, then, Ashbridge's autobiography prefigures the larger project of the Irish American autobiographical writing that was to follow; such writing is a means of social empowerment and has shaped and defined the ethnic **identity** of an often subordinated and religiously isolated minority.

Elizabeth Kaspar Aldrich claims that autobiographical writing in the United States is founded on Benjamin Franklin's journalistic model (17), and, according to Lawrence McCaffrey, many Irish American writers began their careers as journalists and, "following the Irish precedent, Irish American literature emerged from newspaper offices" (30). For example, **Finley Peter Dunne**, who wrote for the *Chicago Evening Post* in the 1890s, provided a social history of the Irish American neighborhood of Bridgeport, Connecticut. The connection between journalism and autobiography in Irish American writing has remained significant, as evidenced by Maureen Dezell's 2002 release, *Irish America: Coming to Clover.* Dezell, an Irish American journalist at the *Boston Globe,* writes about an Irish American identity that runs counter to the stereotypical South Boston model of inebriated bigotry that emerged after the busing riots of the 1970s. In contrast, in *All Souls: A Family Story from Southie* (1999), Michael Patrick MacDonald takes a hard and realistic look at his family's struggles with drug abuse, poverty, **racism**, and suicide, all of which, MacDonald contends, are viewed as embarrassing indicators of the lower-class status that the residents of South Boston vehemently deny. The link between journalism and self-representational narrative is evident too in the works of **Jimmy Breslin**.

The tradition of Irish American autobiography has also been shaped by texts that have focused on regional experiences. For example, Evalyn Walsh's *Father Struck It Rich* (1936) chronicles the experience of an Irish American family in the Northeast as does Frank Leslie's *There's a Spot on My Heart* (1947), a narrative about the Irish upper class in New York. Charles Driscoll's *Kansas Irish* (1943) and *Country Jake* (1946) focus on the author's life in rural Kansas; prolific Irish American novelist Kathleen Norris's 1959 autobiography, *Family Gathering*, chronicles Norris's life in California; and Richard O'Malley's *Mile High, Mile Deep* (1971) is the narrative of the author's life in Montana. At the heart of all of these narratives is each author's sense of identity as primarily Irish American and who must find a specific place and create a community within various and vastly different regions of the United States.

Within the genre of Irish American autobiography there is also the conflicting tension between an **assimilation**ist ideology—the desire for Irish Americans to represent themselves as successful members of the middle and upper classes—and outsider status. Tom Hayden, who was a political radical who protested the Vietnam War and later wrote *Irish on the Inside: In Search of the Irish Soul* (2001), is cautious of the sentimentality that often characterizes Irish American historical writing focusing on the heroic deeds of radicals. Instead, Hayden's memoir constructs a connection between the Irish in the United States and the Irish in Ireland, in part because Hayden refuses to claim kinship with the conservative Irish American community where he grew up in Detroit. In contrast, many famous Irish American actors, politicians, and athletes have written autobiographies in which they claim an Irish identity while simultaneously discussing the success that they have had in the United States. Singer Rosemary Clooney's 1977 autobiography, *This for Remembrance*, and *'Tis Herself: A Memoir* (2004), the autobiography of Golden Age Hollywood actor Maureen O'Hara, are two examples.

Perhaps the most famous and most critically acclaimed work of Irish American autobiography to date is Frank McCourt's Pulitzer Prize winning *Angela's Ashes* (1996), which became a major motion picture in 1999. McCourt chronicles his childhood experiences of abject poverty in Limerick, Ireland where he moved from Brooklyn with his family when he was only four years old. The narrative focuses primarily on McCourt's life in Ireland during his childhood and teenage years and concludes with the author's return to the United States. The work was almost unanimously well received within the Irish American literary community and was touted as an indictment of Irish parochialism and one man's escape from the tyranny of a poverty-ridden existence in Ireland. Such a reading presents the complicated nature of Irish American identity that is apparent on some level in the majority of Irish American autobiography. Irish Americans are at once eager to maintain a sense of connection to one's country of origin and to be accepted as American, although a history of racism and religious bigotry have made such a stance precarious to maintain.

Critical reception of McCourt's sequel to *Angela's Ashes*, *'Tis* (1999), was more varied and less glowing. *'Tis* begins where *Angela's Ashes* ends, with McCourt's life in the United States. The tone is bitter; the narrative voice is that of an adult and not a child. But McCourt's resounding success has largely depended upon the long history of Irish American autobiographical writing chronicled above that has at once shaped and made sense of Irish American identity. McCourt's work is, in many ways, a kind of culmination; *Angela's Ashes* is a combination of the lyrical and oral traditions that inform Irish literature in general and an examination of the poverty, stereotypes, and religious ideologies that have been sources both of conflict and pride for the Irish in America. In the continual examination of the evolving nature of ethnic American identity and in the seemingly eternal quest for an Irish American communal sense of belonging, the success of *Angela's Ashes* points to the increasingly visible position of the Irish in America at the start of the twenty-first century.

Further Reading

Aldrich, Elizabeth Kaspar. "'The Children of These Fathers': The Origins of an Autobiographical Tradition in America." *First Person Singular: Studies in American Autobiography*. Ed. A. Robert Lee. New York: St. Martin's Press, 1988.

Levy, Eric P. "The Predicament of Individuality in *Angela's Ashes*." *Irish University Review: A Journal of Irish Studies* 32.2 (2002): 259–64.

McCaffrey, Lawrence J. *Textures of Irish America*. Syracuse: Syracuse UP, 1992.

Laura Wright

IRISH AMERICAN DRAMA Irish American drama has made significant contributions to the continuously evolving world stage. As an ethnic hybridized art form composed of its Irish past and American future, Irish American drama has contended with the problem of creating its own artistic and cultural **identity**.

This unique theater faces an inescapable history that is rooted in a distant homeland painted in memory, myth, and legend, for few other countries can boast, like Ireland, of having produced such a list of literary lions in drama as William Butler Yeats, George Bernard Shaw, James Joyce, Oscar Wilde, Samuel Beckett, Dion Boucicault, Sean O'Casey, John Millington Synge, and Lady Gregory. This sense of ancestry maintains a profound effect on the development of an independent Irish American drama, which includes playwrights like the great modernist **Eugene O'Neill**. Contemporary Irish plays by Brian Friel, Frank McGuinness, and Marina Carr on American stages appear nearly as legendary as the works by their homeland masters.

As a closely allied immigrant group in a new world, Irish Americans, as early as the nineteenth century, faced the problem of asserting their own unique cultural identity. Although Irish American dramatists remain respectful of their past culture, they have sought their own path leading to inclusion into the American fabric. A reflection of societal and cultural pre-occupations, Irish American drama is the paradoxical story of cultural independence and **assimilation**.

The initial contributions to Irish American drama in the early decades of the twentieth century were easily identified by stereotypes onstage. A theater marked by farce and melodrama was filled with amusing Irish caricatures and stereotypes: the stage drunk, country bumpkin, nonsense philosopher, scandalous women, politically naïve populace, and other comical creations. These exaggerations of the Irish American people were often perceived as insults and did not play without vociferous protest by theatergoers. Irish American audiences in cities like New York, Boston, and Chicago witnessed a steady diet of farce and melodrama that exaggerated and ridiculed aspects of their **ethnicity**. The curious character from the Emerald Isle had become an amusing stock role on the boards.

E. W. Townsend's *McFadden's Row of Flats* (1903), a musical review reminiscent of the Mulligan Guards episodes popular in the 1890s, presented an unflattering pastiche of the Irish working class. The young daughter, Mary Ellen, was denounced as too immoral for an Irish Catholic young lady. Other stereotypes included the typical Irish drunk who finds the pub easier than his home or a job. Audiences protested vociferously with moral indignation the ethnic derision perceived in *McFadden's Row of Flats*. A decade later, Anne Nichols's *Abbie's Irish Rose* sparked similar ethnic confrontation in its portrayal of a young Jewish man's decision to wed an Irish girl. Despite the cultural uproar, *Abbie's Irish Rose* experienced a long run on Broadway in the 1920s.

An event that triggered significant change in Irish American drama occurred in 1911 when the Irish Players, on loan from Dublin's famed Abbey Theatre, began a five-month tour in the United States. The Irish Players brought to American stages the finest comedies and tragedies by William Butler Yeats, John Millington Synge, George Bernard Shaw, Lady Gregory, Lennox Robinson, and other Emerald Isle playwrights. The troupe was hopeful that, in translating the splendor and success of its Irish repertory to what they anticipated would be a sympathetic American public, they would be able to reach the American masses (who were subjected largely to the fare of crude melodrama and farce) and not merely the elite theatergoers. The Irish Players also hoped to fund the dwindling financial assets of the Abbey Theatre in Dublin.

The troupe's goals were jeopardized in New York with the performance of Synge's notorious *Playboy of the Western World*, a staple at home. The play centers on Christy Mahon, a young vagrant and antihero who boasts of patricide and deceives his sweetheart Pegeen Mike and the rest of the community about his ancestry. The possibility of romance for the two young lovers is dashed as Christy's real background and his lies are discovered.

Pegeen is in love with the daring man who she thought had killed his father, but her love fades when she discovers that his father is alive. The New York performance met with immediate outrage over what audiences perceived as an unfaithful depiction of the Irish national character. Irish American audiences deplored the vilification of the Irish people. Newspaper headlines led the fray in defending Irish society in both America and Ireland. Despite encountering such cultural and political hostilities, the troupe's run was successful onstage and at the box office, although it was the elite theatergoers who attended performances and not the popular audiences anticipated by the Irish Players.

Unexpectedly, it was the art form of theater that ignited social debate on the changing Irish American identity offstage as well as onstage. Synge's *Playboy of the Western World* became another port, a metaphoric embarkation, for Irish Americans who sought to define their own roots in a new land. This art-life altercation produced a social reference based on Irish American assimilation into the American landscape rather than on differences to align with Ireland. The debate further redefined the Irish American theater public as unified politically and culturally, with the clout to assert its own American identity. The disputation also underscored the problem of transporting artistic expression from one culture to another.

The third significant occurrence in the development of Irish American drama centered on the emergence of Eugene O'Neill (1888–1953) as America's leading playwright in the first half of the twentieth century. A young O'Neill, inexperienced in playwriting, sat in the audience of the Irish Players' New York performance in 1911. He was struck by the authentic realism and social commentary in plays by Shaw, Synge, Yeats, Lady Gregory, and other distinguished Irish dramatists of the time. Born into an acting family and raised Irish Catholic, O'Neill grew up in theater life. His father was a skilled tragedian in the stock melodrama and farce popular in the first two decades of the twentieth century.

It was witnessing the Irish Players that propelled the twenty-three-year-old O'Neill to write plays. But O'Neill would not follow the traditional Irish plots or themes staged by The Irish Players. O'Neill's vision for drama was to fuel a new American voice and eschew what he saw as the provincial ideas belonging to Ireland. Instead, O'Neill's drama would more clearly echo the Swedish dramatist August Strindberg in his evocation of quintessential modern themes probing alienation and fragmentation from the social body. Strindberg's tragic themes in the realism of *Miss Julie* and his expressionism in *The Ghost Sonata* became O'Neill's model. Rather than the conventional problems of Irish identity, freedom, and economics, O'Neill's plays sought a universal drama set in his American roots.

Several years later, in 1916, O'Neill helped to originate the experimental Provincetown Players in Provincetown, MA. His first plays *Bound East for Cardiff* (1916) and *The Long Voyage Home* (1917), dramas chronicling a seafarer's travails and produced by the Provincetown Players, led to his success on New York and other stages. His early themes on the American stage probed unfamiliar subjects and metaphysical conflicts, including the raw side of derelicts, prostitutes, and God's indifference to humankind.

O'Neill's contributions as an Irish American dramatist extended into the 1940s. He is remembered for such evocative plays as *Anna Christie* (1922, awarded the Pulitzer Prize), *The Hairy Ape* (1922), *Desire Under the Elms* (1925), *Strange Interlude* (1928, Pulitzer Prize winner), *Mourning Becomes Electra* (1931), *The Iceman Cometh* (1939), and *Long Day's Journey into Night* (written in 1941; first performed posthumously and awarded the Pulitzer Prize in 1956).

O'Neill, ignoring melodrama and polite drawing room theater, turned to the roots of ancient Greek tragedies. *Mourning Becomes Electra* transforms the framework of Aeschylus' powerful *Oresteia* trilogy into the conflict of an American family during the Civil War. O'Neill translates the Greek house of Atreus into a nineteenth-century New England home where Lavina's murder of General Mannon after his return from the Civil War ignites the tragedy involving the daughter and son. For the first time, the American stage saw the American past as a point of intersection with Greek mythology.

O'Neill's plays are highly experimental in their stark realism and exploratory expressionism. *Long Day's Journey into Night,* O'Neill's enduring autobiographical masterpiece, exhibits the playwright's daring techniques and innovative concepts. The play depicts the agonized relationship between the four members of the Tyrone family. The father is an aging and disappointed actor; the mother is addicted to drugs; the older son is a resentful alcoholic; and the younger son embodies the disillusioned youth of America. Defeat for the characters hangs in the air as palatable as the play's heavy ocean fog. For *Long Day's Journey into Night* and other plays, O'Neill remains recognized as America's greatest contribution to world theater. He was awarded the 1936 Nobel Prize for Literature and received four Pulitzer Prizes.

Contemporary Irish and Irish American drama is marked by the 1978 staging of Brian Friel's *Philadelphia, Here I Come* in New York. The play shuns Irish stereotypes and focuses on the present-day idea of the Irish diaspora. It tells the story of the young Irishman Gar who has decided to immigrate to the United States In the hours before Gar leaves his homeland, audiences witness the main character's turbulent ambivalence about his expatriatism. Friel portrays Gar as two separate characters seen onstage—Private Gar and Public Gar. Public Gar is the person the other actors know and see; Private Gar, unseen by the cast but visible to audiences, is the incorporation of the hidden thoughts, worries, and concerns of leaving Ireland behind that Public Gar keeps to himself. The gripping psychological impact of *Philadelphia, Here I Come* in its New York debut resulted because Gar, who struggles with his identity as he leaves his homeland for a new world, represents the millions of Irish Americans who have left behind their country in search of a new life in America. Friel ends his play with Gar leaving Ireland. It is the Irish American audiences who are able to complete Gar's journey to a new world in the West vicariously. The open-endedness of the play—whether Irish Americans discover fulfillment or disillusionment, or if they find America hollow and return to Ireland—remains problematic.

Contemporary American stage has been substantially influenced by the work of many other Irish American playwrights. Jason Miller (1939–2001), a noted Irish American playwright, won critical acclaim for *That Championship Season* (1973). Miller's Broadway play tells the story of a team of former high school basketball players and their coach who reunite twenty years after their state championship season. The drama has been viewed a one of the most significant plays of the 1970s for its honest treatment of America's hollow emphasis on winning in sports at all costs. *That Championship Season* ran for 844 performances on Broadway, garnering Miller a Pulitzer Prize for playwriting and a Tony Award for best play. Miller's other notable plays include *Barrymore's Ghost,* a monologue about the famous actor; and *Circus Lady,* a realistic comedy set in East Harlem about a desperate woman who finds that her destiny is no longer within her control.

A trio of playwrights including Bendan Connor, Tom Dunn, and Dan Callahan teamed up to write the popular comedy *Who Killed Woody Allen* (2001), a celebrity spoof and murder mystery set at the fictional funeral of **Woody Allen**. Another newcomer to the list of fashionable Irish American plays includes Donald Dewey's *Batteries* (2002), a short black comedy set in a New York City subway car.

Irish repertory theaters in metropolitan centers have fused a unique cultural identity between Ireland and America through the stage. The Irish Repertory Theatre in New York City specializes in Irish and Irish American dramatic works. In addition to the standard Irish plays by Dion Boucicault, Friel, and Yeats, the company presents Irish Americans such as O'Neill. The Irish Repertory Theatre of Chicago has mounted the Irish Tom Murphy's *Bailegangaire* (1989), a haunting memory play, reminiscent of the later Yeats and Beckett, that explores how three female family members clash with past memories. The Chicago company has also staged Stewart Parker's *Pentecost,* the story of four friends and a ghost who are brought together in a run-down row house in Dublin during the 1974 work stoppage. Also brought to Chicago from Ireland was Marina Carr's *By the Bog of Cats* (1998), the story of a young mother who waits for the return of her own long-absent mother.

The heritage of Irish American drama can be assessed as a struggle for both cultural and artistic identity and freedom. These last two are inseparable in the Irish American context, as this ethnic group has sought to retain its ancestry while accepting cultural **assimilation** into the American society. The rejection of Irish stereotypes onstage has opened the art form of the theater to a more meaningful portrayal of the diasporic Irish American in a mythic America. Friel suggests that the dreams fueling the Irish march

West may merely be another mythic encounter. O'Neill's mature repertory, particularly *The Hairy Ape* which attacks modern industrial capitalism, and Jason Miller's *That Championship Season* present universal themes that are largely devoid of traditional homeland Irish notions. This sort of theater culminates in a theater of universal import.

Further Reading

Harrington, John P. *The Irish Play on the New York Stage, 1874–1966.* Lexington: U of Kentucky P, 1997.

Llewellyn-Jones, Margaret. *Contemporary Irish Drama and Cultural Identity.* Bristol, UK: Intellect Books, 2002.

Sternlicht, Stanford. *A Reader's Guide to Modern Irish Drama.* Syracuse, NY: Syracuse UP, 1998.

Michael David Sollars

IRISH AMERICAN NOVEL   Recent years have brought much critical debate over the "Irishness" of modern novels written by Irish American authors. Some scholars assert that the Irish American novel has lost its Irish **identity**, but many experts in Irish American literature, as well as Irish American authors themselves, contend that the Irish American novel continues to explore Irish **ethnicity** through themes found in Irish American literature for nearly two hundred years. By exploring themes of religion, family, history, and politics through realism and humor, Irish American novelists continue to make significant ethnic contributions to American literature. From the first Irish American novel, *The Irish Immigrant,* published in 1817, to modern novels such as *Very Old Bones* (1992), there continues to be Irish American novelists for whom their Irishness plays a critical role in the way they view and write about the world.

From the beginnings of Irish American literature, historical events have played a critical role in defining the content of the novel. Before the Irish Potato Famine and subsequent influx of Irish immigrants to the United States, most Irish American novels were satirical, and many were published anonymously. But the events in Ireland from 1845 to 1848 would have a profound impact on the Irish people, something that would then translate into Irish American fiction and change the Irish American novel significantly. From 1845 to 1847, much of the potato crop in Ireland failed, and in 1848, as the Irish struggled to cope, virtually the entire potato crop failed. During the famine, about one million Irish died of starvation and related diseases, and between 1846 and 1855, 1.6 million migrated to America. Unfortunately, the Irish who came to America faced discrimination, poor housing, and violent neighborhoods. Certainly, such meaningful struggles would find their way into the fiction of the new Irish Americans.

Between 1845 and 1875, about twenty Irish American novels were written about what it was like to be Irish in America. Written primarily for an Irish American audience, the novels of this period were didactic and emphasized the importance of keeping the faith in Catholicism during trying times.

According to leading researcher of Irish American fiction, Charles Fanning, the plots and themes of the famine generation were highly predictable. In *The Irish Voice in America: 250 Years of Irish-American Fiction*, Fanning describes five patterns found in most novels of the famine generation. Novels predictably described the difficult life in Ireland and the difficult decision to migrate to the United States followed by humiliation and degradation once the characters arrived in America. Ireland is viewed as a pastoral home, "only temporarily despoiled by the British invaders" (Fanning 76). Novels of the famine generation also emphasized correct and incorrect ways of dealing with the hardships the Irish people faced: one could do the right thing and keep the faith in the Catholic religion or do the wrong thing and lose faith, which usually led to an early death. Fanning adds that the morals of these novels would be pointed out with "directness and emphasis, often four or five times in the last few pages" (Fanning 76).

Key novelists Father Hugh Quigley and Mary Anne Sadlier exemplify the predictable patterns of the famine generation. Quigley's novel, *The Cross and the Shamrock* (1853), emphasizes the importance of keeping the faith, and his novel, *The Prophet of the Ruined Abbey* (1855), focuses on Irish freedom in the homeland. Sadlier is known for her romances about the Irish **immigration** to America. Her novels, such as *The Blakes and the Flannagans: A Tale Illustrative of Irish Life in the United States* (1855) and *Bessy Conway; or, the Irish Girl in America* (1862), were sentimental and didactic and, like other novels of the period, predictable. Sadlier's novels, however, offer accurate portrayals of the day-to-day life of domestic servants of the period as well as the social climate in the United States for the Irish after immigration and have thus recently been studied for these important contributions.

Following the generation of famine fiction authors, many American novelists began to emphasize more realistic portrayals of life, but Irish American novelists debated whether or not it was appropriate to write more realistic works of fiction. As a national debate emerged over whether literature should reflect Christian morality and respectability or honest realism, Irish American novelists, many of whom were children of famine immigrants, struggled to find a voice. Irish American novels from 1876 to 1914 reflect the confusion of the period. Irish American novelists were torn between offering morality tales or realistic portrayals of the Irish American experience as new generations of Irish were being born in America. These novels would often be a mix of realism and romanticism, beginning with accurate and realistic depiction of the Irish American ethnicity but concluding with tidy and moralistic endings or vice versa. Catholic leaders within the Irish American communities would ultimately have great influence on Irish American fiction of this period, emphasizing the importance of good, moral fiction. But even with this struggle, important advances were made. Irish Americans were gaining respect and power, and this period reflects a rise in the number of Irish American novelists who sold well and were accepted even outside of the Irish American community.

Unfortunately, this newfound respect for Irish American culture would be short-lived. The fourth generation of Irish American novelists includes **F. Scott Fitzgerald**, whose most famous work, *The Great Gatsby* (1926), does not directly address his Irish ethnicity. Fitzgerald was not alone is this detachment from Irish themes. As the United States was about to enter World War I, the Irish began a revolution in Dublin. This revolution against the British (our allies during World War I) was not popular with many Americans. President Wilson even went so far as to make public comments questioning the loyalty of Irish American citizens. So as America joined World War I, asserting individual Irish ethnicity could be viewed by some as an act of disloyalty.

However, these events did not prevent all Irish American novelists from addressing their ethnicity. According to Daniel E. Casey and Robert J. Rhodes, as Fitzgerald "sheds his Irish identity" (270) in his novels, the novels themselves are still, to a certain extent, autobiographical. Fitzgerald and other novelists of this generation would struggle to move beyond and leave behind the "Irishness" that prevented them and the previous generation of writers from exploring life realistically. But some argue that even Irish American authors who did not overtly address Irish ethnicity in their novels, still address themes important in the Irish American culture. Critic William Shannon points out that Fitzgerald's themes often center around the "relationship between men of lower social background and women of high status or great wealth" (Fanning 249), something which would have been quite familiar to a well-to-do Irish American of Fitzgerald's generation who was still seen as an outcast in Protestant culture.

An Irish American author whose defection away from his Irish American identity was more complete was John O'Hara. O'Hara began publishing during the 1930s and was a prolific writer, producing fifteen novels and numerous short stories. O'Hara seldom addressed his ethnicity in his work, and scholars now criticize this, as it may have actually left a void in his fiction. Although O'Hara was one of the most successful authors of his day, he has now fallen into virtual obscurity. O'Hara refused to have his work anthologized and scholars in Irish American criticism contend that his work is agitated by the fact that he never confronts issues surrounding his ethnicity.

At least one Irish American novelist, **James T. Farrell**, overtly addressed his heritage in his fiction during this period. Novelist, literary critic, and short story writer, Farrell did much to preserve the "Irishness" of the Irish American novel for his generation and, perhaps most significantly, the generations of Irish American authors to come. But Farrell struggled throughout the early part of his career to gain the respect that would only come much later. Charles Fanning writes, "No major American writer has been worse served by criticism than James T. Farrell" (261). After the publication of his novel *Studs Lonigan* (1935), Farrell would continue to write for forty years without critical recognition. Farrell eventually began to gain much-deserved respect for his work near the end of his life in the late 1970s. Farrell's novels address the impact of Catholicism on the Irish culture through the experiences of ordinary Irish American characters. Farrell was among the first to write Irish American novels grounded within American realism.

Shortly after the publication of Farrell's first novels in the early 1930s, a new generation of Irish American authors emerged. In the late 1930s and 1940s, Irish American novelists began, like Farrell, to bring forth their Irish identity in their works. The novels during this period offered realistic examinations of the Irish American culture, setting the stage for an Irish American realistic tradition that continues into the twenty-first century. It is also during this period that regional differences become more pronounced in Irish American literature. While a majority of Irish Americans lived in New England, many settled much further west, as far as Louisiana, Texas, and California. According to Casey and Rhodes, "after World War II, regional differences became more pronounced. The Bostonians, heirs to the Old-World values, established the genteel tradition of the Yankee Irish" (271). But Irish Americans in the South, where they were a small minority, emphasized their religion over their Irishness. **Flannery O'Connor** was just such a writer, and her work is noted for its Catholic influences. Novels such as *Wise Blood* (1952) and *The Violent Bear It Away* (1960) emphasize religious belief through surreal and grotesque situations and plot. Charles Driscoll's *Kansas Irish* (1943) tells the story of an Irish American man who makes his way to the prairies of Kansas, where he works the land fiercely and dominates his family. J. F. Powers writes about the Irish in the Midwest in his novels, *Morte d'Urban* (1962) and *Wheat That Springeth Green* (1988). In these novels, Powers offers realistic yet witty and humorous depictions of Catholic priests.

As the Irish novel developed in the latter half of the twentieth century, it became less continuous; thus, some critics have asserted that the Irish American novel is no more, that Irish American fiction is simply American fiction. And although experts in Irish American fiction acknowledge that the "Irishness" has grown fainter in the Irish American novel, scholars and authors alike argue that there are unique qualities to Irish American fiction. The Irish ethnicity has continued to be explored in the novel throughout the latter part of the twentieth century, and there are still more novelists for whom their "Irishness" plays a critical role in their works, both explicitly and implicitly.

Edwin O'Connor's novels, published throughout the 1950s and 1960s, established a reputation for O'Connor as kind of spokesman for the Irish American people. *The Edge of Sadness* (1961) won for O'Connor the Pulitzer Prize. The novel masterfully portrays middle-class, Irish American Catholics as O'Connor tells the stories of three generations of an Irish American family. In O'Connor's novels, he makes advances with style and theme that would ultimately serve as a bridge between realists like Farrell and modern Irish American authors.

Thomas Flannagan wrote Irish American novels throughout the late 1970s, 1980s, and 1990s in which he directly explores Irish themes through

Irish characters. Flannagan's work has been highly acclaimed. His first novel, *The Year of the French* (1979), has been compared by critics to Tolstoy's *War and Peace*. In *The Year of the French*, Flannagan depicts Ireland's unsuccessful uprising against the British in 1798. Flannagan powerfully describes the strife between impoverished Irish tenant farmers and their wealthy and absent landlords. Flannagan's *The End of the Hunt* (1994) focuses on another uprising for independence by the Irish, the 1916 Easter uprising. In this work of historical fiction, Flannagan's central characters are often directly involved in the fight for an independent Ireland.

Novelist, essayist, and playwright, **William Kennedy** is one of the most influential and prolific Irish American authors of the twentieth century, and Kennedy's Irish heritage plays out directly in his novels. Kennedy, whose literary career spans thirty years with works published well into the 1990s, is considered by many to be the culmination of generations of struggles and progress in Irish American literature. He is "surreal in a way that Farrell was not" and "realistic in a way that O'Connor was not, and he wanted to explore different dimensions of Irish-American life" (Fanning 351). Kennedy's novels address important events in Irish American history, and his characters come from lower- or middle-class Irish American backgrounds only to work their way up in the world and achieve economic success; Kennedy often explores the same characters or different generations of characters. Kennedy's novels include *The Ink Truck* (1969), *Ironweed* (1983), and *Very Old Bones* (1992).

The decades of the 1980s and 1990s and the first years of the twenty-first century have brought even more diversity to the Irish American novel. Even though many Irish American novelists descended from Ireland many generations ago, there are still others who are themselves first-generation immigrants, coming to the United States in the 1980s and 1990s. As the "Irishness" of the Irish American novel continues to come under question, there is a plethora of new work and new criticism published, much of which directly addresses Irish ethnicity. The novels of authors such as **Elizabeth Cullinan** and **Alice McDermott** exemplify the power of the modern Irish American novel.

Elizabeth Cullinan explores the Irish American family and the power of the Catholic Church in her novels *House of Gold* (1971) and *Change of Scene* (1982). Cullinan is noted for her honest but hopeful portrayals of the destructive aspects of Irish American life. Alice McDermott's 1991 novel *At Weddings and Wakes* tells the tale of an Irish American family and examines questions of Irish heritage. McDermott's fourth novel, *Charming Billy* (1998), winner of the National Book Award for that year, tells the story of a charming, Irish American man who dies from alcoholism, and closely examines Irish American culture and what happens when Irish Americans try to break away from it.

But for even those novelists who do not directly address Irish themes or utilize Irish American characters, Ireland remains a "source-country."

Charles Fanning points to Vincent Buckley, poet and son of Irish immigrants who explains the power of Ireland as a "source-country." According the Fanning, Ireland "provides an artist with images, history, language, manners, myth, ways of perceiving, and ways of communicating" (358). Indeed, this may provide a new way of looking at authors of Irish descent but who do not directly explore their ethnicity in their novels.

Although it may be more difficult to determine the Irish dimension in American literature, there continue to be many novelists who directly address the Irish American culture in their works. These novelists explore and redefine their ethnicity by writing about their history, their faith, and their familial networks. The diversity of themes and methods only adds to the strength of the Irish American novel. The Irish American novel has experienced much growth in the one hundred and fifty years since the famine and the formulaic famine fiction. Irish American authors continue into the twenty-first century to have a powerful impact on American fiction. (*See also* Irish American Autobiography)

Further Reading

Casey, Daniel J., and Robert E. Rhodes, eds. *Modern Irish American Fiction: A Reader.* Syracuse, NY: Syracuse UP, 1989.

Fanning, Charles. *The Irish Voice in America: 250 Years of Irish-American Fiction.* 2nd ed. Lexington: UP of Kentucky, 2000.

O'Connell, Shaun. "That Much Credit: Irish-American Identity and Writing." *Massachusetts Review* 41.1–41.2 (2003): 251–68.

Crystal McCage

ISLAS, ARTURO, JR. (1938–1991)   Mexican American novelist, poet, and professor. Arturo Islas Jr. was born to Arturo Islas and Jovita La Farga on May 25, 1938, in El Paso, Texas. His parents named him to honor the memory of the first Arturo Islas, who was an intellectual, poet, and hero shot dead by a Federalist bullet in the Mexican Revolution of 1918. In many ways, Islas lived up to this memory, becoming himself a poet, novelist, and intellectual who cleared new paths of expression and thinking in the late twentieth century.

Born the first of three sons, Islas (or "Sonny," as his family called him) grew up in a racially divided and divisive El Paso during the late 1930s and 1940s. This was a time when signs stating "No Mexicans Allowed" were posted in shop windows and when the public swimming pool was only open to Mexicans just before emptying and cleaning. The Islas family—especially the paternal grandmother, Crecenciana Sandoval Islas—espoused bicultural Anglo and Mexican values and encouraged bilingual Spanish/English fluency, providing Islas with the tools necessary to side-step prejudice from an early age. So, while many of his Mexican American peers struggled with English-only classes in elementary school, Islas excelled. Although Spanish was spoken at home, Islas became an avid reader and writer in English from an early age. If he wasn't under the great oak at the back of the family's house on Almagordo Street, he was to be found at the library or with this grandmother doing homework. Any spare time he had, he spent as an alter boy at the local parish.

Islas's childhood became even more ascetic after he contracted the polio virus just after turning eight years old and just before returning to school after summer break. The polio was caught early enough to curtail an untimely death, but not fast enough to prevent the uneven growth of his legs; even after a surgery during his teenage years, he would not only have to buy two separate pairs of shoes to match the different sizes of his feet, but he would walk with a decided limp for the rest of his life.

Throughout high school, Islas's passion for knowledge continued unabated; he excelled especially at science and English. Although a shorter left leg left him with a limp, this didn't stop him from dancing a mean jitterbug at school socials. His charm and good looks made him extremely popular. Graduating El Paso High as class valedictorian in 1956, Islas became the first Chicano to attend Stanford on an Alfred P. Sloan scholarship. Although Islas entered Stanford with the idea of becoming a neurosurgeon, by the time he graduated in 1960 with a degree in English and minor in religion (Phi Beta Kappa), it was with the firm conviction that he would pursue literary studies and creative writing. That fall, Islas returned to Stanford to embark on his PhD studies in English. Here he studied with Ian Watt, Wallace Stegner, and Yvor Winters—the most influential of his mentors. However, during the height of the **Civil Rights Movement** and worker and student protests worldwide (Mexico, Paris, and Czechoslovakia), he decided to take some time out of the program to explore life outside the ivory tower. After working for more than a year, including as a speech therapist at the Veterans Administration hospital in Menlo Park where Ken Kesey had also worked, Islas suffered from an ulcerated intestine that led to a brush with death and, after three major surgeries, an ileostomy. After recuperating from his surgeries and learning to live with a colostomy bag, Islas finished his PhD and secured a tenure track position in the English department at Stanford in 1971.

During the next five years on the Stanford campus Islas developed pathbreaking courses on Chicano/a literature, established a Chicano/a literary journal, worked to open scholarly spaces for incoming Mexican American undergraduates, and wrote reams of poetry as well as his first novel, *Día de los muertos/Day of the Dead*. Much of his writing during this period not only textures the experiences of a Chicano, but absorbs his full exploration of life as a gay man living in a San Francisco bursting at the seams with same-sex exuberance, an exploration that included cruising and the frequenting of S&M clubs and bath houses. In 1976 the university recognized Islas's creative work and tremendous dedication to teaching and his students by promoting him to associate professor. During this period, he dedicated much time to writing, revising, and sending out the manuscript of *Día de los muertos* to try to secure a contract with a New York publisher. By the early 1980s,

Día de los muertos had been rejected by over thirty different publishers; letters from publishers such as HarperCollins and Farrar Strauss & Giroux attest that editors objected to his excessive use of Spanish (a quick glance at the original manuscript shows the contrary) and/or to his too-strong presence of a gay Chicano protagonist. Islas finally published the novel, much transformed, as *The Rain God* in 1984 with a small local publisher, Alexandrian Press in Palo Alto. It immediately achieved a word-of-mouth eminence within university and high school classrooms and journalistic acclaim in such newspapers as the *San Francisco Chronicle* and the *Los Angeles Times.* In a review for the *El Paso Herald-Post,* fellow El Pasoan (and Stanford PhD alumni) Vicki Ruiz celebrates Islas's shaping of fully developed "poignant women characters . . . who live, love and endure," and concludes, "Whether outspoken or shy, these *mujeres* share an inner strength on which they rely to keep their families together." And friend and professor at the University of California at Santa Cruz, Paul Skenazy, writes in his review for the the *Oakland Tribune* that Islas's autobiographical fiction transforms "family legend into a subtle, quiet fiction that challenges the assumptions we too often bring to ethnic literature [and whose] protest in the novel is more plaintive than outraged." He also notes that it is a novel that ultimately, "unravels the knotted strands of belief, social experience and cultural myth that become destiny." Yale's Héctor V. Calderón compared the novel to Juan Rulfo's *Pedro Paramo* and García Márquez's *One Hundred Years of Solitude,* championing it (and opposing it to **Richard Rodriguez**'s *Hunger of Memory*) for its delicate and complex expression of the Chicano experience.

Islas had finally realized his dream of publishing a Chicano novel that spoke with great subtlety and nuance not only to the ins and outs of a Chicano family's life, but also to the interiority of a gay Chicano. That the novel did well—it was translated into Dutch as *De Regen God*—spurred Islas on to write the next novel. During a visiting professorship (1986–1987) at the University of El Paso, Texas, Islas wrote a draft of the novel he ultimately titled, *La Mollie and the King of Tears.* In a sharp turn from the mythopoetic voice of *The Rain God,* he uses a fast paced first-person narration told from the point of view of Louie Mendoza—a pachuco-styled musician from El Paso living in San Francisco's mission. Islas employs the noir genre to frame Louie's adventures and his coming to terms with his past (a lost daughter), his brother's queer sexuality, and his internalizing of self-destructive values. When Islas sent the manuscript out, he again met with great resistance. The novel was eventually posthumously published in 1996 by the University of New Mexico Press—a press that had rejected the manuscript when he had first sent it.

While Islas's experience with trying to get *La Mollie* published met with dead-ends, *The Rain God* was selling well; too well, in fact, for the small Alexandrian Press to keep up with demand. Islas knew that he needed to reach back out to New York, so he signed on with famed literary agent,

Sandra Dijkstra, who shopped it around for paperback rights and also secured him a contract with William Morrow to write a sequel. With his advance contract (and, later, a contract with Avon to publish *The Rain God* in paperback) in hand, Islas began typing out the story of characters from the fictionalized town of "Del Sapo" (an anagram of El Paso that also playfully translates from the Spanish as "From the Toad") and set earlier (1950s–1960s) than *The Rain God*. Between late 1987 and early 1989, the novel that would be published as *Migrant Souls* took shape. Here, Islas focuses less on the Angel family and the gay character Miguel Chico and more on the women in the family—especially that new generation of women, like Miguel Chico's cousin, Josie Salazar, willing to act and speak against the family's restrictive sexist and racist codes of conduct. The protagonist of *The Rain God* still appears, but less as consciousness that controls the flow of events and more as a secondary figure that can relate to the other outcast characters from the sidelines. Here again, Islas blurs the border between biographical fact and narrative fiction; his intertextual play—figures from *La Mollie* appear as minor characters and French lesbian writer Colette as well as Chicano authors Rolando Hinojosa and Americo Paredes appear in disguised form—serves as a metafictional device that announces its fictionality. Upon publication, *Migrant Souls* proved another success for Islas. It sold out within a month and ranked at the top of *San Francisco Chronicle*'s best-seller list. Anglo and Chicano writers and scholars alike sang its praises. Poets **Denise Levertov** and **Adrienne Rich** gave it their seal of approval. Chicano scholar Roberto Cantú identified it as a dramatic move away from an Us/Them understanding of Chicano and Anglo **race** relations. For Cantú, Islas "advances other narrative dimensions to a higher aesthetic level" to open his readers' eyes to different ways of understanding complex social relations and hybrid cultural phenomenon.

Although mostly known for his two novels, *The Rain God* and *Migrant Souls*, Islas's creative drive and output was immense. We see this not only with the posthumous addition of *La Mollie and the King of Tears* to his opus, but also with the many unpublished short stories, poetry, and beautifully wrought scholarly essays that are now published with Arte Público Press. Though Islas's life was radically cut short when he died of AIDS-related pneumonia on February 15, 1991, his impact as a gay Chicano writer, teacher, and intellectual has been tremendous. Many of his former PhD students, including José David Saldívar and Rafael Pérez-Torres, are now leading scholars in Chicano/a studies. His unyielding drive to confront and overcome a bigoted publishing industry and his dedication to crafting rich and nuanced Chicano/a (gay and straight) poetry and narrative fiction has stretched wide the horizon of the American and world literary landscape. (*See also* Mexican American Gay Literature, Mexican American Novel)

Further Reading

Aldama, Frederick Luis. *Critical Mappings of Arturo Islas's Narrative Fictions.* Tempe, AZ: Bilingual Review P, 2004.

————. *Dancing with Ghosts: A Critical Biography of Arturo Islas.* Berkeley: U of California P, 2004.

————, ed. *Arturo Islas: The Uncollected Works.* Houston, TX: Arte Público Press, 2003.

Frederick Luis Aldama

ITALIAN AMERICAN AUTOBIOGRAPHY   The writing of autobiographies by Italian Americans is quite a recent phenomenon in the scheme of American literary history. The number of published autobiographies is few in comparison to other major ethnic groups and can be attributed to a number of cultural obstacles within southern Italian culture which most Americans of Italian descent had to confront before they could publicly speak and then write about themselves. These obstacles include distrust of the written word (an Italian proverb warns: Pensa molto, parla poco e scrivi meno: Think a lot, speak little and write even less), the immigrant's distrust of social and educational institutions that represent the ruling classes, and a lack of parental encouragement for children to pursue literary careers due to the need to earn money as soon as one is old enough to be employed. Helen Barolini offers an explanation for why Italian immigrants did not encourage their children to write in her "Introduction" to *The Dream Book*, "When you don't read, you don't write. When your frame of reference is a deep distrust of education because it is an attribute of the very classes who have exploited you and your kind for as long as memory carries, then you do not encourage a reverence for books among your children. You teach them the practical arts not the imaginative ones" (4). The institutions of Italy, the Church as well as the state, maintained power over the peasant of southern Italy by controlling literacy. And so, many immigrant families initially distrusted similar cultural institutions in America.

In spite of institutional barriers and the low priority given to writing by Italian Americans on the whole, a number of authors have emerged to document the Italian American experience and create a literary tradition out of a strong oral tradition. In this respect, Italian American writers have much in common with writers who come from Native American and African American traditions. The strong storytelling traditions that we find in Italian American oral culture are filled with tales that give the reasons for traditional rituals and provide information about how to live one's life. They also enable us to examine the evolution of the Italian American's self-concept and its progression into public life.

The idea of speaking of one's self as independent of the community into which one was born is a recent development in Italian American culture. Telling the story of self in public was not part of any public cultural tradition that can be found south of Rome (the region from which come over 80 percent of the Italians who migrated to America). In the Italian oral tradition, the self is suppressed and is not used as a storytelling subject in the communal settings of Italy, where one function of such stories was to create a temporary respite from the harsh realities of everyday peasant life. Traditional stories served both to entertain and to inform the young, while reminding the old of traditions that have endured over the years. Personal information was expected to be kept to one's self.

Although more often than not the models for the structure of Italian American autobiographies come from the dominant Anglo American culture, the content found within those structures is shaped by a home life steeped in oral culture. Very often, American writers of Italian descent point to oral tales as the impetus for the creation of their own stories. In retrospect many of these writers realized that the stories provide the very keys to their self-**identity**. Much of **Jerre Mangione**'s *Mount Allegro* (1943) deals with the stories his family told; **Diane DiPrima** recalls in *Recollections of My Life as a Woman* (2000), her autobiography, that her grandfather Domenico told her stories that have stayed with her. **Gay Talese** recounts quite a number of stories told by his family in *Unto the Sons* (1992).

The earliest immigrant autobiographies document a remaking of the Italian self into an American self. The foreign-born "I" takes on the role of spokesperson for other Italians and argues for acceptance as the "you" that represents the established American who is the autobiographer's model reader. In the immigrant experience we can locate the sources of an autobiographical tradition that pits Italian culture against American culture, creating a tension that drives the narrative. This tension is found in the overriding theme of these immigrant narratives that is the flight to a better world or a promised land, a theme found in many immigrant autobiographies and **African American slave narratives**. Accounts of entering America and facing new challenges for survival become the primary subjects of early autobiographies such as Constantine Panunzio's *The Soul of An Immigrant* (1921) and *Pascal D'Angelo's Son of Italy* (1924), and as-told-to autobiographies such as *Rosa, the Story of an Immigrant* (1970).

Those autobiographies of the children and grandchildren of immigrants, in opposition to immigrant autobiographies, document the remaking of the American self as Italian American. What we often find in the autobiographical work of Italian Americans who are children and grandchildren of the immigrants is an intense politicization of the self. Frequently this politicized expression emerges in combative voices, representative of the intense struggle that Italians faced in becoming Americans.

In *Unto the Sons* (1992) Talese turns to the story of his family's coming to the United States and in the process tries to capture images of the forces of history that have shaped modern Italy and America. His retelling of ancient myths, of St. Paolo di Francesco's miracles and accounts of the evil eye, are combined with excerpts taken right out of his Uncle Antonio Cristiani's diary, interviews of living relatives and research from a number of written sources. What Talese didn't experience himself, he reconstructed using the techniques of fiction writing that scholars point to as his contribution to the concept of New Journalism.

The early chapters focus on Talese's youth, as an "olive skinned" kid in a "freckled-face" Ocean City, New Jersey, during World War II. This section introduces the conflict that second-generation Italian Americans know all too well: "There were many times when I wished that I had been born into a different family, a plain and simple family of impeccable American credentials—a no-secrets, nonwhispering, no-enemy-soldiers family that never received mail from POW camps, or prayed to a painting of an ugly monk, or ate Italian bread with pungent cheese." From there we move into his father's story in Maida, a village in the toe of the Italian boot, and from there to his father's **immigration** to America. The story then shifts back to his great-grandparents. Toward the end Talese becomes a character, like the others in his own book. The book ends by circling back to the opening.

Frank Lentricchia, one of America's foremost literary critics and professor of English at Duke University, has written an autobiographical work titled *The Edge of Night* (1997) that represents a move away from the more traditional approaches found in the *Diaries of Mario Cuomo* (1984), and the autobiographies of Lee Iacocca and Geraldine Ferraro which both employ cowriters. Lentricchia's *Edge* focuses on a period covering a little over a year of his life, refuses to speak for an entire culture, and concentrates on his own personal struggle to form an identity composed of a working-class childhood and middle-class adulthood. What makes Lentricchia's entry into autobiography significant is his use of irony, marking a new and exciting dimension to Italian/American writing. In *The Edge of Night*, with its title taken from a 1950s television soap opera, Lentricchia combines meditations on Yeats and Eliot, subjects of much of his earlier writing, with accounts of his past and imaginative flights into the absurd. The opening epigraph from Pirandello points to the plurality of the individual who is the subject of writing: "A character really has his own life, marked with his own characteristics, by virtue of which he is always some one. Whereas a man . . . a man can be no one." Connected to this is another epigraph, taken from Martin Scorcese's *Raging Bull*, which opens the first section: "Even you don't know what you meant by you." Anyone looking for the "real" Lentricchia will no doubt be frustrated in this work. The "I" in this text is plural; it floats upon wave after wave of memory-made fiction and fiction-made memory. Like the poets of the Italian crepuscular tradition, Lentricchia parodies high culture through popular culture. Through this work he bridges diverse influences of his life; Yeats and Eliot become equals to his grandparents.

Creating an American identity was difficult for Italian American men, but the process for Italian American women would prove even more difficult. Helen Barolini explains that the shift from one culture to another created an identity crisis for the Italian American woman that she then passed on to her children who, "unwilling to give themselves completely to the old ways she transmitted, end up, in their **assimilation**ist hurry, with shame and ambivalence in their behavior and values" ("Introduction" 13). This shame and ambivalence often become the very building blocks of Italian

American women's writing. What we often find in the autobiographical work of Italian American women, especially in the work of those who are children and grandchildren of the immigrants, is an intense politicization of the self, rare even among men in the old world. Frequently this politicized expression emerges in combative voices, representative of the intense struggle Italian American women have waged in forging free selves within the constraints of a patriarchal system.

Though Barolini has not written an autobiography per se, she has provided us with a sense of one through her various essays (many of which are collected in *Chiaro/Scuro* (1999) and with *Festa: Recipes and Recollections* (1988). Her writings reveal the plight of the woman in the immigrant home and create a sense of how traditions both survived and died in the experience of succeeding generations. Barolini believes that the Italian American women can contribute to a revitalization of American literature. And in her "Introduction" to *The Dream Book,* she tells us this might begin with writing about the self in the manner of keeping journals and writing memoirs and autobiographies.

> [Q]uite missing, as yet, are the honest and revealing stories of women's inner lives. . . . Redefining the self not as mirrored by society's expectations but in one's own authentic terms is essential for an integrated literary expression. Autobiography, when it is honest and not a camouflage, can be a powerful declaration of selfhood and a positive step toward establishing an incontrovertible voice. (51–52)

One of the earliest of these powerful autobiographies is Diane di Prima's *Memoirs of a Beatnik* (1969). In the first major autobiography by an Italian American woman, di Prima does something a "good" Italian American woman was not expected to do: she talked about her sex life in public. *Memoirs,* which begins with di Prima recounting the loss of her virginity and closes with her first pregnancy, represents a definitive fracturing of the public silence of Italian American women. In her most recent memoir, *Recollections of My Life as a Woman* (2001), di Prima returns to the troubled times before she left home (when *Memoirs* begins) and struggles to uncover and process the family secrets that have haunted her. Like many other Italian American women writers, di Prima uses the figure of her grandmother as a symbolic source from which she draws her ethnic identity. She weaves her memoir out of journal entries, unsent letters, accounts of dreams, quotes from other writers, poetry, and stories told by her grandfather, a variety of forms which interrupt the narrative flow and remind us that memory comes in pieces.

Louise DeSalvo, a professor of English at Hunter College in New York City, has made a career of connecting writers' lives and their works, and turned her attention toward her own life in *Vertigo: A Memoir* (1996), a powerful testament to the belief that reading can change your life. This "unlikely narrative" is a verbal montage of a life lived in pieces that come together only through writing. A father away at war, a sister's suicide, and a mother's depression and life in an enclave of women-managed households form the basis for DeSalvo's early traumas. She seeks salvation in the local library and fashions her identity through rebellion and pursuit of academic excellence. DeSalvo uses language as a "scalpel" to "exorcise" what has happened in her life. She has learned the secret of writing and how it enables the scribe to live life more fully by living it twice: She writes, "language, I have learned, by writing about this, gives birth to feeling, not the other way around" (105).

Mary Cappello's memoir, *Night Bloom* (1999), opens with a meditation on humor that dissolves into a contemplation of fear. Cappello tells the story of her family, her own lesbian sexuality, and her journey as a professor and writer. She uses excerpts from a journal her mother's father kept to give us a sense of a dialogue across generations and to reveal missing links caused by assimilation.

New versions of Italian American autobiography have come into being through the journalistic essays of Maria Laurino (*Were You Always an Italian* [2000]), the literary criticism of **Edvige Giunta** (*Writing with an Accent* [2002]), and the travel writings of Paul Paolicelli (*Dances with Luigi* [2000] and *Under the Southern Sun* [2003]) and Mark Rotella (*Stolen Figs* [2003]). These writings are characterized by reconsiderations of the Italy of the authors' ancestors and the establishment of new connections to contemporary Italian culture, suggesting that as long as there is an Italy, as long as there is a United States, there will be an Italian American literature and in that literature, a wealth of autobiographies that will continue to redefine what it means to be Italian in the United States.

Further Reading

Boelhower, William. *Immigrant Autobiography in the United States.* Verona, Italy: Essedue Edizioni, 1982.

Gardaphe, Fred L. "Autobiography as Piecework: The Writings of Helen Barolini," *Italian Americans Celebrate Life: The Arts and Popular Culture.* Staten Island, NY: American Italian Historical Association, 1990. 19–27.

Parrino, Maria, ed. *Italian American Autobiographies.* Providence, RI: Italian Americana Publications, 1993.

Patti, Samuel J. "Autobiography: The Roots of the Italian-American Narrative." *Annali d'Italianistica* 4 (1986): 243–48.

Fred Gardaphe

ITALIAN AMERICAN FILM   Italian American cinema comprises both American films *depicting* Italian Americans and American films *directed by* Italian Americans. In more than a century of film production, Italian Americans have been constantly racially typecast, at worst, as lacking emotional restraint, obsessively seeking physical pleasures, and naturally affiliated with organized crime, and, at best, as champions of family allegiance, passionate sentimentality, and ingenious cunning. Invariably the setting of these representations has been the city of New York and its surroundings, where Italians' alleged moral and cultural differences have encouraged both aversion and admiration.

Before the release of D.W. Griffith's *Birth of a Nation* (1915)—the most controversially racist American film of the silent era—the American film industry (still based in New York) devoted several films to Italian characters, ranging from early representations of Mafia-related urban crimes and vendettas as in *The Black Hand* (1907), *The Italian Blood* (1911), *The Musketeers of Pig Alley* (1912), *The Last of the Mafia* (1915), and *The Alien* (1915) to representations of musical talent as in *The Organ Grinder* (1909) and "ethnic" crafts and occupations as in *The Italian Barber* (1910).

After 1915, although the dominant emphasis was still on crime stories, a different tendency emerged. Such sentimental melodramas of love and tragedy set in New York's Lower East Side as *The Italian* (1915; originally titled *The Dago*) and *The Sign of The Rose* (1915), both starring the famous Italian impersonator George Beban, told stories of sudden family death and public injustice that established a first-time emotional identification between American audiences and Italian racial types. In the late 1910s and early 1920s, this unprecedented intimacy allowed for the emergence of new Italian male and female characters engaged in passionate love stories which prepared for the emergence of Hollywood's first superstar, Rudolph Valentino. Daring adventurer and seducer, refined lover and exotic liberator of sexual customs, Valentino expanded the boundaries of romantic love in the direction of sensual playfulness and interchangeability of gender roles in such films as *The Sheik* (1921) and *Blood and Sand* (1922). Biographically coded as an Italian nobleman, protagonist of a Horatio Alger success story in 1920s Hollywood, Valentino was never fully equated with an average immigrant. That he could become an exotic object of sexual desire beyond undue fears of miscegenation tells of a resilient yet malleable racial difference, for years represented as dysfunctional, improper, and even pathetic, and now turned sensually appealing.

Prohibition and, later, the Depression encouraged a new, sinister kind of closeness between the Italian types and the American audiences. At the sound of gunshots and tire-squealing black cars, Mafia stories of brutal violence, social deviancy, and quick prosperity turned the once-appalling gangster into a sympathetic figure. Despite their expected resolution, films like *Little Caesar* (1931), *Scarface* (1932), *The Bowery* (1933), *Fury* (1936), and *Underworld* (1937) challenged sexual and morality codes and offered "American" dreams of self-determination and success to a population oppressed by hardship and indigence. The 1930s also signaled the first appearance of films directed by Italian Americans which were not, however, about Italian Americans. Such interclass romances as Gregory LaCava's *The Age of Consent* (1932) and Frank Capra's *Mr. Deeds Goes to Town* (1936) staged a form of assimilation to American values and lifestyles without any open reference to ethnic difference.

World War II added to the general requirement of **assimilation** that of national and ideological loyalty. In a climate of nativist diffidence fueled by the cold war investigations of the House Un-American Activities Committee (1947), the few film productions of the period depicting Italian Americans were intersections between old gangster films and emerging noir and thriller narratives. In them, a new main character makes his appearance: the private investigator. Not a champion of morality, he—like the gangster—is equally solitary, cynical, and at odds with society's established rules. Several of the films' titles refer most explicitly to a sense of insecurity and internal threat pervading the cities where Italians lived in large number, New York and Chicago: *The Naked City* (1948), *The Street with No Name* (1948), *Dark City* (1950), *Where the Sidewalk Ends* (1950), *The Asphalt Jungle* (1950), *The Naked Street* (1953), and *While the City Sleeps* (1956). A few works drew the line between good and evil *within* New York's Italian American community; two of the most representative were Robert Siodmak's *Cry of the City* (1948) and Henry Hathaway's *Kiss of Death* (1949). More progressive films, such as Nicholas Ray's *Knock on Any Door* (1949), exposed the responsibility that American society as a whole has in the failings of the Italian American community, but many more films continued to look, like a mediocre ethnographer, at the Italian American urban ghetto as a corrupted and criminal environment in and of itself. These films include Howard Hawks's *Big Sleep* (1946), Abraham Polonsky's *Force of Evil* (1949) and *Johnny Allegro* (1949), John Huston's *The Asphalt Jungle* (1950), and William Wyler's *Detective Story* (1951).

The typical Italian trait of family loyalty and attachment to Old World customs signals in this period a dangerous sign of a failure to assimilate as in Joseph Mankiewicz's family drama *House of Strangers* (1949), starring Edward G. Robinson. A similar point, but with an opposite tone, was made in Delbert Mann's *Marty* (1955), starring Ernest Borgnine, winner of an Academy Award for his interpretation of an Italian American butcher whose love life with a non-Italian woman is obstructed by his possessive mother and by the local Italian community.

The 1950s and 1960s witnessed a further development of Italian American ethnic and social marginality. In tune with contemporary portrayals of young alienated antiheroes (Marlon Brando, Montgomery Clift, and James Dean), Italian American characters experienced a repeated mood of isolation, exclusion, and occasional rage, as in the romantic, military melodrama *From Here to the Eternity* (1953) starring Frank Sinatra. The fame of real-life boxers (Primo Carnera, Jake La Motta, and Jimmi Durante) added another setting to the representation of Italian Americans, the questionable and often illicit world of boxing, positioned between the criminal underworld and the world of business as in Robert Wise's *Somebody Up There Likes Me* (1958) with Paul Newman as the unsympathetic Rocky Graziano. Decades later, Sylvester Stallone's *Rocky* (1976) staged a narrative of redemption in contrast to Martin Scorsese's *Raging Bull* (1980), set between the 1940s and the 1960s, which explored instead dynamics of social ambition and self-destruction.

At the end of the 1950s, after a series of celebrated Federal Bureau of Investigation (FBI) arrests of mob leaders in upstate New York, several films and a television series popularized Mafia narratives into a nation-wide film fixation. Mostly set in New York and Chicago, these films included *The Brothers Rico* (1957), *Al Capone* (1959), and *Pay or Die* (1960). Between 1959 and 1963, the ABC network broadcast the successful and lasting television series *The Untouchables,* starring Robert Stack, which was viciously nicknamed either *The Italian Hour* or *Cops and Wops.*

The 1960s cinematic rendering of Italian Americans was still very much geared toward the representation of Italians as dangerous outsiders, not destined to assimilation due to the explosive violence of their social milieu (family and "the street"). Yet some changes began to occur. The city, New York in particular, began to appear as a fast self-renovating modern environment which challenged the Mafia's traditional habits and even broke family allegiances, as in Martin Ritt's *The Brotherhood* (1961); endangered the taboo of interracial attraction, as in John Cassavettes's *Shadows* (1960); or disputed female passivity against family pressures in the intraracial romance *Love with a Proper Stranger* (1964) by Robert Mulligan. Not surprisingly, at the end of the decade, Francis Ford Coppola made *The Rain People* (1969) about a woman, Natalie Ravenna, who refuses her role of wife and mother and decides to leave not just New York, but the East Coast, and freely and aimlessly journey westward.

In the 1970s, the refrain of Italians' self-segregating and anti-assimilationist stance and forthright illegality remained at the center. The best example of the dramatic antagonism between Italian Mafia groups and American legality were Coppola's **Godfather** (1972), starring Al Pacino and Marlon Brando, and *Godfather II* (1977), starring Pacino and Robert De Niro. The former grossed more than a hundred million dollars, a first in the history of American cinema. At the same time, however, American cinema focused on a few characters' new adaptive efforts and ensuing divisions *within* the Italian community. Although still obsessively relying on the platform of the law, *Serpico* (1973) opposed an Italian American detective to Italian American Mafiosi. In the 1970s, another form of separation from old destinies was symbolized by the abandonment of one's own neighborhood or—possibly as an effect of **feminism**—through a reformulation of gender relationships, as in Martin Scorsese's *Mean Streets* (1973), starring De Niro, and John Badham's *Saturday Night Fever* (1977), starring John Travolta; both films engaged in a moral trajectory of punishment and redemption.

Throughout the 1980s and early 1990s, the Italian **ethnicity** became a touristy, consumerist, and very fashionable currency of American culture. Norman Jewison's fairy tale *Moonstruck* (1987), starring Cher and Nicholas Cage, recapitulated, with good craft and in humorous tones, a number of ethnic stereotypes about New York Italian Americans' lifestyles and romantic habits. Between the late 1980s and the early 1990s, a series of original films focused on romance inside and outside the Italian American community. Nancy Savoca's *True Love* (1989) for instance, exposes the impossibility of romantic happiness between two soon-to-be-married Italian Americans from the Bronx in the context of their friendships and family and community ties. In the aftermath of dramatic racial tensions between African Americans and Italian Americans, Spike Lee's *Do the Right Thing* (1989) explored the bonds and differences between an Italian family, which run a pizzeria in the black section of Bedford-Stuyvesant, Brooklyn, and the surrounding black community. Lee would return to the same subject with his 1991 film *Jungle Fever,* centered on the long-prohibited taboo of interracial romance between an Italian woman from Bensonhurst and a black man from Harlem.

The 1990s have somewhat institutionalized the myth of Italian American criminality, with an assortment of approaches ranging from the glamorous to the parodic. With *Goodfellas* (1990) and *Casino* (1993), Scorsese has continued his inside exploration of the New York Italian American criminal community and has exposed the Mafia's efforts to move to legitimate business enterprises, such as the Las Vegas gambling industry—a narrative trajectory also present in Coppola's *The Godfather III* (1990). Rather than portray the experience of a hyphenated American group, these major studio productions have aspired to more generally comment on the greedy and intrinsically corrupted fabric of the American dream. Aside from Mike Newell's daringly unglamorous *Donnie Brasco* (1997), centered on the story of a policeman's undercover penetration into the low circles of New York Mafia, a vast number of films, including parodies and television series, have used Mafia characters and narratives for their profitable aesthetic and commercial marketability. They include the films *The Freshman* (1990), *The Lost Capone* (1990), *Dick Tracy* (1990), *Mob Justice* (1991), *Bugsy* (1991), but also *Hoffa* (1992), *Federal Hill* (1994), and even Woody Allen's *Bullets Over Broadway* (1994), and the television productions *Gotti* (1996), *The Last Don* (1997), and *Bella Mafia* (1998).

Meanwhile, a series of independent productions have offered a wider and more complex picture of the Italian American experience. Quite nonconformist and much more interested in subverting standard narrative conventions are two films, both set in the 1950s: John Turturro's *Mac* (1992), a family story of three brothers working in construction and dealing with old values and new success, and Stanley Tucci's *Big Night* (1996), a family story of two brothers and their restaurant, of traditional gastronomic values and their perhaps necessary commercialization.

Since 1999, the representation of Italians' distinctiveness in American cinema has been dominated by the extraordinary success of the cinematic Home Box Office (HBO) television series **The Sopranos**, developed by Italian American David Chase. Beyond the lightness of such comedies as *Married to the Mob* (1998), starring Michelle Pfeiffer, and *Analyze This* (1999) and

Analyze That (2002), with De Niro and Billy Crystal, *The Sopranos* has regained the artistic gravity of older Coppola and Scorsese films by combining the old components of Italians' excessive *physicality* (violence, sensuousness, excitability), family disputes, and antisocial instincts with a dazzling aesthetic of black humor and metacinematic references. Upgrading, but also following the most constant narrative of Italian American cinema, *The Sopranos* once more has shown that, at least in the movies, Italian Americans continue to have a hard time leaving the old neighborhood, real or imaginary. (*See also* Italian American Stereotypes)

Further Reading

Bondanella, Peter. *Hollywood Italians: Dagos, Palookas, Romeos, Wise Guys, and Sopranos.* New York: Continuum, 2004.

Hoster, Anna Camaiti, and Anthony Tamburri, eds. *Screening Ethnicity: Cinematic Representations of Italian Americans in the United States.* West Lafayette, IN: Bordighera, 2003.

Lavery, David, ed. *This Thing of Ours: Investigating "The Sopranos."* New York: Columbia UP, 2002.

Messenger, Chris. *"The Godfather" and American Culture: How the Corleone's Became "Our Gang."* Albany: State U of New York P, 2002.

Giorgio Bertellini

ITALIAN AMERICAN GAY LITERATURE   Homosexuality has traditionally been perceived in literature and culture as incompatible with family life. Nonetheless, Italian American gay writers have used this incompatibility continuously in their writings and, along with the coming-out novel, sexual exploration and celebration, and testimonial literature emerging from the AIDS crisis, the family remains a principal theme in gay literature. Like other gay writers, Italian American gays have produced literature with themes emerging from the grassroots liberation movement (the Stonewall Rebellion), which marked the first gay riots in American history. The literature of this revolutionary time also includes the subject of sexual exploration in the city and/or pastoral or magical places of retreat, and sexually transgressive writing, including material on pornography and sadomasochism. Post-Stonewall Italian American gay literature often portrays the conjunction between urban gay **identity** and gay male relations to biological families. Writers such as **Felice Picano**, **Robert Ferro**, and **Victor Bumbalo** reflect in their works both a depiction of the adventures of gay life and the relations between gay protagonists and family and mainstream culture.

One of the most influential leaders of the gay movement during the 1970s was Felice Picano. Author of several novels, short stories, and poetry, Picano founded, in 1977, one of the early gay publishing houses in New York City, SeaHorse Press. He collaborated later with two other small gay presses to form Gay Presses of New York (GPNY), and edited an early landmark anthology called *A True Likeness: Lesbian and Gay Writing Today*

(1980). One of the press's most acclaimed publications, **Harvey Fierstein**'s *Torchsong Trilogy,* was instrumental in putting mainstream audiences in contact with gay issues. In 1985, Picano published his first volume of memoirs, *Ambidextrous,* which focuses on his childhood years, sexual awakening, and same-sex experimentation. Following three commercially successful novels, Picano published *The Lure* (1979), a coming-out story and a classic thriller set in Manhattan. An openly gay novel, this work combines the marginal (a homosexual subculture) with the mainstream (a fast-paced thriller), thus creating a generic hybrid which is, as Will Meyerhofer explains, "the finest example of the gay thriller, a classic" (302). Picano's protagonist, Noel Cummings, agrees to go undercover in the gay subculture of bars and clubs in order to trap a serial killer of gays (and others). Experimenting with style and form, Picano brings together recurring themes of coming out, gay lifestyle, and the city as sanctuary. Cummings comes out as gay (falling in love with the very man he agreed to bait), but he also comes to realize that, however controversial the gay subculture might be, it is not corrupt like the New York City Police department and its covert brother, the Mafia.

Picano's work at the gay press and his affiliation with the Violet Quill Club (a gay writers' club that included such members as Robert Ferro, Andrew Holleran, and Edmund White) helped create a post-Stonewall era in which homosexuality was placed at the center of literary focus. Robert Ferro's work also emerges from the 1970s with its unapologetic focus on gay identity. His autobiographical fiction (published in the last five years of his life) includes portrayals of homosexual integration within an Italian American family, and insists on the consistency between homosexual love and ethnic family unity. In Ferro's *The Family of Max Desir* (1983), the title character, a gay man in his thirties, seeks acceptance from his Italian American family regarding his relationship to Nick, his lover. As in many Italian American narratives, the death of the mother produces a domestic crisis, which ultimately culminates in the father's complicated acceptance of his son's homosexuality. *The Blue Star* (1985) and *Second Son* (1988) continue to use themes from gay literature (e.g., coming-of-age) alongside Italian American themes (e.g., using Italy as a geographical location of romance and sanctuary).

Ferro's untimely death from AIDS-related illness in 1988 was tragic, the epidemic itself shifting artistic and behavioral priorities in gay communities throughout the country. Victor Bumbalo's work as a playwright in the early 1990s is a case in point. The plays *Adam and the Experts* (1990) and *What Are Tuesdays Like?* (1994) focus on the AIDS epidemic and its effect on the gay community. Shifting from an earlier focus on Italian American family in humorous conflict (in his 1984 *Niagara Falls and Other Plays*), Bumbalo uses the forum of the theater to counter images of passivity often associated with what was then a death sentence. Instead, Bumbalo produces testimonial work, or, as Adam puts it in *Adam and the Experts,* "I want the universe to know that I was here. That we all were here."

Philip Gambone's 1991 collection of short stories, *The Language We Use up Here,* also examines AIDS, but includes as well topics of concern to gay men in their thirties. Gambone has published work that has appeared in many anthologies, including the *Men on Men* series edited by George Stambolian (which also included the late Sam D'Allesandro's stories about AIDS). Writing autobiographically in *Fuori: Essays by Italian/American Lesbians and Gays* (1996), Gambone explores how his ethnic self—being raised in the language of the *gentiluomo* (gentleman)—intersects with the adopted language of the urban gay male: "It's a polyglot tongue . . . contain[ing] the coarse saltiness of my grandmother's Neapolitan carnality . . . [and] all the dialects of Gay Speak: the queeny, the bitchy, the witty, the campy, the trashy, the stylish" (80).

Recent writing such as Jim Provenzano's book on gay sexuality and wrestling (*Pins,* 1999), Philip Gambone's novel *Beijing* (2003), and the short works featured in *Hey Paesan! Writing by Lesbians and Gay Men of Italian Descent* (1999), which includes Rob Nixon's "Avondale," Paul Attinello's "Reitalianization," and Tommi Avicolli Mecca's "Call Me Latin," reflect a complex understanding of gay male identity. Neither wholly assimilationist in their desire be accepted by mainstream culture nor completely transgressive in their marginality, gay Italian American writers continue to explore gay sexuality in multiple contexts with the continued influence of cultural identity in the mix.

Further Reading

Capone, Giovanna (Janet), Denise Nico Leto, and Tommi Avicolli Mecca, eds. *Hey Paesan! Writing by Lesbians and Gay Men of Italian Descent.* Oakland, CA: Three Guineas Press, 1999.

Dewey, Joseph. "Robert Ferro." *Contemporary Gay American Novelists: A Bio-Bibliographical Critical Sourcebook.* Ed. Emmanuel S. Nelson. Westport, CT: Greenwood Press, 1993. 128–39.

Massa, Suzanne Hotte. "Victor Bumbalo." *Contemporary Gay American Poets and Playwrights: An A-to-Z Guide.* Ed. Emmanuel S. Nelson. Westport, CT: Greenwood Press, 2003.

Meyerhofer, Will. "Felice Picano." *Contemporary Gay American Novelists: A Bio-Bibliographical Critical Sourcebook.* Ed. Emmanuel S. Nelson. Westport, CT: Greenwood Press, 1993. 298–308.

Tamburri, Anthony Julian, ed. *Fuori: Essays by Italian/American Lesbians and Gays.* West Lafayette, IN: Bordighera, 1996.

Woods, Gregory. *A History of Gay Literature: The Male Tradition.* New Haven, CT: Yale UP, 1998.

Mary Jo Bona

ITALIAN AMERICAN HUMOR One important feature of Italian American humor is the recent addition of an Italian American figure to the time-honored tradition in American literature of the comic rustic philosopher. Ethnic writers such as Finley Peter Dunne and Langston Hughes have long been associated with this time-honored tradition in American literature (begun by such figures as Samuel Clemens, Washington Irving, and Seba Smith), and the literary character type became transformed from nineteenth-century rustic comic to twentieth-century urban/ethnic social critic. In the 1980s and 1990s, Fred L. Gardaphe's Italian American comic narrator "Moustache Pete" or "Baffo Pietro" directed his own comic barbs at mainstream American society. Through this comic figure, whose pithy sayings are compiled in the 1999 book, *Moustache Pete Is Dead: Evviva Baffo Pietro*, Gardaphe's satiric attacks on a number of social ills, such as the exploitation of labor, invasion of privacy, and greed, are voiced. Like all of his non-Italian predecessors, Baffo Pietro pokes fun at American icons using the dialect of his native tongue, punning on the Fourth of July as "Il Forte Gelato" or "strong ice cream."

Postmodern Italian American authors take into account this notion of the ethnic comic narrator as well. For example, **Don DeLillo**'s post–cold war epic *Underworld* features the humorous scene of Matt Costanza relating fond memories of his brother reading comics to him and his neighborhood friends, which forms a metaphor for the ethnic comic narrator as envisioned by DeLillo. Nick reads action comics to the neighborhood children while seated on the toilet, acting out voices and sound effects to thrill and entertain them; the most memorable aspect of Nick's performance is the scatological and involuntary noise he makes on the "glory seat" (210). This "funniest sound in nature, sending a happy awe across the faces of his listeners" makes Nick, narrator of both these comics and a significant portion of this novel, a comedian. And the location of his comic performance, in a poor New York City neighborhood populated primarily with Italian Americans and other ethnics, renders Nick a representative ethnic comic narrator. For, as the text explains, "Who else would read the comics to them?" (210) Like such well-known **trickster** figures as **Finley Peter Dunne**'s Martin Dooley, Fred Gardaphe's Baffo Pietro, and **Langston Hughes**'s Jesse P. Simple, DeLillo's ethnic narrator is as marginalized as his audience of children crouching in the tenement bathroom. The fact that Nick reads sitting on the toilet demonstrates to readers that corresponding life experiences of human fallibility create the strongest attraction and help to form a real bond between the comic narrator and his readers and is "better than anything he might deliver from the panelled pages." This ethnic audience's "happy awe" is an empirical identification with the comic figure who involuntarily reveals the flawed humanity he shares with his audience.

Most Italian American fiction shows shifting rhetorical uses of humor, from pre-World War II portrayals of self-mockery and self-approbation in **Pietro Di Donato** and **Jerre Mangione** respectively, to the comic social critique achieved by later figures such as Susan J. Leonardi. A self-confessed "half-and-half," Jerre Mangione mocks the provincial habits of Italian Americans in his book *Mount Allegro.* Bringing to light such familiar figures as the black-clad and veiled feuding Italian American aunts who are not speaking to each other anymore, Mangione's text demonstrates the capacity of Italian Americans to laugh at themselves and reinforces stereotypes of ridiculous behavior. Di Donato also both mocks Italian American figures in 1939's *Christ in Concrete,* and portrays them as mocking each other. Poverty-stricken Italian laborers and midwives alike drink and party in Di Donato's urban exposé, calling each other "Snout-Nose," "holes askew," and much worse.

Later Italian American authors turned their satirical sights to the world outside little Italy. For her part, Leonardi poignantly and humorously confesses the struggle Italian American women experience by not conforming to the stereotype of the "White, thin, Anglo-Saxon, pretty, popular type of girl . . . God likes best" (Leonardi 229) in her tale of a young girl's call to life in the sisterhood, *Bernie Becomes a Nun.* This tendency to focus outside the immediate community contrasts with self-mocking uses of humor found in earlier Italian American authors.

Finally, postmodern Italian American authors such as Michael Martone bring the self-reflective and critical tendency in Italian American humor around full circle. They call into question the processes through which the idea of Italian American **identity** is formed. Martone represents, through surreal and exaggerated juxtaposition, the haphazard forces and processes which he contends form Italian American culture. We see this suggestion in his short story "Ten Little Italies of Indiana." "Settled by Bakunin Anarchists fleeing Boston in the wake of the Sacco and Vanzetti trial[s], the Italian community of Columbus stealthily blended in with the Hoosier natives of this town by dyeing their hair blond and changing all family names, en masse, to 'Streeter'" (23). The opening images are evocative: the fallout of the Sacco and Vanzetti trials was indeed to make Italian Americans paranoid about their ethnic safety; however, the contrast between the ironic adverb "stealthily" and the bizarre spectacle (even if it is an historical fact) of a large gathering of Italian American bleached blondes named Streeter is quite hilarious. Martone's joke suggests that the more one tries to mask ethnic identity, the more obvious it becomes. There is a juxtaposition of forces and activities above that creates a chaotic, at best serendipidous, sense of the Italian American community.

Further Reading

Di Donato, Pietro. *Christ in Concrete.* Indianapolis: Bobbs-Merrill, 1939.

Gardaphe, Fred L. *Moustache Pete Is Dead: Evivva Baffo Pietro.* West Lafayette IN: Bordighera Press, 1997.

Giaimo, Paul S. "Ethnic Outsiders: The Hyper-Ethnicized Narrator in Langston Hughes and Fred L. Gardaphé." *MELUS* 28.3 (2003): 133–48.

Leonardi, Susan J. "Bernie Becomes a Nun." *The Voices We Carry: Recent Italian-American Women's Fiction.* Ed. Mary Jo Bona. New York: Guernica, 1994. 205–32.

Mangione, Jerre. *Mount Allegro.* Boston: Houghton-Mifflin, 1948.

Paul Giaimo

ITALIAN AMERICAN LESBIAN LITERATURE

Lesbian writing, like gay writing, did not achieve cultural visibility until the 1960s and early

1970s, transcending the pre-Stonewall era of portraying lesbians as self-hating and tragic figures. Likewise, Italian American women writers, responding to the liberation movements for women and blacks, began investigating the silences of their cultural group often within the context of their own families. Like other lesbian writers of the 1970s and 1980s, Italian American lesbians began also to define a community unto themselves. In this sanctuary, women were free to develop an alternative reality separate from heterosexual norms, but more culturally visible than the world of bars and private homes necessary for lesbians in the 1950s and 1960s. Three writers of fiction feature characters whose lesbianism is a salient feature of **identity**, but their narratives move beyond traditional lesbian novels in which the awakening process and the acceptance of one's lesbian identity are central.

Dodici Azpadu's novel *Saturday Night in the Prime of Life* (1983) examines the dire consequences of naming oneself as lesbian in an Italian American family. Symbolically annihilating the lesbian daughter, the family in Azpadu's novel suffers as a result of their old-world Sicilian mother's studious avoidance of her first-born daughter, the one family member left who can speak the Sicilian dialect with her mother. Although *Goat Song* (1984), Azpadu's second novel, does not use ethnic markers to identify one of the lesbians, the racial term "olive" peppers Azpadu's fiction and her decision to make this lesbian an orphan without knowledge of ethnic origins may be the author's way of exploring racial ambiguity and loss of homeland for Sicilians. In a similar manner, Rachel Guido deVries's 1986 novel, *Tender Warriors*, examines the issue of lesbianism from the vantage point of an Italian American family. In this book, the lesbian daughter is reintegrated into the family after other members have been estranged following the mother's death. The lesbian character is neither the center of the novel nor its narrative consciousness, suggesting deVries's interest in the interdependence of many Italian American families.

One of the most prolific and experimental writers, **Carole Maso,** is the author of six novels and three nonfiction works. In Maso's first novel, *Ghost Dance* (1986), the author incorporates Italian American identity and lesbianism as interlacing strands in a narrative about the complicated identity of the first-person narrator, Vanessa Turin. This novel is insistently concerned with the protagonist's family, as she must invent a story to make sense of her mother's untimely death and her father's later disappearance. Subsequent novels, especially *The Art Lover* (1990), *The American Woman in the Chinese Hat* (1995), and *Aureole* (1996), continue the nontraditional narrative structure and examine both lesbian and gay identities. For Maso, the erotic is central to her identity as a writer and her endless linguistic experiments in prose. Overtly sexual, *Aureole* is Maso's most compelling lesbian work, resisting categorization as Maso explains in her book of essays, *Break Every Rule: Essays on Language, Longing, & Moments of Desire* (2000): "The impulse in these pieces is to free myself from constraint, from preconception. The flight is from boundaries—linguistic, sexual, intellectual. The longing is for freedom" (116).

Perhaps the longing for freedom also manifests itself in the production of anthologies, collections, and mixed-genre work, all of which have shaped the writings of lesbians. For example, anthologies such as *Fuori: Essays by Italian American Lesbians and Gays* (1996) and *Hey Paesan!: Writing by Lesbians and Gay Men of Italian Descent* (1999) bring together short works by such Italian American lesbian writers as Giovanna Capone, Theresa Carilli, Maria Fama, Vittoria Repetto, Denise Nico Leto, Mary Russo Demetrick, **Mary Cappello**, and **Mary Saracino**. Saracino's 1993 novel, *No Matter What*, examines the illicit love a mother experiences with a Catholic priest. Mary Cappello has published a memoir, *Night Bloom*, conjoining theory and poetic prose about her Italian American family, especially her grandfather, whose own poetic journal (in English and Italian) reveals the unabated poverty and suffering of immigrants during the Depression. Mary Bucci Bush, whose short story "Planting" appears in *The Voices We Carry: Recent Italian American Women's Fiction*, earlier published a collection of stories, *A Place of Light* (1990), which portrays the lives of rural working-class families in upstate New York. Italian American lesbian writers often use sexual identity as the starting point for their examination of Italian American history, working-class lives, linguistic experimentation, and cultural marginalization.

Liberally showcased in *Hey Paesan!* and the 1990 issue of *Sinister Wisdom*, Italian American lesbian poets have gone on to publish books of poetry such as Rachel Guido deVries's *How to Sing to a Dago* and Maria Fama's *Identification*. In her effort to make audible the voices of Italian American women poets, Rose Romano founded and published the journal *la bella figura* (1988–92), culminating in her anthology, *la bella figura: a choice* (1993). In her first book of poetry, *Vendetta*, Romano makes a life-sustaining connection between the heritage of her Italian grandmother, sitting at the "head of the table," her "own boss," and lesbian identity; both are Italian American, heads of households, their own bosses ("To Show Respect"). In her second book, *The Wop Factor*, Romano recaptures the painful historical episodes of violence against Italian Americans in such poems as "Dago Street" and "The Family Dialect." Celebratory poems such as "There Is Nothing in This World as Wonderful as an Italian-American Lesbian," exposes the similarities between generations, males and females, and heterosexuality and homosexuality.

Sexual identity continues to inform the voices of many works of Italian American lesbians. They include Sandra Scoppettone's portrayal of a lesbian detective in *Everything You Have Is Mine* (1991), Mary Beth Caschetta's stories of complicated relations within family and community (including Italian immigrant voices) in *Lucy on the West Coast* (1996), and Diane DiMassa's angry and violent Hothead in her cartoon series, *Hothead Paisan: Homicidal Lesbian Terrorist* (1999). For Italian American women, the topic of lesbian sexuality most often intersects (and conflicts) with patriarchal family identity. Finding a voice within both families—sexual and familial—remains a preeminent strategy of liberation for these writers.

Further Reading

Bona, Mary Jo. *The Voices We Carry: Recent Italian American Women's Fiction.* Montreal: Guernica, 1994.

Capone, Givoanna (Janet), Denise Nico Leto, and Tommi Avicolli Mecca, eds. *Hey Paesan!: Writing by Lesbians and Gay Men of Italian Descent.* Oakland, CA: Three Guineas Press, 1999.

Capone, Janet, and Denise Leto, eds. "Il viaggo delle donne." *Sinister Wisdom* 41 (Summer/Fall, 1990). Special Issue.

Carilli, Theresa. *Women as Lovers: Two Plays.* Toronto: Guernica, 1996.

Tamburri, Anthony Julian, ed. *Fuori: Essays by Italian/American Lesbians and Gays.* West Lafayette, IN: Bordighera, 1996.

Mary Jo Bona

ITALIAN AMERICAN NOVEL In 1993 novelist and essayist Gay Talese (*Unto the Sons,* 1992) generated considerable controversy by publishing an essay in the *New York Times Book Review* asking "Where Are the Italian American Novelists?" A number of scholars have worked tirelessly to refute the absence implicit in Talese's question, and have suggested various paradigms for the development of this tradition; **Fred L. Gardaphé**, for example, has suggested one theoretical structure based on philosopher Vico's notion of history, and **Helen Barolini** offers one based, in part, on Karen Horney's psychoanalytic work, asserting that self-alienation leads to development and achievement rather than repression. Whatever the paradigm, however, all agree that developing a culturally specific approach to analyzing the Italian American novel is imperative.

As noted by many scholars, Italian American literature finds its roots in a primarily oral tradition, which immigrants brought to America in the form of proverbs, stories, and songs. The earliest works composed by Italian Americans closely identified with oral culture and *la via vecchia* (the old way); autobiography, such as Constantine Panunzio's *Soul of an Immigrant* (1921) and *Rosa: The Life of an Italian Immigrant* (1970), and autobiographical fiction focused on the content and themes which grow directly and immediately out of the immigrant experience. In her seminal study *The Italian American Novel: A Document of Two Cultures* (1974), Rose Basile Green argues that the first literary "steps" are *necessarily* autobiographical. The motif of journey and the struggles associated with finding one's way in a culture that is often, at best, tepid in its acceptance, at worst, openly hostile, formed the narrative impetus of these early works. The next dominant phase comes out of the second generation—the children of immigrants—torn between the security of *l'ordine della famiglia* (literally, the order of the family, with all of the traditional values that implies) and the seductions of **assimilation**. In these narratives, generational conflict and miscommunication, self-hatred, and shame are dominant themes. Finally, we see third- and later-generation writers of Italian descent fashioning a new response to their *italianità*, a response based on what Richard Gambino in *Blood of My Blood* terms "creative **ethnicity**"—a move of self-determination, away from direct engagement with immigrant experience and conflict. Frequently, the novels of these writers are characterized by a desire to "recover" the past and to reconnect with the lives of ancestors and their traditions.

Establishing a home and a new identity is a motif common to many immigrant narratives; countless narratives, poems, dramas, and autobiographies explore the exhilarating and painful aspects of this quest for Italian American writers. However, the relationship of Italian American narrative's tradition to "**canon**ical" or "mainstream" American literature is a difficult one to determine. Many scholars of Italian American literature have cited repeatedly the frustration of efforts to identify Italian American narrative tradition and to produce critical scholarship in the face of "silence"—both the imperative within Italian American culture itself, and that of the publishing industry and academia. The catch-22 of publication for Italian American writers is that the writing must look "ethnic" in order to garner any interest, yet is frequently dismissed as narrow or parochial; thus, many early narratives within the tradition went out of print almost immediately. Many preeminent twentieth-century American critics, such as **Irving Howe** and **Leslie Fiedler**, often dismissed literature by and about immigrants with the label of "local color" or "regional" literature, consigning it to the bin of "minor" works in the literary canon. Additionally, the lack of literacy among the first waves of Italian immigrants, coupled with a variety of economic, social, cultural, and psychological barriers (discussed extensively by Barolini in the introduction to *The Dream Book: An Anthology of Writings by Italian American Women* [1985]), ensured Italian American writers a slow entrance into the American literary tradition. Models for the earliest writers were difficult to find, in part because so many of them lived in cultural and economic circumstances that did not encourage reading; for most immigrants, culture (including learning more English than was necessary for basic survival and reading for pleasure) was a luxury to be sacrificed to the imperative for financial security. Early works such as Bernardino Ciambelli's *I Misteri di Mulberry Street* (1893) were composed with an American audience in mind, setting forth stereotyped images of Italian immigrants. More realistic portrayals of Italian immigrant experience, such as Luigi Ventura's *Peppino* (1913), had a difficult time securing an audience and quickly went out of print. Nonetheless, even the earliest autobiographical works demonstrate connections to the Anglo American literary tradition; Panunzio, for example, thematically informs each chapter of his autobiography with an epigraph taken from works by canonical writers such as Matthew Arnold and William Wordsworth. Similarly, many Italian American writers cite encounters with canonical figures such as Dostoevsky, Charles Dickens, Ernest Hemingway, and William Faulkner as significant to their writing. Many contemporary Italian American novelists also cite authorial kinship with writers from other ethnic traditions, seeing in the formation of the canons of Jewish American, African American, Asian American, and Chicano/a literature a model for their own writing.

One of the earliest narratives to meet with some degree of popular and critical success is Garibaldi LaPolla's *The Grand Gennaro* (1935). Set in Italian American Harlem of the 1890s, this narrative confronts the immigrant drive for American wealth and success and its often heavy price; Gennaro Accuci, the novel's eponymous protagonist, battles his way to economic success and political power, only to be murdered by a friend/business associate whom he had cheated. Another important early work, in terms of both its critical and popular success, is **Pietro di Donato**'s *Christ in Concrete* (1939), a highly autobiographical narrative of the gruesome death of Geremio, an Italian bricklayer, on a construction site and its consequences for his sensitive, intelligent eldest son, Paul. The best known of more recent narratives is probably **Mario Puzo**'s ***The Godfather*** (1969); although its popular success earned Puzo a powerful place in the literary world, the problems it poses as a romanticized representation of the Mafia stereotype have been the subject of much critical debate. Other significant figures include **John Fante** (*Wait Until Spring, Bandini* [1938]), and postmodern figures such as **Don DeLillo** (*Americana* [1971], *Libra* [1988], and *Underworld* [1997]) and **Gilbert Sorrentino** (*The Sky Changes* [1966] and *Blue Pastoral* [1983]).

A distinctly female narrative tradition also exists, though many works, such as Antonia Pola's *Who Can Buy the Stars?* (1957), **Octavia Waldo**'s *A Cup of the Sun* (1961), **Diana Cavallo**'s *A Bridge of Leaves* (1961), and Marion Benasutti's *No Steady Job for Papa* (1966) went out of print for lack of an audience. One of the earliest writers identified with this tradition is Frances Vinciguerra (born in Sicily in 1903), who published her first work, an historical novel titled *The Ardent Flame* (1927), under the anglicized name **Frances Winwar. Mari Tomasi**, though producing only two novels, is a powerful figure in the formation of this tradition. Her first novel, *Deep Grow the Roots* (1940), is distinctive in that it is set entirely in Italy, narrating the lives of rural inhabitants in the period just prior to Mussolini's invasion of Ethiopia; it was named in the *New York Herald Tribune*'s list of the ten best novels of the year, and led to Tomasi's inclusion in the American Booksellers' Association's list of the ten most promising new writers. Her second novel, *Like Lesser Gods* (1949), was inspired by the community of immigrant stonecutters in Tomasi's hometown of Barre, Vermont. Helen Barolini, who has devoted considerable effort to claiming a place for Italian American literature, has written two novels, *Umbertina* (1979) and *Love in the Middle Ages* (1986). The former is regarded as the first Italian American novel by a woman that explicitly treats the intertwining themes of gender and ethnic identity; employing the conventions of the sweeping historical epic, she chronicles the lives of four generations of Italian American women and traces out the political, social, and economic factors that shape their lives. Contemporary figures include **Tina DeRosa** (*Paper Fish* [1980]), **Carole**

Maso (*Ghost Dance* [1986]), Josephine Gattuso Hendin (*The Right Thing to Do* [1988]), Agnes Rossi (*Split Skirt* [1994]), and **Rita Ciresi** (*Blue Italian* [1996]).

The majority of these writers came directly out of or descended from the massive wave of southern Italian **immigration** during the late nineteenth and early twentieth centuries, and it is the cultural, social, and political history of these people most evident in Italian American narrative. Italy was not unified as a nation until the *Risorgimento* (uprising) succeeded in ending 200 years of Bourbon rule over the areas south of Rome—collectively known as the *Mezzogiorno*—in 1860. The goal of the uprising and the subsequent unification of southern and northern Italy was to end centuries of the brutal oppression of the South, as well as to develop a national **identity** for what had previously been a loose federation of regions marked by significant cultural and political differences. Ironically, however, unification gave the industrialized North, the center of the unification movement, greater control over the agricultural South, inflicting a new set of oppressive power structures to bear down on the *contadini*'s already difficult lives. Additionally, Northern Italians regarded themselves as physically, culturally, linguistically, intellectually, and morally superior to Southerners. Thus, Southern Italians began emigrating in droves; in *La Storia: Five Centuries of the Italian American Experience*, Ben Morreale and Jerre Mangione note that between about 1870 and 1920, Italy's population was reduced by nearly a third.

In addition to these historical conditions, a number of significant cultural values have shaped Italian experience and the narratives growing out of Italian American experience. The first is the strength and integrity of the family, the bulwark against the oppressive powers of Italy's political and religious institutions; families perform the same function for immigrants foundering in a culture of rugged individualism, prejudice, and economic struggle. The peculiar nature of Italian Catholicism is also worth noting; pagan in its roots and deeply sensual in its expression, it conflicts with the more ascetic version favored by Irish Catholics in America, a conflict that informs a number of the novels, which not only represent the real struggles between Irish and Italian immigrants, but also the larger struggle to assimilate into American culture. Next, work as a measure of moral worth and commitment to Americanization is a significant theme; despite massive documentation of the commitment of Italian immigrants to the value of hard work, images of Italians as lazy, drunken, hotheaded criminals and anarchists persist in popular culture, and writers construct narratives to contradict these negative images. Finally, education played a primary role in the immigrant experience; most Italian immigrants were torn between the recognition of education's role in social and economic success and a deep distrust of its assimilative powers, which usurp the family, and of words and intellectual life in general. The complex net formed by these circumstances and values gives the Italian American narrative its shape. (*See also* Italian American Autobiography, Italian American Stereotypes)

Further Reading

Bona, Mary Jo. *Claiming a Tradition: Italian American Women Writers.* Carbondale: Southern Illinois UP, 1999.

Cammett, John M., ed. *The Italian American Novel.* Proceedings of the Second Annual American Italian Historical Association Conference. Staten Island, NY: American Italian Historical Association, 1969.

Gardaphé, Fred L. *Italian Signs, American Streets: The Evolution of Italian American Narrative.* Durham, NC: Duke UP, 1996.

Giunta, Edvige. *Writing with an Accent: Contemporary Italian American Women Authors.* New York: Palgrave, 2002.

Green, Rose Basile. *The Italian-American Novel: A Document of the Interaction between Two Cultures.* Cranbury, NJ: Associated UP, 1974.

Peragallo, Olga. *Italian-American Authors and Their Contribution to American Literature.* New York: S. F. Vanni, 1949.

Pipino, Mary Frances. *"I Have Found My Voice": The Italian-American Woman Writer.* New York: Peter Lang, 2000.

Tamburri, Anthony Julian. "In (Re)cognition of the Italian/American Writer: And Categories." *Differentia* 6–7 (Spring–Summer 1994): 9–32.

Viscusi, Robert. "A Literature Considering Itself: The Allegory of Italian America." *From the Margin: Writings in Italian Americana.* Ed. Anthony Julian Tamburri, Paolo Giordano, and Fred L. Gardaphé. West Lafayette, IN: Purdue UP, 1991. 265–81.

Mimi Pipino

ITALIAN AMERICAN POETRY   In reading Italian American poetry though a prismatic lens that allows us to see the different nooks and crannies of our **ethnicity** as it has changed over decades and across generations, we see it transform from a dualistic discourse to a multifaceted conglomeration of cultural processes transgressing Italian, American, and Italian American cultural borders. As a category then, Italian American poetry spans the history of Italians in the United States, from 1880 to the present, highlighting the various waves of **immigration**, acculturation, and **assimilation** that Italians have experienced. Italian American poetry thus figures as an ongoing written enterprise that establishes an imagistic repertoire of signs, at times *sui generis,* creating variations that represent different versions—dependent on one's generation, gender, and/or socioeconomic condition—of what can be perceived as the Italian American signified.

Indeed, one might even make an attempt to see its origins dating back to the early part of the nineteenth century in verses included in Joseph Rocchietto's prosimetrum *Lorenzo and Oonalaska* (1935). But the gap between that moment and what we readily consider the beginnings is substantial.

A self-described "pick and shovel poet," Pascal D'Angelo (1894–1934) represents one of the first-generation poets to overcome the trials and tribulations of immigrant life. Learning English on his own, he composed some of the first poetic renditions of the Italian American immigrant experience. Written mostly in free verse, his poetry combines notions of the lofty with the mundane in a swirl of images contrasting the idealized with the harsh reality of daily life.

Emanuale Carnevali (1897–1944) is one of the first to articulate the conflict of hopes and disappointment often confronted by members of the immigrant generation. Unlike D'Angelo, Carnevali met with literary success early on. His poetry articulates his headlong collision with his adopted culture. Unable to overcome the daily travails of the immigrant situation, Carnevali returned to Italy after less than a decade spent in the United States. "Sorrow's Headquarters," "The Return," and "The Sick Man's Hymn" exemplify his disillusioned spirit. Carnevali's poetry places him among the notable poets, especially those nonconventional writers of the American avant-garde; his disdain for rhetorical conventions is reflected specifically in his lyric style of free verse. Often courted by the cultural elites, his poetry appeared in numerous journals including *Poetry*.

From the coal mines of Canada and the United States to the seminary (earning a BA) to radical social politics (e.g., Lawrence textile strike of 1912), **Arturo Giovannitti** (1884–1959) was considered in his time to be the greatest Italian American poet. His only collection of poetry, *Arrows in the Gale* (1914), laments the exploitation of immigrants and the injustices placed upon the working class. Although some of Giovannitti's poetry reflects a formal style, his compositions in *Arrows in the Gale* are written in free verse in long rhythmic prose paragraphs, accompanied by an impelling, austere, realistic style.

The most celebrated of Italian American poets, John Ciardi (1916–86), the son of immigrants, was the first Italian American writer to rise to national prominence. Not explicitly Italian American, Ciardi's early writings nevertheless exhibited general sentiments readily associated with his ethnic group. The title of his first collection, *Homeward to America* (1940), winner of a Hopewell Award in 1939, sets up the dichotomy of the old and the new worlds, where America is now home. Further still, the overall collection questions the possibility of a bright future while fearing the darkness that may await. His Italian heritage may also be seen in his translation of Dante's *Divine Comedy*, which has few equals still for its lyrical quality in English. With close to fifty books of poetry, criticism, and translations, Ciardi made an indelible mark on American literature. His vademecum *How Does a Poem Mean?* remains fundamental reading for an understanding of the poetic process. Full-time lecturer and radio commentator, Ciardi also edited the *Saturday Review*, where the early poetry of Felix Stefanile and Lewis Turco appeared.

Felix Stefanile (1920–) and Lewis Turco (1934–) are two more award-winning representatives of immigrant offspring who have sunk roots in the American literary landscape. Stefanile's career as a poet, prose writer, essayist, and translator spans over fifty years. From *River Full of Craft* (1956) to *The Country of Absence* (2000), Stefanile's poetry has consistently sung the highs and lows of the human condition in venues such as the *Saturday*

Review, Poetry, Sewanee Review, and the *Formalist.* Be it the fig tree, the aroma of fresh bread, or the bocce ball court on Lewis Avenue, one finds references to his Italian heritage and its encounters with U.S. mainstream culture. Stefanile found himself at the forefront of the New Formalist movement in U.S. poetry, as his editorially mercurial magazine, *Sparrow* (1954–2000), dedicated its last decade to the sonnet. Like other talented poets of Italian descent (Jonathan Galassi, Michael Palma, and Stephen Sartarelli), Stefanile has translated numerous Italian poets into English, including Cecco Angiolieri, the Futurists, and Umberto Saba.

With a dozen poetry books to his name, Lewis Turco is among the most prolific of first-generation, U.S.-born poets. Turco's verse is informed by a strong dose of opposition that, early in his career, revolves around a discourse on both a personal and literary identity. Turco blends his strident concern for language with his much-impassioned content; metaphor remains an important key in this regard for his readers. Though not explicitly Italianate, "The Ice House," for instance, may be seen as a metaphorical rendition of the disappearing Italian America he knew as a child. Turco has also written books of literary criticism and "how to" books on poetry (*The New Book of Forms* [1968/1986]) and fiction (*Dialogue* [1989]).

Jerome Mazzaro figures in this category of formalist writing, being a type of self-reflexive traditionalist with a parallel career in critical writing. Other members of this generation worthy of inclusion in an Italian American inventory are John Tagliabue and Gerard Malanga. Whereas Tagliabue periodically invests his poetry with imagery of his Italian American-ness, analogous to Stefanile, Malanga is much more reserved with respect to an explicit ethnic repertoire; like Turco, Malanga engages in a poetry of oppositional veneration.

With a migratory experience unlike his predecessors, and closer in age to Ciardi and Stefanile, Joseph Tusiani (1923–) belongs to a different category of cultural being; he moved to the United States as an adult with a university education. (Others in this general category of biculturalism and bilingualism would include Peter Carravetta, Rita Dinale, Giose Rimanelli, Paolo Valesio, and Pasquale Verdicchio.) With an Italian classical education—weaned as a poet on the likes of Carducci, Pascoli, and D'Annunzio and an avid reader of Dickens, Hawthorne, Browning, and Dickinson—Tusiani arrived with immense cultural wealth. His polycultural experiences contributed to a poetry that has, over the years, mediated the rhetorical extravagance of Italy and the linguistic economy of the United States. But Tusiani is a complex figure; he is the only Italian American poet who consistently writes in four different languages—English, Italian, Latin, and his native dialect. With such a vast linguistic inventory, Tusiani also exhibits a large thematic repertoire from the culturally specific, immigrant experience to the more general motifs of solitude and nostalgia that afflict the human condition. He has authored approximately forty books of poetry, prose, and translations.

Glossing through our category of Italian American poetry, we find the Beat Generation. Lawrence Ferlinghetti, **Gregory Corso**, Philip La Mantia, and **Diane di Prima** are four names that come to mind. Of the first three, Ferlinghetti is the most readily recognized. His poem "The Old Italians Dying" is a swan song to the old Italian neighborhood of San Francisco's North Beach, where flight from the city and gentrification have radically transformed it. Furthermore, his City Lights Publishing house has been instrumental in getting out not only Italian American Beats, but also numerous Italian poets in English translation.

Diane di Prima (1934–) is one of the most prolific writers of the nonconformist generation of the 1960s. Not steeped in an explicit repertoire of Italian American thematics, her poetry does reflect her heritage. Poems such as "Backyard" and "April Fool Birthday Poem for Grandpa" stand as excellent examples of reconciling an ideological and formalistic avant-garde attitude with her Italian heritage. Whereas most Italian Americans flirt with historic Italian anarchy, di Prima embraces it wholeheartedly, whether that anarchy is specifically Italian American, as in "April Fool . . . ," or more universal, as in "Rant," a creative/ideological manifesto. Diane di Prima exemplifies on a more general scale the counterculture that had its roots in the 1950s and blossomed in the 1960s, with more than one dozen books of poetry, two autobiographies, and numerous chapbooks and pamphlets.

Similar to some of her predecessors, **Maria Mazziotti Gillan** (1940–) is also deeply involved in publishing. Editor of *Footwork: The Patterson Literary Review*, she also directs SUNY Binghamton's Creative Writing Program. She coedited *Unsettling America* (1994), the first anthology of contemporary multicultural poetry of the United States that includes—for the first time— a significant number of talented Italian Americans. Mazziotti Gillan's poetry often speaks to the trials and tribulations of the gender issue and a woman's struggle to overcome; often, these themes revolve around issues of the Italian American family. Mazziotti Gillan is very much aware of her style, which in a poem may start out as quite simple and, when necessitated by her narrative, turn into a more complex mode of verse writing. Having won numerous awards for her writing, her self-reflexivity as an Italian American woman is apparent from her earliest collection, *Flowers from the Tree of Night* (1980), to her latest, *Where I Come From: New and Selected Poems* (1994).

A third Italian American voice that shares the gender dilemma is **Daniela Gioseffi** (1941–). Along with her creative writing (poetry and prose), her sensitivities to issues of gender and prejudice are evidenced by her two award-winning, best-selling edited volumes, *Women on War* (1988) and *On Prejudice: A Global Perspective* (1993). Characterized as "one of Whitman's daughters," Gioseffi writes poetry of the more spiritual type, exhibiting an impressive breadth of reading and eloquence. A stylist of sorts, Gioseffi's poetry speaks to the most intense issues of our times inviting her reader to share in her outrage and wisdom. Be it *Eggs in the Lake* (1979) or her later poetry collection, *Going On* (2000), her work is accompanied by a compelling unreservedness for those things she holds dearly, social and political commitments that date back to the Civil Rights Movement.

Considered by *Esquire* to be one of the "Best of the New Generation," **Dana Gioia** (1950–) is known as a poet, critic, translator, editor, and chairman of the National Endowment for the Arts. Although his poetry does not explicitly exhibit Italian American themes, a hue of his ethnic background is present. Work and money seem to occupy a good part of his earlier poetry, where the initial desire to succeed financially—a possible inheritance from the immigrant generation where economic amelioration equaled individual amelioration—transforms itself into the burdensome. But, like the other poets in this Italian panorama, regardless of thematic specificity, Gioia is a poet of great sophistication and elegance. A major participant in the New Formalist movement, Gioia once stated that although "many American poets reject European influences as distractions from the search for a native voice, most Italian-American poets view Europe—sometimes in its Modernistic aspects and sometimes in its older traditions—as a potential source of strength." I would suggest that the same can be said for Gioia: as translator of Italian poetry on a broad scale, he has surely absorbed from the masters of older traditions some of their rhyme and meter.

Along with Ciardi and Gioia, **Jay Parini** (1948–) figures as one of the most prominent Italian American names associated with U.S. poetry. Poet, novelist, critic, professor, radio commentator, and editor, Parini has entered the mainstream of American letters like few others. He may not enjoy the glittering fanfare of a **Mario Puzo** or **Gay Talese**, but he may have, in his own right as poet especially, surpassed them. Parini's poetry exhibits an immense erudition and familiarity with the master poets. Yet, his thematics are very much of the everyday type that transcend ethnic/racial epistemes and carry universal appeal. Be it the hard work of miners, the praises of family elders, or the desire to delve into one's ancestry, any U.S. reader of Parini's can readily identify with the subjects and, at the same time, marvel at his craft as poet. Identified with one of the best writing schools in the United States, Bread Loaf, and editor of the *Columbia Anthology of Poetry* (1993), Parini, like very few Italian Americans involved in the literary world, is a true cultural broker, contributing to the greater history of U.S. literature and to what eventually becomes the traditional **canon**.

These are a few of the poets who have made an indelible mark along the trajectory of what we may consider lyric Italian America. Others too numerous to mention here would be added to a more complete inventory. Vincent Ferrini (1913–) honed his literary skills at a young age while also working as an instructor of literature for the WPA project from 1935 to 1940. A prolific writer since 1941, whose poetry is steeped in social issues of industrialization, Ferrini figures as the logical successor to Giovannitti. Next to Ciardi, Henry Rago (1915–69) figures as one of the first to break into mainstream literary America. His poetry appeared in numerous, prestigious journals over the years throughout the United States and in England (the *New Republic*, *Commonweal*, and *Horizon*). Having published his first poem in *Poetry* when he was sixteen, he later went on, with great success, to edit the journal. A third voice of the pre–World War II poets is Elda Tanasso (1917–). With poetry published in *Voices, Lyric, Columbia Poetry*, and *New English Weekly* (England), she also had poems in *Poetry* at the early age of twenty.

Other poets of the later generation whom we may label "baby boomers," those born after World War II, would surely include award-winning David Citino and W. S. Di Piero, the latter also in the category of translators looking back to Italy, as we saw in Gioia, Galassi, and others. In a similar vein, one finds Paul Vangelisti, celebrated poet, novelist, publisher, and translator whose elegant editorial successes include Red Hill Press and Sun & Moon Publishers. Others, still, include Mary Jo Bona, **Peter Covino**, Gerry LaFemina, Stephen Massimilla, Jane Tassi, and Luisa Villani.

In an attempt to reconcile the ethnic with the general cultural milieu, the more technically conscious and, at times, wistful poets such as Sandra Gilbert and Diane Raptosh deserve their own entry. Likewise, the religious poetry of a Peggy Rizza Ellsberg would be a necessary inclusion to encompass the larger picture. In a different vein, Rose Romano has earned her own place in the history of Italian American poetry both for her own austere creative work and her unselfish editorial activity dedicated to giving voice to the Italian American lesbian, female, and gay voices that would remain otherwise silent.

Finally, there are those who have sunk roots into the American literary soil and, consequently, consider themselves too American to be ethnic. This, perhaps, appears to be the most intriguing aspect of all—namely, poets who uproot their poetry through a poststructuralist, deconstructive lens in order to demonstrate further how the U.S. literary scene is, also, a conglomeration of different voices. All this figures as a pluralistic process of artistic invention *and* interpretation which, by its very nature, cannot exclude the individual—artist *and* reader/viewer—who has found an *ars poetica* that does not violate the several components of her/his individual identity, thus (re)creating, ideologically speaking, a different repertoire of signs.

Further Reading

Barolini, Helen. *The Dream Book. An Anthology of Writings by Italian American Women.* New York: Schoken, 1985.

Gioia, Dana. "What Is Italian-American Poetry?" *Poetry Pilot* (December 1991): 3–10. Republished with a brief postscript in *Voices in Italian Americana* 4.2 (1993): 61–64, followed by a "Response" written by Maria Mazziotti Gillan (65–66).

Giordano, Paolo A., and Anthony Julian Tamburri, eds. *Beyond the Margin. Readings in Italian Americana.* Madison, NJ: Fairleigh Dickinson UP, 1997.

Tamburri, Anthony Julian, Paolo A. Giordano, and Fred L. Gardaphé, eds. *From the Margin: Writings in Italian Americana.* 2d ed. West Lafayette, IN: Purdue UP, 2000.

Anthony Julian Tamburri

ITALIAN AMERICAN STEREOTYPES   The bulk of Italian American immigration occurred during the last two decades of the nineteenth century and the first decade of the twentieth century. Like each new group of immigrants, the Italians were stereotyped according to the perceived differences between their culture and the predominant Anglo-American culture—and, to a lesser extent, between their culture and the cultures of the earlier immigrant groups. Many of the stereotypes of Italian Americans have faded with **assimilation**, but several have shown remarkable staying power.

Because the Italians were the first Mediterranean people to immigrate in large numbers to the United States, they were viewed as racially suspect. In his study, *White on Arrival: Race, Color, and Power in Chicago, 1890–1945* (Oxford UP, 2003), Thomas A. Guglielmo chronicles how Italian Americans were initially regarded as "colored" and were finally categorized and treated as "white" only at the height of the efforts to maintain the rigid segregation of Chicago's African American population within just two of the city's districts.

The heavy labor performed by Italian immigrants in many American industries has been the main topic of Italian American fiction treating the immigrant experience. Nonetheless, the stereotypes of the Italian American as lacking a "Protestant work ethic" range from the quaintly condescending image of the peasant inclined to fanciful daydreaming to the very negative characterization of the Italian American criminal as someone who has no stomach for "regular work."

The Roman Catholicism of almost all Italian immigrants has led to their being stereotyped as a people predisposed to exotic superstitions. Although the Irish Americans had already established a significant Catholic presence in the cities of the Northeast, the Italian Americans were commonly viewed as being even more sinisterly papist. The labor activism among Italian American workers and the notoriety of some Italian American anarchists—most notably, Sacco and Vanzetti—seemed to confirm the worst WASP suspicions that Italian Americans could never be completely assimilated, that they would never completely accept American institutions.

Before **Mario Puzo**'s blockbuster novel *The Godfather* (1969) and Francis Ford Coppola's even more highly acclaimed film adaptation of the novel (1972), organized crime in America had a more multiethnic face in fiction and on film, as it had in practice. Just as the Jewish gangs and the Italian mob had long collaborated in New York and just as the Chicago Outfit came to include many German, Irish, and Polish mobsters, the American crime film from the 1920s to the release of *The Godfather* (1972) can hardly be said to have focused exclusively on Italian Americans. For every film featuring an Italian American gangster such as Edward G. Robinson's Rico in *Little Caesar* (1931) or Paul Muni's Tony Camonte in *Scarface* (1932), there were many films such as *The Roaring Twenties* (1939) that featured non-Mediterranean toughs such as James Cagney and Humphrey Bogart in the leads. Indeed, *The Godfather* had a tremendous impact on American popular culture precisely because, in the immediate aftermath of the Appalachin debacle when FBI agents accidentally raided a top-level Mafia convention, it seemed to provide major revelations about the workings of a then largely unknown criminal underworld.

Since the publication of Puzo's novel (1969) and the release of Coppola's film (1972), the "crime film" has become largely the "Mafia film." *Miller's Crossing* (1990) and *The Road to Perdition* (2002) notwithstanding, the Italian American mobster has become the focal figure of the genre and, ironically, as American as the cowboy. Indeed, although it was attacked as malicious stereotype when *The Godfather* was initially released, Marlon Brando's characterization of Vito Corleone has come to be seen as a mythic and essentially positive portrayal of a figure who stands almost anachronistically in contrast to the much more sordid mobsters portrayed in such subsequent films as *Goodfellas* (1990), *Casino* (1995), and *Donnie Brasco* (1997), and in the television series **The Sopranos** (1999–).

Of course, much of the appeal of *The Godfather*—and perhaps the saving grace of *The Sopranos*—is the emphasis on the family that provides a corollary to the emphasis on "the family" or the criminal organization. In these two types of families can be found the most enduringly positive and negative stereotypes of Italian Americans. For every film like *The Godfather*, there may not be a *Moonstruck* (1987), but when an advertiser wants to exploit the associations of a hearty, old-fashioned family gathering, the family is usually eating Italian.

And if Italian Americans have long been associated with hearty appetites for food, they have also been associated with great romantic passion and sexual energy. Although this amorousness was initially stereotyped negatively, it has for a long time been represented in a largely positive manner. From Rudolph Valentino (1895–1926) to *The Rose Tattoo* (1955) to *Moonstruck* (1987), and even in a film such as *Rocky* (1976), the Italian lover has had more staying power than even the Godfather.

Further Reading

Barreca, Regina, ed. *A Sitdown with the Sopranos: Watching Italian-American Culture on T.V.'s Most Talked-About Series.* New York: Palgrave, 2002.

Beck, Bernard. "The Myth That Would Not Die: The Sopranos, Mafia Movies, and Italians in America." *Multicultural Perspectives* 2.2 (2000): 24–27.

Bondanella, Peter. *Hollywood Italians: Dagos, Palookas, Romeos, Wise Guys, and Sopranos.* New York: Continuum, 2004.

Guglielmo, Thomas A. *White on Arrival: Italians, Race, Color, and Power in Chicago, 1890–1945.* New York: Oxford UP, 2003.

Italian American Stereotypes in U.S. Advertising. Pamphlet. Washington, DC: The Order Sons of Italy in America, 2003.

Misurella, Fred. "The Truth behind the Fiction of Italian-Americans." *Christian Science Monitor* April 15, 2002: 9.

Willis, Ellen. "Our Mobsters, Ourselves." *The Nation* 272.13 (April 2, 2001): 26–31.

Martin Kich

IYER, PICO (1957–)   Indian American travel writer, novelist, essayist, journalist, political commentator, and cultural and literary critic. Best known for his travel writing and keen social and cultural observation, Pico Iyer is an "ethnic" writer who belongs to the world. His most famous pieces, *Video Night in Kathmandu: And Other Reports from the Not-So-Far East* (1988) and *The Global Soul: Jet Lag, Shopping Malls, and the Search for Home* (2000), look toward cosmopolitan citizenship and establish Iyer as an author whose work brings attention to cross-cultural existence and jarring contradictions of the global age.

Iyer's reputation as a travel writer drawn to the contact zones of clashing cultures rests on such works as *Video Night in Kathmandu, Falling Off the Map: Some Lonely Places of the Earth* (1993), *The Lady and the Monk: Four Seasons in Kyoto* (1991), *Tropical Classical: Essays from Several Directions* (1997), and *Sun After Dark: Flights Into the Foreign* (2004). All the volumes share Iyer's unique perspective that bridges East and West. Born to Indian parents, educated at Eton and Oxford, and dividing residence between California and Japan, Iyer is a "global soul" who participates in multiple cultures yet does not belong to any. *Video Night* is a delightful collection of essays about the East and Southeast Asia, where the flicker of neon and the pop of Coca-Cola meet the quiet of Buddhist temples and the poverty of city slums. Iyer's reflections on Nepal, Tibet, Hong Kong, and India, among others, offer telling examples of incongruent, eccentric, and often humorous blends of global trends and local cultures. The book comments on the growing westernization of Asia and the changing perceptions of the "Far East," whose remoteness is reduced by contemporary technology, international travel, and global markets. *Falling Off the Map* retains the same flair for the absurd and the peculiar, observed this time in some of the most isolated corners of the world (Iceland, North Korea, Paraguay), whereas *The Lady and the Monk* is a more personal account of the author's stay in a monastery in Kyoto and an affair with a Japanese woman. The text depicts female confinement in a marriage of convenience and examines the modes of effective communication between lovers, whose cultural particularities get lost or distorted in translation. Iyer continues to explore the same topic of the possibilities and limitations of cross-cultural romance in his fiction. *Cuba and the Night* (1996) brings together a cynical American journalist and a vibrant Cuban senorita, and *Abandon* (2003), a generic hybrid of Western picaro tradition and Persian mystical romance, follows contrasting fellow Californians as they quest for a heretical Islamic manuscript and discover passion and abandon in the foreign terrain.

Iyer received significant critical acclaim for *The Global Soul,* an eclectic piece of personal narration, social observation, and cultural criticism. The book's opening image of Iyer's burnt-down house and resulting homelessness becomes a metaphor for the rest of the book and its exploration of rootlessness and cultural displacement of the present moment. The world of *The Global Soul* is one of transience, congested airports, casual encounters, digital frenzy, cultural "mongrealization" of Western urban centers, and allegiances that go beyond the nation and **ethnicity**. Iyer ventures to offer his vision of a more cosmopolitan future, seeing in the multicultural mosaic of places like Toronto the possibility of an effective international community. He also expresses his views on contemporary culture and the future of globalization in his journalistic work. Since the initial contributions to *Time* magazine in 1982, his articles have appeared in a wide variety of magazines, including *Harper's, The New Yorker,* the *New York Review of Books,* the *New York Times, Sports Illustrated, Condé Nast Traveler,* and *Shambala Sun.* His wide interests are evident in work that includes a piece of literary criticism, "On the Promise of New Canadian Fiction" (*Harper's* June 2002); an inquiry into contemporary migrancy "Why We Travel" (Salon.com); and a speculation about spirituality as a grounding counterpart to the (dis)comforts of cultural and geographic displacements, shared in a number of interviews with fellow exile, the Dalai Lama.

The work of the prolific Pico Iyer, an insightful observer of global (dis)connections, is significant in that it calls for redefinitions of the present understanding of home, citizenship, and cultural and national identities. Moreover, in its resistance to an "ethnic" label, his work challenges us to find new literary classifications that would acknowledge the growing literary interest in representing transnational, global, and international experiences.

Further Reading

Yamamoto, Traise. "'As Natural as the Partnership of Sun and Moon': The Logic of Sexualized Metonymy in *Pictures from the Water Trade* and *The Lady and the Monk.*" *Positions: East Asia Cultures Critique* 4.2 (1996): 321–41.

Ljiljana Coklin

J

JACKSON, ANGELA (1951–) African American poet, playwright, and fiction writer. Angela Jackson's unique position in **African American poetry** is indicated by the fact that two states claim her as their poet: Mississippi and Illinois. Jackson was born in Greenville, Mississippi, and though her family left the South for Chicago when she was still a child, a sense of the South and southern language mingled with that of Chicago and results in a rich experience in language and cadence for her readers.

Jackson, influenced by **Gwendolyn Brooks**, Hoyt Williams, and **Margaret Walker**, emerged as a poet during the **Black Arts Movement** of the 1960s and 1970s. Though her poetry may not be considered as overtly political as much of the Movement's poetry, she did share with other writers of the Movement a commitment to creating art for a black audience without an apologetic stance for failing to imitate Euro-American forms and models. Jackson's writing focuses on various aspects of African American life, with many of her pieces centering on a particularly southern experience.

Jackson's works include collections of poetry, *Voodoo/Love Magic* (1974), *The Greenville Club* (1977), and *Solo in the Boxcar* (1985). She turned to fiction in the late 1970s publishing such works as "Dreamer" and "Witch Doctor" in 1977. She also began adapting her poetry for the stage producing such plays as *Witness!* (1978), *Shango **Diaspora**: An African-American Myth of Womanhood and Love* (1980), and *When the Wind Blows* (1984). Her recent works include *Cowboy Amok* (1992), *Dark Legs and Silk Kisses: The Beatitudes of Spinners* (1993), and *And All These Roads Be Luminous* (1997).

Whether she is writing about institutions, individuals, love, or biblical figures, Jackson takes every day events and lifts them from the mundane to an extraordinary experience in language. Her subject matter is diverse, her metaphors potent. Jackson defines her domain as the dwelling in and between high and popular culture, subverting popular culture as a poet and posing moral and ethical questions.

In "Doubting Thomas," Jackson takes a biblical tale with which many are familiar and poses profound theological questions without seeming to do so. Her voice and manner are so clear and urban that her conclusions seem more common sense and street sense than theological. Poems such as "Monroe, Louisiana" and "George, By All Means, a Farmer" pay homage to a South that is rural, ordinary, familial, and familiar.

Her mastery for transforming the ordinary into the sublime is revealed in particularly poignant and provocative poems such as "The Love of Travellers," which, while bearing witness to the conflict between urban development and nature, also comments metaphorically about the scars we are left with even after the "meticulous mercy" of those who enter and leave our lives.

Further Reading

Kaganoff, Penny. "Dark Legs and Silk Kisses." *Publishers Weekly* 240.38 (September 20, 1993): 68.

Chandra Tyler Mountain

JACKSON, ELAINE (1943–)   African American playwright and educator. An actor in search of more multitextured, challenging roles for black women, Elaine Jackson determined to create characters that would satisfy this need. She began writing during the politically fraught and generative 1970s, when the feminist and Black Power movements collided and converged. Along with contemporaries such as **Ntozake Shange**, **Aishah Rahman**, and Alexis DeVeaux, Jackson is thematically preoccupied with constricted women's roles, the struggle for self-definition, and the authentic expression of personal, social, and artistic freedom. With humor—broad and subtle, wry and wrenching—and a canny ear for quirky, dramatically potent dialogue, Jackson experiments with form while making the lives of black women her primary theatrical focus.

Born in Detroit and educated at Wayne State University, Jackson pursued her interests in both theater and education. She majored in speech and education at Wayne State, then launched a successful stage career, acting in numerous productions in Detroit, California, and New York. She soon evinced her talent for writing, which gradually became her preferred medium of expression. Her first play, *Toe Jam*, was selected for inclusion in the 1972 *Black Drama Anthology*, an influential, even ground-breaking collection that showcases the range and vitality of **African American drama**tic arts. The anthology was edited by playwright **Ron Milner** and Woodie King Jr., producer, director, and founder (in 1970) of New York's New Federal Theatre and the National Black Touring Circuit. King remains a dynamic mainstay in African American theater circles, known for spotting, supporting, and promoting the work of gifted artists. King and Milner knew Jackson from her early acting days in Detroit and championed her unique mix of talents. *Toe Jam*'s appearance in the collection gave Jackson wide exposure, critical attention, and acclaim. The young playwright found her niche in the company of such notables as **Langston Hughes** and **Amiri Baraka**.

Cockfight (1976), a satiric look at marriage, premiered in 1978, beginning Jackson's long association with New York's American Place Theatre. Concerned with myopic versions of beauty, *Paper Dolls* (1979) was first staged as a reading at the American Place Theatre in 1982. The special domain of women on the verge of motherhood is explored in *Birth Rites* (1987). Jackson's work continues to be produced at community theaters and colleges throughout the country. In the aftermath of the September 11 tragedy, King's New Federal Theatre in concert with The New York City Arts Coalition's "Take Back Our City" campaign presented a series of thirty staged readings in memory of the Trade Tower victims. Jackson, a long-time city resident, was a featured playwright, along with Baraka, Milner, **Walter Mosley**, **Ossie Davis**, and others.

Jackson received the Rockefeller award for playwriting for 1978 and 1979, the Langston Hughes playwriting award in 1979, and a National Endowment for the Arts award for playwriting in 1983. An educator for many years, Jackson lives with her husband and her actor/musician son in New York, where she teaches high school English.

Further Reading

Barreca, Regina, ed. *The Penguin Book of Women's Humor*. New York: Penguin, 1996.

Brewer, Mary F. *Race, Sex, and Gender in Contemporary Women's Theatre: The Construction of "Woman."* Brighton, England: Sussex Academic Press, 1999.

Wilkerson, Margaret B., ed. *Nine Plays by Black Women*. New York: New American Library, 1986.

Kate Falvey

JACOBS, HARRIET (1813–1897) African American autobiographer and slave narrator. Jacobs's *Incidents in the Life of a Slave Girl* (1861) is one of a very few existing female **slave narratives**. She wrote it, as she explains in her preface, "at irregular intervals, whenever I could snatch an hour from household duties," while living as an escaped slave in the North, and published it under the pseudonym "Linda Brent." The autobiography borrows from the genre of sentimental domestic fiction and is often read as a novel; indeed Jacobs's editor, the **abolition**ist Lydia Maria Child, noted in her preface to the narrative that "some incidents in her story are more romantic than fiction."

Jacobs, however, assures her readers that "this narrative is no fiction." Crafting her autobiography for the cause of abolition, Jacobs used the techniques of the sentimental novel to reach her audience of nineteenth-century white women. Her appeal to sympathy and use of sentimentality is almost a seduction of the reader. She wanted not only to retain credibility but also make palatable the details of her sexual abuse at the hands of her master and her sexual transgression in taking a white lover. The middle-class northern mothers might respond to the narrator's repeated depiction of their shared maternal identities—her appeal to them early in the narrative, for example, to "contrast *your* New Year's day with that of the poor bond-woman." But Jacobs feared alienating some whose, as Child put it in her preface, "ears are too delicate to listen" to the stories of a fallen woman. Referring to herself in both the first- and third-person, she negotiates the tensions between revelation and concealment, public and private, and her individual life and that of a representative "slave girl" as her title has it. Mixing genres, Jacobs opens up significant silences and dwells in the created space between modes.

Her textual gaps are in fact analogous to the famous garret space. The story follows Brent through childhood and into early womanhood, when her master, Dr. Flint, attempts seduction and rape. She chooses to take a white lover, Mr. Sands, in order to reassert control of her body and thwart Dr. Flint. She bears two children, hoping that her lover will purchase and manumit his secret family, but Dr. Flint's refusal to sell them drives her to attempt escape. An aborted flight leads her to inter herself into a crawl space above her grandmother's house for seven years, to wait out Flint. From the tiny garret she manipulates him with letters apparently mailed from the North, almost creating him as a character in an epistolary novel. He had used her literacy against her by writing her vile notes and whispering obscenities in her ear, and now she turns his tools of language against him.

Her "loophole of retreat," as she calls the hiding place, is thus both a prison and a refuge: as a "living grave," so described in *Incidents*, it literalizes the state of slavery, which is to be beyond "the pale of human beings," and is itself a "living death," in Jacobs's words. Like her self-inflicted confinement, the process of telling her story is painful: "she wept so much and seemed to suffer such mental agony," remembered her friend Amy Post in October 1859, and Brent characterizes memory as distressing throughout the autobiography. But Jacobs also locates power and renewal in invisibility. Like **Ralph Ellison**'s Invisible Man, who retreats to a basement space reminiscent of her attic, she uses her retreat away from society to fashion a subversively *present* absence. A sister of the Victorian "madwoman in the attic," Brent lives in the interstices of the American house divided, embedded in cracks of its institutions, and watches and works for the destruction of the edifice of slavery. The autobiography and the hole, as sites of memory, are ultimately protective and aggressive spaces in the margins of hegemonic discourse, from which Brent emerges, as though from a chrysalis, as the writer Jacobs. (*See also* African American Autobiography)

Further Reading

Carby, Hazel V. *Reconstructing Womanhood: The Emergence of the Afro-American Woman Novelist.* New York: Oxford UP, 1987.

Foreman, P. Gabrielle. "The Spoken and the Silenced in *Incidents in the Life of a Slave Girl* and *Our Nig*." *Callaloo* 13.2 (1990): 313–24.

Kaplan, Carla. "Narrative Contracts and Emancipatory Readers: *Incidents in the Life of a Slave Girl*." *Yale Journal of Criticism* 6.11 (1993): 93–119.

Nudelman, Franny. "Harriet Jacobs and the Sentimental Politics of Female Suffering," *ELH: English Literary History* 59 (1992): 939–64.

Zoe Trodd

JAFFE, DANIEL M. (1956–) Jewish American author, anthologist, translator, and humanist. In his work, Daniel M. Jaffe develops a detailed analysis of modern Jewish American **identity** and culture by observing it through the lens of a wide variety of experiences and locations. Both in his fiction and nonfiction, and in his contributions as a translator and anthologist, Jaffe explores how religious and secular values simultaneously enable and traumatize our quest for an authentic self. Interlocking humor, anger, sexuality, political commentary, and emotional honesty, Jaffe manages to convey the complexities of a society in which the commitment to tradition and the need for new answers are constantly intersecting, a concern he shares with other Jewish American writers like **Cynthia Ozick**, **Isaac Bashevis Singer**, and **Philip Roth**.

The experiential richness of Jaffe's work is directly connected to his education and professional interests. At Princeton University (AB, 1978) he majored in politics and concentrated in Russian studies, writing a prize-winning thesis about the struggles of Soviet Jews to emigrate to Israel. While at Harvard Law School (JD, 1981) he continued his involvement with political issues, studying Soviet law and campaigning for the rights of persecuted Soviet human rights dissidents. After working as a corporate-securities lawyer in Boston, he became a full-time writer, earning an MFA at Vermont College (1997). It is this diverse background that allows him both to translate Dina Rubina's *Here Comes the Messiah!* (2000), a novel portraying Russian émigré life in Israel, and to compile an impressive array of international voices for his anthology of Jewish fabulist fiction *With Signs and Wonders* (2001).

Jaffe's personal essays, included by various editors in Jewish anthologies such as *Kosher Meat* (2000), *Found Tribe* (2002), and *Mentsh* (2004), emphasize the predicament of a Jewish man that wrestles to attain an individual stance in front of the conventional expectations of his friends and elders. Among his fiction published in many journals (e.g., *The Greensboro Review*, *Christopher Street*, *Green Mountains Review*, and *The James White Review*), Jaffe's most recent project (2003–04) is an ongoing series of biblical-themed short stories written for *The Forward*, one of the most important American Jewish newspapers. These stories effectively combine a deep respect for the past with a call for the inclusion of alternative lifestyles and points of view within the Jewish community. Dave Miller, the main character in Jaffe's novel *The Limits of Pleasure* (2001), is torn between the moral obligations imposed on him by his late grandmother, a Holocaust survivor, and his desires as a gay man. By daringly juxtaposing sacred and erotic imageries, the novel presents a courageous portrait of a middle-aged man who slowly learns to define his Jewish identity on his own terms. Dave's capacity to find hope in the middle of conflict is a quality that also defines Jaffe's writing as a whole. (*See also* Jewish American Gay Literature)

Further Reading

Kramer, Micaela. "Of Moonflowers and Magic: Fabulist Fiction by Way of the Midrash." *The Forward* (June 8, 2001): 11.

Purkey, Brad. "Bookends." *Liberty Press* 9.1 (September 2002): 18.

Rinn, Miriam. "Imagine . . ." *Jewish Standard* (May 25, 2001): 31.

Wilson, Martin. "What's Next." *Lambda Book Report* 10.9 (April 2002): 30.

Leo Cabranes-Grant

JANDA, VICTORIA (1903?–)   Polish American poet. Victoria Janda is the first female American poet of Polish descent to write in English and to receive critical notice. Born in Poland in the first years of the twentieth century, Janda spent most of her life in the Minneapolis/St. Paul area where she became a founding member of the Polanie Club, the oldest Polish American women's cultural organization in the United States. Publishing her poems in popular journals and newspapers, she eventually published three volumes of poetry: *Star Hunger* (1942), *Walls of Space* (1945), and *Singing Furrows* (1953). All three of these books were published by the Polanie Club.

Along with her friend the short story writer Monica Krawczyk, also a member of the Polanie Club, Janda was the literary voice of the organization. She reviewed books at meetings, served as president, and influenced the club in a literary direction. She also served as president of the League of Minnesota Poets, belonged to the National League of American Pen Women, and was nominated for the Pulitzer Prize in 1954.

Janda's interests were broad. In addition to three books of poetry, she published fiction and poetry in journals and magazines. In an address to the National League of American Pen Women, Janda spoke to America's diversity and to its literary future: "We are now beginning to appreciate that a culture of any country is made up of different cultures created by different people." She was among the first to call attention to the literary contributions of American writers of Polish descent. She was also well acquainted with Polish literature, as witnessed in her essay "From the Parochial School to the Polish Library."

Janda's poetry is itself an excellent example of the emerging ethnic Polish self and the voice of the ethnic woman in America. However, some of her poems are neither ethnic- nor gender-specific. She writes about nature and love, and in the style of the British romantics she composes occasional poems dedicated to friends and those she admires. Janda is a solitary singer who hopes that "beyond her final silent hour" her story will echo back to earth. She wishes to climb, to seek, to strive, and to transcend. Images of soaring appear frequently in her poems. *Star Hunger,* her first collection, opens this way: "I would in April madness/Fly on my wing-shod feet/My face upraised to thunder/Along the busy street/To snare the wind's wild sweetness." The opening poem in her second collection is titled "Trailing Wings" and begins, "When April comes because she must/Trailing her own wings through the dust/Left colorless by winter's wake/What difference can it ever make/To such as you?" In these lines, Janda reveals the voice within as that of a woman out-of-love, unhappy, melancholy, and alone. The unidentified "you" which the speaker often addresses in these poems is untrustworthy and disappointing. In a sequence of poems called "Shadows of a Lyre," Janda writes, "But when my song turned to your curious eyes/It lost its youthful treble in your cold/Unfriendly gaze." And in a sonnet cycle called "Late Summer," she cuts to the quick, explaining the predicament of a woman in love: "And men will say-what they will say of me/But only you will know my bitter part/On your cold breast I could not warm my heart."

In her best poems, Janda shows American readers that the cares and thoughts of the Polish immigrant—Janda came to the United States when she was three—reflect those of people everywhere. The voice in her poetry speaks to, for, and about American women in the same sense that the voices of Ann Bradstreet, Catherine Sedgwick, and Emily Dickinson had spoken before her. In each of her books, however, Janda includes a section specifically addressing her Polish heritage. These poems are quite different from her other poems. Except for the fact that the speaker is a woman, they are not about gender. The Polish poems are of two types. She writes many describing Poland's wartime suffering. In these poems, Poland is a symbol of courage and dignity, an innocent victim, and a defender of freedom: "The first for liberty to pledge your vow/The first to raise your loyal fearless hand." Other poems celebrate Polish historical and cultural icons, such as Marie Curie-Sklodowska. In "Strange Mountains" she alludes to many of the defining figures in Polish literature. Throughout her Polish poems, Janda describes her Polish heritage as the context and motivation for her own work.

Some of Janda's Polish poems are idealized memories of the Polish highlands where she was born. She talks about "remembered highlands, only seen/with infant unrecording eyes." Even so, she instinctively knows the Highland's beauty, peace, and mystical allure. In "Mountain Magic" she writes, "We walked between the raindrops-when it rained, not to get wet." In "Strange Mountain" she suggests that her ancestry is the inspiration for the romantic yearnings expressed throughout her poems. At one point she connects the solitary wanderer's urge to "climb and search" to the same impulse within the Highland people. She expresses a desire to fly to the Polishness within her, "The heritage that held me . . . compelled me . . . /To go my way in song . . . /to weep and laugh through time/ . . . to sing and climb."

Although an air of melancholy and loneliness pervades these poems, Janda does not present herself as someone caught between two cultures—a theme typical to immigrant literature. Janda is as secure in her American **identity** as she is in her Polish one. She is not a divided self but rather a dual self-enriched by two cultures. Interestingly she speaks of herself as an American and as a Pole, but not as a Polish American. Like the soaring speaker of her poems, Janda seems to have transcended **ethnicity** and to have become bicultural without being bifurcated. Her poetry thus flies in the face of conventional thinking about the stages of ethnicity and assumptions about immigrant literature.

Further Reading

Gladsky, Thomas S. *Princes, Peasants, and Other Polish Selves: Ethnicity in American Literature*. Amherst: U of Massachusetts P, 1992.

Gladsky, Thomas S., and Rita Gladsky, eds. *Something of My Very Own to Say: American Women Writers of Polish Descent*. Boulder, CO: East European Monographs, 1998.

Thomas S. Gladsky

JANSON, DRUDE KROG (1846–1934) Norwegian American novelist and essayist. Unlike many Norwegian American authors, Drude Krog Janson's writings rarely foreground the hardships and complexities of **immigration** and **assimilation**. Janson's work instead most often conveys her interest in **feminism** and other social causes and in the psychology of women's lives and relationships. Janson joined her husband, **Kristofer Janson**, a charismatic Unitarian minister and well-respected writer, in Minneapolis with their six children in 1882. Enthusiastic at immigrating to a country she believed more tolerant of religious and gender rights than Norway, the move spurred Janson's development into a significant female voice in **Norwegian American literature**. Her first publications include essays and translations on women's suffrage in *Saamanden*, a journal founded by her husband, and in *Nylænde*, a Norwegian feminist periodical.

Janson's first novel was *En saloonkeeper's datter* (1887; *A Saloonkeeper's Daughter*, 2002), its title implying Janson's concern for the status of women and the social conditions of immigrants. Astrid Holm, daughter of a once prosperous Norwegian emigrant who has sunk to keeping a saloon, is traumatized by her grim urban milieu, but continues to hold to her dream of becoming an actress. After being unjustly ostracized from Minneapolis's pretentious Norwegian American middle-class through false gossip, Astrid seems destined to be a victim to social forces. Invigorated by a meeting with the visiting Norwegian author Bjørnstjerne Bjørnson, however, Astrid is ultimately able to build a fulfilling life as a Unitarian minister and temperance speaker. Borrowing from genres current in both American and European literature, *En saloonkeeper's datter* is part realistic urban immigrant fiction documenting ills associated with rapid industrialization, while also incorporating elements of naturalism, sentimental romance, the temperance novel, and New Women's and Social Christian novels.

Although not a major theme of her writing, Janson experienced her own serious problems of **assimilation**. The suffering of working-class immigrants she witnessed as a minister's wife greatly dispirited her, as did the materialism she observed in the Norwegian American middle class. Well-educated, with liberal religious and social views, and from a prominent Norwegian family, Janson was also never culturally at home in the Norwegian American community; she had more contact with Norwegian literary circles than Norwegian American ones and counted Bjørnson among her friends. Janson and her husband also grew apart as life in America altered them, and in 1892 she returned to Norway. Janson and her husband divorced in 1897.

Janson's next two novels are partially set in the United States. In *Tore: Fortælling fra prærien* (1894, Tore: A Tale from the Prairie) the jilted Tore marries another suitor and immigrates to Minnesota. The autobiographical *Mira, et livsløb* (1897; Mira, a Life Story) follows Mira as she marries an idealistic student of theology and moves to the United States, but comes to be filled with self-reproach at the marital and other problems her actions cause. Her final novel, *Helga Hvide* (1908), is set entirely in Norway. Janson died in Copenhagen in 1934.

Further Reading

Røssbø, Sigrun. "Drude Krog Janson, Norwegian-American and Norwegian Author." *Essays on Norwegian-American Literature and History: Proceedings from a Seminar on Norwegian-American Literature, June 26–30, 1984*. Ed. Dorothy Burton Skårdal and Ingeborg R. Kongslien. Oslo: NAHA Norway, 1986. 49–60.

Thorson, Gerald. "Disenchantment in Two Minneapolis Novels from the 1880s: Tinsel and Dust." *Minnesota History* 55.4 (1997): 211–22.

Sue Barker

JANSON, KRISTOFER (1841–1917) Norwegian American writer. Kristofer Janson was an established author in Norway when he immigrated and settled in Minneapolis in 1882 with his wife, Drude Krog Janson, and their children to work as a Unitarian minister among the dominantly Lutheran Norwegian immigrants in the rapidly growing city. He had already visited the United States on a lecture tour in 1879 and 1880 and published a book in praise of American liberalism, *Amerikanske forholde* (1881, American Conditions). His first American fiction was published in three volumes with the common title *Præriens saga* (1885; The Saga of the Prairies). Here, as in so much of his writing, women's rights is a central theme. Janson saw religious fundamentalism as one of the main obstacles to the liberation of women, and stories such as "Wives Submit Yourselves Unto Your Husbands" (which was also published in English translation in 1885), where the main character is driven to suicide by the support given to her tyrannical husband by the Lutheran church, caused much controversy in the immigrant society. Two historical novels—*Femtende Wisconsin* (1887, The Fifteenth Wisconsin), about soldiers in a largely Norwegian Civil War Regiment, and *Vildrose* (1887, Wild Rose), a melodramatic story about the Sioux uprising in Minnesota in 1862—are marred by sentimentality and contrived plots.

Far more successful is *Bag gardinet* (1889, Behind the Curtain), inspired by the then internationally popular "mysteries" genre, characterized by a plot that takes the reader "behind the curtain" of a variety of social classes in a specific city. The characters of *Bag gardinet* are from the highest reaches of Minneapolis society to the most miserably poor. The causes of labor and women are voiced by several characters, but the novel's social criticism is obfuscated by its extremes of melodrama and its secondhand accounts of labor conditions. By the time he wrote his next novel, however, Janson had studied the latter more thoroughly. *Sara* (1891) is a naturalistic novel strongly influenced by Helen Campbell's 1887 study of the working conditions of women in urban America in *Prisoners of Poverty*. Janson's indignation in his descriptions of Sara's attempts to make a living by selling her labor and not her body affect his style, giving the reader a sense of the stench, the misery, and the pain of factories and settlements in Chicago. By the time the novel was published, however, the marriage of the Jansons was breaking up and they both returned to Europe in 1893, thus interrupting two promising American literary careers and joining the many European immigrants who chose to return to their homeland after years in the United States. (*See also* Norwegian American Literature)

Further Reading

Draxten, Nina. *Kristofer Janson in America*. Boston: Twayne, 1976.

Øverland, Orm. *The Western Home: A Literary History of Norwegian America*.
  Northfield, MN: The Norwegian-American Historical Association and
  Champaign: U of Illinois P, 1996. 157–69.

Orm Øverland

JAPANESE AMERICAN AUTOBIOGRAPHY   The Japanese started to arrive in America in the nineteenth century, though no Japanese American autobiographies were written until the early twentieth century. The first notable autobiographies were written by women, and just as noteworthy more autobiographies thematize the Japanese American **internment** experience in World War II. What follows is a brief discussion of major Japanese American autobiographers and their works produced in the past eight decades.

Two early autobiographies were written by women. Etsu Inagaki Sugimoto (1874–1950), an immigrant, wrote one of the earliest Japanese American autobiographies, *A Daughter of the Samurai* (1925), which looks back at the narrator's childhood in her home country of Japan while recounting the kind of education she received and the social and cultural customs that the Japanese practiced that she witnessed. The values that she was inculcated in are loyalty, bravery, and honor that characterize the spirit of samurai. The second part of the autobiography focuses on Sugimoto's life in California with her Japanese merchant husband and her forced return to Japan after her husband's death. The narrative ends with her permanent return to the United States with her daughters. Sugimoto makes no mention of **racism** in the United States, though implicit criticism of her adopted country can be found in the autobiography. Another early autobiography is Kathleen Tamagawa's (1897–1979) *Holy Prayers in a Horse's Ear* (1932). The child of a marriage between a Japanese man and an Irish woman, Tamagawa writes about her parents' interracial marriage and her own biculturalism, her acclimation to a life in Japan where her father took his family to Yokohama as a silk buyer, and her own marriage to a white American and the couple's global travels.

Monica Sone (1919–) published *Nisei Daughter* in 1953. Inspired by the Chinese American **Jade Snow Wong**'s autobiography *Fifth Chinese Daughter* (1945) that narrates a young girl's growth in San Francisco, Sone's autobiography deals with essentially the same time period as its Chinese predecessor, though its geographical locale is mostly set in Seattle where Japanese Americans were ordered to evacuate. Sone recounts almost idyllic memories of her childhood life on the waterfront of Seattle where her parents owned a small hotel, but contrasting this peaceful prewar life are the hardships and humiliating ordeals Sone's family suffered at the concentration camps—first at Puyallup and then at Minidoka. Sone returned to the internment camp to visit her parents a year after her departure for college. Sone wrote the book partly to educate readers about her Japanese American family and their community, partly to denounce the government's racist and oppressive mistreatment of a people, and partly to describe the realization of her bicultural heritage and the development of her own cultural and racial identity. Also scrutinized are the psychological aftermaths of camp life on Nisei Japanese Americans like Sone herself and how they internalized racialized victimization.

Daniel Inouye (1924–) wrote *Journey to Washington* (1967), with the assistance of Lawrence Elliott before his reelection to the United States Senate, chronicling the growth of a young Japanese American boy into a war hero and eventually a prominent legislator. The book narrates Inouye's childhood experience up to the point of his entry into national politics. The dominant themes are patriotism, loyalty, and heroism. Inouye expresses an unequivocal American **identity** when Pearl Harbor called on Americans to join the fight against fascism. A strong sense of determination, resilience, and optimism is clearly conveyed throughout the narrative. Whether faced with racial problems in school or racial hatred following Pearl Harbor or life-threatening situations in World War II, Inouye remains determined to succeed in his American dream through a hard work ethic and belief in American ideals and values.

Jim Yoshida (1921–) collaborated with Bill Hosokawa, himself an autobiographer, in writing *The Two Worlds of Jim Yoshida* (1972). Yoshida's is very different from other Japanese American autobiographies written about Japanese American experiences right before, during, and immediately after World War II, for the majority of them focus upon the evacuation and internment of Japanese on the west coast. Yoshida's work deals with a unique experience of an American of Japanese origin detained in his ancestral country with which the United States was at war and for which he was forced to serve under its flag. It is the story of a man without a country. When World War II broke out, Yoshida took his father's ashes to Japan where he was drafted to fight in the Japanese Imperial Army in China. The two worlds Yoshida refers to are apparently the United States and Japan, between which he was emotionally torn while physically stuck in Japan. The autobiography delineates two major issues: Yoshida's conscription and service to the Japanese army, and his legal battle with the United States government to reclaim his American citizenship. To atone for what he was forced to do during his Japanese years, Yoshida volunteered his service to his birth-country by willingly joining U.S. troops in Korea to fight another war in the early 1950s.

Jeanne Wakatsuki Houston (1935–) and James D. Houston (1934–) started to collaborate on Jeanne's personal experience of internment at Manzanar in the late 1960s and published *Farewell to Manzanar: A True Story of Japanese American Experience During and After the World War II Internment* in 1973. The autobiography presents first-hand accounts of the internment experience at one particular concentration camp during World War II. While the book focuses on the family of the Wakatsukis, it also attempts to include the experience of Japanese Americans beyond the circles of family and friends. As is true of other similar accounts of the wartime incarceration, *Farewell to Manzanar* does not merely recount or denounce the internment, but it takes on the onus of exploring and confronting the role of racism in the U.S. government's implementation of a race-based decision. The Houstons contrast the different lifestyles that the Wakatsukis lived before, during, and after the internment and the war. Jeanne's story is chronicled in her struggles with her racial and cultural identity as well as in her efforts to assimilate into the mainstream culture. Her struggles are characterized by a desire for acceptance in a racially divided society. The end of *Farewell to Manzanar* stages Jeanne's return to the concentration camp with her husband and their three children, thereby providing both a physical and psychological closure to what she believes to be a shameful experience.

Bill Hosokawa (1915–) is known for two autobiographies: *Thirty-five Years in the Frying Pan* (1978) and *Out of the Frying Pan: Reflections of a Japanese American* (1989). Hosokawa's personal experience of internment during World War II, his encounters with racial discrimination, and the Asian American experience in general are the principal concerns of many of his newspaper columns that he eventually collected into *Thirty-five Years in the Frying Pan* and *Out of the Frying Pan*. Hosokawa digs to the bottom of the Japanese American internment that he himself, his wife Alice, and their son

Michael endured at Heart Mountain by tracing both the political and racial motivations of the government's decision to incarcerate Japanese Americans. Hosokawa investigates the causes of such mistreatment by scrutinizing the links between **race** and political status in the United States and the reasons why the Bill of Rights applies to certain citizens and not others like his family and his ethnicity under war circumstances.

Yoshiko Uchida (1921–92) published an autobiography, *Desert Exile: The Uprooting of a Japanese-American Family*, in 1982, followed by another, *The Invisible Thread: An Autobiography*, in 1991. Both narratives recount the Japanese American internment experience. *Desert Exile* delves into issues of identity, racial and cultural heritage, and the psychological effects of this racially motivated exile of Japanese Americans. Uchida not only narrates her blissful childhood lived among different ethnic groups and her racially more aware years during college, but also examines her ambivalence about being American in Japan and being Japanese in America. *The Invisible Threat* recaptures the essence of Uchida's first autobiography except that it was written for a younger audience and with new perspectives informed by Japanese Americans' redress movement. In the latter Uchida expresses her positive views of Japan and affirmatively reiterates her Japanese American identity.

David Mura (1952–) is a Sansei poet writing autobiographies. He published *Turning Japanese: Memoirs of a Sansei* in 1991, followed by *Where the Body Meets Memory: An Odyssey of Race, Sexuality & Identity* in 1996. *Turning Japanese* was not first written as a book; it was a collection of essays published previously on various topics such as cultural identity, racial politics, and sexuality from the viewpoint of a Sansei. *Where the Body Meets Memory* delves into basically the same issues that Mura explored in his first autobiography, with emphasis on race, sexuality, and identity, though the book includes stories about his parents and grandparents, which makes it more of a memoir than an autobiography.

Another poet writing autobiography is **Garrett Hongo** (1951–), who takes the name of his birth village for his narrative: *Volcano: A Memoir of Hawaii*. Hongo left Hawai'i at the age of six and settled down in Los Angeles with his parents—a move that his memoir concentrates on. Hawai'i seems like a paradise lost to the narrator who is now on a quest for self-identity through researching his family history and the land that is the site of that history. Thus history and geography occupy prominent places in the autobiographical narrative.

George Takei (1937–) is an actor writing autobiography. Known as Sulu to fans of the TV series *Star Trek*, Takei wrote *To the Stars: The Autobiography of George Takei, Star Trek's Mr. Sulu* (1994), which reflects his ethnicity as well as his career path. Like **Frank Chin**'s novel *Gunga Din Highway* (Takei was cast in Chin's televised play *The Year of the Dragon* in 1974), *To the Stars* examines the important issue of representation of Asians in Hollywood on TV and in films. As a former internee in World War II, Takei also looks into the Japanese American internment and its effects on his parents. Even though Takei's book focuses on the self and his family, his message about subverting Asian American stereotypes and self-representation forms an important theme throughout the narrative.

Further Reading

Ghymn, Esther Mikyung. "Yoshiko Uchida's Positive Vision." *The Shapes and Styles of American Asian Prose Fiction*. New York: Peter Lang, 1992. 67–89.

Goodsell, Jane. *Daniel Inouye*. New York: Thomas Y. Crowell, 1977.

Holte, James Craig. "Monica Sone." *The Ethnic I: A Sourcebook for Ethnic-American Autobiography*. Westport, CT: Greenwood Press, 1988. 161–66.

Huang, Guiyou, ed. *Asian American Autobiographers: A Bio-Bibliographical Critical Sourcebook*. Westport, CT: Greenwood Press, 2001.

Lim, Shirley Geok-lin. "Japanese American Women's Life Stories: Maternality in Monica Sone's Nisei Daughter and Joy Kogawa's Obasan." *Feminist Studies* 16.2 (Summer 1990): 289–312.

Okamura, Raymond Y. "Farewell to Manzanar: A Case of Subliminal Racism." *Amerasia Journal* 3.2 (1976): 143–47.

Rayson, Ann. "Beneath the Mask: Autobiographies of Japanese-American Women." *MELUS* 14.1 (Spring 1987): 43–57.

Sakurai, Patricia A. "The Politics of Possession: The Negotiation of Identity in America in Disguise, Homebase, and Farewell to Manzanar." *Sakurai, Privileging Positions: The Sites of Asian American Studies*. Pullman: Washington State UP, 1995. 157–70.

Sumida, Stephen H. "Protest and Accommodation, Self-Satire and Self-Effacement, and Monica Sone's Nisei Daughter." *Multicultural Autobiography: American Lives*. Ed. James Robert Payne. Knoxville: U of Tennessee P, 1992. 207–43.

Yamamoto, Traise. "Nisei Daughter, by Monica Sone." *A Resource Guide to Asian American Literature*. Eds. Sau-ling Cynthia Wong and Stephen H. Sumida. New York: Modern Language Association, 2001. 151–58.

Guiyou Huang

JAPANESE AMERICAN NOVEL   Language, generation, and the periods before and after World War II are useful reference points in Japanese American literature. Before World War II, Japanese writing in English appeared primarily in journalistic forms rather than the literary. In the late 1920s Issei writers published poems and stories in Japanese language newspapers in Hawai'i and on the West Coast of the United States. Issei-owned newspapers such as the *New World-Sun* and *Kashu Mainichi* served as important publishing forums and professionalizing contexts for Nisei writers. These publications enabled the examination of international issues and domestic **race** relations that defined Japanese as a specific ethnic group, and contributed to a growing awareness of generational differences between foreign-born Issei and their American-born Nisei children. Novels of the early twentieth century emphasized Japanese culture and generally constructed it as "exotic" and "foreign." According to Elaine Kim, prewar

Issei novelists were often members of the Japanese aristocracy, and envisioned themselves as "living bridges" between Japanese and American cultures. A case in point is Etsu Sugimoto's autobiographical novel *A Daughter of the Samurai* (1925), which portrays a romanticized "old Japan" under siege by modernization while simultaneously expressing admiration for American progress and modernity. Some writers from elite backgrounds in Japan focused on Japanese laboring classes in the United States. Yone Noguchi's *The American Diary of a Japanese Girl* (1912) takes the form of a fictionalized diary written in broken English to narrate the story of a young Japanese woman's search for work in the United States.

The evacuation and detention of over 120,000 Japanese Americans during World War II had a particularly strong impact on the Nisei, for whom the **internment** raised troubling questions of racial **identity** and nationality. During the internment Japanese American writings in English appeared in camp newspapers and literary magazines but were censored by government officials. Stan Yogi suggests that Hawaiian Nisei writers took up the novel in their exploration of Japanese American history and culture in the period immediately following World War II (134). He attributes the earlier emergence of the postwar Japanese American novel to the large population of Japanese Hawaiians on the islands who did not experience the displacement and dispossession of internment to the same extent as those in the continental United States and Canada. Postwar Japanese Hawaiian novels, including **Shelley Ota**'s *Upon Their Shoulders* (1951), **Margaret Harada**'s *The Sun Shines on the Immigrant* (1960), and Kazuo Miyamoto's *Hawaii: End of the Rainbow* (1964), offer varied perspectives on **immigration**, **assimilation**, and internment in Japanese American history.

Nisei writers of the 1950s increasingly took up the bildungsroman, or novel of formation, that conventionally follows an immigrant protagonist's journey of education and enlightenment and culminates with assimilation into the nation and the development of self-knowledge. According to Lisa Lowe, Asian American bildungsroman narrate an immigrant's desire for assimilation and upward mobility, but simultaneously expose the racial and economic contradictions of the incorporation of Asian immigrants into the nation. Lowe further argues that the bildungsroman became an important vehicle for Nisei writers to question celebrations of the postwar period as a triumph of American democracy and gave voice to the **racism** and anti-Japanese hostility that denied full citizenship and the possibility of hyphenation to Japanese Americans. **Monica Sone**'s autobiography *Nisei Daughter* (1953) illustrates how Japanese Americans were encouraged to reject Japanese culture and to internalize the conflation of Japanese **ethnicity** with disloyalty to America. One scene shows her protagonist Kazuko burning her Japanese language books and expresses the sense of alienation and anger that it produces for her. The novel offers a critical view of the equation of American identity with the negation of Japanese culture, but also refers to feelings of anger and resistance, exemplified by Kazuko's refusal to burn a Japanese doll from her grandmother.

John Okada's *No-No Boy* (1957) is a poignant exploration of the trauma of internment in Japanese American historical memory. For Nisei writers like him, the representation of Issei, Nisei, and Sansei became intertwined with competing interpretations of the internment. The novel centers on Ichiro, a "no-no boy" who defies the "loyalty questionnaire," which required Issei and Nisei to renounce loyalty to Japan and to state their willingness to serve in the U. S. armed forces. Okada depicts Ichiro's fraught attempts to accept his decision and rebuild his life in the context of postwar anti-Japanese hostility and the fragmentation of the Japanese community in Seattle. Through interior monologues and characters that represent different sectors of society and responses to internment, the novel explores the persistence of the wartime opposition of "Japanese" and "American" identities and its individual and collective impact on Japanese Americans. Okada also uses the figure of Kenji, a crippled war veteran, to question the false conflation of military service with the successful incorporation of Japanese American men into postwar American society.

The **canon**ization of Okada's novel by Asian American writers of the 1970s illustrates the convergence of the recovery of Japanese American novels with the production of a tradition of resistance in Asian American writing. Japanese American novels became key to efforts to challenge the Japanese American Citizens League (JACL) position, exemplified by Bill Hosakawa's memoir *The Quiet Americans* (1969), which stressed the willingness of Japanese Americans to prove their loyalty to the United States through internment. During the late 1970s Japanese American groups in the United States and Canada began to explore possibilities for Japanese American monetary reparations, which encouraged Nisei to speak out against the internment. Although writings on internment by non-Japanese, including wartime reports in *Life* magazine and Karen Kehoe's novel *City in the Sun* (1947), were published during the war, many Japanese American novels were not recognized or widely read until the 1970s. For Asian American writers of the 1970s the internment experience served as a catalyst for artistic production rather than a deterrent. According to the *Aiiieeeee!* anthology editors, the problem was not a lack of writings by Japanese Americans but rather the limitation of publishing forums (xliii).

The recovery of internment novels by Asian American writers of the 1970s coincided with the articulation of masculine Japanese American identities. By casting the "no-no boy" as the emblematic figure of Japanese American identity, Asian American writers of the 1970s also generated male-centered models of Asian American literature. In the 1980s Japanese American female novelists took up the theme of "breaking silence" in female-centered representations of internment and its long-term effects. Joy Kogawa's *Obasan* (1981) explores the complexities of Japanese American history and memory through notions of speech and silence, complicating traditional associations of speaking with resistance and emancipation and silence with repression and shame. The novel narrates the story of three generations of Japanese Canadians through letters, dreams, diary entries, and private memory, and brings together a private trauma of childhood sexual abuse with the public violence of internment. Kogawa's works have also helped to generate discussion on the specificity of Japanese Canadian histories of immigration and racialization. Marie Lo cautions against U.S.-centered accounts of Japanese Canadian literary history, but suggests that Asian Canadian writings need to be considered in terms of both national and transnational histories of racialization and colonialism (99).

The postmodern novel has helped to reconfigure the Japan-United States trajectory as well as the emphasis on the West Coast of the United States. Although the bildungsroman continues to be an important literary model, contemporary writers have looked to other genres for inspiration. In the1980s and 1990s women have primarily authored Japanese American novels, and many have seen critical and financial success in the literary marketplace. Some novels refer to historical themes of internment and dislocation and feature female protagonists and "feminist" themes. **Cynthia Kadohata**'s *The Floating World* (1989) takes up an archetypal "American" genre, the "road novel," to portray the nomadic existence of a Japanese American family during the 1950s. Her second book, *In the Heart of the Valley of Love* (1997), continues to explore the theme of displacement in a futuristic landscape of Los Angeles. **Karen Tei Yamashita**'s magical realist novels explore the Japanese **diaspora** in Brazil, which emerged in part from the 1924 Oriental Exclusion Act, which barred Asian immigration to the United States. *Brazil-Maru* (1992) is the story of Japanese immigrant laborers on Brazil's coffee plantations. *Tropic of Orange* (1997) is a novel that explores the effects of the North American Free Trade Agreement on both sides of the U.S. -Mexico border. Hiromi Goto's *A Chorus of Mushrooms* (1995) shifts the focus from urban communities to three generations of Japanese Canadian women in a prairie town. Although postwar Japanese American writers tended to downplay Japanese life and culture, some contemporary novelists have made conscious attempts to engage Japan. For example, Ruth Ozeki's *My Year of Meats* (1998) connects Japanese female protagonists in the United States and Japan through excerpts from Sei Shonagon's *Pillow Book*.

Japanese Hawaiian writers have utilized the bildungsroman genre and pidgin English to narrate stories that highlight the "local" context of Hawai'i. **Milton Murayama**'s *All I Asking for Is My Body* (1959) explores racial, ethnic, and class struggle in Hawai'i during the 1930s and 1940s, particularly the complicity of filial obligation with the systematic exploitation of Japanese and Filipino plantation laborers. Like Murayama, **Lois Ann Yamanaka** contradicts the stereotypical image of Hawai'i as an idyllic paradise, and instead foregrounds the poverty and hard living conditions on the islands. Set on the island of Moloka'i, *Blu's Hanging* (1997) is narrated by the eldest daughter of the Ogata family, who assumes responsibility for her siblings after their mother's death. In June 1998 protests erupted at the Asian American Studies Association (AASA) meeting in Honolulu when the novel was presented with AASA's 1997 national fiction award. Criticism centered on Yamanaka's portrayals of Filipinos and perpetuation of stereotypes of Filipinos as sexual deviants and resulted in the rescinding of the award and the resignation of the Association's executive board. Candace Fujikane argues that local and national medias' focus on the story of censorship has obscured the context of local Filipino protests against systemic local Japanese racism in Hawai'i. For Fujikane the protests need to be understood in relation to ideologies of race and ethnicity that maintain the political and economic dominance of white and local Japanese settlers in Hawai'i (161).

Contemporary Japanese American novelists continue to explore the internment experience and its implications for civil liberties. In response to attacks on the World Trade Center on September 11, 2001, expanded law enforcement and intelligence legislation has refocused attention on the Japanese American internment. Both critics and supporters seized upon the example of Japanese American internment to counter and justify the targeting of groups and individuals perceived as possible terrorists and threats to national security. Published in the aftermath of the Patriot Act, Julie Otsuka's *When the Emperor Was Divine* (2002) uses notions of loyalty and disloyalty to explore the long-term effects of internment for a single family. Narrated by multiple, unnamed protagonists, the novel diverges from previous narratives that revolve around an individual. As Otsuka suggests, novels continue to provide ways of exploring conflicts and intersections of past and present, identity, and community that continue to trouble Japanese American writers.

Further Reading

Chan, Jeffrey Paul, Frank Chin, Lawson Fusao Inada, and Shawn H. Wong. "An Introduction to Chinese-American and Japanese-American Literature." *Aiiieeeee! An Anthology of Asian American Writers*. New York: Penguin Books, 1974. xxi–xlviii.

Fujikane, Candace. "Sweeping Racism Under the Rug of 'Censorship': The Controversy over Lois Ann Yamanaka's *Blu's Hanging*." *Amerasia Journal* 26.2 (2000): 158–94.

Kim, Elaine H. *Asian American Literature: An Introduction to the Writings and Their Social Context*. Philadelphia: Temple UP, 1982.

Lo, Marie. "Obasan." *Resource Guide for Asian American Literature*. Ed. Sau Ling Wong and Stephen Sumida. New York: Modern Language Association, 2001. 97–107.

Simpson, Caroline Chung. *An Absent Presence: Japanese Americans in Postwar American Culture, 1945–1960*. Durham, NC: Duke UP, 2001.

Yogi, Stan. "Japanese American Literature." *An Interethnic Companion to Asian American Literature*. Ed. King-Kok Cheung. Cambridge: Cambridge UP, 1997. 125–55.

Cynthia Tolentino

JASMINE   **Bharati Mukherjee**'s novel *Jasmine* (1989) occupies a prominent position in South Asian American literature and focuses on a theme central to the tradition: migration and settlement. The novel traces the travels of the eponymous heroine who arrives from India to settle in the United States. Through a series of self-transformations, which are frequently propelled by acts of violent disruption, Jasmine is Americanized. Jasmine's migration from east to west is reproduced in her movement from the East Coast to the West Coast of the United States; it is when she heads out from the Midwest for her last destination, the California frontier and, in particular, the University of California at Berkeley—a symbol in the novel of free thought and untroubled **multiculturalism**—that Jasmine realizes an unfettered American selfhood.

Jasmine's journey may be charted according to the names she adopts along the way. The novel begins with a brief flashback to Jasmine, as Jyoti, during her childhood in Punjab. This early moment is important to the novel's narrative for it establishes a crucial theme: individual will vs. fate, where the first signifies the possibility of self-creation and Americanization and the second implies that tradition, **ethnicity**, nationality, and immigrant are essential and unalterable attributes of oneself. When Jyoti is seven years old, an astrologer foretells her widowhood and exile. Jyoti rejects this with a passion, and in doing so, she suffers a wound and is scarred on the forehead. Resisting the notion that her beauty is now marred and that as a woman she will be shunned, she asserts that her scar is a third eye through which she can view invisible worlds.

As a young woman, Jyoti marries Prakash, a political revolutionary who is also a master of creating electronic equipment using odds and ends—similar to how Jasmine will succeed in her journey by creating and recreating herself by building on materials and contexts available to her. It is Prakash who gives her the name Jasmine. Soon Prakash is murdered in an episode of communal violence. Carrying through with Prakash's plan study in the United States, Jasmine follows unpleasant underground routes to the New World, landing upon a Florida shore. She is brutally raped; she kills her rapist, burns her luggage from India, and continues on her way "traveling light." En route, a Quaker woman who befriends and helps her names her Jazzy.

In Manhattan, Jasmine is a nanny to Duff, daughter of a Columbia University professor named Taylor. Taylor renames her Jase; she now leaps into an intellectual, cosmopolitan life where her exoticism is valued. But in order to elude her husband's killer who is pursuing her, Jase flees to a small provincial town in Iowa. She moves in with Bud, an aging banker, and is now Jane, a middle-class housewife downplaying her foreignness. Jane distinguishes herself from other migrants who remain "hyphenated" in contrast to her own "genetic" assumptions of American identity. Bud is shot and left handicapped. Soon after, Taylor and Duff stop on their way to Berkeley. Feeling "greedy and reckless with hope," Jasmine leaves Bud to join them.

Jasmine has enjoyed a wide readership, from the mainstream to professional literary critics. It has been controversial, as well. For some, it offers an optimistic perspective on **immigration**, where Jasmine rejects marginalization and struggles and alters to secure her place in the New World. For others, the novel does not adequately question the complexities of cultural and class differences, America as a place of possibility and mobility, or the myth of the melting pot. The answer may lie in the age-old dilemma presented initially: Is it our will or destiny that determines our existence? (*See also* South Asian American Literature)

Further Reading

Nelson, Emmanuel S., ed. *Bharati Mukherjee: Critical Perspectives*. Westport, CT: Greenwood Press, 1993.

Ray, Sangeeta. "Rethinking Migrancy: Nationalism, Ethnicity, and Identity in Jasmine and The Buddha of Suburbia." *Reading the Shape of the World: Toward an International Cultural Studies*. Ed. Henry Schwarz and Richard Dienst. Boulder, CO: Westview, 1996. 183–201.

Wickramagamage, Carmen. "Relocation as Positive Act: The Immigrant Experience in Bharati Mukherjee's Novels." *Diaspora* 2.2: 171–201.

Krishna Lewis

JASON, SONYA (1927–) Rusyn American writer of novels and stories and freelance journalist. *Concomitant Soldier* (1973) and *Icon of Spring* (1993) mark Sonya Jason's journey as a twentieth-century American woman with a palpable ethnic heritage. Her essay "From Gunpowder Girl to Working Woman" (*Newsweek*, February 23, 2004) describes the dramatic change for her and so many American women during World War II. *Helper* (1994), true stories about welfare and probation with fictitious names for the characters, and *Professional Angel: A P.O.'s Story* (2001) draw on Jason's experiences as a social worker, probation officer, and journalist.

The cover illustration for *Concomitant Solider* conveys its strong antiwar theme: a peace symbol in which four divisions of the circle by a plowshare are depicted a woman, a soldier, a military medal, and gravestones. The novel begins with the attack on Pearl Harbor. From then on, not only World War II but also American involvement in Korea and Vietnam through late 1968 drastically affect Lia Raven, her family, and friends. When Lia's brother is killed in the Battle of the Bulge, the family is forever wounded. Lia's husband, having fought in World War II, returns to fight in Korea; he fathers a Japanese son who dies. He and Lia separate, and she raises their twins, Diane and David. In Vietnam, Diane's young husband becomes a quadriplegic—perhaps not by chance as at first thought. His suicide adds to Lia and her family's devastation. In a principled rejection of the military action in Vietnam as an unjust war, David refuses induction and is tried and sentenced to jail, yet gives hope for a wiser America. Through all the men's tragedies, Lia—woman, daughter, sister, wife, and mother—suffers no less, yet lives and struggles for an authentic America and its promise of life and freedom for all.

Icon of Spring is Jason's memoir of her 1930s Rusyn American childhood among various ethnic groups. Like so many during those Depression years, Jason's family has little, yet family, neighbors, and friends with human goodness, trust, and religious faith help one another in their daily struggles to survive and even thrive. Occasions such as birth, marriage, Christmas, and Easter bind the community that lives like an extended family. Against America's own dramatic changes during that era, Jason's narrative is a religious icon of spring-like hope, exemplified in her own surviving rheumatic fever.

Professional Angel recounts the search of investigative reporter, ethnic American Kelly Johanson into the death by drug overdose of her niece Carly Sokol. Working undercover as a probation officer, Kelly witnesses the human devastation of prison life and the drug culture for juveniles alienated from their families—themselves often dysfunctional. In her probation work, she learns that you cannot always judge others by externals. Through her efforts, prominent lawyers manipulating adolescents through drugs for sexual favors for themselves and others are found guilty of Carly's death, certain probation department personnel are exposed as drug dealers, and violated juveniles strive to become better individuals through her caring presence in their lives. (*See also* Carpatho-Rusyn American Literature)

Gerald J. Sabo

JAZZ   An indigenous American music created by the descendants of enslaved Africans, jazz has inspired literary artists because of the legendary lives and personalities of its major musicians and because of trademark elements such as improvisation, poly-rhythms, riffs, and scat singing. Since 1919 many poets have written jazz poetry, and since the 1950s a few poets and musicians have collaborated in recording poetry recitals with jazz accompaniment.

History

Jazz originated during the first decade of the twentieth century in New Orleans, Louisiana. It evolved out of four major influences: a style of piano music called ragtime; a type of black folk music, the country **blues**; the call-and-response music in black churches; and the music played by marching brass bands. The first great jazz band was that of Joe "King" Oliver, a band in which the trumpet virtuoso Louis Armstrong got his start. Oliver and Armstrong's music was later named New Orleans Jazz. White musicians copied this music and called it Dixieland Jazz. By the 1920s both kinds of music had spread to Chicago and New York, and in the 1930s jazz evolved into Swing, played chiefly by big bands. The best Swing bands were the black bands of Count Basie, Duke Ellington, and Fletcher Henderson, but the best advertised and best paid were the white bands of Benny Goodman, Woody Herman, and Artie Shaw.

Louis Armstrong conducting for NBC, 1937. *Courtesy of the Library of Congress.*

In response to the white commercialization of jazz, the saxophonist Charlie Parker, the trumpeter Dizzie Gillespie, and the pianist Thelonius Monk created a new and very difficult form of music that white musicians could not easily imitate and exploit. This happened in the 1940s, and the new music was called Be-bop. Bop was not as popular as Swing because it was difficult to dance to. The 1940s also saw a revival of New Orleans and Dixieland Jazz. This very danceable, good-time music became popular with young people not only in the United States but also in Europe before it was eclipsed by rock and roll.

As Be-bop began to fade in the early 1950s, pianist Dave Brubeck, baritone saxophonist Jerry Mulligan, and other white musicians working on the West Coast developed Cool Jazz, a serene sounding music, seemingly more influenced by the baroque music of Johann Sebastian Bach than by the African American jazz tradition. In the mid-1950s, the pianist Horace Silver, the drummer Art Blakey, and other East Coast musicians reasserted the black tradition in jazz by turning Be-bop into Hard Bop, which was less complicated, more hard-driving, and more blues-influenced.

Jazz in all its forms reached the peak of its popularity in the late 1950s but then suffered a serious decline in the 1960s. Two things kept audiences away. One was rock and roll, which had become popular when Elvis Presley started recording in 1956 and even more so after successful British groups such as the Beatles and the Rolling Stones spawned similar bands in the United States. The other debilitating development was the emergence of Free Jazz, a form of music championed by the saxophonist Ornette Coleman. It dispensed with fixed chord progressions and fixed rhythms and was appreciated only by musicians. By the end of the 1960s most radio stations were no longer playing jazz, and most jazz clubs had closed. This crisis drove the trumpeter Miles Davis to collaborate with rock and roll musicians and to create a hybrid form of music called Fusion, which enjoyed brief popularity in the 1970s. Like most rock and roll, Fusion relied heavily on electronic amplification of the sounds of all instruments, even the horns.

Jazz began to pull out of its crisis in the middle 1970s with a return to a hard-swinging acoustic music called Straight Ahead Jazz. This form of jazz is a combination of elements from the Swing, Be-bop, and Hard Bop eras. One of the driving forces behind this development was the veteran tenor saxophonist Dexter Gordon who had spent the doldrum years from 1962 to 1976 in Europe, where jazz was more popular than in America. Many young musicians enthusiastically embraced Straight Ahead Jazz. Among them were the trumpeter Wynton Marsalis and the tenor saxophonist Joshua Redman. The growing popularity of Straight Ahead Jazz led to a modest resurgence of all kinds of jazz during the 1980s and 1990s. This resurgence was modest because jazz has become high art and is appreciated more by the white middle class than by the African American community from which it originally sprang.

Form

The African heritage of jazz can be heard chiefly in the musicians' use of syncopation and counter rhythms. To this day West African drummers are unequaled at laying down several different rhythmic patterns simultaneously. While this is a skill that only the best modern jazz drummers have been able to master, a more basic skill that even gifted amateur musicians can attain is the ability to make the music "swing"; that is, to create a tension between the basic beat of the tune and the melody they are playing. This is the tension that makes audiences want to tap their feet or snap their fingers. As the title of a Duke Ellington tune says, "It [jazz] don't mean a thing, if it ain't got that swing."

Improvisation, in most jazz forms, is limited by the structure of the tune, called "theme" or "head," and its chord progression or "changes." The most common structures in jazz tunes are 12 bars (AAB), 16 bars (AB or AABA), or 32 bars (AB or AABA). One run-through of such a pattern is called a "chorus." The theme is usually played by the ensemble at the beginning and at the end of the piece, and in between the musicians take turns improvising. Jazz musicians don't just embellish the melody of the theme but memorize its chord progression and use it to create melodies that have very little to do with the original tune.

Two elements in jazz that have been of special interest to poets are riffs and scat singing. Riffs are short phrases that are repeated—usually by the ensemble, but sometimes also by the soloist—and interspersed in the improvisations. Scat singing happens when jazz singers improvise by singing not words but nonsense syllables such as "shoo-be-doo-be-doo" or "oop-bop-sh'bam," the latter being the title of a tune written by the great Be-bop trumpeter Dizzy Gillespie.

What distinguish the improvisations of jazz musicians from the improvisations of musicians in classical music is not only that their improvisations swing but that they rely heavily on so called "blue notes." In the key of C, these notes are E-flat and B-flat. They are called blue notes because they were the notes emphasized in the old-time country blues, which many consider to be the true source of jazz. An improvisation that doesn't stress blue notes will simply not sound "jazzy."

A trait that jazz musicians share with composers of classical music is their desire to pay homage to those from whom they learned. Thus New Orleans and Dixieland trumpet players like to quote Louis Armstrong phrases, Straight Ahead musicians keep quoting Charlie Parker's Be-bop phrases, and contemporary drummers often quote licks from forebears such as Max Roach and Art Blakey.

Jazz and Literature

Many literary artists have used jazz musicians as protagonists in their fiction and treated them as admirable counterculture figures. Perhaps the best known examples are the piano players in the short stories "Powerhouse" (1941) by Eudora Welty and "Sonny's Blues" (1957) by **James Baldwin** and the **blues** singer Ma Rainey (an historical figure) in **August Wilson**'s play *Ma Rainey's Black Bottom* (1984). Jazz musicians also figure prominently in a number of novels by contemporary writers, for instance, in **John Edgar Wideman**'s *Sent for You Yesterday* (1984), Xam Wilson Cartier's *Be-bop, Re-bop* (1987), and Nathaniel Mackey's *Djibot Baghostus's Run* (1993).

In jazz poetry there is a closer symbiosis between jazz and literature than in jazz fiction. Jazz poetry began shortly after jazz was first recorded. There are basically two kinds of jazz poetry—one that does not require the cooperation of jazz musicians and one that does.

The first kind is simply poetry about jazz or jazz musicians and attempts in various ways to capture the qualities of the music. An early example is **Carl Sandburg**'s "Jazz Fantasia" of 1919. In that poem the speaker urges a group of black musicians to "batter on your banjos, sob on your cool winding saxophones" and to "go husha-husha-hush with the slippery sandpaper" (probably a reference to a washboard being used as a percussion instrument). In 1926 the black poet **Langston Hughes** set the standard for the use of jazz elements in poetry when he published his collection *The Weary Blues*.

Recordings of the second type of jazz poetry—the kind being recited to jazz music—were first made in the 1950s by the white Beat poets Kenneth Patchen, Kenneth Rexroth, Lawrence Ferlinghetti, and **Jack Kerouac**. In most of these recordings there is little connection between what the poets are reciting and what the musicians are playing. A notable exception is Jack Kerouac's *Blues and Haiku* (1958). On that recording the improvisations of the saxophonists Al Cohn and Zoot Sims succeed in capturing the mood of the poems that Kerouac is reciting.

In 1958 Langston Hughes, who had been reciting his poems to jazz accompaniment since the 1930s, finally recorded some of his poems. His *Weary Blues* contains some of the finest examples of jazz poetry. These jazz poems stand out both because of the way they capture the quality of jazz and because of the way the musicians interweave their improvisations with the poetry.

Hughes's comments on his jazz poetry provide a good definition of that art form. In the "Introduction" to his book of poems *Montage of a Dream Deferred*, Hughes says that just like Be-bop his poetry contains "conflicting changes, sudden nuances, sharp and impudent interjections, broken rhythms, and passages sometimes in the manner of the jam session, sometimes the popular song, punctuated by riffs, runs, breaks and disc-tortions [sic]." And in the liner notes for his recording of *Weary Blues*, Hughes says about his collaboration with jazz musicians: "I tell my musicians, and I've worked with several different groups, to improvise as much as they care to around what I read. Whatever they bring of themselves to the poetry is welcome to me. I merely suggest the mood of each piece as a general orientation. Then I listen to what they say in their playing and that affects my own rhythms when I read. We listen to each other."

The most intimate melding of poetry and jazz occurs when there is a match not only of the moods but also of the structures of the poetry and the music. This happens when poets write their poems to fit specific jazz patterns or musicians write jazz tunes to fit specific poems. For one thing many jazz poems follow the standard AAB structure of the 12-bar blues. Also, musicians such as Duke Ellington, Billie Holiday, Charlie Mingus, and Archie Shepp have written poetry to fit jazz tunes of their own. Here the borderline between jazz and poetry disappears, and some scholars argue that such poems are only jazz poetry when they are recited or chanted, but when they are sung, they are jazz lyrics.

Some well-known contemporary poets who have produced jazz poetry are **Jayne Cortez**, **Nikki Giovanni**, **Michael Harper**, **Amiri Baraka**, **Don Lee**, **Sterling Plumpp**, **Sonia Sanchez**, and A. B. Spellman. Collections of jazz poetry can be found in *Moment's Notice: Jazz in Poetry and Prose*, edited by Art Lange and Nathaniel Mackey, and in the two volumes of *The Jazz Poetry Anthology*, edited by Sascha Feinstein and **Yusef Komunyaka**.

Further Reading

Feinstein, Sascha, and Yusef Komunyaka, eds. *The Jazz Poetry Anthology.* Bloomington: Indiana UP, 1992 and 1996.

Hartman, Charles. *Jazz Text.* Princeton, NJ: Princeton UP, 1991.

Hughes, Langston. *Montage of a Dream Deferred.* New York: Holt, 1951.

Lange, Art, and Nathaniel Mackey, eds. *Moment's Notice: Jazz in Poetry and Prose.* Minneapolis: Coffee House Press, 1993.

Oliphant, Dave. *The Bebop Revolution in Words and Music.* Austin: U of Texas P, 1994.

Wallenstein, Barry. "Poetry and Jazz: A Twentieth Century Wedding." *Black American Literature Forum* 25.3 (1991): 595–620.

Ward, Geoffrey. *Jazz: A History of America's Music.* New York: Knopf, 2000.

Eberhard Alsen

JEFFERS, LANCE (1919–1985)   African American poet, critic, and fiction writer. Born and raised in Nebraska, Lance Jeffers moved to San Francisco at the age of ten. He joined the army in 1942 and served in Europe in World War II. Later he embarked on an academic career after receiving BA and MA degrees from Columbia University and pursuing additional graduate work at the University of Toronto. He taught at California State College at Long Beach, and in 1971 took up the position of chairperson of the English Department at Bowie State College in Maryland. In 1974 Jeffers began teaching at North Carolina State University, where he remained until his death.

Jeffers published short stories and poems in numerous journals and anthologies, including *The Best American Short Stories—1948* and the two noteworthy collections, *Black Voices* (1968) and *New Black Voices* (1972), edited by Abraham Chapman. His work continues to appear in more recent anthologies, such as *Trouble the Water: 250 Years of African-American Poetry* (1997). Jeffers's work also includes the poetry volumes *My Blackness Is the Beauty of This Land* (1970), *When I Know the Power of My Black Hand* (1975), *O Africa, Where I Baked My Bread* (1977), and *Grandsire* (1979), and the novel *Witherspoon* (1983).

Jeffers was a member of the black literary left that in the1940s and 1950s included **John Oliver Killens**, **Julian Mayfield**, Lloyd Brown, and **Douglas Turner Ward**. Although he was from an earlier generation, he often is treated as a poet of the **Black Arts Movement** since he is among those who helped to shape a more positive, reconstructive image of blackness in a time of national transformation.

In the essay Jeffers contributed to *New Black Voices*, he identified African American literature as an appeal to conscience and an assertion of the will to freedom. His poems often speak of a black nation; however, unlike the political postures of some authors who embraced black power, his nationalism was neither narrow nor deterministic. In "There is a Nation" he refers to a nation in his soul, a nation fashioned of song, a nation that ties together the sorrow songs (**spirituals**) of **W. E. B. Du Bois**'s *The Souls of Black Folk* with the **blues**, **jazz**, and poetry itself, the literary form most analogous to black music. And poems such as "O Africa, Where I Baked My Bread," in which he discovers Africa in San Francisco and in the piano playing of Earl "Fatha" Hines, exhibit Jeffers writing in an Afrocentric tradition that extends back to the early nineteenth-century.

Further Reading

Laryea, Doris. "A Black Poet's Vision: An Interview with Lance Jeffers." *CLA Journal* 26 (June 1983): 422–33.

Rambsy, Howard. "Facing Unknown Possibilities: Lance Jeffers and the Black Aesthetic." *Step Into a New World: A Global Anthology of New Black Literature*. Ed. Kevin Powell. New York: Wiley, 2000. 195–200.

Ward, Jerry W., Jr. "Lance Jeffers on the Art and Act of Fiction." *Black American Literature Forum* 18 (Winter 1984): 169–173.

Robert Elliot Fox

JEN, GISH [LILLIAN C. JEN] (1956–)   **Chinese American novel**ist, short story writer, and essayist. Gish Jen's place in contemporary Asian American fiction rests on two important novels, *Typical American* (1991) and *Mona in the Promised Land* (1996), and acclaimed short stories such as "In the American Society" (1986), "Water Faucet Vision" (1987), and "Birthmates" (1994). Frequently included in contemporary textbook anthologies, "In the American Society" revitalizes an old theme in immigrant literature: the cultural dislocation and exclusion experienced by new émigrés caught "Between Two Worlds" ("Personal Journeys") in the suburbs of post–World War II America. Published during the height of U.S. **multiculturalism** debates, Jen's remarkable first novel, *Typical American,* is a sustained treatment of the contemporary process of becoming American, and was named a finalist for the national Book Critics Circle Award and a *New York Times* book of the year. Drawing upon the situation of her own parents, Jen constructs the story of a new kind of Asian American immigrant—that of reluctant émigrés from China's privileged classes who find themselves stranded in the United States in the early 1950s, following the victory of Mao's Communist Revolution in their homeland (Cheung 54). The middle-class Changs gradually become what they initially resisted—"typical American"—seduced into pursuit of the American dream of endless possibilities by glib Grover Ding, a corrupt, self-made millionaire. Ralph Chang's attempts at self-making are thwarted by bleak realization of his own and America's limitations. "It's an American story," Jen provocatively asserts in the novel's opening. *Typical American* demands its place in our national narratives of self-definition. Such powerful immigrant stories of *becoming* American are inseparable from what it means to *be* American today. The fictional Changs are not the perpetually foreign "other"; they are also "us."

Gish Jen with her nine-month-old daughter. *AP/Wide World Photos.*

"Birthmates," selected for *Best American Short Stories 1995* and John Updike's *Best American Short Stories of the Century* (1999), examines the cost of survival in materialist, racist U.S. society. A hostile, inhuman workplace intolerant of disruptions—even one occasioned by the family catastrophe of losing a beloved child—require Art Woo to deaden his emotions and, thus, lose his wife. Jen's unique talent for blending tragedy and comedy are displayed in Woo's misadventures in a multicultural welfare hotel, where antic children and a poor black woman serve as catalysts for resurrecting his buried emotions and recalling him to life.

American-born Lillian C. Jen was raised in Yonkers and Scarsdale, New York, by ambitious Chinese parents determined to assimilate into mainstream U.S. culture, achieve socioeconomic prosperity, and provide the best education possible for their daughters. Even so, her parents pressured Jen to conform to traditional gender expectations of a "nice" Chinese girl Americanized to the extent that she use her expensive Harvard and Stanford educations to marry well and land a lucrative professional career. Accepting **assimilation** as a fact of American life, young Jen learned to appreciate the rewards, as well as the losses, of cultural change—especially for a Chinese American female. Jen's writing aspirations and verbal humor were nurtured by growing up "half Jewish" in Scarsdale (Salz 136); coming of age in the United States during the turbulent 1960s nurtured not only Jen's distrust of institutional authority but also her resistance to traditional Chinese gender roles. Ironically, when Jen fled Stanford Business School and her parents' expectations, she chose China (her parents' homeland) as her destination. As an American "foreign expert" on temporary assignment in China, Jen began to understand her **identity** as a complex and conflicted commingling of Chinese and American strands. Jen would later conclude that this first experience of China was necessary preparation for writing *Typical American* (Lee "Gish" 219). After she returned to the United States, Lillian Jen joined the Iowa Writers' Workshop in the early 1980s, and to her parents' dismay recreated herself as Gish Jen, the writer.

Gish Jen's earliest short stories did not feature Asian American characters. The protagonist's **ethnicity** is not central to Callie Chang's tragicomic attempts to become a Catholic martyr, recounted in "The Water-Faucet Vision," an *American Short Stories 1988* selection. From the mid-1980s Jen's work has steadily attracted critical accolades, prestigious prizes, and fellowships; but Jen has resisted critical and marketplace tendencies to label her an "Asian American" writer and restrict her to stereotypical themes, such as preserving one's ethnic heritage, expected of hyphenated Americans. Jen refuses to accept reductive equations that judge cultural difference as always good and assimilation as always bad. Busting through such reductive formulas, *Mona in the Promised Land* presents a new kind of assimilation narrative. Ralph and Helen Chang, introduced in *Typical American*, are now situated in affluent Scarshill and immersed in intergenerational conflict with their wayward youngest daughter Mona. Her adolescent experiments in American self-invention and identity formation punctuate Mona's spirited coming-of-age story. Rebelling against restrictive paradigms of model minority and traditional Chinese girl, Mona embraces assimilation's liberating possibilities presented by America's complex dynamics of ethnicity blending. Her Chinese parents are appalled when Mona decides to switch to Jewish. For Mona Changowitz, being American means the freedom to choose whomever she wants to be.

Jen continued her experiments with subject and form in the 1999 short story collection *Who's Irish?* More recently Jen obtained a 2003 Fulbright teaching fellowship in China, hopeful that she, her elderly Chinese immigrant parents, and her growing Chinese-Irish American children may revitalize connections to their Chinese heritage. In 2003 the American Academy of Arts and Letters awarded Jen a coveted Strauss Living Award to support her newest work in progress. (*See also* Chinese American Novel)

Further Reading

Cheung, King-Kok. *An Interethnic Companion to Asian American Literature.* Cambridge: Cambridge UP, 1997.

Furman, Andrew. "Immigrant Dreams and Civic Promises: (Con)Testing Identity in Early Jewish Literature and Gish Jen's *Mona in the Promised Land.*" *MELUS* 25 (2000): 209–26.

Lee, Rachel C. *The Americas of Asian American Literature: Gendered Fictions of Nation and Transnation.* Princeton, NJ: Princeton UP, 1999.

———. "Gish Jen." [Interviews 1993, 1996.] *Words Matter: Conversations with Asian American Writers.* Ed. King-Kok Cheung. Honolulu: U of Hawai'i P. Los Angeles: UCLA Asian American Studies Center, 2000. 215–32.

"Personal Journeys: A Conversation with Gish Jen." Interview with Bill Moyers. *Between Two Worlds.* Prod. Public Affairs Television, Thomas Lennon Films, Thirteen/WNET, New York. Videocassette. Films for the Humanities & Sciences, 2003.

Salz, Martha. "Writing About the Things That Are Dangerous: A Conversation with Gish Jen." *Southwest Review* 78 (1993): 132–40.

Cora Agatucci

JEROME, V. J. [ISAAC JEROME ROMAINE] (1896–1965)   Often described as the rigid and terrifying cultural commissar of the American Communist Party, the Russian Polish Jew V. J. Jerome started his literary career writing poems, yet rose to national prominence, thanks to his polemical critical pieces. His literary judgments embody the typical tension in leftist aesthetic theory between the autonomy that should be granted to the artist and the political guidance that the Party as the vanguard of the working classes should provide.

Born in Poland, Jerome moved to the United States in 1915 when he was nineteen years old. He supported himself with odd jobs while he attended the City College for several years. Jerome was already a left-wing militant when, in 1919, he left college to marry fellow radical writer **Frances Winwar**, an immigrant of Italian origins. Their marriage lasted until 1924, the year Jerome joined the Communist Party. Jerome then started a relationship with the influential Communist Rose Pastor Stokes. They married in 1927, but the couple was soon separated when Stokes's cancer forced her to go to Germany for treatment; she died in 1933. In the meantime Jerome had earned a BA at New York University. His early intention was to write fiction, and he thus set out to compose poems on the resistance of African Americans to **racism**. He also started a play on the slave **Nat Turner**. Yet in 1933 Jerome began his collaboration with Sam Don, the editor of the *Communist*, thus shifting his interest to polemical writing. In 1935 Jerome became editor of the *Communist* (later called *Political Affairs*), a position that he would maintain for the following two decades.

Between the 1930s and the late 1950s, Jerome contributed important literary essays to the debate on proletarian literature, such as "Toward a Proletarian Novel" (1933), "Edmund Wilson: To the Munich Station" (1939), "The Intellectuals and the War" (1940), "Culture in a Changing World" (1948), and "The Negro in Hollywood Films" (1950). In 1937, the same year of his marriage to fellow comrade Alice Hamburger, he was appointed head of the Communist Party's cultural commission. As he stated in his essay on Wilson, Jerome firmly believed in Marxism as the scientific theory and practice of the proletariat, which was "made operative through the leadership of the Communist Party." His literary essays and reviews were extremely zealous in finding deviations from the political norms. Yet he was an equally severe critic of his own literary writings; this led him in his later years to an increasing fear of not being able to successfully end all his projects. He also felt frustrated at his having dedicated so much of his time to literary and political theorizing and so little to creative writing. Jerome's portrait as Communist commissar is further complicated by the inconsistency in his artistic tastes. While he privately collected modern art, he was also a passionate advocate of Soviet Socialist Realism.

Jerome's career was increasingly marred by the onslaught of McCarthyism. His pamphlet "Grasp the Weapon of Culture" (1952), published shortly after he refused to testify before the House Un-American Activities

Committee, became the "overt act" under which Jerome was prosecuted and convicted for the violation of the Smith Act. Indicted with other Communist leaders and intellectuals, such as the novelist Dashiell Hammett, Jerome was accused of "conspiracy to teach and advocate the overthrow by force and violence" of the U.S. government. His trial in New York's Foley Square Courthouse lasted for nine months, which Jerome spent writing poetry and correcting proofs of his autobiographical memoir, *A Lantern for Jeremy* (1952). Jerome was finally convicted to three years at Lewisburg Penitentiary and served his sentence between 1954 and 1957. When he came out of prison, he found the Party lacerated by Khrushchev's revelations over Stalinist crimes. Yet he did not take part to the bitter ideological dispute that took place in the late 1950s as he left for Poland in 1958 and lived in Moscow from 1959 to 1961, where he edited Lenin's *Collected Works*. Returning to the United States in 1962, Jerome started to work on several fiction projects as well as on the sequel to *A Lantern for Jeremy*. Yet he suffered from increasingly failing health due to a brain tumor that caused his death in 1965.

Jerome's cultural leadership of the Communist Party showed his belief in the key role that the Party should assume in the political evaluation of a work of art. His model was clearly influenced by his admiration for the Soviet model of state-sponsored literature. Jerome set the prevailing mode for evaluating American radical literature between the 1930s and the 1950s, one that judged its success in relation with the more pressing interests of the working classes.

Further Reading

Foley, Barbara. *Radical Representations: Politics and Form in U.S. Proletarian Fiction, 1929–1941*. Durham, NC: Duke UP, 1993.

Wald, Alan M. *Exiles from a Future Time: The Forging of the Mid-Twentieth-Century Literary Left*. Chapel Hill: U of North Carolina P, 2002.

———. *Writing from the Left: New Essays on Radical Culture and Politics*. London and New York: Verso, 1994.

Wixson, Douglas. *Worker-Writer in America: Jack Conroy and the Tradition of Midwestern Literary Radicalism, 1898–1990*. Urbana and Chicago: U of Illinos P, 1994.

Luca Prono

JEWISH AMERICAN AUTOBIOGRAPHY   The dual nature of the term "Jewish American autobiography" offers an immediate indication of the characteristic tensions of the genre. The Jewish American autobiographers have typically chronicled the difficult negotiation between their Eastern European Jewish heritage and the demands of the new life in America. As the example of many writers below suggests, the attempt to maintain Jewish cultural and religious traditions after arrival in America has to varying degrees failed. The self-questioning form of the autobiography enables the Jewish American writer to address the effects of the new demands on the individual in the face of pressures to assimilate into American life. Moreover, the form allows the writer to discuss other elements of their new life that may have filled the void when maintenance of Jewish tradition became untenable.

Although Jews had been present in small numbers in the United States since early colonization, large-scale **immigration** began in the late nineteenth century, especially following widespread persecution in Eastern Europe. It was not long before a number of these immigrants began recording and disseminating their experience of adjusting to the new country. While these earliest forms of Jewish American autobiography frequently follow a more or less set pattern of narrating the passage—generally from Eastern European *shtetls* (ghettoes)—to arrival in America, there is considerable variation in the nature of the writer's experience.

With *From Plotzk to Boston* (1899), **Mary Antin** produced one of the earliest works to employ this pattern. This impressionistic account of life in Jewish Poland followed by her family's emigration was written in Yiddish from the age of eleven. Antin expanded this early work into *The Promised Land* (1912), which became the first widely commercial success for Jewish American autobiography, selling 85,000 copies by the time of Antin's death in 1949. Antin recalls life in Eastern Europe as deeply divided and restrictive, with a constant undercurrent of **anti-Semitism**. *The Promised Land* describes Antin's growing awareness of the contrasting freedom and opportunity existing for the immigrants in America, which replaced the rigidity of Jewish tradition and the repression of gentile anti-Semitism. Although largely celebratory, Antin's account also gestures toward the emotional sacrifices necessary to succeed in the New World. Her father's decision to break with the traditions of Jewish life and the hardships initially endured by the family, especially the women, lend the book an occasionally more somber tone. In general, however, *The Promised Land* represents a plea for Jews to assimilate into the welcoming New World of America. Antin maintained her advocacy of **assimilation**, believing that discarding the restricting and old-fashioned ties of Jewish tradition offered wider opportunities for success in America. In later life she also became a supporter of Zionism, maintaining that there was no conflict between the two positions.

For Antin and other early immigrant autobiographers such as **Abraham Cahan**, the acquisition of the English language as a replacement for Yiddish was vital in terms of acculturation. In order to succeed in the New World, language was just one among many cultural traditions that required adjustment. Cahan's experiences, as recounted in his autobiographical and semiautobiographical works, represent an illuminating counterpoint to Antin's accounts. Following political persecution, Cahan emigrated from Russia to America in 1882, at the age of twenty-two. In 1897 he founded the *Jewish Daily Forward*, a popular Yiddish-language newspaper, which he edited for nearly fifty years. As with **Isaac Bashevis**

Singer's works, Cahan's autobiography (produced in five volumes between 1916 and 1936) was written in Yiddish. The first two volumes, abridged and translated into English as *The Education of Abraham Cahan*, describe the physical and emotional journeys of his early life. Cahan moved from the Jewish shtetl to the city, from Russia to America, and from religion to secularism and socialism. As Cahan becomes more acclimatized to both the opportunities and obstructions of America, the old country becomes a fading memory, while his autobiography describes his life as a teacher, lawyer, socialist orator, and journalist. Cahan is more widely known for *The Rise of David Levinsky*, which although presented as a novel contains highly autobiographical elements. The text describes Levinsky's rapid acculturation into successful American commercial life, followed by an alienated feeling that his materialistic acquisitiveness has left him morally bankrupt. As Alvin H. Rosenfeld suggests, Levinsky presents an ostensibly similar narrative to Antin's *The Promised Land*, but "[i]n place of the buoyancy and confidence that accompany Miss Antin's rebirth in America, Cahan's narrative is marked by heavy notes of brooding, depression, puzzlement and general spiritual malaise" (137).

One might surmise from this distinction that the different perspectives on the opportunity afforded by the New World is marked by gender—Antin, after all, clearly had more to gain in coming to America in terms of self-fulfillment. Despite reservations, the autobiographical works of **Anzia Yezierska** are also notably more positive about the experience of immigration than Cahan. Although it would be a mistake to take her various accounts of immigrant Jewish American life as autobiography, there nevertheless remains an important autobiographical dimension to Yezierska's works. *Bread Givers* (1925), for example, clearly draws on her family's experience of life in New York's Lower East Side. In particular, *Bread Givers* identifies the necessity of its female protagonist's rebellion against the restrictive patriarchal tradition that had clearly survived the passage from Eastern Europe to New York. Following *Bread Givers*, Yezierska wrote *All I Could Never Be* (1932) and *Red Ribbon on a White Horse* (1950), both of which veer between autobiography and fiction. Although, like Mary Antin, Yezierska describes the attempts of the Jewish girl to fight for an independent existence in America, her works suggest a greater sympathy for aspects of Jewish cultural tradition. In her works the tensions between the greater opportunities of American life and the importance of Jewish cultural heritage are rendered with greater equivocation.

Another autobiographer of life on the Lower East Side was **Michael Gold** (Itzok Isaac Granich), most notably in *Jews Without Money* (1930). Born in the Lower East Side, Gold was for a number of years a highly influential figure in proletarian literature through his position as editor of *New Masses*. *Jews Without Money*, which underwent fourteen printings in the first two years of its publication, consists largely of sketches of the poverty experienced by Gold during his adolescence and young adulthood in the

Jewish community. Contrasting sharply with the success stories of Antin, *Jews Without Money* depicts, sometimes sentimentally, the desperate poverty of Jewish tenement life. The text is less concerned with cultural and religious aspects of Jewish life, instead focusing upon the political and economic exploitation of the working-class ghetto dwellers by rich capitalists. Illustrating this preoccupation, Gold ends the work with a political rally at Union Square where he is converted to the cause of revolution and Communism. Bernard Sherman argues that the vividness of the book's characters is "marred by the narrow limits of the Marxist viewpoint" in which Gold passionately believed (77). Despite its generally crude aesthetic, however, *Jews Without Money* is an important document of immigrant poverty and the extremes of life in the new urban environments. Moreover it became a template that other writers seeking to explore the exploitation of the working masses in 1930s America found impossible to ignore.

Another political radical, although an anarchist rather than a communist, Emma Goldman published a two-volume autobiography, *Living My Life*, in 1931. Like Gold, although she had abandoned the tenets of Judaism, one might argue that her political idealism was informed by her Jewish background. *Living My Life* was written while Goldman was in exile in St. Tropez. This followed her deportation from America to the Soviet Union for her political views following World War I. Disillusioned with the degree of state control in the Soviet Union, Goldman left after two years and traveled in Europe. Beginning with Goldman's journey from Russia to Rochester, New York, her early failed marriage, followed by her arrival in New York at the age of twenty, *Living My Life* details both her anarchist political ideals and the various activities these led to, while being equally candid regarding her personal relationships. Goldman is frank in her description of her nine-year passion for Ben L. Reitman, for example, while simultaneously providing the reader with a forceful critique of American society and government.

Another account of first-generation Jewish American experience is provided in two autobiographical volumes by Ludwig Lewisohn, *Up Stream* (1922) and *Mid-Channel: An American Chronicle* (1929). These works, perhaps more acutely than any others, document the extreme difficulty and the vicissitudes involved in negotiating an identity for the immigrant Jew in the first half of the twentieth century. *Up Stream* begins in Germany where, even prior to embarking for America, the family considered themselves to be Germans before being Jewish. Relocating to South Carolina in 1890, Lewisohn describes his childhood attempts to become an American and shrug off his German Jewish heritage. As part of his assimilation, Lewisohn first converts to Methodism, then becomes a teacher of literature, after which he repudiates Christianity in favor of evolutionary theory. Failing to secure a post at Columbia University because of anti-Semitism, Lewisohn's bitterness was deepened when his loyalty to America was later questioned at the outset of World War I and he was forced to resign another university post. *Mid-Channel* describes how these experiences helped to turn him from support of assimilation toward advocating cultural pluralism, citing his belief that assimilation actually leads to exclusion. Later still, following a ten-year period living in Europe, the experiences of the German Jews under Hitler led Lewisohn to repudiate cultural pluralism and become a powerful advocate of Zionism.

Lewisohn's experiences as an academic and an intellectual predate those described in a number of mid-twentieth-century autobiographies. Again, the tension between the author's Jewish and American identities is often foregrounded in these accounts. Irving Howe's short autobiographical essay, "The Lost Young Intellectual," for example, memorably depicts a family seder (the traditional Passover meal) that he attends and finds his burgeoning intellectual life at odds with family tradition: "He whose head may have been buzzing a few hours back with Kafka or Existentialism or the theory of permanent revolution or Chagall's technique . . . where does he fit in now?" (155). **Alfred Kazin**'s *A Walker in the City* (1951) lyrically explores the similar tensions that develop as the Jewish American intellectual departs from his cultural roots. The autobiography is structured around the return of Kazin to his native Brownsville—a suburb of Brooklyn—following his earlier escape to the intellectual milieu of Manhattan. In Brownsville, Kazin revisits the scenes of his childhood, such as his old school, and writes about the memories these locations evoke, including his discovery of America and in particular its literature. As with earlier Jewish American writers, Kazin's escape from the traditional Jewish world is affected through education and the proficient acquisition of language, granting access to wider, non-Jewish American culture. The narrative centers on the familiar struggle between Jewish tradition and the need to succeed in the world of gentile America. This is felt as a tension between the young man described, who wants to leave the Jewish world and succeed in the intellectual world of Manhattan, and the older man writing, who looks back with nostalgia and some regret at his deracination and the lost tradition of orthodoxy. Kazin wrote two further volumes of reminiscence, *Starting Out in the Thirties* (1962) and *New York Jew* (1978). The former describes Kazin's joining the intellectual Manhattan crowd following the economic hardships of the Depression, while the latter is an account of his life among the intellectual elite from the 1940s onward, which also explores his ambivalent and complex relationship to his Jewishness.

Similar to Kazin's narrative in content, if not tone, is Norman Podhoretz's *Making It* (1967), a disarmingly candid account of the rise of a precocious slum child from Brownsville, through Columbia and Cambridge Universities, to become editor of the influential Jewish cultural and literary magazine *Commentary*. In its depiction of the struggle for success among the intellectual "family," as Podhoretz terms it, *Making It* illustrates his assertion, made at the outset, that "[o]ne of the longest journeys in the world is the journey from Brooklyn to Manhattan," and is also a revealing memoir of the Manhattan intellectual scene in the 1950s. *Making It* received a lukewarm response from the same intellectual world Podhoretz was describing, many reviewers apparently resenting the unabashed celebration of success and wealth as both crassly materialistic and an "exhibition of the 'pushy' Jew at his most excessive" (Rosenfeld 146). Kazin's and Podhoretz's autobiographies relate the tenuous links maintained between the authors and their Jewish roots, even in the face of assimilated American success. Allen Guttman usefully observes crucial differences of tone; however, in the celebration of success that comprises *Making It*, which is "the story of a proudly brash young man who made it; the literary convention is that of Rousseau's Confessions rather than Kazin's nostalgic memoir" (92). Following the uneasy reception of *Making It*, Podhoretz's political views, previously of the liberal left, turned toward the right, as described in memoirs such as *Breaking Ranks* (1979). More recent works, such as *Ex-Friends: Falling Out with **Allen Ginsberg**, Lionel and Diana Trilling, **Lillian Hellman**, Hannah Arendt, and **Norman Mailer*** (1999), as the title suggests, elaborate on his shift in political and aesthetic views and his alienation from the liberal intelligentsia.

In addition to a number of fictional works that draw heavily on material from his life, **Herbert Gold** produced an autobiography titled *My Last Two Thousand Years* in 1972. While his earlier autobiography, *The Fathers: A Novel in the Form of a Memoir* (1967), provides a compelling portrait of the relationship between Gold and his Russian Jewish father, the later autobiography begins with Gold's childhood and alienated adolescence as a Jewish immigrant in the Midwest. The text describes Gold's struggle to achieve his own ambitions in the new country, rather than those of his parents. While Gold succeeds as a critic and novelist, as with other immigrant Jews, it is at some personal cost—a number of failed relationships and an ambivalent and disillusioned relationship to both his American and his Jewish heritage. As with Lewisohn, Gold's encounter with emotionally and physically traumatized **Holocaust** survivors in postwar Europe led him toward greater reconciliation with his Jewishness, a process reinforced by later visits to Israel.

In terms of form, most of the autobiographies discussed hitherto are relatively straightforward chronological accounts. By contrast, *Family Chronicle* (1969), the autobiography of Objectivist poet **Charles Reznikoff**, takes a far freer approach. In a skillful act of ventriloquism, the book is divided up into three sections: the first of which tells the story of Reznikoff's mother, Sarah, in her own voice; the second his father, Nathan: and the third Reznikoff himself. Another very representative tale in terms of content, the narrative tracks the family from poverty and hardship in Russia followed by emigration to America. More years of hardship follow, as Reznikoff reflects upon how his parents strove to provide for the family through the needle trade in the harsh Jewish ghetto environment of early twentieth-century New York City.

A number of the works discussed above, for instance those of Yezierska, Cahan, and Gold, may be characterized by a marked generic hybridity as they blur the line between fiction and autobiography. Late twentieth-century examples suggest that this is a continuing trend. **E. L. Doctorow**'s *World's Fair* (1985), for example, draws heavily upon his own experiences as a Jewish child in New York. Meanwhile **Henry Roth**'s *Call It Sleep* (1934), a fictional work with elements of autobiography, was followed sixty years later by the *Mercy of a Rude Stream* series (1994–98), which deftly traverses the continuum between fictional invention and unadorned autobiography.

Philip Roth has perhaps been at the forefront of this trend, much of his later work playfully testing the boundaries between fiction and autobiography. From the middle period of his writing career, Roth developed the alter ego character of Nathan Zuckerman, who has appeared in a number of his works, starting with *The Ghost Writer* in 1979. In these later works, Roth has used this character and other metafictional devices both to blur the distinctions between fiction and autobiography and to explore contemporary Jewish American identity. As Mark Shechner suggests of these later works, "If Roth's books are not precisely autobiographies, neither are they fictions in quite the same manner that Shakespeare's plays or Dickens's novels are fictions," and he describes them instead as "fables of identity" (225). Roth has also produced two more ostensibly autobiographical works: a memoir about the relationship with his father, *Patrimony: A True Story* (1991), and *The Facts* (1988). The latter further obscures distinctions between fact and fiction through Roth's book ending the memoir with letters on the text exchanged between himself and Zuckerman. The work concludes with a lengthy letter from Zuckerman to Roth, protesting omissions and distortions of the "truth."

Roth's metafictional autobiographies are the latest in a long tradition of inventive and earnest explorations into what it means to be a Jewish American. From dealing with the trauma of emigration from Eastern Europe and arrival in the New World, through explorations of the immigrants' involvement in radical politics and the liberal intelligentsia, to more recent investigations into modern Jewish **identity**, Jewish American autobiography has constantly sought to negotiate between the demands of tradition and those of the new, opportunity-laden country. Immigration to and acculturation in America has resulted in, as Rosenfeld argues, "a complex new creature" (145). This new creature continues to be thoroughly examined through the rich storehouse of Jewish American autobiography. As Leslie Fiedler has suggested, "The autobiography of the urban Jew whose adolescence coincided with the Depression, and who walked the banks of some contaminated city river with tags of Lenin ringing in his [sic] head . . .has come to seem part of the mystical life history of a nation" (65). Although the Jewish immigrant has not always found it desirable to become thoroughly assimilated into American life, one might argue that Jewish American autobiography nevertheless comprises an indispensable element in American literary culture.

Further Reading

Fiedler, Leslie. *Waiting for the End: The American Literary Scene from Hemingway to Baldwin*. London: Jonathan Cape, 1965.

Guttman, Allen. *The Jewish Writer in America*. New York: Oxford UP, 1971.

Holte, James Craig. "The Representative Voice: Autobiography and the Ethnic Experience." *MELUS* 9 (1982): 25–46.

Howe, Irving. "The Lost Young Intellectual." *Commentary* (October 2, 1946): 152–63.

Rosenfeld, Alvin H. "Inventing the Jew: Notes on Jewish Autobiography." *The American Autobiography: A Collection of Critical Essays*. Ed. Albert E. Stone. Eaglewood Cliffs, NJ: Prentice Hall, 1981. 133–56

Shechner, Mark. *After the Revolution: Studies in the Contemporary Jewish Imagination*. Bloomington: Indiana UP, 1987.

Sherman, Bernard. *The Invention of the Jews: Jewish-American Education Novels, 1916–1964*. New York: Thomas Yoseloff, 1969.

Alan Gibbs

JEWISH AMERICAN GAY LITERATURE   The development of gay Jewish literature in the United States has closely paralleled the evolutionary path of gay American literature in general. Whereas Jewish American literature as a whole experienced a flowering in the late 1950s and 1960s, the works written then rarely addressed gay themes or included gay characters. A decade after the gay liberation movement began with the Stonewall riots of 1969, gay literature started developing in the United States as a body of work. It was then that gay Jewish literature—poetry, drama, memoir, and fiction—also began to emerge in a significant way, just as lesbian Jewish literature was doing.

This gay Jewish literary emergence from the late 1970s onward also paralleled the proliferation of gay and lesbian Jewish congregations throughout the United States. In turn the literature itself helped foster a growing sense of identity among American gay Jews as well as an acceptance of gay Jews by non-gay segments of the Jewish community, most particularly by the Reform and Reconstructionist movements. Increased mainstream Jewish attention to the lives of gay and lesbian Jews has helped foster greater interest in and creation of Jewish American gay literature.

These literary works reflect a broad range of experience and **identity**. Some gay American Jews are religious or lead culturally traditional lives, whereas others are secular or do not practice any Jewish traditions whatsoever. Similarly some gay Jewish literary texts focus expressly on the intersection of gay and Jewish identities, their parallels, compatibilities, and conflicts, whereas others reflect primarily gay experience in which characters' Jewishness remains incidental to their senses of self and the lives they lead. Mirroring the dominance of Ashkenazi Jews (those of Central and East European ancestry) in the United States and in Jewish American literature, Jewish American gay literature has rarely presented the lives of

Sephardi (Spanish and North African), Mizrahi (Persian and Mid-Eastern), or Falasha (Ethiopian) Jews in America.

The themes that pervade this literature variously echo themes found in other Jewish American and gay American literatures: the sources of one's definition as Jewish (does Jewish society decide or does the individual?); inner conflict between a nontraditional lifestyle and one based on traditional cultural-religious values; conflict with family and community over breaks with tradition, particularly over choices not to marry a Jewish woman and raise Jewish children; **assimilation** into broader American culture; comfort with one's sexuality; parallels between homophobia and **anti-Semitism**; reactions to the **Holocaust** and to the devastation of AIDS; and alienation from and persecution by broader society.

Poetry

The greatest exception to the minimal gay Jewish presence in American literature prior to the late 1970s was the poetry of **Allen Ginsberg**, widely acknowledged as one of America's most important poets. Ginsberg frequently wrote poetry echoing Hebrew biblical forms and Jewish prayer, and containing Jewish motifs and allusions as well as explicit references to homosexual-identified people sharing space with other Americans. Most well-known are "Howl" (1955–56), a statement against American conformity and cold war politics, and "Kaddish" (1957–59), an elegy to Ginsberg's late mother in which he explores his Jewish heritage and refers to his own homosexuality. His *Cosmopolitan Greetings: Poems 1986–1992* (1994) contains Jewish-themed and gay-themed poems side-by-side.

David Bergman's *Cracking the Code* (1985) likewise contains several gay-themed poems alongside ones exploring Jewish themes, as does **Edward Field**'s Lambda Literary Award–winning collection, *Counting Myself Lucky: Selected Poems 1963–92* (1992). **Kenny Fries**'s collection *Anesthesia* (1996) does similarly, and also includes individual poems mixing issues of gay and Jewish identity.

Drama

Drama is the genre of Jewish American gay literature that has probably reached the largest audience, thanks especially to the works of **Harvey Fierstein**, **Tony Kushner**, and **Martin Sherman**. Their plays not only achieved high critical acclaim, but also have sometimes been translated into film.

Fierstein's Tony Award–winning *Torch Song Trilogy* (1982), the three component acts of which were first performed in 1978 and 1979, depicts the life of a gay Jewish drag queen who struggles to find love, raise a child, and create a family on his own terms. Fierstein's *Forget Him* (1982) chronicles a gay Jewish man's search for the perfect match. Kushner's plays often include gay, Jewish, and gay Jewish characters participating in the sociopolitical issues of the day, and suggest the coincidence of interest shared by gays and Jews as frequently marginalized members of society. In *A Bright Room Called Day* (1985), for example, gay and Jewish characters join others in condemning the rise of Hitler and drawing parallels to American society and politics under President Reagan. The two plays composing *Angels in America*: *Millennium Approaches* (1991) and *Perestroika* (1992) extend these themes and approaches to show the lives of gay Jewish characters and others struggling with AIDS, as well as issues of individual faith and moral responsibility in the modern era. *Angels* earned numerous awards, including two Tony Awards, two Drama Desk Awards, and a Lambda Literary Award. Sherman's *Bent* (1979), which won the Drama Critics Circle Award and others, draws different parallels between gay and Jewish experience by portraying a gay man imprisoned in a Nazi concentration camp who pretends to be Jewish so as to avoid the "worse" label of "homosexual." And in his *A Madhouse in Goa* (1989) an isolated gay Jewish character struggles to cope with his loneliness while other characters seek escape from their fears.

Other significant gay Jewish plays include William Finn's *The Marvin Songs*, a trilogy of musical plays (1979, 1981, and 1990) following the life of a married Jewish man who confronts his gayness and its implications for relationships with wife, son, and lover. Likewise important are three plays showing the lives of gay Jewish men whose lives have been changed by AIDS: William M. Hoffman's *As Is* (1985), which won the Drama Desk and Obie Awards, and **Larry Kramer**'s *The Normal Heart* (1985) and *Destiny of Me* (1993), which won the Dramatists Guild Marton Award and others.

Memoir

Perhaps the earliest memoir of growing up gay and Jewish in the United States is *Under the Rainbow* by Arnie Kantrowitz (1977), detailing the life of a man initially closeted, but later visibly active in the nascent gay rights movement. Lawrence D. Mass, Kantrowitz's partner, later wrote his own memoir, *Confessions of a Jewish Wagnerite* (1994), in which he compares and contrasts the evolution of his attitudes toward gay and Jewish aspects of self. **Lev Raphael**, known primarily for his gay Jewish-themed fiction, published *Journeys and Arrivals: On Being Gay and Jewish* in 1996, a collection of autobiographical essays analyzing the difficulties and rewards of claiming both gay and Jewish identities. In 1997 the comedian Jaffe Cohen published a humorous gay Jewish coming-of-age memoir, *The King of Kings and I*, and the poet Kenny Fries published *Body, Remember*, a memoir exploring the intersection of his gay, Jewish, and disabled identities.

The first anthology of autobiographical essays about Jewish American gay experience and identity was *Twice Blessed: On Being Lesbian or Gay and Jewish* (1989), edited by Christie Balka and Andy Rose, a book including both men's and women's perspectives. More than ten years later, other similar anthologies containing men's and women's writings appeared: *Queer Jews* (2002), edited by David Shneer and Caryn Aviv, and *Mentsh: On Being Jewish and Queer* (2004), edited by Angela Brown. Two anthologies edited by Lawrence Schimel present Jewish men's perspectives exclusively: *Kosher Meat* (2000), a collection of erotic-themed personal essays and short fiction, and *Found Tribe: Jewish Coming Out Stories* (2002), which includes one of the few pieces of gay Sephardi-Jewish American literature.

Fiction

Several American novels involve gay characters who are either secular Jews or whose Jewishness is incidental to the plot and themes developed. Paul Goodman's *Parents' Day* (1951) and **Sanford Friedman**'s *Totempole* (1965) are rare examples of pre-Stonewall novels that include a gay Jewish character. Other notable novels focusing primarily on characters' gayness rather than their Jewishness include Larry Kramer's extremely popular *Faggots* (1978), **Robert Glück**'s *Jack the Modernist* (1985), Gene Horowitz's *Privates* (1986), Stan Leventhal's *Mountain Climbing in Sheridan Square* (1988), and **David Feinberg**'s Lambda Literary Award–winning *Eighty-Sixed* (1989) as well as his *Spontaneous Combustion* (1991).

In still other works of fiction, however, a major character's gay and Jewish identities are treated as equally central to the character's sense of self and to the work's plot and theme. *A Fairy Tale* by S. Steinberg (1980) is a comic novel about a gay Jewish man's conflicts with his matchmaking aunt. Harlan Greene's *Why We Never Danced the Charleston* (1984) depicts a gay love triangle involving a Jewish man in 1920s Charleston. *Years From Now* (1987), a novel by **Gary Glickman**, portrays a gay man who insists upon maintaining a traditional Jewish life similar to that of his non-gay relatives; and Glickman's *Aura* (2004) shows gay and straight Jewish characters sharing life and transitions in post-1960s New York City. Bernard Cooper's *A Year of Rhymes* (1993) tells the story of a Jewish boy's gay sexual awakening as he learns that his older brother is dying from leukemia; Lev Aryeh Stollman's Lambda Literary Award–winning *The Far Euphrates* (1997) is likewise partly the story of a Jewish boy's gay sexual awakening.

Raphael, who regularly wrote gay Jewish-themed short stories throughout the 1980s, won a Lambda Literary Award for *Dancing on Tisha B'Av* (1990), a ground-breaking collection combining gay- and non-gay themed short stories about Jewish American life. He followed this in 1992 with the novel *Winter Eyes*, the coming-of-age tale of a sexually explorative young man whose **Holocaust**-surviving parents hide their Jewishness. The theme of hiding also dominates Richard Hall's *Family Fictions* (1991), a novel comparing the life of an openly gay man with that of his mother, who struggles to hide her family's Jewish origins.

In Geoffrey Linden's *Jigsaw* (1974), a gay character wrestles to reconcile his Jewish heritage with his gayness. Likewise the protagonist of

Douglas Sadownick's *Sacred Lips of the Bronx* (1994) strives to integrate his gay lifestyle and his Jewishness while discovering passion and love with a gay Puerto Rican man. **Daniel M. Jaffe**, who regularly published gay Jewish-themed short stories throughout the 1990s, also explores the inner conflict between gay and Jewish identities in his novel *The Limits of Pleasure* (2001), which uniquely braids religious, cultural, and sexual rituals, imagery, and values. Michael Lowenthal's *The Same Embrace* (1999) sets this identity conflict outside the individual—the novel depicts a gay Jewish man who struggles to bring about reconciliation with his newly Orthodox, homophobic, identical twin brother.

Through its handling of themes relevant to gay and Jewish audiences, Jewish American gay literature is flourishing despite its relatively recent emergence. The numerous awards earned by these works suggest recognition of their importance to American culture as a whole.

Further Reading

Levin, James. *The Gay Novel in America.* New York: Garland, 1991.

Martin, Robert K. *The Homosexual Tradition in American Poetry.* Austin: U of Texas P, 1979.

Nelson, Emmanuel S., ed. *Contemporary Gay American Novelists.* Westport, CT: Greenwood Press, 1993.

———, ed. *Contemporary Gay American Poets and Playwrights.* Westport, CT: Greenwood Press, 2003.

Shatzky, Joel, and Michael Taub, eds. *Contemporary Jewish-American Dramatists and Poets.* Westport, CT: Greenwood Press, 1999.

Woods, Gregory. *Articulate Flesh: Male Homoeroticism and Modern Poetry.* New Haven, CT: Yale UP, 1987.

Daniel M. Jaffe

JEWISH AMERICAN LESBIAN LITERATURE The development of a specifically Jewish American lesbian literature can be linked to various parallel movements within both the Jewish community and the gay, lesbian, and bisexual rights movement. Although the Jewish community has often claimed to be excluded from mainstream American society, especially in the earlier half of the twentieth century, lesbians have often claimed that they are excluded from the rituals and traditions of the Jewish community. As a result Jewish literature has often dealt with themes of tradition, culture, migration, and **assimilation**; while lesbian authors explore these subjects from the unique perspective of double marginalization, accepting the challenge to redefine their lives as Jewish women within the new and changing parameters of lesbian identities.

In the past Jewish American lesbian writers usually wrote from a secular viewpoint, expressing their Jewishness as a cultural or ethnic **identity** rather than subscribing to the traditional Jewish belief system. This reflects the fact that religious ceremonies and traditions are often focused on the rites of passage that define heterosexual lives, such as marriage and childbirth. The Orthodox and Conservative branches of Judaism continue to believe that the Torah specifically forbids homosexual acts in the book of *Leviticus*. However, the Reform and Reconstructionist branches of Judaism believe that there should be a new interpretation of *Leviticus*, which is more open-minded and free from a condemnation of modern homosexuality. Lesbianism is never specifically mentioned in the Torah or any holy book of the Jewish faith, and male homosexuality is only rarely commented upon. For this reason, as well as a dedication to the tradition of Jewish liberalism, Reconstructionist congregations have enacted complete acceptance of gay, lesbian, and bisexual members. Both the Reform and Reconstructionist branches of Judaism in America have also been among the first religious groups in the country to accept lesbians into their congregations, allowing them to become members of the clergy and holding commitment ceremonies for lesbian and gay couples.

Early Jewish American Lesbian Literature

One of the first mentions of lesbianism in twentieth century Jewish literature appeared in a play written by a man. Scholem Asch's play *God of Vengeance* (1922) portrayed life in a brothel where the daughter of the brothel owner falls in love with one of the prostitutes working for her father. The play was so controversial at the time that its cancellation was demanded and the show's star was put into jail for one night. The first Jewish lesbian main character in a novel written by a female was Jo Sinclair's Debbie Brown, one of the protagonists of her novel *Wasteland* (1946). The novel significantly described the interplay of both a lesbian and a Jewish identity because Brown helps her brother come to terms with his Jewishness by recommending a psychotherapist who has already helped her to accept that she is a lesbian. The novel proved to be very successful, winning the Harper prize and remaining on the best-seller list for months.

Gertrude Stein was another figure of importance in the 1940s, living in France with her long-time partner Alice B. Toklas. Stein came from a middle-class Jewish family that had lived in Pittsburgh and San Francisco. She did not explicitly engage the question of Jewishness in her work, and by moving to France she became an exile by choice, distancing herself from her family and upbringing. She was well accepted by the intelligentsia and literati of the day and her home with Alice became a salon for many artists and writers, some of whom were homosexual. She had a brief association with international expatriate lesbian literary circles, including that of Djuna Barnes, but soon isolated herself from them out of discomfort with affiliating herself with a community of lesbians. If Stein's work was concerned with resolving her lesbian identity and sexuality, her novels were written in a new modernist style that made these themes incomprehensible to many readers. Today lesbian literary theorists read Stein's work with an eye to finding codified clues of her lesbian identity and the way she viewed her lifelong partnership with Alice. In her novel *Ida, A Novel* (1941), she explores the idea of "twinning"; Ida creates more possibilities for herself by creating an exact double who can reenact the transgressions of sexuality and identity that Ida cannot allow of herself. *Tender Buttons* (1911) and *The Autobiography of Alice B. Toklas* (1932) are also of interest to lesbian literary scholars.

During the 1940s when America was in the midst of upheaval from World War II, Jewish lesbian authors were able to write narratives about their lives as gender roles became more fluid out of necessity. After the war, just as women who had been working in factories were expected to return to their previous domestic activities, Jewish lesbians were no longer free to express their viewpoints. The 1950s in America were marked by a distrust of anyone who did not conform, and cold war doctrines equated homosexuality with subversion. At the same time, Jews, gays, and foreigners were being targeted as possible communists, creating a climate of fear within both the gay and Jewish communities. There was very little literature by lesbians made public in this decade, and the few lesbian characters that there were appeared mostly in pulp novels.

Modern and Contemporary Jewish American Lesbian Literature

By the end of the 1960s, many groups that had been marginalized were fighting for equal rights. At the same time as political protest was changing society, new communities of people were unapologetically telling their stories in novels, autobiographies, and memoirs. Lesbians and other "queer"-identified communities still felt afraid to tell their stories or write novels about their lives because they were still subject to mistreatment, exclusion, and public ridicule. Empowered by the successes of the African American **Civil Rights Movement**, a group of homosexuals socializing in a Greenwich Village bar in New York City chose to fight against police harassment, throwing rocks and shouting at police who had come to raid the bar. This was the first time that homosexuals had fought back without shame, and the incident became known as the Stonewall Rebellion—a moment that many mark as the birth of the gay rights movement.

After Stonewall, gay and lesbian literature of all types flourished. For Jewish lesbians, this often meant reclaiming their Jewish identity and becoming more involved with Jewish life and religion. Even more than their male colleagues, Jewish lesbian authors were revitalized by the gay rights movement and the feminist movement of the 1970s, emerging with the desire to reinterpret Jewish teachings and reinscribe Jewish rituals in their own lives. As a corpus, post-Stonewall and postfeminist work of Jewish lesbians often present readers with a mixture of poetics and politics. In the 1970s politicized lesbianism was portrayed as an alternative to a woman's life being defined by compulsory heterosexuality and the patriarchal control that is sometimes a dominant force in Jewish culture. In a few short years Jewish lesbians went from being almost completely invisible within both the gay and Jewish communities to expressing their beliefs and telling their life stories freely. Feminist poet and essayist **Adrienne Rich** is one of the most influential Jewish American lesbian writers to emerge during this period; her early work detailed the negative effects of male domination of women, including *Leaflets* (1969), *The Will to Change* (1971), and *Diving into the Wreck* (1973). Her later work, while not strictly autobiographical in nature, is clearly influenced by her political views. In *Twenty-One Love Poems* (1976), *A Wild Patience Has Taken Me This Far* (1981), *An Atlas of a Difficult World* (1991), and other volumes of poetry, Rich has only reaffirmed her commitment to improving the lives of women through her poetry and activism. Her contribution to lesbian literature has been widely recognized, and she has received many awards from both gay and lesbian and Jewish organizations.

Another Jewish American lesbian writer who combines politics with poetry is Warsaw-born **Holocaust** survivor **Irena Klepfisz**, whose collection *Dreams of an Insomniac: Jewish Feminist Essays, Speeches and Diatribes* (1990) takes a pro-Jewish stance that nonetheless makes the case for a new understanding of the Palestinian relationship with Israel. Having gone through the traumatic experiences of war, oppression, and **immigration**, Klepfisz believes that these experiences may be shared through the bonds of women's communication, overreaching racial and ethnic divisions. Other lesbian writers view their Jewish identity as a collection of symbolic cultural practices, which have been inherited from their parents, such as eating certain foods or celebrating Jewish holidays in a certain way. For these women the project of making Jewish lesbian families visible is paramount. **Leslea Newman** is best known for her groundbreaking children's book *Heather Has Two Mommies* (1989), the first children's book about an openly lesbian family. She has also written several collections of short stories, including *A Letter to Harvey Milk* (1988), which was also about the problems that arise when religion and sexuality are in conflict. Her other books include *Good Enough to Eat* (1986), *In Every Laugh a Tear* (1992), and several volumes of poetry. Contemporary with Newman's work was the publication of what was to become the seminal anthology of writing by Jewish lesbians, *Nice Jewish Girls* (1989), collected by Evelyn Torton Beck, whose introduction to the anthology dealt with the subject of **anti-Semitism** in the lesbian community. Like the work of Irena Klepfisz, Beck is seeking a cross-ethnic reconciliation between lesbians of different backgrounds. Sarah Schulman is a lesbian author who addresses the issue of AIDS. Although she does not always write about both lesbian and Jewish subjects, her novels *The Sophie Horowitz Story* (1984) and *Girls, Visions and Everything* (1986) have Jewish characters dealing with their sexualities. In recent years Jewish American lesbian fiction has become increasingly commercial, reaching wider audiences that are not necessarily made up of Jews or lesbians. Although some critics may view this as a factor contributing to the de-radicalization of Jewish lesbian political positions, others will see this as an indication that the struggles of the earlier Jewish and lesbian rights movements have successfully increased the visibility and the acceptance of both Jews and lesbians.

Further Reading

Alpert, Rebecca T., Sue Levi-Elwell, and Shirley Idelson, eds. *Lesbian Rabbis: The First Generation*. New Jersey: Rutgers UP, 2001.

Balka, Christie, and Andy Rose, eds. *Twice Blessed: On Being Lesbian, Gay, and Jewish*. Boston: Beacon Press, 1989.

Beck, Eveyn Torton. *Nice Jewish Girls: A Lesbian Anthology*. Boston: Beacon Press, 1989.

Boyarin, Daniel, and Daniel Itzkvitz, eds. *Queer Theory and the Jewish Question*. New York: Columbia UP, 2003.

Shneer, David, and Caryn Aviv. *Queer Jews*. New York: Routledge, 2002.

Michelle Erfer

JEWISH AMERICAN MUSICALS The musical originated in the United States in the nineteenth century and became a distinct genre in the 1920s. New York City—the famous Broadway—is the birthplace of this hybrid form. Neither "high" art like European opera nor "low" popular entertainment, the American musical combines music, dance, spoken scenes, and acting. It is often considered a product of "middle-brow" culture.

The majority of genre-defining composers, lyricists, and producers of American musicals were Jews, most of whom categorized themselves, like composer Richard Rodgers, as "Jewish for socioethnic reasons rather than because of any deep religious conviction" (Most 12). John Bush Jones estimates that "since the 1920s at least 90 percent of the book writers, lyricists, and composers of Broadway shows have been Jewish" (205). Thus, when we speak of the "American musical," we are generally speaking of the works of Jewish artists like Irving Berlin (Israel Baline), George Gershwin (Jacob Gershowitz), Ira Gershwin (Israel Gershvin), Jerome Kern, Oscar Hammerstein II, Lorenz Hart, Richard Rodgers, Leonard Bernstein, and Stephen Sondheim.

The American musical emerged from various predecessors: the extravaganza, the revue, vaudeville, the minstrel show, but also European operetta and opera. Its triple allegiance—to European operatic forms, to African Americans music and dance, and to popular culture in general—adequately expresses the cultural position of the majority of American Jews involved with their production. Finding themselves between the Old World European traditions and the influence of modern life in America, Jewish American artists played a leading role in inventing a new form of popular theater.

Literary critic Andrea Most reads the history of the American musical as the story of Jewish acculturation. The musical is a theatrical form especially suited for Jewish immigrants and their children; it allowed them to envision and celebrate American identities. The musical stage functioned as a microcosm, a staging ground for an exploration of American values as first- and second-generation Jews imagined them. The majority of shows produced in the period between the 1920s and 1950s "articulates a vision of a utopian liberal society, which by the end of the play is perceived as more tolerant, egalitarian, or just than the status quo" (Most 3). Significantly, this utopian liberal society contradicted sociopolitical realities. Anti**immigration** sentiments, xenophobia, and **anti-Semitism** often caused Americans to stigmatize Jews. Jewish musical theater sought to counteract negative perceptions by presenting an ideal America—a place where everybody was accepted.

The Jewish American musical developed in three stages. In the foundational stage (from the nineteenth century until the 1920s) Jewish "coon" shouters, blackface performers, and comedians reigned the popular stage. The second stage (encompassing the time between the 1920s and the 1950s) was an era of acculturation and influence. The third and final stage (beginning in the 1950s) is the period of the Jewish-themed musical.

The years between 1900 and 1930 were a time of rapid social change in urban centers, especially New York. Jewish immigration and African American migration to the cities of the North coincided with an increasing interest in ethnic entertainment. The genteel Victorianism of the nineteenth century gave way to a more open and eclectic climate of cultural production. Aided by phonograph, radio, and film technology, growing numbers of Americans flocked to "ethnic" music, comedy, and dance. It was the music of African Americans in particular that announced a new era of cross-cultural and inter-ethnic exchange.

For many Jewish entertainers, appropriating black music and culture became an economic necessity as well as a personal investment. Extending the participation of Jews in nineteenth century blackface minstrelsy (where white actors wore burned cork and parodied African Americans), performers such as Sophie Tucker, Eddie Cantor (Edward Iskowitz), and Al Jolson (Asa Yoelson) portrayed racist caricatures of "blackness," pandering to audience preferences and redefining their own identities in the process.

According to Angela Most, Al Jolson (in the 1927 movie *The Jazz Singer*) and Eddie Cantor (in the 1928 musical *Whoopee*) demonstrated that Jews were especially equipped to master modernity's demand of ethnic flexibility by reinventing themselves within the context of racist ideologies. By stressing performative virtuosity, these actors shifted the view from ethnicity to meritocracy: Participating in the depiction of multiple ethnicities on stage and screen qualified them as Americans, and at a time of 100 percent Americanism and the nativist movement, the entertainment industry remunerated ethnic talent of those who celebrated America as the land of democratic ideals.

The first period of Jewish American musicals saw the staging of Sigmund Romberg's *Sinbad* (1918, starring Jolson), George and Ira Gershwin's *Lady, Be*

Good (1924, with Fred and Adele Astaire), Samson Raphaelson's *The Jazz Singer* (1925), and early works by Kern, Hammerstein II, Rodgers, and Hart.

In the era of acculturation and influence, Jewish writers, lyricists, composers, producers, and theater owners were involved in almost every successful Broadway production. The most prominent musicals of that era are: *Show Boat* (1927), George and Ira Gershwin's *Girl Crazy* (1930, featuring Ethel Merman on "I Got Rhythm"), *Babes in Arms* (1937), *Porgy and Bess* (1935), *Oklahoma!* (1943), *Carousel* (1945), *Annie Get Your Gun* (1946), *South Pacific* (1949), *The King and I* (1951), *West Side Story* (1957), and *The Sound of Music* (1959).

Show Boat, based on an **Edna Ferber** novel (music by Kern and libretto by Hammerstein II), introduced several new elements to the American musical. As one of the first shows to qualify as "serious" entertainment, *Show Boat* told the story of Gaylord Ravenal and Magnolia and commented on controversial topics like miscegenation, gambling, racial bigotry, and alcoholism. The musical was set in the 1880s and used the popular entertainment on river cruises as its setting.

Kern and Hammerstein II produced one of the first successful musicals that dealt with uniquely American conflicts. The show spotted an integrated cast, even though one of the characters (Queenie) was played by Tess Gardella in blackface. A 1932 revival was made famous by Paul Robeson's performance as Joe and his rendition of "Ol' Man River." Besides including many hit songs ("Can't Help Lovin' Dat Man," among others), the musical's integration of dialogue and music broke new ground.

Porgy and Bess, George Gershwin's 1935 folk opera (libretto by Ira Gershwin and DuBose Heyward) is another milestone of the Jewish American musical theater. During the Depression years, *Porgy and Bess* provided much-needed work for African American singers and actors. Gershwin's use of African American folk and popular songs as the basis for a serious musical play proved to be a major artistic achievement. Despite allegations of ethnic stereotyping—the characters on Catfish Row are gamblers and prostitutes—*Porgy and Bess* has achieved **canon**ical status: Its songs have been performed by countless **jazz** artists, and the play itself is still staged regularly.

Show Boat and *Porgy and Bess*, indicative of the second stage of the Jewish American musical, displaced Jewish **ethnicity** by depicting black characters and scenes from African American life. Similarly, Lorenz Hart and Richard Rodgers's *Babes in Arms*; Rodgers and Hammerstein II's *Oklahoma!*, *South Pacific*, and *The King and I*; as well as Irving Berlin/Dorothy and Herbert Fields's *Annie Get Your Gun* rarely featured Jewish characters or themes. But Jewish writers and composers constructed visions of Americanness that can only be understood through the lens of socioethnic Jewishness. Even though themes and characters were rarely marked as "Jewish," their values often expressed those of their creators.

Babes in Arms expresses anxieties over a growing anti-Semitism and antiliberalism in the 1930s. Displacing their allegiance to President Franklin D. Roosevelt's New Deal policies, Rodgers and Hart present a group of children who aim to make money by staging a play so that they do not have to attend a New Deal youth project. The kids symbolize America's underprivileged, and they fight for personal and collective freedom by demanding equal opportunity and racial, ethnic, and religious equality. This vision of tolerance, inclusiveness, and black civil rights "illustrates the basic features of American Jewish liberalism" (Most 70).

Produced during World War II, *Oklahoma!* is set in the midwestern Indian territory before it became the state of Oklahoma. Promoting ethnic diversity as evidence of American democracy, the musical demonstrates Rodgers and Hammerstein II's vision of Jewishness as an ethnic trait (aiding **assimilation**) rather than a racial category (complicating assimilation). Although the show did not include a Jewish character, Most points out that Persian peddler Ali Hakim is coded as "Jewish" and essentially "white," while Jud Fry, who is coded as dark and evil, dies in the end (Most 108). Changing the locale from the city to the country and going back in time to the turn of the century, *Oklahoma!* tells the love story between Curly and Laurey, which ends up happily when the foreign influence (Jud) is killed and American utopia restored.

Amending the indirect approach to staging Jewishness are the Gershwin brothers' political satires. Unlike their earlier musicals (*Oh, Kay!* in 1926 and *Funny Face* in 1927), *Strike Up the Band* (1930), *Of Thee I Sing* (1931), and *Let 'Em Eat Cake* (1933) addressed political situations such as shady election campaigns, corruption, and economic hardships without doing so from a specifically Jewish perspective. Kurt Weill's contributions to American musical theater are similarly political. After emigrating to the United States in 1935, Weill wrote eight musicals, among them the antiwar show *Johnny Johnson* (1936, libretto and lyrics by Paul Green) and *Knickerbocker Holiday* (1938, book by Maxwell Anderson). The latter, though set in seventeenth-century New Amsterdam, contained critical references to Roosevelt and European dictators. With the onset of Nazi rule in Germany and the threat of another world war, political satire soon gave way to more patriotic and uplifting material. Overtly political musicals have never fared too well on Broadway, as can be seen in the meager reception of Marc Blitzstein's jazz opera *The Cradle Will Rock* (1937) and George S. Kaufman and Moss Hart's *I'd Rather Be Right* (1937).

In the third stage of the Jewish American musical, Jewish characters and issues are no longer displaced. In the wake of a new self-consciousness and security over mainstream acceptance as Americans and the ensuing postwar vogue in literature (**Philip Roth**, **Saul Bellow**), many Jews on Broadway began to address specifically Jewish themes. Musicals such as *Milk and Honey* (1961), *A Family Affair* (1962), *I Can Get It on for You Wholesale* (1962), and *Funny Girl* (1964) depict love relationships between Jewish characters, include scenes set in Israel, commentary on Zionism, and portray the struggles of Jewish Americans during the Depression years (Jones 205–11).

Fiddler on the Roof (1964) is the most successful of these shows—it ran over three thousand times on Broadway. It was adapted from Sholom Aleichem's stories (book by Joseph Stein) and revolves around generational conflicts between dairyman Tevye and his daughters. Set in the Russian village of Anatevka in 1905, the musical dramatizes Tevye's struggle to preserve Jewish traditions in a rapidly changing world. Religious rites (Sabbath prayer) and social events (weddings) present Jewish life in Russia in a very warm and positive light, while the music (lyrics by Sheldon Harnick, music by Jerry Bock) used traditional Jewish music to underscore the show's benevolent look on Jewish life and history.

After the moderate success of *Wonderful Town* (1953) and *Candide* (1956), Leonard Bernstein's *West Side Story* (1957) finally became a hit show (lyrics by Stephen Sondheim, libretto by Arthur Laurents). Fashioned after Shakespeare's *Romeo and Juliet*, *West Side Story* portrays the rivalry between a gang of young Puerto Rican immigrants (the Sharks) and the "American" Jets, which complicates the budding love between the main characters Tony and Maria. Besides appealing to a large audience, *West Side Story* criticizes the elusiveness of the American dream for ethnic outsiders and disadvantaged white juveniles. Bernstein's musicals were lauded for their sophistication, an honor shared by Stephen Sondheim, whose score for *Sunday in the Park with George* (1984) won the Pulitzer Prize.

Further Reading

Jones, John Bush. *Our Musicals, Ourselves: A Social History of the American Musical Theatre*. Hanover, NH: Brandeis UP, 2003.

Most, Andrea. *Making Americans: Jews and the Broadway Musical*. Cambridge, MA: Harvard UP, 2004.

Daniel T. Stein

JEWISH AMERICAN NOVEL   Although **Abraham Cahan**'s *The Rise of David Levinsky* (1917) is considered the first major novel by an American Jewish author, Jewish American fiction moved from relative obscurity to international recognition only after World War II, when writers like **Saul Bellow**, **Bernard Malamud**, and **Philip Roth** began to publish best-selling novels.

Then at a Modern Language Association convention in 1974 Sanford Pinsker, **Sarah Blacher Cohen**, Bonnie Lyons, and Daniel Walden decided to publish a journal to address this emerging phenomenon. They passed the hat at the convention and raised a few hundred dollars, asked friends and colleagues for more funding, and in the spring of 1975 the first issue of *Studies in American Jewish Literature* (*SAJL*) was published, with five articles and two book reviews in forty-four pages.

With Walden as editor, they began publishing two issues per year, including a 1979 special issue about **Henry Roth**'s *Call it Sleep* (1934) and its influence on American literature. By now their journal had seventy-five pages and cost six dollars a year; they had a book review editor, Irving

Malen, and eight more scholars on the editorial board: Stanley Cooperman, **Leslie Fiedler**, Sheldon Grebstein, Allen Guttmann, **Irving Howe**, Moses Rischin, Ronald Sanders, and Lillian Schlissel. In 1981 State University of New York Press became *SAJL*'s publisher. At ten dollars per year for individuals and twenty-five dollars for institutions, a typical issue would now run to 185 pages and include as many as seventeen articles, four book reviews, and interviews by or with Jewish writers and critics. And then in 1987 Kent State University Press signed on as publisher with *The World of Cynthia Ozick*, an issue containing fourteen articles and **Cynthia Ozick**'s autobiographical "The Young Self and the Old Writer."

In 1993 in his "Introduction" to Volume 12, *The Changing Mosaic: From Cahan to Malamud, Roth and Ozick*, Daniel Walden described how the "Jewish mosaic" of the late nineteenth century had changed into a "new world" in the 1940s and 1950s, and was now evolving again, because the first and second generations were passing on, and because the **Holocaust** was becoming an increasingly important aspect of American Jewish writing.

Since 2001 *SAJL* has been published by the University of Nebraska Press, and the journal continues to be animated by the founding concept that American Jewish literature is a vibrant body of works that continues to change and evolve. It also recognizes the fact that a significant percentage of modern Jewish literature, like early Yiddish literature from Eastern Europe, continues to explore the reality that many Jews still feel a basic "otherness," a sense of separation from American culture, which continues to affect Jewish writers and their work. And last but not least, *SAJL* continues as an invaluable source on which the literary movers and shakers have been and are today.

SAJL frequently highlights the works of women writers, who began playing an important role early on and whose literary output continues to grow. Fiction written by Jewish American women frequently portrays women as survivors, and the guardians of survival, who are extraordinarily determined to choose life, to persevere, and to endure. This concept is also prevalent in Holocaust literature. And another powerful and recurrent theme in recent Jewish American women's literature is their desire to be no longer excluded from participation in their faith's religious rites; nationally known cantor Debbie Friedman's new songs, Ruth Brin's innovative Midrash, and *Lilith* magazine are examples of the creativity released by this movement.

But although "tradition" (believed to be given by God and interpreted and codified by rabbis) once served as the framework for Jewish experience, within which all of life was contained and ordered, many contemporary Jewish American writers (both men and women) feel that tradition has been thinned out by many modern day Jews' ignorance and lack of interest in their tradition and weakened by secularization. An increasing percentage of Jews, for example, no longer join synagogues or attend Shabbat services, and some become Unitarians or create *chaverim* (which turn into "chat groups"). However, despite the fact that critics (such as Alvin Rosenfeld writing in *The Progress of the American Jewish Novel*) had sensed a "new energy" on the horizon (because books like *Portnoy's Complaint* (1969) were administering the coup de grace to "schlemiel fiction" that featured Jewish men as alienated antiheroes and nonachievers and depicted the Jewish woman as merely a subservient wife, mother, and keeper of a kosher home), tradition hasn't completely disappeared; it's beginning to surface again in contemporary Jewish writing.

A popular new group of mostly women writers in the 1980s, for example, created novels that focused on one of the major sources of tension within the contemporary Jewish community—conflict between **feminism** and secular humanism on the one hand, and Orthodox Judaism on the other. Observant Jews tended to be portrayed as religious fanatics in novels and short stories that were often wildly comic in their spiritual content, including twenty-one-year-old **Allegra Goodman**'s *Total Immersion* (1989); Norman Kotker's *Learning About God* (1988); Rhoda Lerman's *Good Year* (1989); Deena Metzger's *What Dinah Thought* (1989); Nessa Rapoport's *Preparing for Sabbath* (1981); **Tova Reich**'s *Sara* (1997) and *Master of the Return* (1998); Steve Stern's *Lazar Malkin Enger's Heaven* (1986); **Anne Roiphe**'s best-seller *Lovingkindness* (1987); and Lynn Sharon Schwartz's *Disturbances in the Field* (1983). Although male authors such as Phillip Roth were writing best sellers focused on Jewish men who were vulnerable, flawed, and fully human—he also zeroed in on their nastiness and warts—Goodman looked at the "good side" of life. She was confident that the pressures of contemporary Jewish life could still be the stuff of fiction, and that the final chapter on **assimilation** had yet to be written. She also discovered that each of us sees history through our own eyes when she wrote about Hawai'i's Jewish community and received letters from many readers saying she was really writing about their community when she described the smell of kosher meat jetted in from California and Lubavitch students far away from their homes in Crown Heights trying to conduct Yom Kippur services. As Sanford Pinsker says, it makes no difference where Goodman sets her stories, because in her novels "a Jew is a Jew."

Meanwhile, of course, the other key theme in Jewish American women's writing is the struggle to define a positive Jewish female **identity** after a century of assimilation and more than three decades of feminism. Some still downplay or ignore their Jewish identity in novels whose plot lines focus on gender and class, but writers such as **Marge Piercy** (one of today's most successful Jewish women novelists) are defining a new genre. In her first novel *Going Down East* (1969), the two central characters Anna and Leon "look Jewish" but don't define themselves as "Jews" and have non-Jewish lovers. Many readers and critics who were instantly drawn to her as a new and wonderful novelist didn't even realize that Piercy was Jewish, and in *Days of Knowing* (a collection of essays edited by Sue Walker and Eugenie Hamner that focuses on Piercy's use of language, her political ideology, and her representation of feminism) none of the essays consider her **ethnicity** as important or refer to her foray into writing about Jewish identity in the early 1990s in *Gone to Soldiers* and *He, She, and It* (whose heroines celebrate their Jewish identity, feel "connected" to each other, and tend to look on non-Jews as "others").

Piercy defines Jewish identity as almost anything an individual chooses, but the definition can also be shaped from others who assign that identity, which is why some members of the Jewish community still feel a basic "otherness," a sense of still being separate from the rest of American culture, despite the fact that Jews have moved into the mainstream in the arts, sciences, and corporate America; very few "hide" their Jewishness when it is time to use "vacation days" to celebrate Jewish holidays; and more than fifty years have passed since developers were advertising new suburban neighborhoods that were "not available to members of the Jewish faith." It still isn't easy to "be Jewish," of course, as Jewish life in the United States becomes increasingly fragmented—Conservative, Reform, and Reconstructionist congregations are in the majority, but a growing number of Orthodox Jewish men wear black hats and coats, have long beards and *payess*, and father large numbers of children. And although hundreds of thousands of Jews still imagine an "authentic" Jewish life as *Fiddler on the Roof* (1971) or *Yentl* (1983), they tend to avoid visibility in religious or cultural practices that would tell their neighbors or their coworkers that they are Jews.

And last but not least, Jewish feminists like **Hortense Calisher** and **Grace Paley** create characters who are alienated from, but drawn to, a heritage from which they are excluded, so to speak, but which plays an important role in their personal lives. Piercy addressed this ambivalence in a recent interview when she said that her novel *Braided Lives* (1982) was close to being autobiographical because she had grown up in Detroit with a Jewish mother and a Welsh father, she was "picked on" by the "other whites," and although her father told her that she wasn't Jewish, when he left for work her mother would tell her that of course she was Jewish! She depicts herself in a Jewish character called Jill Stuart who continues to struggle with definitions of "womanhood" and "working-class" because she loves her Jewish grandmother, but when she goes to work "being Jewish" clearly means "difference" and "otherness." And the same is true of Jacqueline, a French girl in Piercy's *Gone to Soldiers* who joins the Resistance during World War II and risks her life to save Jewish children by escorting them over the mountains to Spain. Jacqueline says she's dedicated to this dangerous activity because "I am a Jew"—and when she ends up in Auschwitz, she decides that "if I am to be myself, entire, authentic, I must find a way of being Jewish that is mine." For the first time in her life, Jacqueline embraces her Jewishness in religious terms by joining her friend Daniela in lighting makeshift candles and reciting prayers on Friday night, secretly celebrating Passover, and quoting the Book of Ruth—"Whither thou goest, I will go, and thy God will be my God." Daniela dies in a "death march" as the war is ending, but Jacqueline recovers in an American-run hospital, where she dedicates herself to being a Jew and to building a Jewish homeland so Jews would never again be stateless. When she arrives in Detroit on a speaking tour sponsored by a Zionist group, she's reunited with her younger sister who survived because she had been sent to the United States. They decide to make *aliyah* to Israel, where Jews are not "others"; but Piercy recognizes that this vision of a unified Jewish "self" in a Jewish homeland raises new problems, and the last line of her novel foreshadows the future of the Middle East: "The end of one set of troubles is but the beginning of another."

Midrash (biblical texts) is also finding its way into Jewish fiction. Popular authors who have integrated biblical texts into their novels include best-selling authors such as **Chaim Potok**, Pamela White Hadas, **Hugh Nissenson**, Cynthia Ozick, and **Isaac Bashevis Singer**, who in 1965 also began writing books for Jewish children. His children's books focused on Jews' faithfulness to their religion and their unquestioning belief in tradition, and he subsequently became the first author of children's books to win both the Nobel Prize for Literature and the National Book Award. In a review of Potok's best seller, *My Name Is Asher Lev* (1972), Henry Ahrens called Potok "the author we love to argue about" because he wrote about the life of Hasidic Jews in modern secular America, creating a world where faith is the undeniable "core" of the lives of Jews; but challenges to their faith are also a way of life. The "double lives" of Potok's characters are central to the plot in almost all of his novels, just as they are in **E. L. Doctorow**'s *The Book of Daniel* (1971) and a growing number of Jewish novels published in recent years. The best writers of the 1930s and 1940s didn't seem to be concerned with their Jewish identity when they were creating the plot for a novel, and many members of the second generation of East European Jews in the United States who have come of age since the 1950s define "Jewishness" as a secular culture created by "Jews in flight from Judaism," who think it's sufficient to express their religion by using doilies decorated with the Star of David, eating ethnic food, and identifying with the state of Israel. However, books such as Nissenson's *Pile of Stones* (1965) and *In the Reign of Peace* (1972), Ozick's *Pagan Rabbi* (1971), and Potok's *The Chosen* (1967) made it clear that many popular Jewish American writers were going beyond personal and social awareness and inclusion to an unprecedented depth of spiritual concern. A literature of theological imagination was emerging, moving beyond "schlemiel fiction" to where questions that in the past had to be answered by the Bible were now part of real life. And perhaps most important in this genre, once again, is Isaac Bashevis Singer. Singer has combined the natural and the supernatural in his colorful accounts of dybbuks, ghosts, fantasies, and coincidences in order to create novels that are plausible and compelling because they depict suffering Jews who struggle to find, maintain, or recover their religious beliefs, even during pogroms and the Holocaust—a pathway also depicted by contemporary novelists such as Graham Greene and William Styron, as well as Singer and **Allegra Goodman**.

Singer has said he believes God is a "silent God" and that sometimes his relationship with God has been protest, not belief, because Jews have always lived in a world that was a "jungle" full of violence and murder. Singer's *The Slave*, for example, first published in English in1962, was the story of a learned and devout Jew sold into slavery during the seventeenth-century anti-Semitic riots in Chmielnicki, Poland. Jacob has lost everything—his freedom, his wife, his children, his community—but he is still a Jew, and although he doesn't have a prayer shawl or phylacteries, he struggles to maintain his faith by reciting his daily prayers from memory while he tends his master's cattle. He refuses to eat non-kosher meat, and lives on vegetables, fruits, and bread; he works harder on weekdays so he won't have to forage for his cattle on the Sabbath. Later, in *Enemies, A Love Story* (1972) and *Shosha* (1978), Singer writes about Holocaust survivors who also abandoned their faith, but eventually made peace with their new lives and returned to their religion.

And to return to fiction based on the Holocaust, this growing postwar genre more or less began with novels like Bellow's *Mr. Sammler's Planet* (1969) and moved on to Jerzy Kosinski's *The Hermit of 69th Street* (1988). Many works of Holocaust fiction have tended to skip over survivors' day-to-day adjustment to their new surroundings, and how Holocaust memories inevitably shadow their present lives—themes prevalent in collections of interviews with survivors—because the authors have had to struggle with a multitude of other "requirements" as they wrote novels that sought to fathom and communicate the incoherence of the Holocaust, to expose the world's complicity, and to give significance to the memory of the dead, an identity to the survivors, and a respect for the past! And perhaps because estrangement and distancing from the traditional Jewish community were becoming the "rule" in late-twentieth-century Jewish life and literature, Bellow and Kosinski focused on disrupted family units as a metaphor for the wounds caused by the Holocaust. Sammler's family members, for example, are reunited in a piecemeal manner, and are more like acquaintances than relatives. And even more interesting is that the women in both novels are not nurturing women; they are ornamental. In short these are "male tales" told in a male enclave where among other things death and disintegration continue to exist; Kosinski's hero survives the Holocaust, but he is murdered by a street gang in New York City.

And of course memory has always been very important in Jewish novels' plot lines. As Jews we continue to have a sense of peoplehood derived from our culture and history, so it is not uncommon for Jewish novels to begin with "Once upon a time." Jewish authors such as Henry Roth, **Isaac Rosenfield**, and **Michael Gold** typify this focus on memory in novels such as Gold's *Jews Without Money* (1930), Roth's *Call It Sleep* (1934), and Rosenfield's *Passage From Home* (1946), which begins with the phrase "I remember the year" and then centers on how important Jewish tradition is in binding together generations that are otherwise separated by the gulf of experience. In his autobiography, Meyer Levin explains his confusion regarding his parents' awkward English and Old World mores, but he also focuses on their companionship with other Jews and the importance of "family," which is always the central component in his novels' plot line. And of course some well-known historians such as Sanford Pinsker believed that Jewish American fiction had played itself out by the 1980s as there were only so many ways one could bash "overprotective Jewish mothers, their benighted husbands, and their whining sons and pampered daughters!" However, Philip Roth's *Goodbye, Columbus* (1959) had already unleashed a controversy that has raged ever since about what is or is not "good for the Jews." Although Roth was only twenty-six years old when *Goodbye, Columbus* was published, he won the prestigious National Book Award that year and became a household name. And then in 1971 Cynthia Ozick became a trailblazer with *The Pagan Rabbi and Other Stories*, whose characters are grounded in Jewish ideals and passionately committed to Jewish values; and now we have novelists **Tillie Olsen** and Grace Paley as models of inspiration and excellence and younger voices such as Allegra Goodman.

Another one of today's growing trends, of course, is intermarriage, which is also finding its way into many novels by Jewish authors. One of the first was **Ben Hecht**'s *A Jew in Love* (1931), which focuses on the "psychological acrobatics" of a self-hating Jewish man who has a brief affair with a gentile woman during which he uses an assumed name to hide his Jewishness. When his book became a best seller, the B'nai B'rith publicly accused Hecht of being a "Jewish defamer of Jews," and the rabbis in Cleveland, his hometown, denied him burial rites in their Jewish cemeteries.

And on a similar note, many scholars believe that Faye Kellerman has really brought Jewish fiction into the twenty-first century. The main character in her first four novels was Detective Sgt. Peter Decker of the Los Angeles Police Department, whose teenage Jewish birth mother had given him up for adoption. He was adopted by a Baptist family, but as an adult he not only returned to Judaism but also became an Orthodox Jew! In the first novel, *The Ritual Bath* (1986), Decker investigates a rape and murder, and when he finds the killer he joins the victim's family in a celebratory Orthodox-style dance! Kellerman's next three plot lines focus on the sexual relationship developing between Decker and Rina Lazarus, a Jewish woman who witnessed the rape. In the course of the investigation, they fall in love—but they don't marry until the fourth novel in the series, *The Day of Atonement* (1991), which is another immersion in the family life of the Orthodox Jewish community!

One of the newest genres in Jewish fiction is "black humor," which some authors have even used to depict the Holocaust. Paul Mazursky's film *Enemies: A Love Story* (1989) is a desperate "bedroom farce" based on Isaac Bashevis Singer's novel of the same name, and **Art Spiegelman** creates a "comic view" of the Holocaust in his continuing best sellers, *Maus: A Survi-*

vor's Tale (1986) and *Maus II: And Here My Troubles Began* (1991), where Spiegelman's cartoon drawings also illustrate another one of the recurrent themes in Holocaust literature—the continued suffering survivors have imposed on themselves because of the guilt they feel for having lived through the hell of the Holocaust while all their family members and friends were dying.

That leads once again to the Jewish American's perpetual quest for a sense of self and independence, a topic addressed by Mark Schechner who points out that many of his college students thought the recurring themes in Jewish fiction were sex, selfishness, and misogyny and that "shikse-lust" was becoming an ongoing part of Jewish American young people's lives. But then they discovered writers like Bellow, **Joseph Heller,** and Bernard Malamud, whose novels suggested that Jewish American intellectuals were focusing on the personal crises of conversion and self-renewal. Schechner says that you could go home to your Jewish community and your family, and "you had to, because your *latkes* were getting cold!" He also points out that the "double perspective" of exile and return and/or rebellion and reconciliation has kept Jewish American culture alive, because books written by the rebels who have succeeded continually enrich the Jewish life from which they have removed themselves.

And last, but certainly not least, although Israel has become increasingly important in American Jews' identity and communal self-expression, it continues to play a remarkably minor role as a theme in American Jewish fiction. However, two best-selling authors, Philip Roth in *The Counterlife* (1986) and Anne Roiphe in *Lovingkindness* (1987), base their plots on Americans who have made *aliyah*. Roiphe's heroine is on the lunatic fringe of Jewish society, but many readers in the twenty-first century continue to identify with her heroine, the twenty-two-year-old daughter of a feminist intellectual who drifts from a life of drugs and rebellion in New York City to Jerusalem where she enrolls in an ultra-Orthodox yeshiva and finds her haven from uncertainty in an arranged marriage! Roth depicts Israel in a much more acceptable way; his hero is an affluent dentist from suburban New Jersey who realizes that although American Jews now enjoy a secure, tolerated existence, equal rights, and freedom from harm he should embrace a life of religious nationalism and return to Judaism by living as a Jew in a Jewish land. (*See also* Holocaust Narratives)

Further Reading

Angoff, Charles, and Meyer Levin. *The Rise of Jewish American Fiction*. New York: Simon and Schuster, 1970.

Baumgarten, Murray. *City Scriptures: Modern Jewish Writing*. Cambridge, MA: Harvard UP, 1982.

Finkelstein, Norman. *The Ritual of New Creation: Jewish Tradition and Contemporary Literature*. Albany: State U of New York P, 1992.

Fried, Lewis, ed. *Handbook of Jewish-American Literature*. Westport, CT: Greenwood Press, 1988.

Lichtenstein, Diane. *Writing Their Nation*. Bloomington: Indiana UP, 1992.

Pinsker, Sanford. *Jewish-American Fiction, 1917–1987*. New York: Twayne, 1992.

Shapiro, Ann R., ed. *Jewish American Women Writers: A Bio-Bibliographical Critical Sourcebook*. Westport, CT: Greenwood Press, 1994.

Shatzky, Joel, and Michael Taub. *Contemporary Jewish American Fiction: A Bio-Bibliographical Critical Sourcebook*. Westport, CT: Greenwood Press, 1997.

Rhoda G. Lewin

JEWISH AMERICAN POETRY   Jewish-identified American poets who write for a general audience form the basis for this category. Although there is much discussion among critics, such as **Harold Bloom**, **John Hollander**, and **Cynthia Ozick**, as to the nature, sorrows and possibilities of Jewish poetry, concentration on the poetry itself as a genre or as a unit is not prevalent. Joel Shatzky and Michael Taub's 1999 sourcebook *Contemporary Jewish-American Dramatists and Poets: A Bio-Bibliographical Critical Sourcebook* is among the first to deal critically with what is indeed a constant and consistent phenomenon in American literature throughout much of its history—the poetic writing of Jews.

Only recently have Jewish poets been grouped together in anthologies, and that may be one of the reasons why there are few theories about the tradition. The editors of the best-known anthologies, Steven Rubin (*Telling and Remembering*, 1997) and Jonathan Barron and Eric Selinger (*Jewish American Poetry: Poems, Commentary and Reflections*, 2000), do not always select the same poets. Although Rubin's is a much more comprehensive anthology, twenty-five of his poets are not in Barron's, twelve of Barron's writers are not in Rubin's, and many more Jewish American poets of note are in neither. This also indicates something of the great number and wide variety of Jewish poets. The selection here is somewhat arbitrary and excludes many noteworthy writers.

While any survey of this size cannot encompass all the recent discussions of Jewish American poetry or all the poets, it is possible to delineate some of the trends. A survey of these poets, writing from the eighteenth century until present times, seems to indicate two interesting unifying principles. First, most do not write so as to speak to or represent Jews, but consider themselves within the framework of the United States. That is, they are not writing with a political or religious agenda, and if they have a social or aesthetic agenda, it is only secondarily related to their Jewishness. Second, most of them are to a greater or lesser extent aware of the existence of another significant language, Hebrew or Yiddish, and as a result seem to perceive the English language and/or American culture as a tool to be used and examined rather than as an absolute and automatic lens through which to observe the world. The results are poetries that scrutinize the social and moral elements of the society in which they are created, that replenish and even revolutionize the language, and that question their own identities and points of reference.

Many of the poets display fervent individuality and a general defiance of category. Therefore, their relationships to their Jewish backgrounds are extremely variable and complex. Nevertheless, the few poets selected here may be seen as dealing representatively with the dilemmas of the times and their Jewish circumstances.

The defiance of category is not necessarily an absence of category. **Allen Ginsberg** is often associated with the Beat movement, **Louis Zukofsky** with the Objectivist movement, **Charles Bernstein** with the Language poets (having cofounded the influential journal $L=A=N=G=U=A=G=E$), and **Alicia Ostriker** with Midrash (the retelling and interpreting of the stories of the Bible which became an extremely popular genre in recent years). But if these associates have anything in common it is the fact that they themselves founded the movements thus changing the possibilities of American poetry. These poets contributed to the tradition of American poetry by helping to create it.

First Poets

Although there are earlier poets, most notably Penina Moise (1797–1880) of Charleston whose *Fancy's Sketch Book* (1833) was the first book of poetry by a Jew to be published in America, the first Jewish poet to receive general recognition was **Emma Lazarus** (1849–1887). From her early poems, Lazarus showed concern with Jewish subjects, and this concern was fueled by the massive pogroms in Europe during the 1880s, causing large numbers of Jews to flee to the shores of the United States. Her *Songs of a Semite* (1882) is the most well known of a number of books published between *Poems and Translations* in 1866 and her early death in 1887.

These Jewish subjects are evident even in her most generally known, non-specifically Jewish work. "The New Colossus" (1883) was written for an auction to raise money for the pedestal of the Statue of Liberty, and the last lines were placed on that very pedestal in 1901. By 1945 the entire poem was placed over the Statue of Liberty's main entrance. The poem that has come to signify the entire tradition of American **immigration** and the celebration of **multiculturalism** is also a clear expression of the Jewish voice. The contradictions and balances between classic Greek culture and modern, the longing of the immigrant and the morality of the welcoming resident, and the feeling of freedom in the new world and oppression of the old are all registered in the poem and central to Lazarus's concerns.

Yiddish Poets

As much as Lazarus may express the secularized Jew living in the non-Jewish society and translate the Jewish experience to an American morality, there were numerous poets in the antithetical position of the immigrants who Lazarus so extolled. These were the immigrants who in the end of the nineteenth century and the beginning of the twentieth were reluctant to part with the rich language of Yiddish even as they became immersed in American culture. Some used the perspective of Yiddish to examine their situation. Morris Rosenfeld describes the harsh conditions in the textile industry in "The Sweatshop" (1910), and in "My Little Boy" (1887) and tells of the long sweatshop hours that prevent a father from experiencing his child.

Others also found the perspective of Yiddish a means of experiencing innovation. These include Mani Leib (1883–1953), Moyshe-Leyb Halpern (1886–1932), Celia Dropkin (1888–1956), Malka Heifetz Tussman H. Leivick (1888–1962, best known for his play "The Golem"), Anna Margolin (1887–1952), A. Leyeles, and Jacob Glatstein. Anna Margolin who wrote in Yiddish may represent in many ways an entire community of Jewish immigrant writers who developed a great association with the American society and culture and yet maintained their unique insularity and point of view, both culturally and linguistically. Her poems exhibit a deep knowledge of imagism and employ techniques of alliteration and assonance rather than the more common rhyme of Yiddish. "Girls in Crotona Park" takes the local habitation and using the brush of imagism paints figures of classic and empty beauty.

With this background of innovation and perspective, it is not surprising that the modernist Jewish poets found many unrecognized possibilities in the English language. As Maeera Schreiber has noted, the Objectivists, with many Jewish poets at their lead, attempted to universalize American poetry. **Charles Reznikoff**, Louis Zukofsky, **Carl Rakosi**, and **George Oppen** wrote of need for a greater vision. Reznikoff's "Kaddish" (1936) emphasizes the sensitivity of the Jews who have suffered, Zukofsky's "Poem Beginning 'The'" (1926) responds to Eliot's pessimism for culture in "The Waste Land" (1922), offering a more relative view of culture and civilization with the infusion of new blood. Zukofsky grew up in a Yiddish-speaking home, and in this poem pays tribute to the new beginnings of his family in contrast to Eliot's despair of the world that was lost with World War II.

Modernism in English

The innovation and creativity of **Gertrude Stein** (1874–1946) has long been acknowledged, but her connection with Jewish culture is complex and controversial. Born in Pennsylvania, she moved to Paris in 1903 and did not return to the United States for thirty years, choosing instead to create the culture of modernism. Although she maintained friendships with American poets such as Ezra Pound and William Carlos Williams, her own poetry shows more the influence of her painter associates such as Pablo Picasso; *Tender Buttons* (1915) employs language in the manner Picasso used paint, for its aesthetic and structural value. Although most critics are uncomfortable with her apparent rejection of Judaism, her ambivalent attitude to Nazism in World War II, and other disconcerting details of her life and politics, Maria Damon relates her sense of identity as flexible and fluid to her Jewishness. If it is a form of Jewishness, it is one of attitude and innovation, not identification and theme.

Formalism

Whereas Stein is noted not for her work but for her influence, **Howard Nemerov** (1920–91) is an antithetical case. Well known and highly praised, Nemerov was poet laureate from 1988 to 1990 (to be followed by a number of other Jewish poets) having been awarded fellowships from the Academy of American Poets and the Guggenheim Foundation, a National Endowment for the Arts grant, and the National Medal of the Arts. He was poetry consultant to the Library of Congress in 1963 and 1964 and chancellor of the Academy of American Poets from 1976 until his death. He published twenty-six books of which thirteen are poetry. His formalist style contains an irony of cosmic proportions and provokes the reader to examine many elements of life. However, despite this popularity and respect in the world of poetry, he was hardly influential and little has been written about his work. Of his very productive career, proportionately little is on Jewish themes. Nevertheless, "Moses," "Pharaoh's Meditation on the Exodus," "Ahasuerus" (from his 1958 book *Mirrors and Windows*), and many others are gems. *Collected Poems* (1977) was awarded the Pulitzer Prize, the National Book Award, and the Bollingen Prize.

The Beat Movement

Nemerov grew up in New York of an upper middle-class family with two sisters, one of whom was the photographer Diane Arbus. Graduating from the Society for Ethical Culture's Fieldstone School, he went on to study at Harvard (BA, 1941), and in World War II served as a pilot in the Royal Canadian unit of the U.S. Army Air Force. After the war, having earned the rank of first lieutenant, he returned to live the life of an academic. Outwardly at least, Nemerov lived the model American life. Allen Ginsberg (1926–97) on the other hand grew up in New Jersey with socialist parents; his mother, a Russian immigrant, had frequent bouts of psychotic behavior that ended with her death in a mental institution. Ginsberg rejected the successful life of marketing researcher to become a free spirit.

There are other differences as well. Nemerov rarely foregrounded his Judaism and always seemed first a poet of the mundane life of screen doors and tree surgery; Allen Ginsberg, however, often introduced himself as poet, Jew, and Buddhist, and he saw in his expansive spiritualism a means of transforming his own reality as well as the world. Central to his poetry is the need to breaking arbitrary rules and create alternative ways for others to follow. Ginsberg's reading of "Howl" in 1956 is said to have been the beginning of the Beat movement in literature; *Howl and Other Poems* (1956) and *Kaddish* (1961) made Ginsberg's Jewishness hip. And indeed even Ginsberg's long beard in the sixties seemed to emphasize not only the hippie movement but also the connection between Jew and the spiritual alternative to society. Despite the fact that Ginsberg was uneducated in Judaism and his relationship to his religion was more tentative than the title of his second book would suggest, he became a model for the sixties Jewish intellectual.

Feminism and Beyond

Adrienne Rich (1929) is a crucial figure in the Jewish experience in twentieth-century poetry. From her first writings until today she has influenced poets everywhere with her evolving conceptions of **feminism**, motherhood, Judaism, and politics. Rich began to overtly define herself as a Jew after she had become known as a feminist poet with the essay "Split at the Root: An Essay on Jewish **Identity**" (1982). This concern has developed and expanded in almost all of her work. From her first well-received book *A Change of World* (1951) in which poems such as "By No Means Native" hint subtly at a Jewish connection, Rich has been exploring Jewish identity and responsibility with growing intensity and widening concern. In *An Atlas of a Difficult World: Poems 1988–1991* (1991), Rich's own changing attitude toward Jews and her Jewishness is mixed with her attempts to understand the complexities of the changing political situation in Israel, the many significances and effects of the Holocaust, the psychology and sociology of **assimilation**, and the intricacies and relevance of the rituals of religion. With its emphasis upon recent events as well as the immediate personal situation, *The School Among the Ruins* (2004) struggles for both a global and intimate vision.

Recent Jewish Themes

Recent years have seen an upsurge of interest in poetry centered on Jewish subjects. Two of the clearest themes are the Bible and the **Holocaust**.

Midrash, or Torah exegesis, has long been a fertile ground for poetry, but it has become a popular tool for finding the voice of women in what appears a patriarchal text. Many women writers, such as Alicia Ostriker, **Enid Dame**, **Marge Piercy**, **Ruth Whitman**, Marge Piercy, and Jacqueline Osherow, have seen in poetry a way to develop dialogues with the Bible. Alicia Ostriker (1937–) may be credited as one of the popularizers and promoters of this genre. Although she had been writing and publishing for many years, Ostriker came to prominence as both a poet and a critic in 1986 when her prize-winning volume of poems *The Imaginary Lover* was published at the same time as her revolutionary feminist critical text *Stealing the Language: The Emergence of Women's Poetry in America* in which she focuses attention on women's poetry. *The Nakedness of the Fathers: Biblical Visions and Revisions* (1994), her book of feminist Midrash, reconceives biblical stories from "the Beginning" to Job. *Green Age* (1989) includes a seven-poem meditation on the many roles of women in Jewish history and culture. Concomitantly, Enid Dame (1943–2003) published her monologues about Adam's first wife, Lilith. *Lilith and Her Demons* (1989) was concerned with Midrash, with reinterpreting biblical texts, one which developed in her later works and her coauthored anthology *Which Lilith?: Feminist Writers Re-Create the World's First Woman* (1998).

Poetry about the Holocaust began to appear even before the Holocaust was over—one example in Yiddish, Kadya Molodovsky's "*El Khonun*/God of Mercy," 1945—but has always been problematic as a genre. Questions concerning entitlement, distance, and the possibilities of aesthetics in the face of unspeakable horror have been discussed at length but not settled with any possibility of finality. Nonfiction is less problematic because the element of aestheticism and distance is less obvious in prose, but in poetry the idea of artificiality and therefore exploitation of the explosive subject is more plausible. Numerous anthologies and critical analyses of the topic have nevertheless appeared and many Jewish poets have found it impossible to avoid the subject.

Language Poetry and Other Alternatives

Charles Bernstein, Bob Perelman, and Ammiel Alcalay are three of the many identified with the attempt to objectify and postmodernize poetry, de-emphasizing the concept of the personality of speaker and focusing on language as a tool and a value in itself. Despite the sense of disconnected poetics, however, the Jewish element is very strong. Charles Bernstein has made significant connections between this concept of language poetry and Judaism, noting that Jewish mysticism focuses on language "in its material form: not what language represents or means or signifies, but what it is in itself" ("Poetry and the Sacred," 1999). In "Anagrammatica" he deconstructs the letters of the name of the renowned philosopher Walter Benjamin, finding in every reconstruction the word "Jew"; and his association of the structure of a poem with the vaudeville joke in "Of Time and the Line" indicates he has incorporated unrecognized influences.

Future Trends

Since the recent attention on a flourishing experience that has been in existence for well over a century, it is to be expected that a greater awareness of the Jewish poetic community will be evident in future writing, and that indeed Jewish poetry may be more apparent as a genre. Considering the recognizable influence poets of Jewish concerns have had on the entire poetry tradition in the United States, it is to be hoped that the tendency will not be toward secularization and isolation. (*See also* Yiddish Literature)

Further Reading

Barron, Jonathan, and Eric Selinger, eds. *Jewish American Poetry: Poems, Commentary and Reflections*. Hanover, NH: U of New England P, 2000.

Bernstein, Charles. "Anagrammatica, Excerpts from Doctrine of Similarity (13 Cannons)." *Forward* (March 5, 2005).

Bloom, Harold. "The Sorrows of American Jewish Poetry." *Figures of Capable Imagination*. New York: Seabury Press, 1976.

Dame, Enid, Lilly Rivlin, Henny Wenkart, and Naomi Wolf. *Which Lilith?: Feminist Writers Re-Create the World's First Woman*. Northvale, NJ: Jason Aronson, 1998.

Damon, Maria. "Gertrude Stein's Jewishness, Jewish Social Scientists, and the 'Jewish Question'." *Modern Fiction Studies* 42.3 (Fall 1996): 489–506.

Finkelstein, Norman. *Not One of Them in Place: Modern Poetry and Jewish American Identity*. Albany: State U of New York P, 2001.

Fishman, Charles M., ed. *Blood to Remember: American Poets on the Holocaust*. Lubbock: Texas Tech UP, 1991.

Florsheim, Stewart J., ed. *Ghosts of the Holocaust: An Anthology of Poetry by the Second Generation*. Detroit: Wayne State UP, 1997.

Grossman, Allen. "Allen Ginsberg, The Jew as an American Poet." *On the Poetry of Allen Ginsberg*. Ed. Lewis Hyde. Ann Arbor: U of Michigan P, 1984.

Gubar, Susan. *Poetry after Auschwitz: Remembering What One Never Knew*. Bloomington: Indiana UP, 2003.

Hollander, John. "The Question of American Jewish Poetry." *What Is Jewish Literature?* Ed. Hana Wirth-Nesher. New York: Jewish Publication Society, 1994.

Howe, Irving, Ruth R. Wisse, and Khone Shmeruk, eds. *The Penguin Book of Modern Yiddish Verse*. New York: Viking, 1987.

Lichtenstein, Diane. *Writing Their Nations: The Tradition of Nineteenth-Century American Jewish Women Writers*. Bloomington: Indiana UP, 1992.

Pacernick, Gary. *Meaning and Memory: Interviews with Fourteen Jewish Poets*. Columbus: Ohio UP, 2001.

———. *Sing a New Song: American Jewish Poetry since the Holocaust*. American Jewish Archives, 1991.

Rubin, Steven. *Telling and Remembering*. Boston: Beacon Press, 1997.

Schreiber, Maeera Y. "Jewish American Poetry." *The Cambridge Companion to Jewish American Literature*. Eds. Hana Wirth-Nesher and Michael Kramer. Boston: Cambridge UP, 2004.

Shatzky, Joel, and Michael Taub. *Contemporary Jewish-American Dramatists and Poets: A Bio-Critical Sourcebook*. Westport, CT: Greenwood Press, 1999.

Karen Alkalay-Gut

JEWISH AMERICAN STEREOTYPES Taking their cue from the most famous stereotypical Jewish character of all—Shylock, the usurer of Shakespeare's *The Merchant of Venice* (c. 1596–97)—American writers tended to depict Jews as money-hungry and miserly. Although Jews often appear as ruthless and shrewd self-made businessmen in American literature, the image is somewhat more complex, since the self-made man was also lauded as a symbol of American individualism and capitalist success. This ambivalence about representations of the Jew extends to Jewish American literature. Although Jewish stereotypes first appeared in works by non-Jewish writers, after World War II it was often Jewish American writers themselves who evoked such fixed images. The prevalence of anti-Semitic stereotypes in Jewish writing is sometimes viewed as symptomatic of self-hatred, but many Jewish American writers also called upon stereotypical images in order to overturn and challenge them.

Jewish Stereotypes in American Literature

In works of early American literature, such as Susanna Rowson's play *Slaves in Algiers* (1794) and Royall Tyler's novel *The Algerine Captive* (1797), Jewish men appeared in stereotypical roles as bankers and merchants. In the nineteenth century, anti-Semitic images were often present in American literature, perhaps most notoriously in the writings of Nathaniel Hawthorne. In *The English Notebooks* (1856) Hawthorne described a Jewish couple he encountered while traveling in London. Explicitly connecting the man to other stereotypical Jewish figures, including Shylock, Judas Iscariot, and the Wandering Jew, Hawthorne expresses his dislike for Jews through the unflattering description. The Jewish woman, in contrast, is described as beautiful, but in a distinctly exotic way. In *The Marble Faun* (1860) he similarly drew on exotic stereotypes of Jewish women in his depiction of Miriam, who is portrayed as a "belle juive," or beautiful Jewess, a figure who becomes associated with temptation.

In the United States, Jews were also viewed as dirty and alien threats to the nation. In response to an influx of **immigration** in the late nineteenth century, nativists argued for the need to keep the country free of contamination, thus leading to stereotypical renderings of the immigrant population, such as those who resided in Jewish ghettos. A number of anti-Semitic slurs occur in Henry James's descriptions of swarming hordes of Lower East Side Jews in *The American Scene* (1907). In contrast to German Jews, who exhibited an eagerness to assimilate (what became known as the *alrightnik* attitude), the Eastern European Jews of the ghettos were seen as unassimilable masses and exotic specimens. Treatises such as Madison Grant's *The Passing of the Great Race* (1916) and Lothrop Stoddard's *The Rising Tide of Color* (1920) expressed fears of the invading Jew who would multiply and overtake the Nordic population. The belief that Jews were an inferior **race** was also manifest in works of fiction such as Jack London's *Martin Eden* (1914).

At the turn of the century and into the twentieth century, economic and social stereotypes of Jews persisted. They were depicted as money-obsessed, vulgar, and pushy parvenus. In literary representations, Jewish men and women wore ostentatious clothing and jewelry. Physical features such as red hair and oversized, hooked noses further contributed to such negative portraits. In Frank Norris's *McTeague* (1899), the red-headed Polish junk dealer, Zerkov, marries a servant girl, Maria, in order to get his hands on a set of gold dishes her family once owned. The Jew's money-hungry instincts turn murderous as he ultimately kills his wife in pursuit of the illusory dishes. In Edith Wharton's *The House of Mirth* (1905), the Jewish character of Simon Rosedale, a wealthy financier, appears as the quintessential social climber; he conflates his desire for a position in high society with his desire for a gentile woman, becoming an unscrupulous suitor of the novel's protagonist Lily Bart. In turn-of-the-century New York, Jews like Rosedale were identified by their conspicuous wealth and attempted displacement or infiltration of the aristocratic upper classes.

Jews play a similar role in the work of **F. Scott Fitzgerald**. The character of Joseph Bloeckman in *The Beautiful and the Damned* (1922) echoes Rosedale. A persistent suitor of Anthony Patch's beautiful wife Gloria Gilbert, Bloeckman represents the Americanized Jew (a threat to the social order) who finds success as a Hollywood film mogul, ultimately changing his name to Black. In *The Great Gatsby* (1925), Gatsby's business partner Meyer Wolfsheim is described in terms of his nasal features and his corruption. Said to be the man who fixed the 1919 World Series, Wolfsheim epitomizes the stereotype of the Jewish gangster. One year later in *The Sun Also Rises* (1926), Ernest Hemingway created the character of Robert Cohn, a prototypical outsider Jew, who pursues the same gentile woman coveted by the protagonist, Jake Barnes.

Stereotypes of Jews in poetry and drama are often viewed as even more pernicious than those that appear in prose. Jews make several appearances in the poetry of T. S. Eliot and Ezra Pound, who have been criticized for their **anti-Semitism**. Like one of his influences Henry Adams, Eliot used Jews as scapegoats for the ills of modern Western society. The stock figure of the stage Jew, who appeared in British and American drama, was played as a grotesque caricature. In the tradition of Shylock, the stage Jew was marked by his orientalized dress, a prominent nose, a heavy accent, and his characteristic lust for money.

In many of these cases Jewish men were portrayed as feminized, a stereotype that has its roots in European anti-Semitic discourse. To inscribe Jewish difference on the body, economic and racial stereotypes were translated into gendered terms. The intent was to deprive the male Jew of his power by identifying him with the feminine. Such feminization is evident, for example, in Simon Rosedale's fastidious concern with fashion or Robert Cohn's decision to take up boxing in order to prove his masculinity and counteract his inferior status as a Jew.

Not only were Jews seen as subverting the social order, but also they were considered to be ideologically and politically subversive. It is no accident that the communist lawyer in **Richard Wright**'s *Native Son* (1940) is a Jew. In ethnic literature Jews often appear as chameleon-like figures, who desire to fit in at all costs. In **James Weldon Johnson**'s *The Autobiography of an Ex-Colored Man* (1912), the Jew comes to represent the expert assimilator, who can blend in with the dominant culture. **Rebecca Leventhal Walker**'s memoir *Black, White, and Jewish* (2001), which describes the biracial author's experiences growing up in the New York Jewish world of her father, has been accused of perpetuating stereotypes about the materialism of assimilated upper-middle-class Jews.

Stereotypes in Jewish American Literature

Although Walker ultimately rejects her Jewish **identity** because she associates it with the white hegemony, she may well fit into a tradition of Jewish writers who are held responsible for upholding anti-Semitic stereotypes. **Abraham Cahan**'s descriptions of newly arrived immigrants, as in *Yekl* (1896), are sometimes seen as reinforcing the traditional view of Jews as uncultured greenhorns. Jewish women were crudely stereotyped as "ghetto girls" and portrayed as gaudily overdressed. The ghetto girl was seen as trying too hard to capture the man who would secure her economic future and satiate her consumerism. In **Anzia Yezierska**'s *Salome of the Tenements* (1923), Sonya Vrunsky first appears as a materialistic vamp who schemes to marry Anglo-Saxon millionaire John Manning. But when Manning continually objectifies her as exotic, savage, and primitive, Sonya divorces him and makes it on her own as a fashion designer, partially undoing the stereotype of the consuming Jewish woman. Like many Jewish American novels, *Salome* incorporates stereotypes of Jews, but also works to overturn (or at least soften) them. For example, the ironically named Honest Abe is a greedy pawnbroker, but Yezierska paints his difficult past in order to make him more sympathetic.

In Jewish American literature the distinct stereotypes associated with men and women were interconnected. The feminization of Jewish men was due to the allegedly domineering behavior of Jewish women. Often accused of perpetuating stereotypes, **Philip Roth** has come under attack for his negative portrayals of Jewish women. In *Goodbye Columbus* (1957), Roth created Jewish American Princess (JAP) Brenda Patimkin, with her sense of entitlement, nose job, and wealthy suburban lifestyle—all provided courtesy of her hardworking father. The JAP also famously appeared as the title character in **Herman Wouk**'s *Marjorie Morningstar* (1955). In Roth's *Portnoy's Complaint* (1969), Sophie Portnoy is the quintessential overbearing Jewish mother. Exemplified by Roth's protagonists Neil Klugman and Alexander Portnoy, the emasculated Jewish man is subdued by the materialistic needs of the JAP and the overprotective demands of the Jewish mother. The stereotype of the Jewish man as neurotic and weak in character similarly appears in the work of **Woody Allen**. These Jewish men usually lust after gentile women, as Roth's and Allen's protagonists do. Such unflattering portrayals are often attributed to Jewish self-hatred, but the self-hating Jew itself has become a powerful stereotype; one of its most famous renderings occurs in **Budd Schulberg**'s *What Makes Sammy Run* (1941), the story of a Jewish movie mogul—not unlike Bloeckman—who goes to great lengths to separate himself from his Jewish past. In American literature by both Jewish and non-Jewish writers, the dominant anti-Semitic stereotypes stem from the Jew's perceived ability to mold to the dominant society and the resulting need to maintain differences between the Jew (as "other") and "real" Americans.

Further Reading

Cheyette, Brian, ed. *Between "Race" and Culture: Representations of "the Jew" in English and American Literature.* Stanford, CA: Stanford UP, 1996.

Erdman, Harley. *Staging the Jew: The Performance of an American Ethnicity, 1860–1920.* New Brunswick, NJ: Rutgers UP, 1997.

Harap, Louis. *Creative Awakening: The Jewish Presence in Twentieth-Century American Literature, 1900–1940s.* New York: Greenwood Press, 1987.

———. *The Image of the Jew in American Literature: From Early Republic to Mass Immigration.* 2nd ed. Syracuse, NY: Syracuse UP, 2003.

Mayo, Louise. *The Ambivalent Image: Nineteenth-Century America's Perception of the Jew.* Teaneck, NJ: Fairleigh Dickinson UP, 1988.

Prell, Riv-Ellen. *Fighting to Become Americans: Assimilation and the Trouble between Jewish Women and Men.* Boston: Beacon Press, 1999.

Lori Harrison-Kahan

JEWISH AMERICAN THEATER   The Jewish American theater is not in itself a separate dramatic genre since Jewish American playwrights create plays dealing with all subjects and ethnic groups. **Arthur Miller** (1915–2005), for instance, a noted Jewish American playwright, wrote a powerful drama about an Italian American family in *A View from the Bridge* (1955) and **Clifford Odets** (1906–63) wrote about another Italian American family in *Golden Boy* (1939). However, there certainly is a significant body of work in the American theater that can be characterized as dealing with Jewish American themes. Many of these deal with the **Holocaust**, Israel, and life in Europe, as well as the Jewish experience in the United States. The roots of the theatrical tradition for Jewish American playwrights, however, go back to Europe in the late nineteenth century.

Yiddish Theater

There was always a need for entertainment among Eastern European Jews at weddings and bar mitzvahs in what was known as the *shtetl* (little town) in which many Jews were confined in Poland and Russia. Songs and dances were performed both by members of the community and professional entertainers known as *klezmorim* whose music provided the festivities with appropriate gaiety. Today there is a revival of *klezmer* music, which is becoming popular even among gentile audiences in the United States.

A form of theatrical entertainment traditionally evolved from the festival of Purim, which commemorated the saving of the Jews from the evil Haman, the prime minister of what was then Persia. It was through the intervention of Esther, later the wife of the Persian King Ahasuerus

(Xerxes), and her Uncle Mordecai that the Jews were not destroyed. Purim is thus a joyous occasion, and many parodies of the story were performed by "Purim Shpielers" (Purim actors) for Jewish audiences many generations before their arrival in the United States.

The Yiddish Theater in America, therefore, had a rich tradition on which to build when the first Yiddish-speaking dramatists arrived in New York during the great migration between 1880 and 1920. Among the earliest was Jacob Gordon (1853–1909), who was born in Russia and emigrated to New York City in 1891. Among his most successful plays were *Gott, Mensh un Taivl* (God, Man and the Devil) and *Yiddisher Kenig Lear* (The Jewish King Lear), a version of Shakespeare's play that, unlike many of the English versions at the time, had tacked a happy ending on the tragic one that Shakespeare had written.

A second early arrival to the Yiddish stage in America was David Pinski (1872–1959), who was born in Russia and settled in the United States in 1899. His earliest work depicts the sufferings of Jews in Russia, and his later efforts were more symbolic, including *The Eternal Jew* and *Shabbetai Tzevi*, a play about a notorious "False Messiah" who had a large following in Eastern Europe in the seventeenth century.

Another was H. Levick (1886–1962), the pen name of Levi Halpern, who was born in Russia and exiled to Siberia when a young man because of his revolutionary activities. He came to the United States in 1913. His most famous play *Der Golem* is a dramatization of the first "Frankenstein" story about Rabbi Judah Löw of Prague who created a monster to protect the Jews from an anti-Semitic plot in sixteenth-century Bohemia.

One of the most influential Yiddish playwrights who emigrated to the United States was Peretz Hirschbein (1880–1948) who before coming here in 1911 had already in 1908 organized a Yiddish theatrical company that toured in Russia and Poland with plays of other Yiddish dramatists as well as himself. Among his most famous plays was *Di Griene Felde* (The Green Fields), which reflected the lives of common Jewish people.

Yet as important as the playwrights were to the Yiddish theater, equally significant were the great actors and actresses who performed these plays. Many of them made the transition from Second Avenue (the heart of the Yiddish theater on the Lower East Side of Manhattan) to Hollywood, such as Muni Weisenfreund (1897–1967), who changed his name to Paul Muni, and Morris Carnovsky (1897–1992). Even James Cagney, the great Irish American actor, revealed that he got his start in the Yiddish theater when he was a teenager.

The towering figures of the Yiddish theater, however, were the great actor-producers: Jacob P. Adler (1855–1926), Maurice Schwartz (1887–1960), and Boris Thomashevsky (1866–1939). These three dominated the Yiddish theater from the early 1900s through the Golden Age (which ended about the time of World War II), producing the plays of Gordon, Pinski, Leivick, and Hirshbein, as well as many more less-prominent Yiddish dramatists.

Boris Thomashevsky came to the United States from the Ukraine in 1881 and organized the first Yiddish theater in New York City shortly thereafter. He started his career by writing his own plays, but soon produced others and became one of the idols of Yiddish theater audiences. Jacob P. Adler arrived in New York City from Russia in 1888 and established himself as one of the leading actors as well as the father of two other performers who would prove to be very influential not only in Jewish American theater but in American theater in general. The more prominent is Stella Adler (1901–92), who with Harold Clurman (1901–80), another Jewish American theater figure, organized "The Group Theatre" in the early 1930s. From this school of acting came what is still known as "the Method" which is derived from the teachings of Konstantin Stanislavsky (1863–1938). Among its practitioners are such star performers as Marlon Brando, Al Pacino, Robert de Niro, and Meryl Streep, as well as many younger actors of stage and screen.

Maurice Schwartz, however, was probably the most successful of the Yiddish theater figures in that he established his own dramatic company in 1918 called the Yiddish Art Theatre. In the next thirty years he produced over 150 plays for Yiddish-speaking audiences, not only by Yiddish playwrights but also by the great European dramatists, such as Ibsen and Chekhov. Among the playwrights represented in his company were Sholem Aleichem, Sholem Asch, and I. J. Singer, as well as Hirschbein and Leivick.

The Second Avenue theater district in New York City at times rivaled Broadway for its popularity with New York City theater goers, a large proportion being Jewish. Although it barely survives today, there are still Yiddish-speaking fans who attend the occasional performances of Yiddish theater. And its enduring quality can be seen in the continued popularity of the musical *Fiddler on the Roof*, which although written for Broadway clearly uses some of the traditions of the Yiddish theater in its story based on the tales of Tevye the Milkman, written by Scholem Aleichem, and the jokes and music as well. In the 1930s, however, native-born Jewish American dramatists began exploring the American theater as an avenue to express their own view of the Jewish experience in the United States.

The Jewish American Theater

It is difficult to define the Jewish American theater as it has grown from the 1930s to the present day by the number of Jewish American playwrights that have been or are presently active in the American theater. The volume on *Contemporary Jewish American Dramatists and Poets* (Greenwood, 1999) lists the names of twenty-four dramatists who can be categorized as Jewish American playwrights whose works have come into prominence after World War II. More could be listed but even among the ones included, their credentials for this definition could be disputed.

However, given the definition of Jewish American playwrights as those of a Jewish background who have written about issues concerning Jewish culture, one could point out at least a dozen who fit this definition well enough to constitute a category for Jewish American theater. Still it should be stated that the earliest forms of Jewish American theater can be best seen not in what are called "straight plays" but in the American musical theater, a category in itself. Among the most prominent of these are Jerome Kern (1885–1945) who wrote the classic musical *Showboat* (1927), Irving Berlin (1888–1991) among whose standard hits are "God Bless America" and "White Christmas," and George Gershwin (1898–1937) whose *Porgy and Bess* (1935) is one of the first and arguably the greatest American operas. None of these Jewish American composers, however, wrote about Jews in their works or on Jewish themes. They were composing for a general American audience on Broadway and were particularly careful not to deal with subjects that would diminish their appeal.

The first prominent Jewish American playwright whose works are still performed occasionally, **Elmer Rice** (1892–1977) wrote *The Adding Machine* (1922) under the influence of the German Expressionist playwrights who had just come to prominence in Europe. But it wasn't until his *Street Scene* (1934) that Rice introduced Jewish characters into his work.

It was shortly thereafter, however, that Clifford Odets presented a serious portrait of a Jewish American family in his drama *Awake and Sing!* (1935), which was produced successfully by the Group Theatre. The play centers on the Bergers, a working-class family run by its matriarch Bessie whose father Jacob represents the social conscience of the family. It is Jacob who juxtaposes the traditional and progressive Jewish values that Odets saw being eroded by the economic opportunism of Bessie's brother, the successful Uncle Morty. Bessie's son Ralph ends the play by rejecting his family's materialism and promising that he will continue in the more idealistic path shown by his grandfather. Odets wrote a second play with a Jewish American milieu, *Paradise Lost* (1936), but little of his subsequent work returns to Jewish American material.

Arthur Miller's work is discussed in greater detail elsewhere in this volume, but his contribution to the Jewish American theater is worth noting here as well. Although his most famous play, *Death of a Salesman* (1949), is not specifically about a Jewish family, the values that are presented by the protagonist's son Biff Loman adhere to Jewish ethical precepts involving a rejection of the crass materialism represented by his father Willy. Most of the rest of Miller's work involving Jewish themes centers on the Holocaust: *After the Fall* (1964), *Incident at Vichy* (1965), the screenplay *Playing for Time* (1980), and *Broken Glass* (1990). But his play *The Price* (1968) has a Jewish character in it, Gregory Solomon, who presents a moral center in a dispute between two brothers about their responsibility toward each other and their father.

Among the younger generation of Jewish American playwrights, several women are prominent, among them **Wendy Wasserstein** (1950–) and **Emily Mann** (1952–). Wasserstein, who was born in New York City and is a graduate of Mount Holyoke and the Yale Drama School, made a hit with her play about five women who have a reunion six years after their college graduation, *Uncommon Women and Others* (1977). The distinctively Jewish figure among them, Holly Kaplan, is the most introspective, wondering what kind of future she should have—that of mainstream America or something "uncommon." But in a later work *Isn't It Romantic?* (1979), Wasserstein centers on a much more ethnically Jewish figure, Janie Blumberg, who is confronted by what was then known as the "generation gap" between her parents who had grown up during the World War II and her own values which lead her to seek a more independent life than her mother has. *The Sisters Rosenzweig* (1992), one of Wasserstein's more recent plays, is probably her most "Jewish," even though the central character, Sara Rosenzweig, is trying to break away from her Jewish roots.

It should be noted that in these and other plays by Jewish American dramatists, the more profound aspects of Jewish life involving religious, Zionist, and Old World values and cultural traditions are slighted and the more familiar characteristics involving food, occasional Yiddish expressions, and other elements that are presently being adopted in general American culture "define" Jewish Americans. This can be attributed both to Jewish **assimilation** into American life and the decline in the valuing of ethnic traditions in a more materialistic society that is typical of the cultures of many ethnic groups.

Emily Mann was born in Boston and educated at Radcliffe College from which she graduated in 1974. She has extensive experience as a director as well as a playwright. Mann's dramatic approach uses a documentary style in such works as *Annulla* (1985), which is an "interview" with seventy-four year old Annulla Allen who was a survivor of the Holocaust, and her best-known play, *Still Life* (1980), which involves a Vietnam War veteran who compares his killing of a Vietnamese family to what the Nazis did to the Jews. But Mann's emphasis is on social issues that transcend a particular ethnic center, such as *Greensboro* (1996) about the killing of five labor organizers in Greensboro, North Carolina, in 1979 by the Ku Klux Klan.

Better known to the general public, however, are the Jewish American comedy playwrights **Neil Simon** and **Woody Allen**. Simon (1927–) is probably the most successful playwright in the American theater for the last forty years with hits such as *Come Blow Your Horn*. It was not until the last twenty years, however, that he focused on people with a specific Jewish background as he did in his semi-autobiographical trilogy: *Brighton Beach Memoirs*, *Biloxi Blues*, and *Broadway Bound*, the first and last of which center on the Jerome family which strongly resembles the family in which he grew up in Brooklyn.

Both Simon and Allen, in fact, along with Mel Brooks—noted more for his movies, such as *The Producers* (1968), *Blazing Saddles* (1974), and *Young Frankenstein* (1974), until his recent musical version of *The Producers* (2001)—worked at approximately the same time on the immensely successful "Show of Shows" introducing television audiences to Jewish humor that they would later see on the Broadway stage. It is through television, in fact, that elements of the humor of the Jewish American theater can now be seen by a general audience in such popular shows as *Seinfeld* and *Will and Grace*.

Woody Allen (1935–) is best known as a screenwriter and director of such hits as *Play It Again, Sam* (adopted from his play) and *Annie Hall*. One of his earliest works is *Don't Drink the Water* (1968), which played on Broadway for a year-and-a-half. But Allen has only written three full-length plays, of which *Play It Again, Sam* (1969) has a distinctively Jewish character, Allan Felix, who is in the typical mold of Allen's "losers." The self-deprecatory character of Allen's Jewish figures has been the subject for much criticism by members of the Jewish community. Yet it is this quality that is in evidence in much Jewish humor.

Another category of Jewish American playwrights are those who are known for their work that does not center on Jewish American issues and yet are accepted as part of that ethnic group. The most prominent of these is **David Mamet** (1947–). Mamet was born in Chicago, and it is through the Chicago-based theater company (the St. Nicholas Players, which he formed) that some of his earliest plays were produced.

Mamet's earliest successes in Chicago were *Duck Variations* and *Sexual Perversity in Chicago* (1974), followed by his first Broadway play *American Buffalo* (1977), starring Robert Duvall and, in a revival, Al Pacino. Mamet is known as a master of spoken dialogue and opened up what was acceptable on the stage with his frequent use of four-letter words in many of his works. He has won the Pulitzer Prize for *Glengarry Glen Ross* (1984), his play about the real estate business, and his created controversy in *Oleanna* (1992), a play about what he feels to be the abuses of sexual harassment accusations.

Until recently there was little awareness among the theater-going public that Mamet was even Jewish, although oddly enough several of his early plays were on Jewish themes: *Mackinac* (1974), about a Jewish trader in early America, and *Marranos* (1975), about a group of Portuguese Jews attempting to escape persecution. Neither has been published, but in the late 1990s Mamet turned to dramas centering on Jewish characters in his trilogy *Old Neighborhood* (1997), the first play of which had the unambiguous title of *The Disappearance of the Jews*. Mamet's recent efforts in Jewish-based drama are part of a pattern shown in Simon and Miller who have gone back to their Jewish roots after establishing themselves with main-stream plays.

There are many other Jewish American playwrights whose work deals with ethnic and religious themes, although they are not as well known as the ones already mentioned. Among one of the more successful in the medium of television was **Paddy Chayefsky** (1923–81), who wrote several plays on Jewish themes such as *The Tenth Man* (1959), about an exorcism in modern-day New York City, and *Gideon* (1961), about a Biblical hero who fought for the Hebrews against the Midianites. But Chayefsky is probably best known for his teleplay and movie *Marty* (1955), about an Italian American butcher. It won an Oscar for Earnest Borgnine in 1955.

Among contemporary playwrights the most controversial is **Harvey Fierstein** (1954–) whose autobiographical *Torch Song Trilogy* (1978–79) broke new ground as a play that centers on an openly gay male. **Tony Kushner** (1956–) wrote the two-part drama *Angels in America* (1990) and received more awards than practically any other American play when it was given the Tony Award, the New York Drama Critics Circle award, and the Pulitzer Prize after its Broadway opening in 1993. Like Fierstein in one respect, Kushner's work centers on gay themes, although both dramatists reflect their Jewish background in many of their characters.

There are many other Jewish American playwrights who have flourished in the American theater over the last thirty years including **Jon Robin Baitz**, **Israel Horovitz** (certainly one of the most innovative of modern dramatists), James Lapine, **Donald Margulies**, **Elizabeth Swados**, and Murray Schisgal. Their works reflect various levels of Jewish American culture as well as religious tradition, although most of them tend to be secular. However, it is difficult to categorize a specially "Jewish American theater" in the twenty-first century as it had been quite easy to describe the Yiddish American theater since it was self-defining by the language it used and the audience to which it appealed. Although **ethnicity** has become a major cultural issue in the United States in the last thirty years, the creative figures who express their ethnic vision often move toward a more universal view of the human condition, just as happened with the first ethnic writers who strove to be accepted by the majority of Americans two generations ago. (*See also* Jewish American Musicals, Yiddish Literature)

Further Reading

Cohen, Edward, ed. *New Jewish Voices—Plays Produced by the Jewish Repertory Theatre*. Albany: State U of New York P, 1985.

Cohen, Sarah B., ed. *The Drama Review. Jewish Theatre Issue* 24.3 (1980).

———, ed. *Jewish American Women Drama*. Syracuse, NY: Syracuse UP, 1997.

Landis, Joseph. *The Great Jewish Plays*. New York: Avon Books, 1972.

Lifson, David. *The Yiddish Theatre in America*. New York: Thomas Yoseloff, 1965.

Schiff, Ellen. *Awake and Singing: Seven Classic Plays from the American Jewish Repertoire*. New York: Penguin Books, 1995.

———. *From Stereotype to Metaphor: The Jew in Contemporary Drama*. Albany: State U of New York P, 1982.

———. *Fruitful and Multiplying: Nine Contemporary Plays from the American Jewish Repertoire*. New York: Penguin Books, 1996.

Joel Shatzky

JIM CROW   The phrase "Jim Crow" is derived from the title of an early nineteenth-century song by the white minstrel performer Thomas "Daddy"

Rice; the demeaning intent of the racist caricature of African Americans that minstrel theater entailed became associated, through the use of this term, with efforts to limit the power of blacks in the period which spanned the withdrawal of federal troops from the South in 1877 to the **Civil Rights Movement** of the 1950s and 1960s. After 1877 the southern states enacted laws which subordinated blacks and perpetuated white supremacy, thus supplanting the Constitutional amendments and federal laws that legislated civil rights, male suffrage, access to public facilities, jury service, and property ownership for African Americans.

In its narrowest application, Jim Crow refers to the legally enforced segregation of blacks and whites put into effect in the South after 1877. However, Jim Crow also refers to any practice of systematic **racism**, whether legal or extra-legal, which enforces the political and economic as well as the social subjugation of African Americans, including: disenfranchisement; exclusion from juries; antimiscegenation laws; racist terror and violence, including lynching and the establishment of white supremacist groups such as the Ku Klux Klan; exclusion from unions and skilled work; and sharecropping or debt peonage which bound workers to the land and white landowners in conditions of virtual **slavery**.

Following the Reconstruction period, black and white Americans were legally segregated in public transportation, schools and facilities, housing, and the workplace. By 1890 *de jure* segregation was in place throughout the South. In 1896 the Supreme Court ruled in *Plessy* v. *Ferguson* that so-called separate-but-equal facilities justified segregated railroad cars; this ruling was evidence of the extent to which federal civil rights were severely restricted if not invalidated by judicial decisions, and it became a precedent for segregation laws as a whole. The 1954 Supreme Court school desegregation ruling in *Brown* v. *The Board of Education* signaled the beginning of the Civil Rights Movement and the end of *de jure* Jim Crow, even if de facto segregation and discrimination continue to exist in both the North and the South.

The documentation of Jim Crow and the struggle over the most effective political and cultural response to it are defining elements of African American literary production. For many writers, critics, and theorists within the tradition, the effects of the enforced separation of black and white Americans for much of the nation's history and the nature of a distinct if shared or hybrid African American cultural tradition that developed, in part, out of this experience are central issues and debates in their work. (*See also* Race)

Further Reading

Litwack, Leon F. *Trouble in Mind: Black Southerners in the Age of Jim Crow*. New York: Knopf, 1998.

Packard, Jerrold M. *American Nightmare: The History of Jim Crow*. New York: St. Martin's, 2002.

The Rise and Fall of Jim Crow. Programs 1–4. Prod. Sam Pollard. Video recording. California Newsreel, 2002.

Woodward, C. Vann. *The Strange Career of Jim Crow*. Commemorative ed. New York: Oxford UP, 2002.

Wormser, Richard. *The Rise and Fall of Jim Crow*. New York: St. Martin's, 2003.

Robin Lucy

JIMENEZ, FRANCISCO (1943–)   Mexican American writer who has chronicled his own life as a migrant child in America in two story collections, *The Circuit* (1997) and *Breaking Through* (2001), and two picture books. Jimenez is also an academic, the author of *The Identification and Analysis of Chicano Literature* (1979) and other critical works. Entering the field of creative literature later in life, Jimenez has, nevertheless, garnered more critical acclaim and distinguished awards than most authors earn in a lifetime.

Perhaps it was listening to and absorbing his father's story talents that gave Jimenez the ability to produce spare, unadorned, but graceful, easily flowing prose, filled with poignant memories, spirited characters, and illuminating insights about Mexican sensibilities, value systems, and cultural strengths. His mother's deep faith and physical resilience, wedded to his father's optimism and belief in human equality, plus Francisco being the middle child of eight siblings produced a childhood filled with hardship but strong family bonds and academic aspirations.

Papa leads the family through a barbed-wire fence and into California when Francisco is only five, and he leaves his small village in Guadalajara because there is no school there and no way to provide adequately for his family. What awaits this family are years of living through backbreaking work, picking cotton and strawberries, never any house of their own, and one misfortune after another. For Francisco, however, there is also the chance to experience and involve himself in a wider world and finally to move fully into it; by the end of the second volume, he has attained a full scholarship to Santa Clara University.

The Circuit takes Francisco from his first days of school, where he sits drawing butterflies because he has no inkling what his English-speaking teacher is saying, to the day, as an eighth grader, when just as he is ready to recite the assigned portion of the Declaration of Independence about all men being created equal, an **immigration** officer arrives to arrest him and send his family back to Mexico. *Breaking Through* takes up where *The Circuit* leaves off, with Francisco and his older brother returning to California to attend and finish high school and with family life and school days weaving together later, when the family is reunited, to produce Jimenez's overarching theme: growing up between two worlds—Mexican migrant child and American immigrant—and learning to navigate between these worlds, integrating and blending the best of both.

Jimenez's picture books emerge from stories in *The Circuit*. In *The Christmas Gift* (2000), Francisco (Panchito) wants a red ball for Christmas but gets only candy instead, the result of his father giving his last dime to a man whose wife has embroidered a white handkerchief. Papa's love for his wife, and for others trying to survive in hard times (the man's wife is expecting a baby), is not lost on Panchito. In *La Mariposa* (1998), Panchito gives his prize-winning butterfly drawing to his classmate Curtis, who has previously wrestled him to the ground to retrieve the coat (given to Panchito by the school principal) that Curtis lost earlier in the school year. The butterfly metaphor runs through this book, and both story collections, as Francisco's transformation from Mexican migrant child to bicultural, bilingual adult (breaking through his cocoon) and flying (journeying) into the world. The coat (itself a metaphor of the pull and tug between American and Mexican for the prized land of Mexico), the butterfly, and the embroidered handkerchief reveal Jimenez's talent for weaving deep and subtle meanings through such remarkably clear and straightforward prose.

Throughout these books, Jimenez emphasizes the trenchant power of love: No family is really poor when filled with such love as this one; no child—even a migrant child—ever lacks schooling if he loves words and stories and knowledge as much as Panchito does. Loss of innocence (some people in American are more "equal" than others, Panchito learns) and the migrant child's quest for self are underlying themes of all these stories, with education providing the stability and permanence that the constant journeying of migrant life precludes. (*See also* Mexican American Autobiography)

Further Reading

Barrera, Rosalinda. "Secrets Shared: A Conversation with Francisco Jimenez." *New Advocate* 16 (Winter 2003): 1–8.

Barrera, Rosalinda, Ruth Quiroa, and Cassiette West-Williams. "Poco a Poco: The Continuing Development of Mexican American Children's Literature in the 1990s." *New Advocate* 12 (Fall 1999): 315–30.

Carger, Chris. "Talking with Francisco Jimenez." *Book Links* (December 2001/January 2002): 14–19.

Nina Mikkelsen

JOANS, THEODORE "TED" (1928–2003)   African American Beat poet, musician, surrealist, performance artist, world traveler, and art collector. Ted Joans was born July 4, 1928, in Cairo, Illinois. As the son of a **jazz** musician, Joans was forced into music at the age of twelve when his father, a riverboat musician, gave him a trumpet and left him on the streets of Memphis, Tennessee. The elder Joans's work on the rivers gave birth to the myth that Ted was born on a riverboat.

Joans studied trumpet and painting at Indiana University, and in 1951 he received a bachelor of fine arts degree. In that same year he moved to Greenwich Village in New York City and became involved with the Beat Movement, though that fact is not always mentioned when the Beat poets are discussed. But Joans was there during the heyday of the movement (1955–65) along with **Jack Kerouac**, **Allen Ginsberg**, **Gregory Corso**, **Amiri Baraka**, and **Bob Kaufman**—the stars of the movement whose names are better known than Joans's.

It is not widely reported that Joans was instrumental in raising money to assist the Beats in publishing their poems in their little magazines. Nor is it frequently documented that Joans's poems were not published in any of the magazines. Joans's obscurity as a Beat poet, however, did not totally prevent him from acquiring a following. He received a fair amount of exposure in write-ups in popular magazines such as *Time, Life, Ebony,* and *Sepia,* which caused many nonacademics to become interested in him and his artistic creations.

Even though Joans is not always acknowledged as one of the Beat poets, he is usually recognized as the first individual to artfully merge jazz and poetry on the bandstand. And when his first book of poetry was published in 1957, Joans was at last given full recognition as a Beat poet, as well as recognition as an important member of one of the most significant counterculture movements of the twentieth century. When the Beat movement became over-commercialized in the early 1960s, Joans became less interested in it and left the United States.

Some sources report only that Joans moved to Europe. More accurately, however, he first went to Africa, specifically, to Timbuktu, Mali, and from there, to Tangier, Morocco. He later traveled to Europe and lived in the cities of Paris, Copenhagen, and Amsterdam. Joans also lived in Harlem, New York, an experience which contributed to a greater presence of African American themes in his work after the Beat movement began to wane.

Joans was interesting not only as a musician, poet, and traveler, but also as a pictorial artist and art collector. During his years at Indiana University he had studied surrealism, which characterized his paintings and some of his poems. In 1961 Joans published *All of Ted Joans and No More,* and in it he makes references to Andre Breton, renowned French surrealist poet. While living in Africa, Joans collected African artwork, which he sold to support himself when he returned to the United States.

Joans wrote more than thirty books exhibiting a wide range of styles and themes. *Black Pow: Jazz Poems* (1969), for example, is at times revolutionary while employing the fiery "burn-baby-burn" rhetoric of the day. And in *Afrodisia* (1970), Joans's preoccupation in the "Africa" section is the African landscape and revolution; in the "Erotica" section sex and eroticism are his concerns.

Becoming an expatriate when he was a young man, Joans died on foreign soil. His life ended in his apartment in Vancouver, Canada, on May 7, 2003. He and his companion, artist Laura Corsiglia, moved there in protest of the acquittal of four white New York police officers who killed an African immigrant in 1999. Standing in the entrance of his apartment building, Amadou Diallo was holding in his hand a wallet, which the officers allegedly mistook for a firearm. Their mistake caused them to open fire on Diallo. After their acquittal an angry Joans left the United States, vowing never to return.

In his last years Joans suffered from diabetes, and from financial difficulties. He read his poems and sold his personal papers to libraries in order to survive.

Further Reading

Fabre, Michel. "Ted Joans: The Surrealist Griot." *From Harlem to Paris: Black American Writers in France*. Champaign: U of Illinois P, 1993. 309–23.

Gates, Henry Louis, Jr. "Ted Joans: Tri-Continental Poet." *Transition* 48 (Spring 1975): 4–12.

Joyce Russell-Robinson

JOHNSON, CHARLES RICHARD (1948–)   African American artist, cartoonist, short story writer, essayist, screenwriter, academic, martial arts expert, and philosopher. Charles Richard Johnson's novel ***Middle Passage*** (1990) brought him wide recognition. After working as a journalist, publishing satirical cartoons lambasting **race** relations in America, and earning a PhD in philosophy, Johnson has focused on creative writing and teaching. In his philosophical fiction, Johnson explores moral ambiguities and ethical dilemmas while striving for socially responsible art. Challenging traditional modes of black representation, championing the works of black writers, and sounding a strong, often controversial, voice on **multiculturalism** and race relations, Johnson interrogates the philosophical issues surrounding identity while fiercely opposing any fixed definition of the black American experience.

Being and Race: Black Writing Since 1970 (1988), *In Search of a Voice* (1991), *I Call Myself an Artist* (1999, Rudolph Byrd, ed.), and *Turning the Wheel: Essays on Buddhism and Writing* (2003) detail Johnson's phenomenological aesthetic for black fiction, his thoughts on the moral obligations of the writer, and his reflections on the way Eastern philosophy has informed his creative process. Johnson aims to create well-rounded black and white characters, forging an aesthetic that values ambiguity and open-endedness. For Johnson writing and reading are ethical acts inextricably bound with the quest for freedom, a universal experience, and according to Johnson the subject of all black literature.

Johnson published two political cartoon collections, *Black Humor* (1970) and *Half-Past Nation Time* (1972), while an undergraduate at Southern Illinois University. He also created fifty-two fifteen-minute episodes of a PBS drawing show called *Charlie's Pad*.

In 1972 while studying with John Gardner, Johnson wrote his first novel to be published, *Faith and the Good Thing* (1974), the black folk tale of Faith Cross, who upon the death of her parents sets out to find herself and the "Good Thing"—truth, beauty, goodness, and life's meaning. Along the way she seeks guidance from a *grigot* figure, the Swamp Woman, who tells the story of Kujichaglia. Like the story the Swamp Woman tells, *Faith and the Good Thing* responds to perennial questions: "Who *am* I? What can I *know*? Where am I *going*? Where have I *been*? and much worse, *What* am I?" As in Johnson's subsequent works, the novel explores the nature of the self from the perspective of phenomenological philosophy and the religious quest, both of which involve "conjurin'," the exploration of the Good Thing, which is "*absolutely* nothin'" and "*particularly* everythin'."

Charles Richard Johnson. *AP/Wide World Photos.*

While a PhD student at the State University of New York at Stony Brook, Johnson researched **African American slave narrative**s and worked on *Oxherding Tale* (1982), a novel Johnson labored seven years to write that appropriates Eastern philosophy and deals with the questions of freedom and bondage. The novel is based on the *Ten Oxherding Pictures* of twelfth-century Zen artist Kakuan Shien, which form a parable of the self, epitomized by an ox seeking enlightenment, *"moksha,"* the name Johnson uses for the novel's last chapter. *Oxherding Tale* tells the story of George Andrews, a biracial slave who confronts his desires and comes to understand that the self is "a palimpsest, interwoven with everything."

In *Sorcerer's Apprentice* (1986), written between 1977 and 1982 while working on *Oxherding Tale*, Johnson tells eight stories from different perspectives—everything from the slave narratives that frame the book, to a man's martial arts transformation, to a children's fable told from the perspective of a watchdog in a pet store, to an encounter between a black doctor and a space alien. All the tales deal with the difficulty of capturing the black experience, the elusive nature of reality, and the possibility that Buddhism may help reconcile dualistic notions of race and identity.

The novel *Middle Passage* (1990), written between 1982 and 1989, is Johnson's masterwork for which he received the National Book Award—the first African American man to do so since **Ralph Ellison** garnered the prize for **Invisible Man** in 1953. Johnson distilled years of exhaustive research on sea writings, the slave trade, and slave narratives into three stories: a love story between a freed slave turned vagabond thief and a Boston school teacher, a story of the slave trade and the horrific conditions slaves endured while traveling from Africa to America, and the story of a mad sea captain. At the center of the novel and telling the tale is Rutherford Calhoun, who after a murderous slave insurrection completes the ship's log.

Johnson's next novel *Dreamer* (1998) tells the story of **Martin Luther King Jr.**'s last two years through the perspective of Matthew Bishop, a young King follower, and includes Chaym Smith, King's look-alike and alter ego. Johnson presents a philosophic King who dreams of refashioning the social order to right the inequalities brought by life's contingencies—the arbitrary way difference and opportunities are doled out. Johnson offers both an idealistic and a realist King. *Dreamer* also chronicles the decline of the **Civil Rights Movement** and the void that opens after King's assassination.

Soul Catcher (2001) is a collection of twelve original stories dramatizing the text *Africans in America: America's Journey through Slavery*, a companion Johnson coauthored with Patricia Smith for a television series of the same name. The tales look at American history—political, economic, and cultural—from the perspective of the black experience, describing how it defines the story of America.

Johnson has written over twenty screenplays, has reviewed numerous books for such publications as the *New York Times*, the *Los Angeles Times*, and *Quarterly Black Review* and has received both a National Endowment for the Arts grant and a Guggenheim Fellowship. He holds the Pollock Professorship for Excellence in English at the University of Washington.

Further Reading

Byrd, Rudolph P. *I Call Myself an Artist: Writings by and about Charles Johnson*.
   Bloomington: Indiana UP, 1999.
Nash, William R. *Charles Johnson's Fiction*. Urbana: U of Illinois P, 2003.

Blake G. Hobby

JOHNSON, E. PAULINE [TEKAHIONWAKE] (1861–1913)   Native American (Mohawk) poet, performer, and journalist. E. Pauline Johnson was one of the best-known stage performers of her generation, touring Canada, England, and the United States at the turn of the century, reciting her poetry, and telling tales of the First Peoples.

Johnson was born in Ontario, Canada, to George Johnson, a Mohawk chief, and Emily Howells, an American woman of British descent. Johnson turned to writing to help support her family after her father died in 1884. One of her earliest successes was "A Cry from an Indian Wife" (1885). In this poem the female speaker sends her husband off to battle against whites encroaching upon their land.

In 1892 she began reciting her poetry publicly, performing the first half of her program in a ball gown and the second half in a buckskin dress. The most famous poem in her repertoire, "The Song My Paddle Sings" (1892), was later included in her first collection, *White Wampum* (1895), and later printed in many poetry anthologies. In this key example of Johnson's nature poetry, the speaker dismisses the wind and takes up her paddle, describing the exhilaration of passing through rapids and the peace of drifting in still waters.

The majority of Johnson's poems contain strong, independent female characters. In "Ojistoh" (1895), another of Johnson's most frequently recited poems, the wife of a Mohawk chief tells of her capture by Huron enemies and her subsequent escape after seducing and stabbing her captor. Her love poems, such as "The Firs" (1886), "Fasting" (1887), and "My English Letter" (1888), provide unflinching examinations of female desire, both requited and denied. Most notably "The Idlers" (1890) provides a highly eroticized description of the lover's masculine beauty as he lounges in the speaker's canoe and she gazes down upon him.

Johnson's strong female narrators also appear in her nonfiction prose pieces, often written for magazines such as *Rudder* that catered to outdoor enthusiasts. In these essays Johnson shares details of her own adventures, as in "Canoe and Canvas" (1896). In others she provides advice and encouragement to young women, advocating the physical and social benefits of rigorous exercise in the open air, as in her series "Outdoor Pastimes for Women" (1892–93).

In a remarkable piece of literary criticism, "A Strong Race Opinion: On the Indian Girl in Modern Fiction" (1892), Johnson condemns the inability of most writers to create realistic images of Native women. She criticizes the use of generic "Indian" characters with no recognizable tribal distinctions and the tired stereotype of the selfless girl who seems consumed by a "suicidal mania" in her readiness to betray her people and sacrifice her life on behalf of the white hero, who inevitably marries his white sweetheart. She closes by calling for more realistic, varied portrayals of native women who might be allowed to win the game of love occasionally. The native women appearing in Johnson's short stories often serve as answers to her own call. Most notable among these is Esther, the heroine of "As It Was In the Beginning" (1899) who kills her white lover Laurence after he betrays her by agreeing to abandon her and consider marriage with a white woman. Another of her heroines Christie from "A Red Girl's Reasoning" (1893) leaves her white husband Charlie after he expresses revulsion at the idea that her parents were not married according to Christian law.

In 1906 Johnson retired from her career as a public performer. Here she wrote essays and stories for *Boys World*, some of which were later collected in *The Shagganappi* (1911). Many of these, such as "Wolf Brothers" (1910), offer positive images of Native boys who exhibit courage and honor. She also wrote many essays and short stories for *Mother's Magazine*, of which seven later appeared in the posthumous collection *The Moccasin Maker* (1913). Johnson began collecting stories of the Squamish people from Chief Joe Capilano [Su-á-pu-luck] and his wife Mary Agnes [Líxwelut]. Fifteen of these stories comprise *Vancouver Legends* (1911). *Flint and Feather* appeared in 1912, a year before Johnson died of cancer, combining all the poems from her first two books of poetry with twenty-five previously uncollected poems. (*See also* Native American Stereotypes)

Further Reading

Strong-Boag, Veronica, and Carole Gerson. *Paddling Her Own Canoe: The Times and Texts of E. Pauline Johnson*. Toronto: U of Toronto P, 2000.

Jennifer A. Gehrman

JOHNSON, HELENE (1906–1995)   African American poet. Considered among the finest of the young poets of the **Harlem Renaissance** by such figures as **James Weldon Johnson** and **Wallace Thurman**, Helene Johnson published only thirty-four poems in her lifetime, leaving her poetry career behind after her marriage. However, the lyricism, nature imagery, and **race** consciousness of her best poems continue to draw enthusiastic readers. The 2000 publication of *This Waiting for Love: Helene Johnson, Poet of the Harlem Renaissance*, containing her published and unpublished works along with a collection of letters, pictures, and a chronology of her life, has helped reestablish her place in the Harlem pantheon.

Johnson was born and educated in Boston. Along with her cousin, the novelist Dorothy West, with whom she was raised, Johnson spent summers on Martha's Vineyard in a cottage next door to the artist Lois Mailou Jones. Johnson's "The Road" appeared in Alain Locke's 1925 landmark *The New Negro*. Three of Johnson's poems won honorable mentions at the April 1926 *Opportunity* awards; Johnson and West moved to New York City the following January.

Johnson and West became good friends with **Zora Neale Hurston** early in their time in Harlem. Johnson worked at the Fellowship of Reconciliation, an international organization for world peace, and for a while for Hurston. Wallace Thurman depicted Johnson and West as Hazel Jamison and Doris Westmore in the novel *Infants of the Spring* (1932), his satire on the Harlem Renaissance.

Opportunity, Vanity Fair, the *Messenger, The Saturday Evening Quill*, and *Fire!!* published Johnson's work. In her poetry Johnson would move across a range of styles, from the formal sonnet to black vernacular, but her preference was free verse. She often delivers rich, evocative images of nature in her poetry, although not always for the expected effect. For instance in "A Southern Road" (1926) she seems first to celebrate the lush beauty of the landscape found along a southern road, but ends with the sight of a lynched figure hanging from a blue gum tree, suggesting the betrayal of God's creations. On the other hand "The Road" compares its subject to the African race, ending with a rallying cry to refuse to be trodden down.

People play at least as strong a role in Johnson's poetry as does nature, as in "A Missionary Brings a Young Native to America" (*Harlem*, 1928), "Poem," and "Sonnet to a Negro in Harlem" (*Caroling Dusk*, 1927). The latter two especially celebrate the identity of urban African American males and linger over physical descriptions. Love was a frequent subject in Johnson's poetry and was sometimes delivered with a sharp sense of humor, as in "He's About 22. I'm 63." Central to most of her poetry is a strong vein of cultural pride, as evidenced in "Magula" (*Palms*, 1926). Here Johnson speaks to an African person whom a missionary is trying to convert. The narrator urges Magula to listen instead to her poetry and to the natural surroundings, rather than to follow a creed that will not allow Magula to dance.

Johnson married William Hubbell in 1933; they had one daughter, born in 1940. The last poem published during her lifetime "Let Me Sing My

Song" appeared in *Challenge* in 1935. Verner D. Mitchell's edition of her poetry collects the thirty-four poems of the Harlem Renaissance era, as well as thirteen unpublished poems written from the 1960s through the early 1980s. Johnson died in Manhattan in 1995.

Further Reading

Mitchell, Verner D., ed. *This Waiting for Love: Helene Johnson, Poet of the Harlem Renaissance*. Amherst: U of Massachusetts P, 2000.

Kathryn West

JOHNSON, JAMES WELDON (1871–1938) African American novelist, poet, songwriter, autobiographer, historian, educator, and activist. Not only was James Weldon Johnson the elder statesman of the **Harlem Renaissance**, but he was also a Renaissance man. In addition to writing beautiful, innovative poetry and provocative, influential prose, Johnson was a school principal (1894–1900), founder of a newspaper (*Daily American*, 1895), the first African American admitted to the Florida Bar (1898), the lyricist of "Lift Every Voice and Sing," which is considered the "Negro National Anthem" (1900), United States Consul to Venezuela (1906) and Nicaragua (1909), editor of the *New York Age* (1914), executive secretary for the NAACP (1920–30), and a professor at Fisk University (1930–38). Johnson's writing challenged literary conventions and racial stereotypes; his public activism challenged ignorance, institutional discrimination, and mob violence.

Johnson's most famous and influential literary work is *The Autobiography of an Ex-Colored Man* (1912). Many critics argue that Johnson revolutionized the autobiographical form and directly influenced the literature of the Harlem Renaissance and the following generation of authors, particularly **Ralph Ellison**, **James Baldwin**, and **Ann Petry**. Johnson rejected the melodramatic tradition of previous novelists and autobiographers, choosing instead to describe realistically the complexities of African Americans' social and psychological struggles. Johnson's modernist protagonist is an unreliable narrator and a complex psychological figure who neither exemplifies the stereotypical lazy buffoon or animalistic criminal nor strives blindly for the white, middle-class ideal. The intelligent, introspective, and conflicted "ex-colored man" learns to appreciate African American culture but chooses to pass for white, showing that American **racism** causes self-denial and that racial identities are merely social constructions.

In *The Autobiography*, Johnson's protagonist thinks he is white until a teacher and America's "one-drop" policy identify him as black. He then spends the rest of the novel searching for an **identity**, alternating between wanting to connect with his African American heritage and passing for white to avoid experiencing shame, discrimination, and violence. His physical travels take him through the South, the North, and Europe, while his philosophical travels allow him to analyze the different people and attitudes he encounters. At one point he witnesses a lynching, causing him to criticize white Americans' inhumanity and African Americans' helplessness.

Johnson's protagonist explores the complex psychology of how African Americans view themselves and their **race**. He is proud when he hears sermons and folk songs, but he is angry when an African American he trusts steals his money and ashamed at his people's inability to resist exploitation and abuse. The narrator wants to be the model African American and disprove the negative stereotypes, but in the end he finds life as a white man easier. When he falls in love with a white woman, he feels a violent revulsion for his "African blood." He chooses what he considers the cowardly route by turning his back on his race, a choice that also denies his children the chance to explore their own racial heritage.

Unlike the "ex-colored man," Johnson embraced his African American identity and was a proud spokesman for his race. Although Johnson's poetry reflects his classical European education, he often tackled political issues. "Mother Night" and "Sleep" follow the tradi-

James Weldon Johnson, c. 1910. *Courtesy of the Library of Congress.*

tional sonnet form and utilize universal, nonpolitical themes. "Brothers" and "The White Witch" on the other hand protest white American's remorseless lynching and groundless fears of miscegenation. "Fifty Years" celebrates the Emancipation Proclamation's fiftieth anniversary by arguing that African Americans deserve social equality and full participation in American society. "Lift Every Voice and Sing" honors African Americans who struggled during slavery and those who continue to struggle against prejudice and for a better future. Johnson's brother Rosamond put the poem to music, and the song inspired and unified the African American community and became the unofficial "Negro National Anthem."

Johnson's dialectical poetry avoids the clichés of the African American dialectical tradition. Instead he created a new African American poetic idiom by using free verse and contemporary words and phrases to capture the essence of how actual people in his community speak. For example, the simple speaker in "Sence You Went Away" is realistic and dignified—not a caricature. In *God's Trombones: 7 Negro Sermons in Verse* (1927) Johnson uses the living speech of the African American preacher to celebrate the beauty and power in his community. In addition Johnson edited several ground-breaking anthologies: *The Book of American Negro Poetry* (1922), *The Book of American Negro Spirituals* (1925), and *The Second Book of Negro Spirituals* (1926). These anthologies helped give African Americans a greater sense of pride in themselves and their community. They also introduced important new poets to the public and encouraged white readers to discard their stereotypes and recognize African Americans as intelligent, creative contributors to American civilization.

Johnson's nonfiction also shows his commitment to racial pride and upliftment. *Black Manhattan* (1930) details the history of African American social and cultural development in New York City from 1626 to 1930. Johnson records the progress his people made as they helped settle the region, rebelled against slavery, founded newspapers and churches, established theater companies and political organizations, and formed a strong community, Harlem, in which they could prosper. Johnson identifies significant contributions African Americans have made to American culture and why the future looks bright for his people.

Johnson's autobiography *Along This Way* (1933) begins as a friendly self-analysis and becomes a serious political commentary, which criticizes racism and suggests significant social changes. It expresses the positive qualities of African American life, dispelling the myth of racial inferiority and calling attention to the many African Americans who held positions of responsibility and authority in the United States, Latin America, and the Caribbean.

In *Negro Americans, What Now?* (1934) Johnson urges African Americans to understand their choices, recognize their individual and communal strengths, and map out a better future. He proposes advancement through education, voting, and economic cooperation. James Weldon Johnson challenged literary conventions, fought social injustice, and inspired African Americans "to march on till victory is won."

Further Reading

Fleming, Robert. *James Weldon Johnson*. Boston: Twayne, 1987.

Levy, Eugene. *James Weldon Johnson: Black Leader, Black Voice*. Chicago: U of Chicago P, 1973.

Matthew Teorey

JOHNSON, SIMON (1874–1970) Norwegian American novelist. Johnson came to North Dakota as a young child and always loved the prairie landscape of his youth. His reading of Norwegian literature gave him an idealized image of the land of his birth while his admiration for writers such as "Longfellow, Emerson, Holmes, yes, even Owen Wister" (as he puts it in his unpublished autobiography) gave him a veneration for what he thought of as the New England tradition. He lived on the family farm until he was employed by a temperance association at the age of twenty-six and also began to submit verse to newspapers and literary journals. His first novel *Et geni* (1907; A genius) is a rather crude prohibition tract, while *Lonea* (1909), in spite of its sentimentality, is valuable for its realistic descriptions of life among settlers on the prairie. *I et nyt rige* (1914; In a new kingdom; translated as *From Fjord to Prairie*, 1916) is a collective narrative of a North Dakota settlement from homesteading days to an established rural society. In a volume of four stories (1917) he turned to contemporary life and wrote critically of the success of the Nonpartisan League in the election of 1916.

Johnson's most ambitious work is also his most embarrassing failure— the two related novels *Falitten paa Braastad* (1922; The bankruptcy at Braastad) and *Frihetens hjem* (1925; The home of freedom). In their reviews **Waldemar Ager** criticized the first for its idealized characters, and **Ole E. Rølvaag** ridiculed the second for its flawless hero and melodramatic villains. Driven by his childhood experience of poverty in Norway, Jens Braastad has carved a small empire out of the one-time wilderness. But as his farm thrives, his family disintegrates; his wife is an invalid and his son a drunkard. His idealistic daughter disapproves of all he does but tries to remain loyal. The bankruptcy at the Braastad farm is of the spirit. Through a contrived and melodramatic plot, Braastad eventually sees the folly of his ways and is reunited with his estranged family. The idealistic Olaf, son of a poor farmer, departs for a lengthy visit to Norway and the home of his ancestors at the close of the novel. While the first of the two novels is mainly concerned with the materialism and spiritual decay of Norwegian Americans, the second sets the idealism of its hero Olaf, whose American patriotism has been strengthened by his visit to Norway, against the excesses of the World War I Americanization movement—it is treacherous to speak languages other than English. Granted a public hearing by the court after the war, Olaf, who has married the daughter of Braastad, is vindicated after he demonstrates that not only is a Norwegian American a true American but that the United States is a land of many cultural traditions. *Frihetens hjem* is Johnson's last published novel. He continued to write, however—four novels, an autobiography, several short stories and two volumes of poetry—leaving them at his death with the archives of the Norwegian American Historical Association. (*See also* Norwegian American Literature)

Further Reading

Øverland, Orm. *The Western Home: A Literary History of Norwegian America.*
  Northfield, Minnesota: The Norwegian-American Historical Association, and
  Champaign: U of Illinois P, 1996. 267–78.

Orm Øverland

JONES, EDWARD P. (1950–) African American fiction writer. Edward P. Jones's very first book, *Lost in the City* (1992), a collection of fourteen stories, won the PEN/Hemingway Award and was a finalist for the National Book Award. His first novel *The Known World* (2003) was also highly acclaimed. It was listed on the *New York Times* Editor's Choice and won the National Book Critics' Circle Award for fiction. In 2004 he won the Pulitzer Prize for fiction and was one of the recipients of the prestigious MacArthur grants.

Jones, born and raised in Washington, was educated in local public schools, Holy Cross College, Massachusetts, and earned his master's degree in Fine Arts from the University of Virginia. Despite the publication of several of his stories that were later collected in *Lost in the City,* he continued to work for a financial magazine, writing on the side, and occasionally teaching creative writing.

For *Lost in the City,* Jones drew upon his experiences of growing up in Washington, DC to portray often forgotten African American communities. Modeled after James Joyce's *Dubliners, Lost in the City* portrays a wide array of characters, each different from the other, yet all bound by their race and their struggle with their environment against poverty, crime, failed dreams, envy, and false pride. **Racism** is a pervasive fact in their lives, yet not the focus of Jones's stories; he depicts distinct individuals of all ages and temperaments realistically. There are children nurtured by their family and community, young men embroiled in crime, enticing impressionable youth, old people living in precarious conditions in city-subsidized housing, middle-class men and women defeated despite their academic achievements, and vulnerable women hurt in their elusive search for love. Some of these characters truly get lost in the city while others eventually reach their destination. Most of the stories are told in third person, allowing Jones to step back and create the world that he knew well. When a rare first person narrator is brought in, it is only to emphasize the limited understanding of the character.

In *The Known World* Jones shifts the setting to the antebellum South and explores a little known aspect of **slavery**, the existence of black slave owners. The novel is set in Manchester County, Virginia, in the 1840s. His imaginatively rendered descriptions and frequent references to the U.S. Census data and other historical scholarly studies create the illusion of a real geographical area, very much like William Faulkner's imagined Yoknapatawpha County.

The fact that a small number of free blacks owned slaves in the South has been confirmed by recent scholarship. Slaves skilled in masonry, carpentry, shoemaking, and other highly prized crafts were often hired to local landowners and businesses and were sometimes helped by their owners to buy their freedom, and with the continuing goodwill of the master eventually bought their own family members. In strictly legal terms, the family members then became the property of the new owner. Some freed slaves, however, bought other slaves as commercial assets. Jones uses this little known historical fact to weave a complex world of the 1840s to the 1860s.

The novel begins with an account of the death of thirty-one-year-old Henry Townsend whose freedom was bought by his father and whose previous owner helped him to set up his own farm. At his death Henry owned fifty acres and thirty-three slaves. The novel is not centered on his achievements entirely, but focuses primarily on the pernicious effects of slavery on human relationships. The sprawling world of Jones's novel encompasses not only masters and slaves but also others on the fringes: the spurned white women embittered by their men's extramarital relationships, slave women victimized by their masters, the poor whites barely eking out a living, illiterate law enforcers asserting their authority over the blacks, conscientious white men uncomfortable with the notion of enslaving another human being yet carrying out the law in the name of their godly duty, Native Americans—a step above the slaves in the social hierarchy, but treated with equal disdain—and new immigrants considered undeserving of justice.

In form and structure *The Known World* draws its inspiration from the Victorian novels. The circuitous plot has looping episodes, shifts from past to present and even a glimpse of the future, and frequent digressions in twelve chapters bearing long titles, each with three sections following the pattern set in Chapter 1, "Liaison. The Warmth of Family. Stormy Weather." An omniscient narrator steers the readers through this richly populated world. The genial, controlled, narrative voice introduces the characters, informs the readers of their past, and in may instances even lets them have a glimpse of the future; other times the narrator allows the readers to be direct observers of events and even share the thoughts of the characters. Jones creates no stereotypes of blacks or whites. William Robbins, the most powerful man in the county, is replete with contradictions. He guards and treats his property as a typical plantation owner would, yet he dearly loves a slave (freed later) and the two children he has with her. He values Henry yet does not set him free, but lets his father Augustus toil for years to pay for his son's freedom. Sheriff Skiffington, a devout Christian, never questions the cruel punishments of runaway slaves and condones their masters' acts. The novel is peopled with flesh and blood individuals filled with complexity and contradictions.

Power and control, at the core of master-slave relationship, are hard to relinquish whether the master has white or black skin. Henry, his wife Caldonia, and Fern Elston, an educated free black woman, all may seem enlightened in some ways but continue to own their human property. Henry's lofty aspirations to run a model plantation with slaves living like a family make little difference to those who are in his power.

Jones's controlled tone of quiet outrage, subtle humor and irony, vivid—almost poetic—language creates an emotional effect of the devastation that slavery causes and makes the novel a biting indictment of slavery and its corrupting influence on the lives touched by it. As the epigraph, a line from the spiritual—"My soul's often wondered how I got over . . ."—indicates his book is a tribute to the invincible spirit of his forebears that helped them survive the ordeals of slavery. The success of his fiction has established Jones's reputation as one of the best contemporary writers.

Further Reading

Maslin, Janet. Review of *The Known World* by Edward P. Jones. *New York Times* (August 14, 2003): Section E, 1, 7.

Yardley, Jonathan. Review of *The Known World* by Edward P. Jones. *Washington Post Book World* (August 24, 2003): 2–3.

Leela Kapai

JONES, GAYL (1949–)   African American writer and poet. As one of the first writers to address explicitly the devastating effects of sexual violence on black women, Gayl Jones is a pioneering voice in African American letters. Her first-person accounts of women involved in cycles of sexual and racial abuse are rooted in the **blues** tradition and the practice of oral storytelling. Her numerous novels and poetry collections depict the psychological consequences of sexual exploitation and explore the unstable boundaries of desire and violence.

Educated at Connecticut College and Brown University, Jones achieved critical acclaim when she was only twenty-six years old with her first book *Corregidora* (1975). This nonlinear novel was hailed for its penetrating portrait of a woman struggling to understand her family's history of enslavement and sexual abuse. Ursa is a blues singer descended from a line of women who were all impregnated by the same man—Corregidora, a Brazilian slaveowner. The Corregidora women obsessively tell the young Ursa brutal stories of their incest in an attempt to counter the failure of historical records to account for the atrocities of slavery. By instructing Ursa to "make generations" as a way to preserve the memory of their sexual abuse, they convert the female body into a form of documentation. Raised with a perception of men as domineering rapists, Ursa pursues an affair with Mutt Thomas that enacts a destructive cycle of abuse. Jones interrogates the nature of the Corregidora women's resistance by examining the role of their sexual desire and the obedience they demand from Ursa and her mother. In her exploration of the intersection between possession and love, Jones refuses to present Ursa as a tragic victim, but rather describes a woman who is conscious of her contradictory emotions and urges.

After accepting an assistant professorship at the University of Michigan, Jones published another powerful and controversial novel, titled *Eva's Man* (1976). In this fragmented narrative, Jones describes the life of Eva Medina, a woman who has been incarcerated for the murder of a man she also castrated. Sexual aggression and exploitation permeate the text as Eva is haunted by childhood memories of being propositioned and threatened by men. Enraged by a world that perceives her primarily as a sexual object, Eva lashes out through violence and descends into madness. While *Eva's Man* was praised for its emotional force, some critics found the main character to be inaccessible and exaggerated. June Jordan expressed concern that such a disturbing representation could lead to misperceptions about black women in general. In all of her novels, Jones mines the complexities of extreme psychological states as she seeks to present her characters independent of authorial judgment.

In 1983 Jones fled to France after Bob Higgins, a man she met in Ann Arbor and whom she later married, was convicted of a weapons charge after threatening a group of gay activists. While in Europe, Jones published three books of poetry, *Song for Anninho* (1981), *The Hermit-Woman* (1983), and *Xarque and Other Poems* (1985), in addition to a work of literary criticism titled *Liberating Voices: Oral Tradition in African American Literature* (1991). In this book Jones compares oral storytelling practices of African American writers with that of **canon**ical authors such as Geoffrey Chaucer and Miguel de Cervantes. Orality has been a major component of her own work, which is often cited for its exemplary use of black speech patterns and rhythms.

Jones and Higgins eventually returned to the United States in order to care for Jones's mother. However, due to a book review for *The Healing* (1998), the police were able to track down Higgins who had been making violent threats. In a dramatic encounter with the Lexington, Kentucky, police, Higgins committed suicide and Jones was subsequently placed in a psychiatric facility.

Despite the tragic events of Jones's personal life, her recent work has continued to garner critical acclaim. *The Healing* was nominated for a National Book Award and *Mosquito* (1999) received favorable reviews. Both novels offer a more hopeful representation of women as they explore the nature of healing and the strength derived from community involvement. *The Healing*'s focus on transformation and rebirth coupled with *Mosquito*'s emphasis on self-definition demonstrate Jones's evolving understanding of the complexities of black, female identity. (*See also* African American Novel)

Further Reading

Coser, Stelamaris. *Bridging the Americas: The Literature of Paule Marshall, Toni Morrison, and Gayl Jones*. Philadelphia: Temple UP, 1995.

Robinson, Sally. *Engendering the Subject: Gender and Self-Representation in Contemporary Women's Fiction*. Albany: State U of New York P, 1991.

Stephanie Li

JONG, ERICA (1942–)   Jewish American author of eight novels, six volumes of poetry, a biography of Henry Miller, a memoir, and a large number of essays on contemporary social and political issues. Erica Jong's foremost literary achievement is the successful adaptation of the European picaresque novel best represented in English by Fielding's *Tom Jones* to the social needs and sexual desires of a late-twentieth-century North American, feminist, cosmopolitan Jewish consciousness.

Jong is a popular writer. The enormous success of her first novel, *Fear of Flying* (1973), three million copies of which were sold in the first year of its publication, made Jong into a literary celebrity and a spokesperson for the emerging women's movement of the 1970s. Yet her persistent joyous celebration of female sexuality in all its permutations has created a critical backlash. Jong has been faulted for a lack of intellectual seriousness, and her work dismissed for its apparent vulgarity and tastelessness. Notwithstanding such critical disdain, Jong's writing continues to attract a wide readership both in the United States and elsewhere in the world.

The diversity of Jong's writing belies its fundamental unity. Her practice when writing may be summarized as telling the same story differently in every work. As Jong says in her memoir *Fear of Fifty* (1994), all her work is essentially about herself. Nowhere is this self-mythologizing impulse clearer than in Jong's early trilogy, *Fear of Flying*, *How to Save Your Own Life* (1977), and *Parachutes & Kisses* (1984). In these novels, as in all her other writing, Jong obliterates the distinctions between fact and fiction and incorporates into her work her sexual interests and exploits, her literary preoccupations, her family relationships, and her cultural and religious concerns. *Flying* moves from Isadora's first failed marriage to a brilliant psychotic to her second failed marriage to an emotionally unresponsive Chinese American psychiatrist. *Life* details Isadora's lesbian encounters, and then her passionate affair with a younger writer from an old left family. *Kisses* begins with Isadora's third divorce, but focuses on her need as a single mother for stability and love. The trajectory of these novels is as much of Jong's life as it is of Isadora's. Jong's family, friends, and miscellaneous lovers are given only flimsy fictional cover.

Jong is an equally strong presence in her other novels, her essays, her poems, and her biography of Henry Miller, *The Devil at Large* (1993). *The Devil* is in fact almost as much about Jong as it is about Miller. Miller was an early promoter of Jong's work. Jong now offers a passionate defense of Miller's right to self-expression against a new wave of feminists who, in Jong's view, would like nothing better than to censor his work as well as her own. Clearly, Jong's discussion of Miller's literary career and her appreciative critical assessment of what his place ought to be in the American literary **canon** is equally Jong's assessment of her own literary career and her own claim to canonical status. Jong implicitly justifies her dual focus by emphasizing that she and Miller believe passionately in the creative possibilities inherent in sexual adventure, they are at their best when they give full and frank expression to their sexual interests, and they suffer the same neglect from establishment critics who judge literature worthy only when it expresses the restrained values of the cultural elite.

What distinguishes *Fear of Fifty* (1994), Jong's autobiographical memoir, from Jong's other prose work is not its autobiographical bent, which is present in all her writing, but its sense of urgency. Mid-life for Jong is when time grows short. In place of Jong's buoyant fictional alter egos is a more earth-bound Jong, who worries about the approach of death. In *Fifty*, Jong finds hope and solace in her protean assertions of self, that autobiographical impulse to which she is addicted. Jong's sexual and imaginative fecundity allow her to be mother, daughter, lover, wife, writer, spokesperson for her generation, and time traveler to the Renaissance in *Shylock's Daughter*

(1987) and to classical antiquity in her latest novel *Sappho's Leap* (2003). The multiple roles Jong embraces and the continuities of blood and word they create provide Jong with a sense of secular transcendence.

In her essay "Mothers, Daughters and the **Holocaust**," written for Holocaust Remembrance Day 2002, Jong contemplates the appalling human propensity for killing other human beings, a condition that includes but is not limited to the German efforts to exterminate the Jews. Jong can provide no explanation for this terrifying aspect of the human condition. In essence, though, Jong's writing is her answer. It is her way of affirming the exuberant abundance of life, and so thwarting the impoverishing finality of death. (*See also* Feminism)

Further Reading

Templin, Charlotte. *Feminism and the Politics of Literary Reputation: The Example of Erica Jong*. Lawrence, KS: UP of Kansas, 1995.

Bernice Schrank

JORDAN, JUNE (1936–2002)   African American poet, novelist, essayist, political activist, feminist, and educator. June Jordan's prolific career, including authoring twenty-eight books in various genres, secures her place in the African American tradition. Jordan has contributed greatly to the literature of resistance, and her political and literary sensibilities have won her much recognition and critical acclaim. She is best known for her novel *His Own Where* (1971) and collections of poetry.

Jordan was born in New York City in 1936 to Granville and Mildred Jordan, immigrants from Jamaica and Panama. Her father was a nightshift postal worker and her mother was a nurse. When Jordan was a girl, her home life was a source of distress for her because of her father's physical abuse and her mother's denial. Despite this rough upbringing, Jordan's relationship with her father was also positive; he raised her like a son and taught her to box. This instilled a sense of confidence in Jordan and encouraged her to set goals and to pursue an education.

Jordan attended Northfield High School for Girls in Massachusetts and Barnard College. In 1955 she met Michael Meyer, a Columbia University student, and they married. Jordan continued her education at the University of Chicago from 1955 to 1956. In 1958 Jordan gave birth to her only child Christopher David Meyer. Jordan found her interracial marriage in the social climate of the 1950s and 1960s challenging, and in 1965 her marriage ended in divorce. In 1969 Jordan published her first book of poetry. During this time she was deeply committed to writing about the African American experience and to fostering urban renewal. These two themes intersect in her only novel and well-known work *His Own Where* (1971). In this work Buddy Rivers, a sixteen-year-old boy, attempts to find safety and love among the cruelties of the city. Because he is abandoned by his mother and his father is hit by a car and injured, Buddy must mature quickly.

While visiting his father in the hospital, Buddy meets the love of his life, Angela Figueroa, the daughter of his father's nurse. Angela's parents disprove of the relationship, and when Angela's father learns of the liaison, he beats Angela severely. Angela escapes to Buddy's house and he delivers her to the hospital. After the beating Angela is sent to a shelter for girls and her siblings are initiated into the foster care system. Eventually the relationship between Angela and Buddy is consummated and they plan for their future. The story ends in a cemetery, where the lovers plan to build a life and a family together. The irony is that the safe place of Buddy's longing—"his own where"—turns out to be among the dead. The novel leaves the characters believing that life is full of possibilities. This theme of the novel, coupled with the motif of how language and physical space shape one's environment, leaves the reader hopeful as well. After all, if the characters can believe in love among ruins and death, then the reader can afford the luxury of faith in urban renewal.

Throughout her thirty-three-year career, Jordan published twenty-eight books of poetry, political essays, fiction, and a memoir. Her political essays include *Affirmative Acts: Political Essays* (1998), *Poetry for the People: A Blueprint for the Revolution* (1995), and *Technical Difficulties* (1994). Some of Jordan's best-known works of poetry are *Kissing God Goodbye: Poems 1991–1997, Naming Our Destiny: New and Selected Poems* (1989), *Living Room* (1985), and *Things That I Do in the Dark* (1977). In 2000 Jordan published her memoir *Soldier: A Poet's Childhood*. Her works include personal and political themes as well as rage at injustices, violations of personhood, and other forms of oppression. Throughout her career Jordan expanded her repertoire of resistance writing from strictly the African American community to the third world and beyond. Jordan relates to the issues of many oppressed groups and writes about the Palestinian struggle, discrimination faced by lesbians, and violence against women.

Jordan's writing warns of the dangers of a culture that proliferates **racism**, classism, sexism, and heterosexism. Jordan resists the notion that one suffering is worse than or more poignant than another one. Perhaps because of her bisexual and bicultural roots, Jordan is hesitant to place her oppression ahead of or behind that of other groups. Jordan's resistance writing is ultimately the expression of her faith in the power of language to create the possibility for redemption in the future—a world characterized by equality and social justice.

Throughout her distinguished career, Jordan received numerous awards. These include a Rockefeller Foundation Grant, the National Association of Black Journalists Award, and the Massachusetts Council of the Arts Fellowship. Jordan's other awards consist of a National Endowment of the Arts Fellowship, a New York Foundation for the Arts Fellowship, the Lila Wallace Reader's Digest Writer's Award, the Women Who Dared Award from the National Black Women's Health Project, and the PEN Center USA West Freedom to Write Award. Jordan died of cancer in 2002.

Further Reading

Brogan, Jacqueline. "From Warrior to Womanist: The Development of June Jordan's Poetry." *Speaking the Other Self: American Women Writers*. Ed. Jeanne Campbell Reesman. Athens: U of Georgia P, 1997.

Eagleton, Mary. "Working Across Difference: Examples from Minnie Bruce Pratt and June Jordan." *Caught Between Cultures: Women, Writing & Subjectivities*. Ed. Elizabeth Russell. Amsterdam, Netherlands: Rodopi, 2002.

Carrie J. Boden

JOY LUCK CLUB, THE   **Amy Tan**'s novel *The Joy Luck Club* (1989) remains a landmark in Asian American literature. Tan's book has become a narrative model for other writers to follow. Its complex portrayals of mother-daughter relationships reveal the depth of familial bonds as well as intricate cultural and generational differences. The popularity and critical aftermath of Tan's book have contributed greatly to the recognition and validation of Asian American fiction in American literature.

The novel opens in San Francisco two months after the death of Suyuan, the main narrator Jing-mei's mother. As the central symbol, the "Joy Luck Club" was initiated by Suyuan in Kweilin during the Japanese invasion of China. Four young women took turns hosting parties, serving and consuming foods for good fortune, playing mah jong, and telling stories about good times in the past and hope for the future. Such an extravagance during wartime becomes the means by which these women raise their spirits and keep at bay fear, despair, and miseries. The San Francisco version of the club started in 1949, when Suyuan, An-mei Hsu, Lindo Jong, and Ying-ying St. Clair met at the First Chinese Baptist Church. Over the years the mothers have been hosting and attending the club where they can recall memories of China and talk about their American-born daughters.

Through Jing-mei's framing narrative, Tan's novel covers considerable temporal and geographical territory. Essentially episodic, the chapters allow each character to tell her story in a first-person narrative. The four pairs of mothers and daughters' love for each other, together with their misunderstanding based on cultural and generational gaps, fills Tan's novel with richness and tenderness. The book ends with the reunion of Jing-mei and her twin half-sisters whom Shuyuan lost during her flight to Chungking in war-torn China. At the airport in Shanghai, Jing-mei finally understands her mother's love and hope for her.

Well-received with more than four million copies sold, *The Joy Luck Club* has been translated into at least twelve languages. In 1993 a stage adaptation by American playwright Susan Kim was performed in China; a feature film, directed by Wayne Wang, based on Tan's screenplay was released in America. (*See also* Chinese American Novel)

Further Reading

Bloom, Harold. *Amy Tan's "The Joy Luck Club."* Philadelphia: Chelsea House, 2002.

Braendlin, Bonnie. "Mother/Daughter Dialog(ic)s In, Around, and About Amy Tan's *The Joy Luck Club*." *Private Voices, Public Lives: Women Speak on the Literary Life*. Ed. Nancy Owen Nelson. Denton: U of North Texas P, 1995. 111–24.

Shear, Walter. "Generation Differences and the Diaspora in *The Joy Luck Club*." *Critique* 34.3 (Spring 1993): 193–99.

Shen, Gloria. "Born of a Stranger: Mother-Daughter Relationships and Storytelling in Amy Tan's *The Joy Luck Club*." *International Women's Writing: New Landscapes of Identity*. Ed. Anne E. Brown and Marjanne E. Gooze. Westport, CT: Greenwood Press, 1995. 233–44.

Xu, Ben. "Memory and the Ethnic Self: Reading Amy Tan's *The Joy Luck Club*." *MELUS* 19.1 (Spring 1994): 3–18.

Lan Dong

K

KADI, JOANNA (1958–)   Writer, cultural critic, poet, musician, and activist focusing on working-class, feminist, and ethnic concerns. Of Lebanese racial and cultural heritage, Joanna Kadi was born and raised in Oshawa, Canada, and has worked closely with Arab communities in Canada and the United States, addressing and fighting against anti-Arab **racism** and various forms of class oppression and violence.

She is the editor of *Food for Our Grandmothers: Writings by Arab-American and Arab-Canadian Feminists* (1994), a groundbreaking anthology that features the work of a group of women writers with various backgrounds, ethnicities, sexualities, and experiences. Uniting these women is an Arab/Middle Eastern heritage that plays a major role in their **identity** formation and their search for a role in their societies, whether living in the Arab world or abroad. In her introduction to this anthology, Kadi emphasizes the importance of forging alliances between Arabs and other communities of color in the United States and Canada in order to combat racism and ethnic invisibility, and to effect social change. *Food for Our Grandmothers* has been hailed as one of the first anthologies to give voice to Arab American and Arab Canadian women writers, thus ensuring the inclusion of their diverse voices in the ethnic literary canon as necessary representations of the Arab American and Arab Canadian experience. Contributors to the anthology include **Lisa Suhair Majaj**, Therese Saliba, **Naomi Shihab Nye**, and Laila Halaby.

Kadi is the author of *Thinking Class: Sketches from a Cultural Worker* (1996), which, like *Food for Our Grandmothers*, was published by South End Press. *Thinking Class* is a book of essays that traces the intersections of racial, sexual, and class oppression, portraying the struggles of the middle class from a personal and communal perspective, and simultaneously working to find a place for gays and lesbians, as well as intellectuals and writers, within these middle-class communities. The book deftly handles a variety of themes, including education, capitalism, oppressive stereotypes, country music, and writing as a means of resistance, among others, all analyzed through Kadi's discerning feminist lens and filtered through her personal experience of growing up and living in racist, homophobic, and sexist environments, in both Canada and the United States.

Her essays and short fiction have been published in books such as *Working Class Women in the Academy: Laborers in the Knowledge Factory* (1993), anthologies (*The Poetry of Arab Women* [2001]), and journals including *Colors, Sojourner: The Women's Forum, Sinister Wisdom,* and *Hurricane Alice.*

Kadi has performed publicly and lectured widely in the United States, where she has taught at several institutions, including the Center for Arts Criticism in Minneapolis and at the University of Minnesota. She currently resides in Florida. As a musician, she plays several instruments, such as the *derbeke* (the Arabic hand drum), the *jembe* (the West African standing drum), the piano, and the fiddle. (*See also* Feminism)

Further Reading

Handal, Nathalie, ed. Introduction. *The Poetry of Arab Women: A Contemporary Anthology.* New York: Interlink, 2001. 1–62.

Majaj, Lisa Suhair. "Two Worlds: Arab-American Writing." *Forkroads: A Journal of Ethnic-American Literature.* 1.3 (1996): 64–80.

Carol Fadda-Conrey

KADOHATA, CYNTHIA (1956–) Japanese American novelist and science fiction writer. A third-generation Japanese American (a Sansei), Cynthia Kadohata was recognized as an Asian American writer with the publication of her first novel, *The Floating World* (1989). The three other works that followed—*In the Heart of the Valley of Love* (1993), *The Glass Mountains* (1996), and *Kira-Kira* (2004)—distinguish her from other Asian American writers in exploring Japanese American experiences in the genre of science fiction or fantasy.

Partly shaped by her own family life experience after World War II, Kadohata's *Floating World* tells the story of the Fujiitano family of Japanese Americans in the United States in the 1940s and 1950s. The novel centers on twelve-year-old Olivia, the first-person narrator, who spends her childhood and adolescence in what her grandmother calls *ukiyo,* or "floating world," traveling with her family from the Pacific Northwest to Arkansas as her father looks for jobs. Recounted through Olivia with great sensitivity and genuineness, the drifting through the Pacific Northwest in a world of unstable employment is filled with descriptions about family, memory, guilt, and a young woman's coming of age. Olivia describes her grandmother's death, her strong feeling of guilt about it, her job at a chicken-sexing factory, her first boyfriend, her second, and her encounter with her father's ghost. Her journey culminates in a scene when Olivia watches her grandmother die without helping her. Interestingly, it is her sharp-tongued, hot-tempered grandmother who has the main impact on shaping impish, perpetually dislocated Olivia.

Like *The Floating World,* with emphasis on ancestral legacy and a search for the meaning of existence, Kadohata's second novel, *In the Heart of the Valley of Love,* however, is more concerned with class than **race**, and with the future instead of the past. This novel explores human relationships in a Los Angeles of 2052, a deteriorating area where the stars have faded behind pollution; where rich and poor are deeply polarized; where riots and arrests are daily occurrences; and where water, food, and education cannot be taken for granted. Amid the political and social upheaval of a "dystopian" Los Angeles, the protagonist, nineteen-year-old Francie, courageously searches for love and meaning. Francie, a child of multiracial parents, lives in a small house with her Auntie Annie and her aunt's lover, Rohn. Witnessing the power of their love, Francie is able to stay optimistic and hopeful among chaos and decay. Yet, after Rohn mysteriously disappears, Francie, in a passive, detached manner, becomes accustomed to a meaningless existence until she and her boyfriend, Matt, discover a box, a symbol of redemption that returns a capacity to hope and to love.

A mixture of science and fantasy, *The Glass Mountain* is set in sector Bakshami of a planet called *Artekka.* Narrated by the female protagonist, Mariska, *The Glass Mountain* opens with a depiction of the grimness of the life in Bakshami, the land of "dustfire," where wind blows all day, dust rises like steam from the fields, and dogs groan all night. But adored by her parents and engaged to be married to the most attractive man in the sector, Mariska feels safe until the appearance of a stranger with pale skin and a long face. Her world is torn apart. The book documents Mariska's journey, her becoming a heroine, her adventures seeking her parents beyond the safety of her village, and her finding peace in a time when her village is threatened by an approaching war.

Kadohata's latest work, *Kira-Kira*—her debut in children's literature and the winner of the 2005 Newbery Medal—deals with the Japanese American experience in post–World War II America, as does her first work, *The Floating World.* Told by ten-year-old Katie Takeshima, *kira-kira,* the Japanese word for "glittering," captures the family's sustaining love and highlights the bond between Katie and her teenage sister Lynn. It's Lynn who teaches Katie the word *kira-kira* to show her the glittering beauty of the stars, and to appreciate everything glittering in everyday life, from the sea to people's eyes, from puppies to colored Kleenex. Moreover, when the family moves from their Japanese community in Iowa to a small town in rural Georgia, where they are among only thirty-one Japanese Americans, it is also Lynn who explains to Katie why some children won't talk to them at school and why people stop them on the street to stare. Lynn warns her about the prejudice and prepares her to encounter it. When Lynn becomes deathly ill, the whole family begins falling apart, and the roles of the two sisters are slowly reversed. After Lynn's death, Katie fully takes on the role of her sister. Insisting that there is something glittering in the future, she offers, at the end, a glittering sense of hope. (*See also* Japanese American Novel)

Further Reading

"Cynthia Kadohata." *American Diversity, American Identity.* Ed. John K. Roth. New York: Henry Holt and Company, 1995. 603–6.

Sarkar, Sheila. "Cynthia Kadohata and David Wong Louie: The Pangs of a Floating World." *Hitting Critical Mass: A Journal of Asian American Cultural Criticism* 2.1 (1994): 79–97.

Fu-jen Chen

KANG, YOUNGHILL (1903–1972)   A pioneering figure in **Korean American literature**. His fictional autobiography *East Goes West: The Making of an Oriental Yankee* (1937) provides a variety of academic disciplines with valuable insights into the early Asian immigrant history and its literary formation as a representative Asian American literature preceding to the new wave of immigration in the 1960s.

Kang's educational background in Korea ranges from the traditional Confucian classics to the Western classical literature, such as Shakespeare, at Christian schools established by American missionaries. Like his fictional persona, Chungpa Han, Kang arrived in the United States in 1921 at the age of eighteen just before the decades-long ban on Asian **immigration** was enacted. Attending Harvard and Boston University while working at menial jobs, he published in 1931 *The Grass Roof,* a novel based upon his childhood experiences in a northern region of Korea, with extended explanations of Korean culture and realities of his country under Japanese colonial ruling before his immigration to America.

Picking up the story where his first book leaves off, *East Goes West* depicts a Korean immigrant's struggle to carve out a place for himself in America. In Kang's chronicling of the narrator, Han's trials and tribulations, his search for a spiritual home is never successful. Like his fellow immigrants, Han finds himself forced into manual labor despite his knowledge and education. Working as a farm hand, cook, salesman, and lowly assistant to an impostor in guise of an evangelical minister, he comes to recognize his limitations in America as a racial and cultural minority. One of the ways Kang manages to win readers' sympathy for his agonized narrator is to render the weight of discrimination and hardship relived by humor. This "comic relief" is also Kang's measure of making charged topics such as racial prejudice and hostility toward immigrants more "digestible" to American readers. But Han's gentle humor as a means of survival has an ironic lingering effect as his life is revealed to be more and more hopeless regardless of the amount of effort he puts into his work.

As a mediation on the possible modes of harmonizing "East" and "West," several characters are presented in the book. Jum, one of Han's fellow Korean immigrants, is a personification of acculturation. He believes that he can be an "authentic" American by catching up with American way of life. He is a beau to a white woman who dances at a Harlem nightclub. Rejecting his Korean heritage, Jum dreams of being accepted into America symbolized by his girlfriend's white body. But he marries a Korean woman and settles in Hawai'i after he was rejected by his white girlfriend. Another Korean who influences Han's American life is Kim, an aristocratic and cosmopolitan intellectual in exile. Kim, who has already spent sixteen years living in Europe and America, is well versed in Western literature and philosophy as well as in Eastern classics and arts. To Han, he is an ideal person who can naturally incorporate Western values into his Eastern tradition. Kim's search for acceptance, however, is frustrated by the color line: The family of the white woman he loves never allows him to see her, and then he commits suicide. After seeking recognition from the American society through his study and hard working, Han finally decides to find his belonging in his love for Trip, a young white college graduate. The book ends with Han, disillusioned of his romance with Trip, still groping for his "spiritual home" in America.

Given Kang's life-long effort to obtain citizenship and its failure despite his relatively successful career as a writer, professor, and his marriage with a white woman, Kang's book seems to squint toward **assimilation**. While he deals with issues of the quest for self-**identity** and the restless confusion that are the very staples of the immigrant genre, Kang never fundamentally challenges American ideals. However, Kang, marking a new beginning in Asian American literature, presents a nuanced critique of racial prejudice and discrimination against immigrants beneath his optimistic view of life and sense of humor.

Further Reading

Chu, Patricia P. *Assimilating Asians: Gendered Strategies of Authorship in Asian America.* Durham, NC: Duke UP, 2000.

Kim, Elaine H. *Asian American Literature: An Introduction to the Writings and Their Social Context.* Philadelphia: Temple UP, 1982.

Lee, Sunyoung. "The Unmaking of an Oriental Yankee." *East Goes West: The Making of an Oriental Yankee.* New York: Kaya, 1997. 375–99.

Palumbo-Liu, David. *Asian/American: Historical Crossing of a Racial Frontier.* Stanford, CA: Stanford UP, 1999.

Seongho Yoon

KAPLAN, JOHANNA (1942–) Jewish American novelist and short story writer. Author of prestigious award winners *Other People, Other Lives* (1975) and *O My America!* (1980), Johanna Kaplan is one of the few contemporary Jewish American women writers who cannot be classified feminist. Though she often writes about immigrant and urban Jews, her characters are complex and universal. Unlike writers who break with Jewish tradition, often celebrating sexual, political, and social change, Kaplan mourns the loss of "yiddishkeit" (Jewishness) in America. Like distinguished authors **Cynthia Ozick** and **Allegra Goodman**, she examines the absurdities of contemporary life, ironically reflecting on the contrast between a discarded Jewish heritage and a materialistic, hedonistic America.

The daughter of Polish immigrant Jews, Kaplan was raised in New York City, the setting for much of her fiction. A graduate of the High School of Music and Art, she received a BA from New York University in 1964 and an MA in special education from Teachers College, Columbia University, enabling her to teach emotionally disturbed children in Mount Sinai's Psychiatric Department, from where she retired. Remarkably, while working full-time in a stressful environment, Kaplan produced *O My America!*, which Diane Cole and others have described as a classic satire of twentieth-century Jewish American life.

Other People's Lives, a novella and five stories, introduces quirky characters, urban settings, and unpredictable resolutions. Though her characters are flawed, Kaplan's criticism is reserved for those who abuse the young and attack the "outsider." Thus in the novella, the reader sympathizes with Maria, a German immigrant with a hospitalized dying husband and a child. Though a gentile, Maria's simple wisdom and decency lift her above her snobbish Jewish neighbors who ridicule her German past. Ironically, it is the German non-Jew who suffers as the outcast in this story. "Baby Sitting" mocks the egotistical, pseudo-artistic Ted Marshak and his wife, Sunny, who neglect their children for their bohemian pursuits. The story foreshadows Kaplan's satire, *O My America!*, in which Ezra Slavin, consumed by his own intellectual ambitions and greed, becomes a cult figure for America's rebellious youth of the sixties. Rejecting his traditional Jewish background, Slavin hypocritically preaches free love and libertarianism, while tyrannizing his own family. Married three times, Slavin psychologically damages all but the eldest of his six children, Merry, daughter of his Yiddish-speaking first wife, Pearl, whom he divorces. Only Merry, a blend of the Polish Jewish past and the Jewish American present possesses the sensitivity and strength to emotionally survive in America. Though she judges her father, she forgives him and is one of the few who sincerely mourns his death at the end.

Replete with Jewish characters and themes, *O My America!*, winner of the Jewish Book Award and the **Edward Lewis Wallant** Award, and nominated for the National Book Award, is an American novel, comparable to **F. Scott Fitzgerald**'s *The Great Gatsby* (1925). Ashamed of his lower class lineage, Slavin, like Jay Gatsby, sheds his past, reinvents himself, and, in chasing his American dream, loses all. After all the conspiring and self-indulgence, Ezra dies from a massive heart attack, betrayed by his own desires, whereas Gatsby, mistakenly murdered by a jealous husband, also fails in his quest for acceptance. Despite cultural differences, one a Jewish immigrant, the other a Midwestern "hick," both lack a core, a solid **identity**, and both romanticize about conquering America.

In subsequent stories, New Yorkers of all backgrounds—Hispanic immigrants, tired teachers and social workers, glib urbanites, a panorama of ethnic and assimilated characters—compete for the same breathing space. An autobiographical essay, "Tales of My Great-Grandfathers" (*Commentary* July–August 2000), a blending of fact and fable, of religious mysticism and deep faith overcoming intense **anti-Semitism**, spiritually elevates the reader and inspires hope. Kaplan tells of two great-grandfathers, Rabbi Jacob Meir of Minsk, whose generosity to the poor and "miracle" works were legendary among Jews and gentiles. By contrast, her father's nameless grandfather had been kidnapped by the Russians and held until age eighteen when he began twenty-five years of compulsory duty in the Czar's army. Ripped from his family and community and forcibly baptized, this grandfather, at age forty-three, found his way back to his birthplace, where he married a poor Jewish orphan girl. Incredibly, he took his bride back to Siberia to form a tiny Jewish congregation. Each great grandfather in his own way provides the heroic figures absent from *O My America!* and many of the short stories. Drawing on her ancestral past, Kaplan has discovered the strength eluding so many of her American characters.

Further Reading

Adams, Alice. Review of *O My America!. New York Times Book Review* (January 13, 1980).

Cole, Diane. "Ez Slavin's Journey, Our Journey." *The Jewish Week* (June 6, 2003).

Girgus, Sam. *The New Covenant: Jewish Writers and the American Idea.* Chapel Hill: U of North Carolina P, 1984. 6–7.

Evelyn Avery

KARMEL, ILONA (1925–2000) Jewish American novelist. Ilona Karmel was born in Krakow, Poland, on August 14, 1925, and died of leukemia on November 30, 2000, in Massachusetts. A survivor of the **Holocaust**, she lived her teenage years in both the Krakow ghetto and forced-labor camps during World War II, writing poetry during her imprisonment. Both of her legs were crushed when inmates in her camp were ordered to lie in the road before an oncoming tank at the war's end.

Karmel convalesced at a Swedish hospital for three years. She immigrated to the United States in 1948 and obtained her BA at Radcliffe College. She then spent ten years in Germany, returning to the United States in 1978 with her husband, a physicist and philosopher, Francis Zucker. She taught writing and humanistic studies for the Massachusetts Institute of Technology for seventeen years, retiring in 1995.

The narrative found in Karmel's novels is exceptionally rich, provocative, and poetic in its use of extraordinary metaphors and similes. The major themes on which she focuses include Semitic appearance, women's bonding, and the rendering of terror during the Holocaust. She provides vivid imagery within her descriptions of the senseless inhumanity suffered by the European Jews during World War II. Her characters despair over their inability to correct their misfortunes, but also exemplify the strength and adaptability of the human spirit, which will ultimately find a way to endure.

Her first novel, *Stephania* (1953), was inspired by her own hospitalization experience in Sweden. The story spans a year in the lives of three women, Stephania, Thura, and Froken Nilsson, sharing a hospital room as they receive treatment for physical disabilities. The recovery process transcends the mere mending of body parts to include learning to accept of limitations. Stephania's sometimes tough exterior can be attributed to the harsh existence and losses she experienced while residing in a Jewish ghetto during World War II. She and her sister, Barbara, experience a coming-back-to-humanness after the **Holocaust** as they are once again able to live their lives "in freedom." Stephania is often depicted as isolated, disconnected, and generally ostracized, sometimes because she is Jewish, other times because of her disfigurement. Karmel illustrates a powerful link between body, mind, and spirit in the recovery process of these characters.

In *An Estate of Memory* (1969), four Jewish women are held in concentration camps in Nazi-occupied Poland, and their gendered experience of the Shoah is central, especially because Aurelia is pregnant, often a death sentence. Tola, Barbara, and Alinka save the life of the baby girl by smuggling her out of the camp aided by three risk-taking men, an outcome dependent on the women's bonding. Their mutual support, however, is fraught with the tension of individual struggle to survive. Striving for normalcy and validity within the dehumanized camp atmosphere, they try to replace the family ties they had cruelly lost. Living through the horrors of the Holocaust, they rely upon the comfort of their pre-war memories to ward off feelings of dehumanization inflicted upon Jews within the camps by the Nazis as well as other Jews. One of the principal ethical dilemmas Karmel dramatizes is how to maintain humanity and pride when forced to behave in selfish ways for physical survival. She is concerned with complicity in or defense against soul murder, the aim of Nazi mockery being to induce the cooperation of the scorned.

Clarity is at times purposely clouded by the author in an attempt to mirror the disorientation of forced laborers, who were usually afforded no explanations, and to whom information regarding the war's progress and their own futures was murky, threatening, and uncertain. Misinformation abounded during World War II. Even German soldiers were led to believe that rumors of the extent of atrocities were *greuelpropaganda* ("atrocity propaganda"). Thus, Karmel answers an overriding post-Holocaust preoccupation: how to find a language commensurate with the scope and inhumanity of these events. Classed among the growing literature of trauma, imprisonment, and testimony, Karmel's deeply metaphoric rendering of barbarity and survival makes *Estate of Memory* one of the most highly recommended works of Holocaust fiction. (*See also* Holocaust Narratives)

Further Reading

Ezrahi, Sidra DeKoven. *By Words Alone: The Holocaust in Literature.* Chicago: U of Chicago P, 1980.

Heinemann, Marlene E. *Gender and Destiny: Women Writers and the Holocaust.* Westport, CT: Greenwood Press, 1986.

Kremer, S. Lillian. "Holocaust-Wrought Women: Portraits by Four American Writers." *Studies in American Jewish Literature* 11.2 (1992): 150–61.

Tobe Levin

KATZ, JUDITH (1951–) Jewish American novelist. Thus far, Judith Katz has produced two magnificent novels, *Running Fiercely Toward a High Thin Sound* (1992) and *The Escape Artist* (1997). Both works are structurally intricate and chronicle the power and persistence of Jewish women's love for one another, despite the corrosive effects that a history of exclusion and homophobia has had upon female-female relationships.

Katz grew up in a fairly traditional Jewish household; however, like many feminists of her generation, she primarily identified with lesbian and women's communities as a young adult. After attending a lesbian seder at Smith College, she felt that her flight from Jewishness left gaps that needed to be filled. Indeed, her novels represent the desire to write a home and a history for the Jewish lesbian.

Running Fiercely Toward a High Thin Sound is a fractured postmodern novel marked by multiple narrators, an abundance of dream work, and the representation of alternative dimensions of reality. The protagonists of this part-Gothic, part-visionary novel are the women of the Morningstar family: three sisters—Nadine, Jane, and Electa—and their mother, Fay. Nadine is the other of this family; we learn in the prologue of the novel narrated by Jane that Nadine used Sabbath candles to burn her hair and face; the scar that results is an emblem of the damage resulting from her outcast status. Her mother considers her a *dybbuk*, an evil spirit; Nadine assumes the last name of Pagan, a textual sign that she is figured as a threat to Jewish tradition. Yet she also embodies tradition as the impassioned and skilled player of her great-grandfather's beloved violin; indeed, Nadine's voice in the novel is the music of this violin. Significantly, at the end of the novel, Nadine returns home to her birth family on the first seder night of Passover. When the door is opened for Elijah, Nadine enters. Thus the text suggests, in keeping with biblical tradition, that the fiery rebel may have a prophetic role to play.

Electa's wedding is the central realistic narrative event of the novel. Devastated by Nadine's disappearance (though unwillingly to admit the role that her abuse played in that flight), Fay views this wedding as a life preserver. Jane, Electa's maid of honor and a lesbian majoring in women's studies, tries to be a good daughter and sister but is horrified by the part she must play in this patriarchal drama. Electa's name perhaps underscores that this family has an affinity for Greek tragedy; it also suggests that, by representing normative heterosexuality and the Jewish marriage plot, she is the elected or chosen daughter. However, as an uninvited guest hiding in the Ark that holds the Torah, Nadine—the outcast lesbian, the wild beast—momentarily takes center stage at the wedding. Poignantly, Nadine wishes that the rabbi, rather than viewing her as an abomination, would cradle her as he would a Torah scroll and strive to decipher the wisdom and intricacies contained within her. Significantly, in one of the later alternative-world sections narrated by Rose, Nadine's lover, a women's-only wedding takes place and Nadine is carried through the crowd as if she were a beloved Torah scroll. Even as *Running Fiercely Toward a High Thin Sound* represents a vision of a repaired world symbolized by a Nadine who is no longer scarred, it also mournfully acknowledges a broken world of pain and exclusion. Katz's writing of *Running Fiercely* was supported by a grant from the National Endowment for the Arts, and the novel received the Lambda Literary Award for Fiction.

The narrator of Katz's second novel, *The Escape Artist,* is Sofia Teitelbaum, a young girl from Warsaw whose family thinks that they are sending her off to Buenos Aires to be the wife of a wealthy man; in fact, however, they have handed her over to a violent and disgruntled pimp, Tutsik Goldenberg, who installs her in his sister's Jewish whorehouse. Sofia narrates her story to Hankus (also known as Hannah Lubansky), her lover and, at the point of this telling, her partner in freedom.

Sofia is initiated into the life of a prostitute through direct sexual lessons provided by the women of the house, especially the proprietress, Perle Goldenberg. Significantly, Perle's desire for women and the means by which she earns her living conflict with her desire for Jewish respectability, learning, and piety. In order to reconcile her spiritual yearnings with the life of her body, she arranges to return to Eastern Europe in order to marry a famous rebbe. In sharp contrast to Perle, Sofia catapults herself into a woman-loving future with the aid of Hankus, the literal and figurative escape artist of the title. Hankus is the only survivor of a pogrom and has made her way to Buenos Aires living as a man. When Sofia and Hankus become lovers, their joining enables them to reclaim their histories and thus their selves, a profoundly painful and joyous process. In a dream that recalls the women's-only wedding sequence in *Running Fiercely,* Sofia is in the whorehouse surrounded by all the women in her life, including Tamar, her girlhood friend and her first love. After a women's waltz of healing, Tamar passes Sofia to Hankus, and the two of them are left standing alone as a couple. By the end of the novel, the final segment of this dream has become a part of their history: Hankus's talents for disguise and escape enable her to liberate Sofia from the whorehouse so that the two of them can ultimately flee to Moisesville, the promised land of the Pampas.

Katz is a visionary writer who manages to merge the Jewish prophetic tradition with lesbian feminism. As such, she represents a vital voice of the contemporary Jewish literary renaissance. (*See also* Jewish American Lesbian Literature)

Further Reading

Ludger, Brinker. "Judith Katz." *Contemporary Jewish-American Novelists: A Bio-Critical Sourcebook.* Eds. Joel Shatzky and Michael Taub. Westport, CT: Greenwood Press, 1997. 166–173.

Schifrin, Daniel. "A Stranger Among Us." *Baltimore Jewish Times* (April 30, 1993): 68.

Helene Meyers

KAUFMAN, BOB (1925–1986)   African American poet and an architect of the Beat poetry movement. The details of Kaufman's life are difficult to locate, and critics are divided about his parental heritage. Most recent considerations assert that Kaufman fabricated his upbringing as a child of a Jewish father and a Catholic mother who was descended from slaves and who passed on voodoo practices. James Smethurst contends that Kaufman's fictitious background speaks to the value that Kaufman placed on connecting with marginalized people. Regardless of his personal history, Kaufman was a preeminent figure of the Beat movement, and his broadside, *Abomunist Manifesto* (1959), warrants equal consideration with **Allen Ginsberg**'s *Howl* as a seminal Beat work. Kaufman also cofounded *Beatitude* magazine with Ginsberg in 1959.

Abomunist Manifesto seems to have been inspired by the finding of the Dead Sea Scrolls and is a condemnation of people's failure to learn from history. The poem is also an antimanifesto that scoffs at the idea of devising a belief structure. Ultimately, the poem speaks out against the cold war, accruing nuclear weapons, and society's pretense of concern for spirituality. This poem was included in Kaufman's first volume of poetry, *Solitudes Crowded with Loneliness* (1965), which his wife, Eileen, collected and submitted for publication. This volume also included "Bagel Shop **Jazz**," which was nominated for the Guinness Poetry Award and published in volume four of the *Guinness Book of Poetry* (1961). "Bagel Shop Jazz" depicts the setting and people characteristic of the Beat movement, and like many of his poems, pays tribute to jazz as a medium for a new kind of expression.

Thematically, the poems in *Solitudes Crowded by Loneliness* are connected by their attention to the conflict between the honesty and dishonesty of governments and other public organizations. Several of the poems also pay tribute to those who toiled against conformity, including Hart Crane and Albert Camus. Kaufman's second collection of poetry was titled *Golden Sardine* (1967). The poems in this collection focus on the themes most characteristic of the Beat movement, including the desire for truth and the necessity of social revolution. Poems in this volume highlight jazz's influence on Kaufman's poetic language. Kaufman's third volume of poems, *The Ancient Rain: Poems 1956–1978* (1981) comprises poems primarily written between 1973 and 1978 after a ten-year vow of silence. The selections in this volume tend to focus more on spirituality than his previous work and speak to his tendency to shun notoriety.

Kaufman's influence is easily detected in the poetry of the **Black Arts Movement**, in many of the poems included in *Black Fire* edited by LeRoi Jones (**Amiri Baraka**) and **Larry Neal**, and in later work by such artists as **Ishmael Reed**, **Jayne Cortez**, and David Henderson.

Further Reading

Damon, Maria. "Unmeaing Jargon/Uncanonized Beatitude: Bob Kaufman, Poet." *South Atlantic Quarterly* 87.4 (Fall 1988): 701–41.

———, ed. "Bob Kaufman: A Special Section." *Callaloo* 25:1 (2002): 103–231.

Lindberg, Kathryne. "Bob Kaufman, Sir Real." *Talisman* 11 (Fall 1993): 167–82.

April Conley Kilinski

KAUFMAN, GEORGE SIMON (1889–1961)   Jewish American playwright. George Kaufman's grandparents were from Germany, and came to the United States, like many immigrants, seeking a better life. As a young man, Kaufman was known for his sharp wit, which he employed well as a humorist and satirist. At the age of fourteen, Kaufman cowrote his first play, *The Failure.* In 1907 he graduated from Pittsburgh Central High, working as a salesman before taking on a job as a newspaper columnist with the *Washington Times* in 1912. Kaufman worked for the *Washington Times* for a year before being fired for being Jewish. His next job was with the *Chicago Tribune,* where he became the drama editor. In 1917 Kaufman became drama editor for the *New York Times,* a job he kept until 1930. On March 15, 1917, Kaufman married Beatrice Bakrow, who would introduce him to many key figures in theater and the arts. Kaufman later became a member of the Algonquin Group. Beatrice died in 1945, and in 1949 Kaufman married actress Leueen MacGrath.

Kaufman cowrote most of his plays with others. Such plays include *Dulcy* (1921) and *Beggar on Horseback* (1924) written with Marc Conelly; *The Royal Family* (1927) and *Dinner at Eight* (1932) with **Edna Ferber**; *Once in a Lifetime* (1930), *You Can't Take It with You* (1936), and *The Man Who Came to Dinner* (1939) with **Moss Hart**; and *The Solid Gold Cadillac* (1953) with Howard Teichmann. Kaufman also wrote and cowrote plays and musicals for the Marx brothers and with George and Ira Gershwin. One of the plays he wrote with Morrie Ryskind with music and lyrics by the Gershwins, *Of Thee I Sing,* won a Pulitzer Prize.

Many of the plays Kaufman cowrote have themes related to the lives of actors and playwrights. *Cocoanuts,* for example, is about a group of friends who work as silent film actors until the "talkies," or films with sound, revolutionized the motion picture industry. These actors go to Hollywood, hoping for success. There they find that the least likely to succeed among them is the most impressive to the people with clout in the business.

Hart and Kaufman's play *You Can't Take It with You* is about a young couple who are engaged: Alice, the member of a bizarre but happy and loving family, and Tony, the son of a Wall Street businessman. Tony is the vice president of his father's company, and Alice works as Tony's secretary.

Members of Alice's family include Penny, her mother, who writes plays because she received a typewriter in the mail by mistake; Grandpa, who throws darts continually and gets letters from the government about not paying income tax; Essie, who does ballet around the house; and Paul, who likes to explode fireworks in the basement and also enjoys typesetting. Other figures in the household include Rheba, an African American cook and maid; Donald, her friend; Mr. Kohlenkov, Essie's Russian ballet instructor; Mr. De Pinna, who helps with the fireworks; and so on. The families have difficulty getting along because of their differences in values and background. The theme of the play is that life is short and should not be spent working at a tedious occupation.

Kaufman's most important contribution to theater was his ability to speak out against the establishment, using satire and humor as a means of making his point.

Further Reading

Goldstein, Malcolm. *George S. Kaufman: His Life, His Theater.* New York: Oxford UP, 1979.

Meredith, Scott. *George S. Kaufman and His Friends.* Garden City, NY: Doubleday, 1974.

Pollack, Rhoda-Gale. *George S. Kaufman.* Boston: Twayne Publishers, 1988.

Teichmann, Howard. *George S. Kaufman: An Intimate Portrait.* New York: Atheneum, 1972.

Stephanie Fischetti

KAZIN, ALFRED (1915–1998) Jewish American literary critic and writer who was connected with the "New York" intellectuals, a group of writers, commentators, and social gadflies (often politically engaged and active) existing mainly in the 1930s and 1940s. This group wielded enormous influence on the cultural beliefs of the country. Kazin, however, was never quite as enamored with Marxism as most of that group was. His first and major work was *On Native Grounds* (1942). He also wrote *A Walker in the City* (1951), *The Inmost Leaf* (1955), *Contemporaries* (1962), *Starting Out in the Thirties* (1965), *Bright Book of Life* (1973), *New York Jew* (1978), *An American Procession* (1984), *Writing Was Everything* (1995), and *God and the American Writer* (1997).

On Native Grounds is a close interpretation of modern American experience and writing (especially prose). It attempts to map out a course of American literature from its earliest uncertain and stressful beginnings to the mid-twentieth century. In this analysis, an account of the vital spirit of American writing and history is revealed. A native and democratic energy appears in both his criticism and in the writings he examines, as well as a realistic social commentary. He also covers the revival of historical fiction and carefully examines documentary literature.

He believes that although our American literature is, and was, in large part a revolt against gentility and repression, and a run toward freedom, it is more than that. Modern literature—as does almost all literature—expresses life. Our literature was rooted in the transformation of our society, especially after the Civil War. Society was being remade, and in the process a new moral code arose. For Kazin, morality means, inter alia, the relation of people to their society. So if society was drastically changing, so were the people and their morality. Our new literature was formed around the year 1890, when America stood between one society and another, one moral code and another. And the change was becoming oppressive. A literature of protest was beginning, leading to the Utopian literature that followed. All this was molded by the struggles of modern life. Kazin realizes that although the greatest single fact about modern American writing is the total absorption of most writers in every aspect of the American world, it is also their deep alienation from it that creates the best writers.

This twofold realization leads him to focus on the estrangement and yearning in many of our writers, as they remold life in the United States. He claims our modern authors have learned to live with this alienation, but he is more interested in seeing through it to the basic principle of experiencing all this on native grounds. That is, to speak of our literature as a struggle against evil and angry tyranny, and toward emancipation is quite true, but it leaves out, in many cases, the great depth of suffering, violence, and even tragedy that lies at the heart of our native land. Along with this, Kazin understands that all of our great writers seem driven to reinvent or rediscover the country in every generation. It is as if they have to cry out "America, America" because we have never known it or grasped its true meaning.

He believes there are numerous factors causing this yearning and horror. Excessively rapid growth, our vast landscape, the furious drive West, the strange Eastern sensibility, American pragmatism, our unique feeling about time, and our belief that all our accomplishments are fragile combine to create this unsettled sensation.

Kazin also discusses American critics. Two fanaticisms appear to dominate the critical ranks. One is a purely sociological, and the other a strictly "esthetic" criticism. He believes that an arid snobbery and insensitiveness have marred and weighed down serious critical work. We cannot separate a study of literature in relation to society, from a study of what literature is in itself. Nor can we study literary texts where we make them devoid of any connection with people's lives. Literature is not produced by society, but by individuals and their emotions. Criticism, which is one of the most fundamental and important communications between people, cannot be a merely scholastic enterprise, nor can it be merely a political or sociological weapon. Choosing either path exclusively will ruin both literature and eventually society. True criticism begins with books, but must link them to the world if it is to speak to us and help us understand the world and ourselves. (*See also* Jewish American Autobiography)

Further Reading

Dajir, Antonio. "My Fellow American," *American Scholar* 68 (1999): 30.

Rosen, Jonathan. "Alfred Kazin's Tie," *American Scholar* 68 (1999): 24.

Robert J. Toole

KECKLEY, ELIZABETH (1818–1907) African American seamstress and memoirist. Keckley was born in Dinwiddie Court-House in Virginia. Her parents were slaves on neighboring plantations. Keckley was separated from her father when he was sold away and remained with her mother, Agnes Hobbs, on the plantation of Colonel A. Burwell in Virginia. Keckley is best known as a seamstress and confidante to Mary Todd Lincoln, a relationship that is chronicled in her only written work, *Behind the Scenes, or Thirty Years a Slave, and Four Years in the White House* (1868). The autobiography is an interesting mix of genres and represents an image of an independent African American woman whose narrative stands as a complex representation of a changing nation.

Keckley's autobiography is a skillful merger of nineteenth century genres including the slave narrative and memoir. Critics have also identified the autobiography as an insider/outsider text that examines the lifestyles of wealthy white patrons from a servant's perspective. Indeed, the title of the narrative points to the various genres that Keckley uses. As the title indicates, Keckley endured thirty years as a slave. However, unlike most **slave narratives**, which focus almost entirely on the narrator's period of enslavement, Keckley narrates her experience in only three chapters. Despite the brevity of her discussion of **slavery**, Keckley narrates the type of suffering that was familiar to many female slaves. After relocating to North Carolina to live with her owner's son, Keckley was forced into a sexual relationship with a white man and as a result gave birth to her only child, George.

After returning to Virginia, Keckley reunited with her mother and moved to St. Louis to begin to work for Burwell's daughter and son-in-law. Keckley's new owners experienced a series of financial hardships that threatened to separate Keckley from her mother. In an effort to prevent her mother from being put out to service, Keckley employed her considerable talent as a seamstress to support both her family and her owner's family

Her hard work led to a series of events that radically changed the scope of both her personal and professional life. Keckley met and eventually married her husband James. By 1855 she was also able to purchase her own freedom, as well as the freedom of her son. By 1860 Keckley had enrolled her son in Wilberforce College and decided to leave her husband, whom she had deemed to be unfit for marriage. With her newfound independence, Keckley moved to Baltimore and then to Washington, DC in an effort to support herself as a dressmaker. Her talents were widely recognized and she established an influential clientele, including Mr. and Mrs. Jefferson Davis. These elite connections eventually garnered the attention of First Lady Mary Todd Lincoln, with whom she shared a long professional and personal relationship.

The "behind the scenes" that Keckley refers to in her title is an adequate representation of the way in which Keckley uncovers the inner lives of Washington's most elite residents. Unlike the early section of the narrative, Keckley reveals very little about her private life. She instead takes the opportunity to critique the hypocrisy of white America. One of the most interesting moments in the autobiography involves Keckley's efforts to help Mrs. Lincoln in the aftermath of President Lincoln's assassination. Keckley attempted to help Mrs. Lincoln settle debts for her extensive wardrobe. After rejecting Keckley's attempts to plan a fundraiser, the women traveled to New York to sell Mrs. Lincoln's wardrobe. The trip failed to yield monetary results, but did indeed fuel the scandal surrounding the widow's reputation. Keckley intended for her autobiography to polish Mrs. Lincoln's tarnished reputation, but the book severed the relationship between the two women.

The publication of the autobiography caused a controversy. Reviews of the text portrayed Keckley as a traitor and her business suffered. Keckley returned to a very private life and taught domestic arts at Wilberforce. She also worked for the Home for Destitute Women and Children. Keckley's son was killed in the Civil War and her income came from a pension she received as the mother of a fallen solider. She died in 1907. (*See also* African American Autobiography)

Further Reading

Fleischner, Jennifer. *Mrs. Lincoln and Mrs. Keckley: The Remarkable Story of the Friendship Between a First Lady and a Former Slave.* New York: Broadway Books, 2003.

Merish, Lori. *Sentimental Materialism: Gender, Commodity Culture, and Nineteenth Century American Literature.* Durham, NC: Duke UP, 2000.

Sorisio, Carolyn. "Unmasking the Genteel Performer: Elizabeth Keckley's *Behind the Scenes* and the Politics of Public Wrath." *African American Review* 34 (2000): 19–39.

Michelle Taylor

KELLEY, SAMUEL L. (1948–)   African American dramatist. Kelley was born on June 23, 1948, in Memphis, Tennessee, one of eight children. After receiving his PhD from the University of Michigan in mass communications in 1979, he accepted a position at the State University of New York College at Cortland, where he has been teaching for the past twenty-five years and is professor of communication studies.

Unlike many of his contemporaries in black theater, Kelley has explored other themes besides the "**race** issue" in his work. His first full-length play, *Pill Hill,* is about a group of black mill workers living in Chicago between 1973 and 1983. The play takes place over this period in which six friends meet at five-year intervals and recount their successes and failures after getting out of the steel mill where they had originally met. The oldest of the six, Charlie, and Joe, one of the youngest, never actually leave the mill. Of the others, Ed becomes a lawyer; Al and Tony, salesmen; and Scott, a drug dealer. Through these characters, Kelley portrays a cross section of the post–World War II African American society in which the younger generation is trying to establish its own values and identities in mainstream society. Kelley also adapted a short story by **Charles W. Chessnut**, which he titled "The Blue Vein Society," about a former slave who is confronted by the woman he had married before Emancipation.

In the past decade, the dramatist has written plays about a variety of subjects, such as racial profiling in *Driving While Black* (2000); here an African American family is terrorized by a white racist policeman who is determined to "find something" in order to arrest them. In one stirring scene, the mother of the family is humiliated in a strip search by a female guard. A more recent work, *Faith, Hope and Charity* (2003), is Kelley's portrayal of the life of the great civil rights activist and educator Mary McCloed Bethuen. He is presently working on a play about the effects of Parkinson's disease on a white family.

The most evident theme in most of Kelley's works is black people's need for a sense of location in a world in which they cannot feel complete control over their lives. Kelley does not merely reveal **identity** crises but the whole dynamic of living in a "white man's world" without becoming obsessed with it. Although many of Kelley's characters in his plays are African Americans, their problems and issues carry a universal resonance.

Further Reading

Gussow, Mel. "Success and Failure in Black Struggle to Rise." *New York Times* (December 3 1992): B8.

Mazer, Cary. "Pill Hill." *Philadelphia Inquirer* (February 8, 1991): C2.

Shatzky, Joel. "Samuel Kelley." *African American Dramatists*. Ed. Emmanuel S. Nelson. Westport, CT: Greenwood Press, 2004.

Joel Shatzky

KELLEY, WILLIAM MELVIN (1937–) African American author of novels and short stories. Although associated with the militant **Black Arts Movement**, Kelley has frequently articulated the primacy of art over polemics. His anger is clearly shaped by a disciplined talent.

His father was editor of the *Amsterdam News* but Kelley was raised in the Bronx and attended the Fieldstone School run by the American Ethical Culture Society. When he graduated in 1957 he went to Harvard, where he studied literature under Archibald MacLeish and John Hawkes. He received the Dana Reed Prize for creative writing in 1960. In addition to his writing career, he has served as a college educator for many years at institutions such as the State University of New York College at Geneseo and the New School for Social Research. Among his numerous literary achievements, he has won the John Hay Whitney Foundation Award and the Rosenthal Foundation Award.

William Melvin Kelley. *Courtesy of the Library of Congress.*

His first novel, *A Different Drummer* (1962) tells the story of Tucker Caliban, a man possessed by the spiritual heritage of his forebears. His martyred great-grandfather, "the African," inspires him to renounce his life as a Southern sharecropper, and in a broadly symbolic act Caliban seeds his land with salt rock, kills his livestock, and burns his home while his wife Bethrah looks on. He also shatters the grandfather clock that had made its way to New World on the same slave ship as his great-grandfather. Caliban is out to create his own New World; to do so he must leave the Old South. In order to free himself psychologically from the tentacles of **slavery**, he migrates North, with the intention of reinventing himself and providing a new life for his family.

Dancers on the Shore (1964) a collection of sixteen short stories, contains the frequently anthologized "The Only Man on Liberty Street," a tale of interracial love in the Old South bravely confronting the intimidation of racist white thugs—until Maynard Herder, the protagonist, is afraid to put his racially mixed child's life at risk; and "Cry for Me," the story about a great **blues** artist, Wallace Bedlow, who performs and dies at Carnegie Hall.

A Drop of Patience (1965) is a well-written novel about a blind musician, Ludlow Washington, and his struggle between finding love with a woman and finding his place in the evolving world of **jazz**. Like **Ralph Ellison**'s invisible man, it is "as if the blindness were not in Ludlow's eyes at all, did not keep Ludlow from seeing, but from being seen." People fail to see Luddy because he is black and blind. The novel raises the question: "What you think white folks want from us?" When Ludlow falls in love with Ragan, a white woman who dumps him, he decides that society wants blacks to be docile. Similar to Tod Clifton, who sells grimacing paper dolls in *Invisible Man*, Ludlow engages in symbolic self-mockery when he appears on stage in minstrel makeup. At the end of *A Drop of Patience*, Luddy is finally "rediscovered" and showered with critical acclaim for his innovative musicianship, but he rejects the world of New York and must decide where to go next. Although

Catherine Juanita Starke sees Ludlow as a victim of environmental determinism, he is a complex, richly textured human being who has cultivated his talent, parlayed it to fame, and who now stands at a crossroads considering a variety of positive, hopeful options.

dem (1967) is about "them" (white people), a novel centering on a fantasy of revenge. Black Cooley fathers white Tam's child not because he loves her but because he wants to settle an old score: four hundred years of slavery visited on blacks by whites in this country. As a result of that abusive history, black women have given birth to racially mixed babies while humiliated black men have stood by impotently. Now Cooley turns the tables by befriending Mitchell Pierce's wife, Tam, and leaving the white couple's lives in shambles. The novel, often utilizing surrealistic techniques, is more experimental and less accessible than *A Drop of Patience.* It also makes for slower reading as it doggedly dissects the psyche of Mitchell Pierce—his warped values, his prejudices, his pathetic desires. Part of the story involves a detour into the idiotic world of daytime soap operas as Mitchell becomes addicted to "Search for Love" and obsessed with its star, Nancy Knickerbocker. As such, it is a bitter satire about "them" and their selfish ways. Whites think they carry the burden of civilization, but they make a farce of it. *dem* was Kelley's most ambitious novel to date but it was less engaging than his earlier work.

His final novel (as of this writing), *Dunfords Travels Everywheres* (1970) pushes stylistic experimentation further than *dem.* Taking off from James Joyce's *Finnegan's Wake,* the novel delves into layers of consciousness and makes extensive use of allusion, symbolism and word play. Chig Dunford, schooled at Harvard (as was Kelley), is both contrasted and compared with the street smart Harlemite Carlyle Bedlow, who, despite his different life experiences, shares a racial brotherhood with Chig. In dealing with his characters' interconnectedness, Kelley attempts to contribute to the development of a black aesthetic.

Although he ceased to publish fiction after 1970, he produced a video, *Excavating Harlem,* which won a grant from the New York Foundation for the Arts, 1989, and an award from the National Institute of Arts and Letters. He has taught at the Taos Institute of Art and currently teaches at Sarah Lawrence College, Bronxville, New York.

Further Reading

Hogue, W. Lawrence. "Disrupting the White/Black Binary: William Melvin Kelley's *A Different Drummer.*" *CLA Journal* 44.1 (September 2000): 1–42.

Starke, Catherine Juanita. *Black Portraiture in American Fiction.* Basic Books: New York, 1971. 120–23, 152–55, 228–30.

Sundquist, Eric J. "Promised Lands: *A Different Drummer.*" *TriQuarterly* (Winter–Summer 2000): 107–8, 268–84.

Leonard J. Deutsch

KENAN, RANDALL (1963–) African American novelist, short story writer, and nonfiction writer. Born in Brooklyn, New York, Kenan was raised in rural Chinquapin, North Carolina, a community on which he has modeled the setting of his first novel and many of his short stories. After receiving his BA in English and creative writing from the University of North Carolina at Chapel Hill in 1985, Kenan worked as an editor at Knopf before launching his writing career. Kenan resists classification, given the wide range of genres in which he works, yet his overriding preoccupations—the deep and abiding sense of place, community, and tradition in the South, the power of language, the honest and frank portrayal of sexuality and **racism**, and the juxtaposition of the real and the supernatural—are apparent in much of Kenan's writing.

Kenan's first novel, *A Visitation of Spirits* (1989), established him as a major new voice in Southern writing. Like William Faulkner and **Ernest J. Gaines**, two novelists with whom he is often compared, Kenan creates a mythical world as the setting for this novel. Tims Creek, North Carolina, clearly the fictionalized version of Chinquapin, where Kenan grew up, displays all the strengths and weaknesses of a close-knit, traditional, rural Southern community. Horace Cross, the sixteen-year-old protagonist, is tormented and alienated by his growing awareness of his homosexuality, and the novel chronicles his downward spiral into despair and finally suicide. Attempting to escape his pain, Horace tries to turn himself into a red-tailed hawk through ritual sorcery and incantation, but he fails to transform and free himself. Instead, he experiences a nightmarish journey, compelled by a voice in his head to roam naked and crazed through Tims Creek to significant scenes of his past. Torn by the opposing impulses of his sexual desires and the repressive religious morality of his family and community, Horace cannot reconcile these two extremes within himself, nor can he choose between them and deny an aspect of his being. Horace's ultimate suicide demonstrates the destructive power of racial, sexual, and moral intolerance on the fragile psyche of a confused young black man.

Kenan shifted to the short story in his second book, *Let the Dead Bury Their Dead* (1992), twelve stories set, like his first novel, in the fictional world of Tims Creek. Nominated for the National Book Critics Circle Award, *Let the Dead Bury Their Dead* includes some of the same characters in Kenan's first novel. The title story is a history of Tims Creek, ostensibly written by the Reverend James Malachai Greene, who plays an important part in *A Visitation of Spirits*. Other stories display Kenan's attraction to the Southern grotesque ("Clarence and the Dead") as well as the influence of magical realism ("The Things of This World"), linking him to such writers as Toni Morrison. The presence of death and the experience of loss dominate this collection, and Kenan continues to explore the explosive power of sexual desire and social judgment.

Kenan's biography for young adults, *James Baldwin* (1994), is the first volume in the Lives of Notable Gay Men and Lesbians series and the first written for younger readers that openly discusses **James Baldwin**'s sexual orientation, tying his sexual **identity** to the larger issues of Baldwin's self-representation, his life, and his works. As a gay black man, Kenan writes with sympathetic understanding about the homophobia and racism that Baldwin encountered, yet he does not focus solely on Baldwin's homosexuality; instead, it becomes simply another part of Baldwin's complex personal and literary development.

Walking on Water: Black American Lives at the Turn of the Twenty-First Century (1999) is Kenan's nonfiction exploration of African American culture. Attempting to answer the question of what it means to be black in America at the close of the twentieth century, Kenan interviews African Americans in black communities across the United States and in Canada, from all classes and all walks of life. *Walking on Water* artfully combines oral history, sociological and political inquiry, and Kenan's personal and communal self-exploration.

Noted for his wide-ranging versatility, his mastery of storytelling, and his powerful evocation of character and place, Randall Kenan depicts the sorrows and obsessions of human existence with humor, sensitivity, and compassion. (*See also* African American Gay Literature)

Further Reading

Harris, Trudier. *The Power of the Porch: The Storyteller's Craft in Zora Neale Hurston, Gloria Naylor, and Randall Kenan.* Athens: U of Georgia P, 1996.

Ketchin, Susan. "Randall Kenan: Ancient Spells and Incantations." *The Christ-Haunted Landscape: Faith and Doubt in Southern Fiction.* Ed. Susan Ketchin. Jackson: UP of Mississippi, 1994. 260–302.

Michele S. Ware

KENNEDY, ADRIENNE (1931–) African American playwright, mystery novelist, short story writer, and autobiographer. Adrienne Kennedy's importance for African American literature lies primarily in her highly personal, ultraexperimental dramas that typically explore painful areas of the psyche that many people, black and white, would prefer not to face. Often difficult, sometimes obscure, Kennedy's plays are daring, demanding, extraordinary, and illuminating.

Born Adrienne Lita Hawkins in Pittsburgh, Pennsylvania, Kennedy's childhood was spent mainly in a pleasant, multiethnic neighborhood in Cleveland, Ohio. This gave her a sense of how people from different cultural backgrounds could get along together. However, she was told many stories about violence and **racism** by her mother, an early warning that she could not count on finding such peace elsewhere. In fact, when she later attended Ohio State University, she encountered racist hostility so great that it became a primary source for the violent imagery in her plays, including one titled *The Ohio State Murders* (1992).

Shortly after her college graduation in 1953, she married Joseph Kennedy and received another lesson in the cruelty and violence of the world when he was sent to Korea less than six months later. In 1960 she accompanied her husband and their first child to Europe and Africa at the time when Patrice

Adrienne Kennedy. *Courtesy of the Library of Congress.*

Lumumba, widely viewed as a hero of African independence, was murdered. This trip sparked her first major play, *Funnyhouse of a Negro* (1962). Shortly after her return to New York, Kennedy submitted her play for admission to Edward Albee's play-writing course and two years later he co-produced it Off-Broadway. In 1964 it won her an Obie for Distinguished Play.

Funnyhouse of a Negro is both individualistic and representative of Kennedy's early work. The central character in this play is a black woman named Sarah who has four other "selves" representing her: Queen Victoria, the Duchess of Hapsburg, Jesus, and Patrice Lumumba. The splitting of her character into different genders, races, nationalities, and religions implies the multitude of conflicts within her. Her appreciation and love for white European culture are mocked by her awareness that the racist forces within this culture reject her. She also seems to have internalized racist standards and to judge herself by them. Her female selves express a fear of being raped, but she is also the male selves who do the raping. Sarah's father had been given a mission by his mother to preach Christianity to the Africans, but the Jesus self in the play seems cruel and untrustworthy. Divided like this, Sarah is unable to construct a whole self that would save her and hangs herself.

Kennedy, while subject to the same torments as Sarah, transcended them and attained wholeness by writing so openly about them. Her excruciatingly painful writing was also very liberating for her. Throughout *The Alexander Plays* (1992) centering on Suzanne Alexander (in many ways a stand-in for Kennedy herself), she refers often to Frantz Fanon, the Martiniquean psychiatrist who analyzed the psychic wounds inflicted on the colonized in *The Wretched of the Earth*. By making such references, Kennedy demonstrates her awareness of how her personal psychological explorations in such plays as *Funnyhouse of a Negro, The Owl Answers* (1965), *A Rat's Mass* (1966), and *A Lesson in Dead Language* (1970) have political and philosophical dimensions as well.

Her most overtly political play, *An Evening with Dead Essex* (1973), was inspired by a 1972 incident in which a black man named Mark Essex gunned down three policemen and several other people as a protest against racism and the Vietnam War. The police retaliated by riddling his body with more than a hundred bullets. Kennedy's play is staged as if it were a final rehearsal with a black director, black actors and a white projectionist. During the supposed rehearsal, the director and actors are preparing for the next night's performance by discussing what they know about Essex's life and death and expressing their opinions about him. They increasingly identify with his motives, since their own lives have made them feel a similar rage against the discrimination and injustice of American society and the racist underpinning—white against nonwhite—of the conflict between the United States and Vietnam.

In focusing on his life, they explore the psychological background of Essex's act. As Kennedy presents it in her play, Essex's childhood has many parallels with her characters' upbringing—and her own. The director and actors emphasize Essex's Christian home and the patriotic songs they all sang in their youth as well as the public events that altered their perspectives, such as the killing of the Kent State student protestors and Nixon's lies. The final impression is that the characters and Kennedy view Essex as a martyr and they seem poised to emulate him.

Another significant feature of Kennedy's childhood as she described it in her memoir *People Who Led to My Plays* (1988) was her love of American popular culture and this feature dominates her play *A Movie Star Has to Star in Black and White* (1976). Kennedy blends scenes from three classic black-and-white movies—*Now Voyager, Viva Zapata,* and *A Place in the Sun*—with scenes from the life of a black writer named Clara and her family. Actors resembling the ones in the classic movies speak lines that are obviously taken from Clara's life and its major events, nearly all of which can be matched to those in Kennedy's own life. These events include her middle-class childhood in Cleveland, her marriage to a man who is sent to Korea shortly after their wedding, and her parents' divorce when she is an adult. Even a play supposedly written by Clara contains lines from Kennedy's *The Owl Answers.*

The effect of Kennedy's mingling of movie illusions involving the lives of white characters with the realities of the life of a black woman character based on the author is twofold. The way Clara projects her thoughts into the mouths of white actresses playing scenes in movies she admired suggests that she may have immersed herself too completely in these white fantasies and lost her sense of **identity** and of the real, black world around her. However, this projection may equally be viewed as the triumph of an imaginative black author who can subvert the images of a hostile white society to suit her own personality and purposes.

Autobiography and experimentalism continue to dominate Kennedy's writings up to the present. *The Deadly Triplets: A Theatre Mystery and Journal* (1990) demonstrated her mastery of the classic detective novel since it contained two solved puzzles. However, the central character was obviously modeled on herself, and the novel was published together with a journal that calls attention to the parallels and contrasts between her life and her fiction. *June and Jean in Concert* (1995) dramatized her memoir *People Who Led to My Plays,* but she divided her experiences between two twins, one of whom dies and returns as a spirit to interact with the living sister. Her play *Sleep Deprivation Chamber* (1996), cowritten with her son Adam, depicted Adam's unprovoked beating by a white policeman and his family's attempt to gain justice, along with several dream sequences.

Among the finest living experimental writers, Kennedy remains capable of astonishing and enlightening us with more great works to come. (*See also* African American Drama)

Further Reading

Bryant-Jackson, Paul K. and Lois More Overbeck, eds. *Intersecting Boundaries: The Theatre of Adrienne Kennedy.* Minneapolis: U of Minnesota P, 1992.

Carter, Steven R. "Adrienne Kennedy." *African American Playwrights: A Sourcebook.* Ed. Emmanuel S. Nelson. New York: Greenwood Press, 2004. 265–82.

Steven R. Carter

KENNEDY, WILLIAM (1928–) William Kennedy was born in Albany, New York, in 1928, and attended Siena College before pursuing a career in journalism. He worked for a short time as a sports reporter for the *Glen Falls Post Star* and was drafted into the U.S. Army in 1950. He worked for an army newspaper in Europe and, upon discharge, he returned to the United States and went to work for the Albany *Times-Union.* In 1956 he went to work as a reporter for a small newspaper in Puerto Rico and ultimately became managing editor of the *San Juan Star* in 1959. While in Puerto Rico, he took a creative writing course with **Saul Bellow** and then, in 1963, returned to Albany to devote his time to writing fiction.

Upon his return to Albany, he published a series of articles about the city (collectively republished in 1983 as *O Albany!*) that earned Kennedy a Pulitzer Prize nomination. The articles covered various aspects of Albany's history from the seventeenth century through the 1950s and focused on the experiences of the Irish immigrants who settled the city. Kennedy used many of the details gleaned during the writing of these articles to provide a backdrop for his first novel *The Ink Truck* (1969). The novel details a strike in an unnamed Albany newspaper office and received great critical acclaim.

In 1975 Kennedy published the first installment of his "Albany cycle." Set in the Irish Catholic neighborhoods of Depression-era Albany, *Legs* was the story of gangster "Legs" Diamond. He followed this with *Billy Phelan's Greatest Game* in 1978. The novel introduced the Phelan family, an extended Irish American family that was to appear in five subsequent novels. Billy, a small-time gambler, becomes embroiled in a plot to kidnap the son of an Albany politician. Critics praised the work for its rich and dramatic dialogue.

The third installment of the "Albany Cycle," *Ironweed*, was published in 1983 and was the winner of both the Pulitzer Prize and the National Book Critics Circle Award for fiction. This novel marked a change in tone and, indeed, set new expectations that readers would bring to subsequent works of Kennedy's. A much "darker" work than its predecessors, the novel follows Francis Phelan, Billy's father, an alcoholic and a vagrant fleeing from his own set of personal demons. Once a major league baseball prospect, Francis accidentally kills one of his infant sons and his guilt drives him to an almost ghostly existence on the fringes of Albany society. Occasionally resurfacing to visit the family he left, Francis wanders through the dives

William Kennedy. *AP/Wide World Photos.*

and hobo jungles of upstate New York. *Ironweed* was praised for its (at times) Joycean narrative and its exploration of notions of destiny through the character of Francis Phelan, as well as the setting of Albany. The success of *Ironweed* allowed Kennedy to pursue his long-time interest in film. He collaborated on the screenplay of *The Cotton Club* with Francis Ford Coppola in 1986 and scripted the film adaptation of *Ironweed* in 1987.

Although originally conceived as a trilogy, the "Albany Cycle" expanded to include a fourth installment in 1988 with the publication of *Quinn's Book*. The novel explores Albany in the nineteenth century through the rather picaresque misadventures of a Phelan ancestor, Daniel Quinn. Although horrific in some of its detail, the work is lighter in tone than its predecessor but (perhaps because of this) did not garner the critical acclaim or sales figures of *Ironweed*.

In 1992 Kennedy published *Very Old Bones*, a work set in the Albany of the 1950s. The novel chronicles the life of Orson Purcell, the illegitimate son of artist Patrick Phelan. Working for Phelan while living in his house and desirous of achieving Phelan's admission of paternity, Owen suffers a mental breakdown but is ultimately accepted by the Phelan family and belatedly by Patrick. The novel explores concepts such as belonging, the nature of art, and redemption, and it features a chapter in which an aging Francis Phelan visits the family to some rather mixed and wholly heart-breaking responses from Phelans too young to recall him.

Kennedy's next installment of the Albany cycle was *The Flaming Corsage* in 1996. The work spans a period from the 1880s through shortly after the turn of the century. It follows the rather turbulent courtship and marriage of Katrina Taylor and Edward Daugherty and begins in a New York hotel room with the bloody "love nest killings" of 1908. The plot moves back and forth between the killings and the courtship of Edward and Katrina, two characters who touch the lives of the Phelans. As the playwright Edward's career becomes more and more successful, Katrina withdraws from the world. Both characters engage in multiple adulteries (Katrina with a young Francis Phelan). Like *Ironweed*, the novel is unsparing in its depictions of some of Albany's seedier environs.

Although best known for his novels, Kennedy has achieved much success in other genres. He published the acclaimed book of essays *Riding the Yellow Trolley Car* in 1993. Covering a variety of topics, the book was well received and sold quite well for a representative of its genre. Additionally, Kennedy published two children's books, *Charlie Malarkey and the Belly Button Machine* (1986) and *Charlie Malarkey and the Singing Moose* (1993), both of which were coauthored with his son Brendan. In 1996 Kennedy's first play, *Grand View*, was staged at the Capital Repertory Theatre in Albany.

In 2002 Kennedy returned to fiction with the publication of his seventh installment in the Albany cycle, *Roscoe*. Although much of the cycle has dealt with such themes as loss and redemption, family, and sin, *Roscoe* is decidedly light in tone. The story of a Democratic politician in mid-twentieth century Albany, the novel was panned by many reviewers as containing predictable plotlines and stock characters. Still, other critics were more forgiving and praised the scope of the work. (*See also* Irish American Novel)

Further Reading

Gillespie, Michael Patrick. *Reading William Kennedy.* Syracuse, NY: Syracuse UP, 2002.

William Carney

KENNY, MAURICE (1929–)   Native American (Mohawk and Seneca) poet, short story writer, essayist, and playwright. Maurice Kenny is a prolific and significant author and has over twenty-five collections of poetry, fiction, and essays to his credit, as well as numerous inclusions in other works. He is the recipient of a National Public Radio Award for Broadcasting, his book *The Mama Poems* won the American Book Award in 1984, and in 2000 he received the Elder Recognition Award from the Wordcraft Circle of Native Writers and Storytellers. His books *Blackrobe: Isaac Jogues, b. March 11, 1607, d. October 18, 1646* (1982) and *Between Two Rivers: Selected Poems 1956–1984* (1987) were nominated for the Pulitzer Prize.

Critics have compared Kenny with Walt Whitman and William Carlos Williams, and his works are informed by a quest for self-**identity** and self-definition contextualized by his Mohawk ancestry. Kenny has stated his philosophy: "I am committed to the earth and the past; to tradition and the future. I am committed to the people and poetry" (Ruppert 456). His later narrative poetry, exemplified by his masterpiece *Blackrobe: Isaac Jogues, b. March 11, 1607, d. October 18, 1646* (1982) and *Tekonwatonti/Molly Brant* (1992), revises native history by giving voice to the silent players of Indian–white history and exposing the complexity of cultures in conflict. The songlike qualities of his poetry are reminiscent of traditional chants of the Iroquois longhouse.

Born in Watertown, New York, on August 16, 1929, to a Mohawk father and a Seneca mother, Kenny's first thirteen years were spent in the wild foothills of the Adirondack Mountains. This setting inspired Kenny to write his earliest poems as odes to nature. Kenny's parents' divorce in 1942 uprooted the family, and Kenny moved with his mother to New Jersey where he first encountered urban American life. A troubled adolescence forced Kenny to bounce from home to home, and he lived at various times with each parent and an older sister in New Jersey; Watertown, New York; and St. Louis, Missouri.

Maurice Kenny. *Photo by Paul Rosado. Courtesy of Maurice Kenny.*

At seventeen, Kenny first read the poetry of Walt Whitman, and found that Whitman's rhythm, language, and equation of himself with his natural surroundings evoked traditional native oral patterns and appealed to his own sense of musicality. Whitman became a literary hero to Kenny, and his writings served to inspire Kenny's subsequent works. Undoubtedly, too, Whitman's homoeroticism also stirred Kenny, who was discovering his own homosexuality, which he revealed in writing for the first time in his article "Tinselled Bucks: An Historical Study in Indian Homosexuality" (1976) in *Gay Sunshine*, UC-Berkeley's gay liberation journal, and in the poem "Winkte" (a Dakota two-spirited person) found in *Only As Far As Brooklyn* (1979). Kenny would later condemn Whitman's silence on U.S.–Native American policies in his critique "Whitman's Indifference to Indians" (1987).

At the age of twenty-three, Kenny enrolled at Butler University in Indianapolis and began writing seriously, but several professors discouraged his efforts and suggested that he abandon poetry for prose, asserting that Kenny's poetic voice lacked rhythm. Dejected, he next enrolled at St. Lawrence University in upstate New York for only one year, but there he came to the attention of novelist and anthologist Douglas Angus, who encouraged Kenny to resume writing poetry. The following year, Kenny left St. Lawrence for New York City, where he was accepted to Columbia University; Kenny, however, never attended classes at Columbia, opting instead to work at a bookstore, where he met many of the leading modern and postmodern literati of the day.

In 1953 Kenny enrolled at New York University, where he found a mentor in poet and critic Louise Bogan, who at the time of their meeting reviewed poetry for *The New Yorker*. Bogan's lyrical sensitivity and insistence upon specificity profoundly influenced Kenny's writing. In 1958 Kenny published his first collection of poetry, *Dead Letters Sent, and Other Poems: Love to Lesbia* followed in 1959.

In the 1960s Kenny wandered throughout the United States, the Caribbean, and Mexico, and worked for a short time writing obituaries for the *Chicago Sun*. He ultimately returned to New York City, where he worked as a waiter until 1974. A heart attack that year compelled him to return to writing seriously, and in 1976 his poem "I Am the Sun"—a response to the Wounded Knee confrontation of 1973 and patterned after a Lakota ghost dance—was published in *Akwesasne Notes*; in that year, he also established Strawberry Press to publish the works of Native American writers. Since then, he has been published almost continually, and has maintained a career as writer-in-residence and professor at several universities and colleges. (*See also* Native American Poetry)

Further Reading

Barron, Patrick. "Maurice Kenny's *Tekonwatonti, Molly Brant:* Poetic Memory and History." *Melus,* 25 (Fall/Winter 2000): 31–64.

Bruchac, Joseph. *Survival This Way: Interviews with American Indian Poets* (Sun Tracks Books, No 15). Tucson, AZ: U of Arizona P, 1990.

Landrey, David."Maurice Kenny: Remembering Molly." *Talisman: A Journal of Contemporary Poetry and Poetics* 11 (1993): 293–95.

Ruppert, James. "The Native American Short Story." *The Columbia Companion to the Twentieth-Century American Short Story.* Ed. Blanche H. Gelfant and Lawrence Graver. New York: Columbia UP, 2001.

Swann, Brian, and Arnold Krupat, eds. *I Tell You Now: Autobiographical Essays by Native American Writers.* Greenwich, CT: Brompton Books Corp., 1989.

W. Douglas Powers

KEROUAC, JACK (1922–1969) Franco American novelist, poet, and nonfiction writer. Viewed as a cultural phenomenon during his lifetime because of his role as "father" of the Beat generation, Jack Kerouac is now considered one of the most important twentieth-century American writers. His novel *On the Road* (1957), once a source of scandal and outrage, has become an American classic widely taught in high schools as well as universities. Moreover, his way of life, theories about spontaneous prose, and literary experimentalism have influenced a host of other writers.

On the Road portrayed actual people and events in Kerouac's life, but with a mythic, larger than life quality that has given the book its enduring appeal. The people and events he made legendary were among the chief inspirations for the Beat movement. Central characters Sal Paradise (Kerouac) and Dean Moriarty (Neal Cassady) embodied the conventionality eschewing, kick-seeking, drug-taking, sexually adventurous, and spiritually questing attitudes that came to be the hallmarks of the Beats. As Kerouac used the term, "Beat" had three primary meanings: (1) an honesty he found in post–World War II hipsters that came from being too beaten down to bother with lies; (2) the rhythm in **jazz** that could lead to spiritual visions; and (3) the root word of "beatific," a quality he deemed profoundly important. In his later years, when he became bitter over the debasement of his beliefs by the media and his supposed followers, what hurt him most was the neglect of his concern for beatitude.

Whereas many of his best-known works, such as *The Subterraneans* (1958), *The Dharma Bums* (1958), and *Desolation Angels* (1965), focused on his involvement with fellow Beat writers, including **Allen Ginsberg**, William Burroughs, and **Gregory Corso**, his main interest was in converting his life story into literature, as Marcel Proust did, and he wrote many novels about his childhood and youth in Lowell, Massachusetts. In his Lowell novels, such as *Doctor Sax (1959)* and *Maggie Cassidy* (1959), he showed the same blend of honesty and mythologizing as in his other works. Even though Kerouac strongly emphasized his French Canadian working-class background, he also pointed up how multiethnic his Lowell neighborhood was.

Considering that Kerouac spoke only a French Canadian dialect until he was six, his later command of English may seem astonishing. In his early work, such as *Orpheus Emerged* (2000) and *The Town and the City* (1950), he used formal, often elegant English. After being inspired by Neal Cassady and jazz to take a less controlled approach, Kerouac developed his practice of spontaneous writing, launching into a description or narrative without revisions. He insisted that the first thought was the most honest. This resulted in looser, more creative language, and many passages in his writing sound like scatting. Some of the most striking passages of this sort occur in his prose works *Visions of Cody* (1972) and *Old Angel Midnight* (1993) and his poetry *Mexico City Blues* (1959).

Part of Kerouac's French Canadian heritage was his lifelong belief in Catholicism. However, he also became a serious student of Buddhism and struggles in many works to harmonize his second religion with his first. For example, in *The Dharma Bums*, which narrates Ray Smith's (Kerouac's) encounter with Japhy Ryder (Gary Snyder), a poet who shares his interest in Buddhism, Smith/Kerouac defends his continuing belief in Catholicism and its compatibility with Buddhism against Ryder's rejection of Christianity. In *Visions of Gerard* (1963), based on the life and death at age nine of his older brother Gerard, Kerouac depicts him as both a Buddhist and a Catholic saint.

During his final years, Kerouac became overwhelmed by alcoholism, but retained his ability to write. His powerful novel *Big Sur* (1962) recounted his unsuccessful attempt to escape from his public persona as King of the Beats and dry himself out in an isolated cabin loaned to him by poet/ publisher Lorenzo Monsanto (Lawrence Ferlinghetti); his subsequent drinking binges, paranoia, and nervous breakdown; and the vision of the Cross followed by the sense of the Buddhist golden eternity that renewed him—temporarily.

His last major work, *Big Sur* shows Kerouac still mining the materials of his life for literature, no matter how painful that material might be. This integrity and honesty are his most important artistic legacy. (*See also* Franco American Literature)

Further Reading

Nicosia, Gerald. *Memory Babe: A Critical Biography of Jack Kerouac.* Berkeley: U of California P, 1983.

Theado, Matt. *Understanding Jack Kerouac.* Columbia: U of South Carolina P, 2000.

Steven R. Carter

KESSLER, MILTON (1930–2000) Jewish American poet and educator. Milton Kessler's importance lies in his wide range of styles and ability to bring vibrancy and color to everyday occurrences, his Jewish roots, and life's inherent struggles. A poet of international acclaim, Kessler published six volumes of poetry, received numerous awards, and taught for over thirty years at the State University of New York (SUNY) campus at Binghamton.

Milton Kessler was born in Brooklyn, New York, in 1930. Raised in the Bronx, his Jewish childhood was one of humble beginnings. Despite dropping out of high school at age fifteen, he found inspiration in the arts and music, especially in singing. Kessler worked in the garment industry, among other odd jobs, and married Sonia Berer in 1952 before entering the University of Buffalo. Kessler went on to earn his master's at the University of Washington, he studied at Ohio State and Harvard University, and he was awarded the Robert Frost Fellowship in poetry in 1961.

Kessler's life as an educator began at Queens College in New York and continued for over thirty years at SUNY-Binghamton, where students and colleagues considered his teaching legendary. Through his energy, booming bass-baritone voice, and love for poetry and literature, Kessler worked to inspire his students. He founded the university's creative writing program and promoted the arts vigorously. Kessler also taught throughout the United States and abroad in England, Israel, Belgium, and Japan.

In his first volume of poetry, *A Road Came Once* (1963), Kessler set forth many of the themes he would return to through out his career, including an intense awareness of suffering, both his own and that around him. Kessler spoke of his early work as ornamental and worked to project the words through his poetry in a kind of music. The range of his work, including both lyric and dramatic poems, was complimented and noted as original and mature. Kessler's published his second work, *Called Home* (1967), as he struggled to establish his teaching career at Binghamton, write poetry, and support his family. As Kessler continued to write and confront struggles, loneliness, and suffering, his collaboration with the artist Robert Marx continued on his next limited edition, *Woodlawn North* (1970).

Kessler's second full-length volume of poetry, *Sailing Too Far* (1973), continued to confront painful experiences and moments of anguish and loss, but his style and confidence showed new strength. Through his ability to catch each fleeting moment before it passed, Kessler successfully ties his Jewish life (and his childhood and family) together in his poetry and finds both strength and solitude. About this time, Kessler spoke of both wanting to improve the world and the need for his private world of poetry—a sort of exile. The lyricism and music were still painful at times, but simple and powerful.

The Grand Concourse (1990) was published in Kessler's sixtieth year. The volume confronts violence and vulnerability again but reflects a continued maturation. Kessler's subjects are familiar (morality and family continuity) and his poems are conversational and wide-ranging in style. Kessler wrote while on the move, in notebooks, with his eyes open and, at one point, found himself waving ships into New York harbor. The resulting poem, "Thanks Forever," was chosen as part of the "Poems on the Underground" to be on London's subway cars and was seen by as many as two million people a day.

Kessler died in April 2000, and *Free Concert: New and Selected Poems* (2002) was published posthumously. *Free Concert* includes all of the old themes and introspection and highlights Kessler's use of sound, weight, and language to create a soft music around the simplest moments. Edited and introduced by two of Kessler's former students, many of the poems were selected, with the assistance of his family, from his notebooks. Over seventy-five of his notebooks, along with notes and letters, have been assembled in the Library of Congress manuscript collection.

Further Reading

Schonbrun, Adam, and D. Jones, A. "Walking the Grand Concourse with Milton Kessler: A Critical Reception and Interview." *Studies in American Jewish Literature* 9.2 (1990): 242–54.

Mark E. Speltz

KILLENS, JOHN OLIVER (1916–1987) African American novelist, crusader against **racism**, cofounder of Harlem Writers' Guild, and vice president of the Black Academy of Arts and Letters. Killens in his four major novels—*Youngblood* (1954), *And Then We Heard the Thunder* (1962), *'Sippi* (1967), and *The Cotillion, or One Good Bull Is Half the Herd* (1971)—brings to light the sordid realities of the African American experience. In the first three novels, he exposes the evils of white racism, but in the fourth the dangers of black classism. He published a collection of autobiographical essays titled *Black Man's Burden* (1965) as well as a biographical novel titled *The Great Black*

John Killens. *Courtesy of the Library of Congress.*

Russian: A Novel on the Life and Times of Alexander Pushkin (published posthumously in 1989). He disagreed with the philosophy of nonviolence preached by **Martin Luther King Jr.**, preferring **Malcolm X**'s philosophy of retaliation against the perpetrators of violence toward blacks. In 1964 he and Malcolm X founded the Organization for Afro-American Unity.

Growing up in the Georgia of the 1920s and 1930s, Killens encountered numerous incidents of white racism. His parents—Charles Miles and Willie Lee Killens—sparked his interest in African American literature, and his great-grandmother told him stories about the sufferings of the black people during **slavery**. He attended a segregated public elementary school and then Ballard Normal School, a missionary school. Thereafter, he studied at Edward Walters College in Jacksonville, Florida, and Morris Brown College in Atlanta, Georgia. In 1936 he moved to Washington, DC, and obtained a clerical position with the National Labor Relations Board. He continued his studies by taking evening classes at Howard University and obtained his bachelor's degree. In 1939 he joined the Robert Terrel Law School, but in 1942 he abandoned his legal studies to join the Army. He served in the United States Amphibian Forces in the South Pacific. When World War II ended, Killens rejoined the Labor Relations Board, this time in New York. He married Grace Ward, whom he had first met in the student movement. The couple lived in Brooklyn. In 1948 Killens enrolled in writing courses at Columbia University and New York University to prepare himself for a career as a writer. He used his writings to wage a relentless war against racism. From 1965 to 1987 Killens taught at a number of universities. He died of cancer on October 27, 1987.

Killens's novels are replete with incidents of racism and how black people respond. Sometimes they give in, and at other times they stand up for their rights. For example, while Laurie Lee in *Youngblood* whips her son Robby to save him from being sent to a reformatory, she refuses to accept the "compromise" offer of the reformatory consignment for her son when Robby is falsely accused of raping the white girl, Betty Jones. Jesse Chaney in *'Sippi* occasionally bows down to white folks to avoid trouble but cannot tolerate their abuse of black women. Joe Youngblood refuses to allow Mack Turner to continue to cheat him of a part of his weekly wages. Killens also furnishes examples of black persons who are strong enough to resist racism. Richard Myles from *Youngblood* and Chuck Othello from *'Sippi* exemplify strong characters. Corporeal Solly Sanders in *And Then We Heard the Thunder* faces discrimination in both at the training camp and during the South Pacific theater operations. Not only is Sanders severely beaten by the white police of Ebbensville, Georgia, but he is also thrown out of the Australian Red Cross Club. In *Cotillion,* Killens expounds that blacks need not imitate whites to reclaim their dignity. They need to respect their black selves. Daphne, the Caribbean mother of the heroine, stops idolizing whites only when she finds whites indulging in promiscuous behavior. Yoruba Lovejoy under the tutelage of the African Ben Ali Lumumba begins to take pride in her black beauty.

Killens's Pushkin is proud of his African heritage and hates serfdom in Russia and slavery in America. In the essay "The Black Man's Burden," included in his autobiographical work, Killens avers that his mission as a writer is to "deniggerize the earth"—to win back for the black people their basic humanity and dignity. (*See also* African American Novel)

Further Reading

Wiggins, William H. "The Structure and Dynamics of Folklore in the Novel Form: The Case of John O. Killens." *Keystone Folklore Quarterly* 17 (Fall 1972): 92–118.

Harish Chander

KIM, MYUNG MI (1957–)   Experimental poet and professor of creative writing, Kim was born in Seoul, Korea, and immigrated to the United States at the age of nine. Her highly experimental poetry deals with her experiences in Korea, issues of language and displacement, human suffering during war, and **diaspora**. Many of Kim's poems seem autobiographical: The references to war, **immigration**, and the displacement caused by the imposition of another language are issues that she has had to negotiate in her own life. Her first collection of poems, *Under Flag* (1991), presents a series of historically specific scenes of the U.S. occupation of Korea blended with dreams and hallucinations. There is a strong sense of grief in the poems, because of the devastation of war and the displacement that it entails. Her next two collections of poetry, *The Bounty* (1996) and *Dura* (1998), center on the question of learning and translating language and being empowered to manipulate it. In *The Bounty,* she begins by suggesting that it is a "study book" and proceeds to write the fourteen consonants of *hangul* (the Korean alphabet) as though to teach the reader. Yet the words and phrases that develop from these consonants transcend traditional forms of poetry, leading the reader along a complex path of the discovery of the ways language and power are related. *Dura* is a long poem, divided into seven parts, that centers on Korean and English words and what they might mean. She then challenges the reader to "Translate: 38th Parallel," to illustrate the intricacy of our intellectual conceptualization of language in relation to historical events. Her most recent collection of poems, *Commons* (2002), recognized as her most outstanding, retakes many of these themes but attends more closely to how the transcultural presence alters what is around it. Again, taking as a point of departure a series of words or phrases, she explores the relation between languages and issues of **colonialism**, immigration, war, and loss. The poems hover between shared and deeply personal experiences, and continue to highlight the poet's intense engagement with language itself.

Language is Kim's most recurring poetic concern. Believing that poetry is how one participates in language, she employs language as a site for questioning ethnic identity, processes of immigration and translation, and relations of interdependence and power. Kim's work has often been classified in relation to the Language poets, because of the ways she negotiates the structures of language to engage issues of culture and power. Nonetheless, her main concern is to try and illustrate a third possibility that arises when two language structures—Korean and English—collide within one person. Through poetic strategies such as ellipsis, fragmentation, blank spaces, and original metaphors, Kim challenges not only conventional ways of representing ethnic **identity** but also the lyric "I" of conventional poetry. In important ways, she suggests that the persona of the poem is constituted by the languages she possesses, which, at the same time, positions her in specific ways in the world and in history.

Further Reading

Chiu, Jeannie. "Identities in Process: The Experimental Poetry of Mei-mei Berssenbrugge and Myung Mi Kim." *Asian North American Identities: Beyond the Hyphen.* Ed. Eleanor Ty and Donald C. Goellnicht. Bloomington: Indiana UP, 2004. 84–101.

Lee, James Kyung-Jin. "Myung Mi Kim." *Words Matter: Conversations with Asian American Writers.* Ed. King-Kok Cheung. Honolulu: U of Hawai'i P, 2000. 92–104.

Rocío G. Davis

KIM, RICHARD E. (1932–)   Korean American novelist and the most well-known Korean immigrant writer since **Younghill Kang** (1903–1972). Critically acclaimed, Richard Kim gained worldwide attention with his first novel, *The Martyred* (1964), which still remains the only Asian American work ever nominated for a Nobel Prize for literature. His experience in the Korean War as a military officer and the presence of Christianity in his family background had a deep impact on his literary career.

Set in the North Korean capital of Pyongyang immediately after the Korean War, *The Martyred* explores the themes of religious belief, salvation, and human nature in the form of a mystery novel. The narrator, Captain Lee, working with a U.S. Army Counterintelligence Corps unit, is assigned to a task to investigate the kidnapping and execution of twelve Christian ministers by retreating North Korean soldiers during the war. Its main plot concerns the knotty questions of who begged for mercy in return for the disavowal of his faith and who was the real martyr? Fourteen ministers were arrested and tortured into denying the existence of God. Then, twelve are executed and two spared. One of the two survivors goes insane under the weight of his traumatic experience and the other surviving minister, Reverend Shin, is presumed to have betrayed the others. By making Revered Shin confess his betrayal, the American military intelligence agency attempts to escalate the twelve executed ministers to the place of martyrs. But a captured North Korean high-ranker states, contrary to Captain Lee's expectations, that Reverend Shin was spared from the execution because he was the only one who remained firm in his faith, unlike the others who denied God and pleaded for mercy. However, Revered Shin confesses to Captain Lee, who confronts the Reverend with the facts garnered from the North Korean officer that the twelve ministers were real martyrs and that he recanted his faith during the interrogation to save his life. By manipulating his confession and deliberately drawing the blame onto himself, Reverend Shin makes an effort to help others to keep their faith not because he believes in God but because he wants others who are too weak to bear the "truth" not to be dejected. With the question of who is the martyr remaining to be resolved by readers, *The Martyred* delves into the meanings of religion, faith, and truth.

His second book, *The Innocent* (1968), reminds some readers familiar with Korean history of the 1961 military coup d'état in South Korea. It was lead by Park Chung-Hee, who subsequently held the country under his despotic rule for eighteen years. The book could be also read as a nuanced commentary on the Vietnam War. However, Kim's second novel, in spite of its controversial sympathetic view of the military leaders, deals with moral issues and existential human dilemmas as a follow-up to his debut, as he contended that the book is not about a historical event itself but about universal human issues: can evil deeds that we sometimes cannot help doing to be truly moral be justified?

The Lost Names: Scenes from a Korean Boyhood (1970) is a fictional memoir of Kim's boyhood and adolescence years in Korea and Manchuria from 1932 to 1945 at the height of Japan's colonial occupation of Korean Peninsula. The title of the book refers to the Japanese policy of forcing Koreans to change their Korean names into Japanese ones. Organized in seven vivid scenes, the book merges personal memories with a traumatized history in its simple but moving depiction of an unbending spirit in face of excruciating experiences through the voice of a young boy. Kim also published a book of photo-essays, *Lost Koreans in China and the Soviet Union* in 1989.

Kim's novels, which touch upon human dilemmas with deep universal resonance, expanded the tight sphere of early immigrant literature beyond the issues of family, community, acculturation, and belonging. His works are compared by some critics with those of nineteenth-century Russian writer Fyodor M. Dostoyevsky and French existential writer Albert Camus. Kim's literary achievement forms a bridge between early immigrant Korean writers and a new generation of Korean American writers after the **immigration** of the 1960s. (*See also* Korean American Literature)

Further Reading

Kim, Elaine H. "Korean American Literature." *An Interethnic Companion to Asian American Literature.* Ed. King-Kok Cheung. New York: Cambridge UP, 2000. 15691.

Valdes, Mario J. "Faith and Despair: A Comparative Study of a Narrative Theme."*Hispania* 49.3 (September 1966): 373–80.

Seongho Yoon

KIM, YONG IK (1920–) Korean American writer. Born in rural Korea, Kim became a successful short story and novel writer in English, his adopted language. He told an interviewer that he was a storyteller even before he learned how to write. It was in Korean schools and college in Japan that he learned English. After the Korean War, he moved to the United States and received a bachelor's degree from Florida Southern College and a master's from the University of Kentucky, and did further study at the University of Iowa. He was a professor of English at a number of schools, including the University of Korea and Duquesne University.

His short stories appeared in many of the most prestigious American magazines, such as *The New Yorker, The Atlantic Monthly, Harper's Bazaar,* and *Mademoiselle.* Kim's novels were printed by major publishers, often with graceful illustrations by artists like Park Minjia, who was also born in Korea. His best-known novels, like *Blue in the Eye* (1964), *The Happy Days* (1965), *Love in Winter* (1969), and *The Shoes from Yang San Valley* (1970) are novellas centering on young protagonists and are often categorized as young adult fiction.

The title of *Blue in the Eye* refers to the distinct color in the protagonist Chun Bok's eyes, which make him stand out in a Korean small town. His family survives because they own a powerful ox that the young boy takes to work other farmer's fields. His mother must negotiate to place her son within the local school, where he is often ridiculed, but where he meets a very kind girl, Jung Lan. Sang Do, the first-person narrator of *The Shoes from Yang San Valley*, tells his story of affection for Soo, the daughter of the town's shoemaker, and his life as a refugee after an attack during the war. *Happy Days* is a sentimental meditation on a bucolic Korean adolescence, and *Love in Winter* is a charming narrative of adolescent love and longing.

Though Kim's work has elicited little critical recognition, he remains an important early figure in the development of Korean tradition in American literature. (*See also* Korean American Literature)

Further Reading

Kim, Elaine. "Korean American Literature." *An Interethnic Companion to Asian American Literature.* New York: Cambridge UP, 1996. 156–191.

Michael W. Young

KIMMELMAN, BURT (1947–)   Contemporary Jewish American poet of exceeding precision and power, whose truncated lines and terse descriptions merge haiku-like simplicity with philosophical depth. His technique of paring down perception to the purity of immediate observation is derived in part by the Objectivists and Imagists, and his heritage can be also traced through such diverse post–World War II poets as William Bronk, Lorine Niedecker, **Joel Oppenheimer**, and Paul Blackburn. But no matter his possible influences, Kimmelman has a vision all his own, one that can be described as an ecstatic clairvoyance arranged around objects and people both acutely present and simultaneously dissolved into the reserve of memory.

In the volumes *Musaics* (1992), *The Pond at Cape May Point* (2002), and *Somehow* (2005), Kimmelman is attuned to the visual arts, particularly painting and sculpture, as a useful field of contemplation for his composition. The relationship between text and image is critical to the trajectory of his work, informing how texture, the materiality of the word, and orality create the means for the poet's dialogic encounter with the world. Moreover, this nexus of forces provides him with the delicately inlaid filaments for aesthetic and metaphysical discovery. A poem like "8.6.86 Tate Gallery/ Gaudier-Brzeska's Pound, The Hieratic Head" offers an instructive glimpse into this method with its melding of artistic perception and an appeal to transcendent wisdom. Such verse almost seems intent on embracing the visionary, although it always patently connects to its subjects so that they become ends in their own right, radiated by the poet's speculation. Kimmelman has noted his need to both escape and to reflect on the pressures of history, and, in isolating "a moment of time," he imbues a note of longing, a rhetoric of hope, to these interpretative glances of the world and the unworldly.

Unlike many contemporary poets, whose survey of subjects often succumbs to **identity** politics and overwrought representation, Kimmelman brings poignancy and attentiveness to his various studies. He has devoted an entire cycle of poems to his daughter and her development; by tracking her experiences, he reveals an absorption in the sensuous and perceptual graspings of the human subject and how we cope with "this grammar of sinew and bone." Rather than strive for determinateness, the poet resolves only to deepen his sensitivity and knowledge of identity, refusing the presumption of any conclusion on any subject. In "The End of Nature" he relates the perplexity of existence and the mutuality made of our collective plight by asking how naming invites a singularity of appearance with a need to commune with others as a necessary rite of its being.

In addition to being an acclaimed poet, Kimmelman is a widely published critic, scholar, and literary historian. His specialties include American poetry and poetics and medieval studies, and he has published *The Poetics of Authorship in the Later Middle Ages: The Emergence of the Modern Literary Persona* (1996) and *The "Winter Mind": William Bronk and American Letters* (1998). Burt Kimmelman teaches at New Jersey Institute of Technology in Newark, New Jersey.

Further Reading

Fink, Thomas. Review of *First Life*. *Boston Review* 26.6 (December 2001/January 2002): 4.

Finkelstein, Norman. Review of *Musaics*. *Sagetrieb: A Journal Devoted to Poets in the Imagist/Objectivist Tradition* 11.3 (Winter 1992): 135–41.

Jonathan Curley

KINCAID, JAMAICA (1949–)   African Caribbean/American short story writer, novelist, and essayist. Jamaica Kincaid is one of the most important and original voices of Caribbean **postcolonialism** and postmodernism. Born Cynthia Elaine Potter Richardson, on the tiny island of Antigua (then a British colony) in the West Indies, Kincaid left at age seventeen to work as an au pair in New York. Observing the lives of the wealthy, white, privileged "conquerors" of the world, her sense of being one of the conquered, colonized, exploited, and oppressed became acute. She soon began speaking frankly, dressing outrageously, and living fearlessly as a starving freelance writer until she became a staff writer for *The New Yorker* in 1976, where she worked until 1995. She currently lives in Vermont with her husband and two children.

Kincaid began her fiction writing career as the author of "Girl," a one-long-sentence short story. Her fiction is set in either Antigua or Dominica, her mother's island of origin. *At the Bottom of the River* (1985), a collection of short stories, brought her to the attention of the reading public. From this first collection to her most recent novel, *Mr. Potter* (2002), Kincaid has continued to blur the line between fiction and autobiography. Her characters are identifiable members of her family—or her employers, in the case of the novel *Lucy* (1991). Events and entire passages are repeated from novel to novel, from nonfiction to fiction, sometimes but not always from different points of view. Kincaid's entire oeuvre is an elaborate creation of a history for a family (her family) and a people (Antiguan descendents of slaves) not part of official history. Her style is unique, characterized by short sentences, frequent repetition of words and phrases, and frequent use of parenthetical expressions. Often approaching her subject obliquely, beginning with a long list of things that it is not, Kincaid also takes on the postmodernist project of revealing the void that language disguises. By acknowledging the impossibility of describing experience through language, by admitting that even those events that truly happened are linguistic creations, Kincaid implies that all histories are linguistic constructions and must be evaluated for their constructive or destructive effects.

Annie John (1985), Kincaid's first (highly autobiographical) novel, describes an unusually strong child/mother dyad that breaks up when the title character approaches adolescence. Her mother's shocking betrayal results in the seventeen-year-old Annie leaving Antigua for England. The story both describes an intensely intimate mother/daughter relationship and acts as a metonymy for Antigua's dependent relationship with the colonizing British. *My Brother* (1997), a nonfiction account of Kincaid's visits back to Antigua as her youngest brother was dying of AIDS, reveals the source of Annie John's emotional catastrophe in Kincaid's own life as being the birth of her three younger brothers beginning when she was already nine years old. She felt immediately devalued by her mother and stepfather as being only a daughter, and was forced to drop out of school to take care of her young siblings.

As a postcolonial author, among Kincaid's major themes are the devastating long-term consequences of **slavery** and colonization. Kincaid never flinches at looking straight at her subjects and describing them with a graphic matter-of-factness. In *My Brother,* her portrayal of Devon's AIDS-ravaged body, his nonchalance at spreading the disease to others, and the nonexistent medical care at what passes for a hospital, are vivid laments for the meaningless lives and senseless deaths of the postcolonials who have limited perspective on their own situations. *A Small Place* (1988), a long nonfiction essay, reveals the author's deep, personal, but outspoken hatred toward the slave traders and slave owners, the British colonizers, the present free but corrupt government of Antigua, and the tourists who admire the natural beauty of Antigua but display the cultural blindness and arrogance of first-world colonizers to a people they consider inferior.

Mr. Potter (2002), Kincaid's latest novel, imagines the life of her father, whom she only met as an adult. Like *My Brother,* it is an indictment of the ignorance and lack of perspective of both the formerly enslaved and colonized and of the European and Middle-Eastern immigrants to Antigua. Being poor and illiterate, Mr. Potter knows almost nothing about history, geography, and current events. A Czechoslovak survivor of the **Holocaust** sees only blank ignorance in Mr. Potter, and cannot fathom any similarities in their situations—and neither can Mr. Potter. Like his own father, Mr. Potter has many children he does not love or even know, with many different women. Lack of paternal and maternal love, a legacy of slavery and poverty, is Mr. Potter's only inheritance and only legacy to his children.

In perhaps her most accomplished novel to date, *Autobiography of My Mother* (1996), the main character, like Mr. Potter, is a spiritual and cultural (as well as actual) orphan, but unlike Mr. Potter, she is acutely aware of her circumstances. Xuela Claudette Richardson experiences the world as composed of only victims and victimizers. As a postmodern subject, she rebels against identifying with any and every dominant discourse. Descended from Carib Indians, African slaves, and European colonizers, she positions herself as one of the disinherited, the disenfranchised, and the defeated and refuses to pass on the legacy by refusing to bear children. She cannot identify with the victors and refuses to become a victim. She sees her self-imposed exclusion and alienation as a victory over history, and although this everlasting "No" has saved her from a false identity created by others, it has restricted her ability to be fully human.

Kincaid's incantatory poetic style and her unflinching, unmasking gaze into the deepest levels of the psyche as a product of history ensure her place as a pivotal Caribbean author of the late-twentieth and early twenty-first centuries. (*See also* Caribbean American [Anglophone] Novel)

Further Reading

Bloom, Harold, ed. *Jamaica Kincaid.* Philadelphia: Chelsea House, 1998.

Paravisini-Gilbert, Lizabeth. *Jamaica Kincaid: A Critical Companion.* Critical Companions to Popular Contemporary Writers. Series ed. Kathleen Gregory Klein. Westport, CT: Greenwood Press, 1999.

Barbara Z. Thaden

KING, MARTIN LUTHER, JR. (1929–1968)   African American Baptist minister, civil rights leader of the 1950s and 1960s, orator, essayist, and winner of the 1964 Nobel Prize for Peace. From a family tradition of preaching from both his father's and mother's sides, King was exposed to Christian values and African American Baptist pulpit oratory since his childhood. His relentless struggle for social justice continued a long tradition of protest in African American letters and ensured him a prominent place in the pantheon of American history. In his many speeches and writings, he consistently capitalized on the power of language to effect change and alter the course of history. He potently used strategies of black folk preaching such as call-and-response, rhythmic and dramatic oratory, and typology at the same time generously invoking biblical figures and ideas, African American history and literature, and world and American political history. These elements are notably reflected in three generally celebrated texts, "Letter from Birmingham City Jail," "I Have a Dream," and "I've Been to the Mountaintop."

King wrote "Letter from Birmingham City Jail" on April 16, 1963, as a reply to an open letter by eight white Alabama clergymen who had called upon his nonviolent resistance movement to let local and federal courts deal with the issues of integration in order to avoid inciting civil unrest. He argued that he was prompted by Christian values in his fight for social justice and that American democracy and morality were at stake. He repeatedly reaffirmed that his struggle was anchored in Christian love, brotherhood, and nonviolence.

"I Have a Dream" is King's most celebrated speech. He delivered it on the steps of the Lincoln Memorial on August 28, 1963. The speech fittingly opens with the invocation of Abraham Lincoln, who signed the Emancipation Proclamation in 1863, King's reminder to America that "one hundred years later" (repeated four times) the promise of the Proclamation has not become a reality for African Americans, who, in spite of the Thirteenth, Fourteenth, and Fifteenth Amendments as well as several civil rights acts and the 1954 Supreme Court decision known as *Brown v. Board of Education*, are still victims of violence, segregation, discrimination, and disenfranchisement. He stresses that his struggle is rooted not in "bitterness and hatred" and violence but in Christian love, brotherhood, and nonviolence even in the face of police brutality, generalized injustice, and fatigue. The "I Have a Dream" part envisions an America where the "self-evident" truth of equality and the "unalienable rights of life, liberty, and the pursuit of happiness" will also be a reality for African Americans, and where brotherhood, freedom, justice, and Christian love will triumph. Invoking the words of a Negro spiritual ("free at last"), he projects an Edenic vision by reiterating his belief in the "land of liberty" and his dream that one day all God's children, black and white, of all religious creeds, will be united in freedom regained.

In "I've Been to the Mountaintop," a speech he delivered at the Mason Temple in Memphis, Tennessee, on April 3, 1968, King urged African Americans to be Good Samaritans and support the roadside victims—the garbage workers on strike. He called on African Americans to work together to defeat the modern Pharaoh's attempt to keep them enslaved, arguing that the collective power of black Americans could be used to oppose injustice and violence, achieve victory, and effect change in hiring practices by some companies and by the local government. King ended his speech by suggesting that despite threats on his life, he did not fear for his life. In spite of the general apocalyptic tone of the speech, he compared himself with Moses and asserted that he had been to the mountaintop and had seen the glory of God and the Promised Land of liberty, freedom, and justice for all even though he may not get there with the rest of his listeners. He was assassinated the next day.

At a difficult time when other black leaders had given up on acceptance by white America and were instead promoting black nationalism, King's message of love, hope, inclusion, and racial equality inspired the nation and the world, and the words of this prophet of peace still resonate today with the same compelling voice. (*See also* Civil Rights Movement)

Further Reading

Hansen, Drew W. *Martin Luther King, Jr. and the Speech That Inspired a Nation.* New York: Ecco, 2003.

Miller, Keith D. *Voice of Deliverance: The Language of Martin Luther King, Jr. and Its Sources.* Athens: UP of Georgia, 1998.

Aimable Twagilimana

KING, THOMAS (1943–) Cherokee, Greek, German American writer and critic. Both as an academic and as a teller of **trickster** stories, King counts to the most influential voices of native literature in North America. Thomas King grew up with his Greek German mother in an urban environment, but spent much time with his Cherokee relatives in their community. He continues to move between native and Western cultures, feeling at home in both, and critical toward neither. After receiving a doctorate in English, King has taught at a number of American and Canadian universities, adding to his fiction writing numerous critical works and anthologies that focus on the situation of native literature. Born an American but now Canadian, King looks beyond the arbitrary boundaries of contemporary political borders when analyzing the cultural consequences of the arrival of the European colonizers in North America. Indeed, his rather loose affiliation with his own indigenous roots has given him the liberty to write about native life in general, without specifying the idiosyncrasies of individual Indian nations; an approach that has also spurned critical reactions. His highly humorous style allows King to address painful and difficult topics in a manner that speaks to a wide audience.

In his first novel, *Medicine River* (1989), King uses a small town as the background for a description of the contemporary life of native peoples. Returning to Medicine River after many years in Toronto, the protagonist, Will, soon finds himself lured into staying in the community, starting the town's first native photography store. Focusing on work, love, basketball, and family, the novel emphasizes that native life follows the same trajectories that determine all human cultures. Foreshadowing much of King's later writing, *Medicine River* features an artist coming home after having lived away from his native environment, bringing back with him an aesthetic means of healing. Here and elsewhere, King tells his story on many temporal layers, juxtaposing then and now, often interrupting a story about the present with an anecdotal paragraph set in the past, thus emphasizing not only the importance of history for an understanding of the present, but also the circularity of time, the repetitiveness of life. This strategy also implies that the key to the future lies hidden in the past and that only careful consideration of our background will enable us to make appropriate decisions about the future. In its humanistic approach to general problems of human life, such as the search for a partner or the bonds to parents, *Medicine River* offers allegorical comments about humanity delivered through the means of traditional native storytelling. The attraction of the novel lies more with its pace and witty commentary on life than with a strong narrative drive.

One Good Story, That One (1993) is a collection of short narratives, many of which employ the coyote as the mythological trickster figure responsible not only for creating confusion in human life, but also for pointing out potential ways of healing for the traumatized indigenous populations. In "Borders," King presents an ironic portrayal of the political borders that cut through native spaces. The story has a native woman travel from Canada to the United States in order to visit her daughter. At the border, she declares herself to belong to the Blackfoot nation, which leads to her being stranded between the Canadian and American border stations, a no-man's land that comments on the disenfranchised real life of many native peoples. In "Totem," a museum is haunted by the magical appearance of totem poles. Even though they are cut down, the poles resurface soon after, making their presence felt by laughing, singing, or shouting. The museum director is disturbed by these specters of native culture, but finally (and characteristically for the established art world) decides simply to ignore them. A similar lack of understanding about the significance of native culture leads to more comical confusion in "How Corporal Colin Sterling Saved Blossom, Alberta, and Most of the Rest of the World as Well." For unknown reasons, all the native people in the story undergo a process of paralysis, leaving the local police officer, Corporal Sterling, confused and helpless. Finally, spaceships filled with blue coyote-like creatures appear to carry the stiff natives away, raising the question of whether the native and the Western culture can live together in one country. Corporal Sterling's interpretation of the events functions as a means of satirizing the prejudices that characterize the way native people are seen in contemporary life, dominated by clichés of alcohol abuse, unreliability, and general helplessness. That native culture is not, and has never been, in need of Western redemption also lies at the center of "A Coyote Columbus Story," a retelling of the "discovery" of America that states that both the continent and the native peoples "were never lost," and thus were not in need of being "found" by European discoverers.

In *Green Grass, Running Water* (1993), King continues the process of rewriting history. Throughout the novel, coyote is trying to recount the story of the beginning of time, blending **Native American creation myths** and the accounts set down in Genesis. At the same time, the novel tells of four escaped ancient native elders who roam the continent "fixing things." In the most memorable moment, they magically reverse the final scene of a Western movie so that the white cowboys and soldiers, led by John Wayne, end up dead after a conflict with an Indian tribe, leaving one of the salespersons wondering: "Who would want to kill John Wayne?" Yet another narrative level deals with the everyday lives of five native characters: Alberta teaches at a university and is trying to have a child, unable to decide which of her two lovers, Charlie or Lionel, to choose as a father. Charlie works as a lawyer; Lionel sells televisions. Latisha owns the Dead Dog Café, which pretends to offer dog food, using tourists' preconceived ideas about native diet as an ironic marketing tool. She still suffers from the abuse of her former husband and tries to bring up her three children. Finally, Eli, a retired University of Toronto professor, has returned to his hometown to live in his mother's cabin. He has managed to bring a dam project to a standstill, insisting on his rights to remain in his house, which sits in the dam's prospective spillway. At the end of the novel, an earthquake, caused by coyote singing and dancing a little, cracks the dam open, putting an end to the project as well as washing away the cabin and Eli. King's novel shows how important it is to continue traditions, stresses the value of telling stories, and provides an example of people who have been wronged finding justice. His characters are tenderly portrayed, shown with all their flaws, but given the opportunity to grow and learn. Once again, King writes about the flow of time, already hinted at by the metaphorical title, and about the essential sameness of all human life.

With *Truth and Bright Water* (1999), King returns to the question of borders. Set in the neighboring communities of Truth, a small American town, and the Canadian reserve Bright Water, the novel marks a unique territory for native peoples within the cultural and political geography of contemporary North America. The character who best represents the overall thrust of the novel is the artist Monroe Swimmer, who returns from life in the metropolis to reshape the lives of his relatives. In one of his projects of reclamation, he paints buildings so that they become invisible before the skyline. Starting with the church, signifying the religious colonization of the native metaphysical space, he later moves on to deal with a boarding school, another notorious location for programs of cultural indoctrination. Swimmer also reintroduces the buffalo into the prairies in the form of sculptures. While his actions are mostly symbolic, they emphasize the need to look into both the traditional values of native peoples and the possibilities of contemporary art to heal the trauma caused by the loss of native lands and cultures. The novel also tells of the adventures of Lum and Tecumseh, two young cousins, through one summer. Both boys struggle with the tensions in their families, their dreams of future achievements, and their wish to be integrated into their local community.

Further Reading

Davidson, Arnold E., Priscilla L. Walton, and Jennifer Andrews. *Border Crossings: Thomas Kings' Cultural Inversions.* Toronto: U of Toronto P, 2003.

Shackleton, Mark. "The Return of the Native American: The Theme of Homecoming in Contemporary Native American Fiction." *Atlantic Literary Review* 3.2 (April–June 2002): 155–64.

Gerd Bayer

KING, WOODIE, JR. (1937–)   African American theater personality, editor, producer, and drama critic. Although King has written a few short stories and plays, he is best known for the immensely important role he has played in the development of African American and multicultural drama since the 1960s.

King was born in Mobile, Alabama, and grew up in Detroit. After graduating from high school, he won a scholarship to the prestigious Will-O-Way School of the Theatre in 1958. Four years later he enrolled at Wayne State University, where he did graduate work in theater for four semesters. While receiving formal training in theater arts, King realized the limited options and venues available to black playwrights and actors. This recognition led to his lifelong commitment to the advancement of African American theater.

In 1960 King became the founding member of the Concept-East Theatre; as its director, he staged several short plays inside a Detroit bar. In 1964 he moved to New York City, where he became a forceful presence in the theater scene. In 1966 he successfully adapted **Langston Hughes**'s collection of poetry, *The Weary Blues* (1926), for stage performance. The following year he adapted Hughes's collection of short stories, *The Best of Simple* (1961), for theatrical production.

King's major success came in 1969. He produced *A Black Quartet,* four one-act plays by four major black playwrights of the sixties: **Amiri Baraka, Ed Bullins, Ben Caldwell,** and **Ron Milner.** The following year King founded the New Federal Theatre in New York City. He actively began to mount not only works by African American artists but other ethnic American playwrights as well. This theater remains King's monumental contribution to contemporary multicultural American drama.

In addition, King is a tireless editor. The numerous anthologies that he has edited or coedited showcase the works of an impressive range of dramatists. He has also written teleplays and scripts for television sitcoms, and has produced several documentaries. His scholarly work titled *Black Theatre Present Condition* (1981) remains an indispensable text for students interested in the development of African American drama during the eventful 1960s and 1970s.

Further Reading

Vallilo, Stephen M. "Woodie King, Jr." *Dictionary of Literary Biography.* Vol. 38. Ed. Thadious M. Davis and Trudier Harris. Detroit: Gale, 1985. 170–74.

Emmanuel S. Nelson

KINGSTON, MAXINE HONG (1940–)   Chinese American novelist, creative nonfiction writer, and essayist. Maxine Hong Kingston is known for her compelling literary works that incorporate the long ignored history of Chinese Americans along with her remembrances of her family and ethnic community. Kingston is one of the writers whose works help to build up the foundation of Asian American literature and enable it to be acknowledged as a valued part of American literature. Her writing has inspired younger generations of writers to continue to explore individual struggles over **identity** construction, family stories, and community histories. Written in the genres of fiction and nonfiction, her works have inspired discussion about literary genres and have drawn attention to her insightful and comprehensive illumination of immigrant experiences in America. Her innovative writing has demonstrated the possibility to redefine memoirs and fiction through creating an invented form of narrative, empowered by elements of history, biography, memory, legend, folktale, myth, and anecdote. The complexity and multiplicity of Kingston's books resist the categorization of any single genre or traditionally defined classification, thus shedding new light on American literature.

No other literary works by Asian American writers have achieved as wide acceptance from general audiences and acclaim from critics as *The Woman Warrior* (1976). This book is estimated to be "the most anthologized of

Maxine Hong Kingston. *AP/Wide World Photos.*

any living American writer" and is read by "more American college students than any other living author" (Skenazy and Martin vii). Frequently discussed together with works by such prominent Latina, Native, and African American writers as **Gloria Anzaldúa**, **Leslie Marmon Silko**, and **Toni Morrison**, this book has contributed to the appropriation of oral literature as a medium to inherit, transmit, and invent cultural memory through creating a new American literary form. The debate on the (mis)representation of Chinese tradition and Chinese American culture in Kingston's works has incurred long-lasting interest among scholars and students of ethnic American literature. *The Woman Warrior* and *China Men* (1980) have added the phrase "talk story" into American literary tradition and English vocabulary. Through reshaping the "talk stories" based on her mother's tales, the Chinese community's anecdotes, cultural memory, and Kingston's own experience of growing up with a double heritage, she engages with both her Chinese ancestry and her American presence and seeks for a balance between gender and **ethnicity**. Her writing covers a broad range of themes that are crucial to ethnic literature in particular and hold universal appeal in general. Another book by Kingston that defies categorization is her limited edition work *To Be the Poet* (2002), integrating poetry, essays, and her personalized illustrations.

Born in 1940 in Stockton, California, Maxine Ting Ting Hong was Chinese immigrants Tom Hong's and Ying Lan Chew's first American-born child. Tom was a professional scholar in his home village of Sun Woi, near Canton, before he migrated to America in 1925. In Stockton, Tom worked as manager of a gambling house and then opened his New Port Laundry. His story has been integrated into *China Men*, where Kingston challenges her father's silence through imagining and reshaping his experiences. Shortly after Tom's departure, their two children died young; Chew went to To Keung School of Midwifery in Canton where she received medical training. She later became a doctor and practitioner in her home village. After a fifteen-year separation, Chew was able to join her husband in America, where she worked hard in different jobs helping to support her family. As the principal storyteller in the Hong household, Chew employed her talk stories to transmit Chinese tradition and moral values to her American-born children. The narratives, together with ethical and pedagogic codes, which Kingston received from her mother in childhood, have been embedded in a variety of forms in her writing.

Because Kingston grew up among Chinese immigrants, her first language was Say Yup, a dialect of Cantonese. The Chinese community in the San Joaquin Valley, where Kingston spent her childhood, was an enclave where people knew one another well and exchanged gossip frequently. The warning against misbehavior, which Brave Orchid emphasizes through her story of the "No Name Woman" in *The Woman Warrior,* provides a mirror image of such a close-knit environment. The communal talk stories thus became a rich source of materials that Kingston could reshape and recreate in her memoirs and novel.

Kingston was barely fluent in English at the beginning of her school life. The wordless Chinese American girl in *The Woman Warrior* and the metaphor of the "black curtain" in her limited edition book *Through the Black Curtain* (1987) reflect the young narrator's anxiety about gaining a voice to break the profound silence for herself and for her community. Kingston earned her BA in English from the University of California at Berkeley, where she participated in protests against the Vietnam War and in other political movements in the sixties and met her future husband Earll Kingston. The Kingstons moved to Hawai'i in 1967 and remained there for seventeen years, leading a life that followed their pacifist ideals. Essays collected in *Hawaii One Summer, 1978* (1987) reflect a variety of aspects in her Hawaiian life. Kingston also embeds her life and thoughts over the years of activism and pacifism in her novel *Tripmaster Monkey* (1989) and her recent book *The Fifth Book of Peace* (2003).

China Men (1980)

If *The Woman Warrior* focuses on female narrative of history, memory, and story, *China Men* appears to be a parallel book that honors the male characters' familial and communal experiences. Although it is not canonized, as is *The Woman Warrior, China Men* has gained lavish praise and acceptance from readers and critics, becoming a landmark in Asian American tradition as another book of "mixed genre." It opens in the mid-nineteenth century, roughly the historical period of Chinese immigrants' large-scale arrival in America. In her storytelling and imagination, Kingston portrays the great-grandfathers, grandfathers, fathers, and brothers as heroic characters in order to correct the usually demeaning image of Chinese men in America. By bridging China and America through the history and stories of her family's men, she claims her ancestors' contributions to the development of America and adds another hue to the multicolored portrait of American history.

China Men is composed of six narratives about her male kin, which are interlaced with twelve brief mythical or historical vignettes. "The Father from China" chronicles her father's (BaBa) life as a cherished baby, a smart student, and then a scholar in his home village in feudal China. "The Great Grandfather of the Sandalwood Mountains" is the story of Bak Goong, who works on sugar cane plantations in Hawai'i. "The Grandfather of the Sierra Nevada Mountains" tells the experiences of Ah Goong as a coolie in the transcontinental railroad camps. "The Making of More Americans" portrays a group of male relatives' who have journeyed to America. In "The American Father," BaBa (now called *Ed*) is a laborer doing menial jobs, then a gambling house manager, and finally the owner of a laundry. "The Brother in Vietnam" concludes the odyssey of her kinsmen toward becoming American by recollecting her California-born brother's story as a Vietnam veteran. The brief tales and vignettes interspersed between chapters introduce and contextualize personal, familial, and communal history.

Tripmaster Monkey: His Fake Book (1989)

After two books published as nonfiction, *Tripmaster Monkey* is considered Kingston's first fiction. The reviews and critical responses toward her third book are mostly positive. Diverging from the first-person narrative that dominates her first two books, the story in *Tripmaster Monkey* is told by an omniscient narrator. Shifting from the concern about family and community history, Kingston's novel knits multiple elements around one man's "show." The protagonist, Wittman Ah Sing, a California native and fifth-generation Chinese American in his twenties, seeks his **identity** with his Chinese heritage and American rearing in the roaring political context of the sixties in San Francisco. The characters who surround Wittman are his mother, Ruby Long Legs (a former Flora Dora Girl); his father, Zeppelin Ah Sing (a theater electrician); his wife-to-be, Taña (a painter); among others, all of whom make up the mosaic of the multicultural environment of the American West Coast at the time. These people become the cast of Wittman's play in the book, a performance of multiculture in theater and reality. Wittman is portrayed as a person dwelling between boundaries: cultural, ethnic, and artistic. He holds a BA in English and is also fluent in Chinatown patois. For him, being bilingual is a symbol of his bicultural identity. The manipulation of language, including storytelling and stage performing, is the medium of Wittman's identity pursuit. The denouement is marked by the antihero's unpunctuated monologue.

Instead of Chinese or Chinese American, Kingston's third book receives literary nourishment from a global context. It is enriched by appropriation of such sources as the Chinese mythological Monkey King, an allusion to American poet Walt Whitman and his "Song of Myself," and the rich symbolism and complex structure based on the works of Latin American author Gabriel García Márquez. Like the Monkey King who is the prominent characterization of rebellion, Wittman, a draft dodger, an actor, a playwright, and unemployed, represents a phenomenal image. The play Wittman is developing throughout the book is reminiscent of stories of the bandits in *The Water Margin* as well as the historical legend of the three sworn brothers of the peach garden from *Romance of the Three Kingdoms,* but his play nonetheless has an innovation style reflecting the sixties and Wittman's own rumination of **identity** and **ethnicity**.

The Fifth Book of Peace (2003)

Kingston begins her recent publication with an autobiographical account titled "Fire" that echoes the loss of her fourth book-in-progress, together with her Oakland house and possessions, in a fire in 1991. The second chapter "Paper" interlaces factual and fictional accounts of the mystical "three books of peace" from ancient China. It is followed by a long section called "Water" that chronicles the adventures of Wittman Ah Sing, together with his wife, Taña, and son, in Hawai'i, demonstrating continuity with and development of her novel. The concluding chapter, "Earth," records Kingston's journey with a group of Vietnam veterans to an international Buddhist community in France where they meet expatriate Vietnamese nuns and monks. Written in a space between fiction and nonfiction, Kingston's new book is concerned with political matters centered on peace that are more universal than ethnic. Another experiment in literary form, it not only traverses the boundaries between autobiography and novel as well as between the journalist and the imaginary, this work also plays with continuity and innovation based on her earlier writing. (*See also* Chinese American Autobiography, Chinese American Novel)

Further Reading

Huntley, E. D. *Maxine Hong Kingston: A Critical Companion.* Westport, CT: Greenwood Press, 2001.

Li, David Leiwei. "*China Men:* Maxine Hong Kingston and the American Canon." *American Literary History* 2.3 (Autumn 1990): 482–502.

Linton, Patricia. "'What Stories the Wind Would Tell': Representation and Appropriation in Maxine Hong Kingston's *China Men.*" *MELUS* 19.4 (Winter 1994): 37–48.

Nishime, LeiLani. "Engendering Genre: Gender and Nationalism in *China Men* and *The Woman Warrior.*" *MELUS* 20.1 (Spring 1995): 67–82.

Skandera-Trombley, Laura E., ed. *Critical Essays on Maxine Hong Kingston.* New York and London: Prentice Hall International, 1998.

Skenazy, Paul, and Tera Martin, eds. *Conversations with Maxine Hong Kingston.* Jackson: U of Mississippi P, 1998.

Slowik, Mary. "When the Ghosts Speak: Oral and Written Narrative Forms in Maxine Hong Kingston's *China Men.*" *MELUS* 19.1 (Spring 1994): 73–88.

Shu, Yuan. "Cultural Politics and Chinese-American Female Subjectivity: Rethinking Kingston's *Woman Warrior.*" MELUS 26.2 (1987): 199–224.

Tanner, James T. F. "Walt Whitman's Presence in Maxine Hong Kingston's *Tripmaster Monkey: His Fake Book.*" *MELUS* 20. 4 (Winter 1995): 61–74.

Williams, A. Noelle. "Parody and Pacifist Transformations in Maxine Hong Kingston's *Tripmaster Monkey: His Fake Book.*" *MELUS* 20.1 (Spring 1995): 83–100.

Wong, Sau-Ling Cynthia. "Necessity and Extravagance in Maxine Hong Kingston's *The Woman Warrior*: Art and the Ethnic Experience." *MELUS* 15.1 (Spring 1988): 3–26.

Woo, Deborah. "Maxine Hong Kingston: the Ethnic Writer and the Burden of Dual Authenticity." *Amerasia Journal* 16.1 (1990): 173–200.

Lan Dong

KIRCHNER, BHARTI (1940–) South Asian American writer and cookbook author. Born in Calcutta, Kirchner came to the United States to pursue further studies; she is now settled in Seattle. Originally trained as a mathematician and professionally a computer programmer, Kirchner began writing in earnest in 1990 when she left her job with a major multinational corporation to devote herself to her present career.

A prolific and award-winning author of numerous articles and books on cooking, Kirchner, in *The Healthy Cuisine of India* (1992), joins an emphasis on healthy cooking with an introduction of Bengali cuisine to a Western audience. In her *The Indian Inspired Cookbook, International Table* (1993), she retains a focus on low-fat cooking while emphasizing the blending of diverse cuisines to produce eclectic dishes. Kirchner has to her credit *The Bold Vegetarian* (1995) as well as *Vegetarian Burgers* (1996) as well.

The fictional works of Kirchner frequently provide for an entertaining and captivating reading experience. Food and cuisine as cultural symbols are important to her latest novel *Pastries: A Novel of Desserts and Discoveries* (2003). In *Pastries,* the young protagonist, Sunya, who has grown up in Seattle, questions the authenticity and origin of her Indian self. The answers appear to lie in the focus on the process of life itself. A common preoccupation of South Asian American literature—that of the relation between place and **identity**—is further complicated and made more intriguing in this otherwise light novel by the weaving of Japanese cultural elements with Indian ones.

Earlier, in *Darjeeling* (2001), Kirchner continued the investigation into the bases of South Asian women's ethnic identity in America that she had begun in her first two novels, *Shiva Dancing* (1998) and *Sharmila's Book* (1999). In *Darjeeling,* the relationships between two sisters living in Canada and the United States and their grandmother living in Darjeeling are at the center of a plot that is geared toward the discovery of one's self in the New World alongside origins in the tea estate world of Darjeeling. The author's interest in cooking is evident in the narrative details. In *Sharmila's Book,* the issues of arranged marriage and inter-caste relationships provide for a textured narrative on the topic of the protagonist's attempt to negotiate her position as a South Asian immigrant woman. In her very first novel, *Shiva Dancing,* Kirchner makes transparent the concern with identity-formation by having her protagonist, Meena, be kidnapped, away from her parents and place of birth. She is rescued from her captors by an American couple that brings Meena to San Francisco and raises her. Kirchner's background in computers is evident, as Meena succeeds in tracing her roots back to her childhood using the Internet. However, upon discovering her origins and the traditional woman's life that would have been hers had she not been kidnapped, she rejects that life and the notion that India could be "home." (*See also* South Asian American Literature)

Further Reading

Fry, Donn. "In Life and In Art: In Her First Work of Fiction, Bharti Kirchner Straddles Two Cultures." *Seattle Times* (March 15, 1998): 14.

Reale, Michelle. "Loss and Disappointment Lead to Personal Growth in Kirchner's Latest Novel." *India Currents* (September 3, 2003): 20.

Rubin, Merle. "Migration that Leads to Self-Discovery." *Christian Science Monitor* (March 10, 1998): 14.

Krishna Lewis

KLEIN, ABRAHAM MOSES (1909–1972) Jewish Canadian poet, writer, journalist, and lawyer. Considered one of the most prominent representatives of modern Canadian poetry and the "father" of Jewish Canadian literature, Klein also wrote numerous journalistic works and shorter fiction, translated Hebrew and Yiddish poetry, and published one novel. The relation of the individual and the community and the question of Jewish identity remained his main concerns throughout his work.

Born in Ratno, Ukraine, in 1909 into an Orthodox family that immigrated to Canada probably in the following year, Klein grew up in Montreal's Jewish workers' district. There, experiencing the interface of the anglophone and francophone Canadian cultures, his Jewish heritage and the social tensions of the Great Depression, he was confronted, early on, with the intricacies of a multiethnic society.

After his graduation with a BA from McGill University (in 1930), Klein studied law at the francophone Université de Montréal, which he practiced from 1933. During his time at McGill, Klein published his first poems and became associated with the Montreal Group of poets and writers (among them A. J. M. Smith, F. R. Scott, Leo Kennedy, and Leon Edel) and from then also dates his active interest in Zionism. Later, he was editor of the *Canadian Jewish Chronicle* (1938–55) and was politically active in the Cooperative Commonwealth Federation (CCF; later the New Democratic Party). Having suffered increasingly from mental illness, Klein retired in 1956, withdrew from public life, and ceased writing.

His first collection of poetry, *Hath Not a Jew . . .* (1940), is a document of Klein's critical engagement with Jewish culture. In "Childe Harold's Pilgrimage," he grapples with his doubts concerning the Orthodox faith of his father; in the sequence "Out of the Pulver and the Polished Lens," which is sometimes considered to be his masterpiece, Klein reflects in a variety of poetic forms on Baruch Spinoza's renunciation of Judaism and his turning toward pantheism; Klein's growing unease with regard to the Fascist threat to Jewish existence informs "The Heirloom." In *Poems* (1944), he was to explore further the Jewish question, as he did in his mock epic *The Hitleriad* (1944), which has been much criticized for its attempt to address the emergence of Adolf Hitler in a satire in heroic couplets. In his last collection of poems, *The Rocking Chair and Other Poems* (1948), for which Klein was presented with the prestigious Governor General's Award, the poet concentrates on Quebec, exploring both rural and urban life (as in the bilingual "Montreal") and addressing the problems of the first nations within multicultural Canadian society (in "Indian Reservation: Caughnawaga").

Klein's only published novel, *The Second Scroll* (1951), combines in its main narrative text and the appended commentaries in the Talmudic tradition many aspects of his earlier work. In the novel, a Jewish-born journalist from Montreal, sent to Israel to cover the emergence of the literature of the new state, makes his journey a quest for his uncle Melech, a survivor of the **Holocaust**, whom he follows from Bari and Rome to Casablanca, and, finally, to Israel. But the ever-elusive Melech Davidson, whose name is a messianic allusion and who is meant to be taken as the embodiment of the paradigm of Jewish **diaspora** existence, dies in Israel before his nephew can meet him. However, witnessing Melech's funeral, he is reassured that Melech has now found his final rest in Israel as have, in another sense, the Jewish people.

Two years later, Klein was to pick up this metaphor again in "In Praise of the Diaspora (An Undelivered Memorial Address)" (1953). Acknowledging the vulnerability of the diaspora, of which the cataclysm of the Holocaust had been horrible proof, in his "eulogy" he now emphatically opposed the alleged negation of the diaspora put forward by the "new"' Israeli Jews, and their claims to the exclusive authenticity of their "Jewish" **identity**. Instead, he suggests the diaspora to have been, and to continue to be, a formative experience and inspiration of Jewish life. Yet in spite of this criticism, Klein still believed in Jewish redemption willed by God acting in history of which the foundation of the State of Israel was visible proof to him.

Further Reading

Fischer, Gretl K. *In Search of Jerusalem: Religion and Ethics in the Writings of A. M. Klein.* Montreal: McGill-Queen's UP, 1975.

Hyman, Roger. *Aught from Naught: A. M. Klein's The Second Scroll.* Victoria, BC: U of Victoria P, 1999.

Mayne, Seymor, ed. *The A. M. Klein Symposium.* Ottawa: U of Ottawa P, 1975.

Axel Stähler

KLEPFISZ, IRENA (1941–) Jewish American feminist poet and essayist who writes out of an intense empathy for the oppressed. As the child of victims of Nazi persecution—her father died fighting in the Warsaw Uprising in 1943—she brings the same intensity of memory to the cause of Palestinians in the West Bank and Gaza under Israeli military occupation, to that of women victimized by partners, to the destruction of language and tradition, and to the anguish of the natural world. Klepfisz is a Jewish lesbian antiwar activist, a faculty member at Barnard, a bilingual poet (Yiddish-English), and an anti-Zionist who is fighting for a more secure Israel—in short, a mass of contradictions.

Irena Klepfisz was born in Warsaw, Poland, in 1941. On April 20, 1943, her father, Michal, flung himself on a German machine-gun nest to stop it from trapping a group of Jewish rebels under fire in an attic. Klepfisz spent part of the rest of the war in an orphanage and part in hiding with her mother, Rose, who held false Aryan papers. In 1946 they moved to Sweden and in 1949 to the Bronx, New York, where they lived near her father's old comrades of the Jewish Labor Bund.

Educated in New York City schools, Klepfisz went on to teach both in the Labor Bund's elementary and middle schools and at Barnard. In 1989 Klepfisz colloborated with Melanie Kaye/Kantrowitz to edit *The Tribe of Dina: A Jewish Women's Anthology* (Beacon Press), which included her own essay on nonreligious Jewish ethnic **identity**, "Yidishkayt in America," as well as her translations of a story and a poem by Yiddish writer Fredel Schtok. The year 1990 saw the publication of her book *Dreams of an Insomniac: Jewish Feminist Essays, Speeches, and Diatribes* (Portland, Oregon: Eighth Mountain Press). In 1991, Klepfisz published a poetry collection, *A Few Words in the Mother Tongue: Poems Selected and New 1971–1990* (Eighth Mountain Press).

In the 1970s, Klepfisz wrote both poetry and prose primarily out of the experience of being Jewish and a lesbian. Taken collectively, her work in that period constitutes the foundation of a structure covering the nature of oppression, victimization, and resistance. One of her most enduring images is that of the ape family in the zoo, the combination of confinement and exposure mirroring the psychological effects of the ghetto and concentration camp, the sexual "closet" and the public nature of "outing." She also deals with solidarity among women and the role of the woman poet in supporting and enabling it.

According to Klepfisz herself, the Israeli invasion of Lebanon in 1982 and the infamous slaughter of Palestinian women and children under Ariel Sharon's command in the Sabra and Shatila refugee camps altered her view of Israel and the consciousness of the Jewish people. She came to believe that Israel had become aggressor and oppressor and that Jews could no longer take comfort in the innocence of victimage. Later she visited the West Bank towns of Hebron and Ramallah and was shocked to see that these completely Arab communities were surrounded and controlled by Israeli troops, defeating the logic of the Israel she had known in the 1960s while staying on a kibbutz. When the first *intifada* (Palestinian uprising) began in 1987, she helped found the group Jewish Women's Committee to End the Occupation, which picketed in front of major Jewish organizations and then in front of Zabar's, a popular delicatessen on the "liberal" and heavily Jewish Upper West Side of Manhattan. Despite acrimonious debates on the street, Klepfisz's group has been credited with raising consciousness of the situation in Israel and Palestine. After a new *intifada* began in the fall of 2000, and especially after September 11 brought the United States more directly into the conflict, Klepfisz went back into the streets and the public forums and has again become a leading voice for peace, conciliation, and diplomacy in what is arguably the center of world war. She continues to insist, forcefully and eloquently, that the Palestinian people themselves, not Israel and not the United States, should lead in determining their own future and that this was the only secure route to peace in the region and in the world. (*See also* Jewish American Lesbian Literature)

Further Reading

Gubar, Susan. *Poetry After Auschwitz: Remembering What One Never Knew.* Jewish Literature and Culture Series. Bloomington: Indiana UP, 2003.

Hedley, Jane. "Nepantilist Poetics: Narrative and Cultural Identity in the Mixed Language Writings of Irena Klepfisz and Gloria Anzaldua." *Narrative* 4.1 (January 1996): 30–54.

Rothschild, Matthew. "*Israel Isn't David . . . It's Goliath.*" *The Progressive* (July 2001): 1–6.

Barry Fruchter

KNIGHT, ETHERIDGE (1931–1991) African American poet. One of seven children, Etheridge Knight was born in Corinth, Mississippi; his early years were shaped by the culture of the streets and bars. He was abusing drugs and alcohol even in his early teens and dropped out of school while in the eighth grade. After a stint in the army, which included time in Korea, Knight returned to civilian life in 1957 and embarked on a career in crime. He was sent to jail in 1960 for robbery and it was while in prison that he began to write poetry to heal his internal wounds, to communicate his feelings, and to create a sense of community among his fellow inmates. He met **Gwendolyn Brooks** when she came to read her poetry at the prison; she discovered his talent, actively encouraged him to write poetry, guided and advised him, and wrote the preface to his first collection of poetry, *Poems from Prison* (1968), which was published by the black-owned **Broadside Press** while he was still imprisoned. Shortly after his release from prison in 1968, he accepted a teaching position at the University of Pittsburgh. Subsequently, he taught at a number of other universities, including the University of Hartford and the historically black Lincoln University. He published four other volumes of poetry: *Black Voices from Prison* (1970), *Belly Song and Other Poems* (1973), *Born of a Woman* (1980), and *The Essential Etheridge Knight* (1986). As a poet who was also a brilliant performance artist, he was a sought-after speaker on college campuses and other venues. He received numerous awards, the most noteworthy being the Guggenheim Fellowship (1974)—the so-called genius award.

Knight was a self-taught poet. He extensively read the works of a number of major poets ranging from Walt Whitman and **Langston Hughes** to

Claude McKay and Robert Bly. What makes his poetry unique, however, is his seamless blending of African American vernacular traditions (such as toast, jive, **blues**) with the formal elements of Anglo-American poetry. One of his most frequently anthologized poems, "The Idea of Ancestry" (1968), for example, is an exquisitely crafted work that powerfully and poignantly explores the notion of ancestry in a specifically African American cultural context. Another popular poem by Knight is "I Sing of Shine" (1970), a celebratory toast to Shine, a folkloric **trickster** figure. A stoker on the ill-fated *Titanic,* Shine manages to swim to safety but not before he overcomes three obstacles: a white banker who offers him a million dollars in return for his help in fleeing the sinking ship; the banker's daughter who offers unlimited sex; and a white preacher who invokes the name of God. Shine rejects the offers and, in fact, cuts the throat of the preacher as he swims ashore, leaving the white folks to drown.

Though Knight was widely recognized as a people's poet and as an indispensable artist, his personal life remained deeply troubled. His drug addiction haunted him through much of his life; though he repeatedly sought treatment, he was unable to overcome his addiction permanently. He died at age fifty-nine.

Further Reading

Hill, Patricia Liggins. "'Blues for a Mississippi Black Boy': Etheridge Knight's Craft in the Black Oral Tradition." *Mississippi Quarterly* 36.1 (1982): 21–33.

Johnson, Thomas C. "Excerpts from Notes of an Oral Rhapsodist: An Introduction to the Poetry and Aesthetic of Etheridge Knight." *Worcester Review* 19.1–2 (1998): 79–83.

McKim, Elizabeth Gordon. "Freedom and Confinement." *Worcester Review* 19.1–2 (1998): 140–147.

Emmanuel S. Nelson

KOCH, KENNETH (1925–2002)   Jewish American poet. Kenneth Koch was one of the principal members of the artistic movement of the 1950s known as the "New York School," which also included poets **Frank O'Hara** and John Ashbery. Born in Cincinnati, Koch served in World War II and fought in the Philippines before attending Harvard and then Columbia University, where he earned his PhD. He then became a professor of English at Columbia and a very influential teacher of, and spokesman for, the art of poetic beauty. As part of the New York School, Koch was influenced by the painters of the period—experimental, abstract artists like Jackson Pollack and Willem de Kooning. He later collaborated with visual artists, and his own poetry sometimes stressed the graphic, as with the posthumously published *The Art of the Possible* (2004), where the medium of drawing becomes the essence of the expression.

Koch's work is best defined by its continually adventurous spirit, its search for the possibilities of art through poetry, as well as fiction, drama, and opera librettos. His poetry collections include *Ko: Or, A Season on Earth* (1959), *The Art*

Kenneth Koch. *Courtesy of the Library of Congress.*

of Love (1975), *From the Air* (1979), *One Train* (1994), and *New Addresses* (2000). Extending the influence of his own verse, Koch was a devoted teacher and his writings on poetry include *Wishes, Lies and Dreams: Teaching Children to Write Poetry* (1970) and *The Art of Poetry: Poems, Parodies, Interviews, Essays, and Other Work* (1997).

Koch's poems seem always to stress the capacities for arriving at, and acknowledging with exuberance, what we create. The New York School was avant-garde precisely because they willed new forms, and Koch used his innovations to find shape for human joy, abandon, and wonder. He became a master of many forms, from blank verse to the sestina. Whereas his infamous "Variations on a Theme by William Carlos Williams" was funny, hyperbolic, and playful, more often Koch's parodies were forms of expanding poetic possibility. Koch's parody was a means of extending the original, while demonstrating the original's limitations. His surrealist twists of language likewise sought to find the mystery and musical possibility hidden within the English language. For Koch, there was much to be found in the surprise of attending carefully to the arrangement of surfaces through colliding words and the sensations of experiencing poetry.

Although he is well known as a teacher of poetry to others, it can be said that at his best, Koch is a teacher in his poetry. The title poem of *One Train* speaks of the process whereby what *is* can obscure what *was* and suggests how the poet and poem might keep everything in view. The principle of the simultaneous—event following event, the world caught by the word—plays out through a litany of what might be obscured if we do not look carefully. Two trains, two lines of verse, two places; each one that is present perhaps blinding us to the possibility of the other—unless, says Koch, we are patient, we pause, we wait. The discovery, Koch writes, comes in the patience, which might let one see both past and present together. Thus he gives experience its joyous, wondered word in the poem that follows it. In the multiform cycle from the same collection, "On Aesthetics," Koch transforms simple observations into meditations on what we do and how we make our lives. His attention to the smallest, human gestures gives Koch's poetry the immediacy he was striving to create. To read the best of Koch's work is not to encounter his confessions or some inner life, but to see the shimmering beauty of the world and its language.

When he writes an address to an abstraction, as he does in works like "To World War Two," "To Psychoanalysis," or "To Jewishness," the principle is discovery. In the third of these, he writes of surprise and the magic quality of everyday events and sights, all of which are connected to the speaker's childhood. But these qualities are also essential to his poems. He teases out the resistance to religion while simultaneously expanding the limits of understanding. Koch uses the form of apostrophe less to express some necessary feeling, or to make a statement of his own perspective. Instead, the poem becomes an opportunity to reach out toward meaning and lend it shape. In Koch's poems, language is the path toward realization and recognition.

Further Reading

Hoover, Paul. "Fables of Representation: The Poetry of the New York School." *American Poetry Review* 30.4 (2002): 20–30.

Lehman, David. "Kenneth Koch: The Pleasures of Peace." *The Last Avant-Garde: The Making of the New York School of Poetry.* New York: Double Day, 1998. 203–42.

Daniel Listoe

KOESTENBAUM, WAYNE (1958–) Jewish American poet, essayist, novelist, and professor of English literature. Having earned an MFA in creative writing from the Johns Hopkins University and a PhD in English literature from Princeton University, Koestenbaum is presently a professor at the City University of New York. Known for his willingness to cross boundaries between disciplines and genres, he has distinguished himself not only as a teacher of literature but also as an award-winning poet, a lyrical essayist, and a provocative cultural biographer.

Since publishing the critical and popular success, *The Queen's Throat: Opera, Homosexuality, and the Mystery of Desire* (1993), he has become an active contributor to queer studies and theorizations of gay male **identity**. In this meditation on the intersection of art, sexuality, and the phenomenon of gay "opera queens" and diva worshippers, Koestenbaum writes in a style that will become his hallmark, a melding of the personal and the academic alongside a similar mingling of analysis of high art and mass culture.

A prolific poet and cultural critic, Koestenbaum blends erudition with pop culture savvy not only in *The Queen's Throat,* but also in volumes of poetry such as *Model Homes* (2004) and *The Milk of Inquiry* (2004) and irreverent works of biography such as his exploration of *Andy Warhol,* written for the Penguin Lives series, and *Jackie Under My Skin: Interpreting an Icon*

(1995), about the former first lady. Koestenbaum's *Model Homes* is his tribute to Byron. Using the nineteenth-century poet's famous eight-line rhyming iambic pentameter (known as *ottava rima*), Koestenbaum composes thirteen cantos in celebration of the gorgeous boredom of domestic life. In *Model Homes*, Koestenbaum plays with the Byronic mode by eschewing the Romantic poet's quest for heroism in favor of writing deadpan poems that imagine his own conception or that resurrect great meals from the past. In *The Milk of Inquiry*, another of Koestenbaum's volumes of poetry, he moves to an even more experimental level. In one long poem, "Metamorphoses (Masked Ball)," mythological figures such as Orpheus and Adonis don celebrity masks and perform a series of 115 risqué sonnets. Next to this magisterial work, the poet places spare lyrics and a lengthy poetic exploration of his childhood.

Koestenbaum gained acclaim for his genre-bending portraits of both artist and impresario Andy Warhol and former first lady Jacqueline Kennedy Onassis. In *Andy Warhol*, Koestenbaum provides an account not just of the trajectory of Warhol's artistic production but also takes the reader behind the scenes to see the Andy that was so carefully masked behind the blank Coca Cola bottles and Marilyn Monroe silk screens that occupied the artist's oeuvre. The cultural critic provides an image of Warhol as one of the most successful and prolific artists of the twentieth century *and* as a vanguard shaper of post–World War II popular culture. Koestenbaum's biography of Andy Warhol distinguishes itself from other histories of the 1960s icon by focusing on the films that Warhol produced at his "Factory" as central to his artistic project. As in *The Queen's Throat*, he provides an intimate glimpse into the queer iconography surrounding an art form and its appreciators. By doing so, Koestenbaum repudiates the claim made by a host of Warhol biographers that the artist was somehow asexual; instead, he argues that the icon's sexual identity, while sometimes enigmatic, was central to his art and life.

In *Jackie Under My Skin: Interpreting an Icon*, Koestenbaum maps evernewer terrain as a cultural commentator by providing a first-person account of his relationship with a distant icon. His biographical exercise takes as its point of origin the disjuncture between Jacqueline Kennedy Onassis, the deeply private individual, and Jackie O., the public figure. Koestenbaum provides an irreverent take on America's love affair with hyperfeminine icons such as Jackie O. By writing of the many objects and artifacts that devotees of the former first lady imbue with sacral power and meaning, he provides the reader with a beautifully written account of the cult of celebrity as a uniquely American phenomenon.

Koestenbaum also brings his poetic ear to *Cleavage* (2000), his collection of essays and fragments on fashion, celebrity, and growing up in America. Characterized by his playful relationship to language, Koestenbaum's essays extend from two-page riffs on his early memories of women's cleavage to detailed explorations of Oscar Wilde's trial and imprisonment. In

Cleavage, Koestenbaum takes on the issue of Jewish identity more explicitly than ever before. In the essay "Aryan Boy," he creates a beautiful homage to his father and an articulation of the complex connections between masculinity, homosexuality, and Jewish identity. (*See also* Jewish American Gay Literature)

Further Reading

Kakutani, Michiko. Review of *Jackie Under My Skin*. *New York Times* (May 5, 1995): B9.

Kaufman, David. Review of *Cleavage*. *New York Times Book Review* (March 5, 2000): 19.

Tanner, Michael. Review of *The Queen's Throat*. *Times Literary Supplement (TLS)* (November 5, 1993): 11.

Jennifer Glaser

KOMUNYAKAA, YUSEF (1947–)   African American Pulitzer Prize–winning poet, *Neon Vernacular: New and Selected Poems* (1993), professor, chancellor of the Academy of American Poets (1999), editor, translator. Growing up in the rural South, with the rich influence of New Orleans jazz and blues, followed by military service in Vietnam anchors Komunyakaa's poetry in realism. Oldest of five siblings, he was born on April 29, 1947, in Bogalusa, Louisiana. His career began with a hundred-line poem written as a high school senior. After graduating in 1965, he enlisted in the United States Army, in which he wrote for the military newspaper *The Southern Cross* and later became the paper's editor and received the Bronze Star for his contribution. After his tour of military duty, Komunyakaa took a creative writing course and completed a BA in English and sociology at the University of Colorado in 1975, an MA at Colorado State University in 1978, and an MFA at the University of California, Irvine, in 1980. After gaining literary recognition, Komunyakaa began teaching poetry in New Orleans and married Australian fiction writer Mandy Sayer in 1985.

The Provincetown Fine Arts Work Center (1980), a community of working artists, encouraged Komunyakaa to consider the role of experience in the composition of poetry. He learned to create new, composite images by reflecting on present possibilities and progressing toward encounters with surprise, merging images that previously did and did not exist. For Komunyakaa, reading and composing are intricately linked, and his poetry is influenced by his boyhood reading of the Bible and a long list of poets, including Poe, Tennyson, Shakespeare, the **Harlem Renaissance** writers, **Gwendolyn Brooks**, and **James Baldwin**. His public readings are an extension of that beginning poet's voice heard when Komunyakaa volunteered to write a poem for his graduating high school class. In an upbeat tone, the poetry celebrates the collective human condition.

Komunyakaa intertwines the power of **jazz** and literature, both vehicles for transposing experience into artistic form. The language and rhythm of the poetry, and the poet's use of dualistic images, enable the reader to inhabit

Yusef Komunyakaa. *Photo by Joyce Pettis.*

multiple realities simultaneously. Komunyakaa writes to "find out," to question, and to celebrate. The introspective nature of the work suggests that the poet initially writes for himself, then as the words and images conspire to produce music on the page, Komunyakaa's poetry speaks to a varied audience. Through his connection of ordinary themes and extraordinary re-visioning of those themes, the poet raises questions that provoke readers to discover new ways of seeing the familiar elements of their lives and new ways of experiencing the human condition. Komunyakaa's poetry is surprisingly transparent in its complexity. The poems are equally exploratory of the aesthetic and the repulsive. Komunyakaa's work embraces the risk of opposition in its probing engagement of tough moral issues, and the poet's almost gentle brusqueness mercilessly analyzes the under layers of these issues.

Komunyakaa's work—collapsing the borders separating the human and divine, the ordinary and the spectacular—has been called Wordsworthian. The poetry, constructed of short lines and vernacular language, evokes familiar images of ordinary events and rugged images that reflect the chaos of war. The poetry is grounded in the poet's fluency in both disciplines. Komunyakaa's published work includes self-published *Dedications and Other Darkhorses* (1977), *Copacetic* (1984), *Lost in the Bonewheel Factory* (1979), *I Apologize for the Eyes in My Head* (1986), *Toys in the Field* (1987), *Dien Cai Dau* (1988), *February in Sydney* (1989), *Magic City* (1992), *Neon Vernacular: New and Selected Poems 1977–1989* (1994), *Thieves of Paradise* (1998), *Pleasure Dome: New and Collected Poems, 1975–1999* (2001), and *Talking Dirty to the Gods* (2000).

Copacetic, his first commercially published book, explores the influences of Komunyakaa's childhood. The work exudes the spirit, the music, and the language forms surrounding the writer's youth. *Copacetic* captures the blues, jazz, folk idioms, and restless spirit of a nation trapped between the pain of racial ambiguities and mellow moments of contentment.

I Apologize for the Eyes in My Head is a continuation of the poet's undergirding theme, identity and lived experience. *Toys in a Field* and *Dien Cai Dau* are collections linking the writer's experiences as poet and soldier. Komunyakaa did not immediately communicate his war experience, but the images eventually began seeping into routine activities, such as remodeling. The multilayered phenomena of the violent chaos of war and survival are poignantly documented in the writer's raw imagery. The psychological flux is especially well symbolized by the indefinable internal and external spaces of "To Do Street."

In *February in Sydney, Magic City,* and *Neon Vernacular: New and Selected Poems,* the poet again returns to themes that are reflective of his childhood and to his interest in the impact of music on culture. In a characteristic manner, Komunyakaa's images range from the predictable, interactive patterns of flowers and bees to fragmented remembered conversations, which are, accordingly, less predictable. The poetry then moves forward from these simpler images to embrace the intangible complexities of human existence as introspective interpretations of the chaotic images of war. The poet redefines extraordinary and commonplace events, by purposefully including and excluding sensory and psychological elements to achieve a candid image, capable of illuminating an experience that was previously too close for visualization. (*See also* African American Poetry)

Further Reading

Asali, Muna. "An Interview with Yusef Komunyakaa." *New England Review* 16.1 (1994): 141–47.

Baer, William. "Still Negotiating with the Images: An Interview with Yusef Komunyakaa." *Kenyon Review.* 20.3–4 (1998): 5–29.

Salas, Angela M. "'Flashbacks through the Heart': Yusef Komunyakaa and the Poetry of Self-Assertion." *The Furious Flowering of African Poetry.* Ed. Joanne V. Gabbin. Charlottesville, VA: UP of Virginia, 1999. 130–43.

Stella Thompson

KONECKY, EDITH (1922–) Jewish American feminist writer. A Brooklyn-born dress manufacturer's daughter and sometime suburban mother, Konecky established a lasting place for her writing with her first novel, published in 1974. *Allegra Maud Goldman* revolutionized the twentieth-century American female coming-of-age story. The novel powerfully redefines the bildungsroman, tracing the development of a Jewish girl into an author despite the constrictions of sexism and a materialistic, patriarchal ethnic culture. Kept in print for decades by Dell and the Jewish Publication Society, the novel appeared in a twenty-fifth anniversary edition from the Feminist Press in 2001. With an introduction by **Tillie Olsen** and an afterword by Bella Brodski, this edition underscores the work's artistic power and its importance to feminist activists and writers. In later works, *A Place at the Table* (1989) and *Past Sorrows and Coming Attractions* (2001), Konecky explores new areas: the complexities of women's aging, of madness and motherhood, women's love of other women, the relations between generations, and the importance of friendship and the writer's imagination. Each work is filled with characters of whom it can easily be said that "There wasn't a cliché in her, body or soul" (*Place*).

Konecky's work, articulate and lapidary in style, is rooted in personal experience. Emerging as a writer in the 1960s, in the second wave of American **feminism**, Konecky helped define the terms by which mid-twentieth century women came to understand themselves. The protagonist of Konecky's first novel, Allegra, questions sexist limitations with an acerbic and knowing voice, reimagining the self and the world. Perhaps especially for younger Jewish women writers, like **Alix Shulman**, who reviewed the book for *Ms.* magazine, Allegra modeled an intellectual coming-of-age and search for a cultural heritage. To a considerable degree, the explosion of Jewish women's fiction in the last two decades of the twentieth century may have been ignited by the power of this book, along with others including **Grace Paley**'s *Lives of Women and Men* (1960), **Cynthia Ozick**'s *The Pagan Rabbi* (1971), Alix Shulman's *Memoirs of an Ex-Prom Queen* (1972), **Erica Jong**'s *Fear of Flying* (1973), and **Esther Masserman Broner**'s *A Weave of Women* (1975), as well as the non-fiction feminist works of Betty Friedan, Gloria Steinem, and others.

In *Place*, Rachel Levin reflects on the episodes of her sixty years of life, considering whether, as her mad but wise former writer friend Deirdre puts it, "The feast of life is spread for all . . . but there are ooonly [sic] so many places at the table." Konecky published selected poems in an obscure journal called *Open Places* (1981, 1985) and short stories (later collected in *Past Sorrow*) in a number of journals, including *The Virginia Quarterly, Story Magazine, Cosmopolitan*. Here, couples divorce, children are imprisoned in Mexican jails, lovers are revealed as pathological liars. In these later stories and novels, published around the same time as works by **Lesléa Newman** and **Irena Klepfisz**, Konecky represents an older generation's development of **identity** as lesbians. But plot in these stories, as in all of Konecky's work, is always subordinated to the deep intelligence revealing the complexity of character. As Konecky has said, "I tend to create my characters from the inside out. . . . Interchangeable characters don't belong in a novel, any more than interchangeable friends belong in your life" (Konecky, 1990, 16–17).

The scarcity of publicly available biographical information about Konecky suggests a love of privacy and a reluctance to subsume fiction to a public persona. Konecky attended New York University from 1939 to 1941, resuming her education at Columbia University after bringing up two children, and shortly thereafter beginning her first novel at the MacDowell Colony. She married Murray L. Konecky in 1944; they were divorced in 1965. She dedicated her first novel to her parents, Harry and Elizabeth (Smith) Rubin, *Place* to her children, and *Past Sorrows* to her "invaluable assistant and beloved son Josh." Konecky's publication of *Allegra* brought considerable critical attention; she won fellowships from the Wurlitzer Foundation (1974), the MacDowell Colony (through 1996), Yaddo (from 1969 to 1977), and the New York Foundation of the Arts (1992). A new work, *View to the North,* was published by Hamilton Stone Editions in 2004. (*See also* Jewish American Novel)

Further Reading

Konecky, Edith. "The Breath of Life." *Writer* 103 (1990): 16–24.

———. "Off the Cuff: Beginning." *Writer* 112 (1999): 3–4.

Rubin, Lois. "Two Jewish Girls Come of Age: Gender and Ethnicity in Allegra Maud Goldman and Leaving Brooklyn." *Yiddish* 11 (1999): 70–85.

Shulman, Alix Kates. "A Me Grows in Brooklyn." *Ms.* (April 1977): 37–38.

Wolk, Merla. "Edith Konecky." *Jewish Women in America: An Historical Encyclopedia.* Ed. Paula Hyman and Deborah Dash Moore. New York: Routledge, 1997. 751–52.

Gail Berkeley Sherman

KOPIT, ARTHUR (1937–) Jewish American playwright. Kopit was originally named Arthur Lee Koenig, but his name changed to Kopit when his mother remarried. Kopit attended Lawrence High School in Long Island, and then Harvard University, where several of his plays were produced. In 1960 his first notable play, *Oh Dad, Poor Dad, Mamma's Hung You in the Closet and I'm Feeling So Sad* won an award for best play, and was then produced and published. Kopit won a Rockefeller Grant for this play. He would go on to win a Guggenheim Fellowship in 1967, a Rockefeller Fellowship in 1968, and awards from the National Institute of Arts and Letters in 1971 and the National Endowment for the Arts in 1974. He also won another Rockefeller Fellowship in 1977. Critics commonly associate Kopit's work with that of Irish absurdist Samuel Beckett and Kopit's American contemporary Sam Shepard. His most famous plays were written in the 1960s and 1970s and include such titles as *Wings* (1979), *Chamber Music, Indians* (1968), *An Incident in the Park* (1968), and *The Day the Whores Came Out to Play Tennis* (1964). Later plays include *Nine* (1981), *The End of the World* (1984), and *Y2K* (1999). The subject matter for Kopit's plays has ranged from psychoanalytic farce to the suffering of a stroke victim, and from the dangers of technology to the possibility of nuclear annihilation.

Wings is written from the perspective of a former aviatrix who has suffered a stroke. The play makes use of sound and light effects, and demonstrates the confusion and inability of the stroke victim to process language.

Chamber Music is about a group of women who either are or claim to be famous. Characters include Joan of Arc, Amelia Earhart, **Gertrude Stein**, and so on. These characters are concerned about their plight because they are patients in a psychiatric ward. They decide that the men's ward is responsible for all of their problems and in protest kill Amelia Earhart, attach their signatures to the body, and send it to the men's ward.

Oh Dad, Poor Dad features Madame Rosepettle, a grotesque, illogical, and overbearing woman who keeps two pet Venus flytraps, and pet piranhas that eat Siamese kittens as emblems of her ferocious soul-destroying nature. Her deceased husband has been stuffed by taxidermists and keeps falling out of his coffin in the closet in which he has been hung. Jonathan, the son of Madame Rosepettle is a simple, stuttering, fearful young man who never goes outside because Madame Rosepettle fears that he might get corrupted.

The End of the World was a commissioned play that shows the audience the struggles of a playwright to write about nuclear apocalypse. The play is autobiographical in some ways, and features a character named *Michael Trent* whose experience with writing the play in some ways parallels that of Kopit.

More recently, Kopit wrote *Y2K,* a response to the age of computers and technology. In *Y2K,* Kopit takes the fear of computer hackers and secret agents to its extreme, showing the decline and eventual ruin of a married couple in the business of publishing. The computer hacker involved is obsessed with the couple, and agents from the Federal Bureau of Investigation who seek to catch the hacker are without correct information, so they interrogate the husband and hold him responsible for the hacker's activities.

Kopit's contribution to the American theater of the absurd is unique. Kopit's grasp of the corruption of human beings and their fragile existence in the technological and postindustrial age is what makes him a notable figure in theater. (*See also* Jewish American Theater)

Further Reading

Auerbach, Doris. *Sam Shepard, Arthur Kopit, and the Off Broadway Theater.* Boston: Twayne Publishers, 1982.

Janiszewski, Adam. *The Idea of the Absurd in the American Drama of the Sixties.* Lublin, Poland: Uniwersytetu Marie Curii-Sklodowskiej, 1996.

Stephanie Fischetti

KOREAN AMERICAN LITERATURE   Between the early part of the twentieth century and the mid-1960s, high-profile Korean American literary works were rarely discussed in academic and commercial literary contexts except in certain instances that corresponded to a small number of Koreans who had immigrated to the United States. In the wake of new waves of **immigration** after 1965, however, Korean American writers have been flourishing not only in their numbers, but also in the breadth and quality of their literary works. No longer constrained within the confines of immigrant experiences, such as basic survival, cultural conflicts, and assimilation, the newest generations of Korean American writers have brought about a "renaissance" of Korean American literature since the mid-1990s.

The First Wave of Korean Immigrants and Their Literary Expressions

By 1888, a small number of Korean students, merchants, exiles, and migration laborers began to arrive on American shores, and the first major wave of Korean immigrants was initiated with the Hawaiian sugar plantations laborers during 1903–1905. It was a time of powerful Western imperialistic advances in Asia; moreover, the Korean peninsula was annexed by

Japan—a rising Asian power—in 1910. As a result, a number of Koreans were forcibly relocated or voluntarily emigrated. Korean immigrants, as a people without a country, thought of themselves as exiles as well as immigrants. The plight of Koreans during the colonial period (1910–45), the loss of individual and collective **identity**, and the struggle in adjusting to life in the New World were reflected in early Korean American writing of the age.

Even though *When I Was a Boy in Korea* (1928) by Il-Han New (1895–71) was the first published Korean American work written in English, **Young-hill Kang** (1903–72) is a pioneering figure in Korean American literature. Kang's first book, *The Grass Roof* (1931), is an autobiographical fiction based upon his childhood experiences in a northern region of Korean with extended explanations of Korean culture and realities of his country under Japanese colonial ruling before his immigration to American. Picking up the story where his first book leaves off, Younghill Kang's *East Goes West: The Making of an Oriental Yankee* (1937), a representative Korean and Asian American literary work of the age, depicts a Korean immigrant's struggle to carve out a place for himself. In chronicling the narrator's trials and tribulations, Kang seeks a mediation on the possible modes of harmonizing East and West through a series of vignettes of American life and Korean immigrants' struggle between their Eastern traditions and Western modern values.

Between the Korean War and 1965

The second wave of Koreans arrived between the Korean War (1950–53) and 1965 as war orphans or wives of American servicemen who had been stationed in Korea. But the Korean American community still remained small before restrictive immigration laws were lifted in 1965. Although Korean American writers of this period attempted to maintain strong ties to their country of origin politically and culturally, the variations on the familiar themes of Korean immigrants' writings became more diverse, laying the foundation of post-1965 Korean American literature.

Richard E. Kim, who served in the military during the Korean War, represents the group of postwar Korean American writers. Critically acclaimed and gaining worldwide attention, his first novel, *The Martyred* (1964), still remains the only Asian American work ever nominated for a Nobel Prize for literature. Set in the North Korean capital of Pyongyang immediately after the Korean War, *The Martyred* explores the themes of religious belief, salvation, and human nature in the form of a mystery novel. His second book, *The Innocent* (1968), as a follow-up to his debut, deals with moral issues and existential human dilemmas. Despite Kim's contention that the book is not about a historical event itself but about universal human issues, *The Innocent* reminds some readers familiar with Korean history of the 1961 military coup d'état in South Korea and could also be read as a nuanced commentary on the Vietnam War.

Induk Pahk (1896–1980) is a Korean American writer who paved the way for the tradition of women's writing in Korean American literature through her keen awareness of women's voice in family (Induk is typically a name for men in Korea) and immigration experiences in her three autobiographical works: *September Monkey* (1954), *The Hour of the Tiger* (1965), and *The Cock Still Crows* (1977). Her well-known *September Monkey*, covering her life from her birth in Korea to her success as an educator in America, provides an intriguing possibility for building a bridge between the two cultures.

Most of the works of **Kim Yong Ik** (1920–1955), who, like Richard Kim, taught writing at several American universities, are set in Korea including *The Diving Gourd* (1962), *Blue in the Seed* (1964), and *Kim's Love in Winter* (1969), a collection of short stories. His works clearly demonstrate how much the history of Korea's political and economic debilitation during the tumultuous times of war and colonization, and enforced modernization, still obsessed the Korean American writers.

The Post-1965 Korean American Writing and the Future of Korean American Literature

In 1965 the Immigration Act abolished the discriminatory quota system based on national origin that had restricted the numbers of Asians allowed to enter the United States. The group of new Korean immigrants was relatively well educated and trained in their professions, but language and cultural barriers often forced them to work outside the fields in which they had been trained. The first post-1965 immigrants focused on the basic necessities of finding housing, securing jobs, and providing for their families. As Korean immigrant families began to settle into their adopted country and find relative success, the new generations of Korean Americans have been witness to an especially rich production of Korean American writing. The cultural differences across generations that had become more and more prominent also characterize the Korean American writing of this period. Not only *Il Se* (first generation) and *I Se* (second generation), but also *Il Chom O Se* (generation 1.5) who were born in Korea and moved to the states in their childhood, began to go through a complex process of defining and articulating their own identities from different perspectives that represented each generation's experiences.

One of the Korean American texts widely used in college courses for many years after the Asian American explosion of the late 1970s is *Clay Walls* (1986) by Kim Ronyoung (1951–82), which draws on conflicting ideas of being Korean in California in the decades between the two world wars. *Clay Walls* calls into question the established boundaries of Korean American identities by presenting multiple character perspectives to the reader. Exploring tribulations of a Korean immigrant family, *Clay Walls* focuses its attention on the meaning of "wall," which is expanded to include the many "walls" between men and women, parents and children, nations, and cultures. The similar theme of bridging "walls" between cultures and generations continues be examined in Ty Pak's collection of short stories, *Guilt Payment* (1983).

With different spins and foci on the lives of Korean immigrants in the United States, the following works partake of the characteristic of autobiographical writing in Korean American literature: Margaret K. Pai's *The Dreams of Two Yi-Min* (1989), *Man Sei!* (1986) and *In the New World* (1991) by Peter Hyun (1907–93), **Sook Nyul Choi**'s *Year of Impossible Goodbyes* (1991), and Mary Paik Lee's *Quiet Odyssey: A Pioneer Korean Woman in America* (1990). Without an equivalent, *Dictee* (1982) by **Theresa Hak Kyung Cha** (1951–82) demonstrates an experimental writing style of merging various genres and disrupting literary conventions along with her unique approaches to the issues of history, identity, language, memory, and **feminism**. Challenging conventional patterns of historical and autobiographical writing, Cha's *Dictee* opens up spaces in which Korean American women, who have been silenced by their differences of **race**, gender, and language proficiency, are enabled to articulate themselves. Each fragmented story written in different styles makes readers continuously conscious of how the very act of piecing together fragments to make a coherent narrative sometimes oppresses the voices of the people in "margin."

The new-generation Korean American writing also bore fruitful results in poetry writing. A lesbian and women's rights activist and a writer, Willyce Kim attempts to reject the submissive role of an Asian American woman in her two collections of poems, *Eating Artichokes* (1972) and *Under the Rolling Sky* (1976). **Cathy Song**, a part-Korean and part-Chinese American born in Hawai'i, received the 1982 Yale Series of Younger Poets Award by her first collection, *Picture Bride* (1983). A touching lyric eulogy to her ancestral roots, *Picture Bride* dramatizes history through the lives of the poet's family in Hawai'i. Myung Mi Kim's *Under Flag* (1991) merges the issue of language fluency with the difficulty of overcoming cultural differences through a young immigrant child's life.

Since the mid-1990s, Korean American literature, an initially marginal literature, has established itself as prominent through a combination of critical recognition in the academy and commercial success. **Chang-rae Lee** is the most prominent Korean American writer currently in the literary mainstream. His debut, *Native Speaker* (1995), captures the issues of identity, **assimilation**, language, and a possibility of political affiliation of immigrant groups through a story of Korean American Henry Park, a narrator who builds his career with a shadowy multinational intelligence firm by spying on notable Asians. *Native Speaker* takes the form of both detective novel and political thriller. As a follow-up to his debut novel, Lee, in *A Gesture Life* (1999), continues to delve into the difficulties of assimilation by unearthing main character Franklin Hata's past relationship with a Korean "comfort woman" (women forced into serving the Japanese soldiers sexually) during World War II behind his impeccably judged veneer of his "gesture life."

Nora Okja Keller, a Korean American writer of a mixed heritage, places the comfort women issue in the center of her novel *Comfort Woman* (1997) and discusses the historical and cultural relationship between Korea and the United States through the story of a once-comfort woman and her daughter by an American missionary. Her next novel, *Fox Girl* (2002), set in an "America town" in Korea following the Korean War, continues to look into the inextricable ties between the two cultures and histories as a historical extension of her first novel. In a similar vein, Heinz Insu Fenkl's *Memories of My Ghost Brother* (1996), based upon the author's experiences as a mixed child of an American soldier father and a Korean mother, traces the experiences of rejected children and their families in a military camp/town in South Korea.

Patti Kim's *A Cab Called Reliable* (1998), Susan Choi's *The Foreign Student* (1998), Linda Sue Park's Newbery Medal–winning *A Single Shard* (2001), An Na's *A Step from Heaven* (2002), and Don Lee's short story collection *Yellow* (2003) are notable outcomes of Korean American literature of this period that address various issues in Korean immigrants' lives stemming from the demographic and sociopolitical changes in the Korean American community.

Conclusion

Corresponding to the growing recognition of Korean American literature from the academy and various readerships, recent years have seen the publication of anthologies of Korean American literature, such as *Kori: The Beacon Anthology of Korean American Fiction* (2001), *Century of the Tiger: One Hundred Years of Korean Culture in America 1003–2003* (2003), *Echoes Upon Echoes: New Korean American Writings* (2003), *Yobo: Korean American Writing in Hawaii,* and *Surfacing Sadness: A Centennial of Korean-American Literature 1903–2003*. One of the notable trends in the growth of Korean American literature since the 1990s is that neither the country of ethnic origin nor the country of habitation functions as a singular place for identity formation, thereby calling into question the very assumptions and meanings of identity pivoting on inherited cultural tradition and shared histories of deprivation and discrimination. For example, one may find in Chang-Rae Lee's *Native Speaker* and Leonard Chang's *Over the Shoulder* (2001) a sly subversion of reader's expectations, which are suggestive of a possibility of the establishment of genre writing in Korean American literature. Chang-Rae Lee and Susan Choi have Japanese Americans as central characters in their recent novels. Even the narrator in Chang-Rae Lee's newest novel, *Aloft* (2004), is not Asian American. Gary Pak's fictions are deeply rooted in a local Hawaiian tradition and **Susan Choi,** who views herself more as a Southern writer than as a Korean American writer, exemplify the transformations and divergent claims in Korean American writing and render the definition of Korean American literature quite complex in light of particular contexts and the interest each writer represents. Extended into a larger context of Korean diaspora writing and expanding the boundaries that circumscribe the reading of Korean American writers, Korean American literature is likely to continue to perform on-going negotiations with various readerships and the competing claims of communities where values and meaning are not always collaborative but even sometimes conflicting in moments of historical transformation.

Further Reading

Han, Jae-Nam. "Korean American Literature." *New Immigrant Literature in the United States: A Source Book to Our Multicultural Heritage.* Ed. Alpana Sharma Knippling. Westport, CT: Greenwood Press, 1996. 143–58.

Kang, Laura Hyun Yi. *Compositional Subjects: Enfiguring Asian/American Women.* Durham, NC: Duke UP, 2002.

Kim, Elaine H. *Asian American Literature: An Introduction to the Writings and Their Social Context.* Philadelphia: Temple UP, 1982.

———. "Korean American Literature." Ed. King-Kok Cheung. *An Interethnic Companion to Asian American Literature.* New York: Cambridge UP, 2000. 156–91.

Kim, Kichung. "Affliction and Opportunity: Korean Literature in Diaspora, a Brief Overview." *Korean Studies* 25.2 (2001): 261–76.

Kim, Pyong Kap. "Korean Americans." *Asian Americans: Contemporary Trends and Issues.* Ed. Pyong Kap Kim. Thousand Oaks, CA: Sage, 1995. 199–231.

Lee, Jeeyeon. "Korean American One-Point-Five." *The Asian Pacific American Heritage: A Companion to Arts and Literature.* Ed. George J. Leonard. New York: Garland, 1999. 143–50.

Solberg, S. E. "The Literature of Korean America." *The Asian Pacific American Heritage: A Companion to Arts and Literature.* Ed. George J. Leonard. New York: Garland, 1999. 515–26.

Yu, Pyong-ch'on. "Korean Writers in America." *Korean Journal* 7.12 (1967): 17–19.

Seongho Yoon

KOSTELANETZ, RICHARD CORY (1940–) American writer, editor, and artist of mostly Sephardic Jewish descent. A prolific polymath, Kostelanetz is an important critic and anthologist of the avant-garde and has created a large body of his own experimental poetry, fiction, and text-based art. He was born and has spent nearly all of his professional life in New York City, and its cosmopolitan culture resonates in his work. His lengthy bibliography contains just a smattering of specifically Jewish works.

Kostelanetz got off to a fast start. By age twenty-five, he had edited two books; had published essays in *Partisan Review, Kenyon Review, Hudson Review, Sewanee, New York Times Book Review,* and other journals; and had received a Pulitzer fellowship. By twenty-six, he had taken an MA in American history from Columbia and had been a Fulbright scholar. By thirty, he had written and edited a dozen books.

While at Columbia, he befriended Richard Hofstadter, and later profiled the great historian in his book *Masterminds* (1969). Kostelanetz's best critical and anthological works reveal something of Hofstadter's influence—an adeptness at historical synthesis, an ability to draw from other disciplines. Perhaps the greatest influence, though, comes from the inventive models of inquiry Hofstadter used to examine America's political past; Kostelanetz created his own to study America's cultural present. He recognized the fertile period in the arts after World War II as one of experiment and stylistic plurality. His early works searched for the best methods to document this plurality, for the critical vocabulary appropriate to the period's most challenging works, and for the past masters and the texts most illuminating to the period's diverse esthetics.

Three of his early books—one critical study, one anthology, and one monograph—provide the foundation upon which much of his later works are built. In *The Theatre of Mixed-Means* (1968), Kostelanetz uses a unique approach to examine the experimental theater known as the *happening*. The creators of this new art had come from such different disciplines as music, dance, painting, sculpture, theater, and film; and their works often combined several of these mediums. In a long opening essay, he breaks the works down to their essential elements—space, time, and action—and with these, he establishes a vocabulary and critical framework useful for approaching the entire medium. The creators of this new theater had developed skills in disciplines other than those in which they had trained, and their insight into the form was unique. To get at this insight, Kostelanetz conducted extended interviews with nine of the artists, including John Cage, Anna Halprin, Allan Kaprow, Claes Oldenburg, Robert Rauschenberg, and La Monte Young. The interviews showed subtleties that served to test, even to expose, the limitations of the framework established in the opening essay. This form of inquiry—where a critical framework is established and its limitations revealed within the covers of a single book—is one Kostelanetz uses frequently in his work.

Possibilities of Poetry (1970), an anthology he regarded as "an extended historical-critical essay," uses this form in a different way. In a lengthy introduction, he surveys the great diversity that flowered in North American poetry in the decades following World War II and identifies ten stylistic tendencies, each a departure from the dominant prewar style of English-language poetry, that of T. S. Eliot. He then presents selections from several poets whose work, first, is among the period's greatest, and second, best exemplifies one of these tendencies. Although the book's selections descend from the overview developed in its introduction, the richness of the poems selected and the range of poetries represented reveal the limitations of any sort of overview in a time of such great plurality.

As with the creators of mixed-means theater, many avant-garde artists and writers of the postwar period worked across artistic disciplines to create visual poetry, sound sculpture, kinetic environments, and other works that combined previously distinct types of art. Although this esthetic is a distinguishing characteristic of the period, Kostelanetz found an eminent precursor in the Hungarian-born artist and writer Lázló Moholy-Nagy and the multiple intelligences he exhibited in his posthumously published book *Vision in Motion* (1947). In *Moholy-Nagy* (1970, 1991), Kostelanetz assembled a documentary monograph of selections from the artist's writings on painting, photography, design, sculpture, film, light machines, and education, and complemented these with photographs of Moholy-Nagy's work in each medium and with critical articles pertaining to this work. In his introduction, Kostelanetz argues that Moholy-Nagy should be regarded as one of the seminal artists of the early modern period, his mastery of several unrelated arts having its greatest influence in the postwar period. To describe artists with Moholy-Nagy's breadth, Kostelanetz later coined the term *polyartist*.

Kostelanetz's later books not only build upon these early works, but also are often best understood in their context. Anthologies such as *Esthetics Contemporary* (1978, 1989) and *Classic Essays on Twentieth Century Music* (1996) are filled mostly of writings by artists and musicians, extending the theme introduced in *The Theater of Mixed Means*—that the best insight into the arts of the postwar period often comes from the creators themselves. His pioneering anthologies *Breakthrough Fictioneers* (1973) and *Text-Sound Texts* (1980) contain an exuberant selection of works that draw from such mediums as photography, performance art, and music—pushing literature to its visual and aural edges. These anthologies include work by artists such as Robert Smithson, Eleanor Antin, Vito Acconci, Alvin Lucier, and John Cage—artists all best known for their achievements outside of writing. Similar to *Moholy-Nagy*, monographs such as *An Other E. E. Cummings* (1998) and *The Gertrude Stein Reader* (2003) interpret these early masters to show their contemporary importance. *A Dictionary of the Avant-Gardes* (1993, 2000) contains hundreds of entries on writers, musicians, visual artists, choreographers, filmmakers, and many who fall in between. An entry on Dieter Rot is followed by one on Jerome Rothenberg, followed by one on Mark Rothko, by one on Raymond Roussel, one on Dane Rudhyar, and so on. An artist's most adventurous work is examined alongside works created not only from different esthetics but in completely different mediums. This leads Kostelanetz to judge a work in terms of its ability to emphasize effects indigenous to its medium. The book furthers Kostelanetz's interest in alternative historiography, in looking across the artistic spectrum, and in elevating lesser-known figures and reevaluating well-known ones.

In the early 1970s, Kostelanetz began creating his own inventive poetry, fiction, and text-based art. One-sentence stories, holographic poems, and book-art books are just a few of the forms he has pioneered. Collections such as *Wordworks* (1993) and *35 Years of Visible Writing* (2004) show a range of literary inventiveness without parallel in American letters.

Further Reading

Gomez, Raymond. "Towards a Critical Understanding of Richard Kostelanetz's Single Sentence Stories." *Critique: Studies in Contemporary Fiction* 35.4 (Summer 1994): 229–36.

McCaffery, Larry. "Alternative, Possibility, and Essence: An Interview with Richard Kostelanetz." *Some Other Frequency: Interviews with Innovative American Authors*. Philadelphia: U of Pennsylvania P, 1996: 196–218.

Douglas Puchowski

KRAMER, AARON (1921–1997) Jewish American poet, essayist, and translator. Son of a Ukrainian Jewish father and Polish Jewish mother (both influenced by Eastern European communism), Kramer began writing poetry at the age of six. Because of the maturity of his work, his parents and teachers encouraged him in his endeavors. At the age of twelve, he declared himself to be a "people's poet," and began to publish in journals such as *The New Pioneer* and *The Sunday Worker* on proletarian and racial causes. By the age of fifteen, Kramer was turning into a "young proletarian," and his poems began to appear in *The Daily Worker.* He graduated high school early and was a member of the Communist Youth League. However, one unfortunate block to Kramer's desire for wide recognition of his art was simply accident of birth. He was simply born much later in the century, writing on themes that his predecessors, such as **Langston Hughes**, had tackled nearer the turn of the century, when proletarian causes had been popular. Kramer was an observant poet and garnered many of his ideas from the industrial, economic, and social unfairness that he saw around him during the Great Depression. He also had a very good ear for rhyming and meter. But as fate would have it, his traditional method of poetry was also considered to be passé as radical poets were becoming more firmly entrenched in the free-verse tradition from which they ironically refused to depart! Kramer considered his style more "reader friendly" and accessible to the public. He refused to change to please those that wanted him to conform. The Spanish Civil War of 1937 had a profound effect upon his creativity, and he wrote many poems that criticized the Fascist government of Spain. Further encouraged by his father, Kramer published his first book of poetry, *The Alarm Clock* (1938), at the age of seventeen, during his sophomore year at Brooklyn College.

Kramer studied German and Yiddish in order to read poets in their original tongue. As a member of the American Student Union while in college, Kramer involved himself in political and literary activities. As a member of the Communist Party of the USA (CPUSA), he became involved in antifascist issues concerning Europe, specifically Germany. But the CPUSA proved to be a disappointment for Kramer because the party elected neutrality in the face of the growing world concern with Hitler. His work *Another Fountain* (1940) deals with the political and social ills of the time and contains early critiques on the House Committee on Un-American

Activities, a committee to which Kramer was vehemently opposed. The destruction by the Nazis of the Czech town of Lidice had a deep effect on Kramer, who commemorated the loss of life in his poem "Song of Lidice." As his college years drew to a close, Kramer's deep desires to become an educator were dashed by his political background. He worked for various companies but despised the exploitation he saw in the corporate world.

Kramer's father died at age fifty-three, and this plunged Kramer into more fervent study of Yiddish, a language his father had always wanted him to cultivate. Kramer studied Yiddish cultural heritage and became a renowned translator of Yiddish poetry, specifically of Yiddish-speaking sweatshop workers. His collection of Yiddish poetry *A Century of Yiddish Poetry* (1989) contains poetry of the Left, of Russia, and of the **Holocaust**. He also translated 110 poems by Heinrich Heine from the original German as well as hundreds of other German poems. He continued to write about racial issues in the 1940s, and in 1949 he was the only white member of the Harlem Writer's Club.

During the McCarthy era, Kramer wrote poetry critical of the time in *Roll the Forbidden Drums!* (1954) and became a lecturer and pioneer in the area of poetry therapy for the blind. He received his PhD in English from New York University in 1966. During the 1960s, Kramer was a radio program host in addition to his work as professor of English at Dowling College. His last translation work, published posthumously, was *The Emperor of Atlantis,* an opera written in the concentration camp of Terezin. It continues to be performed to this day.

Further Reading

Gilzinger, Donald, Jr., and Cary Nelson. "Aaron Kramer: American Prophet." *Wicked Times: Selected Poems.* Aaron Kramer. Urbana: U of Illinois P, 2004. xvii–lix.

Rovit, Rebecca, and Alvin Goldfarb, eds. *Theatrical Performance during the Holocaust.* Baltimore: The Johns Hopkins UP, 1999.

Cynthia A. Klima

KRAMER, LARRY (1935–)   Jewish American activist, essayist, novelist, and playwright. A founder of both the Gay Men's Health Crisis (GMHC) and the AIDS Coalition to Unleash Power (ACT UP), Kramer has often drawn the ire of the gay community by criticizing the promiscuity through which homosexuals have often asserted their identity and by being one of the first to suggest that safe sex and monogamy should be practiced to slow the spread of AIDS. He also enraged the Jewish community by comparing the early days of the AIDS epidemic to the early days of the **Holocaust**, saying that homosexuals were doing nothing to save themselves just as many Jews reportedly turned a blind eye during the 1930s as Hitler began putting his "Final Solution" into effect.

As a writer and as a speaker, Kramer has always allowed his personal and political lives to intersect as he has addressed themes of the difficulties people have in loving each other, how people use sex as a weapon, and how people respond to crisis, making great use of angry hyperbole throughout his career. He bears witness to history and provides his testimony, insisting that the rest of us accept personal responsibility for our world just as he feels he has done.

Born to an American Jewish father and a Russian Jewish mother during the Depression, Kramer and his family lived with his mother's parents. He spent much of his time in the grocery that his grandparents owned while his mother was out seeking odd jobs and his father, an attorney, was often away on cases requiring travel. When Kramer was six, his father landed a job in Mount Rainier, Maryland, where the Kramers were part of a Jewish minority. At age eight, Kramer saw his first play; and a love affair began with the theater, a love affair that brought ridicule from Kramer's father, who thought he should be more interested in sports and other more traditionally "masculine" activities. In 1950, the family moved to Washington, DC.

Kramer entered Yale in 1953. Yale had not been Kramer's first choice of schools, but his father, brother, and uncle had all attended, and his father all but forced him to go the university. While there, Kramer became extremely depressed, falling behind in his studies and attempting suicide during his freshman year. Kramer began seeing a psychiatrist and remained at Yale, where he began an affair with one of his male professors in the spring. Kramer ended the relationship but confided in his brother about it. His brother convinced their parents that Kramer should continue seeing a psychiatrist because of his homosexuality. The relationship between Kramer and his brother would later be highlighted in Kramer's plays. Kramer graduated from Yale with a degree in English in 1957 and joined the Army.

Kramer began working in the teletype room of Columbia Pictures in 1958. Though his employment status and job description at Columbia changed often, he worked with the company throughout the 1960s. By the end of the 1960s, Kramer had gone to work for United Artists, where he wrote the Academy Award–nominated screenplay for *Women in Love* (1969). Despite the film's critical success, Kramer did not enjoy the experience and was further disappointed in the industry with the now-legendary failure of the movie musical *Lost Horizon* (1971), for which Kramer had written the screenplay.

Kramer's first play, *Sissies' Scrapbook,* premiered in 1973. The play, about one gay and three straight male friends, was a success in its original run but was destroyed by a hostile Clive Barnes review in the *New York Times* a year later when it was remounted in Greenwich Village under the title *Four Friends.* In 1978 Kramer published *Faggots,* his first novel. Chronicling four days in the life of Fred Lemish, a gay screenwriter dealing with turning forty in the heyday of emotionally detached gay sex in New York in the late 1970s, the novel suggested that promiscuous homosexuals who denied the importance of love in personal relationships were responsible for their own unhappiness rather than the disapproving heterosexual world. The novel sold well but received mixed reviews, with the gay press labeling Kramer as a self-loathing, homophobic homosexual. This criticism would continue to dog Kramer throughout his career, particularly when he began a grass-roots campaign to collect funds to combat the new "gay cancer" that had begun to kill people in Kramer's circle two years after the publication of *Faggots*. Standing outside gay bars in Manhattan and on the beach at Fire Island, Kramer began collecting dollar bills and spare change to research the as-yet-unnamed disease and subsequently began the newest and most important phase in his career—that of an AIDS activist.

Kramer's first published work on the disease appeared in August 1981, in the *New York Native*. Asking for funds for research into Kaposi's sarcoma, the skin cancer that was killing many gay men, Kramer was immediately attacked in the letters column by writers calling him alarmist and homophobic. In January 1982 Kramer and five other men, including novelist Edmund White, formed the GMHC to educate gay men about the disease and its spread. The GMHC set up a telephone information line, published a newsletter, held public information sessions, and established a crisis-intervention program. Although the GMHC became incredibly successful—raising funds, building a volunteer base, and educating the public about the growing epidemic—Kramer's involvement with the organization had ended within a year and a half due to in-fighting and fears within the group that Kramer's aggressive politics and strident attacks on indifferent government officials would hinder the GMHC's efforts. Kramer had been vocal and highly critical of New York City Mayor Ed Koch's lack of attention to the problem and had published the article "1,112 and Counting" (1983) in the *New York Native*. The article not only attacked the government and health care system but also the gay community itself for its lack of assertiveness in fighting the disease. Kramer would later attack Koch again along with the entire Reagan family in his satirical farce *Just Say No* (1988). The GMHC attempted to distance itself from "1,112 and Counting" and from Kramer, and he angrily resigned his position on the GMHC board. The article became one of the most important documents of the AIDS epidemic, and Kramer's experience with the GMHC became the basis of his play *The Normal Heart* (1985).

The original production of *The Normal Heart* ran for over a year at Joseph Papp's Public Theatre—the longest run of any play there—in New York City and has since been produced all over the world. The play is at once virulently polemic and extraordinarily compassionate, dealing with the problems of the GMHC as well as with Kramer's own family issues, especially the difficulties his brother had accepting Larry's sexuality. Kramer derived the play's title from W. H. Auden's poem "September 1, 1939," itself a reference to the day Germany invaded Poland and began World War II while most of the world watched impassively. *The Normal Heart* was revived at the Public in 2004 with Joel Grey and Joanna Gleason in the cast.

In 1987, Kramer, disappointed with the lack of progress he perceived the GMHC had made in the fight against AIDS, called a New York meeting that led to the formation of ACT UP. Decidedly more radical than the GMHC, ACT UP's first act was to stop traffic on Wall Street during the morning rush to protest the FDA's lack of attention to the AIDS problem. This and other similar acts brought ACT UP the national attention that GMHC, despite its many successes, had never managed to attract and led to many victories in the fight against AIDS. ACT UP is also notable for mobilizing young homosexuals in their twenties, a group that had generally been absent from earlier homosexual activist movements.

Kramer was diagnosed with chronic hepatitis B in December 1988, when he entered a hospital for a hernia operation. Upon further testing, Kramer tested positive for the HIV virus. He did not allow his HIV status to halt his activism but instead incorporated it into his activism, implying in his speeches that the movement had let him down and that now he would die.

The autobiographical play *The Destiny of Me* opened Off Broadway in 1992, earning an Obie and a spot on the short list for the Pulitzer. A sequel to *The Normal Heart*, *The Destiny of Me* continues the story of *The Normal Heart*'s Ned Weeks, now sick and trying to get into an experimental treatment program at the National Institutes of Health while once again dealing with his relationship with his brother—events drawn directly from Kramer's life. The play also draws on Kramer's college suicide attempt and violent relationship with his father. It earned Kramer even better reviews than *The Normal Heart* had.

Often referred to as the single most important and certainly the loudest voice of the AIDS movement, Larry Kramer is currently working on his "great American novel," *The American People*. (*See also* Jewish American Gay Literature)

Further Reading

Mass, Lawrence D. *We Must Love One Another or Die: The Life and Legacies of Larry Kramer.* New York: St. Martin's Press, 1999.

Jeffrey Godsey

KUBIAK, WANDA (1892–1968)   Polish American novelist. Wanda Kubiak deals with the adjustment of the Polish immigrants to the American mainstream. She authored only one book, the obscure *Polonaise Nevermore* (1962), published by Vantage Press of New York City.

Polonaise Nevermore takes place in Berlin, Wisconsin. The novel opens with Marya Topolska in 1947, dean of the local women's college. Her mother is sick, and she travels to the old family homestead with her niece, Kathleen O'Toole. Immediately, we are given the contrast of two generations of Polish Americans. Kathleen knows only three words of Polish and appears thoroughly assimilated.

We learn much about the past through the remembering of conversations and stories from the characters' youth. Whereas the novel begins with

Marya, it switches over to her mother, Kathleen's *Busia,* or grandmother, who remembers her past before she dies. The novel goes back in time to Poland and tells of Busia's life there, and her journey to and settling in America. Overall, *Polonaise Nevermore* brings to light what the immigrant generations went through. Each generation loses more and more of the cultural heritage. This incremental **assimilation**—and the gains and losses it entails—is at the heart of the novel.

The novel also shows how important the land was to the immigrant farmers. In their time, the land and the food that came from it were not taken for granted. Also, Kubiak shows how important the Polish Catholic Church is to the Poles and their adaptation to American life. The church goes beyond the religious institution and serves as a social institution that plays a major role in developing character and community. Even though the novel does illustrate the differences many Polish customs brought by the immigrants and the traditions of mainstream America, it shows that many of the new Polish Americans began to realize they were really not unlike the "Yankees." The core values of patriotism and individualism, and faith in religion, were very important among the immigrants as well as the Americans. However, the role of the church is actually cause for concern in a country that does not endorse any single religion, unlike Poland, which is an officially Catholic country.

Kubiak's novel includes actual historic events, and its characters are based on real people. Although the novel takes place in Wisconsin, the setting and culture presented actually reflect an amalgamation of Polish American settlements across the United States. (*See also* Polish American Novel)

Further Reading

Gladsky, Thomas S. *Princes, Peasants, and Other Polish Selves: Ethnicity in American Literature.* Amherst: U of Massachusetts P, 1992.

Gladsky, Thomas S., and Rita Holmes Gladsky, eds. *Something of My Very Own to Say: American Women Writers of Polish Descent.* New York: Columbia UP, 1998.

Weinberg, Daniel E. "Viewing the Immigrant Experience in America through Fiction and Autobiography: With a Select Bibliography." *History Teacher* 9.3 (1976): 409–32.

Wells, Miriam J. "Ethnicity, Social Stigma, and Resource Mobilization in Rural America: Reexamination of a Midwestern Experience." *Ethnohistory* 22.4 (1975): 319–43.

Stephen Oravec

KUBICKI, JAN (1952?–)   Slavic American novelist. In late 1986, Jan Kubicki's first novel, *Breaker Boys,* was published to good notices in several major newspapers. Although he would subsequently receive several National Endowment for the Arts (NEA) grants to support his work on a projected trilogy of novels, Kubicki would be unable to find a publisher for the first of those novels, titled *True Fire,* and would eventually abandon the project. (The novel still remains unpublished.) Although *Breaker Boys* did not have quite the impact of Henry Roth's *Call It Sleep,* Kubicki's stalled career immediately brings Roth's more widely known story to mind. Moreover, there are broad similarities in their novels' treatments of the immigrant experience. In both *Call It Sleep* and *Breaker Boys,* the youthful initiation story provides a suggestive corollary to the immigrant group's broader, gradual **assimilation** into American society and culture.

Set in Jeddoh, Pennsylvania, at the turn of the last century, *Breaker Boys* focuses on the formative experiences of Euan Morgan. Too young to join his father and his older brother in the deep mines, Euan finally gets a job as a breaker boy, picking slate from the mined coal after it has been run through the breakers that reduce it to a saleable size. The breaker boys straddle chutes down which the coal continually cascades on its way to being mechanically sorted by size, and the labor that the boys perform is truly back breaking. Thus, even in this "child's" job, Euan is exposed to many of the hard realities of the adult world, and ultimately he responds by leading the breaker boys in a strike to protest the brutality of their foreman and to assert their right to just treatment.

The story is given added dimension because the Morgan family's place in Jeddoh is rather uncertain. Relative newcomers, they have lived under the shadow of the suspicions directed at Euan's father, Hugh. While working at another mine, he had refused to join in a strike and had continued working, despite being condemned as a scab. So, as Euan becomes more pointedly aware of how the miners and their families are being brutally exploited by the mine owners, and as he tries to find meaning in his brother's death, he embraces the sort of labor radicalism that his father has pointedly rejected. Indeed, he becomes the protégé of the legendary labor organizer Mother Jones.

The novel is rich in historical detail about the machinery, the work practices, and the working conditions of coal mining, about the social hierarchy of company towns, about the daily lives of the laboring poor, about the differences among the ethnic groups who populated the towns and worked the mines, and about the social attitudes that various segments of the community held toward labor activism.

The back cover of the hardcover edition of *Breaker Boys* provides a photo of Kubicki, showing him to be a man of somewhat indeterminate age. On a back flyleaf, where a biographical note on the author typically appears, there is the simple statement "*Breaker Boys* is Mr. Kubicki's first novel." Indeed, an era characterized by anxieties over electronic threats to personal privacy, Kubicki has managed to keep completely private the most basic details of his life story. An extensive Google search reveals neither a birth date nor a place of birth. Although it was fairly easy to locate Kubicki because his name is not commonplace, he suggested that the following be included in lieu of a more detailed biographical profile: "Jan Kubicki no longer writes. He lives in total obscurity somewhere in south-eastern Pennsylvania, where he works as a video artist and portrait photographer" (e-mail to the author, March 10, 2004).

Further Reading

Wood, Susan. "Mining a Culture of Poverty." *Washington Post* (January 19, 1987): D15.

Martin Kich

KUMAR, AMITAVA (1963–) Indian American scholar, poet, photographer, and scriptwriter. Kumar, who teaches in the English Department at Pennsylvania State University, is a prolific and versatile scholar who often uses his own experiences as a postcolonial immigrant to explore themes of **identity**, expatriation, and nostalgia for the past in his writing and criticism.

In an essay describing his 1986 departure from his family home in Patna, India, to travel to the United States and graduate school, Kumar notes that he was "entering the drama that was becoming the reality of thousands, no, more than a million, Indians" ("Leaving My Father's House" 116). This drama—the reality of life in the **diaspora** and the inescapable sense of confusion and loss such a reality entails—is a critical and personal concern for Kumar, who endeavors to address the complexities of hybrid identities through a diversity of media that, refreshingly, appeals to both scholarly and popular readers.

Kumar's list and range of publications are prodigious. He is the editor of several volumes of politicocultural essays, including *Class Issues: Pedagogy, Cultural Studies, and the Public Sphere* (1997), *Poetics/Politics: Radical Aesthetics for the Classroom* (1999), and *World Bank Literature* (2002). Most recently, he has edited a collection of writing from well-known writers of the South Asian diaspora, including R. K. Narayan, V. S. Naipaul, Salman Rushdie, **Bharati Mukherjee**, and Hanif Kureishi, who articulate aspects of the experience of the migrant. *Away: The Indian Writer as an Expatriate* (2004) is Kumar's attempt at compiling a record of Indian literary voices outside of India, and defining the ways in which Indian emigrants, from Rabindranath Tagore to Rohinton Mistry, locate a sense of self and home not in the East or West exclusively, but in the world at large. Kumar has authored three books, including a book of poems, *No Tears for the NRI* (1996); *Passport Photos* (2000), a multigenre book that includes photography, poetry, and criticism regarding belonging and the crossing of cultural borders; and *Bombay-London-New York* (2002), an account of the multifaceted immigrant experience in three global cities through the examination of immigrant literature and Kumar's own knowledgeable perspective based on his personal life. The concept of nostalgia is of particular importance to Kumar in this work, as he speaks to the necessity of observing the ways in which the "soft" emotion of nostalgia may transform into the less harmless "hard" emotion of fundamentalism.

Kumar's nonfiction and poetry have appeared in *The Nation, Harper's, The Kenyon Review, New Statesman, Transition, American Prospect, Toronto*

Review, The Hindu, The Times of India, among other notable periodicals. He is a literary columnist for Tehelka.com and coedits the online journal *Politics and Culture.* In addition, he serves on the editorial boards of *Rethinking Marxism, Minnesota Review,* and *Cultural Logic.* In 1997 the documentary *Pure Chutney,* for which Kumar wrote the script and provided the narration, was produced to critical acclaim as a study of Indo-Trinidadian culture in a postcolonial society. Soon to be published is his current project, titled *Husband of a Fanatic: A Personal Journey Through India, Pakistan, Love, and Hate.* Throughout his expanding body of work, Kumar maintains the need to recognize that those born in the diaspora and who live in and between multiple worlds and identities are, in fact, "the inheritors of our new modernity" ("Leaving My Father's House" 103). (*See also* South Asian American Literature)

Further Reading

Kumar, Amitava. "Leaving My Father's House." *Mementos, Artifacts, and Hallucinations.* Ed. Ron Emoff and David Henderson. New York: Routledge, 2002. 101–16.

———. "World Bank Literature: A New Name for Postcolonial Studies in the Next Century." *College Literature* 26:3 (1999): 195–204.

Dana Hansen

KUMIN, MAXINE (1925–)   Jewish American poet, essayist, novelist, and children's author. Maxine Kumin is best known for her direct, unsentimental poetry about life on her two-hundred-acre New Hampshire horse farm. Her poems, which appear in such periodicals as *Atlantic Monthly, New Yorker,* and *Ploughshares* are frequently anthologized. Inevitably compared with Robert Frost and Henry David Thoreau because she writes of Nature in New England, Kumin nonetheless stands on her own as an unflinching observer of what is gritty and real. Her most frequently anthologized poems are "Woodchucks" and "Noted in *The New York Times.*" Kumin won a Pulitzer Prize in 1973 for *Up Country: Poems of New England, New and Selected* (1972). She served as consultant in poetry to the Library of Congress from January 1981 until May 1982, before the position was renamed *Poet Laureate.* She has also been poet laureate of New Hampshire. Kumin is a self-professed feminist and a proponent of compassionate animal husbandry.

Maxine Winokur Kumin was born in Germantown, Pennsylvania, on June 6, 1925, her parents' only daughter and the youngest of four children. She has loved animals, especially horses, since childhood. The details of her life are well known through Kumin's essays, many of which are collected in *Always Beginning: Essays on a Life in Poetry* (2000) and *To Make a Prairie: Essays on Poets, Poetry, and Country Living* (1979), and the numerous interviews she has granted. Kumin's father was a pawnbroker, and her mother a housewife who had wanted to be a concert pianist. The family were Reform Jews, but for kindergarten through second grade, she was sent next door to the convent school run by the Sisters of St. Joseph because the public school was a mile away. Similarly, her mother, whose family members were the only Jews in rural Virginia, played the organ for Methodist church services while growing up, and then left for Philadelphia at eighteen. Kumin remembers hearing anti-Semitic remarks from the neighborhood children and notes that her father "always referred to non-Jews as his 'Good Christian friends'" (Shomer 533). Kumin has been for many years an avowed atheist, but she has said that her Jewish consciousness is present in many of her poems.

As a child, Kumin was an avid swimmer and at eighteen would have joined a traveling synchronized swim team if her father had not refused to let her go. Kumin graduated from Radcliffe, with a bachelor's degree in 1946 and a master's degree in 1948. As an undergraduate, Kumin was so stung by the criticism of Wallace Stegner, her writing instructor, that she refused to write poems for many years. In 1957, married and the mother of three children, Kumin enrolled in a poetry workshop taught by John

Maxine Kumin. *AP/Wide World Photos.*

Holmes at the Boston Center for Adult Education, where she met fellow budding poet Anne Sexton, also a housewife with young children. Kumin and Sexton quickly became close friends and Holmes's star students. They read and critiqued each other's writing, staying connected via telephone for hours at a time while they worked in their respective homes. Kumin and Sexton later collaborated on four children's books. They remained friends until Sexton committed suicide in October 1974, just after having lunch with Kumin.

Kumin's first collection of poems, *Halfway,* was published in 1961. Her others, in addition to the Pulitzer Prize–winning *Up Country,* are as follows: *The Privilege* (1965); *The Nightmare Factory* (1970); *The Designated Heir* (1974); *House, Bridge, Fountain, Gate* (1975); *The Retrieval System* (1978); *Our Ground Time Here Will Be Brief: New and Selected Poems* (1982); *The Long Approach: Poems* (1985); *Nurture: Poems* (1989); *Looking for Luck: Poems* (1992); *Connecting* the Dots (1996); Selected Poems, 1960–1990 (1997); The Long Marriage: Poems (2001); and Bringing Together: Uncollected Early Poems 1958–1988 (2003). In addition, she has written five novels, five collections of essays and stories, and a memoir.

Kumin has frequently remarked that one cannot make a living by being a poet in the United States, but one can make a living by talking about being a poet. Teaching, writing, and lecturing about being a poet—what Kumin calls "poetry business," or "pobiz" for short—has provided a good living for Kumin. In tribute, she and husband Victor, a retired chemical engineer to whom she has been married since 1946, have named their New Hampshire property "PoBiz Farm."

It was at the farm that Kumin suffered a near-fatal accident on July 21, 1998. An experienced equestrian, Kumin had given up riding some years earlier because of her arthritis and was training for a carriage-driving competition with her favorite horse, Deuteronomy ("Deuter"), an Arabian-Standardbred chestnut gelding. When a logging truck on the nearby road spooked Deuter, Kumin was thrown from the carriage, and the frightened horse continued running. Deuter deftly avoided stepping on Kumin but pulled the 350-pound, four-wheeled carriage over the right side of her body, breaking her neck and eleven ribs, puncturing a lung, and causing other injuries as well. A fellow equestrian who was also an emergency room nurse kept Kumin immobile until the helicopter arrived to transport her, saving her life. Kumin spent three months in a halo, a cage-like restraint designed to keep her neck rigid while it healed. Inside the Halo and Beyond: The Anatomy of a Recovery (2000) is her story of nine months spent in recovery. Buoyed by the support of Victor and their three grown children, Kumin was able to return to writing and teaching six months after the accident. Several years later, however, she still has not regained full use of her right arm.

During the recovery, Kumin feared that she would lose her ability to write, but, as reviews of The Long Marriage attest, that was not the case. The volume contains several poems that had their genesis in Kumin's recuperation, but only one, "Grand Canyon," directly addresses it. Others, such as "Skinnydipping with William Wordsworth," pay tribute to the poets she has admired or, like "The Angel," attest to her political activism. Three poems, "The Ancient Lady Poets," "Three Dreams After a Suicide," and "Oblivion," are about Anne Sexton. Still others address either the literal long marriage of Victor and Maxine Kumin or, as critic Sandra M. Gilbert suggests, "the wedding of life and (or to) art that made this volume and others possible" (370). Kumin's body of work, a marriage of observations about family and friends, animals, vegetable gardens, and life and death, clearly reveals that her life is her art.

Although Kumin usually writes lyrical free verse, she has a firm grounding in prosody. In the various colleges where she has taught as visiting professor, including Princeton, Washington University, and Columbia, she insists that her students learn such forms as the villanelle, the sestina, and the pantoum in addition to the more common sonnet and quatrain. She also insists that her students memorize poems, arguing that if they are ever held as political prisoner the poems will help them keep their sanity. She credits her own memory bank of heavily metered poems for keeping her from panicking during MRI exams.

In addition to her writing, Kumin is known for her support and encouragement of budding writers and for ensuring that those writers have opportunities for recognition. She has conducted readings and writers' workshops across the country. In the poetry workshop she teaches each year in the MFA program at Florida International University, she nurtures students who attend classes in addition to holding full-time jobs. As consultant in poetry to the Library of Congress, she organized readings and lunches to bring attention to women and minority poets, who she felt were being overlooked. In 1998, Kumin and Carolyn Kizer, chancellors of the Academy of American Poets, resigned their posts to protest the racism and sexism in the organization. The academy refused to accept their resignations and the ones that followed, and began to revise its structure to admit more women and minorities. Previously, the great majority of its awards had gone to white males.

In addition to the Pulitzer Prize and a chancellorship in the Academy of American Poets, Kumin has also been awarded the Aiken Taylor Poetry Prize, the Charity Randall Prize, the Poets' Prize, and the Ruth E. Lilly Award. (*See also* Jewish American Poetry)

Further Reading

Craik, Roger. "Poetry Meets Journalism: Maxine Kumin's 'Noted in *The New York Times*'." *ANQ* 17.1 (2004): 46–48.

Gilbert, Sandra M. "Of First and Last, and Midst." *Poetry* 182.6 (2003): 356–75.

Grosholz, Emily, ed. *Telling the Barn Swallow: Poets on the Poetry of Maxine Kumin.* Hanover, NH: UP of New England, 1997.

Howard, Ben. "A Secular Believer: The Agnostic Art of Maxine Kumin." *Shenandoah: The Washington and Lee University Review* 52.2 (2002): 141–59.

Knaff, Devorah L. "Kumin Finds Rhymes and Reasons to Be a Poet." *Press-Enterprise* [Riverside, CA] (February 2, 1996): A16.

Kumin, Maxine. *Always Beginning: Essays on a Life in Poetry.* Port Townsend, WA: Copper Canyon Press, 2000. 195–234.

Ratiner, Steven. "Maxine Kumin: New Life in the Barn." *Christian Science Monitor* (May 13, 1992): 16.

Shomer, Enid. "An Interview with Maxine Kumin." *Massachusetts Review* 37 (1996): 531–55.

Claudia Milstead

KUNITZ, STANLEY (1905–) Jewish American poet. Kunitz is remarkable among American poets not only for his extraordinary longevity, but also for the unusual trajectory of his career. He came into his own as a poet only in his fifties. Then, at the age of sixty-six, he published a breakthrough

Stanley Kunitz. *AP/Wide World Photos.*

book, which he called his "emancipation proclamation." In his seventies, eighties, and even nineties, he has continued to write steadily, producing some of his finest work. Kunitz's vision is essentially tragic, his voice elegiac. But his sense of loss and his acute awareness of mortality are tempered by compassion and by his acceptance of the human condition. His vision and his eloquence have made him a significant presence in twentieth-century American poetry.

Kunitz was born of immigrant Jewish parents in Worcester, Massachusetts. His father's suicide, six months before Kunitz's birth, was a crucial event for the poet, a deep wellspring of longing and loss. His poetry across seven decades is marked by a search for the lost father, and many poems, early and late, come from powerful childhood memories. A gifted scholar, Kunitz attended Harvard at a time when the university imposed a strict quota on Jewish students. While completing his master's degree, he was told that he could not teach English at Harvard because he was a Jew. Shattered by this encounter with institutional **anti-Semitism**, Kunitz for many years pursued a career as a journalist and editor before returning eventually to teaching. While acknowledging "Jewish cultural aspirations and ethical doctrine" as influences on his work, Kunitz once described himself an "American freethinker" grounded in a wide range of intellectual and artistic traditions.

Kunitz's first book, *Intellectual Things,* appeared in 1930, but his second, *Passport to the War,* not until 1944. Neither book garnered major recognition, but his third collection, *Selected Poems: 1928–1958* (1958), won a Pulitzer Prize. Taken together, these three volumes represent what is generally regarded as Kunitz's "early" work, much of it influenced by the densely allusive, elaborately formal style of such seventeenth-century metaphysical poets as John Donne and George Herbert. In *Selected Poems,* some of the intricacy begins to yield to simpler forms, as in the widely anthologized "The War Against the Trees."

It is not until *The Testing-Tree* (1971), however, that Kunitz masters his characteristic "later" style, marked by an extraordinary clarity of image and statement. Much of the emotional distancing in the earlier work gives way in this collection to more direct, open modes of expression. *The Testing-Tree* includes poems ranging from intensely personal pieces about his childhood ("The Portrait," "The Magic Curtain") to works on historical subjects ("The Gladiators," "Around Pastor Bonhoeffer"). In the highly regarded title poem, Kunitz transforms his sense of loss, his longing for the absent father, into a powerful meditation on mortality. And in "An Old Cracked Tune," a song written in the voice of Solomon Levi, a fifteenth-century rabbi and poet, Kunitz's affirms the possibility joy even in the face of loss.

Since *The Testing-Tree*, Kunitz has produced a small but impressive body of poems. In his best work, he draws on colloquial diction and the natural rhythms of speech to achieve an almost paradoxical stateliness of expression, as in "The Wellfleet Whale," one his most frequently anthologized poems, written when he was in his mid-seventies. Important later volumes include *The Poems of Stanley Kunitz 1928–1978* (1979); *Next-to-Last Things* (1985); and *Passing Through* (1995), which won the National Book Award and demonstrates that, even in his nineties, Kunitz retained the capacity to write a powerful, passionate love poem like "Touch Me." In 2000 Kunitz published *The Collected Poems* and was named poet laureate of the United States.

During his nearly eight decades as a poet, Kunitz has also written numerous essays, many of them gathered in *A Kind of Order, a Kind of Folly: Essays and Conversations* (1975). He has also edited collections of poetry by John Keats and William Blake, published widely as a translator, and produced many reference works of literary biography for the H. W. Wilson Company.

Further Reading

Barber, David. "A Visionary Poet at Ninety." *Atlantic Monthly* 277.6 (1996): 113–20.

Hénault, Marie. *Stanley Kunitz.* Boston: Twayne, 1980.

Moss, Stanley, ed. *A Celebration for Stanley Kunitz on His Eightieth Birthday.* Riverdale-on-Hudson, NY: Sheep Meadow, 1986.

———. *To Stanley Kunitz, with Love: From Poet Friends for His 96th Birthday.* Riverdale-on-Hudson, NY: Sheep Meadow, 2002.

Orr, Gregory. *Stanley Kunitz: An Introduction to the Poetry.* New York: Columbia UP, 1985.

Michael Hennessy

KUSHNER, TONY (1956–) Jewish American playwright, essayist, and activist. Tony Kushner's highly intellectual and often lengthy plays deal with complex political and philosophical issues, the struggle of both Jews and homosexuals in modern Western society, and moments of crisis and change in human history, often magically linking such issues and events across historical and even metaphysical boundaries. He has won numerous awards for his work, most notably the Tony Award and Pulitzer Prize for *Angels in America.* Kushner approaches his work in the theater as a cultural and ethical responsibility, and has also been active as a public intellectual, speaker, activist, and nonfiction writer.

Tony Kushner accepts award for *Angels in America. AP/Wide World Photos.*

Tony Kushner was born in Manhattan, New York, on July 16, 1956, but his parents moved the family to Lake Charles, Louisiana, shortly thereafter. Kushner grew up as the child of two classical musicians and one of very few Jews in southwest Louisiana in the 1960s, something that surely shaped his worldview and sense of political activism, as much of his work deals with characters outside the perceived mainstream of American life. His mother was also an actress, and Kushner traces his fascination with the theater to watching her perform when he was a child. He has also spoken of being aware of his homosexuality from a very early age, but he did not explore that part of his identity until he returned to New York City to attend Columbia University as a young man, and did not come out of the closet until he was in his early twenties.

Kushner graduated from Columbia in 1978 and, after several years operating a switchboard at the United Nations, decided to pursue a full-time career in theater and enrolled in New York University's graduate program in directing, earning his MFA in 1984. His mentor was Carl Weber, a specialist in the work of German playwright and dramaturg Bertolt Brecht; both Kushner and his critics cite Brecht as a major influence on his plays. Tennessee Williams, George Bernard Shaw, Herman Melville, Walter Benjamin, William Shakespeare, Henrik Ibsen, and Karl Marx are also often listed among Kushner's influences.

The following year he worked as assistant director of the St. Louis Repertory Theatre, which produced his play *Yes, Yes, No, No.* By 1987 Kushner had returned to New York, where for several years he would work for major arts organizations and teach at several prominent universities, and three more of his plays were produced: Kushner's adaptation of Goethe's *Stella* and his original play *Hydriotaphia: Or, The Death of Dr. Browne: An Epic Farce about Death and Primitive Capital Accumulation* were both performed in New York, and *A Bright Room Called Day,* which had been workshopped in New York in 1985, was performed in San Francisco. *A Bright Room Called Day* tells the story of a group of radicals during the decline of the German Weimar Republic in the 1930s, but also features a parallel Jewish American female character living in the 1980s who links their tale to contemporary issues. *The Illusion,* Kushner's highly regarded adaptation of Pierre Corneille's play *L'illusion comique,* was produced in New York in 1988.

Kushner catapulted to international fame with the production of his next two plays. In 1991 *Angels in America: A Gay Fantasia on National Themes, Part One: Millennium Approaches* was produced in San Francisco and then moved to Los Angeles. It opened at the National Theatre in London in 1992, and then in New York in 1993. The second half of *Angels,* subtitled *Part Two: Perestroika,* followed a similar circuitous path while in development, and opened just six months after *Millennium Approaches,* performed in repertory by the same cast. Both plays, directed by Kushner's close collaborator George C. Wolfe, won many prestigious awards wherever they were produced. *Millennium Approaches* and *Perestroika* each won the Tony Award for Best Play in succession, and *Millennium Approaches* won Kushner the Pulitzer Prize in drama for that year. Talk of a film version soon followed, but for various reasons, production never got beyond the planning stage until Kushner finally adapted the script into a well-received, award-wining television film, directed by Mike Nichols, premiered in December 2003. The labyrinthine plot follows the oddly intertwined lives of a gay man with AIDS named Prior Walter who is visited by an angel who tells him he has been chosen as a prophet; his guilty lover fleeing from the crisis; their friend, an African American gay male nurse who is assigned to care for notorious right-wing lawyer and closeted homosexual Roy Cohn as he secretly dies from AIDS; Cohn's Mormon protégé, who is married and only beginning to come to terms with his own repressed homosexuality and who becomes the lover of Prior's former lover; the Mormon wife, who escapes from her empty marriage with valium; her mother-in-law, who comes to New York to intervene when her son comes out to her but instead winds up transformed by her experience there; the ghost of Ethel Rosenberg (executed for espionage in 1953), who haunts Roy Cohn; and an assortment of other figures symbolic of the complex fabric of American life in the 1980s. The play takes place in New York City, but also in dreams, some shared by characters who have not yet met, and even in heaven, where Prior confronts a confused ruling band of angels abandoned by God and rejects their command that humanity must cease moving and growing and changing (the agenda behind his disease), renouncing his mantle as prophet and demanding instead "more life." The play indicts Ronald Reagan and many other right-wing forces as inhuman and sometimes even evil, but it does not excuse the failings of any of its characters, while at the same time offering grace to even the worst offenders against humanity, sometimes offered by the least likely of the characters they might have oppressed. It is a rare play with an ambitious political, philosophical, and social agenda that asks more questions that it answers; in Kushner's worldview, nothing is simple or easy.

Kushner described his next play as a sort of coda to *Angels in America* inspired by a moment in the earlier work. *Slavs! Thinking About the Longstanding Problems of Virtue and Happiness* debuted to mixed response at the 1994 Humana Festival of New American Plays at Actors Theatre of Louisville and was subsequently produced in New York and London. The play deals with the last days of the old Soviet Union and is set in 1985 Moscow and 1992 Siberia. The central question of the play is posed by a character who also briefly appeared in *Angels,* Aleksii Antedilluvianovich Prelasparianov, the World's Oldest Living Bolshevik, who demands of the Politburo just before his death that they tell him how they plan to live now that they are rejecting the "Beautiful Theory" that has governed their way of life. The play's characters try to find a way to live through and beyond this upheaval in political philosophy in much the same way as the characters in *Angels* learn to live beyond hope in their shattered world.

Kushner's next project was an adaptation of *The Good Person of Setzuan* by Bertolt Brecht, perhaps his greatest influence as a playwright. It premiered at the La Jolla Playhouse in July 1994. Another adaptation followed: *A Dybbuk, or Between Two Worlds,* which was based on Solomon Ansky's play *Der Dybbuk,* opened at the Hartford Stage in 1995 and again in New York in 1997.

In 1996 Kushner contributed another new offering to the Humana Festival, a one act titled *Reverse Transcription: Six Playwrights Bury a Seventh, A Ten-Minute Play That's Nearly Twenty Minutes Long.* The play features several characters drawn from motifs and figures in theater history conducting a funeral for a talented playwright as darkly comic dialogue explores what it means to be a dramatist. In 1998 Kushner contributed an eccentric Freudian comedy set in a psychiatrist's office, titled *Terminating, or Lass Meine Schmerzen Nicht Veloren Sein,* to the collection *Love's Fire: Seven New Plays Inspired by Seven Shakespearean Sonnets.* And Kushner's play *Henry Box Brown, or the Mirror of Slavery* was produced at the National Theatre in London in 1998.

Kushner's next play to receive significant attention from critics and the popular media was *Homebody/Kabul,* which made its New York debut in December 2001. It seemed an almost eerie coincidence that Kushner's play dealing with Afghanistan was in preparation for production when terrorists flew airplanes into the World Trade Center buildings on September 11, 2001, which prompted the United States to go to war against Afghanistan for harboring Al Qaeda leader Osama bin Laden. The first part of the four-hour play is a long monologue by a lonely, eccentric British housewife whose fascination with Afghanistan leads her to travel alone to Kabul in 1998. The remainder of the play deals with the efforts of her husband and daughter to discover the truth about her fate after she disappears in the Taliban-ruled country. Many critics hailed it as Kushner's return to the ambitious epic scope of *Angels in America.*

In response to the Bush administration's addition of Iraq to the country's theaters of war, Kushner began writing *Only We Who Guard the Mystery Shall Be Unhappy.* The first scene, which features First Lady Laura Bush reading a bedtime story to the ghosts of dead Iraqi children, was given staged readings at numerous theaters in 2003.

Kushner collaborated with Broadway composer Jeanine Tesori to write the sung-through musical *Caroline, or Change,* which opened at the Public Theatre in New York in December 2003. The production, directed by

George C. Wolfe, moved to Broadway in April 2004 and was nominated for several Tonys, one of which was won by Anika Noni Rose for her supporting role as a budding teenage activist. The story is Kushner's most autobiographical yet. Caroline Thibodeaux is an African-American maid employed by a Jewish family in Louisiana in 1963, and the play deals with how she and the young son of her employers, among others, deal with the peculiar power dynamics of race and class in the deep South and the many ways, big and small, in which change is coming to their world in the civil rights era. A cast album of the full score (there is virtually no spoken dialogue) was released in summer 2004. In 2005 Kushner's next play, *The Intelligent Homosexual's Guide to Capitalism and Socialism with a Key to the Scriptures*, is set to debut in Los Angeles. He is also developing a screenplay based on the life of playwright **Eugene O'Neill**.

Kushner has written a number of nondramatic essays and books, including a 2003 children's book called *Brundibar*, illustrated by Maurice Sendak, which is also in development as an opera. Two of his best-known prose publications are the 1995 book *Thinking about the Longstanding Problems of Virtue and Happiness: Essays, a Play, Two Poems and a Prayer,* and the 2003 essay collection *Save Your Democratic Citizen Soul!: Rants, Screeds, and Other Public Utterances for Midnight in the Republic.*

While not all of his work has met with critical or audience expectations in the wake of *Angels of America*, Kushner is widely regarded as one of the most inventive, visionary, unique, thought-provoking, and gifted playwrights of his generation, and, as he seems to be entering his most productive stage yet as he enters middle age, his reputation will surely grow and evolve in the years to come. (*See also* Jewish American Gay Literature, Jewish American Theater)

Further Reading

Brask, Per, ed. *Essays on Kushner's Angels.* Winnipeg: Blizzard Publishing, 1995.

Fisher, James. *The Theatre of Tony Kushner: Living Past Hope.* New York: Routledge, 2001.

Geis, Deborah R., and Steven F. Kruger, eds. *Approaching the Millennium: Essays on Angels in America.* Ann Arbor: U of Michigan P, 1997.

Vorlicky, Robert. *Tony Kushner in Conversation.* Ann Arbor: U of Michigan P. 1998.

Laura Grace Pattillo

KWONG, DAN (1954–)   Asian American performance artist. A graduate of the School of the Art Institute of Chicago, Dan Kwong is best known for utilizing an eclectic mixture of music, dance, multimedia, dynamic physical movement, and martial arts during performance monologues, which explore his struggles as a Chinese/Japanese/American male. These autobiographical solo performances focus on the distinct challenges of being a mixed-heritage Asian American facing interethnic discrimination.

Kwong's first show, *Secrets of the Samurai Centerfielder* (1989), explores the challenges of living with the triple **ethnicity** of his American Japanese mother and Chinese father's heritage. Using baseball as a metaphor, *Secrets* details Kwong's rich family history and childhood including the **immigration** of his maternal mother's family, his grandparents' internment during World War II, the divorce of his parents, his "model minority" sisters, and his exclusion from both Chinese and Japanese cliques at school.

Kwong's later performances include *Tales from the Fractured Tao with Master Nice Guy* (1991), *Monkhood in Three Easy Lessons* (1993), *The Dodo Vaccine* (1994), *The Sword and the Chrysanthemum* (1997), *The Night the Moon Landed on 39th Street* (1999), and *Station Wagons of Life* (2000), among others. Although each performance piece differs significantly—for example, *Tales* examines Kwong's dysfunctional family; *Dodo* looks at HIV/AIDS in the Asian American community; and *Night* addresses universal human experiences—Kwong's personal struggles with isolation and cultural self-loathing act as the backbone of each piece and provide the constant against which he explodes stereotypes, working to break the cycle of silence within Asian American communities.

In addition to founding "Treasure in the House," L.A.'s first Asian Pacific American Performance and Visual Art series, Kwong also founded the 1994 performance workshop, "Everything You Ever Wanted to Know about Asian Men But Didn't Give Enough of a S— to Ask," a series of participants' autobiographical performances intended to encourage more men to participate in the arts. Besides publishing various essays and performances, Kwong has also been recognized by the National Endowment for the Arts and the Rockefeller Foundation and has been the recipient of numerous fellowships for his excellence in performance art.

Kwong's 2004 anthology, *From Inner Worlds to Outer Space: The Multimedia Performances of Dan Kwong,* collects some of his best-known performances and includes highlights from the transcript of an ongoing interview carried on between 1999 and 2003 in which he shares his thoughts on the roots of his creative energy and the future of autobiographical solo performance. Hailed by critics as a masterful storyteller, Kwong's innovative solo performances combining autobiography, multimedia, and storytelling identify him as the best-known major autobiographical solo performer in American theater.

Further Reading

Lee, Esther Kim. "Between the Personal and the Universal: Asian American Solo Performance from the 1970s to the 1990s." *Journal of Asian American Studies* 6.3 (2003): 289–312.

Ling, Amy, ed. *Yellow Light: The Flowering of Asian American Arts.* Philadelphia: Temple University Press, 1999.

Lowenberg, Cathy. "A Few Minutes with Dan Kwong." *International Examiner* (April 16, 1996): 17.

Sylvia M. DeSantis

L

LAHIRI, JHUMPA (1967–) Indian American novelist and short story writer. Born in London to parents from India and raised in Rhode Island, Lahiri earned her bachelor's degree from Barnard College and her master's degrees in English, creative writing, and comparative studies in literature and the arts, followed by a PhD in renaissance studies, from Boston University. A fellowship at the Fine Arts Work Center in Provincetown launched Lahiri's career as a fiction writer. Her short stories have appeared in *The New Yorker, Aging, Epoch, The Louisville Review, Harvard Review,* and *Story Quarterly.* Lahiri has taught creative writing at Boston University and the Rhode Island School of Design. Currently, she lives in New York City.

The recipient of a Transatlantic Review 1993 award from the Henfield Foundation and a fiction prize from *The Louisville Review* in 1997, Lahiri published her first collection of short stories, *The Interpreter of Maladies,* in 1999, going on to receive the PEN/Hemingway award for the best debut of the year. The title story of her collection was selected for both the O. Henry Award and *The Best American Short Stories.* In 1999 *The New Yorker* named her as one of the twenty best writers under the age of forty.

The Interpreter of Maladies, which won her the Pulitzer Prize for Fiction in 2000, is a collection of nine stories, seven of which deal with immigrant lives in the United States. The two exceptions, "The Real Durwan" and "The Treatment of Bibi Haldar," are set in Calcutta. However, the protagonists in these two stories—one a sweeper of stairwells, and the other an epileptic young woman—share the common dilemmas of displacement and marginalization. Lahiri's characters, whether it is Mr. Pirzada in "When Mr. Pirzada Came to

Jhumpa Lahiri. *AP/Wide World Photos.*

Dine" or Mrs. Sen in "Mrs. Sen's," are all caught up in situations that offer few explanations and fewer solutions. In "The Interpreter of Maladies," the bored Mrs. Das, who is visiting India with her husband and children, is another discontented character. She steps out of her apathy only to relapse into it when Mr. Kapasi, the interpreter of maladies, is unable to interpret the cause of her unhappiness, even after she has confessed to him a dark secret of her sexual life. Mrs. Sen, a babysitter, becomes desperate when she can neither hold on to the familiar world she has left behind nor adapt herself to the New World she has come to live in and where she "cannot sometimes sleep in so much silence." "A Temporary Matter," a finely crafted and acutely poignant story, illustrates the alienation of Shoba and Shukumar, whose marriage has come to an impasse. A one-hour power cut for five consecutive evenings draws them into an intimacy they hadn't experienced since their baby's death. The reprieve, however, is lost as soon as the electricity is restored. "The Third and Final Continent" is different from the rest of the stories, for here the protagonist has traveled farther in terms of time and experience. Though he is still bewildered, as he says at the end of the story, "by each mile I have traveled, each meal I have eaten, each person I have known, each room in which I have slept," he is at peace for he has found his "final continent" at last.

Written in a direct, unadorned but lucid prose, the stories stand out as a testament to Lahiri's control of the narrative art where there is not a word out of place, not a situation sentimentalized, and not an emotion exaggerated. In exploring the psychological and physical dislocation of her characters, she manages to negotiate and interpret, too, the differences between Indian and American cultures for her readers.

The Namesake (2003), *Lahiri's* first novel, continues with and extends the themes of displacement, alienation, and the search for one's **identity**. Gogol Ganguli, the protagonist of the novel, is born to Indian immigrant parents in Cambridge, Massachusetts. His father names him Gogol after the Russian writer Nikolai Gogol, whom he greatly admired. The boy, however, grows up resenting his name Gogol as much as he hates his Indian culture. Since the given name is neither Indian nor American, the boy changes it to Nikhil in an effort to reinvent himself. He wants to announce to the world,

"I'm Nikhil," but realizes that "his parents, and their friends, and the children of their friends, and all his own friends from high school, will never call him anything but Gogol." Obviously, Lahiri uses the name as a metaphor for one's identity and the crises brought on by its indeterminacy. The farther Gogol/Nikhil goes from his family and his heritage, the farther away he travels from himself. It is only toward the end, actually after his father's death, his failed marriage, and his widowed mother's decision to return to India, that Gogol/Nikhil comes to the point of self-realization, from where his growth may begin. For the first time he recognizes the pain his parents must have gone through "leaving their respective families behind, seeing them so seldom, dwelling unconnected, in perpetual state of expectation, of longing. He had spent years maintaining distance from his origins; his parents, in bridging that distance as best as they could." He is finally at home in his body.

The Namesake makes a fine attempt at understanding the immigrant psyche, which involves more than a physical and cultural displacement. "For being a foreigner, Ashima . . . [begins] to realize, is a sort of lifelong pregnancy—a perpetual wait, a constant burden, a continuous feeling of sorts." Lahiri effortlessly weaves into her narrative scenes of Calcutta that range from crowded streets and buses to posh suburbs and quite bungalows. Not a single discordant note is to be found in her dialogue, for she understands the American idiom and uses it deftly. And what is more, she is a good storyteller. Missing from the novel, however, is the intensity and tension the reader finds so fascinating in her short stories, which affects the delineation of characters in the novel as well. The pace of the narrative slows down when Lahiri strains after details of Indian customs created for the benefit of the American reader. But these are minor points in an otherwise fascinating story.

Jhumpa Lahiri belongs to a newly emerging group of young diasporic writers, such as Monica Ali and Zadie Smith, who write about their peoples back home, about immigrants to the West, and about the mixing of cultures with an ease and unselfconsciousness that places them in the mainstream of English writing. (*See also* South Asian American Literature)

Further Reading

Austen, Benjamin. "In the Shadow of Gogol." *New Leader* (September/October 2003): 31–32.

Bess, Jennifer. "Lahiri's Interpreter of Maladies." *Explicator* 62.2 (2004): 125–28.

Bromwich, David. "The Man without Qualities." *Nation* (October 2003): 36–38.

Farnsworth, Elizabeth. Interview. *PBS Online News Hour.* April 12, 2000.

Kakutani, Michiko. "Liking America, but Longing for India." *New York Times* (August 6, 1999): E2.

Lewis, Simon. "Lahiri's Interpreter of Maladies." *Explicator* (Summer 2001): 219–21.

Lynn, David H. "Virtues of Ambition." *Kenyon Review* (Summer 2004): 160–67.

Munson, Sam. "Born in the USA." *Commentary* (November 2003): 68–71.

Rothstein, Mervyn. "India's Post-Rushdie Generation." *New York Times* (July 3, 2000): E1.

Ruddy, Christopher. "Strangers of a Train." *Commonweal* (December 19, 2003): 18–20.

Sen, Mandira. "Names and Nicknames." *Women's Review of Books* (March 2004): 9–10.

Vijay Lakshmi Chauhan

LAKSHMI, VIJAY (1943–) Indian American short story writer. Lakshmi's debut book of fiction, *Pomegranate Dreams and Other Stories* (2002), is a collection of seven short stories and the title novella. The stories chronicle the hopes, dreams, despair, and the pathos of immigrant Indian women caught between two worlds and their search for the American dream. The book is part of the tradition pioneered by Indian American women writers such as **Bharati Mukherjee**, **Chitra Divakaruni**, **Meena Alexander**, and many others. Like Lakshmi, they are well-traveled women who came to the United States to further their education and who now teach at the college level. *Pomegranate Dreams* moves beyond these pioneering women who wrote about the Indian **diaspora**'s alienation and psychological conflicts in their attempts to assimilate into the American culture. This is a nuanced work on domesticity exploring such universal themes as the parent-child conflict and the disintegration of a marriage, but also incorporating the need to balance divergent cultures, especially when east meets west, which is multicultural.

Lakshmi's short stories are narrated by strong, complex, and well-developed characters that break the stereotype of the immigrant condition and the triumphs and challenges these women encounter in their transition to their new lives. For example, in one short story, "Mannequin," a mother narrates how her teenage daughter does not want her to wear a sari to a school function and tells about her difficulties in going to the store to buy a dress. The title novella, "Pomegranate Dreams," is written from the perspective of a woman looking back on her childhood. Having recently arrived in the United States, she is homesick for her home in Jaipur, India. Now living on a street named Brink Road, a name that is symbolic of her situation, she is trying to cope with missing her grandparents in India, with **racism**, and with being teased at school. This is a lyrical, tender, and understated story exploring the innocence and confusion of childhood.

Except for the novella, all seven stories are narrated by adult women. Three of the stories are narrated by Anu, who is married to a university professor and who is the mother of school-age children who have completely assimilated into American culture and prefer American foods and clothes. The book gently critiques some of the Indian mindsets and situations: the traditional Indian male who does not want his wife to work and wealthy, professional Indians embracing the American dream of financial success and their resulting conflict with spirituality. Some of the stories move beyond the Indian community to compare the experiences of other immigrants—Russian immigrant women, for example. One story deals with adultery; two professionals passionately in love with each other cannot leave their respective unhappy marriages due to their ingrained cultural values. Lakshmi also examines a circumstance many adult immigrants to the West experience, the circumstance of having aging parents in their home country, and one story focuses on an adult child trying to convince a widowed mother to immigrate to the United States.

Lakshmi's contribution to Indian American literature rests on her compelling and engrossing stories that transcend different cultures to incorporate universal themes. (*See also* South Asian American Literature)

Further Reading

Ulrich, Anne D. "Vijay Lakshmi." *Writers of the Indian Diaspora: A Bio-Bibliographical Critical Sourcebook.* Ed. Emmanuel S. Nelson. Westport, CT: Greenwood Press, 1993. 175–79.

Ymitri Jayasundera

LAPINE, JAMES (1949–) Jewish American playwright and director. James Lapine is best known for his award-winning collaborations with Stephen Sondheim, in musicals such as *Sunday in the Park with George* and *Into the Woods.* While occasionally highlighting portrayals of Jewish life, the musicals and dramas of James Lapine are celebrated primarily for their conceptual innovation and visual appeal. In both directing and writing projects, he tends to avoid traditional realism, often incorporating memories, thoughts, and dreams as substantial story elements. He has won numerous honors, including a Pulitzer Prize for drama and multiple Tony Awards.

Lapine earned a Master of Fine Arts degree in photography and design at the California Institute of Arts. While subsequently teaching and working as a graphic artist at the Yale School of Drama, he took advantage of a Yale initiative encouraging teachers and students to work on projects outside their usual fields. Borrowing from his background in the visual arts, Lapine decided to stage **Gertrude Stein**'s poetic *Photograph,* relying heavily on projections at a time when their use in the theater was rare. After a popular run at Yale, *Photograph* opened again at the Open Space Theatre in New York in 1977 and earned an Obie Award.

Following the success of *Photograph,* Lapine wrote and directed two projects with Playwrights Horizons: the play *Table Settings* in 1980 and the one act musical *March of the Falsettos* in 1981, a collaboration with William Finn. Both plays explore the boundaries of Jewish family life through comedy and modest stereotype. The main character of *March of the Falsettos* is a gay man who leaves his family for a young lover, later attempting to balance his two worlds. Lapine and Finn revisited the storyline nine years later with *Falsettoland,* a continuation integrating the AIDS epidemic. The two one-act musicals were combined into a single piece, *Falsettos,* in 1992 at the John Golden Theatre on Broadway. The production received Tony Awards for best score and best book. In 1981 Lapine wrote and directed *Twelve Dreams,* which performed at the Off Broadway Martinson Hall of the Public Theatre. A drama based on a case study of Carl Jung, the play utilized a scrim, projections, and other sound and lighting effects to portray the Jungian dreams of a ten-year-old girl.

Returning to the Playwrights Horizons in 1983, Lapine began a famous partnership, writing the book to Stephen Sondheim's music and lyrics for *Sunday in the Park with George.* One of the still images Lapine had used years earlier in *Photograph* was a projection of the nineteenth-century pointillist painting by Georges Seurat, *A Sunday Afternoon on the Island of La Grande Jatte.* In the musical, Lapine and Sondheim dramatize the subjects of this painting as characters in the life of the artist, Seurat, and as painted figures complaining of the heat on the canvas. The character Seurat builds his painting with both living actors and painted cutouts. The second act satirizes the contemporary art world with the story of another George, the fictional great grandson of Seurat, a light and sculpture artist who loses his vision under the pressure of seeking promotions and commissions. After a workshop production was created and performed at the Playwrights Horizon, *Sunday in the Park with George* opened at the Booth Theatre on Broadway in 1984. The play received a Tony nomination, an Olivier Award, and the 1985 Pulitzer Prize for drama.

The Lapine and Sondheim team also received popular acclaim for their next musical venture, *Into the Woods,* which opened at the Old Globe Theatre in San Diego before moving to the Martin Beck Theatre on Broadway in 1987. The first act of *Into the Woods,* which cleverly and comically weaves together several children's fairytales, was praised by most critics for its inventiveness and fun. The same critics often gave less favorable reviews for the second act, in which the familiar fairytale characters die or discover that life does not continue "happily ever after." Even with the reserved critical attention, however, *Into the Woods* garnered several awards, including Tony Awards for best musical book and best score.

Following Lapine's solo writing and directing project, *Luck, Pluck, and Virtue*, at the La Jolla Playhouse in 1993, Lapine and Sondheim collaborated a third time with the 1994 musical *Passion,* winning the Tony Awards for best musical and best musical book. *Passion* is a story of obsessive love set in 1863 Italy and based on a 1981 Italian film by Ettore Scola. The protagonist, Giorgio, a captain in the Italian army, is pursued throughout the play by Fosca, the ill and homely cousin of his commanding officer. He learns to accept her love as the play ends tragically. Despite the awards, critical reception of *Passion* was harsh. Reviewers faulted Sondheim for a lack of musical variety and Lapine for his plot reliance on love letters and for offering little relief from the story's gloom. A few critics, and Lapine himself, felt that the play was moving but misplaced on Broadway and that it would have fared better with an Off Broadway or opera audience.

In more recent years, Lapine's writing projects have included two more musical collaborations with William Finn, *A New Brain,* produced at the Mitzi E. Newhouse Theater at Lincoln Center in 1998, and *Muscle,* at the Pegasus Players in Chicago in 2001; and the plays *The Moment When,* at Playwrights Horizons in 2000, and *Fran's Bed,* at the Long Wharf Theatre in 2003. While continuing to write, Lapine has also pursued an active and successful career as a film and stage director. (*See also* Jewish American Musicals, Jewish American Stereotypes)

Further Reading

Berg, Joshua. "James Lapine" *Contemporary Jewish-American Dramatists and Poets.* Ed. Joel Shatzky and Michael Taub. Westport, CT: Greenwood Press, 1999. 90–94.

Jacobs, Leonard. "In Focus: James Lapine Retraces His Journey." *Back Stage–The Performing Arts Weekly* 43.27 (July 5, 2002–July 11, 2002): 5, 31.

Thelen, Lawrence. "James Lapine." *The Showmakers: Great Directors of the American Musical Theatre.* New York: Routledge, 2000. 59–73.

Steven Pounders

LA PUMA, SALVATORE (1929–)   Italian American fiction writer. Salvatore La Puma only took up writing fiction full time in his mid-fifties, after careers as an advertising copywriter and real estate salesman.

Born in Brooklyn but a long-time resident of Santa Barbara, California, La Puma has produced three books since the mid-1980s: *The Boys of Bensonhurst* (1987), which won the prestigious Flannery O'Connor Award for Short Fiction and received an American Book Award; *A Time for Wedding Cake* (1991); and *Teaching Angels to Fly* (1992).

Like many others, La Puma uses his Italian American roots as the basis of his writing. Both of his first two books are set in Bensonhurst, the part of Brooklyn where La Puma was raised and which has long had a multiethnic population. With an extreme attention to detail and a masterful portrayal of characters through their Italian-accented English, La Puma vividly recreates the period when the area was heavily Sicilian, during and after World War II. Immigrants and their American offspring are shown struggling in many ways: making ends meet, maintaining Sicilian family values, and taking advantage of new American cultural freedoms—but often in a comical way.

La Puma enjoys poking fun at stereotypes. One that he especially explores is the stereotype of Sicilian *machismo.* Men and boys explore sexual freedom to the limit in both books. Women are desired, pursued, and enjoyed; they rarely say no. In the background sits another stereotype—the Sicilian mama, often embittered, always in black, trying to maintain Sicilian honor and traditions. And La Puma finds lots of material for parody in stories about mobsters. Desire for a job that will pay more than the bare minimum causes teenage boys to flirt with mob-related activity. For instance, fifteen-year-old Ernesto Foppo, breaking a promise he believes he made to his dead father's ghost to not get involved in the mob, agrees to be an accomplice in a hold-up in "The Gangster's Ghost." In another story, two boys, Mike and Vito, go even further, robbing a church. These two stories are good examples of the black humor that characterizes La Puma's earthy style.

The novel *A Time for Wedding Cake* is a parody of the usual portrayal of post–World War II American conformity. Through various ups and downs, two brothers, Mario and Gene, eventually both marry (hence the title) and settle down near each other and their continually warring Sicilian parents. In spite of deaths, accidents, infidelities, infertility—it is hard to keep up with all the action—the brothers remain locked in a darkly comic embrace with each other and their wives.

The third book, *Teaching Angels to Fly*, represents a partial break from the setting and themes of the earlier books. While several stories are set in Bensonhurst and involve Sicilians, others are written in the "magical realism" style associated with Gabriel García Márquez and have other settings. La Puma also explores other tones in his writing, although he remains a master of his usual style.

Christina Biava

LARSEN, NELLA (1891–1964)   African American novelist and short story writer. Nella Larsen was born April 13, 1891, and died March 30, 1964. The daughter of a Danish mother and a West Indian father, Larsen at birth was named Nellie Walker. When Larsen was two years old, her father died. Shortly after his death, Nella's mother married Peter Larsen, a white man of Danish descent. Peter Larsen adopted Nellie Walker, who from that time on used the surname Larsen.

When Larsen's mother and stepfather welcomed the birth of their own biological daughter, color discrimination began to occur in the home. Peter Larsen was embarrassed by Nella Larsen's dark skin and made no attempt to hide his embarrassment from his stepdaughter. Larsen therefore spent as much time away from her all-white family as she could. Finding little joy in her home, Larsen turned to books for comfort and for self-education. Her extraordinary knowledge and book learning would later cause most of her literary and professional associates to assume that she was a college graduate, though she never took a degree.

With her sister, Larsen attended private school in Chicago. From 1909 to 1910, she attended Fisk University, where for the first time in her life, similar to **W. E. B. Du Bois**, she was immersed in African American culture. Unlike Du Bois, however, who upon arriving at Fisk found comfort and embraced his black environment, Larsen did not feel at ease there, or in any other predominantly black community. Leaving Fisk after only one year and moving to Denmark, Larsen audited classes at the University of Copenhagen.

In 1912 Larsen returned to the United States and for the next three years studied nursing at Lincoln Hospital in New York City. She worked in the field of nursing, both as a nurse and supervisor of nurses, for the next six years. First, she was employed at Tuskegee Institute's Andrew Memorial Hospital and later at Lincoln Hospital, where she had received her training in nursing. Larsen also worked for New York City's Board of Health.

In 1920 Larsen's first literary work was published in *The Brownies' Book,* a magazine edited by **Jessie Redmon Fauset**, a writer with whom Larsen developed a friendship. **James Weldon Johnson**, **Langston Hughes**, **Walter White**, and Carl Van Vechten—all writers of the **Harlem Renaissance**— also befriended Larsen. These friendships began developing in 1922 when Larsen took a job in the Harlem Branch of the New York Public Library.

While Fauset was the individual who first published Larsen, White and Van Vechten were the ones who assisted Larsen in having *Quicksand* (1928) published, which was the first of her two novels. These two men persuaded Alford A. Knopf publishers to offer Larsen a contract. With the publication of Larsen's second novel, *Passing* (1929), Larsen's standing as a major author of the Harlem Renaissance was firmly established.

The plots of both of Larsen's novels are quite similar in that they both concern women of mixed **ethnicity**. Helga Crane, the protagonist of *Quicksand,* is the daughter of a Danish American mother and an African American father. Helga struggles for acceptance from her family but does not receive it. She constantly moves from city to city and from country to country in pursuit of acceptance and happiness.

In *Passing* Irene Redfield and Clare Kendry, two African Americans who look white, are at the center of the story. Although both women are "passing," meaning that their skin color allows them to live the lives of white women, Irene passes only now and then. Clare, in contrast, having married a white man who does not know that she is an African American, passes one hundred percent of the time.

In 1928 the Harmon Foundation awarded Larsen a bronze medal for fiction. Her two-time nomination for the Harlem Award for Distinguished Achievement among Negroes in the literature section, in 1928 and 1929, meant that she had won the respect and acclaim of her fellow artists. And Larsen won a Guggenheim Fellowship in creative writing in 1930, becoming the first African American woman to win the award in that category.

The year nineteen thirty did bring Larsen honor on the one hand, but brought dishonor on the other. The award-winning novelist was at the height of her popularity when in 1930 she was accused of plagiarizing "Sanctuary," her short story that had been published in January of that year. Although her publishers accepted her explanation that the similarities between her story and "Mrs. Adis" by the British writer Shelia Kaye-Smith could be attributed to sheer coincidence, an emotionally damaged Larsen lacked the motivation to continue her writing. After "Sanctuary" Larsen published nothing else.

On a more personal level, Larsen's marital difficulties may have contributed to her literary silence. She had married Elmer Imes, an African American physicist involved in pioneering work at Fisk. Although the marriage had been troubled for a while, the couple remained together for the sake of Imes's career. His extramarital affair with a white woman eventually led the couple to divorce in 1933. Imes's involvement with the woman was reported in various black newspapers around the country. Larsen suffered great embarrassment and became despondent. Her embarrassment was exacerbated in 1941 when, after Imes's death, the white woman, carrying the cremated remains of Imes, returned to Fisk and scattered Imes's ashes over the campus.

Mother-in-law issues also plagued the Larsen-Imes marriage. Imes's mother—who looked like a white woman—and Larsen did not get along well. Ms. Imes refused even to visit in the home of her son and daughter-in-law while Larsen was present.

The accusations of plagiarism and the troubles of home undoubtedly had an impact on Larsen's creativity. Larsen's natural tendency towards nervousness and her fondness for privacy may also have made it difficult for her to concentrate and discipline herself for the task of writing.

Some of the biographical details of Larsen's life are difficult to substantiate and others, because of Larsen's unwillingness to discuss the more personal aspects of her life, are difficult to locate. Some sources give 1891 as the year of her birth while others say 1893. Some scholars have speculated that Larsen was elusive about her life quite simply because she felt rejected by her white relatives and found it too painful to discuss her feelings of rejection and sadness. Records from Fisk show that Larsen changed her name from Nellie Marian to Nella Marie, which suggests Larsen's attempt to separate herself from a painful past while also attempting to construct a new identity.

Not a particularly friendly woman, Larsen was an outsider. She was different from most of the other women of her time. For example, Larsen wore short dresses, smoked cigarettes, kept her hair short, and subscribed to no organized religion. Her outsider status and her desire for privacy caused her to live her final days alone and to die alone. Larsen died of a heart attack in her Second Avenue apartment in New York. A friend discovered her body almost a week later.

Even though Larsen was one of the most significant novelists of the Harlem Renaissance, she was all but forgotten until the 1960s when the next great African American artistic movement occurred, namely the **Black Arts Movement**. That movement led to the reprinting of many forgotten African American texts, and *Quicksand* and *Passing* were two of the more popular novels to be rediscovered and reprinted. Since the 1960s, Larsen's novels have continued to be of interest to those studying African American literature, American literature, and women's literature.

Further Reading

Davis, Thadious M. *Nella Larsen, Novelist of the Harlem Renaissance: A Woman's Life Unveiled.* Baton Rouge: Louisiana State UP, 1996.

Joyce Russell-Robinson

LATTANY, KRISTIN [HUNTER] (1931–)   African American novelist. Best known for her 1960s adult and young-adult novels focused on
poor, urban African American communities, Lattany received praise for
creating nuanced works that went beyond one-sided portrayals of social
dysfunction. Having published three novels since 1996, Lattany remains an
active author whose recent works mix popular presentation with pointed
political argument.

Born Kristin Eggleston in Philadelphia, Lattany attended the University
of Pennsylvania and graduated in 1951. In the following years, she worked
as a copywriter, television scriptwriter, and professor of creative writing at
the University of Pennsylvania, publishing several novels under the name
Kristin Hunter. As of 2004, she was the author of thirteen works of fiction,
six for children and seven for adults, and she has won numerous awards,
including the 1996 Moonstone Black Writing Celebration Lifetime Achievement Award.

Critical attention to Lattany's works has focused primarily on her first
novel, *God Bless the Child* (1964). The novel takes its title from a famous
Billie Holiday song, and, as Gerald Early points out, it echoes themes associated with Holiday's life: the rise to riches of an African American woman
who is ultimately destroyed by the limitations of the world around her.
Chronicling the tragic life of Rosie Fleming, the novel recounts the character's struggles to attain the wealth her grandmother observes daily as a
maid to a white family. Struggling to keep three jobs, Rosie literally works
herself to death to achieve the outer trappings of success. Ultimately, the
novel suggests that the "American dream" is deadly to those who are denied
opportunity because of racial and sexual politics.

Lattany continues to explore the relationship between **racism** and success in her two most well-known young adult novels, *The Soul Brothers and
Sister Lou* (1968) and its sequel, *Lou in the Limelight* (1981). Explicit in its portrayal of economic hardship and police brutality as seen through heroine
Louretta's eyes, *Soul Brothers* also foregrounds the positive values of her
community. Because the novel concludes with the sudden success of the
singing group Lou has formed with her friends, many reviewers argued
that its happy ending was unrealistic. However, although the ending may
be contrived, it is less than optimistic: Success drives a wedge between the
group members and their families and friends, reminding the reader that
riches for the chosen few will not solve the socioeconomic problems racism
has created for the community as a whole. *Lou in the Limelight* ratifies this
assessment, as Lou and her fellow band members find themselves manipu-
lated and placed in debt by the unscrupulous white recording industry.
Together, both novels work to illustrate that such dreams of fame and fortune cannot offer the deeper solutions needed for the problems facing the
African American poor.

Such critical confusion over Lattany's use of optimism, humor, and satire
occasionally marked the largely positive reception of *The Landlord* (1966),

noted for its comic style, and *The Lakestown Rebellion* (1978), a fictionalization of a real-life struggle to preserve an historic all-black town from the wrecking-ball. While Lattany's three most recent novels also possess a light touch and popular appeal, they indicate that she still uses this approach as part of her own brand of social protest. For example, *Do Unto Others* (2000) uses the relationship between its generous African American heroine and a scheming, selfish African woman to insist that solidarity between Africans and African Americans is far from given, and African Americans themselves have far too little to share. Continuing this tendency to take issue with received wisdom, *Breaking Away* (2003) chronicles the political education of Bethesda, an Ivy League professor who gradually loses her blinders regarding the racism of her colleagues and the supposedly liberal institution in which she works. Rather than learning to fight back against all odds, however, Bethesda must come to grips both with the **racism** around her and the fatal danger of trying to attain justice from a ruthless white establishment. Lattany's recent novels thus continue what could be considered her trademark style—iconoclastic yet pragmatic political argument, often married to an informal or humorous approach. (*See also* African American Young Adult Literature)

Further Reading

Early, Gerald. "Working Girl Blues: Mothers, Daughters, and the Image of Billie Holiday in Kristin Hunter's *God Bless the Child*." *Black American Literature Forum* 20 (Winter 1986): 423–42.

Harris, Trudier. *From Mammies to Militants*. Philadelphia: Temple UP, 1982.

Neufield, John. Review of *Soul Brothers and Sister Lou*. *New York Times Book Review* (January 26, 1969): 26.

Tate, Claudia. *Black Women Writers at Work*. New York: Continuum, 1983. 79–88.

Jane Elliott

LAURENCE, PATRICIA ONDEK (1942–) Slovak American author, literary historian and critic, and professor. Her professional work and writings have focused primarily on women here and abroad. After serving as deputy director of the Center for the Study of Women and Society at City University of New York (1993–95), Laurence became codirector of the Activist Women's Voices Oral History Project (1995–2003), through which the voices of unheralded activist women in community-based organizations in New York City have been documented. Much earlier, though, it was her Slovak grandfather who intrigued Laurence about her Slovak background. His silence about himself, his shrug to questions, prompted her to explore the meaning of physical work for Slovak immigrants as presented in American literature. The result was "The Garden in the Mill: The Slovak Immigrant's View of Work" (1983), aptly published in **MELUS** (the Journal of the Society for the Study of Multi-Ethnic Literature of the United States). (Interestingly, appreciation of silence in the writings of especially English women authors—Virginia Woolf, Jane Austen, and Charlotte Brontë—significantly informs Laurence's subsequent literary scholarship.)

"The Garden in the Mill" remains a seminal piece concerning Slovak immigrants and Slovak Americans in American literature. Eager to better understand her grandfather, Laurence read whatever American literary writings there were at that time involving Slovak immigrants and Slovak Americans. For "only through the study of literature" could Laurence have her "longed-for dialogue, half-real and half-imaginary, with [her] grandfather and his times." Her resources in writing "The Garden in the Mill" were **Thomas Bell**'s *Out of This Furnace* (1941), Thames Williamson's *Hunky* (1929), Fr. Andrew Pier's autobiography *The Woodlands Above, the Mines Below* (1974), and Peter Oresick's poetry in *The Story of Glass* (1977). Through these authors, Laurence intends to show in her writing what role "work," "machine," and "nature" play in Slovak immigrant lives from the perspective of workers like her grandfather. Machinery does take its toll on Slovak immigrant and Slovak American lives. Yet, as Laurence also illustrates, Slovak laborers so harmonize in working with machines that the latter become extensions of their bodies. Even though machines often intrude upon immigrant lives, "the dehumanization of work and men, the adverse effects of mechanization . . . are not in the Slovak-American experience. Nature and garden imagery is plentiful in descriptions of work, and it is used to reveal the rootedness and connectedness of work and the worker." For these laborers "work is organic." Bosses and machines that replace a worker do disturb the good relation between worker and job. Yet "Slovak-American literature about the immigrant does not present men whose minds and bodies are split, men who are alienated from their work," for whatever hardship in industry the Slovak immigrant worker endures, he is "grounded by his organic connection to work." In writings about and by Slovak Americans, "what is unique is the harmony, the 'garden' that men found in the mills, mines and factories despite the abuses of industry." Laurence's "The Garden in the Mill" remains a salient example of an ethnic writer's blending of autobiography and critical reading to arrive at a deeper understanding of her self and community. (*See also* Slovak American Literature)

Gerald J. Sabo

LAURENTS, ARTHUR (1917–)   Jewish American playwright, screenwriter, novelist, and stage director. Laurents is best known for the books to the musicals *West Side Story* (1956) and *Gypsy* (1959), often called the best book ever written for a musical. He also wrote the screenplays for the popular blockbuster film *The Way We Were* (1973) and for the critically acclaimed *The Turning Point* (1977).

Throughout his career, Arthur Laurents has remained socially committed, addressing serious social and psychological issues, including **anti-Semitism**, the **Holocaust**, the notorious Joseph McCarthy era blacklist, and gay rights. He generally focuses on the individual's need to confront a harsh reality while accepting the responsibility of living in it. His characters progress through journeys of discovery and acceptance, illuminating through their own struggles something about the society they inhabit.

Born in Brooklyn, New York, to a liberal Jewish father with Orthodox parents and a Jewish Socialist atheist mother, Laurents faced anti-Semitism on the streets of New York while going home to a family that taught him to be true to himself and his ideals. After graduating from Cornell University in 1937 with a degree in English, he began writing sketches for a nightclub act as well as episodes for several radio series.

In 1940 Laurents enlisted in the U.S. Army, where he spent five years writing military training films before leaving the Army in 1945 with the rank of Sergeant. Though he never left the States during World War II, the stories he heard from returning soldiers and the prejudice he witnessed stateside laid the framework for his first Broadway play, *Home of the Brave* (1945). The play puts the friendships developed among American soldiers in opposition with anti-Semitism in the ranks. Critically successful and moderately popular, *Home of the Brave* is now considered a classic and was eventually adapted for the screen, though the Jewish character was changed to an African American.

West Side Story opened in 1956 on Broadway with a book by Laurents, lyrics by Stephen Sondheim, and music by Leonard Bernstein. Musical theater auteur and McCarthy informer Jerome Robbins directed and choreographed. Laurents had originally wanted the musical to focus on feuding Jewish and Catholic families on New York's East Side, but he and Bernstein changed the gangs to Puerto Ricans and "Americans" on the West Side after reading of Chicano gang wars in Los Angeles. The musical made stars of its young principles—Larry Kert, Carol Lawrence, and Chita Rivera—and is still widely performed.

Three years later, Laurents made perhaps his most important contribution to the literature of American theater with the book for *Gypsy*, with lyrics again by Sondheim and music by Jule Styne. The musical starred Ethel Merman in her greatest role, the ultimate stage mother in desperate need of personal recognition, and was directed and choreographed by Jerome Robbins, with whom the fervently anti-informer Laurents had a thorny relationship.

Other librettos Laurents created for the musical theater include those for *Anyone Can Whistle* (1964), *Do I Hear a Waltz?* (1965), *Hallelujah, Baby!* (1967), and *Nick and Nora* (1991). Other plays include *Heart Song* (1946), *The Bird Cage* (1950), *The Time of the Cuckoo* (1952), *A Clearing in the Woods* (1957), *Invitation to a March* (1960), *The Enclave* (1973), *Scream* (1978), *The Madwoman of Central Park* (1979), *The Radical Mystique* (1995), *Jolson Sings Again* (1995), *My Good Name* (1996), *Claudio Lazlo* (2001), *Attacks on the Heart* (2002), *The Closing Bell* (2002), and *2 Lives* (2003).

Laurents first went to Hollywood in 1948, where he worked on the screenplays for *The Snake Pit* (1948), *Rope* (1948), and *Anastasia* (1956), among others. In 1973 he conceived and wrote the screenplay for the romantic classic *The Way We Were,* directed by Sydney Pollack and starring Barbra Streisand and Robert Redford. The film, like the play *Jolson Sings Again*, placed a story of interpersonal relationships against the backdrop of the McCarthy era, a time that Laurents finds as shameful as he finds those individuals, particularly Robbins and Elia Kazan, who informed. His next film, *The Turning Point,* inspired in part by his relationship with the ballerina Nora Kaye, was an enormous critical success staring Anne Bancroft and Shirley MacLaine.

Laurents has also had a successful career as a stage director, directing Streisand in *I Can Get It for You Wholesale* (1962), her Broadway debut, and winning a Tony for his direction of the original Broadway production of the musical *La Cage Aux Folles* (1983). (*See also* Jewish American Musicals)

Further Reading

Arthur Laurents. Special issue of *American Drama* 12.1–2 (2003): 1–183.

Laurents, Arthur. *Original Story By.* New York: Alfred A. Knopf, 2000.

Jeffrey Godsey

LAVIERA, TATO (1951–) Puerto Rican American playwright and poet. Tato Laviera was born in Santurce, Puerto Rico, in 1951 and migrated to New York with his family when he was nine years old. Besides having taught writing at Rutgers University, he is deeply committed to helping the community, having worked as the Director of the Community Services, served as chair of the board of directors of the "Madison Neighbors in Action," and sat on the board of directors of the "Mobilization for Youth, Inc."

Although younger than poets like Miguel Algarin, Pedro Pietri, Sandra Maria Esteves, and Jack Agueros, Tato Laviera is often catalogued with them as a **Nuyorican** poet. Adopting the name "Nuyorican" as a reference both to the city and to their Puerto Rican origins, these poets were part of the Beat Generation, which produced such figures as **Allen Ginsberg** and **Jack Kerouac**. The Nuyorican poets drew their experiences, as did the Beat poets, from bohemian city life. Unlike the poets of the Beat era, however, the Nuyorican writers were truly living a life of deprivation as the children of immigrants who spoke little English and were placed at the lowest rung of the socioeconomic ladder.

Laviera has written eight plays, several of which have been presented in New York, including *Piñones* (1979), *La Chefa* (1981), *Here We Come,* (1983), *Becoming Garcia* (1984), and *The Base of Soul in Heaven's Café* (1989). Laviera's plays reveal his interest in what it means to belong to both the Puerto Rican and American cultures. It is with his poetry, however, that Laviera has left an indelible mark on the literary landscape. Laviera straddles both cultures in his poetry, and the title of one of his books, *AmeRícan,* (1986), is a reflection of his concept of himself as neither wholly American nor wholly Puerto Rican. His other books of poetry include *Enclave* (1981) and *Mainstream Ethics* (1989). His most influential work to date, however, is *La Carreta Made a U-Turn* (1979).

La Carreta Made a U-Turn was the first book published by the now renowned Arte Público Press in Houston, founded by Nicolás Kanellos. The success of the book is evidenced by the fact that it is now in its seventh edition and has sold more than 60,000 copies. It is considered by many literary critics to be the poetic work that best embodies the cultural and linguistic ambiguity that Puerto Ricans living in New York often feel. The book's title derives from Rene Marques's 1953 play *La Carreta* (The Oxcart), which describes the Puerto Rican people's transition and movement from the countryside to the urban areas of the capital and eventually to New York City. Laviera picks up the story where Marques left off, in effect adding a fourth act to the play, which he divides into three distinct sections.

The first section, titled *Metropolis Dreams*, picks up Marques's characters in their urban environment. In poems like "angelito's eulogy in anger," Laviera captures the essence of the bilingual Nuyorican by presenting both an English and Spanish version of the text. Laviera also examines the sometimes confrontational relationship between Puerto Ricans in New York and those on the island. In *Loisaida Streets: Latinas Sing*, the second section of the book, the poet captures the sounds and images of the Lower East Side of Manhattan. In "titi teita and the taxi driver," one of the books' forty-two poems with English titles but Spanish texts, a newly arrived immigrant provides a cab driver with an address in broken English. The cab driver offers to take her, albeit at an outrageous price, and thus begins her journey into what will be a punishing world. Finally, unlike Marques's characters, Laviera's characters do not return home, but instead stay in their New York slums in the third section of the book titled *El Arrabal: Nuevo Rumbon*.

Laviera's poetry has appeared in several anthologies including *Herejes y mitificadores: Muestra de poesía puertorriqueña en los Estados Unidos* (1980), *Aloud: Voices from the Nuyorican Poets Café* (1994), and *The Prentice Hall Anthology of Latino Literature* (2002). The continued success of Laviera's work is demonstrated by its increasing appearance in mainstream anthologies such as these. By employing code-switching and powerful imagery, Laviera provides a vivid picture of a new immigrant whose two distinct identities have merged into one, and his work is sure to be relevant to newer generations of readers. (*See also* Bilingualism, Puerto Rican American Drama)

Further Reading

Flores, Juan, John Attenasi, and Pedro Pedraza. "*La Carreta Made a U-Turn*: Puerto Rican Language and Culture in the United States." *Daedalus* 110 (1981): 193–217.

Luis, William. "From New York to the World: An Interview with Tato Laviera." *Callaloo* 15.4 (1992): 1022–33.

Rodriguez de Laguna, Asela, ed. *Images and Identities: The Puerto Rican in Two World Contexts*. New Brunswick: Transaction, 1987.

Eduardo R. del Rio

LAWSON, JOHN HOWARD (1894–1977)   Jewish American dramatist, screenwriter, and political activist. A pioneer in reorienting the American stage, Lawson vigorously championed the theater's obligation to comment on social and political issues. Dubbed "the dean of revolutionary theater," he influenced his contemporaries, notably **Clifford Odets** and John Dos Passos.

As his name suggests, Lawson came from a family eager to assimilate. His father, who left Poland as Simeon Levy, prospered here. At the highly selective Williams College, however, John Howard discovered that **ethnicity** counted. He was denied editorship of the student newspaper because he was Jewish. He took his literary aspirations to Broadway, where his talent was quickly recognized. When the well-known producers George M. Cohan and Sam H. Harris optioned his first play, *Standards* (1915), an indictment of hypocrisy in public behavior, Lawson's father had to cosign the contract because his son had not yet reached legal age.

Neither *Standards* nor the subsequent *Servant, Master, Lover* (1916) was successful. Lawson had somewhat better luck with *Roger Bloomer* (1923), *Processional* (1925), *Nirvana* (1926), *Loud Speaker* (1926), *The International* (1928), and *The Pure at Heart* (1929). Although these plays were produced on Broadway, they have not enjoyed enduring popularity. *Processional* depicts the contrasting effects of a mining strike on the population of a nearby town, displaying a panorama of Americans, some already classic ethnic stereotypes among them. Both *Loud Speaker* and *The International* were mounted by the New Playwrights Theatre, a company Lawson founded in 1926 with four other writers. One of them was Dos Passos, a friend since their ambulance driving days in World War I.

Lawson's most significant play is aptly titled *Success Story* (1932). It tells the tale of the relentlessly ambitious Sol Ginsburg. Enraged by the inequities of capitalistic ethics and impatient with the gradual changes achieved by political activism, Ginsburg takes on the system singlehandedly, only to be corrupted and destroyed by the very corporate structure he opposed.

Success Story was first produced by The Group Theatre, a major force in early twentieth-century American theater. The Group was an egalitarian, left-wing producing company, many of whose actors and directors rose to prominence. In his history of The Group, cofounder Harold Clurman describes the value to the enterprise of Lawson's's talent for dramatizing provocative issues. Another Group member was an aspiring actor named Clifford Odets, who understudied Luther Adler's role as Sol Ginsburg. Waiting vainly to go on stage for Adler, Odets poured his frustrations into the play that became known as *Awake and Sing!* (1935), the earliest quintessential American Jewish play. The imprint of John Howard Lawson is unmistakable in its depiction of the yearning for life not "printed on dollar bills" and in its restless young characters' striving to take on the challenges represented by America's opportunities.

In 1928 Lawson moved to Hollywood. One of the first to write for the "talkies," he turned out some twenty scripts. He cofounded the Screen Writers Guild in 1933 and served as its first president. In 1934 he joined the Communist Party and was considered the head of its Hollywood section. Because the Hollywood Communists were more concerned with creative problems than with propagandizing, they were largely ignored by the Party. Still, Lawson wrote several ideological scripts, like *Blockade* (1938), which portrayed the Spanish Civil War, and *Counter-Attack* (1945), a tribute to the wartime alliance between the United States and the Soviet Union.

These activities earned him a subpoena to appear before the House Committee on Un-American Activities (HUAC) with nine others. Dubbed the Hollywood Ten by the media, they refused to testify, claiming their constitutional rights. They were aware that their recalcitrance would trigger contempt citations, but lost the gamble that the Supreme Court would overturn the decisions as First Amendment violations, ending the Committee's activities. All ten were found guilty. Lawson was sentenced to twelve months in jail and fined $1000. Of course, he was blacklisted, but continued to write under his own name. Indeed, he took pride in the notoriety, asserting his principles—and those, he claimed, of all loyal and grateful citizens of a free country.

Lawson continued to write, revising some of his plays and adding several new ones. He articulated his views that drama must reflect the temper and problems of its society in *Theory and Technique of Playwriting* (1936) and served as associate editor of several left-wing publications. He was actively involved in defending the rights of workers, including his colleagues in professional organizations such as the National Council of the Arts, Sciences and Professors. Lawson died in 1977.

Further Reading

Clurman, Harold. *The Fervent Years*. New York: Hill and Wang, 1957.

Rabkin, Gerald. *Drama and Commitment: Politics in the American Theatre.*
    Bloomington: Indiana UP, 1966.

Ellen Schiff

LAXALT, ROBERT (1923–2001)   Basque American novelist, memoirist, and newspaperman. Laxalt, one of Nevada's major literary figures of the twentieth century, has been unanimously regarded as the voice of the Basque American experience. Although he has written successful fiction dealing with other ethnic groups, in book such as *A Man in the Wheatfield* (1964), and with traditional western subjects, in novels such as *Dust Devils* (1997), he has achieved a well-deserved reputation for his ability to portray the lifestyle of the Basques both in the United States and in Europe.

Robert Laxalt was born in Alturas, California, to Dominique and Therese Laxalt, immigrants from the Basque provinces of the French Pyrenees. His father was a sheepherder and his mother operated a boarding house after their move to Carson City, Nevada. Educated at the University of Santa Clara in California and the University of Nevada-Reno, Laxalt began his writing career as a reporter for United Press. He was also a frequent contributor to *National Geographic.* With seventeen books to his credit, Laxalt received many honors throughout his career, including two nominations for a Pulitzer Prize in fiction for *A Cup of Tea in Pamplona* (1985) and for *The Basque Hotel* (1989). Laxalt was the founder of the University of Nevada Press. He taught creative writing at the University of Nevada-Reno and was also instrumental in forming the Basque studies program at this university.

Laxalt's best-known book is *Sweet Promised Land* (1957), a moving memoir of his father's nostalgic return to his native Basque Country and the archetypal story of the Basque sheepherder in the American West. The instantaneous success of the book as a Basque American epic became a fundamental event in the process of vindication of the figure of the immigrant Basque sheepherder in the United States. The book, already translated into four languages (German, French, Basque, and Spanish), introduced a little-known Basque element of the American West to the wider American public. Additionally, the story was praised as a classic tale of **immigration**, dealing with the universal themes of ethnic pride, struggle for acceptance, and the modern individual's need for a sense of place and **identity.**

Laxalt also demonstrated his artistic talent when depicting the lifestyle of the European Basques in nonfiction books such as *In a Hundred Graves: A Basque Portrait* (1972), *A Time We Knew: Images of Yesterday in the Basque Homeland* (1990), and *The Land of My Fathers* (1999), and also in the novella *A Cup of Tea in Pamplona.* Most of these books are based on the experiences that were lived by Laxalt in the land of his forefathers during two extended pilgrimages in the 1960s. These books reveal Laxalt's affection for the traditional lifestyle of the Basques and a sense of longing for an almost bygone era. However, his nostalgic identification with the land of his ancestors often coexists with his commitment to achieve objectivity in his treatment of the Basques. Because of that, Laxalt does not hesitate to disclose the other side of the Old World Basque life in the 1960s: the drama of poverty in Basque villages, the rigid social barriers, the moral taboos, the political and cultural repression under Franco's regime in the Basque provinces in Spain.

Laxalt consolidated his position as the literary spokesman for the Basque American community with his novella *Time of the Rabies* (2000) and, above all, with his superb trilogy of the Indart family, composed of the novels *The Basque Hotel, Child of the Holy Ghost* (1992), and *The Governor's Mansion* (1995). It is a semiautobiographical trilogy focused on the story of a Basque immigrant family in the United States as told by a second-generation son. The three volumes offer different perspectives on family relations on a Basque household, but they all stress the conflict between ancestral or hereditary bonds and self-made or contractual identity. The three books are written in the same lean and engaging prose that distinguishes most of Laxalt's works. His literary career ended with *Travels with My Royal* (2001), a posthumous autobiographical book in which Laxalt describes his youth in Carson City, his early writing days, and the genesis of his major books. (*See also* Basque American Literature)

Further Reading

Etulain, Richard W. "Robert Laxalt: Basque Writer of the American West." *Portraits of Basques in the New World*. Ed. Richard W. Etulain and Jeronima Echeverria. Reno: U of Nevada P, 1999. 212–29.

Rio, David. *Robert Laxalt: la voz de los vascos en la literatura norteamericana*. Bilbao, Spain: U Pais Vasco, 2002.

———. "Robert Laxalt: A Basque Pioneer in the American Literary West." *American Studies International* 41.3 (2003): 60–81.

David Rio

LAZARUS, EMMA (1849–1887) Jewish American poet. Emma Lazarus's most famous work by far is "The New Colossus" (1883), the sonnet inscribed at the base of the Statue of Liberty. This poem, written near the end of her career, was inspired by Lazarus's concern for Russian Jews fleeing persecution in their homeland and seeking refuge in America.

Emma Lazarus was born into a wealthy Jewish family in New York that traced its history back to colonial America. Her father paid for the publication of her first collection of poetry, *Poems and Translations, Written between the Ages of Fourteen and Sixteen* (1867) when Lazarus was just eighteen years old. This volume contains translations of several works by German Jewish poet Heinrich Heine and French writers Victor Hugo and Alexander Dumas and thirty-five original compositions by Lazarus herself, including a novella in verse form called "Bertha."

After Lazarus sent a copy of *Poems and Translations* to Ralph Waldo Emerson, the two began a friendship that lasted for many years, with the elder poet acting as mentor to Lazarus, recommending reading material and providing advice about her poetry. There was a serious rupture in their friendship when Emerson failed to include any of Lazarus's poems in *Parnassus*, the collection he edited in 1874. Although their correspondence waned abruptly after this episode, Lazarus visited Concord in 1876 at Emerson's invitation and published tributes to Emerson after his death in 1882.

Lazarus's second major publication, *Admetus and Other Poems* (1871), includes poetic retellings of various Greek myths and European folktales, a handful of translations, including the first part of Goethe's *Faust,* and an original cycle of sixteen short poems collectively called "Epochs." Scholars speculate that the heightened sense of emotion and personal reflection evident in "Epochs" may have been occasioned by the scandal that rocked the Lazarus family in 1870. Lazarus's maternal uncle, Benjamin Nathan, was bludgeoned to death in his home, and Lazarus's cousin, Washington Nathan, was suspected (though never convicted) of parricide in the high-profile investigation that followed.

Next, Lazarus turned her hand to biography. In 1874 she published her only novel, *Alide, An Episode of Goethe's Life,* about an early love affair in which the great poet abandons his lover in order to pursue his art. In 1876 she completed a verse drama called *Spagnoletto* about the life of Spanish painter Jose de Ribera (1591–1652). Lazarus returned to poetry and translation in 1881 with the publication of *Poems and Ballads of Heinrich Heine.*

Lazarus began studying and translating the works of medieval Jewish poets in 1877. Influenced by this work, she began taking greater interest in Jewish history and culture. Her interest intensified in 1881, when the persecution of Jews in Russia escalated dramatically, and waves of refugees started to pour into the United States. Lazarus began devoting herself to alleviating the plight of these refugees and visiting them at Wards Island as they arrived. She was appalled at the squalor in which they were forced to live.

Then in 1882 Lazarus read an essay by Russian social scientist Zinaida Alexievna Ragozin, who defended the actions of mobs leading the pogroms against the Jews, condemning the Jews themselves for their alleged greed and disloyalty to Russia. Lazarus immediately published an indignant reply, followed by a series of fourteen additional essays, known collectively as "An Epistle to the Hebrews," exploring the history of the Jewish people, their continued persecution, and the possibility of a Jewish homeland in Palestine. Lazarus also published her fourth collection of poetry at this time, *Songs of a Semite* (1882). The longest poem in this collection, "The Dance to Death," describes the dignity of German Jews in the face of an impending massacre in 1349. Additional poems in this volume celebrate key moments in Jewish history, decry contemporary injustices, and look forward to a renaissance of Jewish culture and pride.

Emma Lazarus. *Courtesy of the Library of Congress.*

Inspired by meetings in England with poet Robert Browning and socialist artist William Morris, Lazarus continued speaking out on behalf of immigrants and also helped to found the Hebrew Technical Institute. She was a veteran activist and spokesperson by 1883 when she composed "The New Colossus" as her contribution to raise money for the construction of a pedestal to support the Statue of Liberty. The poem was read aloud at the dedication of the Bertholdi statue in 1886 and inscribed on the pedestal in 1913, twenty-six years after the poet's death of Hodgkin's disease in 1887. (*See also* Jewish American Poetry)

Further Reading

Vogel, Dan. *Emma Lazarus.* Boston: Twayne Publishers, 1980.

Jennifer A. Gehrman

LEAVITT, DAVID (1961–)   Jewish American short story writer, novelist, editor, book reviewer, and essayist whose works have appeared in publications such as *The New Yorker,* the *New York Times, Esquire,* and *The Paris Review.* He has received numerous honors, including an O. Henry Award, a National Endowment for the Arts grant, a Guggenheim fellowship, and a Visiting Foreign Writer position at the Institute of Catalan Letters in Barcelona, Spain. A graduate of Yale who worked as an editor at Viking-Penguin and who has held several academic posts, he currently serves as Professor of Creative Writing at the University of Florida. When he was twenty-one, *The New Yorker* published his first short story, "Territory" (1982), which, with its openly gay subject matter, shocked many readers and immediately established him as one of the most influential writers of the gay literary movement.

Leavitt captures gay experience while avoiding stereotypes and traditional notions of identity. He does so by creating well-rounded homosexual and heterosexual characters and bringing a striking level of realism to gay literature, one in which things do not always work out as planned, men are not always beautiful, and relationships have complex intellectual and emotional dimensions.

In *Family Dancing* (1984), his critically acclaimed first collection of short stories, Leavitt describes a sexually repressed, middle-class culture ruled by material desires. As with many of Leavitt's works, his characters are often secular Jews who, although they observe rituals, are loosely connected to their tradition. These nine stories include a gay man seeking acceptance from his mother ("Territory"), two different families dealing with broken marriages ("The Lost Cottage" and "Family Dancing"), a daughter imagining she is from another planet after her father's near fatal car accident ("Aliens"), an angry child coming to terms with his gay father and divorced parents ("Danny in Transit"), a mother undergoing radiation treatment ("Radiation"), a family gathering after the father dies ("Out Here"), and a heterosexual woman seeking a gay man's love ("Dedicated").

The Lost Language of Cranes (1986), Leavitt's first novel that was later made into a successful BBC film, is the story of Philip Benjamin and his father, Owen, each coming to terms with their homosexuality. The book captures the 1980s, a time when the increasingly worrisome and mysterious threat of AIDS loomed, and gay culture, although gaining recognition, was still vying for acceptance. The book does an especially good job of representing gay life for a general audience and of eliciting sympathy for all members of the Benjamin family: Philip, whose romances the book chronicles; Owen, the deeply conflicted father who leads a double life; and Rose, the mother who struggles to accept her son's homosexuality. Each seeks a lost language for their complex experiences.

Like the Auden poem from which it takes its name, *Equal Affections* (1989) focuses on a series of unequal relationships in the Cooper family. Louise Cooper, the mother, is dying of cancer. While Louise's twenty-year battle with cancer provides the book's continuity, short narrative divisions, often skipping back and forth in time, create the novel's shifting perspectives. *Equal Affections'* family includes a dying Jewish mother who, in struggling with religious faith, contemplates converting to Catholicism; a computer profes-

David Leavitt. *Photo by Jerry Bauer.*

sor/inventor father who has an extramarital affair; a gay attorney son leading a suburban, monogamous life; and a lesbian folksinger and feminist daughter who, with the sperm of a San Francisco homosexual, artificially inseminates herself.

A Place I've Never Been (1990) is a collection of short stories, the first of which Leavitt began in 1984 while working at Viking Press in New York and subsequently finished, with the help of a Guggenheim Foundation fellowship, at the Institute of Catalan Letters of Barcelona, Spain. Although the stories sometimes describe promiscuous behavior and graphic sex scenes, as in "Ayor," an acronym for "At Your Own Risk," this behavior is always placed in a moral framework. In both "My Marriage to Vengeance" and "Houses," married heterosexuals struggle with homosexual desire. Both stories present characters who, after a brief foray into a homosexual relationship, choose to stay in a heterosexual marriage. Among the collection's other compelling stories are "Spouse Night," in which a man and woman meet in a support group after the deaths of their spouses, and "When You Grow to Adultery," in which Nathan and Celia, characters from *Family Dancing'*s "Dedicated," return.

While England Sleeps (1993) was embroiled in controversy from the moment Bernard Knox, writing for the *Washington Post,* noted parallels with Stephen Spender's 1950 autobiography, *World Within World.* Although *While England Sleeps* takes place in London and Spain during the Spanish Civil War, the novel tells of the passionate affair between Brian Botsford and Edward Phelan, the kernel for whose story lay in Spender's autobiography. Responding to Leavitt's novel, Spender claimed that Leavitt had plagiarized the autobiography. Spender also objected to what he described as pornographic love scenes. After a protracted legal and press battle, the novel was withdrawn and pulped. Leavitt settled the lawsuit out of court and revised objectionable sections of the book, although the love scenes remained untouched. The publishing company, Houghton Mifflin, then reissued *While England Sleeps* with an introduction given in the form of an interview with the author.

In "The Term Paper Artist," the first of the three novellas collected as *Arkansas* (1997), Leavitt plays with the relationship between authors' lives and their works—the cat and mouse game of which literary biography is made. In the novel, a character named David Leavitt writes term papers in exchange for sex with UCLA undergraduate men. As with *While England Sleeps,* "The Term Paper Artist" had a controversial reception. Originally slated to appear in *Esquire,* the story was canned by the magazine's editor in chief, Edward Kosner, who felt the story's sexually explicit language would offend readers. The collection's second novella, "Saturn Street," deals with a writer who delivers lunches to homebound AIDS patients, and the final novella, "The Wooden Anniversary," resurrects Nathan and Celia, who were first introduced in *Family Dancing* and who also appear in *A Place I've Never Been.*

The Page Turner (1998) tells the tale of an eighteen-year-old pianist, Paul Potterfield, who dreams of making the concert circuit, and his love affair with Richard Kennington, a virtuoso pianist. While Potterfield and Kennington fall in love in Rome, the bulk of the novel's action takes place in New York where Potterfield is a student at Julliard. The book also centers on Paul's mother, Pamela, who faces her husband's betrayal and the unexpected discovery that her son is gay. She blames Kennington, whom she also loves. *The Page Turner* was adapted into a successful film, *Food of Love* (2002), by gay Catalonian filmmaker Ventura Pons.

Martin Bauman: Or a Sure Thing (2000) is a story of a young writer who hobnobs with New York literati and looks for the sure thing: the great novel, a sustaining literary career, and a lasting gay relationship. In his search for self-understanding and fame, Martin is plagued by Stanley Flint, Martin's former writing professor who is now a key power broker in the publishing industry. With its thinly disguised personalities and institutions, the novel is a gossip-filled accounting of New York's literary circles and the political machinations of the publishing industry, all of which draw upon Leavitt's own Martin Bauman–like life.

With its nine stories, *The Marble Quilt* (2001) moves from the nineteenth century setting of the first story, "Crossing St. Gotthard," to twentieth century San Francisco, to Florida, to Rome, exploring gay themes and depicting the present gay community in the aftermath of AIDS. Leavitt plays with a variety of stylistics, most notably in "The Infection Scene," a lengthy story shifting from Lord Alfred "Bosie" Douglas, Oscar Wilde's malicious lover, to Christopher, a modern-day gay man living in San Francisco seeking to infect himself with HIV. Both stories show an infected gay community, one at odds with itself.

Leavitt has also authored *Florence, A Delicate Case* (2002), a guide to the city, and has coauthored with his partner, Mark Mitchell, a travel book, *Italian Pleasures* (1996). Together they have also edited three gay literary anthologies: *The Penguin Book of Gay Short Stories* (1994), *The Penguin Book of International Gay Writing* (1995), and *Pages Passed from Hand to Hand: The Hidden Tradition of Homosexual Literature in English from 1748 to 1914* (1997). (*See also* Jewish American Gay Literature)

Further Reading

Guscio, Lelia. *"We Trust Ourselves and Not Money. Period.": Relationships, Death and Homosexuality in David Leavitt's Fiction.* New York: Peter Lang, 1995.

Kekki, Lasse. *From Gay to Queer: Gay Male Identity in Selected Fiction by David Leavitt and in Tony Kushner's Play "Angels in American I-II."* New York: Peter Lang, 2003.

Blake G. Hobby

LEBOW, BARBARA (1936–)   Jewish American playwright. Barbara Lebow, a critically respected author of over twenty-five plays, is known chiefly for exploring themes of disenfranchisement and discrimination, a focus that includes **anti-Semitism**, though not exclusively. Her national reputation derives largely from the success of *A Shayna Maidel* (1985), the story of a **Holocaust** survivor and the family with whom she reunites. *A Shayna Maidel* is the only play of Lebow's to perform Off Broadway, with a fifteen-month run that opened at the Westside Arts Theatre on October 29, 1987.

The play was first produced at the Academy Theatre in Atlanta, a company that has sponsored the openings of many Lebow plays and for whom she has served as playwright-in-residence. The second staging of the play occurred at the Hartford Stage Company. Prior to this, Lebow's work had never been produced professionally outside of Atlanta, but since then her work has been seen at the Jean Cocteau Repertory Theatre, the Philadelphia Theatre Company, The Empty Space, the Berkshire Theatre Festival, and other regional theaters.

Barbara Lebow was born in Brooklyn in 1936 and moved to Atlanta in 1962. When she was ten years old, her family, then living in Manhattan, opened their home for a few months to a group of cousins who had survived concentration camps. Her responses to them later became integral to the character of Rose in *A Shayna Maidel*. Rose is the younger sister of the Jewish family portrayed, a young woman born in Poland, but now completely Americanized. She emigrated with her father at the age of four and was separated from her mother and older sister Lusia, who had contracted scarlet fever and could not go. The American curb on **immigration** during the Depression and the German invasion of Poland separated the family for years. Their mother died in Auschwitz. Lusia lived and, as the play begins, is reunited with Rose and their father Mordechai in New York.

To research Lusia's experiences, Lebow interviewed Holocaust survivors, focusing on the events following their liberation rather than accounts of the concentration camps. She portrays through Rose and Lusia the conflict between the victims of the holocaust and the family members that are distanced from their tragedy. As they strive for assimilation, Lusia copes with survivor guilt while Rose becomes increasingly aware of the mother she has lost and the suffering she has escaped.

Lebow uses memory and fantasy scenes throughout the play, theatrical devices that she also utilizes in other plays such as *Little Joe Monaghan* (1981) and *Cyparis* (1987). She is careful to point out that memory scenes in her plays are not actual flashbacks; they depict past events as they live in the distorted memory of a character rather than past events that are historically accurate. Scenes between Lusia and her childhood friend Hannah are colored by the bias of Lusia's guilt. Fantasy scenes depict imaginary events, such as conversations between Lusia and her deceased mother.

As head of the Academy Theatre's human service program, Lebow has developed a number of plays in development with disenfranchised groups such as prison inmates, the homeless, the disabled, at-risk youth, and individuals with drug addictions. The central characters of her plays are frequently social outcasts, the victims of prejudice or ignorance. In *Little Joe Monaghan*, the title character changes her name from Josephine to Joe and spends her life disguised as a man to escape the stigma of bearing a child out of wedlock. The first act of Lebow's *Trains* (1990) is set on a rail car traveling from New Orleans to Montreal. Growing racial tensions overshadow the relationship of the passengers, a white boy and his surrogate father who is black. The second act takes place on a contemporary railroad track, where two homeless men struggle with issues of personal independence. Homelessness plagues six characters in *Tiny Tim Is Dead* (1991), paired with both drug addiction and physical handicap. In *The Left Hand Singing* (1992), four students disappear on the way to a civil rights event; their parents subsequently spend years searching for them and coping with their loss. Alabama's first female governor, Lurleen Wallace, is the subject of Lebow's *Lurleen* (1994).

Lebow is the recipient of many national and regional grants and awards, including a Guggenheim Fellowship for play writing, a TCG/Pew Theatre Artists Residency, an NEA/TCG Residency, an Atlanta Mayor's Fellowship in the Arts, and a Georgia Governor's Award in the Arts. In addition to her work at the Academy Theatre, she has frequently supervised first productions of her work at other theaters and has served as playwright-in-residence for the Alabama Shakespeare Festival.

Further Reading

Cohen, Sarah Blacher. "Barbara Lebow: *A Shayna Maidel.*" *Making a Scene: The Contemporary Drama of Jewish-American Women.* Syracuse, NY: Syracuse UP, 1997. 73–128.

Sterling, Eric. "Barbara Lebow." *Contemporary Jewish-American Dramatists and Poets.* Ed. Joel Shatzky and Michael Taub. Westport, CT: Greenwood Press, 1999. 102–8.

Steven Pounders

LEE, ANDREA (1953–) African American journalist, novelist, and short story writer. During the next to last decade of the twentieth century, Andrea Lee was hailed as an auspicious journalist and a promising novelist; two decades later, Lee continues to garner the attention of literary critics and the reading public with the publication of her latest work, a collection of short stories. Lee, who received a BA and MA from Harvard University, wrote her first book, *Russian Journal* (1981), while she was a graduate student accompanying her husband, a Harvard doctoral candidate in Russian history, to the Soviet Union in 1978–79. During their ten-month stay, they lived among Russian students at Moscow State University and Leningrad State. Lee's journal entries are not written from the perspective of an African American in Russia; instead they are written from the viewpoint of an American woman in Russia. Indeed readers do not discover that Lee is an African American until page 155, which is more than halfway through the journal. Among the book's most interesting entries are the ones about the month Lee taught a surreptitious English class to Soviet Jews who were preparing to emigrate. *Russian Journal*, which was nominated for a 1981 National Book Award for general nonfiction, received the 1984 Jean Stein Award from the American Academy and Institute of Arts and Letters. Lee, who has contributed articles and short stories to such periodicals as *The New Yorker, New York Times,* and *Vogue,* is the author of two book-length works of fiction: *Sarah Phillips* (1984) and *Interesting Women* (2002). *Sarah Phillips* is a semiautobiographical, coming-of-age novel about a middle-class African American girl during the 1960s and 1970s. The title character may be viewed as a twentieth-century equivalent to the title character of Alexander Pushkin's classic *Eugene Onegin* (1831). Both characters have become bored and disenchanted with their lives. At times, they even appear insensitive to their closest relatives. While taking care of his sick uncle, Eugene, instead of being grateful for their time together, eagerly awaits the old man's death. Sarah, the daughter of a prominent Baptist minister and an elementary school teacher, is also concerned with self. For example, she is so pleased that the clothes that are selected for her to wear to her father's funeral make her look like a beautiful heiress that she concentrates on assuming a glamorous persona rather than grieving for Rev.

Phillips. Sarah, after graduating from Harvard, goes to Paris to escape her ennui. Ultimately, she becomes disillusioned and decides to return to the United States. Lee's third book, *Interesting Women,* is a collection of thirteen short stories. Most of the tales, which have generated favorable comparisons to Colette's narratives, repeat Lee's theme from *Russian Journal* and *Sarah Phillips*—remarkable American women abroad who, like women elsewhere, contend with **identity** issues and relationships. Andrea Lee currently lives in Turin, Italy.

Further Reading

Krishnamurthy, Sarala. "Andrea Lee." *Contemporary African American Novelists: A Bio-Bibliographical Critical Sourcebook.* Ed. Emmanuel S. Nelson. Westport, CT: Greenwood Press, 1999. 267–72.

Linda M. Carter

LEE, C. Y. (CHIN YANG) (1917–) Chinese American novelist. C. Y. Lee's legacy among Chinese American novelists rests largely on his delightful 1957 novel *The Flower Drum Song* and the musicals it generated for the stage. Rodgers and Hammerstein's *Flower Drum Song* opened at New York's St. James Theater in December 1958 and was the first Broadway show to feature Asian American players; the film version, released in 1961, inaugurated the careers of the first generation of Asian American actors, including Nancy Kwan, James Shigeta, and Jack Soo. On October 2, 2001, the Mark Taper Forum in Los Angeles premiered **David Henry Hwang**'s musical to glowing reviews, and after an extension of its initial run, the production moved to Broadway.

C. Y. Lee's work and career, however, have been largely overlooked because of the reception of *The Flower Drum Song* and Rodgers and Hammerstein's musical, which many critics felt perpetuated **Chinese American stereotypes** of Asians. Although his novel was a *New York Times* best seller, it quickly went out of print, and rarely appeared on university reading lists. Ironically, the political climate that fuelled ethnic consciousness-raising in the late 1960s and early 1970s refused Lee's playful depiction of San Francisco Chinatown's social customs. But *The Flower Drum Song*'s evocation of cultural conflict and the invention of new traditions in immigrant life attests to Lee's modernity and remains as relevant for contemporary audiences as it was in 1957. In 2002, forty-five years after its initial publication, Penguin Books reissued Lee's novel.

But as the author of eleven novels and a collection of short stories, many of which have been translated into several languages, C. Y. Lee merits a more nuanced consideration of his work. Although Lee himself identifies his second novel *Lover's Point* (1958) as his personal favorite, several others are worth noting. A number of short stories that originally appeared in *The New Yorker* were published as *The Sawbwa and His Secretary* (1959; re-released as *Corner of Heaven* [1962]), a memoir of his joyful year and a half in Burma as the secretary to the Chinese maharajah. *A Corner of Heaven* was adapted as a miniseries for Taiwanese television and remains popular both in England and Taiwan. *The Virgin Market* (1964) tells the story of a beautiful Eurasian woman raised by a Chinese fisherman and his wife in Hong Kong's impoverished Aberdeen market, and Lee's most recent novel *Gate of Rage* (1991) dramatizes the events of Tiananmen Square and their impact on one family.

Lee's own life offers a window to the historical and political upheavals of the time. Born in Hunan Province and raised in Beijing, Lee traveled to the United States in 1942 after receiving his bachelor's degree to escape the continued political turbulence in China. After a brief stint at Columbia University, Lee enrolled at Yale to study drama with Walter Pritchard Eaton, Eugene O'Neill's mentor, graduating with an MFA in 1947. In 1949 he won a *Reader's Digest* sponsored contest for "Forbidden Dollar," a short story anthologized in *Best Original Short Stories*; the award encouraged Lee to become an American citizen later that year. (*See also* Chinese American Novel)

Further Reading

Shin, Andrew. "'Forty Percent Is Luck': An Interview with C. Y. (Chin Yang) Lee." *MELUS* 29.2 (Summer 2004): 77–104

Andrew Shin

LEE, CHANG-RAE (1965–)   Asian American novelist. With just three novels, Chang-rae Lee has established himself as a major voice in Asian American literature. He is clearly the most prominent Korean American novelist, and it is not an exaggeration to say that the publication of his first novel, *Native Speaker*, in 1995 marked the starting point for the emergence of Korean American literature onto the national scene.

Chang-rae Lee was born in Korea on July 29, 1965. When he was three years old, his parents, Young Yong and Inja (Hong) Lee, immigrated to the United States. They settled in metropolitan New York, where his father established a successful psychiatric practice. In contrast, his mother was a homemaker and never mastered English. Although the family lived first on the Upper West Side of Manhattan and then in New Rochelle, they attended a Korean Presbyterian church in Flushing. So almost from the start, the spheres of Lee's life were defined by paradoxical demarcations— between the lives led by his a professional father and by his homebound mother and between their own family life in prosperous suburban neighborhoods and life in the ethnic, inner-city neighborhoods of most Korean American immigrants.

After graduating from Phillips Exeter Academy, Lee received a BA from Yale University in 1987, worked for a short time as an analyst on Wall Street, and then pursued a graduate degree in creative writing at the University of Oregon, receiving an MFA in 1993. He has since taught in the creative writing program at the University of Oregon.

For *Native Speaker,* Lee received the PEN/Hemingway Award for Best First Fiction and the 1995 Discover Award. In addition, the literary journal *Granta* included Lee in its list of the fifty best American writers under the age of forty.

Chang-rae Lee. *Photo courtesy of Chang-rae Lee.*

The protagonist of *Native Speaker* is Henry Park, a relatively young Korean American who works for a shadowy spy-for-hire company specializing in ethnic and racial investigations. At a point when Park's few, fragile personal relationships have come apart, he is assigned to infiltrate the organization of a popular Korean American city councilman from Flushing who is being touted as a New York mayoral candidate. Almost inevitably, Park's **identity** as a spy is revealed, causing him to confront profound questions about his identity apart from his spying.

Native Speaker has been justly praised for its convincing synthesis of a broad variety of themes. The immigrant's experience is presented as being, at once, archetypically American and marginalizing. The native language is integral to the immigrant's sense of **identity**, to a feeling of personal continuity and stability in the midst of tremendous changes in circumstance, and yet it is also the major obstacle to **assimilation** and success in America. The difficult transition from one culture to another involves continual compromises between very different expectations and between very different ways of articulating them. On the simplest level, the word "native" becomes itself paradoxical, designating both the immigrant's "native" tongue and the new language that his children need to learn to speak as the "natives" do.

Lee has expressed his concern that a novelist who chooses to focus on his **ethnicity** or region is too readily categorized as "ethnic" or "regional"—with both terms suggesting works with less than universal themes and less than lasting import. Consequently, it is hardly surprising that in his second and third novels he has tackled subjects that are pointedly not "Korean American" but that address some of the same themes of identity and dislocation that he explores in *Native Speaker*.

In *A Gesture Life* (1999), Lee provides a penetrating character study of an aging Japanese American man who seems perfectly assimilated but who harbors a secret that has kept him from being truly contented and that in one way or another has had a corrosive effect on most of his personal relationships: While serving in the Japanese army during World War II, he first fell in love with and then abandoned one of the Korean "comfort-women" that the Japanese military had forced into its brothels.

In *Aloft* (2004), Lee presents the story of a middle-aged Italian American man who is aptly, but in the end, perhaps more ironically, named Jerry Battle. His enjoyment of flying solo in his Cessna becomes symbolic of his deepening alienation from the people closest to him—his longtime girlfriend, his debilitated and yet overbearing father, and his impetuous, self-indulgent son—and, more broadly, from the norms of the suburban community and culture that he has allowed to define him. (*See also* Korean American Literature)

Further Reading

Chen, Tina. "Impersonation and Other Disappearing Acts in *Native Speaker* by Chang-rae Lee." *MFS: Modern Fiction Studies* 48 (Fall 2002): 637–67.

Dwyer, June. "Speaking and Listening: The Immigrant as Spy Who Comes in from the Cold." *The Immigrant Experience in North American Literature: Carving Out a Niche.* Ed. Katherine B. Payant and Toby Rose. Westport, CT: Greenwood Press, 1999. 73–82.

Engles, Tim. "'Visions of Me in the Whitest Raw Light': Assimilation and Doxic Whiteness in Chang-rae Lee's *Native Speaker.*" *Hitting Critical Mass: A Journal of Asian American Cultural Criticism.* 4 (Summer 1997): 27–48.

Huh, Joonok. "'Strangest Chorale': New York City in *East Goes West* and *Native Speaker.*" *The Image of the Twentieth Century in Literature, Media, and Society.* Ed. Will Wright and Steven Kaplan. Pueblo, CO: Society for the Interdisciplinary Study of Social Imagery, U of Southern Colorado, 2000. 419–22.

Lee, James Kyung-Jin. "Where the Talented Tenth Meets the Model Minority: The Price of Privilege in Wideman's *Philadelphia Fire* and Lee's *Native Speaker.*" *Novel: A Forum on Fiction* 35 (Spring–Summer 2002): 231–57.

Parikh, Crystal. "Ethnic America Undercover: The Intellectual and Minority Discourse." *Contemporary Literature* 43 (Summer 2002): 249–84.

Song, Min Hyoung. "A Diasporic Future? *Native Speaker* and Historical Trauma." *Lit: Literature Interpretation Theory* 12 (April 2001): 79–98.

Martin Kich

LEE, CHERYLENE (1953–) Chinese American playwright and actress. A native of Los Angeles, Cherylene Lee began acting at age three. One of the first Asian American actors appearing on popular television, she guest-starred on shows such as *My Three Sons, McHale's Navy, Dennis the Menace, The Bachelor Father,* and, later, *M*A*S*H.* Film work includes Rodgers and Hammerstein's *Flower Drum Song* (1961) and *Donovan's Reef* (1963). After volunteering at the La Brea Tar Pits, Lee pursued a bachelor's degree in paleontology from the University of California at Berkeley (1974) and a master's degree in geology from the University of California at Los Angeles (1978). Between degrees, she toured with the musicals, *A Chorus Line, The King and I,* and *Flower Drum Song.*

Themes of **identity**; cultural heritage, transmission, and **assimilation**; and reconciliation as well as justice run strong in her work, which combines science, art, and politics to illuminate the Asian American experience.

Her first poem, published in Seattle's *International Examiner,* responded to the case of Vincent Chin, a Chinese American beaten to death with a baseball bat by two laid-off Detroit autoworkers in 1982. That case later became the subject of one of Lee's most successful plays, *Carry the Tiger to the Mountain* (1998).

An early break came with the production of *Wong Bow Rides Again* in San Francisco in the East West Players' 1986–87 season. Three more of her plays have received production there, including *Arthur and Leila*, which explores the tension between contemporary and traditional Chinese culture and values through the conflict-ridden relationship of an aging Chinese American brother and sister; *Carry the Tiger to the Mountain*, which has been called an agitprop treatment of Vincent Chin's murder that asks audiences to identify with the emotional journey forced upon Vincent's mother, Lily Chin, and to contend with issues of justice in America; and *Mixed Messages*, which premiered in the fall of 2004.

Mixed Messages was inspired by Census 2000, which offered people more ethnic categories for identifying their background than ever before and revealed the mixed-**race** classification as a rapidly growing population. In *Mixed Messages*, a nine-thousand-year-old human skull from the La Brea Tar Pits becomes the locus for a physical anthropologist and Chumash tribe descendant's battle over the skull's classification: research fossil or Native American ancestor. Their confrontation with their own identities as people of mixed race pits culture against science, heritage against **ethnicity**.

Lee's other major work includes *Antigone Falun Gong* (2004), which maps Sophocles' *Antigone* onto a story about Chinese nonviolent dissent, and *The Legacy Codes* (2003), inspired by the story of Wen Ho Lee, the nuclear weapons scientist charged with downloading atomic secrets at Los Alamos and giving the information to the Chinese government.

Among her many honors, Lee has earned a TCG/NEA Playwriting Residency, a Kennedy Center Fund for New American Plays grant, a Rockefeller MAP grant, a California Arts Council Playwriting Fellowship, and a Wallace A. Gerbode Play Commission. (*See also* Chinese American Drama)

Further Reading

Kaplan, Randy Barbara. "Cherylene Lee (1953–)." *Asian-American Playwrights: A Bio-Bibliographical Critical Sourcebook*. Ed. Miles Xian Liu. Westport, CT: Greenwood Press, 2002. 175–84.

Jennifer Lynn Lavy

LEE, DON L.   *See* Madhubuti, Haki R.

LEE, GUS (1946–)   Chinese American author of autobiographical novels, courtroom dramas, and a memoir, as well as an ethicist and leadership consultant. Gus Lee's work features strong Chinese American male protagonists in several genres. His first novel, best-seller *China Boy* (1991), is based on his own childhood experiences of trying to survive the brutal street-life of San Francisco's impoverished Panhandle district.

Through his six-year-old protagonist, Kai Ting, Lee first honors his mother and sisters for their courageous escape from China during the Japanese invasion. The only American-born member of his formerly wealthy, traditional Chinese family, he lovingly recounts his warm, albeit brief, childhood as the only son. This sheltered world collapses when his mother dies, and young Ting is forced to face the violence of the neighborhood streets. As the only Asian American boy among African and Latino American children, Ting must learn to navigate through the cultural, verbal, and physical landscapes without familial protection or guidance. Not only constantly beaten by the young street fighters, but also physically and emotionally abused by his new (white) stepmother, Ting falls into a world of fear and suffering until he is rescued by Hector, an auto repair shop worker, who fears for the slender boy. Hector convinces Ting's often-absent father that the boy needs to learn how to box in order to survive; he will teach the child street-fighting, but Ting must first learn the basics of boxing from the local YMCA.

The YMCA coaches, with their attention to his body and spirit, become Ting's surrogate fathers. Ting gathers a multicultural family around him, in addition to the coaches, including mother figures who nourish him with food and hugs, best friends like Touissant LaRue who endure the same rough life, and a group of elderly Chinese bachelors who were trained as classical scholars but whose lives as immigrants include poverty and loneliness.

The diversity of Ting's multicultural and multigenerational family highlights the tension between honor and violence as well as the challenges in shaping an ethnic American **identity**. The elderly scholars look to Ting as their hope, their "collective Only Son," and teach him classical Chinese calligraphy and texts, but Ting's father and stepmother want him to become "American," meaning Caucasian, by rejecting Chinese language, food, and culture. Torn between these two binaries, Ting is also trying to survive on the slum streets as one of the African American youths. His battered body and spirit are revived by the YMCA boxing community as he develops his strength and sense of identity.

With the support of his coaches and friends, Ting stands up to the terrors in his life, including the most vicious bully in the neighborhood, his cruel stepmother, and even the loss of his mother and, with her, the brevity of his gentle childhood. Learning to fight enables Ting to survive the harsh Panhandle streets and necessarily mature from boyhood into manhood by the age of seven. While recognizing the importance of self-reliance and independence, this autobiographical novel truly celebrates the diverse surrogate family members who nurture Ting's success.

The theme of honor and violence continues in Lee's award-winning trilogy of autobiographical novels, which also includes *Honor and Duty* (1994) and *Tiger's Tail* (1996). For example, by writing about his stepmother and father, Lee exposes their cruelty while risking damage to his family honor.

Yet he also honors his mother and multicultural surrogate family, thereby complicating ideas about honor, family, and Americanism. These autobiographical novels, as well as his legal suspense works, trace the growth and paths of admirable Asian American male protagonists.

Unlike stereotypical, fictional Asian American men who are featured as one-dimensional buffoons, gang members, drug addicts, or martial arts experts, Lee offers complex male characters who reach across racial, class, and other possible barriers. In overcoming challenges and assaults, these Chinese American men demonstrate spiritual and physical integrity that, in Lee's writings, stem from individual honor as well as communal bonds. From young Kai Ting who tries to balance street-fighting with classical learning to *No Physical Evidence*'s (1998) Joshua Jin who can maneuver powerfully both on the streets as a cop and in the courtrooms as a deputy district attorney, Lee's protagonists ably carve out their own identities and spaces as American men. (*See also* Chinese American Novel)

Further Reading

Shen, Yichin. "The Site of Domestic Violence and the Altar of Phallic Sacrifice in Gus Lee's *China Boy*." *College Literature* 29.2 (2000): 99–113.

So, Christine. "Delivering the Punch Line: Racial Combat as Comedy in Gus Lee's *China Boy*." *MELUS* 21.4 (1996): 141–55.

Karen Li Miller

LEE, JARENA (1783–?) African American autobiographer and itinerant preacher. Jarena Lee was the first African American woman to write a spiritual autobiography and the first African American woman sanctioned by church officials to preach the Gospel. Lee was born February 11, 1783, in Cape May, New Jersey. Though her parents were free, they were poor and when Lee was seven years old, she was placed into domestic service sixty miles away from her home. Shortly after she began her service, Lee told a lie to her employer, and the ensuing guilt compelled Lee to begin searching for salvation and forgiveness. In her autobiography, *The Life and Religious Experiences of Jarena Lee, A Coloured Lady, Giving an Account of Her Call to Preach the Gospel*, published in 1836, Lee describes her journey toward her spiritual awakening. Lee's narrative also describes her belief in a sinfulness that weighed down her soul, so much so that she considered suicide more than once, which she describes as being driven by Satan. Lee frequently suffered from illnesses that were brought about by her overwhelming fear of God's judgment and her struggle with a belief in her inherent wickedness. Her autobiography reveals her search for the denomination that was most suited to her needs, which she found when she heard a sermon by the Rev. Richard Allen, head of the African Episcopal Methodist Church in Philadelphia. Lee describes her marriage to Rev. Joseph Lee, in 1811, and her frustration with her subordinate role as preacher's wife. Lee bristled at the enforced domesticity that restricted her religious activities, which she considered more important. After six years of marriage, Lee was widowed with two small children to raise. Lee's desire to preach was overwhelming, and leaving her young son with other women, she went on the road to preach throughout the Northeast and Mid-Atlantic states.

The significance of Lee's autobiography is twofold. That an African American woman could preach the gospel was very progressive in an age of slavery when most blacks were denied the right to literacy. Lee's narrative also demonstrates the beginnings of women's issues within American society. In her narrative, Lee advocates women cultivating faith communities despite the patriarchal nature of the church. She advocated women's active participation in the pulpit, using Biblical passages as her best argument in her fight to get the church to allow women to preach. Her narrative demonstrates self-validation through individual interpretation of the Bible, and she became a source of hope for other women who wanted to answer the call to spread the biblical word. Lee's narrative ends with the conversion of a cruel slaveholder, who, after hearing her preach, changed his ways for the better. Her inclusion of the slaveholder's story demonstrates Lee's keen awareness of the power a spiritual narrative could have to affect broader cultural issues. (*See also* African American Autobiography)

Further Reading

Andrews, William, ed. *Sisters of the Spirit: Three Black Women's Autobiographies of the Nineteenth Century.* Bloomington: Indiana UP, 1986.

Higonnet, Margaret R., and Joan Templeton, eds. *Reconfigured Spheres: Feminist Explorations of Literary Space.* Amherst: U of Massachusetts P, 1994.

Oden, Amy. *In Her Words: Women's Writings in the History of Christian Thought.* Nashville: Abingdon Press, 1994.

Debbie Clare Olson

LEE, LI-YOUNG (1957–)   Chinese American poet and creative nonfiction writer. Li-Young Lee's position in the growing field of Asian American poetry has mainly evolved from two aspects. First, his compelling writing reflects his cultural, familial, and personal past and its connection with and influence on the present. Second, his poems represent and reinvent images of Chinese immigrants in America that challenge the racial stereotypes.

Born in Jakarta, Indonesia, to Chinese expatriate parents, Li-Young Lee is one of the celebrated Chinese American poets. He has published three collections of poetry, which have established his literary reputation. Published with a foreword by Gerald Stern, his first collection *Rose* (1986) belongs to the *New Poets of America* series. Lee received New York University's Delmore Schwartz Memorial Poetry Award and the 1988 Whiting Foundation Award for this book. Inspired by both classical Chinese poetry and the psalms of the Old Testament, Lee writes in his poems about his family history and particularly about his relationship with his father. The son's love for and striving to understand this godlike father figure, who has lead a varied life as a personal physician to Mao Zedong, a medical advisor to

Sukarno, a political prisoner in Indonesia, and eventually a Presbyterian minister in western Pennsylvania, empower his lyric to be personal as well as spiritual. Moreover, through memories of his earlier experiences of exile, disconnection, and alienation, Lee infuses his poetry with explorations of **identity** construction in a cross-cultural context.

As the 1990 Lamont poetry selection of the Academy of American Poets, Lee's second collection *The City in Which I Love You* (1990) shows a different thematic focus. Selected poems in this book are distinguished by a shifting emphasis from his family to Lee's personal life and ethnic identity, which are challenged, reconsidered, and re-created in his writing. Lee's recent publication is another collection of poetry, titled *Book of My Nights* (2001). In terms of reinventing and representing physical features of Asian Americans, Lee's poetry shares a similar resistance against racial stereotypes with works by other Asian American poets such as **David Mura**, **Cathy Song**, and **Marilyn Chin**. Such examinations can be attributed to Lee's cross-cultural experience that has broadened his views and enriched his poetry. Furthermore, his poetic technique—using a central image to lead the flow of the subject matter and to structure the poem—has successfully added an innovative approach to poetry writing.

In 1990, Lee traveled to China and Indonesia, conducting research for his book of autobiographical prose that became his memoirs *The Winged Seed: A Remembrance* (1995). Using poetic language, Lee traces his family history back to the fifties. After being jailed as a political prisoner, Lee's father, an émigré Chinese, fled Indonesia with his family in 1959 and finally settled down in the United States in 1964. Lee's autobiographical text provides a memorable example for the readers to examine the memories and psychological struggles of the Chinese diaspora from a son's perspective. As important as the mother-daughter dichotomy set up by **Maxine Hong Kingston**, **Amy Tan**, and other Chinese American writers, Lee's narrative of the son's connection to a father figure and to his family illuminates another aspect of what the border-crossing protagonist inherits from his cultural memory. His remembrance also recollects the early years of his life in the United States when he struggled to survive in school with his accented, nonfluent English.

Besides poetry and prose writing, Li-Young Lee also appears in television programs in which he discusses modern poetry and his growth as a poet. In *Voices of Memory* (1989) hosted by Bill Moyers, Lee addresses how his family history, childhood, and multicultural experience affect his poetry writing. Other programs such as *Li-Young Lee* (1995), *Li-Young Lee Always A Rose* (1990), *The Writing Life* (1995), and *Readings and Conversations* (2000) comprise Lee's conversations with **Shawn Wong**, Tom Titale, Michael Collier, and Michael Silverblatt on poetical inspiration and writing, respectively. (*See also* Chinese American Poetry, Chinese American Stereotypes)

Further Reading

Chang, Juliana. "Reading Asian American Poetry." *MELUS* 21.1 (Spring 1996): 81–98.

Lim, Shirley. "Reconstructing Asian-American Poetry: A Case for Ethnopoetics." *MELUS* 14.2 (Summer 1987): 51–63.

Slowik, Mary. "Beyond Lot's Wife: The Immigration Poems of Marilyn Chin, Garrett Hongo, Li-Young Lee, and David Mura." *MELUS* 25.3/4 (Autumn–Winter 2000): 221–42.

Zhou, Xiaojing. "Inheritance and Invention in Li-Young Lee's Poetry." *MELUS* 21.1 (Spring 1996): 113–32.

Lan Dong

LENTRICCHIA, FRANK (1940–) Italian American critic, essayist and novelist. Raised in Utica, New York, by working-class parents who were children of Italian immigrants, Frank Lentricchia was educated at Duke University and began his professional life as a literary scholar and a critic, becoming one of the most widely known figures in the field of American and English literary criticism.

His early publications include books on Robert Frost and William Butler Yeats. In the mid-1970s he begins to pay attention to contributions of Italian American writers. He published two articles in the first two issues of *italian americana*: a short review of a minor poet and an essay that sets the record straight on the origins of Italian American fiction. He attempted to compile and publish an anthology of Italian American writers, but put the work aside after publishers showed a little interest. In 1981 he published *After the New Criticism* (1981), a work that established him as a major voice in literary criticism. In his next study, *Criticism and Social Change* (1983) he brought in anecdotes about his Italian grandfather, personalizing his criticism and signaling a transition into his writing more consciously as an American of Italian descent. He indirectly returned to Italian American literature when he edited an issue of *South Atlantic Quarterly* dedicated to the writing of **Don DeLillo**. Lentricchia located DeLillo in the most American of literary traditions of social criticism, which has been the center of the works of such mainstream luminaries as Ralph Waldo Emerson, Henry David Thoreau, and Mark Twain. What Lentricchia had been working toward in his theory and practice of American literary criticism is precisely what DeLillo does with American literature.

During this time he published his first completely autobiographical work, titled *The Edge of Night* (1997). Lentricchia's imaginative autobiographical narrative focuses on a period covering a little over a year of his life, concentrating on his own personal struggle to form an **identity** composed of a working-class childhood and middle-class adulthood. What makes Lentricchia's autobiographical narrative significant is his use of irony that marks a new and exciting dimension to Italian American writing. *The Edge of Night* transcends any traditional definition of autobiography. Each chapter is the result of a shedding of a self that continues to evolve. In this way, Lentricchia fashions a masterful example of what Italians call *bella figura,* or good front.

His next publication was his first major move into truly fictional territory. *Johnny Critelli* and *The Knifemen* (1996) are two novellas published in one book. What Lentricchia knows well is that creation of art requires imitation as well as originality. In these two works he draws breath from **Mario Puzo**, Edgar Allan Poe, and James Joyce and blood from filmmakers Federico Fellini, Martin Scorsese, and Brian DePalma in his attempt to be unique. *Johnny Critelli* could be about a kid who shares the author's name, who once pitched a one-hitter in a Little League game, who is both subject and object of his own life story, but then again, it could also be about a ghost, as friendly as it is frightening, who is conjured up by those who need to explain their past. *The Knifemen* is not a novel for the easily offended; it's obvious that in this novel Lentricchia is not writing to please anyone but his muse.

In his next fictional work, *The Music of the Inferno* (1999), Lentricchia presents Robert Tagliaferro, an orphan child of unknown racial background who makes a grim discovery shortly after his eighteenth birthday that causes him to run away from his hometown of Utica, New York. The young man takes refuge in a bookstore in New York City where he reads his way through the shelves. His book learning replaces his family and he becomes a composite of all that he's absorbed through his studies. Forty years later, he returns to Utica to uncover some of the town's deep secrets. In this revision of returning home, Lentricchia penetrates the dark recesses of a Little Italy to reveal the sins of Utica's "immigrant merchant princes" who have shaped the city's economy and thus, its history.

Lucchesi and the Whale (2001) continues the author's defiance of commercial fiction. At the story's center is one Thomas Lucchesi, an academic personality, all wrapped up in his writing. Lucchesi talks mostly to himself, and when he does speak to others, it is as though he is lecturing. Through this character Lentricchia presents us with what has become common in his fiction, a man alone in the world. He observes the fractured portions of his life as they crash into each other, as though he views his world through a kaleidoscope. (*See also* Italian American Autobiography, Italian American Novel)

Further Reading

Bliwise, Robert J. "Putting Life into Literature." *Duke Alumni Magazine* (May 1988): 2–7.

Salusinszky, Imre. "Frank Lentricchia." *Criticism in Society.* New York: Metheun, 1987. 177–206.

Fred Gardaphe

LESTER, JULIUS (1939–) African American Jewish author. Julius Lester, born January 27, 1939 in St. Louis, Missouri, is an African American Jewish author, primarily of children's books. He is noted for works of history, fiction, folklore, and autobiography that challenge **racism** and revitalize and reinvent traditional stories, works that often cause controversy by courageously and expertly taking on themes that many authors avoid because of racial sensitivity. Lester has won several major awards for his publications for children, including the Newbery Honor Medal for *To Be a Slave* (1968), National Book Award Finalist for *Long Journey Home* (1972), and both the Caldecott Honor and Boston Globe-Horn Book Award for *John Henry* (1994). He is also a musician, having released several albums in his early career, and he contributed the photographs for the reprint of Jerry Silverman's *Folk Blues* in 1968. Some of his photographs of the Civil Rights Movement are in the permanent collection of the Smithsonian Institution.

Lester, the son of a Methodist preacher, spent his childhood in Missouri, Kansas, Tennessee, and Arkansas. In 1960 he graduated from Fisk University in Nashville, Tennessee, with a BA in English. Rhythmic African American and southern speech patterns are integral to his literary art and clearly contribute to the powerful sense of voice and oral storyteller evident in all of his work. In fact, Lester considered himself a musician as he came to manhood and did not acknowledge that he had a particular expertise in writing until the publication of *To Be a Slave* in 1968.

After college Julius Lester moved to New York, where he was perceived as an angry and extremely vocal young black man of the 1960s **Civil Rights Movement**. His outrage over racism and the political oppression of African Americans found voice in such works as *Look out, Whitey!: Black Power's Gon' Get Your Mama!* (1968) and *Revolutionary Notes* (1969).

While living in New York in the 1960s, Lester hosted the "Julius Lester Program" on WBAI Radio, a Pacifica station. He was accused of **anti-Semitism** in 1968 and 1969 when he allowed a teacher to read a controversial poem written by a fifteen-year-old African American girl; the poem included phrases that are derogatory against Jews. The Anti-Defamation League of B'nai Brith requested that all anti-Semitic content be removed from the program and the FCC investigated the station as a function of its fairness requirements. Lester told his detractors that since the African American community has anti-Semitic feelings, it is the responsibility of the radio station to air these feelings. After its investigation the Federal Communications Commission (FCC) accepted the station's assertion that the feelings expressed in the poem were repugnant to everyone at the station, but that the station wanted to "illuminate a dangerous new form of bigotry, and, by discussion of the problem, aid in its eradication and in developing better relations between the **races**."

Although Lester's cultural, racial, and religious identification was that of Christian African American as he was growing up, he also has white Jewish ancestry. As an adult, when he became a professor in the Afro-American studies department of the University of Massachusetts, Amherst, he examined and embraced this Judaism, an act that probably upset people more than the presumed anti-Semitism of his earlier years. The displeasure over Lester's claim to a Jewish **identity** came to a crisis in 1988 after the publication of *Lovesong*, his spiritual autobiography. Lester stated that **James Baldwin** had made an anti-Semitic statement in a class when he (Baldwin) insisted that the news media should not have reported Rev. Jesse Jackson's disparaging comment about New York City as "Hymietown."

Since Baldwin was perceived as an unassailable cultural icon, Lester's statement outraged members of his department of Afro-American studies. His departmental colleagues voted unanimously to have Professor Lester reassigned to another department. He did leave Afro-American studies and was accepted as a professor in the university's Judaic studies department.

Some critics find a conflict in these two Jewish controversies in Lester's life, but in fact, Julius Lester loves to examine and transform the pain on the edge of politically incorrect status quo. He is unafraid of controversy and insists that he does not regret any of the significant choices and decisions he has made in his life.

Lester applies a rigorous honesty to all of his work and creations, and he is no more likely to avoid giving yelling space for the crying out loud pain of young African Americans reacting to **racism** than he is to avoid spiritual and intellectual paths, such as the path to embracing Judaism, that inspired his intelligence and love.

Lester has written over fifty books and has published scores of essays and book reviews in such publications as the *New York Times* and the *Boston Globe*. His books can be classified into several overlapping areas: African American folk tales (*Uncle Remus*, 1987; *John Henry*, 1994), tales of traditional interest for African Americans (*Sam and the Tigers*, 1996), literary fiction (*What a Truly Cool World*, 1999), historical fiction (*To Be a Slave*, 1968), Jewish midrash (*When the Beginning Began*, 1999), autobiography (*Lovesong*, 1988) and African folk tales (*Shining*, 2003).

Julius Lester and his wife Milan live in Western Massachusetts, where he is a professor of Judaic studies at the University of Massachusetts, Amherst.

Further Reading

Meyer, Adam. "Gee, You Don't Look Jewish: Julius Lester's Lovesong, an African-American Jewish-American Autobiography." *Studies in American Jewish Literature* 18 (1999): 41–51.

Susina, Jan. "Reviving or Revising Helen Bannerman's *The Story of Little Black Sambo*: Postcolonial Hero or Signifying Monkey?" *Voices of the Other: Children's Literature and the Postcolonial Context.* Ed. Roderick McGillis. New York: Garland Publishing, 1999. 237–52.

Carolivia Herron

LÊ THI DIEM THÚY (1972–) Vietnamese American writer and performance artist. Born in Phan Thiet, lê left Vietnam in a boat with her father in 1978. She grew up in Linda Vista, California, moved to Massachusetts, graduated from Hampshire College in 1994, and became a performance artist. *Red Fiery Summer* and *the bodies between us*, her solo performances, have been presented at the Whitney Museum of American Art, the International Women Playwright's Festival in Galway, Ireland, and the Third New Immigrants' Play Festival at the Vineyard Theater, New York City. lê has been awarded residencies from the Lannan Foundation, the Headlands Center for the Arts, and Hedgebrook and a fellowship by the Radcliff Institute for Advanced Study at Harvard University. She was selected by the *Village Voice* as a "Writer on the Verge." She is presently at work on her second novel, *The Bodies Between Us*.

The Gangster We Are All Looking For (2001), her debut novel, focuses on the travails of an immigrant Vietnamese family in America. The narrator is an unnamed young girl who was pulled out from the sea along with her father and four other men. The father takes care of his daughter until the mother who has been left behind in Vietnam joins them. The novel reveals, in flashbacks, the story of the parents who fell in love with each other and married against the wishes of their family. Ma was Catholic, and Ba was a Buddhist and a gangster, though we are not given much information about the kind of gangster he had been in Vietnam. In Alta Vista, where they are living now, Ba works as a gardener and Ma works at a restaurant, but neither has found joy or fulfillment of their dreams. Haunted by the past, Ba grows sorrowful and withdraws into himself, Ma lives with the memories of the sea, and the girl struggles with the memory of her brother who was drowned, "whose body lay just beyond reach, forming the shape of a distant shore."

The strength of the novel lies in its evocative prose and fresh images: "In the morning, the world is flat. Westinghouse Street is lying down like a jagged brushstroke of sunburnt yellow." lê brings to the narrative the fluidity and sensitivity of performing arts. Her rendition of the memory of loss and sorrow, of alienation and dislocation, of tension between the past and the present in *The Gangster We Are All Looking For* offers a blend of memoir and a novel. lê said in an interview that she didn't want to write a memoir because what happens to the narrator, "happens in the world. The experience of displacement is a profound one and is one that so many people have gone through" (Johnson 23). For a novel, she needs to make her characters more rounded and complex.

Like Dao Strom and Monique Truong, lê thi diem thúy is also committed to a portrayal of the Vietnamese experience which is usually neglected in mainstream narrative about Vietnam. It is, as she has stated, "usually about the American GI, while the Vietnamese are part of the landscape. They rarely get particularized as characters" (Mehegan B7). In particularizing this experience, she touches the chords that make immigrant writing so vibrant. On a broader scale, lê has earned a place for herself among writers such as **Sandra Cisneros**, **Maxine Hong Kingston**, and **Jhumpa Lahiri**. (*See also* Vietnamese American Literature)

Further Reading

Baumann, Paul. "Washing Time Away." *New York Times* (May 25, 2003): 26.

Johnson, Sarah Anne." Between Two Worlds." *Writer* (February 2004): 22–25.
Mehegan, David. "Refuge in Her Writing." *Boston Globe* (June 2, 2003): B7.

Vijay Lakshmi Chauhan

LEVERTOV, DENISE (1923–1997)   Jewish/Christian American poet and critic. Levertov published more than twenty volumes of poetry and criticism; her work is especially notable for its adaptation of the principles of American modernism and its explorations of the meaning of faith, the spiritual importance of Nature, and the collision between everyday human experience and wider political concerns. Levertov's work communicates her profound commitment to the poet's role, protesting injustice, protecting the sacred, and interrogating her world.

Born in Ilford, England, Levertov's mother was a Welsh Congregationalist, while her father was Russian, a Hasidic Jew who became an Anglican priest. Levertov's religious inheritance was thus complex and rich, and her poetry is imbued with an inclusive response to matters of belief, acknowledging facets of Judaism, Christianity, myth, and a profound appreciation of Nature. Levertov published her first poem at seventeen, and her first volume, *The Double Image,* in 1946. In 1947 she married Mitchell Goodman, an American writer, and moved to the United States; their son, Nikolai, was born in 1949. She became a full-time poet and teacher at a number of American universities, while publishing translations, works of criticism, and award-winning volumes of poetry.

Levertov became an American citizen in 1956, but was writing in a recognizably American style long before. Her early poetry shows the influence of the English Romantics, whose work she quotes stylistically (for example, "Childhood's End" of 1946) and literally, as in "Memories of John Keats" (1972), which uses fragments of Keats's letters. Nevertheless, the key influences on her poetry are American: the criticism and poetry of the "high" modernists, Pound, H. D. [Hilda Doolittle], and T. S. Eliot, contributed to the precision and Classicism of Levertov's work, while the experimental poets of mid-century, such as Robert Creeley and Charles Olson, influenced her understanding of free forms and shaped her American voice.

More than any of these, however, William Carlos Williams was Levertov's mentor; their published correspondence shows their mutual respect and shared priorities for the practice of poetry. Like Williams, Levertov's poetry displays unsentimental empathy for human experience and an appreciation of Nature as something separate from, but profoundly important to, humanity. In terms of technique, Levertov shares Williams's commitment to free verse forms that offer carefully crafted directives for reading and interpretation.

Levertov believed in poetic craft and in the value of open form, considering free verse the most appropriate technique for expressing the uncertainties of experience. She also believed that the appearance of the poem on the page should offer a precise guide as to how it should be read. "O Taste and

See" (1964) is an exemplary Levertov poem: stylistically free-form, with short lines and a rhythm that emphasizes the sounds of its words alone and in combination, helping the poem to "sing." Both its relatively few words—around three to a line—and its lack of metaphor offer evidence of the influence of the Imagists; it evokes the energy and passion of Williams without copying his technique; it acknowledges an English literary heritage in its rephrasing of Wordsworth but locates its concerns firmly in the contemporary moment. In terms of content, the poem interrogates the meeting-point of the religious and the everyday, acknowledging the reality of physical needs as well as the necessity of spiritual fulfillment.

Levertov was a contemporary of many of the famous "Confessional" poets of the mid-century, but she remained skeptical about the validity of the form; she saw a distinction between poetry that includes elements of autobiography, as her work does, and poetry aimed at purging difficult experiences, that attaches less importance to craft. "Olga Poems" (1964) is a long sequence that explores the life and premature death of Levertov's sister. Although extremely personal in content and conveying intense grief, these are also poems that maintain a high level of craft and are never allowed to become overly sentimental; they express empathy but acknowledge the distance between the sisters, making it possible to read the poems as an act of mourning that does not exclude the reader.

Levertov's style remained distinctive across her career: Her later poetry shows an overall increase in line-length and density of word use as well as in total length. See, for example, the long "Evening Train" (1992) but also "Witness" from the same year; the latter poem retains the brevity of her mid-period work, and in both cases the poems maintain her principles of precision of word, image, and sound, regardless of length. Her concerns remain stable, too: Without ever being an overtly feminist poet, Levertov consistently expressed a critical awareness of the barriers between the sexes, both in intimate relationships (as in "The Ache of Marriage," 1964) and in the public sphere (as in "The Mutes,"1967). Nature remained an enduring subject: "Sojourns in the Parallel World" (1998)—the world of the title being Nature—emphasizes the spiritual relationship between Nature and humanity, the necessity of communion with Nature along with a questioning intellectual life.

Levertov's religious and ethnic heritage informs much of her poetry. "Illustrious Ancestors" (1958), for example, admires the qualities and diversity of her lineage and makes of these a model for her own poetic practice, and "A Map of the Western Part of the County of Essex in England" (1961) considers the impact of her English childhood. When Levertov decided to write, as an intellectual exercise, a Christian Mass for "Doubting Thomas," she found that composing the poem, finally titled "Mass for the Day of St. Thomas Didymus"(1982), had affected a genuine religious conversion. From a life-long position of skeptical pantheism, she became, ultimately, a practicing Catholic. Although many of her poems from the last years of her life reflect the changes in her religious perspective, the work continues to question the meaning of experience, and her faith—as it is reflected in the poetry—remains grounded in its relationship to the human.

Equally important is Levertov's empathy for the outsider, for those positioned as "other" to the dominant order, perhaps as a result of her own experience of being Welsh-Russian in England, Jewish to Christians, Christian to Jews, English in the United States, and female in a male-dominated field. Her empathy for the marginalized, coupled with an intellectual understanding of the victimizer, strongly informs the political content of Levertov's work. Although she worked as a nurse throughout World War II and was well informed about the concentration camps, Levertov did not write about these events until "During the Eichmann Trial" (1961), which expresses horror at the acts of Nazism while recognizing the uncomfortable truth that the Nazis were as human as poet or reader. The Vietnam War provoked Levertov to activism and to overt expression of her political beliefs in her poetry; she shifted her antiwar stance from absolute pacifism to a revolutionary position, abhorring war but believing in the right of protest. "Life at War" (1967) explores the paradox of the human capacity to both love and harm, setting descriptions of war atrocities in Vietnam against examples of human compassion.

Distinctive and passionate, Levertov's poetry and criticism articulate her commitment to a range of issues: political activism, religious faith, Nature, humanity, and poetry itself. Her craft, as much as her subject matter, was sacred to her; she was one of the century's best free verse practitioners. (*See also* Jewish American Poetry)

Further Reading

MacGowan, Christopher, ed. *The Letters of Denise Levertov and William Carlos Williams.* New York: New Directions, 1998.

Wagner-Martin, Linda, ed. *Critical Essays on Denise Levertov.* Boston: G. K. Hall, 1990.

Sarah Graham

LEVIN, MEYER (1905–1981)   Chicago-born Jewish American novelist, journalist, and filmmaker. Throughout his career, Levin contributed several books and articles to the social and political literature of the 1930s and early 1940s and portrayed the Jewish experience in America as well as the founding of Israel. He also played a crucial role in the American publication of Anne Frank's *Diary,* although he was distressed by the rejection of his theatrical adaptation and spent the last twenty-five years of his life filing lawsuits.

Levin graduated from the University of Chicago, where, as a student reporter, he covered the shocking 1924 murder trial of Richard Loeb and Nathan Leopold, who were defended by Clarence Darrow against the charges of killing fourteen-year-old Bobby Franks for the thrill of it. In 1957

Levin would use the Leopold-Loeb murder case for his "nonfiction novel" *Compulsion,* which he also successfully adapted for the stage and which inspired the homonymous movie starring Orson Welles. Upon graduation, Levin went to work full time for a newspaper, an experience that would be the base for his first novel, *Reporter,* in 1929. After two years, *Yehuda* documented the life of a kibbutz in Palestine, making Levin a careful observer of Jewish life.

Because of the critical standards inherited from the cold war, Levin's role as a committed left-wing writer has usually been obscured, and his controversy with Lillian Hellman over the stage adaptation of Frank's diary is usually taken as evidence of his anticommunism. Yet, though Levin later lent support to this characterization, in his autobiographical volume *In Search* (1948), he professed his commitment to the creation of a classless society and his ambition to be viewed as a significant proletarian writer. *The New Bridge* (1933), *The Old Bunch* (1937), and *Citizens* (1940) all show Levin's left-wing leanings, and they described in detail Jewish life in Chicago, both within and without the confines of the ethnic ghetto. Levin wrote that in *The Old Bunch* he wanted to show how the ethnic group was central to determining human relationships. As in *Citizens,* which shares several characters with *The Old Bunch* and fictionalizes the killing of ten steel mill strikers in Chicago on Memorial Day in 1937, this ethnic perspective was combined with the abolition of a central character, which served a clearly political point. The adoption of multiple viewpoints was in itself an affirmation of democracy and allowed Levin to carry out a more complete social analysis. In his article "Novels of Another War" (1940), which was published in the left-wing journal *The Clipper,* Levin emphasized how writers of his generation were documenting a different type of war than the Modernists, whose characters led meaningless lives without any enduring commitments or passions. The politically committed writer of the 1930s documented instead the war of the Great Depression and the battles against economic exploitation and capitalist greed. This article provides evidence of Levin's involvement in the ideological and aesthetic debates about radical fiction fostered by the English translation of Georg Lukakcs's article "Tendency or Partisanship?" (1934).

After World War II, Levin was one of the first American journalists to enter the liberated concentration camps. Wishing to find a voice to document to the entire world the horrors of the **Holocaust**, he judged Anne Frank's *Diary* to be the suitable medium to illustrate the persecution of Jews for a mass audience. Thus, he helped to arrange for its American publication, managing to publish a five thousand word glowing review of the book in the *New York Times.* Anne's father, Otto, granted Levin the rights to adapt the *Diary* for the stage. But Levin's treatment was perceived to be overtly "Jewish," and it was rejected in favor of a play with a more universal message, written by **Lillian Hellman** and the non-Jewish screenplay writers Frances Goodrich and Albert Hackett. For the rest of his life, Levin protested against what he thought was a suppression of Anne's Jewishness and her legacy, and he devoted two volumes to the controversy, *The Fanatic* (1964) and *The Obsession* (1973).

Israel was the main source of inspiration for Levin's later novels, *Gore and Igor* (1968), *The Settlers* (1972), and the latter's sequel, *The Harvest* (1978). For his last novel, though, he returned to his native Chicago: *The Architect* (1982) fictionalized the life of Frank Lloyd Wright. Levin was also a film critic for the *Esquire* magazine and a filmmaker. He directed several features supporting Zionism such as *My Father's House* (1947), the first film to be entirely produced in Palestine, and *The Illegals* (1977), on the Jewish exodus from Poland to Israel.

Further Reading

Foley, Barbara. *Radical Representations-Politics and Form in U.S. Proletarian Fiction, 1929–1941*. Durham, NC: Duke UP, 1993.

Graver, Lawrence. *An Obsession with Anne Frank: Meyer Levin & the Diary*. Berkeley: U of California P, 1997.

Klein, Marcus. *Foreigners: The Making of American Literature 1900–1940*. Chicago: U of Chicago P, 1981.

Levin, Meyer. "Novels of Another War." *The Clipper* 1 (1940): 3–8.

Melnick, Ralph. *The Stolen Legacy of Anne Frank. Meyer Levin, Lillian Hellman, and the Staging of the Diary*. New Haven, CT: Yale UP, 1997.

Rubin, Steven J. *Meyer Levin*. Boston: Twayne Publishers, 1982.

Luca Prono

LEVINE, PHILIP (1928–)   Jewish American poet. For Philip Levine poetry is first and foremost an act of witnessing, a means of expressing the human struggle and giving voice to the oppressed and the forgotten. His own family's descent in social and economic status brought about by his father's untimely death when Levine was only five and, even more so, his encounters with the truly poor—children who wore no socks in the bitter Michigan winter, who stayed home from school because their parents could not afford a winter coat—sparked the sense of moral outrage and commitment to social justice that would become the driving force in his poetry. As Levine relates in his 1994 autobiography *The Bread of Time*, growing up in "a viciously anti-Semitic community in a particularly anti-Semitic era" also politicized him as a young man, as did an affinity with the anti-fascist, anarchist heroes of the Spanish civil war, who would become an important reference point in his poetry.

Levine held a series of industrial jobs in his youth, partly out of necessity as he worked his way through Wayne State University and partly out of a commitment to an oath that he and his twin brother Edward made at fourteen never to enter the propertied middle class. It was at the age of twenty-four, after discovering poetry at Wayne State University, that Levine consciously decided to become a poet. He left for Iowa to study poetry with Robert Lowell in 1953, where he met and married Frances J. Artley in 1954, began publishing poetry, and eventually earned an MFA in 1957. Levine accepted a position teaching poetry at the University of California at Fresno in 1958, where he remained until his recent retirement.

Levine's books through the early 1970s, including *On the Edge* (1963), *Not This Pig* (1968), *Five Detroits* (1970), *Pili's Wall* (1971), *Red Dust* (1971), and *They Feed They Lion* (1972), established his working-class loyalties and status as a distinctly urban poet. Among the most well-known poems in these early collections are "The Horse" (*On the Edge*), which imagines the psychological trauma of the survivors of Hiroshima, and "Animals Are Passing from Our Lives" (*Not This Pig*), the story of a defiant pig (generally understood as a metaphor for the oppressed urban worker) who maintains his dignity and resists his fate of being slaughtered at market. "They Feed They Lion," the title poem of the volume that brought Levine to national prominence, evokes the justified anger of black Detroit that resulted in the **race** riots of 1967.

1933 (1974), named for the year that his father died, marked a turning point in Levine's poetry as he began to look toward his own past for subject material and his tone became less angry and combative. The title poem of this volume alternates between past and present as the poet remembers his father and reflects on how much the world had changed since his passing. In *The Names of the Lost* (1976), Levine linked childhood memories of his extended family with the doomed anarchist heroes of the Spanish Civil War with whom he had come to identify even more strongly after living in Spain for two years (1965–66 and 1968–1969) with his wife and sons.

In *Ashes: Poems New and Old* (1979), Levine sought to come to terms with the losses that he had described in his two previous volumes, to accept their finality and take strength from their communal inheritance. The volumes published over the next few years, *7 Years from Somewhere* (1979), *One for the Rose* (1981), and *Sweet Will* (1985), reflect a maturing Levine whose utopian vision has been tempered by an acceptance of the world with all its imperfections.

The narrative character of Levine's poetry has become more pronounced over time, as the title poem of his 1988 collection, *A Walk with Tom Jefferson* (1988), well illustrates. The Tom Jefferson of this poem is a retired black factory worker who leads the poet through a Detroit neighborhood devastated in the late 1960s, showing him not only destruction, but also the courage of the residents who have reverted to a quasi-rural lifestyle and carried on with the courage of survivors.

Memory, family history, and a continuing commitment to conveying the struggles and triumphs of ordinary people have continued to drive Levine's recent collections, including *What Work Is* (1991), *The Simple Truth* (1994), and *The Mercy* (1999). The title poem of this last collection conveys the combination of fear and excitement that Levine imagines his own mother, who died in 1998, must have felt as a nine-year-old child immigrating to America. (*See also* Anti-Semitism)

Further Reading

Christopher Buckley, ed. *On the Poetry of Philip Levine: Stranger to Nothing.* Ann Arbor: U of Michigan P, 1991.

Levine, Philip. *So Ask: Essays, Conversation, and Interviews.* Ann Arbor: U of Michigan P, 2002.

Nadia Malinovitch

LEVINS MORALES, AURORA (1954–)   Jewish and Puerto Rican feminist, poet, scholar, historian, and activist. Although her Puerto Rican mother and Jewish father, who are communists, were born and raised in the United States, Levins Morales was born in Indiera, Puerto Rico. In 1967, she and her family moved to the United States, and they lived in Chicago and New Hampshire. Levins Morales has a PhD in women's studies and history. She teaches at the University of California, Berkeley and at the University of Minnesota, Minneapolis, writes poetry commentaries for Pacifica Radio's *Flashpoints* news magazine, lectures, and conducts poetry-writing workshops.

Levins Morales's work has appeared in a number of important collections, including *Revista Chicano-Riqueña* (1980), *This Bridge Called My Back* (1983), and *Cuentos: Stories by Latinas* (1983), as well as *Ms.,* the *Women's Review of Books, Bridges, The American Voice,* and numerous anthologies.

One of her most significant contributions to Latina literature is the collection *Getting Home Alive* (1986), which she coauthored with her mother, Rosario Morales. The collection comprises short stories, poems, essays, prose pieces, and dialogues between the two. Some of the prominent themes include identity, especially as a female and a minority, cultural borderlands, class, and familial ties, especially mother-daughter relationships. It is obvious in this collection that Levins Morales's identity as a Puerto Rican Jew is something that she celebrates. In "Child of the Americas," she acknowledges the many and varied elements of her identity and describes herself as a child "born at the crossroads"; in "Old Countries," she celebrates the stories of her ancestors; and in "Puertoricanness," she examines the undeniable growth of her identity as a Puerto Rican, something "she had kept hidden" for many years. In "Class Poem," Levins Morales relates that she is grateful for the sacrifices made by her family that have enabled her to live a middle class life, and she recognizes that feeling guilty about this privilege will not help those who are less privileged; however, it is important to note Levins Morales's definition of privilege. She points out that privilege is not about material items but the love of her family. It is clear that a primary goal of the collection is to give voice to the oppressed; for example, in "A Story," Levins Morales describes a pregnant woman who has been shot and killed by soldiers and whose baby is still moving inside her.

Medicine Stories: History, Culture, and the Politics of Integrity (1998) is a collection of essays that examines the colonized past of Puerto Ricans. In this work, Levins Morales examines the colonization of nations as well as the abuse of individuals. In addition, she discusses her own encounters with abuse as a child. Her life experiences are incorporated into *Remidios: Stories from Earth and Iron from the History of Puertorriqueñas* (1998) as well. The work is a historical and mythical discussion of the meaning of being Puertorriqueña and explores the many women and cultures that have intersected in Puerto Rico, beginning over 200,000 years ago, and the hardships these women have endured. In particular, she examines those Puerto Rican women who have been silenced by their oppressors and disregarded by historians. She also discusses the healing powers of food and herbs that have been shared between generations of women. Levins Morales is one of eighteen Latinas who contributed to the important collection of over sixty essays, stories, poems, and memoirs titled *Telling to Live: Latina Feminist Testimonios* (2001) by the Latina Feminist Group. Although the women come from a variety of backgrounds, they acknowledge their shared experiences, especially those related to their development as thinkers and writers and their struggles to be successful in academia. In 2002 the collection won the Gustavus Myers Award, an award that honors works that examine the causes of bigotry.

Levins Morales's post-9/11 poem "Shema" was shared on the Internet and read at many peace rallies and is the basis for a soon-to-be self-published collection of poems titled *Shema: Writings on Love and War. (See also* Puerto Rican American Poetry)

Further Reading

Benmayor, Rina. "Crossing Borders: The Politics of Multiple Identity." *Centro de Estudios Puertorriqueños Bulletin* 2.3 (1988): 71–77.

Khader, Jamil. "Subaltern Cosmopolitanism: Community and Transnational Mobility in Caribbean Postcolonial Feminist Writings." *Feminist Studies* 29.1 (2003): 63–204.

Rojas, Lourdes. "Latinas at the Crossroads: An Affirmation of Life in Rosario Morales and Aurora Levins Morales's *Getting Home Alive.*" *Breaking Boundaries: Latina Writing and Critical Reading.* Ed. Asunción Horno-Delgado, et al. Amherst: U of Massachusetts P, 1989. 166–77.

Stefanko, Jacqueline. "New Ways of Telling: Latinas' Narratives of Exile and Return." *Frontiers* 17.2 (1996): 50–70.

Diane Todd Bucci

LIFSHIN, LYN (1944–)   Jewish American poet and writing instructor. Labeled the "Queen of the Small Presses" because of her dedication to the small presses that first published her and because of her ability to survive on her own without the support of any major publishing house or institution, Lyn Lifshin is one of the most prolific contemporary poets in the United States. Her poetry has appeared in practically every literary and poetry magazine, and she has contributed to hundreds of anthologies. Lifshin has published more than ninety collections of her own work, along with an autobiography and a "how-to" book for other writers. In addition, she is recognized for editing several highly praised women's writings and for her many poetry workshops and readings. Though her Jewish heritage only comes through in a portion of her vast collections of writings, when she has tackled Jewish topics in her writing, she has shown herself to be a strong Jewish American female voice.

Lifshin attributes her vast collection of published poems to her constant need to write. In fact, she believes that writing is as essential to her being as breathing. Born and raised in Vermont, Lifshin was exposed to poetry at an early age. She skipped several grades in elementary school and landed in a third grade classroom where her teacher had the students reading the works of major British writers; her first poem was written in this class. Along with this teacher, Robert Frost, a customer in her father's store when she was a child, also recognized young Lifshin's talent, praising one of her poems that he was presented.

Despite the support for writing she received as a child, Lifshin also faced obstacles as she pursued a career in writing, especially due to her religion and gender. She felt constrained in her small town, particularly because she was part of one of the town's few Jewish families, and she saw poetry as a way to rise above her circumstances. In graduate school, Lifshin faced more barriers when she was assigned a male advisor who was known to never pass a woman and who continually told her she did not have the right religious background to teach seventeenth-century English literature.

Although her religious and cultural heritage did at times create obstacles for her, Lifshin was not strongly affected by being Jewish until she was much older. Lifshin attributes her first powerful emotions of outrage and terror over **anti-Semitism** and the **Holocaust** to a film that she watched as an adult, rather than to real life experiences. When Lifshin was asked to do a workshop about the Holocaust at a museum in Albany, New York, she felt uneducated on the subject. As a result, Lifshin chose to immerse herself in stories, films, artwork, nonfiction accounts, and poetry about the Holocaust. Because she was so consumed by the subject, Lifshin began to write her own poems about the tragedy, which she published in the book *Blue Tattoo* (1995). Other poems in her collection not only discuss the historical event of the Holocaust, but also address the issue of anti-Semitism in general. For instance, her poem "For Me the Holocaust Started in '33 in a Small Village" comes from the perspective of a child in a school classroom who is degraded and beaten because he/she is Jewish.

Typically, Lifshin's poems are short, containing a few words per line and a small number of lines. As a result, most of Lifshin's poems focus on a single event or emotion. As can be imagined, her vast array of writings covers a wide range of topics. Although Lifshin addresses aspects of her own cultural and religious history in her works, she also explores other past events, such as her exploration of the lives of the women in the Shaker religious communities of early America in the collection *Shaker House Poems* (1976).

Her interest in other cultures can also be noted in her Eskimo poems in the collection *Leaning South*. Some of Lifshin's most popular poems reflect her feminist concerns. Her well-known "Madonna" poems can be found in a variety of works that she has collected throughout her career. In many of these poems, the Madonna figure is used as a metaphor to describe different female archetypes.

From **feminism** to cultural exploration, from cats to Jesus, Lifshin's burning desire to write has spurned a vast collection of literary works that cover an incredible range of topics. She has received numerous awards and has earned considerable recognition for her art.

Further Reading

Fox, Hugh. *Lifshin: A Critical Study.* Troy, NY: Whitiston Press, 1985.

Jessie N. Marion

LIM, SHIRLEY GEOK-LIN (1944–) Chinese American poet, short story writer, novelist, critic, educator, and editor. Lim is a prolific writer who has helped steer the direction of Asian American discourse with her critical writing and her editorial work. Lim has edited or coedited diverse influential Asian American anthologies including *The Forbidden Stitch: An Asian American Women's Anthology* (1990), *Reading the Literatures of Asian America* (1992), and *Power, Race and Gender in Academe* (2000). She has also contributed greatly to scholarship on South East Asian writing in English.

The accessibility of her American Book Award winning memoir *Among the White Moonfaces: An Asian American Memoir of Homelands* (1996) is largely due to the unrelenting frankness with which she imbues her recollections and observations. No one is spared, neither her mother who abandoned the family, nor her father whose feckless existence brought them to the brink of starvation, and not Lim herself, for the choices that she made. Yet she tempers these indictments with remembrances of love, tender moments in which the harshness of betrayal is tinted by bursts of joy. Born in Malacca, then a part of Malaya, Lim had a colonial-style education that stressed the English language as a tool for advancement in a country where dialects and a slew of cultures indigenous and imported proliferate. Her experiences of multiple colonizations in Malaysia, Singapore, and America greatly influenced her imagination and self-making process. As an "other" in both birth and chosen national home-places, Lim as a first generation Chinese American weighs each encounter with prejudice and each blessing, carefully analyzing each experience to explain her sense of global citizenship. A key motif in her work is the issue of travel, of journeys. Be it a high anxiety car ride along the American highways or a return visit to Malaysia, the migratory and diasporic themes are very much in evidence.

Lim's novel *Joss and Gold* (2001) is in some ways a reworking of the themes and issues present in *Moonfaces*. We follow the protagonist Li-An as the conflicts that arise in her personal life parallel the national disturbances of Malaysia's 1969 racial riots and the country's efforts to distinguish itself from the

Shirley Geok-lin Lim. *Photo by Dan Gray. Courtesy of Shirley Geok-lin Lim.*

lingering influences of British colonial rule. **Diaspora** and marginalization also haunt Lim's short story collections, which include *Another Country and Other Stories* (1982), *Life's Mysteries* (1985), and *Two Dreams* (1997).

Crossing the Peninsula and Other Poems (1980) is an intimate collection of poems about gender, **race**, and the complexities and contradictions inherent in constructing **identity**. After becoming the first Asian woman to win the 1980 Commonwealth Poetry Prize, Lim went on to publish *No Man's Grove* (1985), *Modern Secrets* (1989), and *Monsoon History* (1994). In *What the Fortune Teller Didn't Say* (1998), Lim separates her collection of new and old poems into three sections that track the development of immigrant consciousness. Her writing is characterized by an intensity of form as well as the enriching lushness of her Malayan heritage. From the young child enveloped in cultural contradictions, there emerges a woman whose ties to her traditions both aid and hamper her resettling in her new homeland.

It is a challenge to categorize Lim's writing according to a national space. For instance, *Moonfaces* is also separately published in Asia under the subtitle of "Memoirs of a Nyonya Feminist." The subtitle change in context with the region of publication is symptomatic of Lim's transnational appeal. The difficulty of articulating an identity, be it of the self or of a nation or an ethnic group, is presented in the turmoil that is encapsulated in Lim's struggle to situate herself at various times in geopolitical nations that are purportedly multiracial and multicultural. Emotional exile, abandonment, absence, and loss echo in her works, which explore the boundaries of liminal existence and the possibilities imbued in the concept of deterritorialized space.

For Lim, the outsider is a universal character. Like her mother's Peranakan ancestors (Malayan Chinese who have assimilated into Asian ethnic and western cultures), Lim takes pride in the acceptance of the validity of a unique series of identities. Hence, choosing to become an American citizen does not necessarily mean the negation of subscriptions to alternative homelands; nor does it necessarily single out the United States as the space in which the naturalized citizen feels most "comfortable" or, ironically, most "at home." To this end, her works demonstrate a rethinking of how, relationally, American identities are intranational as well as international constructs.

Further Reading

Quayam, Mohammed A. "An Interview with Shirley Geok-lin Lim." *MELUS* 28.4 (Winter 2003): 83–100.

Poh Cheng Khoo

LIMINALITY   A concept deriving from anthropology used to describe the state of a person between two different socially defined modes of being. Cultural studies have begun to use the term more and more to describe those immigrant groups' sense of identity or place within the country they now reside. In the United States, the term has been equally applied to Latin Americans, Asian Americans, Native Americans, and African Americans. Border Theory scholars, in particular, have adapted the term in their studies.

Anthropologist Arnold van Gennep (1873–1957), whose research focused on the rituals of African tribes, first used the term in the early twentieth century. He and Victor Turner (1920–83) both speak of rites of passage and focus their attention on the liminal or "in-between" period during initiation ceremonies. They speak of, for example, puberty rituals: those in which a boy becomes a man or a girl a woman in the eyes of the tribe or society. In those rites there is a formal time-space where the initiands, those undergoing the rite, are slightly more than a boy or girl, but not quite a man or woman. Turner describes the liminal period in these terms: "The liminal period is the time and space betwixt and between one context of meaning and action and another. It is when the initiand is neither what he has been nor is what he will be" (Turner, *Ritual Process*, 113).

Those undergoing the ritual lose all **identity** with which they had been previously associated: Girls lose their girlhood, unmarried persons lose their unmarried rights and privileges, etc. Yet, while the rites are carried out, they have not yet acquired any new status or social definition. It is not until the rite is finished that they acquire a new social position.

Van Gennep demarcates three ritual stages: separation, transition, and reincorporation. During the first ritual stage, the initiands lose the identity with which they associated prior to undergoing the rite. In the second phase, the initiands lose their social status and are seen as dangerous to those observing them. They are dangerous because they are beyond social definition and, as such, no societal proscriptions apply to them: societies are based on social definitions, which the initiands lack. This is the liminal stage. Finally, the last phase of any rite reintroduces the initiands into society with new social definitions and all the rights, privileges and duties, associated with the new status.

During the liminal phase, the initiands are beyond the realm of definition. They are symbolically and sometimes literally both a part of society and outside of it. They are nondefinable in that they no longer have the status they enjoyed prior to the rite, but have not acquired their postritual status; and they are nonmembers of the society because without a working definition as to who they are within their given society, they cannot be counted among the society's members.

Should a rite conclude during the liminal phase, the initiands would exit the rite with no working social definition and be, therefore, lacking in all rights, privileges, and definitions. Boys and men during this period lose all masculine traits symbolically. Girls and women are no longer feminine. Those moving into the "sacred" caste (priests and shamen, for example) are neither considered profane nor holy. This is the space that many immigrant groups to the United States often occupy: They have lost their identities as Cubans, Japanese, etc., and have not yet "become American."

The liminal period is locked in between two more fully defined spaces; it is complex and complicated. It is there, but ought not be. In other words, the liminal space-time in which rituals are conducted, according to Turner and Van Gennep, exists between two more definable stages in development or social acceptance: between being a girl and being a woman, or between being an ordinary woman and being a healer.

Within the United States, many "hyphenated groups" have taken shape in the last half-century or so: Cuban Americans, African Americans, Chinese Americans, etc. Their writings, cultures, and politics have developed their own personas, and they are considered neither what they were (Cuban, African, Chinese, etc.) nor what would be considered "mainstream American." These groups have brought their homelands, hopes, and dreams with them, internally in their minds as well as externally with their clothes and codes of social engagement, and they have settled on the threshold between two different and often opposed cultures. In particular, it is the second and third generations whose identities are often designated as liminal, since they are frequently raised in a home where their parents' or grandparents' customs from their homeland are still practiced within the United States, where these traditions are seen as alien. They are, therefore, products of two cultures and often do not feel entirely comfortable within either environment. (*See also* Border Narratives)

Further Reading

Cruz, Victor Hernandez, et al., eds. *Paper Dance: 55 Latino Poets.* New York: Persea Books, 1995.

Ellis, Larry. "Trickster: Shaman of the Liminal." *Studies in American Indian Literature* (Winter 1993): 55–68.

Gennep, Arnold van. *The Rites of Passage.* Trans. Monika B. Vizendom and Gabrielle L. Caffee. Chicago: U of Chicago Press, 1960.

Naficy, Hamid. "Phobic Spaces and Liminal Panics: Independent Transnational Film Genre." *Global/Local: Cultural Production and the Transnational Imaginary.* Ed. Rob Wilson and Wimal Dissanayake. Durham, NC: Duke UP, 1996. 119–44.

Schechner, Richard. *Between Theater and Anthropology.* Philadelphia: U of Pennsylvania P, 1985.

Turner, Victor. *The Anthropology of Performance.* New York: PAJ Publications, 1987.

————. *The Ritual Process: Structure and Anti-Structure*. New York: Aldyne de Gruyter, 1969.

Alexander Waid

LIMÓN, GRACIELA (1938–) Chicana novelist, teacher, and activist. In a writing career that began in the 1990s, Graciela Limón renders a complex landscape of Latino **identity** as it is shaped by gender, relationship, politics, and cross-border experiences.

Born and raised in East Los Angeles, the daughter of Mexican immigrants, Graciela Limón received her PhD in Latin American Twentieth Century Literature at UCLA in 1975; she previously earned her master's from the Universidad de las Americas in Mexico City. Her first career was spent teaching Latina/o literature at Loyola Marymount College; she retired in 2001.

Limón's first book, *Maria de Belen: The Autobiography of an Indian Woman* (1990), has become difficult to locate. In a first-person narrative, later rewritten as *Song of the Hummingbird* (1996), it relates a native woman's life as she witnesses her civilization being conquered.

In 1990 Limón traveled as part of a delegation to El Salvador to investigate the assassination of Jesuit priests there. Those experiences helped shape her novel, *In Search of Bernabé* (1993). It chronicles a Salvadoran woman's search for her disappeared son, from whom she was separated during the funeral for the assassinated Archbishop Romero. Luz, the mother, travels into Mexico, then Southern California, and finally back to El Salvador. In addition to providing a harrowing picture of the nature and complexities of the civil strife in El Salvador in the 1980s, the novel is notable for its strong sense of the dislocation and lack of welcome encountered by many Central American refugees (those Salvadorans fleeing for their lives in the 1990s were not granted refugee status by the United States). *In Search of Bernabé* won an American Book Award and was named a "critic's choice" by the *New York Times Book Review*. A Spanish translation appeared in 1997.

Less well received was Limón's *The Memories of Ana Calderón* (1994); in it she focuses on migrant life and the struggle to live in two cultures, especially as it is experienced by women. Praised for its perceptions into the motivations of both men and women and its understanding of popular religiosity, it has nevertheless been criticized for the melodrama of its plot. *Song of the Hummingbird* also received mixed reviews. An Aztec princess, in the first person, recounts witnessing the arrival and ascension of the Spanish conquistadores; her tale of life as Aztec royalty, then as slave and concubine, and finally in a convent, is told in the form of her final confession to a priest hoping to convert her.

Also set in Mexico, *The Day of the Moon* (1999; translated and released in a Spanish edition in 2004) traces fifty years in the life of the Betancourt family, from Don Flavio's sudden wealth in a card game through his denial of his native heritage and assertion of Spanish purity. His bigotry deforms the lives of all around him, especially his daughter, who falls in love with a native Rarámuri. While dramatizing the complexities of cultural **identity**, interracial romance, and patriarchy, the novel presents an impressive sense of Mexican history.

Limón returns to more contemporary history in *Erased Faces* (2001), using the Zapatista guerilla uprising of January 1994 as her setting. Weaving through the story the myths of the Lacandón and moving between the barrios of Los Angeles and Chiapas, Mexico, Limón again explores forbidden love and racial politics. From the plight of Central American political refugees who find themselves to be "migrant labor" in the eyes of the United States to explorations of gender and racial oppression in Mexico to the challenges of crossing the U.S. border or being born Mexican in the United States, Graciela Limón has enriched our understanding of Latino experience and uncovered important questions for **multiculturalism**.

Further Reading

Rodriguez, Ana Patricia. "Refugees of the South: Central Americans in the U.S. Latino Imaginary." *American Literature* 73.2 (June 2000): 387–412.

Kathryn West

LITHUANIAN AMERICAN LITERATURE   Lithuanian **immigration** to America happened in two waves: in the first half of the twentieth century, when many Lithuanians left their country for economic reasons, and immediately after World War II, when thousands of Lithuanians fled to Western countries fearing the impending Soviet occupation. From 1864 to 1945 almost 400,000 Lithuanians left their homeland, many of them heading to the United States.

The First Wave of Immigration

The generations that came to America before World War II were mainly workers in industrial centers such as Chicago or Pennsylvania. Although this wave of immigrants proved to be the most numerous and established the Lithuanian press and book publishing, it did not generate significant works of literature. The first Lithuanian books and newspapers were written, edited, and printed by Mykolas Tvarauskas (later he was joined by Jonas Šliūpas) at the end of the nineteenth century. Lithuanian immigrants were more concerned with publishing Lithuanian books and supporting their relatives in their homeland than participating in the cultural life of the American nation. From 1864 to 1904, Tsarist Russia forbade the printing of books using the Latin alphabet in Lithuania (at that time part of the Russian Empire). Lithuanian Americans were helping their home country to fight this ban by printing Lithuanian books in America and smuggling them to Lithuania as well as by supporting different political and cultural activists. Among those who worked and lived in the United States were the author of the first erotic Lithuanian poem, Kleopas Jurgelionis (1886–1963) and the pioneer of Lithuanian **feminism** and realism, Žemaitė, as well as Stasys Santvaras (1902–91), Juozas Tysliava (1902–61), Petronėlė Orintaitė, Marija Černeckytė-Sims (1906–85) Antanas Gustaitis (1907–90), Gražina Tulauskaitė (1908–90), and Alfonsas Tyruolis Šešplaukis. Many writers who worked and lived at that time were concerned with their ethnic identities and the culture of their homeland. Although the members of the community tried to preserve their ethnic **identity**, most of their children assimilated into American culture, and some even changed their names, disappearing in the mainstream of American literature. The first in-depth image of the Lithuanian ethnic community in American literature emerged not in Lithuanian writings but in Upton Sinclair's novel *The Jungle*. This novel raised a huge controversy over how America treated its immigrants. Although Sinclair himself was not Lithuanian, he could be considered the first writer to raise the question of ethnic Lithuanians as a group of immigrants building the American nation.

The Second Wave of Immigration

The most productive period for Lithuanian American culture was between 1947 and the 1980s, when, in an effort to escape the occupation of Lithuania by the Soviet Union and its feared repressions, hundreds of the most talented Lithuanians were forced to run away and start their lives anew in exile. As they came to the United States, they established many cultural organizations and began active lives. The trauma of being displaced and the injustice of history and fate dominate the works of these authors, who longed for their inaccessible home country, which had become a Soviet communist republic. Many of the immigrants never acknowledged the fact of their immigration and considered themselves to be displaced people who were involved in political movements for Lithuania's independence, continuing the tradition of Lithuanian culture abroad and separating it from American reality. Many writers faced language barriers and most of them never considered themselves a part of American culture. They thought they were continuing the traditions of Lithuanian literature that were developed in Lithuania during the interwar period of independence (1918–39). Only after the collapse of the Soviet Union, when return to Lithuania became possible, was the understanding of the Lithuanian community in the United States as an ethnic minority developed and theorized. Some of the writers who survived until Lithuania regained its independence returned to Lithuania, and some continue to work and live in the United States.

In many cases, the notion of national belonging and national identity is connected to the language in which the writer speaks and writes. But the writers who came to America late in their lives were not very productive after being disconnected from their homeland. Their literature was nourished by patriotism for their homeland and was oriented toward its development. Many writers believed that apolitical literature had higher moral and aesthetic values that could be expressed without addressing more direct problems of assimilating subjects. Members of the two oldest generations of this wave of immigration, Vincas Kėrėv-Mickevičius, (1882–1954), Faustas Kirša (1891–1964), Bernardas Brazdžionis (1907–2003), Jonas Aistis (1904–73), Henrikas Radauskas (1910–70), Vincas Ramonas (1905–85), Jurgis Jankus (1906), Antanas Vaičiulaitis (1906–92), Pulgis Andriušis (1907–70), Nelė Mazalaitė (1907–93), and many others, didn't raise the questions of their changing identities and their **ethnicity** in the American context. Some of them (Brazdžionis, Aistis) became prophets and mourners for their nation, often using religious images to express this loss. Some of them (Radauskas) looked for aestheticism as a way to distance literature and art from the pain of the displaced national community.

More productive was the so-called generation of "the Land": Kazys Bradūnas (1907–), Henrikas Nagys (1920–96), Alfonsas Nyka-Niliūnas (1919), Marius Katiliškis (1914–80), and Henrikas Nagys (1920–96). They used the imagery of Lithuania and its landscape to compensate for the loss of the home country in their poetry and prose. Marius Katiliškis was the only writer in his generation who tried placing his subject in American reality, and he offered a rethinking of this subject in regard to his ethnicity and class in his last book, *Monday on Emerald Street*. Katiliškis was one of the first writers to suggest an understanding of American life as a transition from Lithuanian nationalism to American capitalism. The works of other writers of that period embrace a philosophical and lyrical rethinking of imagery of their native land, re-creation of Lithuanian myths and realities in exile, and longing for home. A philosophical rethinking of displacement, of human belonging, and of memories dominates the literature of this generation.

The real move towards American reality in the American Lithuanian tradition starts with the prose and plays of Antanas Škėma (1911–61) and poetry of **Algimantas Mackus** (1932–64). These two were the most influential of the Lithuanian American authors. Škėma's only novel, "The White Cloth" (1958), was the first to narrate a story of immigrants who were disconnected from their nation and had to rebuild their identity abroad. The protagonist of this story, Garšva, is the first Lithuanian character who functions in a multinational and multiracial state as an immigrant. Škėma uses the stream of consciousness style to reveal the subject's psychological makeup and show his internal tensions and contradictions. The protagonist works as an elevator operator in a hotel in America and dreams about his poetry and native land. The subject's identity emerges from different historical and personal events: His witness to the trauma of the Bolshevik occupation of Lithuania, exile, love affairs, and his mother's mental illness makes Garšva a very complex character that is more common to the literature of Western modernism than Lithuanian patriotic romanticism. Garšva enters Lithuanian American literature as the first character approaching the escape from illusions of nationalistic belonging and declaring that death of ethnicity is the most important reality for an exile.

Antanas Škėma's works gave the impulse to a generation of writers known as "Separated from Land," best represented by poets Algimantas Mackus and Liūnė Sutema (1927–), to look for new forms of expression. The term for this generation was coined by famous sociologist Vytautas Kavolis (1930–96), who theorized its poetics and worldview. According to Kavolis, the generation emerged because of mistrust in the "reality" of human existence and because of the inability to "naturalize" displaced lives within certain networks of belonging. Those "Separated from Land" were mostly poets, influenced both by Lithuanian traditional literature and by their American lives. As Algimantas Mackus's poetry shows, it was a generation marked by transition from Lithuanian images to the problems of ethnic identity while assimilating into American culture. In this case, Mackus continued Škėma's work, thinking about the death of ethnicity as the only possible fate of the communities of people who live and work in exile.

Playwrights Algirdas Landsbergis (1924–2004) and Kostas Ostrauskas were also similar to the generation of those "Separated from Land." Although Landsbergis has published some stories, both of them are known as playwrights who continued the tradition of absurd theater to express their new immigrant reality and to talk about the fate of the Lithuanian community in exile. Landsbergis wrote both in Lithuanian and English; however, the problem of Lithuanian ethnicity is addressed in his Lithuanian prose more than in his plays. Landsbergis distances himself from the Lithuanian community and writes about certain national customs and relationships with humor, especially through the critique of marriage outside of the ethnic community. However, like the other authors, he also tends to think about the Lithuanian American community as the Lithuanian community. Kostas Ostrauskas published some plays about the Lithuanian ethnic community and its hermetic condition. In his trilogy, *Once upon a time there was Grandfather and Grandmother*, he addresses the same problem of death that Mackus raised, showing how nationalism imprisons and motivates the lives of communities, which articulate themselves through the loss of the native land.

Younger American Lithuanian Writers

Only the writers who were either born abroad or came to the United States early in their childhood began writing in English and developed a modern understanding of Lithuanian ethnicity in the United States. Among those later writers are Birute Putrius Serota, **Al Zolynas**, Vainis Aleksa, Anthony Petrosky, and Lina Ramona Vitkauskas and also Canadian Lithuanians Irene Maciulyte Guilford, Antanas Sileika, and Raymond Filips.

This generation continued its work by offering the understanding of Lithuanian heritage through their ethnic difference, their "otherness" within American culture. They not only transformed the imagination of traditional Lithuanian images (both Catholic and national) while talking about their American identities, but they also could think about these identities with more distance. For example, Birute Serota, in short stories published in magazines, recodes the relationship of Catholic and Lithuanian identity, showing the emerging conflict of religious and ethnic Lithuanian and American belongings. Al Zolynas and the Canadian Lithuanian authors Raymond Philip, Irene Gilford, and Antanas Sileika theorize their ethnic difference as having the most impact in their American lives in their poetry and novels, although their writings introduce thinking about Lithuanians in the context of transition from strictly patriotic to a multinational community. Their Lithuanian heritage emerges both as their access to a different language and culture and as a way of representing the "otherness" in American culture and juxtaposing it with other cultures. (*See also* Assimilation)

Further Reading

Šilbajoris, Rimvydas. "The Experience of Exile in Lithuanian Literature."
　　Lituanus: Lithuanian Quarterly Journal of Arts and Sciences 18.1 (Spring 1972):
　　48–57.

―――. *The Perfection of Exile*. Columbus: Ohio State UP, 1970.

Rimas Zilinskas

LIU, AIMEE (1953–)　　Part Chinese and part white American novelist. After graduating magna cum laude from Yale with a BA in Fine Art in 1975, Aimee Liu pursued nonfiction writing for fifteen years before publishing novels: *Face* (1994), *Cloud Mountain* (1997), and *Flash House* (2003). Part Chinese, Liu's own mixed race heritage has richly inspired and informed her novels, which focus on interracial marriage, cross-cultural experience, and international history and politics. Aimee Liu served as 2002 president of PEN USA, a writer's organization dedicated to human rights and freedom of expression. She is now PEN USA's executive vice president.

The portrayal of the challenge of interracial marriage characterizes Aimee Liu's three novels. Liu's debut novel *Face* is a quest for **identity** and truth about the character's past. An interracial heritage is a marker of difference and dislocation for Maibelle Chung, a photographer in New York's Chinatown. She struggles with her sense of nonbelonging and difference and wrestles with an identity crisis that is personal, cultural, and psychological.

The theme of interracial, intercultural experience becomes more complicated in Liu's second novel, *Cloud Mountain*. In lyrical, evocative prose, Liu probes powerful and passionate human stories set against the massive sweep of major historical events. The novel depicts racial prejudice in 1900s

California where interracial marriage was against the law. Hope Newfield, an American schoolteacher, and Liang Po-yu, a Chinese scholar and revolutionary, escape the hostile environment by moving to China. They witness and survive political upheavals and violence as well as the Japanese attack on Shanghai. Yet, unable to sustain their relationship in a prejudiced and culturally alienating world, Hope returned to the States with her children in the 1930s before the Communist takeover.

In *Flash House,* the interracial marriage of Joanna and Aidan Shaw is put under greater test and pressure in the cold war era, when personal stories are intricately and inescapably woven with international politics. Set during the cold war era, Aidan Shaw, a journalist in search of truth and covering Indian politics for the West, has to prove his loyalty to America when suspected of being a communist because of his idealism and Chinese heritage. His disappearance and subsequent news of his death set Joan on a search for him in India and China, a complex and arresting adventure filled with intrigue, suspense, secrets, and personal mysteries.

Liu has a penchant for weaving poignant and intriguing personal stories against the epic background of history and politics. Her narrative finesse enables her to realize the potential of fiction as a means of exploring weighty personal and collective histories.

Further Reading

Becker Arlene. "China Revealed in *Cloud.*" *Milwaukee Journal Sentinel* (June 22, 1997): 19.

Figes, Kate. "My Grandmother's Awfully Bog Adventure." *The Independent* (June 19, 1998): 8.

Haysom, Ian. "The Asian Novel's New Identity: Aimee Liu Part of Literature's Hot New Trend." *Toronto Star* (August 14, 1997): C10.

Parets, Meredith. "Flash House." *Booklist* (February 15, 2003).

Persico, Chrissy. "Flash House." *New York Daily News* (February 2, 2003): 16.

Zaleski, Jeff. "Flash House." *Publisher's Weekly* (March 3, 2003): 56.

Jie Tian

LOCKE, ALAIN (1886–1954) African American intellectual, editor, and philosopher, especially influential during the decade of the **Harlem Renaissance**, when he encouraged younger intellectuals such as **Claude McKay**, **Zora Neale Hurston**, or **Langston Hughes**. Locke was born in Philadelphia, and after graduating with honors from the local high school, he went to Harvard, graduating magna cum laude in philosophy in 1907. He then became the first African American to be awarded a Rhodes scholarship, which allowed him to obtain another degree at Oxford in 1910 and spend one year at the University of Berlin. He became a teacher of English, education, and philosophy at Howard University (1912–16), but went back to Harvard to complete his doctorate (1916–17). Immediately after, he resumed his post at Howard University, where he remained for the rest of his career.

His major achievement, upon which his fame rests, is the edition of *The New Negro*, a collection of primary works and essays that he published in 1925. The collection was a revised edition of a special issue of *Survey Graphic*, a sociological magazine, in March 1925. He titled this issue *Harlem: Mecca of the New Negro*, and it included renowned figures of the Harlem Renaissance such as **W. E. B. Du Bois**, Langston Hughes, **Jean Toomer**, **Countee Cullen**, **Anne Spencer**, and **James Weldon Johnson**. The expanded version in *The New Negro* incorporated poetry and fiction by Claude McKay, **Angelina Grimké**, Zora Neale Hurston, and **Jessie Redmon Fauset**; artwork by Aaron Douglas; and several essays by Kelly Miller, Melville Herkovits, E. Franklin Frazier, and **William Stanley Braithwaite**, to name a few. It is considered the foundational manifesto of the movement, born out of a new notion of racial pride for African Americans after World War, also known as representatives of "The **New Negro**." It is a momentous anthology as it gave shape and voice to the diverse tendencies that flourished in the decade of the twenties.

According to Locke in *The New Negro*'s introduction, the primary objective of the anthology was "to document the New Negro culturally and socially,—to register the transformations of the inner and the outer life of the Negro in America that have so significantly taken place in the last few years" (xxv). As a whole, it reflects the wide range of artistic expressions characteristic of the Harlem Renaissance, as it comprises work by some of the most influential artistic and intellectual voices of the era. In the work Locke reflects his belief in the importance of art as a cultural bridge between races and, therefore, as crucial to solving the racial problem in the United States. In this sense, Locke drew many of his ideas from W. E. B. Du Bois's cultural agenda, namely the concepts of double consciousness and **Talented Tenth**. On the one hand, the anthology testifies to the duplicity inherent in African American culture, arguing that its main manifestations are genuinely American but that the manifestations' roots can be traced back to the African legacy that was transplanted to the new land with slavery. On the other, Locke also echoes Du Bois's notion of the Talented Tenth when he depicts the young generation of New Negroes as the educated blacks who could pave the way to intellectual and social parity by means of art.

Apart from this epochal collection, he also edited other volumes in which he demonstrated the wide range of his interests: *Four Negro Poets* (1927), *Plays of Negro Life* with Montgomery Green (1927), *Negro Art: Past and Present* and *The Negro and His Music* (both in 1936), and *The Negro in Art: A Pictorial Record of the Negro Artist and of the Negro Theme in Art* (1940).

But perhaps his philosophical writings are less known, although he was acknowledged as one of the most relevant thinkers of his time. In 1935 he started publishing his philosophical articles, which mainly focused on the concepts of cultural relativism and cultural pluralism. He pointedly emphasized the similarities among different cultures and, through them, their basic equality. With Bernhard Stern, Locke coedited *When Peoples*

*Meet, a Study in **Race** and Culture Contacts* (1942), an anthology on global race relations and reputed to be the best compendium of his later work. When he died from heart disease, he was planning to write *The Negro in American Culture* in order to substantiate his claims on the importance of African American cultural legacy, but the work was left unfinished.

Further Reading

Locke, Alain, ed. *The New Negro. Voices of the Harlem Renaissance.* 1925. New York: Atheneum, 1992.

Mar Gallego

LOPATE, PHILLIP (1943–)   Jewish American essayist, novelist, and poet. Best known for his essays and his role in revitalizing this commercially marginalized form, Phillip Lopate has become recognized in the Jewish American writing tradition for his controversial pieces on the **Holocaust** and other aspects of Jewish life. Although Lopate is acclaimed as a persuasive and provocative essayist, when his essay "Resistance to the Holocaust," in the collection *Portrait of My Body* (1996), went public, it sparked an outcry from the Jewish community in America.

Lopate's view that today's Jews overglorify the Holocaust is pervasive in his works and is at the center of the dissension in the Jewish community. In "Resistance to the Holocaust," Lopate argues that the Jews have excluded all other human disasters in their preoccupation with the Holocaust. This false piety that has been attached to the Holocaust, therefore, has only served to push the tragic event to the outskirts of history. Lopate contends that the Holocaust is no different from any other genocide of the past, but it is merely an example of the evil that fills our world. Glorifying this one tragic event, then, is not the way to prevent its reoccurrence, for it is simply one instance of the malevolence that humans have displayed throughout time.

Some of Lopate's other essays, such as "Invisible Woman," "The Movies and Spiritual Life," and "The Story of My Father," also address Jewish themes with the same frankness and honesty. For instance, in "The Movies and Spiritual Life," Lopate explores the idea of spiritual transcendence that can be found in some films. As a self-proclaimed secular Jew, Lopate tackles the conflict that comes from finding spirituality in things outside of Judaism. On the other hand, in his work "Detachment and Passion," Lopate takes time to examine the more spiritual side of his Jewish background. In it, Lopate discusses his sister's devotion to Buddhism and admits to his own lack of religious attachment. He adds, though, that if he were to follow a spiritual path, it would be Judaism first. Through these and some of his other works, Lopate displays his Jewish education and acknowledges the importance of his Jewish heritage, while challenging commonly held beliefs and ideas about what it means to be a Jewish American man.

Although Lopate often explores his Jewish roots in his works, his vast collection of essays offers commentary on a wide range of other topics. In his first compilation of essays, *Bachelorhood: Tales of the Metropolis* (1981), Lopate looks at life in New York as a bachelor from a variety of perspectives, most of them autobiographical. Topics ranging from his mother's affair and its consequences in his family to an exploration of works written by other bachelors in New York are discussed and examined. Lopate continues this trend of mixing the autobiographical and the literary in his subsequent collections, *Against Joie de Vivre* (1989) and *Portrait of My Body.* These collected works also offer an exploration of a wide variety of topics, from lighter topics like his attack on picnics and an analysis of his own body to more serious subjects like the story of a fellow teacher's suicide, all written in Lopate's characteristically candid and poetic manner.

In addition to compiling his own collections of essays, Lopate has edited a number of well-received anthologies of essays. Eighty essays written by more than fifty different writers, such as James Thurber, Henry David Thoreau, Plutarch, Seneca, Virginia Woolf, and **James Baldwin**, are brought together in the collection *The Art of the Personal Essay: An Anthology from the Classical Era to the Present* (1994). One hundred eight different writers make up his second collection, *Writing New York: A Literary Anthology* (1998), which celebrates one hundred years of New York as a unified city through poems, essays, memoirs, letters, and works of fiction.

Though he is best known for writing and editing collections of essays, Lopate, however, is not limited to this literary genre. As a teacher of creative writing with the Teachers and Writers Collaborative Program in the New York City Schools (1968–80) and at the University of Houston, Columbia University, and Bennington College, Lopate's experiences reveal his versatility. In his third book, *Being With Children* (1975), Lopate creates an autobiographical account of his years of teaching racially diverse inner-city children to write poems, stories, or plays. He describes the difficulties he encountered while dealing with students' choices and needs, and he reveals his own struggles to keep his teaching meaningful and exciting. In this work, Lopate not only divulges his own thoughts and feelings during his experience, but he also takes the opportunity to celebrate the writings of the children he was able to impact through his teaching.

Unlike his third book, Lopate's first two novels, *Confessions of Summer* (1979) and *The Rug Merchant* (1988), are fictional and stray from the autobiographical. In *Confessions of Summer,* Lopate explores the concept of the love triangle, and in *The Rug Merchant* he tackles the problems of culture and environment in New York City through his protagonist Cyrus, a young man who is the son of Iranian immigrants.

Lopate's interest in city life and New York City itself can also be seen in his second volume of poetry, *The Daily Round* (1976). His subjects are people who are New Yorkers and are much like him, and through them he is able to examine the rituals of everyday life in the City.

In Lopate's wide variety of writings, he reveals himself as a watcher of people and a person of great self-knowledge as he examines himself and other individuals in everyday life. As readers, then, we are given the advantage of observing human life as Lopate opens new doors for us and reveals a somewhat different view of humanity in a way that is honest and unabashed.

Further Reading

Corey, Melinda. "Phillip Lopate: New York Storyteller." *Creative Nonfiction* 6 (1996): 116–25.

McIntosh, Sandy. "Fair Game: Phillip Lopate and the Personal Essay." *Confrontation: A Literary Journal* 56–57 (Summer–Fall 1995): 35–46.

Jessie N. Marion

LÓPEZ, JOSEFINA (1969–) Chicana playwright and screenwriter. Josefina López gained both recognition in the Chicana/o community and commercial success in the entertainment industry by using comedy as a means to make social critiques. In her writing, workshops, and community activism, López speaks out for the rights of women, Chicana/os, and immigrants.

López was born in Mexico in 1969. She and her family immigrated to the United States illegally when López was five years old. Though she grew up in East Los Angeles, López did not gain her U.S. residency until the passage of the 1987 Simpson-Rodino Amnesty Law. López attended the Los Angeles County High School for the Arts with the intent to become an actress. As an actress, López longed to play challenging roles written for Chicanas and ultimately decided that she would need to write them for herself. From 1985 to 1988, she took part in the Los Angeles Theatre Center's Young Playwright's Lab. In 1988 the California Young Playwright's Contest and director Luis Torner put López's writing on the stage for the first time with a production of *Simply María, or the American Dream.*

That same year, López went to New York City to work with **María Irene Fornes** in the INTAR Hispanic Playwright's-in-Residence Laboratory and began work on her most successful play: *Real Women Have Curves.* Teatro de la Esperanza produced the world premiere of the play in 1990, and it was so well received that it quickly became the most produced Chicana/o play in the early 1990s. The play was adapted into a television movie in 2002, and López cowrote the screenplay with George LaVoo. The five characters in the play *Real Women* are workers in a sweatshop in Los Angeles, most of whom have just received their legal residency because of the passage of the Simson-Rodino Amnesty Law. The movie entirely leaves out the issue of **immigration**, focusing instead on the exploited labor of Chicanas, the overweight female body, and the main character's struggle to go away to college.

López was a staff writer for the *Culture Clash* television show in the 1990s and has written a screenplay titled *ADD Me to the Party.* She is also a poet, actress, and founder and artistic director of CASA 0101, an art and performance space in the Boyle Heights neighborhood of Los Angeles. López often teaches workshops on writing and digital filmmaking. Her other plays include *Confessions of Women from East L.A.*, *Food for the Dead*, *La Pinta*, and *Unconquered Spirits*. (*See also* Mexican American Drama)

Further Reading

Figueroa, Maria P. "Resisting 'Beauty' in *Real Women Have Curves*." *Velvet Barrios: Popular Culture and Chicana/o Sexualities.* New York: Palgrave Macmillan, 2003. 265–82.

Huerta, Jorge. "Redemption: Looking for Miracles in a Man's Church." *Chicano Drama: Performance, Society and Myth.* Cambridge: Cambridge UP, 2000. 100–39.

Marrero, María Teresa. "*Real Women Have Curves*: The Articulation of Fat as a Cultural/Feminist Issue." *Ollantay Theater Magazine* 1.1 (1993): 61–70.

Ashley Lucas

LÓPEZ TORREGROSA, LUISITA (1942–)   Puerto Rican American memoirist. Born in Puerto Rico, Luisita López Torregrosa was the oldest of six children. As a child, she moved several times because of her father, including to Mexico for a time while he attended medical school. She became the first member of her immediate family to migrate to the United States when she attended an all-girls boarding school in Pennsylvania to finish high school. As a journalist, López Torregrosa worked for the *San Francisco Chronicle* and contributed to prestigious U.S. magazines, such as *Vanity Fair, Condé Nast Traveler*, and *Vogue*, before becoming an editor at *The New York Times*. In 2004 she published the memoir *The Noise of Infinite Longing*, with its portrayal of a family of professionals whose members did not leave Puerto Ricoto seek fortune, but to obtain academic degrees and explore the world, provides a new perspective to the literature on Puerto Rican migration.

Her memoir opens with the 1994 reunion of the six López Torregrosa children following the death of their mother María Luisa in Edgewood, Texas, where she lived with her second husband. As she traveled the world as a journalist, Luisita López Torregrosa became distant from her family. Over the four days of funeral arrangements, she recalls the troubled marriage of her parents and the migration stories of her two eldest siblings, as well as her own, and comes to terms with her past.

López Torregrosa's contradictory vision of her mother María Luisa as a professional woman and as a dutiful wife is at the center of the first two parts of the memoir. Born to a family of professionals, her mother founded a theater ensemble with her brother at age seventeen and then left her town to study law at the University of Puerto Rico. Her sister Ángela Luisa became a popular newspaper columnist, and her brother José Luis was a famous comedian. María Luisa herself became a lawyer and register of deeds. However, she was also an obedient wife, helplessly enamored of an abusive husband with an alcohol problem. She moved from town to town following his footsteps, endured his violent behavior, and failed to protect her children from him.

The third part of the memoir dedicates a chapter to each of the eldest López Torregrosa children: Amaury, an aspiring musician who becomes a teacher in the Bronx; Ángeles, who joins the revolutionary struggle in Nicaragua; and Luisita, a journalist who leaves a good job in Philadelphia to join her lover Elizabeth in Manila. The memoir ends with the author's 2001 return to Puerto Rico to bury her father.

Luisita López Torregrosa's memoir is resolutely unsentimental; the focus is largely on her family. The author's family history is not presented as a success story, and even though there are brief mentions of childhood and early adulthood crushes, her sexual **identity** is not directly addressed until the next-to-last chapter. López Torregrosa's memoir is reminiscent of Marie Arana's *American Chica* (2001), which centers on the turbulent relationship of the parents of a Peruvian American girl who becomes an editor at *The Washington Post*.

Further Reading

Huneven, Michelle. "An Island of Words." *LA Weekly* (May 28, 2004): 32.

Volk, Patricia. "A Place and the Family That Left It But Never Forgot It." *New York Times* (April 23, 2004): A35.

Roberto Carlos Ortiz

LORD, BETTE BAO (1938–) Chinese American novelist, children's book author, and human rights advocate. Bette Bao Lord was born in Shanghai and became a happenstance immigrant in America at the age of eight. She had traveled with her parents on a business trip, and they remained in the United States when the communists wrested control of China from the nationalists. In her autobiographical children's book, *In the Year of the Boar and Jackie Robinson* (1984), through her persona Shirley Temple Wong, Lord shares her experiences as an immigrant girl integrating her Chinese background and language into her American **identity**. Bao's biculturalism is especially significant in her work as a cultural ambassador, interpreter, and writer between both countries.

Spring Moon (1981) remains Lord's best-known work. A sweeping saga, this novel captures the history of the House of Chang from 1892 to the early 1970s, covering family relationships and fortunes changed by the political and cultural upheavals in China. Aristocratic Spring Moon and her revolutionary daughter embody the values of Old and New China, but Lord emphasizes a continued bond, not a severance.

Married to Winston Lord, former ambassador to China, Lord and her husband were assigned to Beijing from 1985 to 1989. As a witness to pro-democracy student demonstrations in Tiananmen Square, Lord frames each chapter of her book *Legacies: A Chinese Mosaic* (1990) with headlines of the protest, juxtaposing this violence with that of the Cultural Revolution. The primary focus of *Legacies* is giving voice to survivors of the Cultural Revolution. During her residency in Beijing, Lord was able to collect the stories of many individuals, either personally or through taped recordings that were passed on to her.

Each chapter presents a new voice, such as "The Scholar" and "The Peasant," and is written in the first person. Lord's use of "I" is powerful in that it not only conveys the story of the individual, but each "I" also represents thousands of others who shared similar sufferings. "The Actress," for example, speaks of her tumultuous childhood education, which taught her to reject her beloved father as an enemy. Her father, who loved poetry, was imprisoned as a "rightist," and his daughter was tormented by her class-mates. To protect herself and her daughter, the actress's mother divorced him. When the actress learned that her father had committed suicide after years of torture, she realized that she had been a perpetrator and victim of an unnatural hatred bred by the political climate of the Cultural Revolution.

Lord also weaves in her insights regarding the social and political developments in China, and she finds hope in the people's strength. Lord's political criticism and human rights advocacy are based on valuing family. As children renounce their parents, spouses divorce, and friends and enemies are difficult to differentiate in *Legacies,* Lord looks to stable, loving family bonds to heal past pains. (*See also* Chinese American Novel)

Further Reading

Natov, Roni. "Living in Two Cultures: Bette Bao Lord's Stories of Chinese-American Experience." *The Lion and the Unicorn* 11.1 (1987): 38–46.

Karen Li Miller

LORDE, AUDRE (1934–1992) African American poet and writer. Self-described "black lesbian, mother, warrior, poet," Audre Lorde celebrated the multiple aspects of her **identity** and affirmed the power of difference in her poetry, essays, and prose writing. She refused to be silenced, despite her marginalized position in society, and confronted the injustices of **racism**, sexism, and homophobia with courage, hope, and eloquence.

The youngest of three daughters, Lorde was born in New York City to parents who emigrated from Granada, the West Indies, with the hope of achieving financial success and then returning home. However, the family remained in the United States, creating a sense of dislocation for Lorde, which strongly contributed to her conception of home as a journey rather than as a single geographic locale. Severely near-sighted, Lorde began speaking when she was five years old, and she later described her early communication as a form of poetry. She published her first poem in *Seventeen* magazine after it was rejected by her Catholic high school's student paper.

Lorde enrolled at Hunter College in 1951, but did not receive her BA until 1959 because she had to support herself throughout her studies. She worked as an X-ray technician, medical clerk, social worker, and factory employee, among other jobs. During the 1954–55 academic year, she studied at the National University of Mexico. In 1961 she received an MA in library science from Columbia University and worked as the young adult librarian at Mount Vernon Public Library. The following year she married lawyer Edwin Ashley Rollins. They had two children, Elizabeth and Jonathan, and divorced in 1970.

After receiving a grant from the National Endowment for the Arts in 1968, Lorde left her position as the head librarian at Town School Library in New York City to become the poet-in-residence at Tougaloo College in Mississippi. Her first volume of poetry, *The First Cities* (1968), is an introspective collection that uses natural images to describe the complexities of human emotion. These poems reflect an acute disillusionment with American ideals and anticipate her later exploration of themes such as dispossession, marginalization, and activist rage. In *Cable to Rage* (1970), Lorde explores marital love, personal deception, and child rearing. Using fresh, powerful language, Lorde examines the fleeting nature of love and suggests that betrayal is a result of the human

Audre Lorde, c. 1975. *Courtesy of the Library of Congress.*

capacity for change. The poem "Martha" contains Lorde's first reference to her homosexuality, a major concern of her later works.

Lorde published most of her critically acclaimed poetry in the 1970s. After receiving a Creative Artists Public Service grant in 1972, Lorde wrote *From a Land Where Other People Live* (1973), which was nominated for a National Book Award. In this collection, Lorde unites political concerns with personal experiences of outrage, discrimination, and self-exploration. Writing about the devastation caused by **racism** in the black community, Lorde protests the domination of white culture. She also examines her identity as a black woman and describes her relationships with other women.

The New York Head Shop and Museum (1974) is often considered Lorde's most radical poetic work. In stark urban images, she decries the deterioration of the city and expresses her anger in a more aggressive style, which is characteristic of the new black poetry movement of 1960s. In *Between Ourselves* (1976), Lorde again uses poetry as a means of channeling her rage against social injustice and as a way to confront personal conflicts and concerns. She received the Broadside Poets Award in 1975.

Coal (1976) was Lorde's first book to be released by a major publishing house. A compilation of poems from her first two books, this collection was read by a wider audience and helped to bring Lorde to national attention. In *The Black Unicorn* (1978), Lorde uses African mythology to assert her blackness and to express her female identity. She celebrates the land, culture, and people of Africa while also emphasizing the multiple aspects of her identity. Much of Lorde's later poetry addresses the mother-child relationship. Lorde offers conflicted representations of the mother; she is both a repressive force linked to conformity and deception and a figure of comfort, love, and identity.

Lorde's first major work of prose, *The Cancer Journals* (1980), is also the first publication about breast cancer by a black woman. As she describes her struggle with the disease and its aftermath, Lorde writes from a fundamental need to express her pain and to share her experience with others. She confronts her fear, anger, and despair with courage and a passionate will to survive. Lorde's decision not to wear a prosthesis following her mastectomy testifies to her rejection of conventional standards of beauty and to her desire to honor her survival physically. *The Cancer Journals* was the winner of the American Library Association Gay Caucus Book of the Year Award for 1981.

Lorde's second major prose work, *Zami: A New Spelling of My Name* (1982), is a "biomythography" that combines aspects of memoir, poetry, fiction, and mythology to describe her artistic maturation and her search for a home space. As the story of a poet's journey to self and voice, Zami focuses upon the development of Lorde's creative sensibility while also imaginatively rewriting experience. The central metaphors in Zami center on images of the home and body. For Lorde, making a home means fashioning a line of descent composed of women who have contributed to her identity, especially as a poet and an outsider. While affirming the physical embrace of bodies and erotic pleasures, she also writes about her mother as a figure of difference and envisions a cultural heritage that validates her lesbianism.

Despite the success of Lorde's poetry, she has become best known in academic circles for her essays on black **feminism** and her reevaluation of difference. In her influential collection, *Sister Outsider: Essays and Speeches* (1984), Lorde asserts her lesbianism and argues for the relevance of feminism to the black community. Essays such as "The Master's Tools Will Never Dismantle the Master's House" and "Age, Race, Class and Sex: Women Redefining Difference" explore the role of difference as a dynamic, enriching force which is too often presented as a threat to social stability. In "The Uses of the Erotic," perhaps her most cited essay, Lorde presents the erotic as a vital source of female power. She argues that the racist patriarchy of American society has oppressed and devalued female creativity. Lorde explains in "Poetry Is Not a Luxury" that empowerment comes from a firm commitment to self-expression.

Lorde combined her socially conscious writing with a strong dedication to community involvement. With **Barbara Smith**, she founded Kitchen Table: Women of Color Press to promote the writings of feminists. She also helped create Sisterhood in Support of Sisters in South Africa and served on the board of the National Coalition of Black Lesbians and Gays. From 1980 to 1987 Lorde was poet and professor of English at Hunter College where she mentored young feminists and students of color. In 1991 she was named the poet laureate of New York.

Following her death in St. Croix in 1992, women and men all over the world held tributes to her. In eulogies and vigils, they remembered a poet and activist who eloquently protested social injustice and passionately claimed the multiple facets of her identity. Lorde's commitment to self-expression and social consciousness have made a significant impact on black feminist thought and critical discourses on **race**, gender, and sexuality. (*See also* African American Lesbian Literature)

Further Reading

Wilson, Anna. *Persuasive Fictions: Feminist Narrative and Critical Myth.* Cranbury, NJ: Associated UP, 2001.

Steele, Cassie Premo. *We Heal from Memory: Sexton, Lorde, Anzaldúa, and the Poetry of Witness.* New York: Palgrave, 2000.

Stephanie Li

LOUIE, DAVID WONG (1954–) Chinese American short story writer and novelist. His début short story collection, *Pangs of Love* (1991), marks David Wong Louie as a promising writer, and his novel, *The Barbarians Are Coming* (2000), further confirms his place in Asian American literary tradition. The majority of Louie's stories center around Asian American male characters who, only appearing to be successful and "Americanized," are aliened from their families and partners. For instance, the protagonists in "Birthday," "Pangs of Love," and "Warming Trends" are physically and culturally separated from their (immigrant) parents. Many of the characters, such as those in "Birthday," "Pangs of Love," "Love on the Rocks," Bottle of Beaujolais," and "One Man's Hysteria—Real or Imagined—in the Twentieth Century," fail to sustain meaningful relationships with (white) women. Whereas the alienation resulting from the cultural and generational clashes is a reiterated theme in Asian American literature, the failure of interracial relationship offers a refreshing critical view of miscegenation and **assimilation** in the multicultural era.

The themes of alienation and displacement also recur in *The Barbarians Are Coming*. The novel features an American-born Chinese character named Sterling Lung, a professional chef whose culinary specialty is French, not Chinese. Working for a white country club and marrying a daughter of a Jewish real estate mogul, Sterling thinks that he has "arrived." However, his "Americanization"—choice of lifestyle, occupation, and partner—disappoints his immigrant parents, particularly his father. Among three chapters of Sterling's first-person solipsistic narrative is a chapter revealing the "American" life of the immigrant father "Lung," from which we learn that the son has actually "inherited" many things from his father, such as a problematic relationship with a white woman and the loss of a son. Like Louie's short fiction, the novel raises the questions about interracial relationships, Asian Americans' upward mobility, and the liberal multiculturalist notion of **ethnicity**.

Like the protagonist in his novel, Louie is American-born Chinese and grew up in the back rooms of a laundry shop, where his immigrant parents worked, in Long Island, New York. Unlike Sterling, Louie writes and teaches, and his works have been acknowledged and have received numerous accolades. His works have been compared with those by other Asian American authors such as **Louis Chu** and **Cynthia Kadohata**. (*See also* Chinese American Novel)

Further Reading

Davis, Rocío G. "David Wong Louie." *Asian American Short Story Writers: An A-To-Z Guide.* Ed. Guiyou Huang. Westport, CT: Greenwood Press, 2003. 173–76.

Eng, David L. *Racial Castration: Managing Masculinity in Asian America.* Durham, NC, and London: Duke UP, 2001. 194–203.

Lim, Shirley Geok-lin. "David Wong Louie." *The Columbia Companion to the Twentieth-Century American Short Story.* Ed. Blanche H. Gelfant. New York: Columbia UP, 2000. 345–49.

Wong, Sau-ling Cynthia. "Chinese/Asian American Men in the 1990s: Displacement, Impersonation, Paternity, and Extinction in David Wong Louie's *Pangs of Love.*" *Privileging Positions: The Sites of Asian American Studies.* Ed. Gary Y. Okihiro, et al. Pullman: Washington State UP, 1995. 181–91.

Shuchen Susan Huang

LOVE MEDICINE   Winner of the 1984 National Book Critics Circle Award for Fiction, **Louise Erdrich**'s first novel is perhaps the most widely acclaimed literary work by a Native American writer in the past thirty years. Set mostly on an Ojibwe Indian reservation in North Dakota, the novel explores the tangled lives of the Kashpaw, Lamartine, and Morrissey families from 1934 to 1984. Each chapter of the novel is told from a different point of view; in fact, several were published first as short stories, including the award-winning "The World's Greatest Fishermen" as well as "The Red Convertible" and "Scales," which had appeared in *The Best American Short Stories of 1983.* Yet the stories also weave together as whole to show the tangled web of love and bitterness built up among these families over the generations.

The novel opens with a chapter describing the death of June Kashpaw, a hard-living Ojibwe woman, once vibrant and beautiful, but now caught in a dead-end life of alcoholism and sexual promiscuity. June's death prompts other characters' memories and their returns home to the reservation. The novel's central plot focus on the love triangle between June's adoptive parents, Marie and Nector Kashpaw, and Lulu Lamartine, Nector's first love. Late in the novel, June's son, Lipsha Morrissey, brings various narrative strands together when he concocts the love medicine of the title to try to rekindle his grandfather Nector's love for Marie. Though the results of Lipsha's love medicine are disastrous, the medicine also works in unexpected ways, healing some of the old wounds opened by June's death.

While the book is satisfying to readers unfamiliar with Ojibwe history or mythology, Erdrich subtley weaves elements of her cultural heritage into the novel, increasing its richness. She depicts certain characters, such as Lulu Lamartine, Gerry Pillager, and Lipsha Morrisey, as trickster figures, closely allied with Nanabozho, the traditional Ojibwe trickster. Her plots sometime mimic stories told in traditional Ojibwe tales: The struggle between Marie and Sister Leopolda can be read in terms of Ojibwe stories about young girls battling Windigos, cannibalistic ice monsters. Similarly, when Lipsha Morrissey cheats at cards to win the Firebird that contains his mother's spirit, we hear echoes of the Ojibwe creation tale in which the trickster battles the great gambler, cheating to win and free the spirit of his people.

Love Medicine explores issues of home, belonging, and survival as it depicts characters often abandoned by families and parents and a group of Americans historically deprived of their homelands. Though the book shows characters who struggle with alcoholism, cultural **assimilation**, and even suicide—the legacy of hundreds of years of oppression—it is nevertheless not a tragic novel. Erdrich's characters may be greedy, jealous, cruel, and irresponsible at times, but they also love intently and live fully.The novel is often humorous and always poetic and lyrical in its language. Images of rebirth and survival counter the hard lives some of these characters live and offer hope for the future. (*See also* Native American Novel)

Further Reading

Hafen, Jane B. *Reading Louise Erdrich's Love Medicine.* Boise, ID: Boise State UP, 2003.

Wong, Hertha D., ed. *Louise Erdrich's Love Medicine: A Casebook.* New York: Oxford UP, 2000.

Susan Farrell

LOWE, PARDEE (1905–?)   Chinese American writer. Lowe is often regarded as a literary pioneer in Chinese American literature. His autobiography *Father and Glorious Descendent* (1943) is one of the earliest published works by American-born Chinese. The book became an immediate mainstream success in the postwar era when Chinese in the United States enjoyed unprecedented popularity because China was viewed as America's ally in Asia during World War II.

Although his book was welcomed as an example of how America's racial minorities can "succeed" through perseverance and hard work at the time of its publication, it became a controversial text in contemporary Asian American academic circles. On the one hand, *Father and Glorious Descendent* is dismissed by many in the field as a "document of self contempt" and a "humiliating book" to the Chinese because Lowe's story reveals an urgent need for acceptance by white society. On the other hand, it is valued as a tribute to the ability of Chinese people to adapt to a foreign land without losing themselves or their culture in a hostile racial climate.

Despite the controversy, the book stands as a significant account that not only relates a crucial aspect of the early Chinese American experience, but also expresses the cultural duality that occurs in most immigrant families.

Throughout the book, Lowe describes trials and tribulations endured by the Chinese American community in California, ranging from such major events as the Great San Francisco Earthquake at the beginning of the century to such everyday occurrences as dealing with widespread racism in a white majority. The autobiography also reveals a typical cultural conflict between father and son, the immigrant and the American-born generation. Having grown up in the home of first generation Chinese immigrants, Lowe reveals his ambivalent attitude toward a root culture represented by his father. While he admires his father for his success as a Chinatown leader, he shows his resentment of him when the father continually speaks of the way traditional Chinese children should act. Like most American-born Chinese children and adolescents, he gradually moves away from his family and community and endeavors to enter mainstream society. For Lowe, living up to being the "Glorious Descendent" and gaining an understanding of racial **identity** proves to be a difficult and painful process. After he endures a job rejection, Lowe experiences a slight shift in perspective. He realizes that he could never have a chance to become fully accepted in white American society because of his darker skin and different ancestry. Further, he sees that half of his identity is Chinese and that he must reconcile with it, even if he initially does not want to. However difficult this shift may be, Lowe eventually develops a mature understanding of his identity as a Chinese American. (*See also* Chinese American Autobiography)

Further Reading

Kim, Elaine H. *Asian American Literature: An Introduction to the Writings and Their Social Context.* Philadelphia: Temple UP, 1982.

Su-lin Yu

LOWENFELS, WALTER (1897–1976) Jewish American author. Lowenfels is largely unread today and remembered chiefly as a literary maverick and political agitator who helped give rise to the proletarian literary movement in the thirties. But his significance to American letters is immense. As editor, poet, novelist, playwright, and political activist, he exemplifies so well not only the principles of social commitment he espoused, but the dizzying virtuosity of such principles across modes, genres, and conventions, and often against convention.

After turning his back on a possible career in the family's butter business, he became a militant leftist, working for the Pennsylvania edition of the *Daily Worker.* Unlike many of his contemporaries, who supported left-wing politics opportunistically and then for only a brief time, Lowenfels would be a lifelong adherent to socialist practices and beliefs. The first literary expression of this political commitment was in his poetry, which he described as "the continuation of journalism by other means." Rather than presenting simple partisan polemics, the poems achieve both a signature personal idiom and sweeping social perspective, and Lowenfels and his poetry garnered the Richard Aldington Award for American Poets in 1930 (shared by e.e. cummings), the Mainstream Share in 1954, and the Longview Foundation Award in 1959.

He moved to Paris in 1926 to join the flowering American expatriate community a year after publishing his first collection, *Episodes and Epistles*. European bohemia was not to his liking, however, and he soon returned to the United States. In 1930 he cofounded with Mitchell Fraenkel the Carrefou Press, publishing the pamphlet "Anonymous: The Need for Anonymity." Long before postmodernists would declare the death of the author, Lowenfels's manifesto strove to incite artists to surrender their authority as owners of their work in the hopes of establishing a proliferating industry of literature that would cleave to social obligations and go against the grain of convention as a collective, faceless presence. It would also, Lowenfels hoped, nullify artistic competition and alienation. He joined the Communist Party the same year that he established the press and sustained his membership until 1953. In 1951 he was unjustly arrested under the Smith Act for attempting to overthrow the U.S. government. Although he would never again maintain affiliation with political parties thereafter, he espoused various causes and joined ad hoc protest groups for the rest of his life.

His play *USA with Music* was written and performed in 1932 and led to an accusation and later a legal suit against George Gershwin for plagiarism. Throughout the thirties and forties, he was extremely prolific, increasingly concentrating on poetry, political pamphlets, and autobiographical writings. By the late fifties, he was considered the foremost editor and anthologist of avant-garde poetry in the country. Older age never stifled his prodigious writings advocating revolutionary action and denouncing political repression. His writing was topical, never nostalgic, and always asserting itself as an immediate intervention into war, humanitarian disasters, and the despair of modern life. Some of the most notable later anthologies of poetry are multinational and multicultural in nature. Among these titles are *Where Is Vietnam? American Poets Respond: An Anthology of Contemporary Poets* (1967), *In the Time of Revolution* (1969), *From the Belly of the Shark: Poems by Chicanos, Eskimos, Hawaiians, Indians, Puerto Ricans, with Related Poems by Others* (1973), and *For Neruda, For Chile: An International Anthology* (1975). Talisman Press released *Reality Prime: Selected Poems* in 1998. Walter Lowenfels died in Tarrytown, New York, in 1976.

Further Reading

Brian Daldorph. "The Politics of His Poetry: Walter Lowenfels's Poetic Response to *U.S. vs. Krugman* (1953–1954), His Smith Act Trial." *Left History: An Interdisciplinary Journal of Historical Inquiry and Debate* 2.1 (Spring 1999): 147–60.

Walter Lowenfels Papers. Department of Special Collections, Olin Library.
    Washington University. St. Louis, MO.

Jonathan Curley

LUM, DARREL H. Y. (1950–)   Asian American writer, playwright, and editor. Most visible as the cofounder and editor of the contemporary

Hawaiian literary journal *Bamboo Ridge*, Darrel H. Y. Lum is also the leading figure in the introduction of local pidgin vernacular to modern **Hawaiian literature**.

Lum's first collection, *Sun: Short Stories and Drama* (1980), contains the story "Beer Can Hat," a first-person pastoral narrative delivered entirely in Hawaiian pidgin dialect. The story is remarkable in both its form and its content; not only does it break with the conventions of dialect previously employed in Hawaiian narratives, in which pidgin was either avoided or reserved for tangential characters, but it furthermore breaks with conventions of subject matter, showing the reader a Hawai'i far removed from stereotypical postcard images. In this way, the works in *Sun*, and its successor *Pass On No Pass Back* (1990), can be seen as a direct response to the call of the famous 1978 "Talk Story" conference for a new Hawaiian literature that was by, for, and about the local population.

Reaction to the use of pidgin in literature has been mixed, and Lum's work has helped to advance and sharpen the focus of the debate. On one side of the issue are those who recall the works of such authors as James Michener, in which pidgin is spoken only by characters whom the audience is meant to view as marginal or degraded. Therefore, any application of pidgin, according to such reasoning, automatically stigmatizes the speaker/narrator and, moreover, sharply limits the audience to those who are familiar with the dialect's idiosyncracies and vocabulary. Those who fall into the opposite camp, including Lum himself, view the use of pidgin as an affirmation of local language and literature (pidgin being the language of both storytelling and daily life) as well as a declaration of independence on the part of a polyethnic culture.

Lum has continued to publish, and his works have been widely anthologized. He has also edited a number of anthologies of local writers, including *Growing Up Local: An Anthology of Poetry and Prose from Hawai'i* (1999). Perhaps Lum's best-known association, though, is with the Hawaiian literary journal *Bamboo Ridge,* of which he is (with Eric Chock) cofounder and coeditor. Some of Lum's best known stories, including "Primo Doesn't Take Back Bottles Anymore" (1980) and "Paint" (1985), first appeared in the journal's pages, and *Bamboo Ridge* has become the cornerstone of the contemporary Hawaiian literary scene.

Further Reading

Sumida, Stephen. *And the View from the Shore: Literary Traditions of Hawai'i.* Seattle: U of Washington P, 1991.

Wilson, Rob. *Reimagining the American Pacific: From South Pacific to Bamboo Ridge and Beyond.* Durham, NC: Duke UP, 2000.

William Curl

LUM, WING TEK (1946–) Asian American poet. One of the most widely read and anthologized of the Asian American poets of Hawai'i, Wing Tek Lum's work has been hailed by critics for its incisive commentary on ethnic **identity** as well as for its advancing of the Chinese American literary tradition.

Lum's most notable early poem, and one of the best starting points for an examination of his work, is 1972's "Grateful Here." The five stanzas that form the poem are, in terms of content, all considerations of various facets of the narrator's ethnic identity, interweavings of memory and action that point to an irresolvable multiplicity. The second stanza, which describes his childhood attendance at a Confucian graveside observance side-by-side with Sunday attendance at a Christian church, is particularly striking in this regard, in that it implies that such a duality is not symbolic of a struggle for a sense of ethnic identity, but rather emblematic of that ethnic identity.

This theme can be found resonating throughout Lum's work, of which "Taking Her to the Open Market" (1979) is another prominent example. Here, the narrator recounts taking his Chinese-born grandmother to the fish market, trying to impress her with his knowledge. He knows what one should look for in a fish: firmness of texture, a certain condition of the eye, and so forth. His grandmother, though, is not impressed, as all of the fish he is selecting—indeed, all of the fish in the market—are dead, completely unlike the fish in the markets of her Hong Kong youth. As in "Grateful Here," there is a sense of both connection and transition, connection in that the narrator feels a strong sense of ethnic identity, transition in the sense that his identity does not correspond precisely to that of his forebears. Indeed, as critic Stephen Sumida has suggested, this sense of historical continuity is central to Lum's significance as a poet. Rather than depicting a clean break with the past or an artificial "rediscovery" of one's cultural heritage, Lum's poetry brings a sense of cultural continuity in which change and loss are inevitable and the struggle for identity is, in fact, a historical constant.

Lum's poetry has been collected in the volume *Expounding the Doubtful Points* (1988), and his individual poems have been widely published and anthologized. He is closely associated with the *Bamboo Ridge* writer's group and has at times been instrumental in the journal's publication. (*See also* Hawai'i Literature)

Further Reading

Sumida, Stephen. *And the View from the Shore: Literary Traditions of Hawai'i.* Seattle: U of Washington P, 1991.

Wilson, Rob. *Reimagining the American Pacific: From South Pacific to Bamboo Ridge and Beyond.* Durham, NC: Duke UP, 2000.

William Curl

LUMPKIN, GRACE (1891–1980) Part-Jewish American, radical novelist of the 1930s who became progressively more reactionary with the advent of McCarthyism and who spent her later life documenting the evils of Communism and preaching for the conversion of Communist militants to Christianity. Lumpkin went *Full Circle* in her lifetime, as the title of her fourth and last 1962 autobiographical novel suggests. Raised in a well-off and deeply religious Southern family, she became one of the most prominent writers of the left with her novels *To Make My Bread* (1932) and *A Sign for Cain* (1935), which offer a utopist vision of multiethnic working-class alliances. She responded enthusiastically to **Michael Gold**'s call for proletarian literature, and she joined the Communist Party after moving to New York. But as McCarthy's witch-hunt spread throughout the United States, Lumpkin named names and returned to her family's religious and reactionary roots.

Lumpkin's first two novels are inextricably linked with the importance that the "Negro Question" assumed in Communist Party's policies in the 1930s and with the southern region of Gastonia, North Carolina, which was the theater of important labor struggles and strikes in the spring and summer of 1929. The resolution of the Communist International on the "Negro Question" in the United States claimed that white comrades should work together with African Americans and that "the Negro problem must be part and parcel of all and every campaign conducted by the Party." The attraction of African Americans into the Communist Party was thought of as essential for the success of a future Communist revolution in America. This multiethnic model was a direct translation of the Soviet one, where ethnic minorities had given their support to the revolution. The Loray Mill Strike in Gastonia gave Lumpkin as well as other radical female writers such as Mary Heaton Vorse, Fielding Burke, and Myra Page the chance to present a cross-racial alliance where racial stereotypes and barriers are overcome in the common struggle to stamp out class oppression.

In *To Make My Bread* and *A Sign for Cain,* Lumpkin stresses the importance of forging cross-racial alliances so that white militants and organizers can include African Americans in their activities and movements. In her works, she also gives women a prominent position to establish the contact between whites and blacks. Women workers share a marginalized and oppressed position regardless of their **race**, which brings them together. *To Make My Bread,* winner of the Maxim Gorky prize for the best labor novel of 1932 and successfully adapted for the stage, describes both the migration of southern farmers to the mills and the workers' rising awareness of the class struggle. Through the friendship between the white organizer Bonnie McClure and the black worker Mary Allen, Lumpkin shows women as the primary agents for the establishment of interracial communication. The novel was also the first to advocate a mutual understanding between the races and to depict cross-racial solidarity useful not only for blacks but also for white workers. The channel of communication opened up by Bonnie and Mary Allen stops blacks from scabbing, thus enabling the workers' victory.

A Sign for Cain focuses on the struggles of two Communist organizers, one black and one white, in a small Southern town in the years following the Gastonia strike. As a subplot, Lumpkin also depicts the political and intellectual growth of a black, working-class woman, Selah, who is able to free herself from the racist context of the South. *A Sign for Cain* is a plea to both white and black working-class communities to educate their respective members in order to bridge the mutual suspicions that may endanger their common cause. Thus, African Americans are represented as having equal agency as whites.

Lumpkin's third novel *The Wedding* (1939) is usually considered a sign of the author's declining support for a socially conscious type of literature in favor of a more controlled style typical of a Victorian comedy of manners. Yet Jessica Kimball Printz has challenged this view, suggesting that the novel should be ascribed to genre of female "dystopian radical fiction." Contrary to the plots of *To Make My Bread* and *A Sign for Cain,* the parallel stories of the middle-class Middleton sisters, Jennie and Susan, reveal the author's growing pessimism about political change and interracial solidarity.

Further Reading

Foley, Barbara. *Radical Representations: Politics and Form in U.S. Proletarian Fiction, 1929–1941.* Durham, NC: Duke UP, 1993.

Hall, Jacquelyn Dowd. "Open Secrets: Memory, Imagination, and the Refashioning of Southern Identity." *American Quarterly* 50.1 (1998): 109–24.

———. "Women Writers, the 'Southern Front,' and the Dialectical Imagination." *Journal of Southern History* 69.1 (February 2003): 3–36.

Printz, Jessica Kimball. "Tracing the Fault Line of the Radical Female Subject: Grace Lumpkin's *The Wedding.*" *Radical Revisions: Rereading 1930s Culture.* Ed. Sherry Linkon and Bill Mullen. Champaign-Urbana: U of Illinois P, 1996. 167–86.

Rabinowitz, Paula. *Labor and Desire: Women's Revolutionary Fiction in Depression America* Chapel Hill: U of North Carolina P, 1991.

Sowinska, Suzanne. Introduction. *To Make My Bread.* Grace Lumpkin. Urbana: U of Illinois P, 1995. vii–xliii.

———. "Writing Across the Color Line: White Women Writers and the "Negro Question" in the Gastonia Novels." *Radical Revisions: Rereading 1930s Culture.* Ed. Sherry Linkon and Bill Mullen. Champaign-Urbana: U of Illinois P, 1996. 120–41.

Luca Prono

LUTHER STANDING BEAR (c. 1868–1939)   Native American autobiographer, activist, and film actor. Writing from the perspective of the last generation of Sioux living in the manner of pre-reservation Lakota, Standing Bear's autobiographical writings convey both his early acceptance of and later disillusionment with the **assimilation** process while dispelling the contemporary stereotype of the Indian as "uncivilized savage." Standing Bear draws on his experiences growing up on the plains of South Dakota in the traditional manner and his childhood spent at Carlisle Indian School in his autobiographical writings.

Standing Bear was apparently born (the exact date is in dispute) the year the Fort Laramie treaty consigned the Lakota to federally designated reservation lands. This treaty influenced the remainder of Standing Bear's life for in 1879,

Luther Standing Bear. *Courtesy of the Library of Congress.*

his father enrolled him in the Indian boarding school at Carlisle, Pennsylvania, where Standing Bear underwent a transformation that changed not only his name (which was Ota Kte—Plenty Kill), but also his hair, which was cut short, and the clothes that he wore. Standing Bear faced all of these changes—some more traumatic than others—with the attitude of a warrior entering the land of a hostile tribe, determined to be brave.

As an adult, Standing Bear worked at various jobs, from teacher to store clerk. He also performed in Buffalo Bill's Wild West Show and later traveled to Hollywood to act in western films; at this time, he formed the Indian Actors' Association. All of his activities were designed to preserve the cultural traditions of the Lakota and to educate white people about his tribe, though later in life, his attitudes about assimilation grew steadily more negative.

Standing Bear tried to accomplish his purposes in his published writings. His first book, *My People the Sioux* (1928), was published when Standing Bear was sixty years old. From this vantage point, he recounts the dramatic changes he observed in his tribe. He also vividly describes Lakota culture and customs in an attempt to preserve them and argues vehemently for universal citizenship for Native Americans (Standing Bear received his own citizenship in 1905). While contemporary critics regard the work as "naïve" and inaccurate, *My People the Sioux* remains an important work for its time, considering the limited opportunities open to American Indian writers.

The book's complex structure belies Standing Bear's simple writing style. He uses the ethnographic form of an autobiography to critique American culture and stereotypes of Native Americans by first offering vivid description of some aspect of Lakota culture. He follows that by either correcting a widely held stereotype or asserting the superiority of Lakota values. Yet he manages these critiques without offending or alienating his readers, primarily white Americans.

Standing Bear continues to discount commonly held stereotypes of his people, but for younger readers, in his second book, *My Indian Boyhood* (1930). Here, he vividly describes daily life and coming of age rituals among Lakota children, providing insight into the tribe's family structure and education. His presentation of these details to a young readership is a clear effort to educate Americans about the Lakota in the hopes of correcting misconceptions and encouraging fair treatment of his tribe.

Standing Bear expands his ethnography from the personal to the community in his next two books. *Land of the Spotted Eagle* (1933) describes the culture of the Lakota people, and here, Standing Bear details the mundane, day-to-day activities of the tribe. By describing the differences in moral philosophy and worldviews between whites and Native Americans, Standing Bear offers up a critique of the less than humane treatment of his people by the Bureau of Indian Affairs.

His fourth and final book, *Stories of the Sioux* (1934) is a collection of folklore, written for the younger readership he addressed in *My Indian Boyhood*. Here, he includes traditional Sioux tales about the natural world and spirituality, recorded in much the same style as he heard them as a young boy.

Clear similarities can be seen between Standing Bear's writing and that of **Charles Eastman** (Ohiyesa) and Gertrude Simmons Bonnin (**Zitkala-Ša**). These Lakota also attended Carlisle and wrote autobiographical works detailing the anguished transformations they endured and their ability to survive and even flourish despite the attempts to assimilate them into mainstream American culture. All three Lakota wrote to vividly express their views about assimilation and the loss of traditional Lakota culture. (*See also* Native American Autobiography, Native American Stereotypes)

Further Reading

Hale, Frederick. "Acceptance and Rejection of Assimilation in the Works of Luther Standing Bear. *Studies in American Indian Literature* 5.4 (Winter 1994): 25–41.

Patti J. Kurtz

M

M. BUTTERFLY David Henry Hwang's play *M. Butterfly* (1988) was the first major success for this Chinese American dramatist, winning the Tony Award for Best Play, the New York Drama Desk Award, the Outer Critics Circle Award for Best Broadway play, and the John Gassner Award for the season's outstanding new playwright. In 1989 the play moved to a hugely successful run in London, establishing Hwang as the first Asian American playwright to attain international acclaim.

Inspired by a newspaper article, *M. Butterfly* is based on the true account of a French diplomat who fell in love with a Chinese opera singer, with whom he had an affair for twenty years. In all that time, the diplomat never realized that his lover was actually a man as well as a spy, even though the Frenchman passed secret documents to her (him) without ever questioning why she (he) needed them. When the truth was finally revealed and his lover betrayed him, the diplomat was convicted for treason.

An inverse version of Puccini's renowned opera *Madame Butterfly*, the play incorporates parts of the score as well as elements of Kabuki theater, and the main character, Rene Gallimard, imagines himself as the opera's central figure and calls the woman, whose real name is Song Liling, his Butterfly. The play is presented in flashback form, framed by Gallimard's first-person narration from his prison cell, where he has apparently, in ritualistic form, mentally replayed the events of his life every night, hoping for a different, happier ending. His narratives are interwoven with the scenes he describes, including the notoriety his case has attained, his youth and troubled sexuality, and his meeting and relationship with Butterfly, as well as the changing political landscape in China. He has come to realize the illusion in which he was living—and recognizes that he in fact sensed the truth during the relationship—but at the end, noting that reality demands a sacrifice, he returns to the world of his fantasy and kills himself in a formalized hari-kari style, acknowledging that death with honor is better than life with dishonor.

M. Butterfly explores ingrained Western stereotypes of the East and incorporates themes of **racism**, sexism, gender, imperialism, and the blurring of truth with fantasy. Like Hwang's other plays, *M. Butterfly* addresses the issue of cultural identity and the many faces people wear; in his other plays, this theme investigates the immigrant's dilemma of how to retain and honor one's cultural heritage while also attempting to assimilate into American life. (*See also* Chinese American Drama)

Further Reading

Berson, Misha. "The Demon in David Henry Hwang." *American Theatre* (April 1998): 14–21.

Brennan, Stephen Vincent, ed. *New Voices of the American Theater.* New York: Henry Holt, 1997.

DiGaetani, John L. "'M. Butterfly': An Interview with David Henry Hwang." *Drama Review* 33.3 (1989): 141–53.

Pao, Angela. "The Critic and the Butterfly: Sociocultural Contexts and the Reception of David Henry Hwang's 'M. Butterfly'." *Amerasia Journal* 18.3 (1992): 1–16.

Savran, David. "David Hwang." *In Their Own Words: Contemporary American Playwrights.* New York: Theatre Communications Group, 1988. 117–31.

Karen C. Blansfield

MACKEY, NATHANIEL (1947–)   African American poet, scholar, editor, and professor. Nathaniel Mackey defines a recent movement in African American poetics that is rooted in the creative responses advanced by **Harlem Renaissance** and **Black Arts Movement** writers to social inequalities. Participants in all three movements have understood the politics of American culture as the key basis for their work, have tested poetry's ability to formally articulate political ideas, and have incorporated elements of traditional African mythologies. However, the work of late-century writers like Mackey advocates culturally inclusive politics as well as postmodernist investigation, grounded in black history, of language's potential for both play and critique.

Mackey gained public recognition after he published his first short collection of poetry, *Four for Trane* (1978). He has published six additional books of poetry and many individual poems. Since 1982 he has edited *Hambone,* a journal that publishes inventive works by writers and artists of all cultural backgrounds. Later he edited *Moment's Notice: Jazz in Poetry and Prose* (1993) with fellow **jazz** poet Art Lange and published *Discrepant Engagement: Dissonance, Cross-Culturality, and Experimental Writing* (1993), a collection of essays that examine trends in literary scholarship and the innovations of Caribbean and

African American poets. He joined the English Department at University of California, Santa Cruz in 1979 and is now a professor of literature and a chancellor of the Academy of American Poets. Mackey also advised poet **Harryette Mullen** during her dissertation work at Santa Cruz. His editing and teaching, like his creative work, have highlighted the intersections between literature, history, and social environment.

Mackey is best known for *From a Broken Bottle Traces of Perfume Still Emanate*, a multivolume epistolary novel, and *Song of the Andoumboulou*, a serial poem included as part of three poetry collections: *Eroding Witness* (1985), *School of Udhra* (1993), and *Whatsaid Serif* (1998). The *Broken Bottle* series so far includes *Bedouin Hornbook* (1986), *Djbot Baghostus's Run* (1993), and *Atet A. D.* (2001). These volumes comprise a chain of letters between the "Angel of Dust" and "N.," letters that consider the musical and philosophical evolution of N.'s avant-garde jazz ensemble. *Song of the Andoumboulou* traces

Nathaniel Mackey. *Photo by Paul Schraub. Courtesy of Nathaniel Mackey.*

African American cultural traditions back to African societal beliefs and mythologies. *Broken Bottle* has inspired music by musician-composer Glenn Spearman; Mackey produced an album, *Strick: Song of the Andoumboulou 16–25* (1995), on which he read to the accompaniment of musicians Royal Hartigan and Hafez Modirzadeh. Both *Broken Bottle* and *Song* challenge the confines of their conventional forms through use of punning, esoteric vocabulary, and analogies between life experiences and jazz performance. Mackey's writings both reflect on the history of human existence and imagine a world shaped by the complexities of African and African American creative practices.

Further Reading

Allen, Joseph. "Nathaniel Mackey's Unit Structures." *Black Orpheus: Music in African American Fiction from the Harlem Renaissance to Toni Morrison.* Ed. Saadi A. Simawe. New York and London: Garland Publishing, 2000. 205–29.

Naylor, Paul. "An Interview with Nathaniel Mackey." *Callaloo* 23.2 (Spring 2000): 645–63.

Jennifer D. Ryan

MACKUS, ALGIMANTAS (1932–1964)   Lithuanian American poet, literary critic, cultural activist, and journalist. One of the most influential Lithuanian American writers, Mackus became a symbol of an entire generation of Lithuanian exiles. He was the first to juxtapose the questions of the loss of the native land with the problems of **assimilation** into American culture.

Mackus emigrated from Lithuania as a child with his parents and studied in Roosevelt College in Chicago from 1957 to 1959. There he was greatly affected by the **Civil Rights Movement** and its critique of the discrimination against African Americans. He worked on a Lithuanian radio program called "Margutis" (The Easter Egg, 1954–1964) and was an editor for the Lithuanian American cultural magazine by the same name. Mackus published three books: *Elegijos* [*Elegies*] (1950), *Jo yra žemė* [*His is the land*] (1959), and *Neornamentuotos kalbos generacija ir augintiniai* [*The generation of unornamented language and the foster children*] (1964). The fourth book, *Chapel B*, dedicated to Antanas Šėkma, a Lithuanian writer who died in a car accident, was published posthumously in 1965, shortly after Mackus died in a car accident in Chicago.

In his early poetry, Mackus used traditional symbols of the homeland and expressed nostalgia for it. However, in his second book Mackus moved away from traditional narratives and offered a complicated view of exiled **identity** seeking to root in any land and believing that God could be a solution for political exiles. In later books he moved on from religious discourses about his situation in exile to expressions of his belief that the system of power that represses certain individuals and displaces them in history is enforced through language and ideologies (religion, nationalism, and **racism**) and is present both in a totalitarian and communist state, as well as in imperialist and racist America. In realizing this, Mackus became the first author to understand and articulate that Lithuanian exiles are destined both to assimilate into American culture and to experience racist forms of exclusion. He continued the work of Antanas Šėkma by showing that the Lithuanian community in exile, in confronting American reality, had to face the problem of the death of their Lithuanian identities because the reproduction of the Lithuanian nation is impossible in exile. According to Mackus, when the big imperial powers share the map of the world, those who are marginalized by these powers face death and discrimination. By looking at those who were discriminated against at a certain time in history, Mackus compared the tragedy of Lithuanian exile to that brought on by genocide and racism. He critiqued nationalism and racism as violent symbolic forms of belonging and exclusion, while admitting that there is no way to escape from one's own national identity, a powerful force that leads to a hermetic existence and self-destruction in exile. (*See also* Lithuanian American Literature)

Further Reading

Šilbajoris, Rimvydas. "Algimantas Mackus—the Perfection of Exile." *Perfection of Exile: Fourteen Contemporary Lithuanian Writers*. Norman: U of Oklahoma P, 1970. 184–217.

Žilinskas, Rimas. "Imagining Lithuanians, Reproducing Americans." *Lituanus: Lithuanian Quarterly Journal of Arts and Sciences* 49.2 (2003): 33–74.

Rimas Zilinskas

MADGETT, NAOMI LONG (1923–) American poet, publisher, editor, and educator. As one of America's leading editors and publishers of Lotus Press in Detroit, Naomi Long Madgett has advanced the literary career of a generation of black and other ethnic minority poets, has celebrated the experiences of black Americans in her writings, and has encouraged a generation of students in her work. With a passion for poetry all her life, she herself was encouraged to continue writing while attending the all-black Sumner High School in St. Louis, Missouri. By age seventeen, she had published her first volume of poetry, *Songs to a Phantom Nightingale* (1941), mostly nature poems, which show the influence of such poets as John Keats, William Wordsworth, and Alfred Tennyson.

An award-winning poet, Madgett has published seven collections of poetry since 1941. Her second volume, *One and the Many* (1956), is an actual record of Madgett's life to the mid-1950s. It reveals her conflicting feelings as a poet as she shifts from her lyric poetry as in "The Ivory Tower" to that of the social concerns of her **race** in "Not I Alone," where she speaks with a strong protest voice against **racism**. In her next volume, *Star by Star* (1965), she continues to explore the black experience in such poems as "For a Child," "Violet," "Nocturne," "Alabama Centennial," "Pavlov," and her most popular 1959 poem, "Midway," where the black speaker represents the voice of all Americans in their struggle for victory at a time when the country is plagued by civil unrest. During this period, Madgett, along with **Dudley Randall**, **Robert Hayden**, **Owen Dodson**, **Ronald Milner**, and Hoyt Fuller, was also a member of Margaret Danner's writer's workshop at Boone House in Detroit from 1962 to 1964.

In 1972 Madgett, three friends, and Leonard Patton Andrews, her third husband, founded Lotus Press in Detroit, which she and Andrews took over in 1974. As the publisher and editor of Lotus Press for nearly two decades, Madgett published the works of such writers as **Samuel Allen**, **James A. Emanuel**, **May Miller**, Dudley Randall, Lance Jeffers, **Haki R. Madhubuti**, **Gayl Jones**, **June Jordan**, **Margaret Walker**, Pinkie Gordon Lane, **E. Ethelbert Miller**, **Toi Derricotte**, Paulette Childress White, Ojaide Tanure, and Selene DeMedeiros. In 1972 Lotus Press published Madgett's *Pink Ladies in the Afternoon: New Poems, 1965–1971*, which describes her life during the late 1960s and early 1970s and addresses her dedication to her career in the midst of civil disorder and the Vietnam War, her approaching middle age, and her deep-seated awareness of her heritage and **identity** in such poems as "Black Woman," "Glimpses to Africa," based upon her trip to Africa with Operation Crossroads, and "Newblack," where the poet argues against the senseless attacks against distinguished black leaders from **Booker T. Washington** to **Martin Luther King Jr.**

In 1978 Lotus Press published Madgett's fifth poetry collection, *Exits and Entrances: New Poems*, which continues and enlarges the autobiography of *Pink Ladies*, reemphasizes the poet's interest in Afro-American themes, and contains her most recent lyrics in poems such as "Family Portrait," "The Silver Cord," "Fifth Street Exit, Richmond," "City Night," "Monday Morning Blues," and "The Old Women." Her next volume, *Phantom Nightingale: Juvenilia* (1981), includes poems that reflect both her formal classroom education and her informal education and her contemporary life, with titles like "Threnody," "Sonnet," "Pianissimo," "Democracy," and "Market Street."

By the 1970s and 1980s, Madgett's work had shifted from a political stance to a more personal tone. *Octavia and Other Poems* (1988) recreates black family life in Oklahoma and Kansas in the early twentieth century and centers on Madgett's great-aunt Octavia Corrnelia Long and several other members of her family, depicting the personal responsibility of women for the welfare of the community. Madgett's latest collection, *Remembrances of Spring: Collected Early Poems* (1993), commemorates her work as an editor and publisher and provides a retrospective examination of a powerful poetic voice and social conscience that has touched her readers' imaginations.

Madgett has been a champion runner in the struggle to promote the creation, distribution, and preservation of African American poetry over two decades. For her commitment and her own love of self-expression, she has been inducted into the Literary Hall of Fame for Writers of African Descent and the Michigan Women's Hall of Fame, and she has received Lifetime Achievement Awards from the Furious Flower Poetry Center and the Gwendolyn Brooks Center for Black Literature. In September 2000 she became the Poet Laureate of Detroit. (*See also* African American Poetry)

Further Reading

Bailey, Leaonead Pack. *Broadside Authors and Artists: An Illustrated Biographical Directory*. Detroit: Broadside Press, 1974.

Redmond, Eugene B. *Drumvoices: The Mission of Afro-American Poetry*. New York: Anchor/Doubleday, 1976.

Thompson, Julius E. *Dudley Randall, Broadside Press, and the Black Arts Movement in Detroit, 1960–1965*. Durham, NC: McFarland, 1999. 152–59, 213–20.

Loretta G. Woodard

MADHUBUTI, HAKI R. (1942–) African American poet, critic, essayist, publisher, activist, and educator. Though he is primarily known as a poet of the **Black Arts Movement**, Madhubuti's dedication to black pride and commitment to helping other African Americans through publishing, education, and activism establish him as someone for whom the personal and artistic are also the political. The primary subject of Madhubuti's work is blackness or Africanness, and he writes about every aspect of black life. Madhubuti actively displayed his commitment to his own Africanness when he changed his name from Don L. Lee to the Swahili name Haki R. Madhubuti in 1973.

Madhubuti's philosophy that art is also an avenue for political awareness and change is reflected in his first two volumes of poetry, *Think Black* (1967) and *Black Pride* (1968). Like Langston Hughes before him, Madhubuti contends that realistic representations of black life and language will help African American readers appreciate and celebrate themselves and their communities. In his early works, Madhubuti incorporates black vernacular into his poems in an attempt to represent spoken language. In this way, Madhubuti seeks to elicit the involvement of African American readers, who are often more familiar with the tradition of verbal storytelling. Madhubuti's early poetry also breaks with many poetic conventions by incorporating startling metaphors, unusual wording, and disjointed reiterations, giving his poetry a sense of motion and vigor.

The poems throughout *Think Black* deal with **racism** ("America Calling" and "Understanding But Not Forgetting"), the dangers of internalizing "white" values ("Back Again, Home"), and the need for consciousness of and action against racism ("Education"). Madhubuti continues these themes in *Black Pride*, where he celebrates his own blackness in poems such as "The Self-Hatred of Don L. Lee" and where he extends this pride to African American role models in "The Wall." Madhubuti also openly criticizes African Americans who do not properly appreciate and value their own blackness in poems such as "The Traitor," "The Negro," and "Contradiction in Essence."

Madhubuti's third volume of poetry, *Don't Cry, Scream* (1969), extends his earlier subjects from the narrow world of his personal experience and relationships to include social activism on a larger scale. Like many African American poets, Madhubuti also views the music of African Americans as one of their most valuable contributions to American culture. This is evidenced by his dedication of the title poem, "Don't Cry, Scream," to John Coltrane.

We Walk the Way of the New World (1970), Madhubuti's fourth collection of poems, demonstrates his broadening view of blackness that also includes Africanness. In this work, he expands his previous themes to include his image for a new world. His fifth volume, *Directionscore: Selected and New Poems* (1971), comprises poems from his first four volumes and five new poems. Madhubuti believes this to be his finest work to date.

Madhubuti published his first work under his new name in 1973 with *Book of Life*, which is divided into two parts. The first part comprises six long poems, which are comparable to the poems in his previous collections. The second part illustrates a change in Madhubuti's approach. Made up of a lengthy prose poem, it reflects the influence of Islam on Madhubuti's values. Most noteworthy, however, is Madhubuti's shift in this volume to Standard English. Madhubuti did not publish another collection of poetry until *Earthquakes and the Sun Rise Missions* (1984), which explores the poet's continued interest in issues such as solidarity and endurance.

Aside from being a prolific poet, Madhubuti is strongly committed to the active pursuit of the ideals outlined in his art. He started Third World Press, which publishes the work of new African American writers, he helped to establish the Institute of Positive Education, where he also served as director, and he was a charter member of the Organization of Black American Culture. Madhubuti's latest works—*Heart Love: Wedding and Love Poems* (1998), which is about love, bonding and friendship, and *Tough Notes: A Healing Call for Creating Exceptional Black Men* (2002), dedicated especially to young black men who have grown up without a father—reflect his ongoing commitment to education and art that have the potential to effect change.

Further Reading

Mosher, Marlene. *New Directions from Don L. Lee.* Hicksville, New York: Exposition Press, 1975.

April Conley Kilinski

MAILER, NORMAN (1923–) Jewish American novelist, essayist, and journalist. Mailer also has published poetry and has written and directed several stage plays and movies. His total output consists of over forty books, and at the age of eighty, he is still publishing. Major themes in his work are sexuality, violence, and political power. Mailer is best known for his novel *The Naked and the Dead* (1948), which is set in the Philippines during World War II, and for his two Pulitzer Prize–winning books, *The Armies of the Night* (1967) and *The Executioner's Song* (1979), which both combine fiction and nonfiction. Mailer's Jewish upbringing does not play a role in any of his writings because he developed a religious philosophy all his own. This religious philosophy evolved into a unique form of Manicheanism that includes a belief in magic, karma, and reincarnation.

Norman Kingsley Mailer was born in Long Branch, New Jersey, on January 31, 1923. His parents were Isaac Barnet Mailer, who was an accountant, and Fanny Schneider, who ran a small business, supplying oil to bakeries and food-processing companies. In 1927 the family moved to Brooklyn. Mailer was a precocious boy. He started writing fiction at the age of seven, and on the occasion of his bar mitzvah, he gave a speech on the philosopher Spinoza. He entered Harvard at the age of sixteen, wrote constantly, and published some of his fiction in the student magazine *The Harvard Advocate.* At a time when Harvard was still a citadel of white, Anglo-Saxon Protestantism, Mailer pugnaciously flaunted his Jewishness. However, some of his Jewish classmates criticized him for not showing any interest in Judaism and for not observing Jewish holidays. In the course of his long career, Mailer has made contradictory statements about his perennial quest to overcome his Jewish upbringing and about his Jewishness as one half of his personality.

When Mailer graduated from Harvard in 1943 with a degree in aeronautical engineering, his mind was not on engineering but on writing the great American novel. The subject for that novel offered itself when he was drafted into the Army and sent to the Philippines. Mailer's experiences as a combat infantryman on the island of Luzon provided him with the material for *The Naked and the Dead*, which many critics consider the best novel to come out of World War II. The worldwide success of the novel made Mailer into an instant celebrity and encouraged him to assume the posture of an intellectual guru, both in his writings and his public appearances.

The Naked and the Dead illustrates two aspects of Mailer's early vision of life: his naturalist belief that history is shaped less by man's endeavor than by the forces of chance and nature, and his infatuation with atheistic existentialism.

Norman Mailer. *Courtesy of the Library of Congress.*

The core of the novel's plot is a doomed reconnaissance mission behind the Japanese lines by a platoon of American soldiers. The mission is defeated as the men try to traverse a steep mountain covered by jungle vegetation. When they are near exhaustion, half way up the mountain, one of them happens to stir up a hornets' nest. The hornets attack the men and make them hurtle down the mountain scattering their equipment and weapons in the jungle.

Mailer illustrates his existentialist ideas through the belief-shattering experiences of Private Joey Goldstein, a deeply religious Jew. Goldstein loses his faith in God but acquires a faith in humanity. Goldstein's new-found faith is reminiscent of the ideas that Jean Paul Sartre expressed in his 1942 essay "Existentialism is a Humanism." The message of that essay is that in the face of the overwhelming forces of chance and nature, humans need to cling not to the antiquated idea of a God but to one another.

After *The Naked and the Dead,* Mailer wrote seven more novels: *Barbary Shore* (1951), *The Deer Park* (1955), *An American Dream* (1965), *Why Are We in Vietnam?* (1967), *Ancient Evenings* (1983), *Tough Guys Don't Dance* (1984), and *Harlot's Ghost* (1991). Among those novels, *An American Dream* and *Ancient Evenings* stand out because they illustrate aspects of Mailer's vision of life that contrast sharply with his Jewish upbringing, his Manicheanism, and his belief in magic, karma, and reincarnation. Although Mailer developed his Manichean outlook in the late fifties, he kept referring to his ideology as "existentialism." He defined as existential any risky situation whose outcome is uncertain, and he believed that the outcome of the battle between the good and evil forces in each person and in the universe could not be foretold.

An American Dream is the first novel in which magic plays an important role and in which Mailer spells out the Manichean ideology that informs all his later writings. Mailer's protagonist expresses the core of his Manichean outlook when he says he believes that "God's engaged in a war with the Devil, and God may lose." The plot of the novel suggests that in America, the Devil is in league with the millionaires who have corrupted the American dream and that Las Vegas is a symbol of this corrupted dream. Magic appears in the novel in the form of several magic objects, of telepathic communication, and of the protagonist acquiring the clairvoyance to predict the cast of dice, a power that allows him to make a fortune in Las Vegas.

In *Ancient Evenings*, Mailer not only toys with the idea of karma and reincarnation—as he had done in a 1960 *Paris Review* interview and on several other occasions—but he also uses reincarnation as a structural device. The novel is set during the nineteenth and twentieth dynasties of ancient Egypt (approximately 1200 B.C.), and it traces the fortunes of the narrator-protagonist through four consecutive incarnations.

Although fiction was always Mailer's first love, the bulk of his work consists of essays and journalism. He achieved his first great success in nonfiction with a 1957 essay titled "The White Negro: Superficial Reflections on the Hipster." Mailer defines the hipster as an antisocial counterculture hero who wants nothing to do with the conformist "square" society that has developed in America since World War II. Mailer calls the hipster a "philosophical psychopath," a "rebel without cause," and a "white Negro" who models his values, behavior, and language after those of African American **jazz** musicians. The essay later became the centerpiece in Mailer's first collection of fiction and nonfiction, *Advertisements for Myself* (1959). His greatest achievement in nonfiction was his Pulitzer Prize–winning reportage of the Vietnam protest march on the Pentagon, titled *The Armies of the Night: History as a Novel/The Novel as History* (1968).

The rest of Mailer's nonfiction covers a wide spectrum of topics, ranging from bullfighting (*The Bullfight*, 1967) and the NASA's space program (*Of a Fire on the Moon*, 1970) to women's liberation (*The Prisoner of Sex*, 1971) and boxing (*The Fight*, 1975). A recurring topic in Mailer's nonfiction writings is presidential politics. He dealt with that topic in several books, the best known being *Miami and the Siege of Chicago* (1968), his analysis of the 1968 Republican and Democratic presidential conventions.

In Mailer's nonfiction, the Manichean notion of the struggle between God and the Devil keeps recurring in the unlikeliest contexts. For instance, in "Ten Thousand Words a Minute," his lengthy ruminations on the heavyweight bout between Floyd Patterson and Sonny Liston, Mailer aligns Patterson with the divine principle and Liston with the forces of darkness (see *Presidential Papers*, 1963). Similarly, in *St. George and the Godfather* (1972)—his account of the conventions that named George McGovern and Richard Nixon the Democratic and Republican presidential candidates—Mailer describes McGovern as being on the side of good and Nixon on the side of evil.

A third major genre in which Mailer worked is a mixture of fiction and nonfiction, sometimes called the nonfiction novel. He achieved his greatest success in this genre with *The Executioner's Song*. That book is a painstakingly researched fictionalization of the life and death of Gary Gilmore, who was convicted of two murders and executed by firing squad in Utah in 1977. Over one thousand pages long, and full of transcriptions of interviews and letters, *The Executioner's Song* is a gripping page-turner that earned Mailer his second Pulitzer Prize. Less successful than the *Executioner's Song* are Mailer's fictionalizations of the lives of Marilyn Monroe (*Marilyn*, 1973), Lee Harvey Oswald (*Oswald's Tale*, 1995), Pablo Picasso (*Portrait of Picasso as a Young Man*, 1995), and Jesus Christ (*The Gospel According to the Son*, 1998).

Mailer's most recent work, *The Spooky Art* (2003), is a collection of essays, interviews, and speeches about the craft of writing. In a chapter on "The Occult," Mailer reaffirms his belief in magic as a form of "Divine or Satanic intervention," and in a chapter on "Being and Nothingness," he admits to a long-standing obsession with the questions of "how God exists," whether he is "an essential or an existential God," whether he is "all powerful," or whether he is "like us, an embattled existential presence who may succeed or fail in His vision." (*See also* Jewish American Novel)

Further Reading

Dearborn, Mary. *Mailer: A Biography* New York: Houghton Mifflin, 1999.

Guttman, Allen. "The Apocalyptic Vision of Norman Mailer." *The Jewish Writer in America.* New York: Oxford UP, 1971: 153–72.

Lennon, J. Michael, ed. *Critical Essays on Norman Mailer.* Boston: G. K. Hall, 1986.

Newman, Paul B. "Mailer: The Jew as Existentialist." *North American Review* 2 (July 1965): 48–55.

Eberhard Alsen

MAJAJ, LISA SUHAIR (1960–) Arab American scholar, poet, and political activist. Lisa Suhair Majaj has published extensively in the field of Arab American, Arab, and postcolonial literature. Born in Hawarden, Iowa, to a Palestinian father and an American mother, Majaj spent her childhood in Lebanon and Jordan. She graduated with a BA in English literature from the American University of Beirut, after which she moved to the United States to pursue her MA and PhD degrees at the University of Michigan.

Majaj has been a forerunner in the study of Arab American studies and literature, raising pertinent questions in relation to this community's racial categorization and examining the position of this minority's literary output within the ethnic **canon**. She underscores the ambiguity inherent in the current racial classification of Arab Americans as whites, noting how the concurrent prejudice and **racism** exhibited toward this group in the United States saddles it with an unsettled racial and cultural **identity**. This split, Majaj points out, is replicated within the Arab American community, with one faction adhering to the white racial classification, and another lobbying for minority status.

The preoccupation of contemporary Arab American writers with such communal concerns is clearly delineated by Majaj in her analysis of poetry and fiction by the likes of **Naomi Shihab Nye**, David Williams, Lawrence Joseph, **Diana Abu-Jaber**, and Pauline Kaldas, among others. Exploring pertinent themes in these writers' work such as memory, nostalgia, tradition, intercultural exchange, and ethnic visibility, Majaj outlines the shift in Arab American literature from the nostalgic and often **assimilation**ist tone characteristic of works from the earlier part of the twentieth century to a more critical one pervading the current Arab American literary arena. Majaj underscores the need for this literature to move toward a more complex identity formation, by which connecting ties can be forged across various racial and ethnic boundaries.

Her critical work appears in various collections such as *Memory and Cultural Politics: New Approaches to American Ethnic Literatures* (1996), *Arabs in America: Building a New Future* (1999), and *Postcolonial Theory and the United States: Race, Ethnicity, and Literature* (2000). She is also the coeditor of *Going Global: The Transnational Reception of Third World Women Writers* (2000), *Intersections: Gender, Nation, and Community in Arab Women's Novels* (2002), and *Etel Adnan: Critical Essays on the Arab-American Writer and Artist* (2002).

Majaj's poetry and creative pieces are imbued with insightful reflections on her bicultural heritage and the arduous struggles that accompany its history. Such work serves to relate Arab American identity with larger issues that extend beyond the personal to embrace the communal, such as Palestinian displacement and exile, suffering emanating from war, and feelings of loss and yearning toward an ancestral homeland. Her creative work has been published in several anthologies, including *Unsettling America* (1994), *Food for Our Grandmothers* (1994), *Worlds in Our Words* (1996), *The Space Between Our Footsteps* (1998), *Post Gibran: Anthology of New Arab-American Writing* (1999), and *The Poetry of Arab Women* (2001), as well as in journals including *South Atlantic Quarterly, Global City Review, Visions International, International Quarterly, Mizna, Al Jadid, Cafe Solo, Women's Review of Books*, and others. (*See also* Arab American Poetry)

Further Reading

Handal, Nathalie, ed. Introduction. *The Poetry of Arab Women: A Contemporary Anthology.* New York: Interlink, 2001. 1–62.

Carol Fadda-Conrey

MAJOR, CLARENCE (1936–)   African American novelist, short story writer, poet, editor, essayist, lexicographer, and visual artist. Largely a postmodernist practitioner of the arts, Clarence Major has devoted his life to creating a collection of works that in many ways celebrate multicultural aspects of the American experience rather than strictly continue the legacy of realism and naturalism focusing on the African American experience that the majority of Major's forebears and contemporaries have established. Because of this and because of his wide range of artistic interests, Major has claimed a unique place for himself in twentieth- and early-twenty-first-century American literature.

Major was both drawing and writing poetry at an early age while living in Atlanta, where he was born. Moving to Chicago with his mother when he was ten helped expose Major to the world of fine art, leading him to study at the Chicago Art Institute while a teenager. Major continued to work on his writing as well, although he did not find significant success, at least in terms of satisfaction, in his work until he moved from the Midwest to New York City in 1966, at the height of the **Black Arts Movement**. Making this move proved to be intellectually stimulating and cataclysmic for Major, who found himself in the artistic company of other poets such as **Audre Lorde** and **Gwendolyn Brooks**, other writers such as **Alice Walker** and Ishmael Reed, and musical artists such as Miles Davis and John Coltrane. In the midst of the excitement and all-around experimentation of the era, Major consciously fashioned a literary style for himself that embraced his own style of postmodernist experimentation, mixed with his own brand of political statement—one that often ran in stark opposition to the more mainstream political statements of his literary peers.

Major's first novel, *All-Night Visitors* (1969), is a work of distinctly black erotica that was first published by Olympia Press. While working on a rewrite for Olympia, Major made some lengthy and significant changes that the Olympia editors subsequently rejected. As publication was his main goal at the time, Major conceded to cutting the changes, much to the chagrin of some of those closest to him. The novel was republished, without the Olympia cuts, by Northeastern University Press in 1998, some time after Major's work had reached critical attention.

Major moved on to further facets of his craft, editing *The New Black Poetry* (1969) and publishing the *Dictionary of Afro-American Slang* (1970). An updated version of this dictionary appeared in 1998 as *From Juba to Jive: A Dictionary of African-American Slang*. Both volumes give serious consideration to a facet of American English that is often pushed aside in the name of standardization. Major continued to work as an anthology editor as well, producing collections such as *Calling the Word: Twentieth-Century African-American Short Stories* (1993) and *The Garden Thrives: Twentieth-Century African-American Poetry* (1996), both of which have helped secure his place as a caretaker of African American culture, a position which can become somewhat ironic when one carefully studies Major's overall **canon**.

Major has taught during most of his writing career and continues to do so, currently as a professor at the University of California, Davis. An early stint at Macomb Junior High School led to Major's editing the volume of student writing, *Man Is Like a Child: An Anthology of Creative Writing by Students*

(1968). Major has credited his teaching with helping to set an ever-important balance to his creative work.

Travel has also been an important part of Clarence Major's life. Visiting and living and working in various countries, including France, Italy, Greece, Liberia, and Ghana, have helped Major to better understand his own citizenship, according to the author himself. This understanding has at times led Major's writing to a significantly multicultural approach which separates Major from many of his contemporaries, who tend to solely focus on African American culture and experience. Major tends instead to look at the American experience as a whole, considering and remarking on the experiences of a variety of Americans rather than on one portion or another of the American experience. This tendency is shown particularly well in the novel *Painted Turtle: Woman with Guitar* (1988), named a Notable Book of the Year by the *New York Times*. The novel focuses on the life of a Zuni woman who is ostracized from her tribe partly due to her questioning of traditional ways. Major returns to the theme of Native American culture with the poetry collection, *Some Observations of a Stranger at Zuni in the Latter Part of the Century* (1989), which can be seen as a companion piece of sorts to *Painted Turtle.* Most recently, Major explores the character of a Chinese American woman in the novel *One Flesh* (2003). It is interesting to note that Major not only crosses cultural barriers but gender barriers as well in the writing of some of his multicultural work.

Major prepared to enter the twenty-first century with his poetry collection, *Configurations: New and Selected Poems, 1958–1998* (1998), which captures a lifetime of work and which was a National Book Award finalist. Major also continues to exhibit his visual art, as he has done since his youth, currently focusing on landscapes, and he continues to hone his writing craft, working out ideas of both experimentation and identity for himself through his pen. Although Major's definition of experimentation changes throughout his works, his commitment to approaching literature from a holistic perspective does not. Major looks to many literary mentors and muses—not solely American and certainly not solely African American—for inspiration and guidance, helping to put Major in a category of his own distinct creation. (*See also* African American Poetry, Multiculturalism)

Further Reading

Bell, Bernard, ed. *Clarence Major and His Art: Portraits of an African American Postmodernist.* Chapel Hill: U of North Carolina P, 2001.

Bunge, Nancy, ed. *Conversations with Clarence Major.* Jackson: UP of Mississippi, 2002.

Fleming, Robert. "35 Years as a Literary Maverick." *Black Issues Book Review* 6.2 (March/April 2004): 54–58.

Terry D. Novak

MALAMUD, BERNARD (1914–1986) Jewish American novelist, short story writer, playwright, memoirist, and essayist. Bernard Malamud was born on April 14, 1914, in Brooklyn, New York, to Max and Bertha Fidelman Malamud. Although Malamud's parents met in the United States, both Max and Bertha had been raised in the Ukraine, and both had fled czarist Russia for New York City around the turn of the century. Shortly after his arrival in the United States, Max found work driving a dairy cart. Eventually, Max managed to become a partner in a grocery store in Brooklyn's Borough Park and moved his family into a nicer part of the city. However, after being cheated by his partner (a situation Malamud would later fictionalize in his 1957 novel, *The Fixer*) Max was forced to move his family again. After a short time spent in Flatbush, the Malamuds finally settled in the Gravesend section of Brooklyn, where Max opened a small delicatessen and grocery store. Although both Max and Bertha worked long hours at the store, the enterprise

Bernard Malamud. *Courtesy of the Library of Congress.*

never became successful enough to provide a comfortable life for the family. The years of suffering and economic failure experienced by Max and Bertha strongly influenced Bernard's outlook on life and became themes that the writer would repeatedly explore in his fiction. In addition to *The Fixer* (1957), Malamud revisits the crippling sense of personal failure resulting from poverty in short stories such as "The Grocery Store" (1943) and "Take Pity" (1956).

After graduating from Public School 181, Malamud attended Erasmus High School, where he quickly became editor of the school's literary magazine, *The Erasmian*. Malamud then attended the City College of New York from 1932 to 1936, where his writing earned him the praise and encouragement of his professors. Upon graduation, Malamud sought work as a public school teacher, one of the few economically secure jobs available during the Great Depression. However, New York City's public school system required that each new teacher obtain a master's degree before becoming a teacher with full benefits. As a result, Malamud began attending Columbia University on a government loan while working part-time in factories, department stores, and as a letter carrier. He also worked as a teacher-in-training for Lafayette High School and taught English to Jewish refugees living in the city. He finally received his MA degree from Columbia in 1942.

In 1940 Bernard Malamud became a "permanent substitute" teacher at his former high school, a position he would hold until 1948. Teaching mostly night classes to recent immigrants, Malamud began working on his (eventually aborted) first novel, *The Light Sleeper*. In 1945 Malamud married Ann de Chiara, an Italian American woman whose ethnic background provided the author with another rich source of cultural material for his fiction. As a writer, Malamud found that teaching high school did not leave much time to pursue his literary interests. In 1949, while teaching evening classes in Harlem, Malamud began applying to teach at colleges around the United States, figuring it would give him more time to work on his writing. Not long after he first contacted the school, Malamud accepted a position to teach freshman composition at Oregon State College in Corvalis, Oregon, where the Malamuds would live until 1961.

While living and teaching in Oregon, Malamud's short stories began appearing in major national magazines such as the *Partisan Review, Harper's Bazaar,* and *Commentary*. He also wrote and published three novels, *The Natural* (1952), *The Assistant* (1958), and *A New Life* (1961), and *The Magic Barrel* (1958), a collection of short stories. In 1958 Malamud received the Rosenthal Foundation Award of the National Institute of Arts and Letters for *The Assistant*. The next year, Malamud won the first of his two National Book Awards for *The Magic Barrel*. In 1961 Malamud left Oregon to accept a professorship at Bennington College in Bennington, Vermont, a position he would hold until his death in 1986.

Much of Bernard Malamud's fiction output draws on the author's experiences as a first-generation Jewish American living among the largely immigrant population in Great Depression–era Brooklyn. Not surprisingly, many of Malamud's early short stories deal explicitly with the difficulties faced by poor Jewish, Italian, and Irish characters in situations not very different from those Malamud experienced himself or observed among his neighbors. *The Natural,* Malamud's first published novel, stands as the only fiction in the author's *oeuvre* not to deal with Jewish characters. Rather, Malamud weaves elements of the Arthurian legend, pulp literature, the Homeric epic, the Grail legend, American baseball lore, the morality tale, and Jungian psychology into powerful exploration of the ramifications of fame and the pursuit of money. With references to Branch Rickey's miserliness, Shoeless Joe Jackson's involvement in the Black Sox Scandal of 1919, and Babe Ruth's extravagances, *The Natural* situates the mythological figure of Roy Hobbs in a distinctively American setting. Hindered by the *hamartia* of traditional Greek and Roman heroes, Roy Hobbs, Malamud's prideful and enormously talented protagonist, struggles to overcome an injury caused by youthful arrogance to become a baseball star in his thirties. Eventually succumbing to avarice, Hobbs's epic failure as a baseball hero has been read as a critique of the pursuit of the American dream.

Despite the novel's obvious departure from Malamud's early preoccupations, *The Natural* does explore many of the themes the author repeatedly explores. Hobbs's absent parents, the youth and ability he squanders, the guilt with which he struggles, and his inevitable failure recur throughout the author's subsequent fiction. Like many of Malamud's early stories, *The Assistant* follows the life of an impoverished immigrant futilely struggling to overcome the hardships of life in the New World. In a situation reminiscent of Max Malamud's, Morris Bober, a hard-working and idealistic Jewish grocer, helplessly strains to run his business while Frank Alpine, his assistant, steals from the store and injures the grocer's family.

Malamud's next book, *The Magic Barrel,* won the National Book Award in 1959, becoming only the second collection of short stories to achieve the honor. Although most of the stories in the collection had been published prior to *The Assistant,* many readers will find strong thematic connections between the two works. In *The Magic Barrel,* Jewish and Italian ghettos provide the settings for stories of unceasing suffering, thwarted dreams, and the occasional instance of spiritual redemption.

A New Life, Malamud's comic third novel, follows S. Levin, a Jewish academic not unlike the author, as he moves from the east coast to the Pacific Northwest to teach at a small liberal arts college. Much to Levin's chagrin, the college has abandoned the ideals of a liberal arts education in favor of a strong scientific curriculum. Though Levin's attempts to alter the strict curriculum result in a comedy of manners, the professor's constant sense of sadness and repeated vocational and sexual failures places *A New Life* on the same thematic ground as Malamud's previous work.

Malamud's second collection of short stories, *Idiots First* (1963), explores many of the same themes as the author's earlier work, but adds a political dimension previously absent from Malamud's fiction. In the collection's final story, "The German Refugee," the narrator describes the tragic life of Oskar Gassner, a German Jewish journalist whose entire existence has been destroyed by the effects of Hitler's control of Germany. The story follows Gassner as he attempts to establish a life for himself in America, having seen his wife murdered, his culture destroyed, and his homeland overtaken by fascism. Like so many of Malamud's other protagonists, Gassner finds that success and happiness are elusive, and he settles into despair, eventually taking his own life.

The Fixer (1966), Malamud's most famous and highly acclaimed work of fiction, takes place in czarist Russia and tells the story of Yakov Bok, a Jewish laborer falsely accused of murder. Set during a period of virulent **anti-Semitism,** *The Fixer* forces the reader to meditate upon the freedom, prejudice, and injustice present in all societies. The winner of the Pulitzer Prize and the National Book Award, *The Fixer* holds a central place in twentieth-century American fiction and established Malamud as one of America's foremost novelists.

Although none of the fiction Malamud would publish during the final two decades of his life would meet with the success of his earlier work, the author published four additional novels and a third collection of short stories, each of which continue to be concerned with the themes of failure and struggle. *Pictures of Fidelman: An Exhibition* (1969) is an experimental picaresque novel made up of six short stories about a failed painter, Arthur Fidelman, as he travels around Italy. In *The Tenants* (1971), a black writer and a Jewish writer struggle to finish their work amid the growing animosity between blacks and Jews in their Brooklyn neighborhood. *Rembrandt's Hat* (1973), a collection of short stories, examines the lives of people whose lives are burdened by familial relationships, prejudice, aging, and artistic struggle. In *Dubin's Lives* (1979), the middle-aged, prize-winning biographer William Dubin struggles to understand himself while pursuing a woman half his age. Malamud's final novel *God's Grace* (1982) envisions a world where humanity's failure to avoid war results in thermonuclear Armageddon. The lone human survivor, Calvin Cohn, eventually settles in a modern-day Garden of Eden and strives to please God. A suitable conclusion to Malamud's career-long exploration of human failure, *God's Grace* ends on a hopeful note only occasionally present in the author's earlier fiction. (*See also* Jewish American Novel)

Further Reading

Avery, Evelyn, ed. *The Magic Worlds of Bernard Malamud.* Albany: State U of New York P, 2001.

Salzberg, Joel, ed. *Critical Essays on Bernard Malamud.* Boston: G. K. Hall & Co., 1987.

Solotaroff, Robert. *Bernard Malamud: A Study of the Short Fiction.* Boston: Twayne, 1989.

Erik Grayson

MALCOLM X [aka MALCOLM LITTLE; Islamic Name EL-HAJJ MALIK EL-SHABAZZ] (1925–1965) African American activist, Islamic minister, lecturer, and founder of the Organization for Afro-American Unity (OAAU). Malcolm X demonstrated his commitment to the cause of African American rights and unity by his tireless work on behalf of the Nation of Islam, and later, the OAAU. Malcolm was the focus of intense media attention, declaring himself as "the angriest black man in America," and provided a pro-active front for the **Civil Rights Movement**, as opposed to **Martin Luther King Jr.**'s passive resistance. Malcolm's premature death at age forty casts him as a legendary figure, and today he is a model for those who seek to reclaim their original African heritage that Malcolm believed had been stolen by whites.

Malcolm Little was born in Lansing, Michigan, to Earl Little who, as an outspoken minister and follower of **Marcus Garvey**, was reportedly murdered by the Ku Klux Klan when Malcolm was six years old. Under the strain of raising the family alone, Malcolm's mother Louise suffered a nervous breakdown and was institutionalized in 1937, and the Little children were parted out to foster homes. Malcolm showed promise as a smart and popular student but left school after the seventh grade when told by a teacher that he could never hope to become a lawyer because he was black. Malcolm then drifted into a life of crime, beginning in Detroit, and moving to New York City, where he became a pimp, drug dealer, and burglar. In Boston, Malcolm, age twenty-one, was arrested for armed robbery and imprisoned; he served six years in the Charlestown State Prison in Massachusetts.

While in prison, Malcolm wrote to Elijah Muhammad, leader of the Nation of Islam, and converted to Islam. He read voraciously and educated himself in history, politics, and philosophy. Upon his release from prison in 1952, Malcolm began to work for the Nation of Islam, taking the name Malcolm X (the "X" standing as a negation of his "slave name" and a symbol of his unknown African heritage). Malcolm was appointed minister of the Nation of Islam's Temple Number 7, in Harlem, in 1954. There, Malcolm recruited for the Nation, declaring his intent to forcefully accelerate the cause of African American civil rights and was a shining example of the Nation of Islam's highest ideals. He also founded the Nation of Islam's official publication, *Muhammad Speaks*, in 1961.

Malcolm X, 1964. *Courtesy of the Library of Congress.*

While Malcolm exhorted the Nation's followers to oppose the constraints of white dominance, dissension began to form in the Nation of Islam's highest office. Malcolm was officially silenced by Elijah Mohammad when, in response to the assassination of President John F. Kennedy in 1963, Malcolm told the press that this was "a case of chickens coming home to roost," meaning that the violence created by white greed had turned on its highest leader. Malcolm had also discovered financial and sexual improprieties on the part of Elijah Muhammad, which led to a final break between the two men.

After the split with the Nation of Islam, Malcolm quickly organized Moslem Mosque, Inc., to continue his work. Also, during this period Malcolm began to research fundamental Islam, and went on his *hajj,* the traditional pilgrimage to the holy city of Mecca that every devout Muslim must take at least once, in April 1964. While in Mecca, Malcolm realized that true Muslims were not divided by **race**, and upon returning to Harlem, he began to reformulate his social position. Taking the Islamic name El-Hajj Malik El-Shabazz, he founded the Organization for Afro-American Unity in 1964, and began to focus his efforts on improving international unity by overcoming the evils of racism. However, his split from the Nation of Islam had not been amicable, and Malcolm received death threats regularly.

In 1962 Malcolm agreed to dictate his life story to **Alex Haley**, and the resulting *Autobiography of Malcolm X* (1965) is a testament to Malcolm's spiritual and social efforts, as well as to the intense pressure he was under during the last years of his life. Though continually under the threat of violence, Malcolm never stopped working, traveling, and lecturing. His home was firebombed on February 13, 1965, but fortunately he and his family—wife Betty Shabazz and their four children—escaped serious injury. Malcolm X was assassinated on February 21, 1965, while lecturing at the Audubon Ballroom in New York City, the identity of his assassins never determined. Since Malcolm had never accepted money for his work (all money beyond living expenses went to the Nation of Islam and, later, to the OAAU), he left his family nearly destitute. Malcolm's death caused the sales of his autobiography to skyrocket, and the book became a best seller, selling more than five million copies. His example in life, as a hard working, devoted spiritual leader, unfailingly honest and committed to the cause of African American unity, survives him in death largely through the *Autobiography,* which was successfully filmed by director Spike Lee in 1992. The film *Malcolm X* was critically and commercially successful (though Lee focused on Malcolm's redemption while downplaying the extent of his criminal activity) and has been listed in the Library of Congress' National Film Registry. The *Autobiography* continues as required reading in college courses around the United States, and has been translated into eight languages. Malcolm's message and philosophy live on through numerous collections of his lectures, in print, on film, and on audio recordings. (*See also* African American Autobiography)

Further Reading

Clark, John Henrik. *Malcolm X: The Man and His Times.* New York: Macmillan, 1969.

Davis, Lenwood. *Malcolm X: A Selected Bibliography.* Westport, CT: Greenwood Press, 1984.

Dyson, Michael. *Making Malcolm: The Myth and Meaning of Malcolm X.* New York: Oxford UP, 1995.

Haley, Alex. *The Autobiography of Malcolm X, as Told to Alex Haley.* New York: Grove, 1965.

Karim, Benjamin. *Remembering Malcolm: The Story of Malcolm X from Inside the Muslim Mosque.* New York: Carroll & Graf, 1992.

Lee, Spike. *By Any Means Necessary: The Trials and Tribulations of Making Malcolm X.* London: Vintage, 1992.

Bill R. Scalia

MALTZ, ALBERT (1908–1985) Jewish American novelist and screenwriter. Albert Maltz belongs to the proletarian tradition and the postimmigrant tradition of Jewish American writers who felt betrayed by the failure of American society to provide equality and freedom for all. Maltz's passionate opposition to **racism** and **anti-Semitism** motivated him to found and edit the journal *Equality* in the late 1930s; it was also a reason he gave for joining the Communist Party. Anti-Semitism in the socialist countries during the cold war period, however, caused his final break with the Party.

Born into a lower-middle-class immigrant family in Brooklyn and educated at Columbia University, Maltz later studied at the Yale School of Drama, where he met George Sklar. His 1930s plays target corruption and war as the inevitable consequences of capitalism. Based on an actual event, a technique often used by Maltz, *Merry-Go-Round* (coauthored by Sklar), attacks the political depravity of a large city, its police brutality, and in essence, the hypocrisy of the entire system. *Peace on Earth* culminates in a murder frame-up and martyr's death (martyrdom recurs in his first two novels). Politically, its antiwar theme is fused with class struggle: a dispute between striking longshoremen and capitalist bosses. *Black Pit*, a psychological "proletarian morality" play, drew a sympathetic portrait of an informer. His short fiction of the period depicts workers dying of occupational diseases and the pride they take in their abilities (the 1949 novel *The Journey of Simon McKeever* returns to these themes); the O. Henry award-winning "The Happiest Man in the World" portrays their obsessive desire to work, as Jesse Fuller, a typesetter unemployed for seven years, prefers certain death at the wheel of a truck carrying nitroglycerin than the inability to feed his family.

Maltz's five novels are examples of the proletarian social novel. This form uses a multi-protagonist structure and generally portrays the contradictions between economic classes through a series of intertwined plot lines related to important events that demonstrate the correctness of a specific political or party position. This is certainly the case with his first, *The Underground Stream* (1940), based on the struggles to organize automobile workers in Detroit in the late thirties, which Maltz covered for the Communist press. The novel is unfortunately so transparently political and supportive of the Communist Party position that its flaws and didacticism are obvious. He solved the problem by embedding the message in his characterizations in *The Cross and the Arrow* (1944), where an apolitical drop-forge worker awarded a War Service Cross in a German tank factory commits an act of sabotage, out of moral indignation induced by the Nazi ideology of racism and inhumanity. Maltz's Marxist belief in the causality of specific historical events precludes a blanket denunciation of the German people, and he establishes two polarities, the Nazi leadership at the tank plant and a more politically ambiguous worker opposition.

Despite his skill as a writer, Maltz is probably best remembered for his work as a screenwriter and his subsequent political fate. In the Hollywood studios of the 1940s, he authored scripts such as *The House I Live In*, *Pride of* the Marines, and Broken Arrow, which spoke out for liberty and equality and attacked racism—the same themes Maltz expressed in his fiction. Maltz believed in the Communist Party's concept of "art as a weapon" but objected to its vulgarization as a doctrine used to straitjacket the writer. As a result, he was attacked by the party and forced to recant his views. With the defeat of fascism, the country turned to fighting Communism, and Maltz was one of the prime targets. Claiming First Amendment guarantees, he refused to testify about his political activities before the House Un-American Affairs Committee and was cited as a member of the "Holly-wood Ten" for contempt of Congress. Convicted, sentenced to prison, and fined, he was subsequently blacklisted. Deprived of his livelihood, unable to work for the studios openly, he went into self-imposed exile in Mexico for eleven years. Due to government prohibitions on known Communists, Maltz found it difficult to find a publisher: A Long Day in a Short Life (1957) was released by a Communist-affiliated publisher, and his last novel A Tale of One January (1966) was never published in the United States.

Further Reading

Salzman, Jack. *Albert Maltz*. Boston: Twayne, 1978.

Goldblatt, Roy. *Payment Is Extracted: Mechanisms of Escape into America in Immigrant and Post-Immigrant Jewish American Fiction*. Joensuu, Finland: University of Joensuu Press. 150–77.

Roy Goldblatt

MAMET, DAVID (1947–) Jewish American playwright. David Mamet has become one of America's most distinctive playwrights as well as one of its most eclectic and prolific. While his reputation rests primarily on his dramatic work, Mamet has also gained increasing fame and recognition as a screenwriter and director, with films such as *The Untouchables, The Postman Always Rings Twice, The Edge, Wag the Dog, The Spanish Prisoner*, and *Ronin*, among others. In addition, he has written adaptations of Chekhov, children's books, poetry, novels, collections of essays, and books on acting and has done some television work.

Much of Mamet's drama presents a scathing indictment of American materialism and commercialism, and his plays are known for their brutal, coarse language, their exploration into the seamy side of American society, and their exposure of callous, conniving behavior in the quest for the American Dream—which, in Mamet's view, involves betrayal, violence, and exploitation in the craving to get to the top. Many of his plays also deal with the difficulties of male-female relationships, and others—such as *The Old Neighborhood* and *Goldberg Street*—delve into an exploration of Jewish identity, often to a semiautobiographical degree.

Although Mamet's early works such as *Sexual Perversity in Chicago* (1974) met with success, the play that essentially launched his career was *American Buffalo* (1975), set in Mamet's native Chicago, premiering at its Goodman Theatre, and starring William H. Macy, a longtime Mamet collaborator. When the play moved to New York, it won an Obie Award as well as the New York Drama Critics' Circle Award, establishing Mamet as a unique and vital voice in American theater. Set in a run-down junk shop, the play centers around a trio of comically inept, would-be thieves who are planning to rob a man who they believe owns a valuable coin collection. Their efforts end in failure and an eruption of physical and verbal violence— a frequent event in Mamet's plays. Like much of Mamet's work, *American Buffalo* exposes the underbelly of the American Dream, illustrating how individual betrayal and sordid business ethics supersede loyalty and integrity in the quest for the almighty dollar. The failure of communication among the characters, who constantly interrupt each other and speak in fragmented dialogue, underscores this lack of solidarity. Such brittle, sparse dialogue, along with the manipulation of language, is another hallmark of Mamet's work.

An apex in Mamet's career came with *Glengarry Glen Ross* (1983), which premiered at London's National Theatre, where it won the prestigious Olivier Award among other honors. When it transferred to Broadway the following year, it garnered another host of awards, including the Pulitzer Prize and four Tony nominations. Again, the play concerns brutal business ethics. Set in a real estate office, it centers around a contest among the salesmen, in which the one to score the most sales will win a Cadillac, the runner-up will receive a set of steak knives, and the others will lose their jobs. Such a scenario sets the stage for fierce competition, with the men pitted against each other. As in other Mamet plays, language is central, as the salesmen use it not as a means of communication but as a tool for manipulation, entrapping unsuspecting clients into false friendships in hopes of selling them worthless plots of land in a romantic sounding Florida locale called Glengarry Highlands. The play culminates with a robbery of the real estate office by one of the salesman (in collusion with another) in a desperate attempt to obtain the premium "leads"—the most promising sales prospects—which the salesman then sells to a rival firm.

While Mamet's plays have often been provocative in their subject matter and language, none has caused as much controversy as *Oleanna* (1992), which coincidentally was produced around the time of the Clarence Thomas/Anita Hill hearings over sexual harassment. In this two-character play, Carol, a student, goes to see her professor, John, about her grade. Initially, Carol is an inarticulate, self-deprecating young woman, concerned about her inability to comprehend the material and obsessed with her own stupidity. John, the pompous if well-meaning professor, offers to tutor her and tries to assuage her low self-esteem, although he is preoccupied with his impending tenure and the purchase of a new house, information which is conveyed through the continual interruption of telephone calls. As the play progresses, however, Carol somehow develops a level self-confidence and a command of language, seemingly through the assistance of a mysterious feminist group. By the end of the play, having demanded the banning of John's book along with others, she charges him with assault, sexual improprieties, and ultimately rape, thus destroying his career. Language again is central to *Oleanna*, as Carol twists John's words against him to validate her accusations of sexual harassment. The incendiary response to this play, which left audiences arguing over who was right or wrong, and even, in some cases, inciting audience members to stand up and yell at the characters, surprised Mamet as much as anyone. Clearly, the play tapped into heated contemporary issues of power, sexual harassment, and gender politics, showing Mamet to be well attuned to the tenor of American society.

While Mamet's body of work is extensive, others of his more prominent plays include *A Life in the Theatre* (1977), a poignant story about an aging actor and his young protégé, which takes place both onstage and backstage; *Edmond* (1985), a harrowing depiction of one man's descent into the American underworld in search of some sense of self-**identity**; *Speed-the-Plow* (1989), which pierces the aggressive, egotistical nature of Hollywood moguls and filmmaking; and *The Cryptogram* (1994), a three-person play which charts the disintegration of a young boy's innocence as well as the end of a friendship and a marriage. The latter play, in which one character is the boy's mother, marks a move toward a greater presence of women in Mamet's plays, a notable shift for a playwright whose work famously centers around the world of men and male domains—to the point that he has often been accused of misogyny.

Several of Mamet's plays have been made into films, with varying degrees of success. In 1979, the Public Broadcasting System (PBS) aired a production of *A Life in the Theatre*, starring Jack Lemmon and Matthew Broderick; in 1992, Mamet's screenplay of *Glengarry Glen Ross* featured an all-star cast that included Al Pacino, Jack Lemmon, Alec Baldwin, Alan Arkin, and Ed Harris; in 1994, Mamet's screenplay of *Oleanna* was produced, with veteran Mamet actor William H. Macy; and in 1996, a film version of *American Buffalo* was released, starring Dustin Hoffman and Dennis Franz. Additionally, Mamet has written and directed a number of original screenplays, including *House of Games* (1987), which starred another Mamet veteran, Joe Mantegna; *Things Change* (1988), also featuring Mantegna; *Homicide* (1990), with both Mantegna and Macy, and *State and Main* (2000), whose cast included Macy, Alec Baldwin, Patti Lupone, Charles Durning, and Sara Jessica Parker. Like his stage dramas, Mamet's films feature familiar themes of deception and betrayal, the lust for money, and the manipulation of language to cheat and deceive, and in *House of Games*, it is actually the woman who breaks into the man's world and who prevails in the end.

Mamet has acknowledged as key influences on his work Samuel Beckett and Harold Pinter, two central writers of Theatre of the Absurd—a term bestowed by critic Martin Esslin on a group of writers who, in his view, shared similar views of the world and shattered conventional dramatic structure. In many ways, Mamet's drama does adapt characteristics of Absurdist theater, including the fragmented and brutal language, the eruption of violence, the mysterious sense of menace, the failure of communication, and the manipulation of language for treasonous purposes. To some extent, then, he is writing in the tradition of his predecessors of the 1950s and 1960s, but he has also established his own distinctive style in his use of these techniques, and unlike the Absurdist writers—whose dramatic styles mirrored the central idea that life is irrational and without meaning— Mamet hews to more conventional structures, particularly the well-made play. Furthermore, whereas Absurdism theatrically illustrates life's mundane and empty routine, Mamet's work takes aim at the weaknesses and shortcomings of American life and ethics, making him a distinctly American writer. (*See also* Jewish American Theater)

Further Reading

Bibsby, C. W. E. *David Mamet*. London: Methuen, 1985.

Bloom, Harold, ed. *David Mamet*. Philadelphia: Chelsea House Publishers, 2004.

Carroll, Dennis. *David Mamet*. London: Macmillan, 1987.

Dean, Anne. *David Mamet: Language as Dramatic Action*. Rutherford, New Jersey: Fairleigh Dickinson UP, 1990.

Hudgins, Christopher C., and Leslie Kane, eds. *Gender and Genre: Essays on David Mamet*. New York: Palgrave, 2001.

Kane, Leslie, *Weasels and Wisemen: Ethics and Ethnicity in the Work of David Mamet*. New York: St. Martin's Press, 1999.

———, ed. *David Mamet: A Casebook*. New York: Garland, 1992.

———, ed. *David Mamet in Conversation*. Ann Arbor: U of Michigan P, 2001.

Savran, David. "David Mamet." *In Their Own Words: Contemporary American Playwrights*. New York: Theatre Communications Group, 1988. 132–44.

Karen C. Blansfield

MANDELBAUM, ALLEN (1926–) Jewish American translator, poet, and essayist. Allen Mandelbaum is widely renowned as one of the most important translators of ancient writers and Dante in the contemporary era and as an essayist and editor of Jewish poetry. He was born in Albany, New York, but spent the early years of his life in a variety of cities—Louisville, Kentucky; Toronto, Canada; Troy, New York; and Chicago, Illinois. At the age of thirteen, he arrived in New York City, where he attained a BA from Yeshiva University and an MA and PhD from Columbia University. Afterward, Mandelbaum taught at Yeshiva University and Cornell University and was a Rockefeller Foundation humanities fellow. In 1951 he was elected to the Society of Fellows at Harvard but primarily lived in Italy during the period. In 1964 he returned to the United States and joined the faculty of the Graduate Center of the City University of New York. There he served as a professor of English and comparative literature and as the chair of the English graduate faculty for more than two decades. Since 1989 he has been the W. R. Kenan Jr. Professor of Humanities at Wake Forest University, a professor (*per chiara fama*) of the history of literary criticism at the University of Torino, and a professor emeritus of English at the Graduate Center of the City University of New York.

Mandelbaum emerged as one of the most influential translators of the latter half of the twentieth century, beginning with his translations of Giuseppe Ungaretti (*Life of a Man*, 1958) and Salvatore Quasimodo (*Selected Writings*, 1960). Mandelbaum's greatest acclaim in translation followed his verse translations of Virgil's *Aeneid* (1972), Dante's *Divine Comedy* (1980–84), Homer's *Odyssey* (1990), and Ovid's *Metamorphoses* (1993). Both widespread adoption of his texts for introductory and advanced scholarship and multiple editions suggest that his translations will shape the study of these authors for the foreseeable future. His translation of the *Aeneid* won the National Book Award in 1973, his translation of the *Metamorphoses* was a finalist for the Pulitzer Prize for poetry, and his translation of *Divine Comedy* garnered international praise. The most frequently acknowledged feature of Mandelbaum's verse translations has been his ability to breathe contemporary life into the classical and Renaissance texts, elegantly translating not only the core narratives but also the music of the original Greek, Latin, or Renaissance Italian into contemporary English. In the *Aeneid*, he has been credited for elegantly reflecting Virgil's complex relationship with Rome. He has been hailed as a worthy successor to heralded translators of the last century and heartily defended against critics by scholars like the late Irma Brandeis.

In addition to translation, Mandelbaum has compiled a formidable body of original work, drawing from a seemingly endless well of literary allusions and conversing in depth with his literary predecessors across centuries and continents. His volumes of poetry include *Journeyman* (1967), *Leaves of Absence* (1976), *Chelmaxioms: The Maxims, Axioms, Maxioms of Chelm* (1978), *A Lied of Letterpress* (1980), and *The Savantasse of Montparnasse* (1988). As an essayist and editor, Allen Mandelbaum has contributed both to scholarship on Jewish writers and to the American tradition in poetry. Notable in this area are "A Millennium of Hebrew Poetry in Italy (1850–1906)" in *Gardens and Ghettos: The Art of Jewish Life in Italy* (1989), eight volumes of the Jewish Poetry Series, the ongoing project *Lectura Dantis* (1998–), critical companion volumes to his translation of the *Divine Comedy, Three Centuries of American Poetry* (1999), and *A Treasury of American Poetry* (2004).

Mandelbaum's work has spawned interdisciplinary treatments as well, including composer Mark Scearce's *Shades of Orpheus*, based on portions of his translation of Ovid's *Metamorphoses*. In addition, the national and international laurels awarded to Mandelbaum's translations and poetry are prodigious and defy brief listing. In 2000 Mandelbaum became the first and only American recipient of the Gold Medal of Honor of the City of Florence. The award for his translation of the *Divine Comedy* was part of the celebrations during the 735th anniversary of Dante's birth. In 2003 Mandelbaum received the Presidential Prize of the President of Italy, and in 2004 he received Italy's highest award, the Presidential Cross of the Order of the Star of Italian Solidarity.

Further Reading

Ahern, John. Review of *The Divine Comedy*. *New York Times Book Review* 9 (April 21, 1985): 12.

Shatzky, Joel, and Michael Taub, eds. "Allen Mandelbaum." *Contemporary Jewish-American Dramatists and Poets: A Bio-Critical Sourcebook*. Westport, CT: Greenwood Press, 1999.

Eric Ashley Hairston

MANFREDI, RENÉE (1962–)   Italian American fiction writer. Renée Manfredi is one of the talented Italian American women writers who gained prominence in the last decade of the twentieth century.

Herself a native of Pittsburgh, Manfredi's family immigrated to the United States from Sicily and southern Italy. She received her MFA in 1991 from Indiana University's creative writing program and is currently an associate professor of creative writing and literature at the University of Alaska at Fairbanks.

Her first book, *Where Love Leaves Us* (1994), is a collection of nine well-crafted stories. The book was a cowinner for the 1993 Iowa Short Fiction Award and won a Best American Novelist Under 40 Award from *Granta Magazine* in 1996. Most of the stories are set in Pittsburgh's Italian neighborhoods in the 1960s and look at second- and third-generation families, especially examining father-daughter relationships.

In "The Projectionist," the focus is on the father, a Sicilian World War II refugee. Twenty years later in the United States, he is becoming unhinged as he watches his world disintegrate during the changing values of the 1960s. His Italian neighborhood is dying, and his daughter is growing distant from him as she starts casually dating a hippie. In "Truants," dad and daughter play hooky together from work/school, keeping it a secret from workaholic lawyer mom.

At times, the father-daughter relationship is, in fact, uncomfortably close; this is most obvious in "Bocci." Set in an Italian Sons and Daughters clubhouse during a social event, rambunctious ten-year-old precocious Ellen wanders around, talking with relatives and leaving religious literature in restrooms. While her doting father and cold mother are dancing upstairs, Ellen's overly familiar manner leads her into a conversation with handsome Carlo, who rapes her in the men's room. As in this story, Manfredi often portrays mothers negatively.

Manfredi's second book is the well-received novel *Above the Thunder* (2004). Here Manfredi continues to explore familial relationships—but successfully breaks away from fathers and daughters to focus on others. The two plots, eventually entwined, involve three generations of women on the one hand and a gay couple on the other. In the first, Anna, a widowed fifty-three-year-old medical technologist in Boston, is similar to some of the mothers in *Where Love Leaves Us*: distant, unloving, and unforgiving. After many years of estrangement from her only child, who continues to struggle with drug addiction, Anna finally meets her granddaughter Flynn for the first time. Flynn is an odd girl, full of imagination and fears resulting from years of neglect and abandonment. Anna grudgingly agrees to take the girl in, only to eventually lose her heart to her. The gay couple, serious Stuart and wild Jack, come apart just as Jack finds out he has AIDS. They meet Anna in an AIDS support group she is helping oversee; Anna finds she has room in her heart for them as well. In spite of its tragic ending, the novel looks deeply into the human heart and finds love and compassion.

Christina Biava

MANGIONE, JERRE (GERLANDO) (1909–1998) Italian American novelist, essayist, editor, literary critic, and educator. Jerre Mangione is one of the pioneering figures in Italian American literature, whose work gives voice to the second-g eration immigrants. His memoirs, *Mount Allegro: The Memoir of Italian American Life* (1943) and *An Ethnic at Large: A Memoir of America in the Thirties and Forties* (1978), and his account of the Federal Writer's Project, *The Dream and the Deal: The Federal Writer's Project 1934–1943* (1972), give a slice of ethnic Americana of the 1920s and 30s and show the difficulties of defining an ethnic writer in America.

Mount Allegro brought Mangione major critical acclaim and public success. The memoir chronicles the joys and tensions of Sicilian communal living in a working-class Italian neighborhood of Rochester, New York. Recreating his childhood through a narrative of the fictive Amoroso family, Mangione's light and humorous tone raises serious questions about growing up ethnic in America. The text manifests the double difficulty of generational and ethnic conflicts, complex translations between cultures, struggles to refute an ethnic stereotype, and attempts to establish one's self independently from one's **ethnicity**. Above all, a text that opens with a bold statement, "When I grow up I want to be an American," it is about the self-consciousness and shame associated with ethnic difference and aspirations to find modes of success that would help one escape an ethnic community and blend with the American mainstream. It is this very subject—Mangione's attempt to become an American and a writer—that is the subject of his next memoir, *An Ethnic at Large.* The text follows Mangione's education at Syracuse University and his move to New York City, where he establishes himself as an author and works as an editor and public relations officer for various government agencies, expressing his strong antifascist sentiment in a number of articles, book reviews, and social and political satire published in *The New Republic,* the *New Masses,* and the *Partisan Review.* The lasting value of *An Ethnic at Large* lies in the fact that it extends beyond the personal experience and includes the generation of emerging ethnic writers who shared Mangione's challenges of the choice of topics and literary approaches, the definition and expectations of audiences, and the designation and location of ethnic writers in America. Mangione further contributes to the ethnic literary scene with his ambitious *The Dream and the Deal.* The book records Mangione's involvement with the Federal Writers' Project in the capacity of a national coordinator and offers a valuable behind-the-scenes look at the making of some of the major figures of American literature, such as **Richard Wright**, **Ralph Ellison**, **Saul Bellow**, and **Zora Neale Hurston**. Apart from exploring the American literary scene, Mangione also sets a number of his works in Sicily. These other nonfiction works include *Reunion in Sicily*, an ethnographic account of his first visit to Sicily, and *A Passion for Sicilians: The World Around Danilo Dolci* (1972), a portrait of an Italian social activist of the 1950s and 1960s. His works of fiction include *The Ship and the Flame* (1948), *Night Search* (1965), *America Is Also Italian* (1969), and *Mussolini's March on Rome* (1975).

Mangione's last major project was *La Storia: Five Centuries of the Italian American Experience* (1992), a comprehensive survey of Italian immigration in America, coauthored with Ben Morreale. The volume documents the Italian experience of

Jerre (Gerlando) Mangione. *Courtesy of the Library of Congress.*

America by combining historical facts with photographic material and vivid personal narratives of the challenges, struggles, and hopes of Italian immigrants. *La Storia* highlights Italian contributions to American society and culture and points out the achievement of prominent Americans of Italian origin, ranging widely from Christopher Columbus to Madonna. The last thirty years of his life, Mangione spent teaching literature and creative writing at the University of Pennsylvania, from which he received an honorary doctoral degree and where he helped institute the Italian Studies program, becoming its first director in 1978. Together with **Pietro di Donato** and **John Fante**, Jerre Mangione is one of the founders of Italian American literature, and his work is a lasting record of Italian **immigration** in America, the struggles to define an ethnic American writer, and the ambivalence that accompanies one's coming to terms with ethnicity in America. (*See also* Italian American Autobiography, Italian American Stereotypes)

Further Reading

Gardaphè, Fred L. "My House Is Not Your House: Jerre Mangione and Italian-American Autobiography." *Multicultural Autobiography: American Lives.* Ed. James Robert Payne. Knoxville: U of Tennessee P, 1992. 139–77.

Ljiljana Coklin

MANN, EMILY (1952-) Jewish American playwright and director. Growing up in the heyday of political ferment, civil rights, and political activism, Emily Mann established her reputation with plays that she calls "theater of testimony," a term borrowed from South African director Barney Simon. She prefers it to the more conventional genre "docudrama," which she feels implies a modicum of fiction, whereas Mann is adamant about having characters speak in their own words and is careful to avoid any nuance of propaganda.

Mann's initial ambitions were to be a musician and composer, but she became attracted to theater in high school, going on to study directing at Harvard, the Guthrie Theatre—where she received a Bush Fellowship—and the University of Minnesota. In 1973, inspired by **Holocaust** survivors' transcripts compiled by her father, a history professor, as part of an oral history project, she traveled to London to meet and interview her college roommate's Czechoslovakian aunt, who had escaped from a concentration camp. That material became the basis for her first play, *Annulla Allen: Autobiography of a Survivor* (1974), which she wrote specifically for actress Barbara Bryne. Mann also drew upon her own maternal ancestors' experiences in Poland, as well as upon a visit to her grandmother's village.

Mann's subsequent "theatre of testimony" plays are often disturbing. *Still Life* (1980) is based on the memories of a Vietnam veteran, Mark, tortured by his role in the My Lai massacres, as well as on interviews with his terrified, abused wife and his mistress. Mark is an artist who paints "still life" portraits, but the title also suggests lives that have been stilled. The play, which Mann found traumatic to write, reconciled a rift with her hawkish father over the war and also confronted the question of how and why people resort to violence, domestically as well as nationally. Staged at the Goodman Theatre, *Still Life* won six Obie Awards.

Execution of Justice (1983) probes the 1978 murders of San Francisco Mayor George Moscone and City Supervisor Harvey Milk by disgruntled ex-employee Dan White, a homophobic Vietnam veteran as well as an ex-policeman and fireman. The trial introduced the notorious "Twinkie Defense," which argued that White's actions were due to an overindulgence of sugar-laden junk food, resulting in a sentence of less than eight years—of which White served only five; a year after his release, he committed suicide. Commissioned by the San Francisco Eureka Theatre, the play premiered in 1984 at the Actors Theatre of Louisville, moving to New York in 1986, marking Mann as the first woman to direct her own play on Broadway and earning the Helen Hayes Award, among other honors.

Having Our Say: The Delany Sisters' First 100 Years (1995) is one of Mann's more uplifting plays, lacking the political edge of her other works, despite the horrific prejudice and suffering underlying it. Adapted from the memoir *Having Our Say* by centenarians Sarah and Elizabeth Delany, the play became a surprise Broadway hit.

Greensboro (A Requiem) (1996) is far grimmer, based on events surrounding a 1979 Ku Klux Klan assault on an anti-Klan rally in Greensboro, North Carolina. Five people were killed and eight wounded, but the crime went unpunished, in large part because of police department collusion.

Despite her obsession with presenting people's words verbatim, Mann—like **David Mamet**, a playwright she much admires—is concerned with transmuting the "testimonies" into linguistic rhythms as well as delineating characters who are dramatically engaging. Besides Mamet, Mann has also acknowledged Brecht as an influence on her audience-awareness approach.

Turning to her own Jewish roots, in 1999 Mann dramatized the novel *Meshugah* by **Isaac Bashevis Singer**, one of her father's favorite authors. While not in the tradition of her "theatre of testimony," the play does confront moral and ethical issues about good and evil and the need to survive.

Meanwhile, Mann was also forging a career as a director, working at regional theaters around the country, and since 1990, she has served as Artistic Director of Princeton University's McCarter Theater. Under her leadership, the McCarter won the 1994 Tony Award for Outstanding Regional Theater, followed by three nominations for work done in 1995.

Among her other projects, Mann adapted August Strindberg's *Miss Julie* (1993), Federico García Lorca's *The House of Bernarda Alba* (1999), and Chekhov's *The Cherry Orchard* (2001), and turned **Ntozake Shange**'s novel *Betsy Brown* into a rhythm and blues opera. She also directed **Anna Deveare Smith**'s one-woman show, *Twilight: Los Angeles 1992* at Los Angeles's Mark Taper Forum, and she wrote the screenplay for *Winnie (The Winnie Mandela Story)*.

After being diagnosed with multiple sclerosis in 1995, Mann continued to work, turning her disease into a positive force, a focus she attributes to a doctor she considers remarkable. The many honors Mann has received include a Guggenheim, McKnight Fellowship, NEA Playwrights Fellowship, NEA Artistic Associate Grant, and Rosamond Glider Award for Outstanding Creative Achievement in Theatre.

Further Reading

Betsko, Kathleen, and Rachel Koenig, eds. "Emily Mann." *Interviews with Contemporary Women Playwrights.* New York: Beech Tree Books, 1987.

Bigsby, Christopher. "Emily Mann." *Contemporary American Playwrights.* Cambridge, UK: Cambridge UP, 2000. 132–64.

Greene, Alexis, ed. "Emily Mann." *Women Who Write Plays: Interviews with American Dramatists.* Hanover, NH: Smith and Kraus. 286–310.

Savran, David. "Emily Mann." *In Their Own Words: Contemporary American Playwrights.* New York: Theatre Communications Group, 1988. 145–60.

Karen C. Blansfield

MARKFIELD, WALLACE (1926–2002) American novelist, short story writer, and literary journalist. Although he has received scant critical attention, Wallace Markfield deserves recognition as a talented chronicler of Jewish American urban life. His three novels on Jewish themes render with wit and affection a largely vanished milieu of candy stores, egg creams, and the intense, striving atmosphere of Jewish New York.

Markfield began his literary career in the late 1940s by publishing short stories in *Commentary* and *Partisan Review*, the leading intellectual journals of the time. Although well regarded as an up and coming writer, it was not until the publication of his first novel, *To an Early Grave* (1964), that Markfield truly made his mark. The story of four New York Jewish pseudo-intellectuals who travel from Manhattan to Brooklyn in a Volkswagen Bug, *To an Early Grave* garnered widespread praise and earned Markfield a prestigious Guggenheim Fellowship. Markfield's novel depicts the impact of the death of Leslie Braverman, a celebrated, middle-aged literary journalist and notorious lothario, on four men: Morroe Rief, a speechwriter for Jewish organizations (as was Markfield); Felix Ottensteen, a hack writer for a Yiddish newspaper; Holly Levine, a pretentious literary critic; and Barnett Weiner, a failed poet and critic. Critics praised the novel's pitch-perfect satire of the New York intelligentsia and especially noted Markfield's ear for the rhythm and tone of Jewish pseudo-intellectual conversation. With considerable humor and fine-tuned sense of aggravation, Markfield paints his characters as witty but ultimately shallow men whose intellectual pretensions block them from honest thought and personal connection. It is only in the realm of trivia and popular culture—movie titles, theme songs, once famous actors and actresses—that the funeral-goers truly come alive, delighting in their ability to recall the heroes of their distant childhood. At the end, after the funeral, it is only Morroe Rieff, the novel's central protagonist, who is able to register anything resembling heartfelt grief for his dead friend, although Morroe's sadness is directed as well at his failed ambitions.

Markfield's next novel, *Teitlebaum's Window* (1971), is arguably his best, although it was not warmly received by critics. It did not help, presumably, that the novel, a bildungsroman about a Jewish boy growing up in Brooklyn during the 1930s, was published soon after **Philip Roth**'s similarly themed controversial *Portnoy's Complaint*. Many critics dismissed the novel as covering the already well-trod ground of urban Jewish boyhood, but unlike the comically bitter tone of Roth's novel, *Teitlebaum's Window* is for the most part a keen, affectionate portrait of Jewish Brooklyn. Told mainly from the point of view of Simon Sloan, a Jewish boy with an inexplicably hateful father and an overbearing, self-centered mother, the novel experiments with diary entries, stream-of-consciousness narration, and a panoramic overview of Jewish street life. Less concerned with plot than *To an Early Grave*, the novel follows Simon from childhood until American engagement in World War II, when then nineteen-year-old Simon enters the army. Although Markfield's experimental narration did not endear the novel to readers and critics, its rich aura of family warmth and intergenerational tension and its poignant depiction of the teeming public life of Jewish city streets mark it as one of the best Jewish American "documentary" novels of the postwar era.

Markfield's third novel, *You Could Live If They Let You* (1974), effectively marked the end of his career as a Jewish writer. Eschewing plot in favor of collage-like pastiche, the story is told from the point of view of Chandler Van Horton, an obviously non-Jewish biographer working on a book about Jules Farber, a famous Jewish comedian. The chapters consist of Van Horton's dreams and book notes, excerpts from Farber's stand-up routine, and send ups of Jewish newsletters and academic studies of Jewish comedy. Although largely ignored by critics, the novel is an engaging tribute to Jewish humor and its impact on American culture.

Markfield published two more novels—an unfinished comedy called *Multiple Orgasms* (1977) and a political thriller, *Radical Surgery* (1991)—but his legacy as a Jewish American writer rests mainly on his early work. On the strength of *To an Early Grave* alone, Markfield deserves prominent mention alongside other, more celebrated Jewish novelists of the postwar era.

Further Reading

Friedman, Melvin J. "The Enigma of Unpopularity and Critical Neglect: The Case for Wallace Markfield." *Seasoned Authors for a New Season: The Search for Standards in Popular Writing.* Ed. Louis Filler. Bowling Green, OH: Bowling Green U Popular P, 1980: 33–42.

Jeremy Shere

MAROTTA, KENNY (1949–) Italian American fiction writer. Kenny Marotta is one of the Italian American writers who became well known near the end of the twentieth century.

Marotta was born in Malden, Massachusetts, and grew up there and in St. Louis. He received his BA degree from Harvard and his PhD from Johns Hopkins. He has taught writing and literature at the University of Virginia in Charlottesville since 1974.

Marotta's father and maternal grandparents emigrated from Sicily, and he uses their experiences and stories as the basis for his writing. He has published two books: *A Piece of Earth* (1985), a novel about two Italian immigrant families in the 1940s, and a collection of interrelated stories, *A House on the Piazza* (1998), a prequel to the earlier novel.

Marotta's strength is his characterization, and both works are centered on the same handful of Sicilian immigrants and their American-born children, whose lives are often conflicted. The compelling *A Piece of Earth* finds American-born Agnes Zammataro and her fiancé, Mike Buonfiglio, struggling against the cultural expectations of their immigrant families. As many first generation daughters, Agnes finds she must strive to exert her independence, especially from her domineering old-world father, Nino. Although she has a job, she is still not trusted with money or with a key to the family's apartment. Mike, living up to his surname (*buon* means "good" and *figlio* means "son"), tries to satisfy the demands of his mother, Madge, who uses the issue of who will take over the care of her aging mother as a means of manipulating him.

Although the stories are angst-ridden, with issues of poverty and old-world superstitions, the overall tone of the novel is quite humorous. This is where Marotta shows his dexterity with Sicilian idioms and discourse styles. Characters are developed by his conveying their thoughts in Italian-accented English, often in the form of questions that reflect a character's twisted logic of a situation. For instance, Madge's spoiled brother Lino, a petty criminal with mob connections, is not above stealing his sister's life savings, but only after he has convinced himself that his sister would, in fact, have wanted him to take it.

While the characters are sympathetically conveyed in *A Piece of Earth*, they are presented more straightforwardly in *A House on the Piazza*. In these stories Marotta takes the characters back to the villages in which they grew up in Sicily, where he explores the cultural and economic forces that shaped them: the poverty, the family honor, and the desire for status. In the final story, "Asphodel," Marotta presents the issue of the immigrants' desire to return to Italy at the end of their working lives. Here we see the immigrant's life transcended: Although Midge and Nino decide to remain, ultimately they can only do so as new people—as Italian *Americans*—who have learned to overcome a lifetime of marital hostilities and relate to one another as free men and women, unbound by tradition.

Further Reading

Albright, Carol Bonomo. "From Sacred to Secular in *Umbertina* and *A Piece of the Earth*." *MELUS* 20.2 (1995): 93–103.

Christina Biava

MARRANT, JOHN (1755–1791) African American author and minister. Searches for John Marrant's life and work most often result in little or nothing. Such omission seems remarkable given the diversity of the literal and figurative sojourns that he recorded in his two major published works. His first major published work, *A Narrative of the Lord's Wonderful Dealings with John Marrant* (1785), reads like an impossible blending of the most popular eighteenth- and nineteenth-century literary genres: the picaresque captivity narrative and confessional. In part, it chronicles his misadventures as celebrated musician, his conversion to Christianity, his near death as a captive, his impressed service in the British Navy during the American Revolution, and his return to his religious devotions. His *Narrative* proved so popular that it ran through at least fifteen different editions. In contrast, his second major published work, *A Journal of the Rev. John Marrant* (1790), tempers such wide-ranging adventures with more fundamentalist arguments. In it he also justifies establishing a religious colony in Sierra Leon for African Americans seeking refuge from persecution in Nova Scotia, where Marrant had maintained his congregation prior to his death. The tension manifest in these two autobiographical narratives informs Marrant's life and times and suggests why he remains to this day an obscure figure in African American literature.

Those critics who recognize his prominence often celebrate his uniqueness, not just as America's first black preacher (a title often given Marrant), but also as an original voice. These critics acknowledge that his 1785 *Narrative* is among the very first published African American books and therefore deserves greater academic attention than it currently enjoys. **Henry Louis Gates Jr.**, who rescued Marrant from obscurity, further validates Marrant's primacy in African American literature when he claims that this narrative "inaugurates the black tradition of English literature" (145). Despite such prominent calls for their inclusion, most anthologies still exclude his works.

Critics like Benilde Montgomery and John Saillant insightfully argue that such exclusion derives from Marrant's indeterminacy: His *Narrative* does not fit neatly into any of the conventional categories used currently by critics. To illustrate their claims, they point to the portion of his first narrative that recounts his captivity among the Cherokee. This portion counters the dominant critical model of captivity narratives, a model that argues that works in the genre originated as typological or ethnographic tracts but had become almost exclusively racist propaganda by the period in which Marrant's *Narrative* first appeared. Instead, Marrant's captivity narrative combines typology with an appreciation for cultural diversity and thereby ultimately testifies to his captors' humanity. While such nonconformity may determine much of Marrant's current obscurity, it also depicts much of the African American experience during Marrant's time and provides scholars today with a rich example from which to extrapolate about the innumerable other African Americans whose stories will remain unknown. (*See also* African American Autobiography)

Further Reading

Gates, Henry Louis, Jr. *The Signifying Monkey.* New York: Oxford UP, 1988.

Montgomery, Benlide. "Recapturing John Marrant." *When Brer Rabbit Meets Coyote.* Ed. Jonathan Brennan. Urbana and Chicago: U of Illinois P, 2003. 158–67.

Saillant, John. "'Wipe Away All Tears from Their Eyes': John Marrant's Theology in the Black Atlantic, 1785–1808." *Journal of Millennial Studies* 1.2 (Winter 1999). http://www.mille.org/journalpublications/winter98/saillant.PDF (accessed November 1, 2004).

Zafar, Rafia. "Capturing the Captivity: African Americans among the Puritans." *MELUS* 17.2 (Summer 1991–1992): 19–35.

Clay Kinchen Smith

MARSHALL, PAULE (1929–) Barbadian American writer and author of five novels and two short story/novella collections, *Soul Clap Hands and Sing* (1961) and *Reena and Other Stories* (1983). Marshall's fiction focuses on females of the African **diaspora** facing conflicts of **identity** and engaging in quests for self. Traveling from America (usually Brooklyn,

New York, where her family immigrated during World War I) to the Caribbean, France, and—in memory—to the Sea Islands of South Carolina, or back to America from Europe or the islands, these women find missing parts of themselves and spiritual sustenance.

Marshall is well known for creating compelling characters, large themes focusing on how Barbadians and Barbadian Americans can survive in a materialistic, avaricious white world, and a strong sense of place for all her work. Rows of leaning Brooklyn brownstones, island shacks, palatial hotel rooms, and small, cramped apartments in Paris or Manhattan all reveal the inner lives—triumphs, dreams, disasters—of those that inhabit them. Houses are especially important in her fiction. The attached row houses of her first and most recent book reflect the strong family and community bonds of the Afro-Caribbean in America who lease and own them. Purchasing property becomes the obsession of many who are caught up in chasing white American dreams to their own detriment (loss of culture, loss of self, and loss of an integrated black identity).

Brown Girl, Brownstones (1959) is a coming-of-age novel that takes Selina Boyce from a ten year old, listening to the talk of the Barbadian American women sitting in her mother's kitchen (oral language raised to an art form when these women talk to release their immense creativity) and trying to save her father's dreams from her mother's wrathful destruction, to a young adult dancer encountering her first racist insults.

The Chosen Place, The Timeless People (1969) focuses on the vagaries of power when a large-scale American research team, headed by Saul Amron, comes to Bourneville, the poor, black section of a small Caribbean island. The islanders learn ultimately they must save one another and themselves with interracial friendships such as arise between the protagonist, Merle Kinbona, and Saul and with Merle's return to Africa to discover family ties and cultural understanding, in the wake of crisis and disorienting events.

Praisesong for the Widow (1983) focuses on Avey Williams, an affluent African American widow in her sixties, who jumps ship from her Caribbean cruise to become reconciled with her "opposite," Lebert Joseph, an old man she encounters in a rum shop on the beach in Granada (Marshall's literary incarnation of the Yoruba trickster Legba, mediator between gods and humans who serves as agent for Avey's rebirth). The gift she receives from him—psychic, spiritual, and political—and brings back to her native land and her community in White Plains is ancestral storytelling. She will share her cultural awakening with others to bring them to a better understanding of how to deal with the oppressive materialism that she sees shattering the spirit of African Americans.

Daughters (1991) is about Ersa Beatrice MacKenzie, who is the symbolic daughter of Celestine, the family housekeeper and her father's earliest lover, and of Astral Forde, the manager of her father's hotel and his long-term mistress, and the real daughter of Estelle, wife of Primus MacKenzie (also the prime minister), the prime mover encircled by female constellations. In *Daughters*, Ersa is searching for a way to live in America where those who categorize her as immigrant erase half her life.

In *The Fisher King* (2000), Marshall introduces an eight-year-old boy, grandson and namesake of Sonny, a famous **jazz** pianist who, years earlier, fled America for fame—and later neglect—in Paris. Sonny, with Barbadian grandfather, African American grandmother, Barbadian American mother, and African father, begins his own quest as the novel unfolds: trying to mend the fractures of **race** and class in this complicated family. Here, as in *Daughters* and *Praisesong for the Widow,* Marshall uses as her dominant narrative strategy a dense, interweaving of back stories to fill gaps of information and family and social history and to explore themes such as the conflict of the dreamer and doer in marital relationships (aggressive females like Selina Boyce's mother, Silla, and Saul Amron's wife, Harriet, who destroy their husbands' dreams in order to shape and design their lives, or males like Primus MacKenzie and Sonny Payne who keep a circle of females all moving to their designs); the loss of innocence, when female trust or male dreams are shattered or young adults encounter racist, classist, or sexist constrictions; the quest for self in a world that sees the black female in generic rather than individual, personal ways; and the need for knowledge of oneself and one's culture—for taking a spiritual journey into the past—in order to understand how one will face the future.

As an ethnic feminist, Marshall emphasizes women, especially mothers and foremothers of female children, telling stories for the transmission of culture, as Avey remembers hearing from her Great-Aunt Cuney in South Carolina as a child in *Praisesong for the Widow.* But men also tell stories in Marhsall's books. In *Daughters*, Primus MacKenzie tells his wife, Estelle, the story of Congo Jane and Cudjoe, co-conspirators in slave resistance and equals in strength and value to one another, a story that Estelle tells Ersa and Ersa tells her lover and friend Lowell, and one that Ersa adopts in her own quest for equity in male-female relations. (*See also* African American Novel, Caribbean [Anglophone] American Novel, Feminism)

Further Reading

Christian, Barbara. *Black Feminist Criticism: Perspectives on Black Women Writers.* New York: Pergamon, 1985.

DeLamotte, Eugenia. *Places of Silence, Journeys of Freedom: The Fiction of Paule Marshall.* Philadelphia: U of Pennsylvania P, 1998.

Pettis, Joyce. *Toward Wholeness in Paule Marshall's Fiction.* Charlottesville: UP of Virginia, 1995.

Skerrett, Joseph. "Paule Marshall and the Crisis of Middle Years: *The Chosen Place, the Timeless People." Callaloo* 6.2 (Spring–Summer 1983): 68–73.

Washington, Mary Helen. "Afterword." *Brown Girl, Brownstones* by Paule Marshall. New York: Feminist Press, 1981. 311–25.

Wilentz, Gay. *Binding Cultures; Black Women Writers in Africa and the Diaspora.* Bloomington: Indiana UP, 1992.

Nina Mikkelsen

MARTÍ, JOSÉ (1853–1895)   Cuban poet, essayist, journalist, and revolutionary. Martí's leadership in the struggle for Cuban independence from
Spain led to his fifteen-year exile in the United States, primarily in New York,
from 1880 until he returned clandestinely to Cuba, where he died in battle in
Dos Ríos on May 19, 1895. Even though Martí wrote as a writer in exile rather
than from the perspective of an ethnic American experience, he occupies an
important place in comparative nineteenth-century American letters.

Martí's essential exile writing—much of which he wrote or published (or
both) in New York—comprises lyric poetry, the children's magazine *La Edad
de Oro* (1889), and essays, chronicles, and other journalism. His poetry features both the traditional *arte menor* (octosyllabic or shorter) verse forms of
Ismaelillo (1882) and the *Versos sencillos* (1891) as well as the hermetic and
densely composed hendecasyllables of the *Versos libres* (1913) and the more
formally varied *Flores del destierro* (1933). Martí wrote prolifically on culture
and current events in the United States and on U.S.–Latin America relations
for Spanish- and English-speaking readers of North and South American
periodicals, most notably for *La Nación* (Buenos Aires), *El Partido Liberal*
(Mexico City), and, published in New York, *La América* and *Patria*. His collected chronicles and essays on the United States fill five volumes of his
Obras completas (27 vols.; Havana, 1963), most under the title *Escenas norteam-
ericanas* (North American scenes, 1881–1891). In exile in the United States,
Martí penned the centerpiece of his thought, "Nuestra América" (*El Partido
Liberal*, January 20, 1891), which delineates the unity and strength of Latin
America vis-à-vis the United States, as well as his acclaimed masterpieces on
the topics of Coney Island, the Statue of Liberty, the Brooklyn Bridge, Henry
Wadsworth Longfellow, and Walt Whitman, among many other widely
anthologized and lesser-known essays and chronicles. Martí's elegant aes-
thetic helped shape the renovation of prose genres in late-nineteenth-century
Spanish American *modernismo*.

José Martí is a pivotal figure in a long tradition of Cuban exile literature
in the United States that includes José María Heredia's canonical ode "Niá-
gara" (1824) and the anthology *El laúd del desterrado* (1858), the latter significantly reissued by **Arte Público Press** as part of the Recovering the U. S.
Hispanic Literary Heritage project (1995; ed. Matías Montes-Huidobro).
Two recent publications offer testament to Martí's enduring relevance for a
potential anglophone readership, both popular and academic, in the
twenty-first century: Esther Allen's authoritative collection and translation
of selected writings of Martí for the Penguin Classics series (2002) and
Anne Fountain's comprehensive scholarly study of Martí's reception of
U.S. literature and writers (2003).

Further Reading

Allen, Esther, ed. and trans. *José Martí: Selected Writings*. New York: Penguin,
    2002. ix–xxv.

Fountain, Anne. *José Martí and U.S. Writers*. Gainesville: UP of Florida, 2003.

Catharine E. Wall

MARTÍNEZ, DEMETRIA (1960–)   Multiethnic   American   poet, journalist, fiction writer, and human rights activist. Martínez's interest in and dedication to issues of human rights heavily influences her poetry, fiction, and journalism. From the beginnings of her publishing career, Martínez has explored the intersections of religion/spirituality, gender, and **ethnicity**.

Martínez claims Spanish, indigenous, Jewish, and Moorish cultural roots. Born in Albuquerque, New Mexico, in 1960, Martínez has inherited her commitment to social justice from her father, who was a bilingual education activist. Martínez attended the Woodrow Wilson School of Public Policy and International Affairs at Princeton University. While there, she participated in writing workshops and took classes in religious social ethics at the Theological Seminary at Princeton. In 1982 she graduated with a BA in public policy. Martínez returned to Albuquerque to join the Sagrada Art School, an organization that encourages artists and writers to dedicate themselves to their work full-time.

Martínez continued to hone her craft over the next six years, publishing the poetry collections *Border Wars* (1985) and *Turning* (1989). During this same period, she began working as a reporter for the *National Catholic Reporter* and then as a religion writer for the *Albuquerque Journal* in 1986. In 1988 Martínez was indicted on charges related to smuggling two refugee women into the United States because she had accompanied a Lutheran minister while carrying out his duties as a Sanctuary worker, helping refugees as they escaped the U.S.-sponsored wars in their Latin American homelands. Under such an indictment, she could have served twenty-five years in prison and been forced to pay $1.25 million in fines. The prosecuting attorney attempted to use Martínez's poem, "Nativity, for Two Salvadoran Woman," as evidence against her. Martínez used a First Amendment defense, arguing that as a journalist, she had the right to witness an event without being obligated to disclose such information to the government. The jury acquitted her of all charges.

Although Martínez did not abandon writing poetry, she shied away from it for the next few years. Her next production was *Mother Tongue* (1994), for which she was awarded the Western States Award for fiction. Martínez drew upon her experiences as a Sanctuary worker, telling the story of a nineteen-year-old woman Mary/María and the man she gives refuge to, José Luis. The novel explores the characters' need to translate and cross ethnic, cultural, and linguistic barriers to understand not only each other, but themselves as well.

Martínez has recently returned to poetry, publishing *Breathing Between the Lines* (1997) and *The Devil's Workshop* (2002), in which she continues her exploration of spirituality and gender. In her forthcoming book of essays, *Confessions of a Berlitz Tape Chicana* (2005), Martínez takes up an issue she explored in *Mother Tongue*, the role of language and translation for people who live biculturally.

Further Reading

Castillo, Debra, and María Socorro Tabuena Córdoba. *Border Women: Writing from La Frontera.* Minneapolis: U of Minnesota P, 2002.

Nancy K. Cardona

MARVIN X (1944–) African American poet, playwright, and activist. Marvin X, who was born Marvin Ellis Jackman, emerged as one of the principal members of the **Black Arts Movement** during the late 1960s. He still remains deeply committed to his radical politics, which informs his artistic vision. His first play, *Flowers for the Trashman,* premiered in 1965; a modified version of the play, with the title *Take Care of Business,* was produced in 1971. The entire action of the play takes place in a prison cell. The protagonist, Joe Simmons, is an African American college student who finds himself in jail after an altercation with white police officers. Joe's angry conversations with his fellow prisoners and his frequent direct comments to the audience allow Marvin X to articulate his own analysis of American racial politics. The most poignant part of the play, however, is Joe's relationship with his father, a trash collector. The father dies on his way to bail Joe out of jail, and Joe's final words are a tribute to his father as well as to other black fathers who, despite the emotional and economic damage racism inflicts on them, struggle to maintain their self-esteem and protect their children from harm. The play emphasizes the "need for loyalty, family solidarity, and action" (Idland 507).

Marvin's next play, *The Black Bird* (1969), reflects his newfound faith in the teachings of Elijah Muhammad and his formal induction into the Nation of Islam. The tone of the play is explicitly didactic. A young man, who is a recent convert to Islam, engages two very young black girls, ages six and seven, in conversation; his goal is to familiarize them with the fundamental teachings of the Nation of Islam so that they will not be deceived by the "white devils" when they grow older.

Marvin X's most recent play, *One Day in the Life* (2001), is an autobiographical work that examines his own personal battles with drug addiction and the enormous damage his addiction has caused him and those close to him. The play was produced by Recovery Theatre—a production company and performance space established by Marvin X. He currently devotes much of his time to address the issue of drug abuse in the inner-city neighborhoods. Theater, he believes, has transformative power and the capacity to heal.

Further Reading

Idland, Michael. "Marvin X." *African American Dramatists: An A-to-Z Guide.* Ed. Emmanuel S. Nelson. Westport, CT: Greenwood Press, 2004. 503–13.

Thomas, Lorenzo. "Marvin X." *Dictionary of Literary Biography.* Vol. 38. Ed. Thadious M. Davis and Trudier Harris. Detroit: Gale, 1985. 177–84.

Trevor A. Sydney

MASO, CAROLE (1956–) Italian American novelist and professor. Maso's prolific literary career began in New Jersey, where she was raised by middle-class parents who gave her hundreds of lessons in such activities as piano, painting, ballet, **jazz**, and fencing. Maso's father was a musician and her mother a nurse. Maso credits her mother as her first and only mentor, who insisted on hard work and loyalty to one's intellect. While completing her BA in English at Vassar in 1977, Maso wrote about fifty pages of prose poems as part of a creative independent study. In order to focus solely on her writing, Maso worked as a waitress, a fencing instructor, and an artist's model, alternating between full-time writing and menial jobs. Maso's first novel, *Ghost Dance* (1986), which she considers her apprenticeship, took seven or eight years to complete. With Maso refusing to compromise her experimental style for marketplace considerations, the novel went unagented for months until the now defunct North Point Press decided to publish it. Since *Ghost Dance* was completed, Maso has been the recipient of many writing awards, including the W. K. Rose fellowship for Vassar alumnae artists (1985) and the Los Angeles-based Lannan Literary fellowship for fiction (1993), which generously honors writers of high literary merit and future potential. Since the early 1990s, Maso has worked as a creative writer, beginning at Illinois State University as a writer-in-residence. Thereafter, Maso was a writer-in-residence at George Washington University (1991–92) and an associate professor at Columbia University (1993). In 1995 Maso became a professor and director of the creative writing program at Brown University.

For Maso, writing is about the search for a legitimate language. *Ghost Dance*, her first novel, explores fundamental questions of **identity**, such as how does one construct a self. Exploring the dispersal and disintegration of a family, Maso introduces Vanessa Turin, first-person narrator and child of German and Armenian ancestry on her mother's side and Italian ancestry on her father's side. In order to answer the question of her family's disappearance, Vanessa heeds and invents the imperative she hears throughout the novel: "Tell me a story." Organized into five sections, the novel explores Vanessa's losses through a multidimensional narrative that adheres to a multileveled logic. Vanessa's status as a third-generation ethnic American makes her a primary candidate for reinventing cultural identities. Her mother, a famous poet and a manic-depressive, dies tragically in an automobile accident, and her father, who has been silenced by his parents' loss of Italian **ethnicity**, leaves the family after his wife's death. A novel of self-awakening and retrieval of cultural consciousness, *Ghost Dance* examines a young woman's struggle to articulate her own identity amid the chaos that has become her family.

The Art Lover (1990), Maso's second novel, is also nontraditional in its narrative technique. Containing three concurrent fictional narratives and a section of autobiographical nonfiction dedicated to Maso's friend Gary, who died of AIDS, the novel's postmodern strategies collapse hard-and-fast distinctions between fiction and nonfiction and reconstruct family narratives that are nontraditional in themselves, delegitimating any one quintessential family story. Revealing influences other than fictive, Maso further dismantles traditional narrative through the use of graphics such as photographs of art, poems, and newspaper clippings scattered generously throughout the narrative. The suffering son, the grieving mother, and the artist as recreator of family history embodied in the Caroline/Carole narrators, haunt the pages of Maso's second novel.

Compared by critics to James Joyce's *Ulysses, Ava* (1993), Maso's third novel, recalls the life of Jewish American Ava Klein on the last day of her life as she dies prematurely from blood cancer. Examining how silence is as much a presence in the novel as any character, Maso's experimental form juxtaposes Ava's thoughts with intervals of silence and white spaces in between the written lines. Recalling her lovers, marriages, and many travels, Ava's fragmentary utterances reveal her to be equally in love with those literary artists that influence her impressionistic memories. According to Maso, she could never have arrived at *Ava* creatively without having first written her fourth published novel, *The American Woman in the Chinese Hat* (1994). Maso's aim in this novel was to dramatize the breakdown of language altogether, with Catherine, the young American writer abroad on a grant, who descends into madness as the narrative advances. Employing alternating first- and third-person points of view, Maso reflects Catherine's split identity. In contrast to Ava's repetitive reflections, Catherine's repetitions reflect a shattering of linguistic possibilities; as Catherine breaks down, so does her language, her fluency.

Understanding that writing for her is a significant human adventure, Maso's fifth book, *Aureole* (1996) is part novel, part poetic diary, with its focus on erotic entanglements between women. Comprised of interpenetrating vignettes, Maso's prose emerges out of her own desire to simulate the language of intimacy in its most erotic and reckless moments. Never one to rest from linguistic risk, Maso's sixth novel, *Defiance* (1998), appears to be more recognizably linear, but her protagonist, Bernadette O'Brien, former Harvard physics professor, is awaiting execution on death row in a Georgia prison for murdering—postcoital—two male students. A child prodigy of a working class Irish American family, Bernadette's ethnic and social status contributes to her refusal to be a victim and to the ruthless revenge she enacts on privileged men.

In her book of nonfiction, *Break Every Rule: Essays on Language, Longing, & Moments of Desire* (2000), Maso reiterates many of her literary mantras, reinforcing her devotion to writing lyrical fiction. Replacing strict definitions of character and plot with recurring patterns and imagery, Maso's *oeuvres* constitute a search to find the right language and form to tell the story of desire. Refusing to play it safe, Maso continues to adhere to her own aesthetic needs, not the prescriptions of mainstream publishers. Writing every day to be well and to revel in the nuances of language, Maso's journal of pregnancy and birth, *The Room Lit by Roses* (2000) chronicles in a ruminative and poetic way Maso's journey toward motherhood. Although never focusing solely on ethnicity as a source of identity, Maso nonetheless uses ethnic subjects within a larger canvas as she explores the multifaceted nature of American selves. (*See also* Italian American Novel)

Further Reading

Bona, Mary Jo. "Rooted to Family: Italian American Women's Radical Novels." *The Lost World of Italian American Radicalism: Politics, Labor, and Culture.* Ed. Philip V. Cannistraro and Gerald Meyer. Westport, CT: Praeger, 2003. 287–99.

"Carole Maso." *Contemporary Authors.* Gale Literary Databases. Entry Updated, 2001.

Innes, Charlotte. "Dancing on a Literary Edge." *Los Angeles Times* (June 23, 1994): E1+.

Maso, Carole. *Break Every Rule: Essays on Language, Longing, & Moments of Desire.* Washington, DC: Counterpoint, 2000.

———. "Interview by Joyce Hackett." *Poets and Writers* 24.3 (1996): 64–73.

———. "Interview by Nicole Cooley." *American Poetry Review* 24.2 (1995): 32–35.

———. "Interview with Steven Moore." *Review of Contemporary Fiction* 14.2 (1994): 186–91.

Mary Jo Bona

MATHEWS, JOHN JOSEPH (1894–1979)   Osage novelist, biographer, and historian. John Joseph Mathews published most of his works prior to the era known as the "Native American Renaissance" (a period beginning in the 1960s and including writers such as **N. Scott Momaday** and **Leslie Marmon Silko**) and produced both fiction and nonfiction texts that commented on the influence white people had on Native American cultures. His first book, *Wah'kon-tah: The Osage and the White Man's Road* (1932), originated from the personal documents of the first federal agent assigned to the Osages, Major Laban J. Miles. It recounts and explores the changes on the Osage reservation during Laban's residency and was the first book by a Native American author to be presented by the Book-of-the-Month club.

Wah'kon-tah was soon followed by Mathews's first and only novel, *Sundown* (1934). The protagonist, Chal Windzer, whose father names him Challenge because he will challenge the white man, is a mixed-blood young man who struggles to distinguish where his **identity** lies between the white and Osage worlds. Believing that the white world is more sophisticated and civilized, Chal disdains his own Osage culture and is embarrassed by the "backwards" ways of his friends while away at college. Chal makes several attempts to find a path of his own, but repeatedly fails at them and at his "destiny." Rather than challenging the white world, Chal would rather assimilate with it at the cost of his own culture. Louis Owens suggests that Mathews, like his contemporary, **D'Arcy McNickle** (whose novel *The Surrounded* also focuses on a young man who is trapped between white and native cultures), analyzes in *Sundown* the negative impact white culture had, and will have, on native peoples.

Mathews's autobiography, *Talking to the Moon* (1945), is often compared to Thoreau's *Walden* because of its beautiful language. Robert Allen Warrior points out that it is a sensitive description of the natural world of the Osage reservation, highlighting how changes to the land (brought about by white "civilization") will affect people.

Life and Death of an Oilman: The Career of E. W. Marland (1951) is a discerning biography of a slightly eccentric yet compassionate oil man who would eventually become governor of Oklahoma. Mathews's last book, *The Osages: Children of the Middle Waters* (1961), is a history of his people from their creation through the Indian wars and to Mathews's time.

Mathews, one-eighth Osage (his great-grandfather married a full-blood Osage woman named A-Ci'n-Ge), was surrounded by and participated in Osage language and culture. He attended the University of Oklahoma, receiving a BA in 1920, and Oxford University, receiving a BA in 1923. He was a pilot during World War I, cofounded the Osage Tribal Museum in 1938, and was a member of the Osage tribal council from 1934 to 1942. (*See also* Native American Autobiography, Native American Novel)

Further Reading

Owens, Louis. *Other Destinies: Understanding the American Indian Novel.* Norman: U of Oklahoma P, 1994.

Warrior, Robert Allen. *Tribal Secrets: Recovering American Indian Intellectual Traditions.* Minneapolis: U of Minnesota P, 1995.

Carrie L. Sheffield

MAZZA, CRIS (1956–)   Italian American writer, editor, and teacher, currently a professor in the Program for Writers at the University of Illinois at Chicago. A prolific writer of fiction and nonfiction, Mazza published her first collection of stories, *Animal Acts,* in 1992. She is also the coeditor of two volumes of *Chick Lit* (1995 and 1996), anthologies of women's literature. Mazza's voice speaks for many silenced and disenfranchised Americans, many of them women. She is an image-maker, leaving readers to draw their own conclusions about American culture and the ravages that gnaw on the fibers of our society.

For example, in *Is It Sexual Harassment Yet?* (1998), Mazza's vignettes present glimpses into the lives of men and women with mutual desires living what seem to be ordinary lives. However, many of the women are subtly or overtly denigrated by inappropriate behavior in ways that could be and often is mistaken for harmless behavior, suggesting that we should more closely examine and actively question whether or not the ordinary is acceptable. What is often ignored and attributed to typical male or female behavior may actually be subtle cases of harassment. These insidious behaviors, perpetrated by the uninformed, the apathetic, and the psychotic, cross boundaries that compromise the comfort and dignity of the victims, devaluing, oppressing, and silencing them.

In a collection of personal essays, *Indigenous: Growing Up in California* (2003), Mazza dispels the California stereotypes of cheerful, carefree blondes on beaches and freeways by presenting the California that framed her upbringing. She remembers an untamed, less inhabited, more rural California. Her rustic California held the excitement and promise of survival, particularly for those resourceful people who could learn to live along with the rhythms of nature, hunting and foraging, growing and playing. Her family is close-knit and hardworking. Her mother was uncommonly free-thinking while supportive, caring, and loving; her father was a master at working the land.

Homeland (2004) is a fictionalized account of Mazza's profound veneration for the California not dominated by cars, roads, and glitz. She demythologizes the stereotypical New Age Californian by presenting the story of the invisible untouchables: homeless migrants, infirmed elderly, and unconventional people. Ronnie, the protagonist, recounts her history with joyless nostalgia as she cares for her father, Enzo, who has recently suffered two strokes. Together but homeless, they embark on a journey to uncover old family secrets and begin healing their wounded psyches. Enzo's convoluted speech and loss of strength make this journey all the more difficult. But Ronnie is undaunted by the challenge. By the end, they both face and exorcise the demons that repress their emotions and render them virtually incapacitated, thus restoring their dignity.

Mazza is not a writer to be overlooked. Her subject matter is a bold reminder to everyone to look in the quietest corners of our environments and notice what ails the often unnoticed.

Further Reading

Caughie, Pamela L. "Introduction." *Is It Sexual Harassment Yet?* Cris Mazza. Normal, IL: Fiction Collective Two, 1998. iv–xx.

Suzanne Hotte Massa

McBRIDE, JAMES (1957–) Autobiographer, novelist, journalist, musician, and composer. Born in 1957 to a white Jewish mother and an African American father, James McBride grew up in Brooklyn's Red Hook housing projects. Having never known his biological father, Andrew Dennis McBride, who died before James was born, McBride developed a close bond with his mother. Following the death of her first husband, Ruth McBride married another African American man, Hunter Jordan, who died when James was a teenager. Frustrated by his mother's struggle to raise twelve children on her own, the rebellious McBride turned to alcohol and drugs as a means of escape. Fortunately, his strong upbringing and fear of incarceration encouraged McBride to alter his reckless lifestyle. At seventeen, he began attending an all-black public school, which cultivated his interests in writing and music. Upon graduation, McBride enrolled in Oberlin College in Ohio, where he received a bachelor of arts degree. After college, he continued his pursuit of higher education and earned a master's degree in journalism from Columbia University.

The recipient of several literary and music awards, McBride oscillates between careers as a writer and a musician. In addition to having worked as a journalist for the *Boston Globe, People Magazine,* and the *Washington Post,* McBride has written for *Essence, Rolling Stone, The Philadelphia Inquirer,* and the *New York Times.* He has also composed music and lyrics for such renowned artists as Anita Baker and Grover Washington Jr. In 1996, McBride published his acclaimed memoir, *The Color of Water: A Black Man's Tribute to His White Mother,* which was awarded the Anisfield-Wolf Book Award for literary excellence. An amalgam of autobiography and biography, *The Color of Water* relates McBride's search for self while attempting to unlock the mystery of his mother's **identity.** The lone white face in a sea of black, Ruth McBride Jordan was respected and admired by her neighbors as a mother who instilled pride and ambition in her children. Her refusal to pigeonhole herself according to **race,** while at times baffling to her young son, offers an intriguing commentary on American society's color consciousness. Following the success of *The Color of Water,* McBride was chosen to coauthor *The Autobiography of Quincy Jones,* which was released in the fall of 2001. Published the following year, McBride's first fictional work, *Miracle at St. Anna,* is an historically based novel that recounts the experiences of four African American soldiers, a band of partisans, and an orphan boy trapped in the Italian foothills during World War II. A tale of hope and courage, *Miracle at St. Anna* speaks to the resiliency of the human spirit and the commonality of the human experience. (*See also* African American Autobiography)

Further Reading

Harper, Phillip Brian. "Passing for What? Racial Masquerade and the Demands of Upward Mobility." *Callaloo: A Journal of African American and African Arts and Letters* 21.2 (Spring 1998): 381–97.

Carol Goodman

McCALL, NATHAN (1954–) African American autobiographer and essayist. Nathan McCall is a respected journalist and oft-requested lecturer, although he is perhaps best known for his autobiography *Makes Me Wanna Holler: A Young Black Man in America* (1994) which follows in the tradition of such African American autobiographical narratives as **Richard Wright's** *Black Boy* (1945), **Claude Brown's** *Manchild in the Promised Land* (1965), and *The Autobiography of Malcolm X* (1965). In *Makes Me Wanna Holler,* McCall chronicles his privileged upbringing in the suburban community of Portsmouth, Virginia, and his growing fascination with the goings-on in the inner city during the tumultuous **Civil Rights Movement** in the 1960s. McCall finds himself at a psychological as well as physical distance from the black freedom struggle as it is occurring simply because he does not live in close proximity to large groups of white individuals. Despite this lack of encounter, the teenage McCall remains aware of the **racism** that marks him and tries to develop an **identity** predicated on the posing and posturing of the inner city "thugs" he envies in contrast to the weaker, more scholarly students he is surrounded by in his suburban enclave. He opts to adopt a "tough guy" mentality, which includes joining a local street gang, robbing convenience stores for lunch because he is too lazy to return home for the meal and, most notably, carrying a gun by the age of fifteen. At twenty years old, McCall is incarcerated for a failed armed robbery at a McDonald's restaurant. During his three-year prison stretch, McCall becomes enraptured by Islamic principles (similarly, one of the key conversion narratives found in *The Autobiography of Malcolm X*). After his parole, McCall studies journalism at Norfolk State University and makes his way to the news desks of some of the country's most prominent newspapers, including the Atlanta *Journal-Constitution* and the *Washington Post*. Critics and scholars alike have hailed *Makes Me Wanna Holler* for its unflinching portrayal of an African American man who paid penance for his transgressions and now cautions other African American males to do likewise. For example, **Henry Louis Gates Jr.**, writing in *The New Yorker*, called the text "a stirring tale of transformation." Four years after the release of *Makes Me Wanna Holler*, McCall published another text, a collection of essays titled *What's Going On?* (1998). Although not as much of a critical or commercial success as its predecessor, the second text continues McCall's aim of pointing out the disparities in racial and ethnic politics in U.S. culture. In addition to that focus, *What's Going On?* extends *Makes Me Wanna Holler*'s tradition of exploring intersections in African American communities, namely in its explication of gender dynamics in these communities (e.g., when McCall discusses his feelings about his actions of raping several women during his teenage, pre-incarceration years). Notably, both of the titles of McCall's texts are culled from Marvin Gaye's landmark album *What's Going On?* (1971), which remarked on racial and ethnic inequalities in cultural praxis.

Further Reading

Jardine, Gail. "To Be Black, Male, and Conscious: Race, Rage, and Manhood in America." *American Quarterly* 48 (June 1996): 385–93.

Pond, Susan Evans. "Nathan J. McCall." *African American Autobiographers: A Sourcebook*. Ed. Emmanuel S. Nelson. Westport, CT: Greenwood Press, 2002. 264–69.

Chris Bell

McCARTHY, MARY (1912–1989)   Irish American novelist, essayist, and autobiographer. Mary McCarthy's scrupulous interest in facts and concern for motives have made her most recognized for autobiography and for fiction in which the ambivalent protagonist serves as a mirror image of herself. The McCarthy family arrived in the United States some generations before Mary's birth; family tradition held that their immigration was due not to the potato famine, but to religious concerns. Although Mary's father married a Protestant, the children received a strongly Catholic upbringing that is apparent in the constant confessions in McCarthy's writing.

After writing book reviews for *The Nation* and *The New Republic* and a theater column at *Partisan Review* in the 1930s, McCarthy turned her attention to

Mary McCarthy. *Courtesy of the Library of Congress.*

fiction at the encouragement of her second husband, the critic Edmund Wilson. The result was *The Company She Keeps* (1942), a collection of short stories tied together through their heroine, Margaret Sargent, who more than occasionally resembled McCarthy herself. These early stories already bear her characteristic style and moral perspective; the endlessly self-critical narration, in which Margaret questions and re-questions her own motives, presents a not-quite-likeable protagonist whose pride sets her up for falls. The most famous story from the collection, "The Man in the Brooks Brothers Shirt," finds the heroine in a one-night stand aboard a railroad car, coping with the shame of both the affair with an unsophisticated midwesterner and the safety pin on her underwear.

If *The Company She Keeps* was McCarthy's great critical success, then *The Group* (1963) was her great popular success. Following eight roommates of the Vassar class of 1933 from their graduation through marriage, childbirth, and finally the death of one of their number, *The Group* continued McCarthy's racy reputation with a scene in which an unmarried character buys a diaphragm. In a narrative voice that blends a third-person perspective with the voices of the Group, the novel explores topics ranging from the etiquette of contraception to the marvels of canned goods. Like Betty Friedan's feminist text *The Feminine Mystique* published the same year, *The Group* shows women with education, aspirations, and faith in modernity attempting to reconcile their college education with traditional women's roles. The book, which sensitively portrays the everyday lives of young women in the 1930s, was too sensitive for some real-life Vassar alumnae and excited some controversy for its resemblances to reality.

McCarthy's self-interrogation was a natural fit with autobiography. She became known for personal essays and several volumes of autobiography, most notably *Memories of a Catholic Girlhood* (1957). A collection of previously published short memoirs, the work is held together by interludes in which McCarthy questions the accuracy of her own memory and the relative truth and falsity of each recollection. Indeed, she writes in the introduction that readers were often apt to question the episodes, because even when they were accurate, they had a fairytale quality. McCarthy and her three younger brothers were orphaned during the influenza epidemic of 1918 and taken in by Dickensian relations who believed in root vegetables and regular beatings. One chapter, "A Tin Butterfly," describes the punishment a ten-year-old Mary received when accused of stealing the prize from her brother's Cracker Jacks. At the end of the story, it is revealed that Uncle Meyers stole the tin butterfly himself, though McCarthy then questions whether she might have unconsciously invented that twist for dramatic effect. Though her father's family practiced what she describes as a "blood-curdling" Catholicism, she writes that the church provided an aesthetic escape from her drab surroundings and continued to serve her in various ways even after she "lost her faith," initially as a deliberate move to gain attention in her Catholic school and then, to her surprise, in earnest. Eventually, she was rescued by her mother's family, and went to live with them in Seattle. *Memories of a Catholic Girlhood* concludes with a surprising recollection of her Jewish grandmother, her mother's mother. In later memoirs she recalls hiding her Jewish heritage deliberately, as there was stigma enough in being Irish Catholic.

Although McCarthy continued to write until her death in 1989, she was by then most notorious for her feud with playwright **Lillian Hellman**, whom she had accused of lying. McCarthy's penchant for criticism—of self and others—endured throughout her life. (*See also* Irish American Autobiogaphy, Irish American Novel)

Further Reading

Kiernan, Frances. *Seeing Mary Plain: A Life of Mary McCarthy.* New York: W. W. Norton, 2000.

Stwertka, Eve, and Margo Viscusi, eds. *Twenty-Four Ways of Looking at Mary McCarthy.* Westport, CT: Greenwood Press, 1996.

Jaime Cleland

McCLUSKEY, JOHN A., JR. (1944–) African American novelist, professor, and editor. McCluskey was born in Middletown, Ohio, in 1944; his father was a truck driver, his mother a domestic. A brilliant student and athlete, McCluskey won a scholarship to attend Harvard University, where he received his BA in 1966. His senior thesis was a sociological examination of the novels of **James Baldwin**, **Ralph Ellison**, **Chester Himes**, and **Richard Wright**. In 1972 he earned his MA at Stanford University.

The January 1973 issue of *Black World* carried McCluskey's first published short story titled "Nairobi Nights." The story is an imaginative exploration of what the judicial system would be like in a futuristic, thoroughly self-contained African American community. In 1972 McCluskey published his first novel *Look What They Done to My Song.* A picaresque narrative that focuses on the formative life experiences of Mack, a young black musician, it maps an artist's incremental discovery of the larger musical tradition of which he is a part. McCluskey sees the novel as his own "comment on the **Civil Rights Movement**, the **Black Arts Movement**, and the Black Power Movement of the late 1960's" (Rowell 915). Deeply influenced by the language of the **blues** and the improvisory techniques of **jazz**, McCluskey's debut novel reveals his efforts "to come up with a language that would resonate with the energy" (Rowell 915) of the 1960s.

McCluskey's second novel, *Mr. America's Last Season Blues* (1983), focuses on the difficulties of Roscoe Americus Jr., a middle-aged athlete. He faces a failed marriage; his attempts to resuscitate his athletic career are unsuccessful. His largest battle, however, is to secure the release of Stone—the son of Americus's girlfriend—who has been falsely accused of murdering a young white man. Here too Americus fails: An indifferent African American community and a racist all-white jury undermine his battle. The novel poignantly depicts a man's heroic struggle in the face of personal and professional defeats.

An editor of several scholarly works, McCluskey currently directs the Department of Afro-American Studies at Indiana University.

Further Reading

Rowell, Charles. "An Interview with John A. McCluskey, Jr." *Callaloo* 19.4 (1996): 911–28.

Trevor A. Sydney

McCUNN, RUTHANNE LUM (1946–)   Eurasian American writer of historical Chinese American fiction and pictorials for adults and children. Ruthanne Lum McCunn brings nineteenth-century Chinese and Chinese American history to life both in her pictorials, *An Illustrated History of the Chinese in America* (1979) and *Chinese American Portraits* (1996), as well as in her fictionalized accounts of historical persons, most notably *Thousand Pieces of Gold* (1989), *Sole Survivor* (1999), *Wooden Fish Songs* (2000), and *The Moon Pearl* (2000). Through historical research, personal interviews, and creative writing, McCunn gives voice to and celebrates the lives of Chinese persons who exemplified a balance of individual courage as well as respect for kinship.

Thousand Pieces of Gold is representative of McCunn's interest in the lives of nineteenth-century Chinese, both those in China and the immigrants in America. In this novel she focuses on those most disadvantaged and abused, young prostitute slaves. The creative biography is based on the life of Lalu Nathoy, whose impoverished father was forced to sell her to bandits during the famine of 1871 in China. Brutally terrorized by the bandits, Nathoy then suffered the humiliation of being auctioned naked at a brothel while potential buyers regarded her only as sexual property. Her buyer was a Chinese merchant who shipped many young women into forced prostitution in the United States. Traders in sexual slavery brought Nathoy to a new owner, a Chinese saloonkeeper in a mining town in Idaho who renamed her as Polly. As a lone young woman among over a thousand men in a frontier town, she survived the dehumanizing violence and degradation with her combination of intelligence and determination.

Eventually a white friend and lover, Charlie, won her in a poker game and freed her. Yet Charlie is not the hero of this creative biography, even though he plays a critical role in freeing Bemis from sexual slavery and ultimately in helping her to buy her own piece of property and home, since persons of Asian descent were not permitted to own land. Bemis garners the reader's admiration as a girl who grew into womanhood and selfhood while facing brutal conditions, including sexual slavery, anti-Chinese violence, and the harsh life of a frontier town.

McCunn's selection of characters and decision to bring them to contemporary attention always deserves appreciation. Her vivid images and language ably convey the challenges that Chinese and Chinese Americans courageously faced in the nineteenth century. In particular, the female protagonists demonstrate great integrity and strength in confronting stereotypes of Asian women as dragon ladies, prostitutes, and dolls. Thousands of early Chinese immigrants suffered abusive treatment, and in her biographies and pictorials, McCunn calls readers to remember, honor, and celebrate the lives of these Chinese American heroes. (*See also* Chinese American Novel)

Further Reading

Cheung, King-kok. "Self-fulfilling Visions in *The Woman Warrior* and *Thousand Pieces of Gold*." *Biography* 13.2 (1990): 145–53.

Terry, Patricia. "A Chinese Woman in the West: *Thousand Pieces of Gold and the Revision of the Heroic Frontier*." *Literature/Film Quarterly* 22.4 (1994): 222–26.

Karen Li Miller

McDERMOTT, ALICE (1953–)   Irish American novelist. Alice McDermott's books chronicle the lives of ordinary, middle-class Irish Catholic New Yorkers in the 1950s and 1960s. Often wistful and melancholy in tone, her novels are admired as meticulously crafted works of realism that evoke the texture and feel of suburban Long Island life and suggest a rich emotional resonance to be found in commonplace events and characters.

McDermott, like many of her characters, grew up in an Irish Catholic family on Long Island. As a girl, she attended Catholic elementary and high schools, enrolling at the State University of New York at Oswego for college in 1971. Her first novel, *A Bigamist's Daughter* (1982), was published after McDermott completed her MA in fiction writing at the University of New Hampshire. It tells the story of Elizabeth Connelly, a young editor at a Vanity Publishing House in New York City whose main job is to soothe the fragile egos of the company's eccentric authors. When Elizabeth becomes romantically involved with Tupper Daniels, a new author writing a novel about a bigamist in a small southern town, she begins to confront her own past, including her suspicions

Alice McDermott. *AP/Wide World Photos.*

about her often absent father's secret life. Despite some critics' objections that the main characters, especially Tupper, seem somewhat implausible, the novel received mostly good reviews; critics praised its accomplished prose and its refusal to cater to romantic illusion.

Written while she was teaching at the University of California at Davis, McDermott's second novel, *That Night* (1987), was a finalist for the National Book Award, the Pulitzer Prize, and the PEN/Faulkner Award. The night of the title refers to a violent encounter between a group of suburban Long Island fathers in the early 1960s and a teenage gang, led by Rick, who has come to reclaim his fifteen-year-old girlfriend Sheryl from her protective family. Narrated by a neighbor of Sheryl's, now grown, but only ten at the time, the novel spirals outward from this central incident, showing how romantic illusions are shattered. The fierce, pure love of adolescence must give way to adult practicality, and this is a loss the novel laments.

At Weddings and Wakes (1991), which unfolds the lives of three generations of an Irish Catholic family in Brooklyn, New York, was also a finalist for the Pulitzer Prize in fiction. The novel is told from the perspective of the youngest members of the Towne family, who are hauled into the city twice weekly to visit their maternal relatives: Momma, the family matriarch, and their mother's three unmarried sisters. The novel probes both the joy and bitterness of family relationships, the strong ties that hold family members together as well as the ways that families constrict their members, obligating them and narrowing their lives.

While well respected in the literary and academic community, it wasn't until the publication of *Charming Billy* (1998) that McDermott won popular acclaim and a wider readership. *Charming Billy*, winner of the 1998 National Book Award, tells the story of amiable alcoholic Billy Lynch. The books opens at Billy's funeral lunch, and his story is told mostly in flashbacks, beginning in 1945 after Billy has returned to Long Island from service in World War II. When Billy is betrayed by Eva, an Irish girl with whom he has fallen in love, Billy's cousin Dennis lets him believe that Eva has died. Dennis's lie shapes Billy into a tragic and singular figure in the community, someone his relatives and friends invest with their own romantic longings, and against whom they measure their own mundane lives. The novel, like much of McDermott's work, explores human frailty— our tendency to lie to ourselves and to each other—but also ways that this frailty can lead to great acts of kindness and love.

A coming-of-age story ripe with the wistful nostalgia of her earlier works, McDermott's fifth novel, *Child of My Heart* (2002), recounts one summer in the life of fifteen-year-old Theresa, who spends her summer taking care of neglected animals and lonely children, spinning fantasies to entertain them and trying to keep out impending disaster. In *Child of My Heart,* as in all of her quiet, yet emotionally evocative novels, McDermott explores the deep spiritual truths that underlie human nature: the way that love mingles with sorrow, the fragility of human relationships, and the human tendency to weave deceptions to make the pain of loss easier to bear. (*See also* Irish American Novel)

Further Reading

Rothstein, Mervyn. "The Storyteller Is Part of the Tale." *New York Times* (May 9, 1987): sec. 1, 13.

Susan Farrell

McDONALD, JANET (1953–) African American autobiographer and novelist. Janet McDonald's first extended contribution to ethnic American literature came with her debut memoir *Project Girl* in 1999, a text that details her arduous journey from a New York housing project, where she grew up, to Paris, where she now works as a corporate lawyer and writer. Although she is likely best known for this compelling memoir, McDonald has also written several novels for young adults, many of which both complicate and further elaborate on her efforts to negotiate her neighborhood, upbringing, successes, and many rebounds with her own sense of self.

McDonald was raised in a traditional nuclear family and was the fourth of her parents' seven children. Her father was a postal worker, whom she revered for his self-learned knowledge and many diverse talents. Her mother stayed at home with Janet and her six siblings and managed most of the household tasks. McDonald writes in her memoir of quickly learning that books could remove her from conditions that were often cramped and filled with noise. She did very well in school, even skipping a grade, and went on to graduate from Vassar College, Columbia University Graduate School of Journalism, and New York University School of Law. None of these achievements were met, however, without increasing bouts with trauma and anxiety that she frequently tried to counteract by writing journals, diary entries, and letters.

Project Girl details the slow transformation that began sweeping over her neighborhood when her community became what she calls the "last stop for the excluded poor." Yet she is also careful to deconstruct the notion that living in the projects equates to being the projects, even as she writes directly and openly about the difficulties that she, her friends, and her siblings faced when trying to thrive in environments that sometimes disavowed one's self-determination and sense of belonging. Although McDonald is now far removed geographically from the projects that she called home, she still identifies with that area of Brooklyn and the struggles and joys that marked her adolescence and young adulthood. Her texts for young adult readers often draw from her experiences growing up and feature protagonists who too must grapple with their sense of worth and power to act as potential change agents in their own lives when little social support is offered.

McDonald's first book of adolescent fiction, *Spellbound,* was published in 2001 and was named an American Library Association best book for young adults. It is the first in a trilogy of novels focusing on African American female teenagers, and was followed by *Chill Winds* in 2002, *Twists and Turns* in 2003, and *Brother Hood* in 2004. In these texts readers find characters who are often trying to bridge different worlds, locate stable identities, and survive amid circumstances and environments that alternate between being harsh and affirming—much, one might say, as Janet McDonald herself did. (*See also* African American Autobiography)

Further Reading

Kennedy, Thomas E. "Up from Brooklyn: An Interview with Janet McDonald." *Literary Review* 44.4 (Summer 2001): 704–20.

McDonald, Janet. "Double Life." *Literary Review* 45.4 (Summer 2002): 679–85.

Amanda J. Davis

McELROY, COLLEEN (1935–)   African American poet, short story writer, speech therapist, educator, and playwright. McElroy studied speech and language and received her PhD from the University of Washington in ethnolinguistic patterns of dialect differences and oral traditions. Her fascination with words and the rhythms of language led her to begin writing poetry in her mid-thirties. McElroy is primarily known for her poetry, but she has also published two collections of short stories, two poetic memoirs, a choreopoem coauthored with Ishmael Reed, and a play about Harriet Tubman.

McElroy was encouraged to write poetry by authors like Richard Hugo and **Denise Levertov**, and she found role models in other black poets including **Langston Hughes** and **Gwendolyn Brooks**. Her first collection of poems, *The Mules Done Long Since Gone* (1973), reflects her interest in the countryside of the Pacific Northwest, and her second collection, *Winters Without Snow* (1979), deals with her divorce from poet David McElroy. McElroy's best-known collections of poetry are *Queen of the Ebony Islands* (1984) and *What Madness Brought Me Here: New and Selected Poems, 1968– 1988* (1990). Though her poems are wide-ranging in subject matter, most reflect her talent as a storyteller and her love for travel. McElroy approaches her poetry like music and claims that she is often influenced by her surroundings as well as her dreams. She also sees **race** as an essential component to all of her writings, though she often treats the subtlety of **racism** rather than focusing on its overt forms.

In her short stories, McElroy strives for a sense of continuity, while creating characters that work against received stereotypes about African Americans. For example, in stories like "Imogene," McElroy explores the individual lives of her black characters, rather than having characters that represent a particular quality or statement about blackness. Additionally, McElroy includes sensuality and humor in her fiction, and stories like "More Than a Notion" and "A House Full of Maude" reflect her interest in the mutability of language.

Queen of the Ebony Isles was picked for the Wesleyan University Press Poetry Series and won the American Book Award in 1985. McElroy also served as editor for *Dark Waters* magazine, and her numerous awards, including a Rockefeller Fellowship, a Fulbright Creative Writing Fellowship, and two National Endowment for the Arts Fellowships, attest to her skills as an author. She was also the first African American woman to receive a promotion to full professor at the University of Washington. Though not as widely known as other African American poets, McElroy has made a significant contribution to American literature.

Further Reading

Broughton, Irv, ed. *The Writer's Mind: Interviews with American Authors.* Vol. 3.
Fayetteville: U of Arkansas P, 1989.

April Conley Kilinski

McGRATH, THOMAS (1916–1990) Irish American poet and novelist. Thomas McGrath turned away from his Irish Catholic ethnic heritage early in life and became a left-wing Communist radical whose nontraditional politics can be found on the surface and at the core of his writing and **identity**. His many works include the novels *The Gates of Ivory, The Gates of Horn* (1957) and *This Coffin Has No Handles* (1988) and the poetry collections *To Walk a Crooked Mile* (1947), *Longshot O'Leary's Garland of Practical Poesie* (1949), *The Movie at the End of the World: Collected Poems* (1973), *Echoes Inside the Labyrinth* (1983), and *Selected Poems: 1938–1988* (1988). His most ambitious work, the poem *Letter to an Imaginary Friend* (1962), evolved over the years. In 1970, *Part II* appeared coupled with the original. Together in 1985, *Part III* and *Part IV* were released. Copper Canyon Press published the collected *Letter to an Imaginary Friend* (1997) posthumously.

Thomas McGrath came from a North Dakota family of Irish Catholic immigrant farmers. They suffered greatly during the Great Depression of the 1930s and were forced to foreclose on their farm. McGrath's politics were founded during this time from those of the laboring farming community striving to stick together against the banks and capitalists. The future writer also turned against Catholicism and organized religion. Ironically,

McGrath served in the U.S. Army Air Forces during World War II. After the war, as the United States became more conservative as a country, McGrath refused to let go of his politically liberal, Communist beliefs that were becoming increasingly unpopular and suspicious. In 1953 McGrath was called before the House Un-American Activities Committee. He refused to cooperate with the committee. Afterwards, McGrath found himself without a job.

This life is the inspirational foundation for McGrath's *Letter to an Imaginary Friend.* The piece is a chaotic, autobiographical poem of considerable length that seeks to attempt to reclaim the past through remembering in order to guide the future. The poem jumps around in time and in the age of the narrator. McGrath calls for a return to nature, and the poem is very much inspired by the works of Walt Whitman and Henry David Thoreau. *Letter to an Imaginary Friend* also recalls modernist Ezra Pound's *Cantos.*

This Coffin Has No Handles, dedicated to "the social revolutionaries," is McGrath's novel dealing with the Marxist class struggle in post–World War II New York City. Though published in 1988, it was originally written in 1947 and 1948. In the novel, McGrath through his pessimistic narrator criticizes the greed of capitalistic New York City, which he sees as a waste. McGrath even puts in a plug for Karl Marx's *Communist Manifesto.* In this novel, everyone is corrupt, from the union bosses, to the cops, to the church. Reform in the unions is needed for the West Side dock workers, and the situation forces people to take a side as the workers strike. At first, the narrator does not want to be a part of it. However, McGrath believes that everyone must take responsibility and get involved.

McGrath's poem "First Book of Genesis According to Marshall," found in *Longshot O'Leary's Garland of Practical Poesie,* rewrites the opening of the book of Genesis from the Bible. Instead of God creating the Earth and all living things as in the Bible, the poem is about the horrors done by political officials who commit their crimes officially and unofficially. On the first day, instead of God creating the heavens and the earth, orphans are drowned. On the second day, workers revolt and are slaughtered. On the third day they are buried. McGrath has horrendous military exploits, elected officials being bought off, and the United States Congress turning on the taxpayers. Throughout this, however, McGrath holds out hope for the poor, working classes. He writes as if a "second coming" is in store in Western Europe, if not in the United States. For McGrath, the second coming is not that of the Christian savior Jesus, but an economic second coming recalling the Bolshevik Revolution. This is the poor revolting against the rich, a staple of Marxist ideology. McGrath turns the West's Christianity against itself, mocking the religious stories by turning them into atheistic, Communist ones.

Further Reading

Gibbons, Reginald, and Terrence Des Pres, eds. *Thomas McGrath: Life and the Poem.* Urbana: U of Illinois P, 1992.

Stern, Frederick C., ed. *The Revolutionary Poet in the United States: The Poetry of Thomas McGrath.* Columbia: U of Missouri P, 1988.

Stephen Oravec

McHALE, TOM (1942–1982) Irish American novelist. The critical response to McHale's novels emphasized the wonderful eccentricity and yet credibility of his characters, the lively invention and yet accessibility of his language, and his ability to invest his storylines, which in summary might read like weird melodramas, with a great deal of subtlety and complexity. McHale's second novel, *Farragan's Retreat* (1972) was a finalist for the National Book Award, and in 1974, McHale received a Guggenheim fellowship for fiction.

Born and raised in Scranton, Pennsylvania, McHale attended a Jesuit high school, and his Irish American background and his family's Roman Catholicism would become essential elements in his fiction. After graduating from Temple University, McHale was employed for a period as a caseworker for the Department of Public Assistance in Philadelphia. The deep impact of the city on his view of the world is palpable in his first two novels. For a brief period, however, McHale would relocate to the rural Midwest to pursue an MFA degree at Iowa State University.

For a first novel, *Principato* (1970) was reviewed quite widely. For over three decades, Joseph Principato has tried to live up to his reputation for being an obstinate individual. His persona has become almost legendary within the Principatos' neighborhood in South Philadelphia, and it has even acquired its own distinctive tag, "The Defiance." So his son, Angelo, is put in an impossible position—to be truly like his father he cannot be at all like him. The consequences of this conundrum are comic, but a good deal of the comedy has its source in discomfort. To complicate matters further, Angelo marries into an Irish American family for whom compliance with social and religious norms is an unquestioned expectation. Thus, being like his father becomes tantamount to willful sinfulness.

Between the publication of his first and second novels, McHale became writer-in-residence at Monmouth College in New Jersey, a position he would hold until his death. *Farragan's Retreat* (1972), his second novel, received even better notices than *Principato* did. Through its depiction of an Irish Catholic clan in Philadelphia, *Farragan's Retreat* mordantly explores the generational conflicts created by the Vietnam War. Simon Farragan is a draft-dodger who has sought asylum in Canada. Worse, he has compounded the disgrace that he has brought upon his family by writing a letter in support of Ho Chi Minh that has been reprinted in the newspapers. After one of his cousins loses an arm and another dies while serving in Vietnam, their distraught parents demand that Simon's father, Arthur, locate Simon and execute him for his twofold betrayal of his family and his nation. Out of this darkly improbable but almost biblical situation, McHale spins a picaresque that lends an absurd geographic dimension to the conflicts between father and son and all that they represent.

The protagonist in McHale's third novel, *Alinsky's Diamond* (1974), is Francis X. Murphy, an American schemer who agrees to lead a motley group of pilgrims who will attempt to walk from France to Jerusalem. Murphy will carry a cross, in which the sponsor of the pilgrimage, Meyer Alinsky, has hidden Suleiman's Pebble, a hot diamond with a colorful history. The novel combines the structure and pacing of a "caper" novel with the attention to character and manners of a social satire.

School Spirit (1976) similarly exploits the conventions of the thriller genre while emphasizing character and theme over plot. The protagonist is a retired football coach named Egil Macgruder. For several decades, he has been troubled by the memory of a bullied player's death in what was explained away as a prank gone wrong. In his late quest to expiate his residual guilt over this incident, Macgruder undertakes a cross-country trip from the Pacific coast to New England, which becomes a means for him to recover some lost aspects of his own character while discovering some broader truths.

Despite its old-fashioned title, McHale's next novel, *The Lady from Boston* (1978), presents a portrait of a contemporary woman who is equally irresistible and unscrupulous. In his final novel, *Dear Friends* (1982), McHale takes an idyllic family setting—a holiday gathering of family and friends at the home of a couple who are expecting their first child—and infuses it with a deepening dread as it is gradually revealed that almost nothing that the presumptive father believes to be true about his life is actually true. The harbinger of the main character's inescapable disillusionment is his accidental witnessing of several strangers' suicides.

McHale himself would die within the year. Conflicting reports on the cause of his death attributed it to a heart attack or to suicide. Regardless of the cause, his death at age forty was certainly premature and a great loss.

Further Reading
Browne, Joseph. "John O'Hara and Tom McHale: How Green Is Their Valley?" *Journal of Ethnic Studies* 6.2 (1978): 57–64.

Martin Kich

McKAY, CLAUDE (1889–1948) African American poet, novelist, and essayist, and one of the most compelling figures of the **Harlem Renaissance**. He was born Festus Claudius McKay in Sunny Ville, Clarendon Parish, Jamaica. He was the youngest of eleven children born to Thomas Francis McKay and Hannah Ann Elizabeth Edwards, members of Jamaica's peasant class.

McKay, sensitive to the poor working class in his island home, turned to writing verse in his youth. Before immigrating to the United States in 1912, McKay published two volumes of dialect verse about his homeland: *Songs of Jamaica* (1912) and *Constab Ballads* (1912). These small collections quickly garnered a reputation for the young McKay in Jamaica. The poems record an emerging lyrical voice sensitive to the Jamaican peasantry who, like workers around the globe, struggle against exploitation for sustenance and identity. At the age of twenty-two, McKay became the first black to receive the medal of the Jamaican Institute of Arts and Sciences.

McKay's idealized depiction of the economic and political struggles of his Jamaican people would transform later into a more direct and defiant protest anthem for blacks and other culturally marginalized people. He left Jamaica in 1912, never to return. The following several decades would see McKay as an existential modernist who was disillusioned by the aftermath of World War I and the race riots in America in 1919. He sought to rediscover a sense of individual and cultural **identity** in America, Europe, and Africa. An expatriate from his beloved Jamaica for the rest of his life, McKay in his writing searched for individual and cultural identity.

Arriving in a racially divided America in 1912, McKay enrolled at the Tuskegee Institute in Alabama, an agriculture and technical college founded by **Booker T. Washington**. The young student with poetic aspirations studied agronomy, but he soon found the curriculum too restrictive and mundane. He also encountered for the first time the vicious face of American **racism** in the country's Deep South. He transferred to Kansas State University later that year, but disillusioned with his studies, he left formal education behind in 1914. He remarked that if he could not achieve a degree, he would "graduate as a poet." He settled in New York where, after a marriage and business venture both failed in less than a year, he embarked on a literary career.

McKay arrived in Harlem at the beginning of an auspicious time for black Americans in the arts, a period first coined the **New Negro** Movement and later the Harlem Renaissance. He struggled financially, working menial jobs while writing. McKay came in contact with Edwin Arlington Robinson, **Waldo Frank**, and others. In 1917 McKay's two sonnets "The Harlem Dancer" and "Invocation" appeared in *The Seven Arts*, published by Frank. In 1919 Max Eastman, who befriended McKay, published the poet's "The Dominant White" and other poems in the *Liberator*, an out-spoken Marxist literary magazine. McKay later adopted the communist ideology and became an editor of the *Liberator*. His poems were also published in *Pearson's* magazine, edited by Frank Harris.

McKay's most enduring poem, "If We Must Die," appeared in 1919 in the *Liberator*. Written in McKay's trademark sonnet form, the poem conveys startling vividness and spontaneous evocation. "If We Must Die," a militant anthem on black resistance and power, was inspired by the violent **race** riots in America during 1919. Although the poem contains no direct language referencing black oppression, and this freedom from temporal references gives the poem its universality and endurance in the arts, the sonnet was instantly recognized as a battle hymn for all people facing maltreatment. The poem's originality reaches beyond racial borders. During World

War II, Winston Churchill included "If We Must Die" in a rallying speech against the Nazis.

McKay left the United States in 1919 to travel abroad. In England during the next two years, he met many fellow writers such as George Bernard Shaw. He published a volume of poetry, *Spring in New Hampshire* (released in the United States in 1922), and the renowned English critic I. A. Richards wrote a preface praising the poetry collection. McKay also worked at the British socialist magazine *Workers Dreadnought*, and a number of his poems appeared in the *Cambridge Magazine*.

McKay returned to the United States in 1922, a momentous year for the young writer and for black art in general. In addition to the U.S. edition of *Spring in New Hampshire*, McKay's added contribution to the Harlem Renaissance was *Harlem Shadows*, arguably his most important collection of poetry. *Harlem Shadows* collects many of his memorable and well-crafted sonnets, including "If We Must Die." *Harlem Shadows* that year appeared along with **W. E. B. Du Bois**'s *Darkwater* and the black actor Charles Gilpin's performance in **Eugene O'Neill**'s *The Emperor Jones*.

Harlem Shadows, according to scholars, virtually ushered in the artistic fervor of the Harlem Renaissance. The decade-long flowering of the Harlem Renaissance in the 1920s witnessed an unprecedented creative explosion in all disciplines of art by African Americans. Work by other artists such as **Countee Cullen**, W. E. B. Du Bois, **Zora Neale Hurston**, and **Nella Larsen** in literature brought attention to the unique culture and expression of black Americans. Folk material, painting, drama, **blues** and **jazz** music, and spiritual songs described the marginality and alienation faced by blacks during the great urban migration from the South to northern cities during the first quarter of the twentieth century. This vanguard movement also included the rise of radical black intellectuals.

Encouraged by this literary success and funding from New York artists, McKay began a twelve-year absence as an expatriate writer in Russia, Western Europe, and Africa. Oddly, McKay traveled abroad during much of the Harlem Renaissance with which he is integrally identified. The years between 1922 and 1934 proved to be the most prolific period for McKay's writing in the genres of poetry, the novel, and essays.

In 1923 in Moscow, McKay became a minor celebrity in postrevolutionary Russia. His artistic and minority status, bolstered by his polemics in support of the proletariat, gained him platforms from which to argue against oppression and capitalism. As a black man, McKay was a novelty in the Russian capital. He found himself, armed with communist leanings derived from his work at *The Liberator* and other Marxist journals, in the midst of the political fervor. The country was still recreating itself after the 1917 Bolshevik revolution, and McKay, who was discerning about people and politics, was easily accepted by the Russian people as a sign of race solidarity. McKay addressed the Fourth Congress of the Communist International, was introduced to Trotsky, and saw the publication of his poem

"Petrograd: May Day, 1923" in *Pravda.* During the same year, the Cotton Club opened in Harlem and **Jean Toomer**'s *Cane* was published in the United States.

McKay's Moscow sojourn also aided his literary accomplishments. In Russia, he compiled a series of essays into book form, *The Negroes in America* (unpublished until 1979). Then he turned to fiction, finishing his first novel, *Home to Harlem* (1928), the story of a black soldier's return to Harlem after World War I. The first novel by an African American to become a best seller in the United States, *Home to Harlem* offers a graphic look at the people, music, and sex that filled the exotic nightlife of Harlem during the initial decades of the twentieth century.

Living in France in latter half of the 1920s, McKay finished his second novel *Banjo: A Story without a Plot* (1929), a sequel to the critically acclaimed *Harlem Nights.* During the same year appeared Countee Cullen's *The Black Christ and Other Poems* and Nella Larsen's *Passing.* McKay's next two works, *Gingertown* (1932), a collection of short stories, and *Banana Bottom* (1933), McKay's third novel, failed to gain an enthusiastic audience. Despite its lukewarm reception, *Banana Bottom,* the story of a young Jamaican girl who has been raped and is befriended by a white couple, continues to be considered McKay's best effort at the novel genre.

Running out of funds, McKay returned in 1934 to an America changed economically by the Great Depression, but unchanged in its racial divide. In New York he worked in the Federal Writers Project and finished his critically acclaimed autobiography, *A Long Way from Home* (1937). Still a socialist sympathizer, he wrote for the *Nation,* the *New Leader,* and the *New York Amsterdam News.* In 1940 he published *Harlem: Negro Metropolis,* a collection of sociological essays. That same year the Jamaican-born writer became an American citizen.

As a black American artist, McKay was not able to support himself with his writing. Working in 1943 at a federal shipbuilding yard, he suffered a stroke that left him in fragile health. Later that year, McKay moved to Chicago where he, a life-long agnostic, converted to Roman Catholicism. In Chicago he taught in the Catholic Youth Organization, but lived in penury and wrote very little. After a difficult battle with high blood pressure and heart disease, McKay, at the age of fifty-eight, succumbed to congestive heart failure in Chicago. His body was returned to New York where he was laid to rest in Harlem.

McKay never returned to his homeland of Jamaica after departing his birthplace as a young man in search of a literary life. His life and writing can be viewed as the search by an expatriate—from both Jamaica and the United States—for his cultural roots. Left unpublished until after his death was his second autobiography, *My Green Hills of Jamaica* (1979), a memory of his native land. McKay is well remembered for his articulate poetry of protest in the sonnet form that inaugurated the rich period of the Harlem Renaissance. McKay continues to appeal to readers worldwide with his resonant message against bigotry and oppression. (*See also* African American Novel, African American Poetry, Caribbean [Anglophone] American Novel, Caribbean [Anglophone] American Poetry)

Further Reading

Cooper, Wayne F. *Claude McKay: Rebel Sojourner in the Harlem Renaissance: A Biography*. Baton Rouge: Louisiana State UP, 1987.

Giles, James R. *Claude McKay*. Boston: G. K. Hall & Co., 1976.

Tillery, Tyrone. *Claude McKay: A Black Poet's Struggle for Identity*. Amherst: U of Massachusetts P, 1992.

Winston, James. *A Fierce Hatred of Injustice: Claude McKay's Jamaica and His Poetry of Rebellion*. London: Verso, 2000.

Michael David Sollars

McKNIGHT, REGINALD (1956–) African American fiction writer and editor. Born into a military family in Germany, McKnight is presently the Hamilton Homes Professor at the University of Georgia where he teaches Creative Writing. Reginald McKnight's stories, often written in first person, relate African Americans' frustration at being located within a society that devalues their cultural cache and have led critics to compare him favorably to **Ralph Ellison** and **James Baldwin**. McKnight's collections and novels present African American male protagonists whose encounters with a white dominated society often lead to self-loathing and doubt. He also successfully combines his experiences in Senegal with black intelligentsia's quests to find themselves in an over romanticized motherland. However, their Western educations prove useless and they are either blind to their epiphanies or they misinterpret them once they occur. Therefore, African American characters find their "twoness" difficult to overcome since they are outside the cultural milieu of both their American and African worlds.

Moustapha's Eclipse (1988), McKnight's first collection of stories, which grew from his master's thesis, received positive reviews and was awarded the Drue Heinz Literature Prize and the Ernest Hemingway Foundation Award. Here he succinctly expresses his views regarding the black middle class and the intraracial conflicts therein by experimenting with a range of voices, including Africans and Americans, black and white. The title story, "Uncle Moustapha's Eclipse," is narrated by Idi, the nephew of Moustapha, a prosperous village farmer and concerns the conflict that arises when an education black American confronts the traditions of African folk culture.

McKnight's first novel, *I Get on the Bus* (1990), continues with a disoriented American in Africa. Evan Norris, the novel's protagonist, leaves behind his girlfriend and travels to Senegal with the Peace Corps from which he later resigns. While there, Evan embarks on a series of out of body adventures; he is haunted by guilt from a murder that never occurred and that he did not commit. In attempting to reject his American influences, Evan becomes seduced by Senegalese culture and Aminata, the daughter of a village marabou, and is forced to realize that his romanticized preoccupation with Africa is detrimental to his existence.

In McKnight's second collection, *The Kind of Light That Shines on Texas* (1992), the narrators' cautionary tales of **race** are stippled with humor, and characters find themselves in a myriad of circumstances. The title story, honored with an O. Henry Award, involves Clint, a young man who reminisces about his experiences as one of only a handful of blacks in a white school in Texas. Through a series of events, Clint overcomes self-hatred and spite and learns that viewing his own blackness as a handicap is inaccurate, inappropriate, and inexcusable. Yet, he must also struggle with the memory of degradation at the hands of racists and understand that such is the price of living in a racially polarized society.

White Boys (1998), McKnight's third collection of stories, also includes a novella written in third person, which gives the collection its title and examines race relations from the point of view of a middle-class African American family on a military base in Louisiana. The protagonist, Derrick Oates, removes snow from the car of Sergeant Hooker, his white neighbor. Derrick is chastised by his father and the neighbor, yet he and Garret, Hooker's son, attempt to forge a friendship until Garret is forced to choose between his father and his friend when his father devises a wicked and racist plan of revenge. Garret chooses to end the friendship in order to save his friend from humiliation; thus, McKnight demonstrates convincingly that racist attitudes negatively and permanently disrupts the lives of whites and blacks alike.

Similar to McKnight's novel *I Get on the Bus*, his second novel, *He Sleeps* (2001), also features an educated African American male who encounters major life-altering experiences while living in Senegal. The main character, anthropologist Bertrand Milworth, initially goes to Africa to research urban legends, but is in fact escaping a failed marriage and attempting to recapture his **identity**. While there he begins having violent, erotic nightmares that offer insight into the answers he seeks, but he is incapable of dissecting and digesting their true meanings.

Further Reading

Ashe, Bertram D. "Under the Umbrella of Black Civilization: A Conversation with Reginald McKnight." *African American Review* 35 (2001): 427–37.

Megan, Carolyn E. "New Perceptions on Rhythm in Reginald McKnight's Fiction." *Kenyon Review* 16 (1994): 56–62.

Walsh, William. "We Are, in Fact, a Civilization: An Interview with Reginald McKnight." *Kenyon Review* 16 (1994): 27–43.

Clarissa West-White

McMILLAN, TERRY (1951–) African American novelist and editor. Terry McMillan was born and raised in Port Huron, Michigan. Her parents, Madeline Washington Tilman and Edward McMillan, divorced when she was thirteen, and her father died when she was sixteen. As a teenager,

Terry McMillan (center) with actresses who have performed in films based on her books. *AP/Wide World Photos.*

McMillan worked in a library, shelving books, and this is how she discovered literature. She was introduced to black writers when she enrolled in an African American literature course at Los Angeles City College. She says that she has been inspired by **Langston Hughes** and **Zora Neale Hurston**. She went on to attend the University of California, Berkeley. It was here that McMillan developed an interest in writing, when she became involved with a new publication, *Black Thoughts*. Her interest in fiction began when she enrolled in a fiction class taught by **Ishmael Reed**. She changed her major from sociology and, ultimately, earned a bachelor of arts degree in journalism. McMillan also received a master of fine arts degree in film at Columbia University. McMillan was awarded a New York Foundation for the Arts Fellowship in 1986, a National Endowment for the Arts Fellowship in 1988, and a Barnes and Noble Writers Award in 1999; she was a Yaddo Colony Fellow in 1982, 1983, and 1985, and a MacDowell Fellow in 1983. She has taught at Stanford University, the University of Wyoming, and the University of Arizona, Tucson. McMillan has a son and she currently lives in northern California.

McMillan began writing her first novel, *Mama* (1987), when she was a single mother in her early thirties and was working as a legal secretary. The novel began as a short story called "Mama Take Another Step." During this time, McMillan was a member of the Harlem Writers Guild. It was here that she was encouraged by other writers to develop the work as a novel. She took a two-week vacation from her job and went to Yaddo, an artists' colony in upstate New York, where she finished her first draft of the novel. When it was finally published, she was told that there were no plans to promote it, so McMillan began doing so herself. She was successful: the first printing sold out, and it went into a second printing. The novel has been compared to **Alice Walker**'s *The Color Purple* (1982) because of the strength of the main character, Mildred Peacock. The story focuses on Mildred's frustration with her poverty-filled life. Mildred does not always make the most responsible life decisions, but she is a hard worker and attempts to propel her five children into better lives. *Mama* received a National Book Award by the Before Columbus Foundation.

McMillan's second novel was *Disappearing Acts* (1989), which is about Zora Banks and the conflicts of her relationship with Franklin Swift. Although Zora is living a successful life as a teacher and singer, she is unhappy with her relationships with men. She develops an interest in Franklin, a construction worker who is an alcoholic. The novel explores the complications of their relationship and has an open-ended conclusion. The novel was adapted into a film by Home Box Office.

Like the works of other African American women writers, including Walker's *The Color Purple,* McMillian's third novel, *Waiting to Exhale* (1992), has been criticized by some for its negative portrayal of black men; however, the novel was on the *New York Times* best seller list for thirty-eight weeks and became a successful film in 1995. McMillan cowrote the screenplay. The novel is told using black dialect and focuses on the lives of four African American women in their thirties who live in Phoenix, Arizona. The women are confronting the challenges of being black women and are coping with the pressures of careers, families, and relationships while searching for a respectable black man to complete their lives. A prevalent theme in the novel is the strength of friendship.

McMillan's fourth work, *How Stella Got Her Groove Back* (1996), was on the *New York Times* best-seller list for twenty-one weeks. In this semiautobiographical novel, Stella is the main character. She is forty years old, and she has a successful career and a teenage son. Stella, however, is dissatisfied with her life. She travels to Jamaica where she tries to revive her "groove," and she falls in love with a twenty-year-old man. Some criticized McMillan's use of stream of consciousness in the novel, but, despite this, the work has been a huge success. The novel became a major motion picture, and McMillan cowrote the screenplay for this film as well.

A Day Late and a Dollar Short (2001), McMillan's fifth novel, portrays the lives of Viola and Cecil Price and their four grown children. The work is told from the perspectives of the parents and each child and explores the obstacles that they encounter, including alcoholism, divorce, incest, and sibling rivalry. A major theme in the novel is that even the most troubled families have an undying strength.

Her sixth and most recent novel is *The Interruption of Everything* (2004), which explores the life of Marilyn Grimes. Marilyn has been the perfect wife and mother but is experiencing the empty-nest syndrome and the other frustrations that go along with being middle-aged. She feels the urge to rediscover her dreams and reinvent herself.

What is significant about McMillan's fiction is that she portrays a variety of African American female characters, including the poor and the upwardly mobile. Additionally, McMillan redefines the traditional family unit to show that there are other ways of finding satisfaction in life. Although some of her works do portray families, often ones that are non-traditional, others show women who are empowered by their relationships with one another.

McMillan also edited the important collection *Breaking Ice: An Anthology of Contemporary African-American /Fiction* (1990), which includes works by established and new authors. (*See also* African American Novel)

Further Reading

Christopher Murray, Victoria. "Everybody Wants to be Terry McMillan." *Black Issues Book Review* 4.1 (2002): 36–39.

Ellerby, Janet Mason. "Deposing the Man of the House: Terry McMillan Rewrites the Family." *MELUS* 22.2 (1997): 105–17.

Diane Todd Bucci

McNICKLE, WILLIAM D'ARCY (1904–1977) Native American author, activist, and anthropologist. Although D'Arcy McNickle is today known primarily for his novels—*The Surrounded* (1936), *Runner in the Sun* (1954), and the posthumously published *Wind from an Enemy Sky* (1978)—he made major contributions to Native American political struggles and also made his mark in the field of anthropology.

Though his heritage was Métis and Irish, McNickle grew up on the Flathead Reservation in Montana, and his parents enrolled him as a member of that tribe in 1905. Like his fictional characters Archilde and Antoine, protagonists of *The Surrounded* and *Wind from an Enemy Sky,* respectively, McNickle attended an Indian boarding school as a youth; he later enrolled at the University of Montana, where he published his first poems and essays.

McNickle's fiction and nonfiction continually revisit the question of Indian and white coexistence, and the possibility for—or impossibility of—communication between these different cultures. While McNickle's career was dedicated to improving the relationship between whites and Indians, his novels suggest the impossibility of real interaction. In particular, the posthumously published novel *Wind from an Enemy Sky* suggests the hopelessness of Indian-white relations, as characters consistently misunderstand and miscommunicate with each other, leading to tragic consequences. In that novel, the fictional Little Elk Indians, whose homeland is threatened by the building of a dam, fight for the return of a sacred medicine bundle, taken from them by missionaries and kept in a Washington museum. In spite of efforts to recover the bundle, its return finally proves impossible, as it has been destroyed by years of neglect. Its destruction, hardly noticed by the museum staff, is devastating for the Indians and shows the lethal effects of white society's indifference and ignorance toward Indian culture.

McNickle himself spent much of his life negotiating between Indian and white worlds. After leaving Montana, he spent time in Oxford, Paris, New York, and Philadelphia and worked briefly at the Depression-era Federal Writers Project. In 1936 McNickle accepted a position with the Bureau of Indian Affairs (BIA), where he helped implement the 1934 Indian Reorganization Act and assisted in restoring land to Indian tribes. Much of his time at the BIA was spent serving under Commissioner John Collier. McNickle admired Collier's Indian New Deal program, which was marked by a move away from prior assimilationist policies and toward increasing tribal autonomy. McNickle himself believed the federal government should gradually cede control of tribal lands and services to the tribes themselves, who would in the process learn effective self-government and administrative skills. McNickle persistently pushed the BIA toward promoting sovereignty and self-government for Indian tribes. However, after Collier's resignation in 1945, the BIA began to return to a more paternalistic relationship with tribes, and although McNickle held out for some time, that shift eventually led to his resignation from the BIA in 1952.

In 1944, as questions arose on a national level about outstanding Indian land claims and tribal autonomy, McNickle became one of the founding members of the National Congress of American Indians (NCAI). The NCAI was a pantribal organization dedicated to promoting the political and cultural rights of Indian people and tribes. After resigning from the BIA, McNickle devoted more of his time to NCAI, which led the struggle against the 1953 federal Termination Act, which threatened the very existence of tribes. McNickle was also increasingly involved in developing workshops and other opportunities for younger Indians and was instrumental in organizing the 1961 American Indian Chicago Conference that led to the foundation of the National Indian Youth Council.

Through NCAI's adjunct organization, American Indian Development (AID), McNickel coordinated a health education project at Crownpoint, near the Navajo Reservation. Faced with opposition both from local whites and Navajo traditionalists, McNickle found support among younger tribal members who, like him, had some experience in white society, but who had chosen to return to their community. McNickle's 1954 novel, *Runner in the Sun*, reflects many of these experiences. Based in part on his historical research, *Runner in the Sun* is a coming-of-age tale for younger readers set close to Crownpoint, among the pre-Columbian Anasazi people. Unlike his other two novels, which focus on conflicts between Indians and whites, *Runner in the Sun* explores tensions between tradition and innovation in a wholly Indian context and reflects McNickle's own changing role. Rather than negotiating between tribal communities and the federal government, his work for AID often involved negotiating between different factions of the same tribe and exploring ways to harmonize tradition and progress, as *Runner in the Sun*'s protagonist Salt eventually learns to do.

Although he was never formally trained in anthropology, McNickle's work with the BIA's Applied Anthropology Unit and his fieldwork with AID, as well as his extensive writing about American Indians, earned him a reputation as a skilled anthropologist. McNickle was also active as an editor, assisting in the publication of numerous works about Native American culture and history. In 1965, he finally received academic recognition in the form of an honorary doctorate and became chair of the University of Saskatchewan's Department of Anthropology. McNickle's nonfiction work includes *The Indian Tribes of the United States: Ethnic and Cultural Survival* (1962, revised as *Native American Tribalism*, 1973) and *They Came Here First: The Epic of the American Indian* (1949), which was among the first accounts of Native American history to be written by a Native American.

McNickle's career was dedicated to promoting tribal autonomy and fostering understanding between white and Indian cultures, goals that, as his novels show, were often elusive. Nevertheless, McNickle was a tireless fighter for Indian rights, and his life and work reflect not only his disillusionment, but also his idealism. (*See also* Native American Novel)

Further Reading

Parker, Dorothy R. *Singing an Indian Song: A Biography of D'Arcy McNickle.*
 Lincoln: U of Nebraska P, 1992.
Purdy, John Lloyd, ed. *The Legacy of D'Arcy McNickle: Writer, Historian, Activist.*
 Norman: U of Oklahoma P, 1996.

Miriam H. Schacht

McPHERSON, JAMES ALAN (1943–) African American fiction writer, essayist, editor, and teacher. Among the most thoughtful and talented of African American writers to emerge during the 1960s, James Alan McPherson published two award-winning collections of short stories before turning his hand to nonfiction, editing, teaching, and other tasks. Like the fiction of his mentor, **Ralph Ellison**, McPherson's writing has earned critical esteem for the originality of its technique as well as for the distinctiveness of its themes and values. As a commentator on the contemporary American scene, McPherson is unique in many respects.

Born in Savannah, Georgia, on September 16, 1943, James Alan McPherson grew up in a working-class black community. Despite the poverty and **racism** of his childhood, McPherson believes that he benefited from many positive influences in his formative years. With the support of his parents, who worked as an electrician and a domestic, he graduated from high school with self-confidence and a belief in racial progress. McPherson earned a BA degree in English from Morris Brown College in Atlanta before attending Harvard Law School, from where he graduated in 1968. At the same time, he began publishing fiction and nonfiction in the prestigious *Atlantic Monthly* magazine. Following law school, he attended the Writers' Workshop at the University of Iowa, where he earned an MFA in creative writing in 1969 and where he has taught for over two decades. He has served as a visiting lecturer at many universities, including Harvard, the University of Virginia, the University of California at Santa Cruz, and Morgan State University. He has also taught at Meiji University and Chiba University in Japan.

From its first appearance, McPherson's fiction gained widespread critical attention with critics such as Robert Bone, Granville Hicks, and **Irving Howe** publishing reviews. Over the years, McPherson has garnered a number of literary awards and fellowships, including the *Atlantic* "Firsts" award for "Gold Coast," a Guggenheim Fellowship in 1973, the Pulitzer Prize for fiction (for *Elbow Room* in 1978), and membership in the American Academy of Arts and Sciences.

McPherson's fiction gained wide recognition at the same time that it resisted the familiar mode of protest writing that dominated African American fiction of the 1960s and 1970s. As McPherson insists, his own background was never limited in terms of **race** or social class. From an early age, he pursued friendships among a diverse group of people. Early jobs in a supermarket and on the Great Northern Railway brought him into contact with Americans from all backgrounds. As a result, the problems that he writes about—essentially personal themes of injustice, hatred, sexuality, aging, and failure—are universal rather than strictly racial in nature, although many, like "An Act of Prostitution" or "A Matter of Vocabulary," have racial inequality as their primary subject matter.

After the publication of his second collection of short stories, *Elbow Room*, McPherson turned increasingly to writing essays and to editing. Among his important early essays were a series of articles that he published in the *Atlantic Monthly,* including two essays on the Blackstone Rangers in Chicago and an essay titled "Indivisible Man," written with Ralph Ellison. His essays have also appeared in *Esquire, Reader's Digest, Playboy,* and the *New York Times Magazine.* His edited works include *Railroad: Trains and Train People in American Culture* (1976), edited with Miller Williams, and *One Hundred Years After Huck: Fiction by Men in America,* a special issue of the *Iowa Review* (1984).

McPherson's recent essays focus on the problems that he sees in contemporary American culture, especially the attitudes of complacency that he refers to as "Moral Dandyism," which he defines as the sense of moral superiority of those who condemn whatever is out of fashion or easily attacked. In their search for a more authentic basis for ethical commitment, McPherson's essays often explore the belief that American society has lost sight of the traditional values that were important in the past. In the final analysis, McPherson must be credited for the originality of his iconoclastic vision and his determination to explore a broad range of cultural traditions.

Further Reading

Blicksilver, Edith. "The Image of Women in Selected Stories by James Alan McPherson." *CLA Journal* 22 (June 1979): 390–401.

Howe, Irving. "New Black Writers." *Harper's Magazine* 239 (December 1969): 130ff.

Perry, Patsy B. "James Alan McPherson." *Dictionary of Literary Biography.* Vol. 38. Ed. Trudier Harris and Thadious M. Davis. Detroit: Gale, 1985. 185–94.

Shacochis, Bob. "Interview with James Alan McPherson." *Iowa Journal of Literary Studies* (1983): 7–33.

Jeffrey J. Folks

MEDINA, PABLO (1948–) Cuban American novelist, short story writer, poet, and essayist. Pablo Medina has lived most of his life in the Northeast since he emigrated from Cuba when he was twelve years old. Unlike some of his compatriots, Medina has always written in English. Some of his longer works include *Pork Rind and Cuban Songs* (1975), *Exiled Memories: A Cuban Childhood* (1990), *Arching into the Afterlife* (1991), *The Marks of Birth* (1994), *The Floating Island* (1999), and *The Return of Felix Nogara* (2000). In addition he has published dozens of essays, articles, short stories, and poems in academic journals and popular magazines throughout the United States.

Like many Cuban American writers, Medina's work shows his preoccupation with the double-edged sword of **assimilation**. Though his characters often eventually undergo a redemptive experience, the road to self-knowledge is treacherous. In *The Marks of Birth,* for example, Medina traces the life of Antón, a Cuban child who attempts to erase his **identity** by losing his Spanish accent, altering his name, and marrying the all-American girl next door. Although his physical metamorphosis is complete, the itching of his birthmark is a constant reminder that his spiritual transformation is impossible. Ultimately, this attempt at cultural erasure collapses, as does his marriage. Ironically, the only thing that survives is his need to return to the land he had so fervently tried to deny.

Pablo Medina's poetry is much like his fiction: unassuming yet powerful. *Pork Rinds and Cuban Love Songs* was the first book of poetry originally written in English published by a Cuban American writer. In it, Medina presents the reader with poems like "The Exile," which depict a speaker's connection to the past, a staple of Cuban American literature. What is not ordinary, however, is Medina's powerful use of imagery—visual, auditory, and tactile. In another offering from the book, "Winter of a Rose," Medina seemingly parallels his novel as he traces the speaker's exile, disillusionment, and eventual renewal.

Perhaps Medina's most compelling work, however, is not his fiction, but his autobiographical memoir, *Exiled Memories: A Cuban Childhhood.* Possibly the pattern for the novel about Anton, which came four years later, this account by Medina of his early years in Cuba is both compelling and disturbing. It attracts the reader as Medina vividly recalls events from his youth in an almost poetic prose; yet it concludes by acknowledging that because of his exile, Medina's self can never be truly reconciled. Although this struggle between two halves of one identity is common in much Cuban American fiction, it is somehow more tragic when there is no created persona, only the author himself, and when that author admits that these two halves can never be reconciled. (*See also* Cuban American Novel)

Further Reading

Borland, Isabel Alvarez. *Cuban-American Literature of Exile: From Person to Persona.* Charlottesville: UP of Virginia, 1998.

Eduardo R. del Rio

MEHTA, VED PARKASH (1934–)   Indian American author. Prolific journalist, autobiographer, and academic, Mehta is one of the most visible Asian American writers. As a staff member of the *New Yorker* since the early 1960s and as author of an eleven-volume autobiography, travel books, political commentary and fiction, Mehta and his writing on India have clearly helped form the American idea of the subcontinent, as well as offered important perspectives on the life and professional career of a blind writer.

Mehta was born in Lahore, India (now Pakistan). At the age of four, a severe bout of meningitis left him blind, which, for Indian children of that time was tantamount to being condemned to begging. His parents persisted in educating their bright son, and at five, Mehta was sent to Bombay's Dadar School for the Blind. At the age of fifteen, he moved to the United States to study at the Arkansas School for the Blind. He received his BA in 1956 from Pomona College and later went on to study at Oxford (1959) and Harvard (1961). He worked for the *New Yorker* from 1961 to 1994, where most of his book first appeared in installments. Mehta has also taught history, literature, and creative writing at Yale, Oxford, Sarah Lawrence College, and Vassar, among others.

His first book *Face to Face: An Autobiography* (1957) narrates his life from childhood until just before he leaves for England. Written at the age of twenty-three, the text signaled Mehta's imaginative insight and potential as a writer. This book became the nucleus of his "Continents of Exile" series, eleven volumes of biography and autobiography that chronicle his family's life, his experiences growing up in India, his education in the United States and England, and his subsequent career. The first two books in the series, *Daddyji* (1972) and *Mamaji* (1979), chronicle his parents' lives before their marriage and present a vivid portrait of middle-class India. Mehta illustrates the fundamental differences between them: His father, a rational Western-educated physician, approaches the world scientifically; his mother is uneducated, childish, loving, and superstitious. *Vedi* (1982) centers on Mehta's blindness and his family's attempts to educate a disabled child in India. This text is a fascinating stylistic negotiation, as the writer

leads the reader to experience his blindness by removing all visual references and encounter the world as the blind child does, through smell,
touch, and taste. In *The Ledge Between the Streams* (1984), Mehta continues
his account of his childhood from nine to fifteen, which includes the dramatic experience of the Partition of India and their family's flight out of
Lahore, as they became refugees; the next book, *Sound-Shadows of the New
World* (1986), recounts his first three years at the Arkansas School for the
Blind, where Mehta engages issues of homesickness and cultural alienation
as he discovers his future vocation as a journalist, after serving as the editor
of the school newspaper.

The next two books in the series center on Mehta's undergraduate years
at Pomona and Balliol College. *The Stolen Light* (1989) and *Up at Oxford*
(1993) are extraordinary in the context of their author's disability and his
cultural and class separation from many of the other students he meets.
Mehta writes in detail about his long and prolific career at the *New Yorker* in
Remembering Mr. Shawn's New Yorker: The Invisible Art of Editing (1998), as a
tribute to William Shawn, the magazine's editor from 1952 to 1987. *All for
Love* (2001) is a retrospective look at four women he fell in love with in his
twenties and at how the difficulties in these relationships made him see
that the determination and drive that allowed him to overcome his disability and be successful as an Indian in permanent exile from his home was
detrimental in the context of romance. Mehta appears to appease his need
for roots and stability in *Dark Harbor: Building House and Home on an
Enchanted Island* (2003), where he recounts the chronicle of building the
house for his wife and their children, an allegory of the story of Mehta's
own personal and professional trajectory. The series concludes with *The Red
Letters: My Father's Enchanted Period* (2004), where, with the excuse of asking his son to help him write a novel, Mehta's father reveals to him a love
affair in which he had engaged just before Ved was born. As Mehta delicately explores this story, he is led to rethink his relationship with his
father, his perspective on his mother, and his notions about their forty-nine-
year-old marriage.

Two central themes recur in Mehta's work: his ambivalent relationship
with India and the fact of his blindness. Mehta has written several books
that analyze the cultural and political context of India. The historical and
political commentary he enacts in *Mahatma Gandhi and His Apostles* (1977)
and the trilogy, *The New India* (1978), *A Family Affair: India under Three Prime
Ministers* (1982), and *Rajiv Gandhi and Rama's Kingdom* (1994), are crucial
perspectives on the volatile situation of the country and the difficulty in
finding solutions. With regard to his blindness, though his disability is
what leads his family to send him abroad, and though his early works foreground his positive and pragmatic attitude towards his blindness, later
works often elide his sightlessness, and he even forbade some of his editors
to make mention of it in the book jackets. As he writes in *All for Love*, one of
the conditions he placed in his relationships was that his girlfriends would

ignore his blindness, act as though it was irrelevant and meaningless. Functioning as a sighted person is also behind his struggle to build a house in Maine in *Dark Harbor*. Interestingly, Mehta's imagery is profoundly visual, particularly in his books about travel in India, which has led people to think that he is sighted.

Apart from his autobiographical works, Mehta has also published travel books, such as *Walking the Indian Streets* (1960, rev. edn. 1971), where he tells of a return visit to India after ten years abroad, and *Portrait of India* (1970, reprinted 1993); essays such as *The New Theologian* (1966) and *John Is Easy to Please: Encounters with the Written and the Spoken Word* (1971); and fiction in *Delinquent Chacha* (1966) and *Three Stories of the Raj* (1986). Mehta's engagement with issues of **immigration** and adaptation, the history of India as seen through one family, his own struggle with blindness, and his long career in journalism make him an important protagonist the field of transcultural writing. (*See also* South Asian American Literature)

Further Reading
Slatin, John M. "Blindness and Self-Perception: The Autobiographies of Ved
    Mehta." *Mosaic* 19.4 (Fall 1986): 173–93.

Rocío G. Davis

MELUS (1973–)   The Society for the Study of Multi-Ethnic Literature of the United States (MELUS) was founded in 1973. Designed to expand the definition, teaching, and literary criticism produced about American literature and to bring together scholars of ethnic studies, the organization was officially recognized as a Modern Language Association (MLA) affiliate society in 1974.

The landmark event historically accorded recognition, as the impetus for the creation of MELUS was the continued refusal of the MLA to schedule panels on ethnic American literature. In retaliation, in 1972, a group convened in the hallways of one of the conference hotels in the city of New York to hear a presentation of a session on African American literature. Responding to the institutional **racism** that seemed to be a part of universities and colleges and to be within the MLA itself, this group planned to continue holding sessions in the hallways and corridors of the conference hotels until the MLA officially recognized the importance of the study of the multiethnic literature of the United States. By 1974, this goal had been achieved.

In addition to the society itself, in 1974 MELUS also produced a journal by that same name. *MELUS,* the journal, first appeared as an unbound newsletter, but under the editorial leadership of Katharine Newman, in 1978, *MELUS* became a scholarly publication with a mission to challenge the boundaries of current American literary criticism, textbook structures, and canon formation while at the same time increasing understanding and awareness and appreciation of the multiethnic nature of American literature.

From 1985 to 1999, under the editorial leadership of Joseph Skerrett, *MELUS* expanded its coverage to include criticism and theoretical concerns and a greater depth of coverage within genres with special topics issues and guest editors. While continuing to publishing feature articles, interviews, and book reviews on topics associated with ethnic and multiethnic American literature, Skerrett also began to include writers from Canada, Mexico, and the Caribbean. MELUS was beginning to go global, with organizations in India and throughout Europe, and in 1998 MELUS-Europe hosted an international conference in Heidelberg.

In 2000 two very important events occurred in the history of MELUS. The journal *MELUS* moved to the University of Connecticut under the editorial leadership of Veronica Makowsky. Under Makowsky's guidance, the journal began to explore new directions in multiethnic literature such as the importance of children's literature in **identity** formation and hybrid **ethnicity**, the study of authors who identify with more than one ethnicity. Also in 2000, MESEA, the Society for Multi-Ethnic Studies of Europe and the Americas was founded as a forum for interdisciplinary multiethnic studies by scholars throughout Europe replacing MELUS-Europe.

As the premiere learned society for the study of the multiethnic literature of the United States, MELUS continues to celebrate the totality of American literature both in the Americas and beyond. (*See also The Heath Anthology of American Literature*, Multiculturalism)

Further Reading

Newman, Katharine. "MELUS Invented: The Rest Is History." *MELUS* 16.4
    (Winter 1989): 99–113.
TuSmith, Bonnie. "On Cultural Contexts, Aesthetics, and the Mission of MELUS."
    MELUS 27.3 (Fall 2002): 3–10.

Darcy A. Zabel

MENA, MARÍA CHRISTINA (1893–1965)   Mexican   American short fiction writer and children's novelist. María Cristina Mena is best known for her series of proto-magical-realist stories commissioned by the editors of *Century Magazine* between 1913 and 1916, a time of increasing political tension between the United States and Mexico. These pieces have since been collected in *The Collected Stories of María Christina Mena* (1997). Mena, whom *The Household Magazine* once called the "foremost interpreter of Mexican life" (qtd in Doherty xxii), has largely been forgotten in the United States, though some critical reconsiderations of her work have materialized since the onset of **multiculturalism** in higher education. She was, along with **María Amparo Ruiz de Burton**, one of the first Chicanas to write in English for American audiences. Born in Mexico City on April 3, 1893, Mena led a privileged childhood until she was forced into exile at fourteen due to the political unrest that heralded the Mexican revolution of 1910. Her mother was Spanish and her father was a wealthy Yucatan businessman with high-ranking connections among the Porfirio Diaz administration. She received a fine convent and English public school education in Mexico before immigrating to New York City in 1907. In New York, she prospered in the highest levels of society and, with her marriage to the Australian writer Henry Kellett Chambers, in elite literary circles as well.

Mena's first two stories, "John of God, the Water-Carrier" and "The Gold Vanity Set," were both published in the November 1913 issues of *Century Magazine* and *American Magazine,* respectively. As in all her work, these stories were meant to enlighten mainstream Americans by offering narratives set in Mexico that featured "authentic" (but always light-skinned) Mexican characters. In her fiction, she neither belittled Mexicans by affirming preexisting **Mexican American stereotypes** nor affronted mainstream audiences with strident **identity** politics. In one instance, she defended the use of cultural detail in her first story for *Century Magazine,* a publication that was simultaneously publishing the rabid antiimmigrant diatribes of the sociologist Edward A. Ross, by convincing her editor that "American readers, with their intense interest in Mexico, are ripe for a true picture of a people so near to them, so intrinsically picturesque, so misrepresented in current fiction, and so well worthy of being known and loved, in all their ignorance" (Doherty xxii). Mena scholars Amy Doherty and Tiffany Ana López argue that this tone, though apparently condescending, was deliberately employed to win over her racist backers, and hence permit the "tricksterism," or cultural subversion, embedded in her best work. Henry Chambers died in 1935, leaving Mena in a debilitating state of mourning until her death in 1965.

Further Reading

Doherty, Amy, ed. "Introduction." *The Collected Stories of María Christina Mena.* Recovering the U.S. Hispanic Literary Heritage Series. Houston: Arte Público Press, 1997. vii–l.

López, Tiffany Ana. "María Christina Mena: Turn-of-the-Century La Malinche, and Other Tales of Cultural (Re)Construction." *Tricksterism in Turn-of-the-Twentieth-Century American Literature: A Multicultural Perspective.* Hanover and London: Tufts UP, 1994.

Mena, María Christina. "The Birth of the God of War." *The Collected Stories of Maria Christina Mena.* Ed. Amy Doherty. Houston: Arte Público Press, 1997. 63–69.

Robert M. Dowling

MENCKEN, H. L. (1880–1956)   Third-generation German American journalist, literary critic, and scholar. Mencken is best known for attacking the American middle class for its lack of culture. He hated things English and loved things German. During World War I, he obstinately rooted for Germany, but during World War II, he was firmly anti-Nazi. In his literary criticism, Mencken championed controversial new American writers, among them the black writers of the **Harlem Renaissance**. A self-taught philologist, Mencken broke new ground with his study, *The American Language* (1919), which he revised and expanded several times.

H. L. Mencken. *Courtesy of the Library of Congress.*

Henry Louis Mencken was born on September 12, 1880, in Baltimore, Maryland. His father and his uncle ran a cigar factory, which had been founded by Mencken's grandfather, who had emigrated from Germany in 1848. Mencken grew up in the German section of Baltimore and attended first a private school and then the Baltimore Polytechnical Institute. In 1899 Mencken began an apprenticeship with the *Baltimore Herald*, and by 1905 he was the paper's managing editor. When the *Herald* folded in 1906, Mencken started his life-long association with the *Baltimore Sun*. In 1908 Mencken began publishing book reviews in *The Smart Set*, and in1924 he started his own literary magazine, the *American Mercury.* Until he suffered a stroke in 1948, Mencken contributed articles and editorials to many different newspapers and magazines and wrote several books. On January 29, 1956, Mencken died in the house where he had grown up.

Mencken's knowledge of German is generally underestimated because Mencken let on that he didn't know the language very well. He claimed that what little German he knew, he learned from listening to his mother speaking to their German maids and to German tradesmen. However, when Mencken became fascinated with the philosophy of Friedrich Nietzsche, he was forced to read most of his works in German since they had not yet been translated. In fact Mencken even published his own translation of Nietzsche's *The Anti-Christ* (1908), and he wrote two books about Nietzsche (*The Philosophy of Friedrich Nietzsche,* 1908, and *The Gist of Nietzsche,* 1910). Moreover, Mencken liberally sprinkled his writings with German words and phrases. He did this occasionally to bait the anglophiles among his readers, as for instance in his pro-German pieces about World War I, which he sometimes ended with "Deutschland Über Alles" ("Germany Above Everything") or "Hoch der Kaiser!" ("Hail to the Kaiser").

On the other hand, Mencken's knowledge of German culture and German literature is generally overestimated. Although Mencken was very fond of the composers Bach, Beethoven, and Brahms and sang in a German *Männerchor,* his knowledge of the works of classic German writers such as Johann Wolfgang von Goethe, Friedrich von Schiller, and Friedrich Hölderlin was very limited. This is probably because his vision of life was rooted in philosophical materialism. He therefore disliked romantic literature and had no use for poetry. He believed that poetry by definition is unrealistic and sentimental. When Mencken died, his personal library contained only sixty books by German authors, most of them minor contemporary writers whose works he had reviewed for *The Smart Set* and the *America Mercury*. Mencken's favorite German writer was the dramatist Gehard Hauptmann, whom he considered one of the two greatest playwrights of his time, second only to George Bernard Shaw.

Mencken's style was strongly influenced by that of the later, misanthropic Mark Twain, but Mencken gave his own style more bite by freely using invective and exaggeration. For instance, he called the average American the "Boobus Americanus," labeled the middle class the "Bouboisie," and referred to the United States as "this glorious commonwealth of morons." In his essay "On Being an American," Mencken expresses his often-stated belief that democracy is nothing but mob rule and that in America "this domination of mob ways of thinking, this pollution of the whole intellectual life by the prejudices and emotions of the rabble, goes unchallenged because the old landed aristocracy of the colonial era has been engulfed and almost obliterated by the rise of the industrial system, and no new aristocracy has risen to take its place, and discharge its highly necessary function" (*Prejudices: A Selection*. New York: Vintage, 1955: 103).

Mencken wrote most of his literary criticism in the form of reviews for *The Smart Set* and the *American Mercury*. An exception is the essay titled "Criticism of Criticism of Criticism." In that essay he declared his opposition to four trends in contemporary criticism—ethical, aesthetic, psychological, and formalistic—and explained that he favored the approach of J. E. Spingarn, who believed that a literary work should be judged by asking what the poet's aim was and how well he accomplished it. Mencken's criticism was extremely influential in the 1920s in paving the way for the acceptance of the fiction of **Theodore Dreiser** and Sinclair Lewis; and **F. Scott Fitzgerald** gave Mencken credit for having created a climate favorable for new fiction. Also, Mencken not only reviewed the work of African American writers—he took a special interest in the novelists **James Weldon Johnson** and Walter White—but he also published black writers in his literary magazine, the *American Mercury*.

Less known but at least as important as Mencken's journalism and literary criticism is his scholarship. In addition to his two books on Nietzsche, Mencken also wrote a book on the dramatist George Bernard Shaw. But his greatest contribution to scholarship is his study, *The American Language: An Inquiry into the Development of English in the United States* (New York: Knopf, 1943). He explains that he originally wrote the book in 1919 because "the American form of the English language was plainly departing form the parent stem," but that he had to rewrite it completely in 1943 because due to the world-wide influence of American movies, "the pull of American has become so powerful that it has begun to drag English with it." Mencken's study of American English remains an important piece of scholarship to this day.

Further Reading

Fecher, Charles. *Mencken: A Study of His Thought*. New York: Knopf, 1978.

Manchester, William. *Disturber of the Peace* [Biography of H. L. Mencken]. New York: Harper, 1950.

Nolte, William H. *H. L. Mencken: Literary Critic*. Middletown, CT: Wesleyan UP, 1966.

Richman, Sheldon L. "Mr. Mencken and the Jews." *American Scholar* 59.3 (Summer 1990): 407–11.

Scruggs, Charles. *The Sage in Harlem: H. L. Mencken and the Black Writers of the 1920s*. Baltimore: Johns Hopkins UP, 1984.

Eberhard Alsen

MERIWETHER, LOUISE (1923–)   African American novelist. Louise Meriwether's three published novels cover wide historical ground—from 1930s Harlem to Civil War Charleston and then to late twentieth-century Harlem—and encompass a corresponding range of narrative styles, from the naturalistic and brutal language in her first novel, *Daddy Was a Number Runner* (1970), to the lyricism and dreamy sensuality of her third novel, *Shadow Dancing* (2000).

Born in Haverstraw, New York, and educated in Harlem's public schools, Louise Meriwether earned her BA in English at New York University and a master's degree in journalism from the University of California at Los Angeles in 1965. Her first novel, *Daddy Was a Number Runner*, narrates events in the life of twelve-year-old Francie Coffin during the years of 1934 and 1935 in Harlem. Meriwether draws partially on autobiography for this novel—Meriwether's father worked as a number runner, an organizer of illegal gambling, to support his family in Harlem—but she is equally interested in recalling national history, in recording the period of African American history in which the hope of the **Harlem Renaissance** began to fade. In the novel, one ray of hope comes from the literature of this era, as when Francie reads **Claude McKay**'s *Home to Harlem* (1928) and thinks, "It was strange to discover that someone had written about these same raggedy streets I knew so well." Francie rejects the options seemingly available to the women she sees around her—prostitution, labor in white homes, or single motherhood under government assistance—but the novel is ambiguous about whether Francie, whose ambitions of going to college are threatened by poverty, sexual predators, and the lure of crime, will be able to escape these fates. *Daddy Was a Number Runner* provides an unflinching depiction of **racism** and violence.

After *Daddy Was a Number Runner*, Meriwether published three books of black history geared toward elementary school students, *The Freedom Ship of Robert Smalls* (1971), about a black Civil War hero; *The Heart Man: Dr. Daniel Hale Williams* (1972), about the black doctor who may have performed the first open heart surgery; and *Don't Ride the Bus on Monday: The Rosa Parks Story* (1973), about the civil rights activist who spurred the

Montgomery bus boycott. The first of these history books, *The Freedom Ship of Robert Smalls*, becomes the impetus for Meriwether's second novel *Fragments of the Ark* (1994), in which the protagonist Peter Mango, whose heroics are based on the actions of Smalls, steals a confederate gunboat for the Union cause. Meriwether's most recent novel, *Shadow Dancing* (2000), is a middle-class love story set in contemporary Harlem, which follows the turbulent romance and marriage of two artists, journalist Glenda Jackson and theater director Mark Abbitt.

Further Reading

Walker, Melissa. *Down from the Mountaintop: Black Women's Novels in the Wake of the Civil Rights Movement, 1966–1989.* New Haven and London: Yale UP, 1991.

Melissa S. Shields

MERKIN, DAPHNE (1954–)   Jewish American essayist, reviewer, journalist, and novelist, born in New York and educated at Barnard College. Merkin's magazine career began in *The New Yorker*'s typing pool. Within two years she was writing reviews for *The New Republic* and *The New York Times Book Review*. Her first published short story won the **Edward Lewis Wallant** Award and became a part of her novel *Enchantment* (1986). Merkin is known for her brash and blatant commentary that frequently defies political correctness, and although readers may find some of her personal explorations offensive in print, her broad-ranging intellect not only brings her experience as a post-**Holocaust** Jewish girl to life, but also invites the post-Holocaust generation as a whole to explore the unique questions of **identity** addressed directly to the historically persecuted **ethnicity**.

Merkin's tone typically offers little hint of restraint. As a journalist, she understands her task does not require an emotional bond be formed between herself and the reader, only between the reader and the subject. Likewise, as a critic, her task is to present her thoughts and opinions, not the thoughts and opinions that will have the most appeal to the most readers. Merkin simply projects her true self, a Jewish woman from an Orthodox Jewish family scarred by the effects of the Holocaust who views the world as a realist willing to probe beneath the polite surface.

Like her biting reviews and articles, the novel *Enchantment* provokes and challenges the reader and in so doing captures the essence of what it is like to grow up with parents dramatically challenged emotionally by their years under Nazi German rule. Merkin's directness and brazenness are best demonstrated through the fantasy of the main character, Hannah Lehman, who imagines her mother, strict, authoritarian, and unemotional, as the chief female officer at the German concentration camp in Auschwitz. This startling fantasy, something that may seem morbid or emotionally twisted, acts as a hallmark for Merkin's prose. *Enchantment* provides those outside the Jewish faith a means by which to understand the depths of suffering initiated by the Nazi regime. The death camps annihilated millions of innocent souls, but went on to scar and emotionally batter not only the survivors, but the children of the survivors as well. Merkin paints a portrait of the generational carnage left in the wake of Nazi terrorism with stunning clarity.

Dreaming of Hitler (1997) provides examples of Merkin's personal daring, wit, and powerful prose. This collection of essays, all previously published in journals including *The New Yorker* and *The New York Times Book Review,* covers a gamut of idiosyncratic topics from sex and marriage to celebrities and diets. Merkin's religious tradition enhances each subject, creating not simply a self-portrait, but a portrait of the present age. Whether probing the personal struggles of an emotionally unavailable mother, unconventional sexual pleasures, a failed marriage, or a lost religion, Merkin cannot escape her ethnicity, her Jewishness, any more than the world can escape the shadow of influence generated by the atrocities of the Holocaust.

The issue frequently arises in her writing, at times with candid recklessness, at other times with poignant elegance. One segment titled "In My Tribe" explores her impression of modern Israel and allows the reader to struggle with her as she attempts to glean personal meaning from the biblical Song of Songs. Sharing her thoughts on the Book of Ecclesiastes takes the reader to the Orthodox household of Merkin's youth and memories of Succot, the Jewish festival of Booths.

Perhaps the title essay and most inventive piece of *Dreaming of Hitler* best demonstrates Merkin's contribution to literature as a Jewish American writer. In this selection, Merkin relates a childhood dream in which she attempts to convince Hitler that he actually does not hate Jews. Deep within her youthful innocence rests a reflection of the true nature of Judaism. Merkin represents in this essay the universal Jew confronting not the man responsible for the near extermination of European Jewry, but the soul of **anti-Semitism**. In view of the catastrophic atrocities, revenge seems the only human response after such inhuman treatment, but instead Merkin attempts to convince Hitler that he does not hate Jews, echoing back through all the genocidal pogroms of European history. Merkin reminds readers that it was the hatred of a **race**, not the actions of a race, that led to mass murder. She reminds readers the answer lies in the wisdom of the Torah, the sacred writings linking Christians and Jews: Thou Shall Not Kill.

Further Reading

Leak, Andrew, and George Paizis, eds. *The Holocaust and the Text: Speaking the Unspeakable.* New York: St. Martin's Press, 2000.

Nadel, Ira Bruce. *Jewish Writers of North America: A Guide to Information Sources.* Detroit, Michigan: Gale Research Company, 1981.

Solotaroff, Ted, and Nessa Rapoport, eds. *Writing Our Way Home: Contemporary Stories by American Jewish Writers.* New York: Schocken Books, 1992.

Wirth-Nesher, Hana, and Michael P. Kramer, eds. *The Cambridge Companion to Jewish American Literature.* New York: Cambridge UP, 2003.

Christine Marie Hilger

MEXICAN AMERICAN AUTOBIOGRAPHY   In reading a novel we are allowed into the writer's creative mind, but in reading an autobiography we are given privileged access into the writer's very soul. Mexican Americans now constitute the largest minority group in the United States, and since much of their literature is autobiographical, one task is determining what should be categorized as fiction and what can be considered autobiography. Autobiographical literature is found in all genres: novels, essays, short stories, poems, plays, biographies, and oral histories/*testimonios.* Autobiographies range from the lyrical-poetic to the sociohistorical with everything in between.

The origin of Mexican American autobiography depends on how the term *Mexican American* is defined, for some sixteenth and seventeenth century Spanish explorers like Bartolomé De Las Casas (*A Short Account of the Destruction of the Indies,* 1552) and Bernal Díaz (*The Conquest of New Spain,* c. 1568) wrote about their travels in the Americas. These works might more accurately be referred to as U.S. Hispanic literature, but even that definition can be problematic. Generally scholars of the Mexican American autobiography focus on works published after 1848, when the Treaty of Guadalupe Hidalgo was signed and when some 80,000 Mexican nationals became U.S. citizens.

Autobiographical writers often address questions of identity: "who am I?" Increasingly, there are autobiographies written by those who are part Mexican, so **identity** issues abound. Some writers wish to preserve history and leave a record for the younger, often more assimilated generation. Many memoirs focus on coming-of-age experiences, which often include immigration, schooling, language-acquisition, **assimilation**, cultural conflict, migrant work, love, sex, and religion. Other narratives are episodic and focus on specific dramatic events; some autobiographies underscore themes of prejudice; a few read like a Chicano rags-to-riches story. More and more, these narratives are written by the moderately famous (actors, politicians, business people, scholars, singers). Memoirs are also produced by war veterans, ex-gang members, gays, prisoners, students, and ministers. Furthermore, Mexico's tripartite identity—Spanish, Indian, and *mestizo* (mixed)—contributes to a complicated sense of identity and loyalty.

Autobiographical works raise questions about truth, exaggeration, embellishment, obfuscation, posturing, and so forth. Since many autobiographies are penned late in the author's life, memory also serves as a significant factor. Some writers record dialogue that may have occurred when they were young, but it is unlikely that they can remember such details verbatim five or six decades later. There is thus the *invention* of words and scenes, though usually these literary conventions are accepted by readers. Sometimes childhood is romanticized or idealized; sometimes past difficulties are exaggerated; important details can be left out or ignored. Writers usually (and sometimes artificially) impose structure, emphasize conflict or change, create themes or resolution, composite characters, and change names (or circumstances) of people. Moreover, in recording a life, the life is not merely explained or presented, but rather a *persona* is developed. Similarly, time and space create restrictions, for it is impossible to record a life in totality: much must, of necessity, be left out. Thus, some of these narratives end while the authors are barely out of their teens, some focus primarily on the latter part of their lives—their successes, some are primarily about their formal education, and some autobiographies give a great deal of background on the lives of ancestors and parents and therefore border on biography.

A few autobiographical works defy genres and are difficult to classify: **Richard Rodriguez**'s works take the form of autobiography, essays, and journalism. Like the work of other Mexican American writers, Floyd Salas's writing is autobiographical, biographical, and fictional. **Cherríe Moraga** and **Gloria Anzaldúa** both inventively combine poetry, essays, stories, journal entries, lesbian politics, and autobiography. Anzaldúa, for example, described herself as a Chicana *tejana*-lesbian-feminist writer. Other autobiographical texts are sociological, political, historical, psychological, or anthropological.

Under the rubric of autobiographical fiction—one of the largest categories within Mexican American literature—we have a number of notable works including: **José Antonio Villarreal**'s *Pocho* (1959), **John Rechy**'s *City of Night* (1963), **Tomás Rivera**'s *. . . y no se lo trago la tierra* (1971), **Rudolfo Anaya**'s *Bless Me, Ultima* (1972), Nash Candelaria's *Memories of the Alhambra* (1977), **Sandra Cisneros**'s *House on Mango Street* (1984), **Arturo Islas**'s *The Rain God* (1984), and Patricia Santana's *Motorcycle Ride on the Sea of Tranquility* (2002); these writers, and myriad others, borrow considerably from their own life experiences.

Early writers of autobiographical narratives include Fabiola Cabeza de Baca, Fray Angelico Chavez, Cleofas Jaramillo, Miguel Otero, Juan Seguin, Leonor Villegas de Magnon, and Luis Perez, among others. In these early writers' works, there is sometimes a romanticized view of the world. Many of these narratives were written by middle-class Mexican Americans who often referred to themselves simply as *Hispanos* or *Mejicanos*—without a hyphen, and there is often considerable class-consciousness as well as an attempt to maintain Spanish (as opposed to Mexican or Indian) roots.

One of the most enduring and endearing Mexican American autobiographies is **Ernesto Galarza**'s *Barrio Boy* (1971), which begins in Mexico during the revolution of 1910. Young Ernie migrates with his mother and uncles and eventually settles in Sacramento, California. The subtitle "The Story of a Boy's Acculturation" presents one of Galarza's concerns, for he believes his own experiences are characteristic of thousands of other immigrants who fled the revolution. The book ends before Galarza begins high school, even though he went on to earn a PhD. Like other works in this genre, this is a poignant, somewhat bittersweet, coming-of-age story that relates the difficulties associated with **immigration** and poverty.

Oscar Acosta's *The Autobiography of a Brown Buffalo* (1972) presents a troubled and complex individual searching for a sense of identity. The autobiographical novel is organized around several trips/quests: Acosta is on an actual road trip, he trips on drugs, and he explores his past via a psychiatrist. These journeys/quests are effectively interwoven within the late 1960s San Francisco counterculture. At the end of the book, in Mexico, Acosta claims to have finally found and accepted himself. The sequel, *The Revolt of the Cockroach People* (1973), chronicles his legal work for the Chicano Civil Rights Movement in Los Angeles. Although at times crude and sexist, Acosta captures the complexities of his culture and his era.

A prominent and controversial book is Richard Rodriguez's **Hunger of Memory**, which was positively reviewed when it appeared in 1981. It is partly a collection of previously published—and carefully crafted—essays that were compiled and edited into book format. As a child, Rodriguez was inadvertently taught to be ashamed of his brown skin, and he once tried to scrape away the dark pigment with a straight razor. Other chapters deal with Rodriguez's assertions that because of his superior education, he is not a disadvantaged minority but rather a middle-class assimilated American. Numerous Chicano scholars think that Rodriguez repudiates his culture, and he has been accused of having a colonized mind. In particular, minorities have been critical of his stance against affirmative action and bilingual education. Despite these critiques, it is acknowledged that Rodriguez is a fine prose stylist. He is an award-winning journalist who has since produced two other collections of essays: *Days of Obligation* (1992) and *Brown* (2002), which discuss topics germane to minorities. One work that might serve as a companion piece to *Hunger of Memory* is Ruben Navarrette's *A Darker Shade of Crimson* (1993) about his experiences as a Chicano at Harvard University. He devotes a few pages to discussion of Rodriguez.

Also of particular significance are the two distinguished autobiographies by Francisco Jiménez: *The Circuit* (1997) and *Breaking Through* (2001), in which he chronicles his family's immigration from Mexico to California, their struggles, deportation, and their return. Despite hardship and prejudice, and because of much diligent work, Francisco manages to excel in school and continue to college. Thus, he is able to break through the cycle of poverty and ultimately become a professor.

Gary Soto is among the more prolific producers of personal stories. He has written at least four autobiographical texts, and his background as an award-winning poet lends his writing a richness of imagery and metaphor. His short stories about growing up poor and Mexican in Fresno, California, are full of grace and humor. *The Effects of Knut Hamsun on a Fresno Boy* (2000) is a highly recommended introduction to Soto's autobiographical prose since it borrows from earlier books and presents new work as well.

Surprisingly there are not many autobiographies by women, and Mary Helen Ponce adds the much-needed female voice to this genre. *Hoyt Street* (1993) is a collection of charming stories set in a small town near Los Angeles in the 1940s and 1950s. These stories primarily detail her years up to the onset of puberty. She relates coming-of-age experiences that are typical of Mexican-Americans growing up at that time. Another notable work is Elva Trevino Hart's *Barefoot Heart: Stories of a Migrant Child* (1999), a sensitively written account that carefully delineates the wearisome world of migrant work. Although she begins by writing, "I am nobody. And my story is the same as a million others," she went on to earn a graduate degree in computer science/engineering from Stanford University. Michele Serros's *How to Be a Chicana Role Model* (2000) is a funny, hip, contemporary, and loosely autobiographical work set in the Los Angeles area. Other significant works include Norma Cantu's *Canicula* (1995) and **Pat Mora**'s *House of Houses* (1997).

Gang memoirs and prison narratives have increased in popularity, and in this category Luis Rodriguez's *Always Running: La Vida Loca: Gang Days in L.A.* (1993) stands out among the best written. One poet who has recently produced prose about his prison experience is **Jimmy Baca**, whose *A Place to Stand* (2001) is an exceptionally moving and dramatic story of a boy who is essentially abandoned by his parents, grows up in an orphanage, and eventually goes to prison on drug charges. While there, he teaches himself to read and thus transforms his life. Mona Ruiz, a former gang member, became a police officer and, with the *Los Angeles Times* journalist Jeff Boucher, produced *Two Badges: The Lives of Mona Ruiz* (1997). Ruiz not only renders gang life from the female point of view, but she also presents episodes from an abusive marriage that she is finally able to flee.

Although Chicano/a literature is primarily a working-class instrument, most writers who have penned their life stories ironically have graduate degrees—including PhDs. Recently there have been a number of autobiographies by former college professors and administrators, including *Luis Leal: An Auto/Biography, Julian Nava: My Mexican-American Journey*, Ramón Ruiz's *Memories of a Hyphenated Man*, and Kevin Johnson's *How Did You Get to Be Mexican?* While many autobiographies are loosely set within the Chicano/a movement of the 1960s and 1970s—and include such themes as poverty, racism, and the migrant experience—increasingly, there are works that lie outside the marginalized-Mexican point of view: writings by Linda Chavez, Julian Nava, David Maldonado, Kevin Johnson, and perhaps Floyd Salas and Miguel Otero are examples. These writers, like some who are part-Mexican, such as Anthony Quinn, Joan Baez, John Rechy, Cherríe Moraga, **Luis Alberto Urrea**, Linda Chavez, and Kevin R. Johnson, do not always identify with traditional Mexican culture.

In contrast, Mexican nationals have come to the United States and written about their experiences, as did Ramon Perez in his depiction of picaresque adventures as an illegal, *Diary of an Undocumented Immigrant* (1989). A more difficult case is Ilan Stavans (*On Borrowed Words*, 2001), a Mexican of Jewish ancestry, now a professor at Amherst College. An eclectic and prolific scholar, Stavans also writes about U.S. Latino literature (among numerous other topics). In a loose sense, some of the work by Perez and

Stavans could be considered Chicano literature. When *Famous All Over Town* by **Danny Santiago** was published, readers thought it was an auto-biographical work by a young Chicano, but it turned out to have been penned by an elderly Anglo social worker named Daniel James. Some writers do not fully accept the designation "Chicano," like José Antonio Villar-real or Richard Rodriguez. Furthermore, as Mexican Americans continue to intermarry we will have more complex categories: among the more interesting, Blaxicans (Black-Mexican) and Mexipinos (Mexican-Filipino), as well as amalgams of other minority groups.

Memoirs by those somewhat well known have been recorded by Anthony Quinn, Linda Chavez, Julian Nava, Joan Baez, Lydia Mendoza, Maria Hinojosa, David Maldonado, Luis Leal, Bert Corna, Miguel Otero, Ramón Ruiz, and others. And while the working-class immigrant autobiography will continue to be popular, there will continue to be more autobiographies by women, those who are middle-class, and those who are not Catholic and by semi-celebrities, politicians, athletes, actors, and scholars. Increasingly, there will be more works that are unorthodox or experimental within the genre—works like Michele Serros's *Chicana Falsa and other stories of death, identity, and Oxnard* (1993). The accelerated output within Mexican American autobiography will also lead to more scholarly research on the subject, for there is a scarcity of full-length works in the field.

Autobiography is usually literary ground zero for those who wish to write; apprenticeship novels are often based on the writer's life. Though many authors feel that their experiences are not unique, Mexican American autobiographies provide a privileged portal into what it means to immigrate, what it means to be marginalized, what it means to suffer, what it means to love, and ultimately what it means to be human.

Further Reading

Bruce-Novoa, Juan. *Retrospace: Collected Essays on Chicano Literature.* Houston: Arte Público Press, 1990.

Flores, Lauro. "Chicano Autobiography: Culture, Ideology and the Self." *The Americas Review* 18.2 (Summer 1990): 80–91.

Jimenez, Francisco, ed. *The Identification and Analysis of Chicano Literature.* Binghamton: Bilingual Press, 1979.

Lattin, Vernon E., ed. *Contemporary Chicano Fiction.* Binghamton: Bilingual Press, 1986

Olivares, Julian, ed. *The Americans Review* [Issue on U.S. Hispanic Autobiography] 16.3–4 (Fall–Winter 1988).

Padilla, Genaro M. *My History, Not Yours: The Formation of Mexican American Autobiography.* Madison: U of Wisconsin P, 1993

Saldívar, Ramón. *Chicano Narrative: The Dialectics of Difference.* Madison: U of Wisconsin P, 1990.

Shirley, Carl R., and Paula W. Shirley. *Understanding Chicano Literature.* Columbia: U of South Carolina P, 1988.

Paul Guajardo

MEXICAN AMERICAN CHILDREN'S LITERATURE   Over the past decade, the field of Mexican American children's literature has expanded dramatically. To be sure, publishers' interest in tapping a lucrative market has facilitated this growth. Yet although market dynamics are integral to any understanding of the astounding growth that has taken place in this genre, they do not fully explain why, in particular, authors such as **Gloria Anzaldúa**, **Luis J. Rodríguez**, **Ana Castillo**, **Rudolfo Anaya**, and Juan Felipe Herrera, all already renowned for their "adult" fiction, criticism, and theory, have begun in greater numbers to write for younger audiences. Collectively, Mexican American writers who publish books for children tend to be motivated by a desire to tell the stories of Mexican American lives in order to validate these experiences. In addition, many of these authors seek to intervene, for the better, in the thinking habits of young readers by facilitating critical thinking about various social issues.

Poet **Francisco Alarcón**, who has published several illustrated collections of poetry for children, suggests the importance of depicting culturally-specific experiences when he explains, "When you don't see your own images through the media or in books, you start thinking you're weird, and your self-esteem gets bruised" (Fernandez E3). In collections such as *Laughing Tomatoes and Other Spring Poems* (1997), Alarcón makes poetry out of daily life and out of the immediate physical environment that may be familiar to children. In effect, the people, landscape, and cityscape that surround young people emerge poetic in their own right. Importantly, the apparent simplicity of the poems in terms of their structure, language, and subjects invites young readers to make poetry about their own surroundings and experiences.

The earliest examples of Mexican American children's literature emanate from this basic desire to validate Mexican American identities. Works such as Elia Robledo Durán's *Joaquín, niño de Aztlán* (1972), Graciela Carrillo's *El frijol mágico* (1974), and Nepthtalí de León's *I Will Catch the Sun* (1973) legitimate Mexican American cultural attributes simply by portraying these attributes. As the authors of these texts strategically contradict the erasure and disparagement of Mexican American **identity** and culture, they attempt to counter the shame young people may feel because they are "different" or because they belong to an ethnic group that historically has had a denigrated standing in the United States. Along these same lines, a number of writers have published adaptations and collections of Mexican and Mexican American folktales in an effort to celebrate and sustain these oral traditions.

A number of writers have devoted themselves to telling hitherto untold stories about the children of migrant, farmworking families. For example, bilingual, illustrated books by Juan Felipe Herrera (*The Upside Down Boy* [2000], *Calling the Doves* [2001]) as well as **Francisco Jimenez**'s novel, *The Circuit: Stories from the Life of a Migrant Child* (1997), depict the sometimes warm, sometimes traumatic nature of life for these children. Herrera and

Jimenez foreground the family as a space of love and security for these children while school and the public realm in general represent intimidating, alien spaces. Though books such as these hold special significance for children for whom **immigration**, **racism**, and social marginalization are a part of their own experience, books such as these can also be valuable for children who come from different backgrounds and who are otherwise unfamiliar with such experiences. For such children, the stories told by Herrera and Jimenez can prompt an empathetic understanding of how some children live and thus enable a critical understanding of racism, poverty, and immigration. This is especially true of Gloria Anzaldúa's controversial work, *Friends from the Other Side* (1993). This illustrated book deconstructs figurations of Mexican immigrants as "wetback" others by emphasizing their moral decency and by inviting compassion for Joaquín, an undocumented boy who worries about eluding the Border Patrol and who struggles to support his mother and himself.

The recent surge in literature for children by established Mexican American writers such as Anzaldúa can be best understood via realization that these writers wield an activist desire to inspire positive changes in readers' attitudes, perceptions, behaviors, and sympathies in relation to a range of contemporary issues. To write for children allows writers of an activist orientation to extend the reach of their efforts to raise others' critical awareness. In turn, they manage to more completely fulfill their commitment to contribute to the well being of their communities.

Ana Castillo, Luis Rodríguez, and Rudolfo Anaya are some of the other noteworthy authors who have crossed over into children's literature. Castillo, who has received acclaim for novels such as *So Far from God* (1993) and *Peel My Love Like an Onion* (1999), offers young readers of *My Daughter, My Son, the Eagle, the Dove* (2000) a reenvisioning of gender roles. In an effort to disrupt the perpetuation of conventional definitions of masculinity and femininity that lead to unhealthy forms of manhood and cripple women's autonomy and self-esteem, Castillo encourages boys to become compassionate men while she asks girls to grow into confident, self-reliant, and brave women. Like Castillo, Rodríguez betrays a special interest in tackling gender issues in his children's books. In *América Is Her Name* (1998), the subjects of racism and the oppression of women and girls within Latino cultures are portrayed critically. In *It Doesn't Have to Be This Way* (1999), Rodríguez interrogates masculinity and gangs. A former gang member himself, Rodríguez suggests that boys can find ways to be men outside of gangs.

To maximize the activist value of their books for children, many Mexican American authors craft their stories so that they provoke both children and adults to think critically about a range of social and cultural concerns. For this reason, some Mexican American illustrated books for children may seem bolder in relation to other illustrated books for children in terms of the issues they engage and their frank manner of engaging them. Ideally, through dual address, both young and old(er) readers can come to better understandings of the problems that haunt their lives and their communities so that they may both participate in the healing of these problems. As children and adults share in the experience of reading about contemporary concerns, they can share with each other their understandings of the issues being addressed and then collaboratively arrive at possible strategies for rectifying them.

Gloria Velásquez is an especially innovative figure within the field of Mexican American children's literature. In her *Roosevelt High School* series (which includes *Juanita Fights the School Board* [1994], *Maya's Divided World* [1995], and *Tommy Stands Alone* [1999]), Velásquez introduces protagonists who tackle the same difficult issues that adolescents face. Issues of discrimination and gender suffuse *Juanita Fights the School Board,* a novel about a girl who is expelled from school for fighting another student who had been hurling racial slurs at her. Although one valuable feature of this first installment in the *Roosevelt* series is its depiction of life for the daughter of farm worker parents, an important feature of the sequel, *Maya's Divided World,* is its depiction of an upper-middle class Mexican American household. Together, *Juanita Fights the School Board* and *Maya's Divided World* portray diversity amongst Mexican American families. Maya's mother is a university professor and her father is an engineer, and because of their commitment to their professions, Maya feels neglected. Eventually, she rebels and runs away from home. *Tommy Stands Alone* is a breakthrough novel that portrays the homophobia, parental rejection, and suicidal tendencies that too many gay adolescents endure. With this novel, Velásquez speaks to gay youth by acknowledging their ordeals, and she simultaneously invites others to reconsider homophobia.

Of course, while well-intentioned authors of literature for children pursue particular political agendas, the issue of literacy development cannot be overlooked. Indeed, it is possible to worry that as Herrera, Anzaldúa, Rodríguez, and others explore the political possibilities of children's literature, the capacity of stories to develop literacy risks being forgotten. Authors thus face the challenge of crafting books that strengthen young readers' reading skills, nurture a love of reading, and convey positive lessons about potentially unpleasant subjects. Herrera creatively tries to accomplish this balance with *Super Cilantro Girl* (2003), a story that disarticulates the validity of border policies as it introduces readers to a Chicana superhero. Questions remain, however, as to whether a writer really can ever perform such a careful balancing act. Moreover, ethical questions automatically accompany any efforts to inscribe a political purpose into a book for children because of a fear of such books functioning as nothing less than tools of indoctrination.

Gary Soto and **Pat Mora**, perhaps the most prolific Mexican American writers of books for children, validate Mexican American experiences and convey positive messages, yet they seem especially concerned with creating enjoyable reading experiences. Relative to some other Mexican American children's books, the works of Soto and Mora tend to be lighter in terms of their politicized content. Soto has in fact professed his commitment to writing short stories and illustrated books that entertain audiences. Indeed, some of his work captures culturally specific experiences, appeals to culturally specific sensibilities, and engages difficult realities, such as racism and poverty. Predominately, however, Soto crafts his works to hold universal appeal. Among his collections of short stories, *Baseball in April* (1990) and *Living Up the Street* (1992) focus on common growing up experiences. Of Soto's many illustrated books, *Too Many Tamales* (1993) has become a Christmas classic because it amuses readers with its playful narration of a girl's worry that she has unwittingly dropped her mother's wedding ring in tamale dough.

Pat Mora, who has been celebrated for her poetry for adults (*Chants* [1984], *Borders* [1986]), has also produced a number of books for young adults and young children. *My Own True Name: New and Selected Poems for Young Adults* (2000) engages the personal issues young adults must face as it also touches upon various social topics. Illustrated books such as *Pablo's Tree* (1994), *The Desert Is My Mother* (1994), and *Tomás and the Library Lady* (1997) cover themes as diverse as family ties, the beauty of nature, and the excitement that can be found in the library. Thus, in contrast to authors who unflinchingly deal with harsh realities in their books for children, Mora emphasizes the freedom and excitement that can also characterize childhood. Rather than suggesting Mora's naïve insistence on protecting tenuous assumptions about childhood innocence, her books simply reflect her different strategy for participating in child readers' lives.

Diversity in writers' agendas has made Mexican American children's literature a very dynamic genre. A survey of the field reveals a panoply of approaches that writers have followed as they participate in the moral and intellectual edification of young people, encourage cultural pride, and provide young people with amusement. Ultimately, such diversity can be seen as healthy and useful. The existence of so many different approaches to the writing of literature for children means that there are ongoing reevaluations within the genre, and this carries the possibility for more enlightened innovations and developments to occur.

Further Reading

Day, Frances Ann. *Latina and Latino Voices in Literature for Children and Teenagers.* Portsmouth, NH: Heinemann, 1997.

Fernandez, Maria Elena. "A New Chapter on Cultural Pride." *Los Angeles Times* (September 24, 2000): E1+.

Phillip Serrato

MEXICAN AMERICAN DRAMA   The roots of Mexican American drama extend far beyond the physical borders and historical formation of the United States. Theatrical performances by Mexican Americans have occurred for as long as formerly Mexican territories have been part of the United States. Mexican American performance traditions derive from a rich array of cultural performances all over the world, including various indigenous performance styles, colonial Spanish religious dramas, Mexican *carpas* (tent shows), Brechtian techniques, Augusto Boal's theater of the oppressed, and various forms of social protest theater in the United States in the 1960s. Since the start of the Chicano Movement in 1965, many Mexican American theater practitioners have chosen to identify as Chicanas and Chicanos, rather than Mexican Americans. For this reason, Mexican American drama from 1965 to the present is most often categorized as Chicana/o drama. From its inception to the present day, Mexican American drama/Chicana/o drama has been a valuable and active part of American drama as a whole.

The earliest Mexican American theater frequently consisted of Catholic morality plays in Spanish performed throughout the southwestern United States as a means of increasing church membership or teaching lessons from the Bible. Mexican American performances also included secular folk dramas, traveling tent shows in Mexican *carpa* style, and vaudevillian *variedades* (variety shows). Nicolás Kanellos and Elizabeth Ramírez are among the scholars who have written about Mexican American drama before 1965.

The Chicano Movement began with the United Farm Workers (UFW) union's first major act of social protest: the Great Delano Grape Strike of 1965. **Luis Valdez**, the son of migrant farm workers and a native of Delano, convinced the UFW leader César Chávez that theater could be used as a means to further the strike. Valdez founded El Teatro Campesino (The Farmworkers' Theatre) by bringing together a group of unionized farm workers as a company of actors. On the first day of rehearsal, Valdez passed out scripts he had written for a political skit. When he discovered that most of his actors were illiterate, the scripts were tossed aside, and a theater of improvisation was born. Valdez would create scenarios, and the actors would improvise short scenes that encouraged workers to join the union and support the strike. The *acto* (short political skit) became the signature format of El Teatro Campesino because it was a portable and effective medium of performance. The troupe performed in the fields and on the beds of trucks so that they could reach their target audience and escape quickly if angry growers threatened them.

El Teatro Campesino quickly began performing about issues beyond the strike, and as their popularity grew during the Chicano Movement of the late 1960s and early 1970s, *teatros* (Chicana/o theater companies) began appearing all over the United States. Groups such as Teatro de la Esperanza (Theatre of Hope), Su Teatro (Your Theatre), Teatro de los Pobres (Theatre of the Poor), and many others fed the Chicano Movement by rallying groups of people to various causes associated with the Movement. Chicana/o performances during this time period argued in favor of bilingual and ethnically specific education for Chicana/o students, explored Chicana/o **identity**, and protested against the Vietnam War.

have wreaked upon farm workers and their families, while simultaneously embodying the will to resist these oppressions.

Cerezita's family suffers from a variety of social and physical maladies. Cerezita's mother refuses to let her out of the house. Her father deserted the family long before the play begins. Her sister's baby is dying because of birth defects caused by the pesticides, and her gay brother contracts HIV during the course of the play. Moraga has been criticized for addressing too many issues in a single play, but she has also been praised for weaving together deeply meaningful social issues that in reality do have enormous impacts on one another. *Heroes and Saints* examines the corporeality and spirituality of a farm worker community, as the limbless protagonist watches the children around her die. The play addresses life and death with rich metaphors and symbolism melded to urgent social issues.

Just as the sexist tendencies of the early Chicano Movement had previously shut out the voices of women, the homophobia of the movement prevented the voices of queer playwrights from being heard. **Guillermo Reyes**, Oliver Mayer, Monica Palacios, Cherríe Moraga, and **Luis Alfaro** are among those who have been writing on queer themes in Chicana/o theater since the 1980s. Though Guillermo Reyes is of Chilean American descent, academics and theater practitioners often include his work in discussions of Chicana/o theater because so many of his characters are Chicanas and Chicanos.

The premier of Reyes play *Deporting the Divas* took place in March of 1996 at the Celebration Theatre in Los Angeles, California. The play's main character is a Chicano named Michael González who works as a U.S. border patrol agent. He also struggles with his homosexuality, especially when he discovers his attraction to Sedicio, an undocumented immigrant who broadens Michael's mind and tolerates his profession. Michael has an ongoing daydream of his ideal mate: a transvestite tango queen named Sirena Angustias. Michael's wanderings between fantasy and reality reflect his fragmented identity as a gay Latino, and the conflicts in the play over immigration issues serve to question labels such as "illegal" and "undocumented" when applied to thinking, feeling human beings who are no less a part of U.S. society and economy than native-born citizens.

Several of the original *teatros* from the 1960s and 1970s remain active today, including El Teatro Campesino and Teatro de la Esperanza. Groups such as the Latino Theater Company, the Chicano Secret Service, and Latins Anonymous have written and produced popular performances in the time since the end of the heyday of Chicana/o *teatros*. However, the three-man *teatro* **Culture Clash** is currently the Chicana/o theater group that finds the most consistent and widespread commercial success in the regional theaters. Since 1994 Culture Clash has been working on a continuing project they call Culture Clash in AmeriCCa. Regional theaters around the country have commissioned the trio to write interview-based plays about their cities, as a means of exploring interactions between different ethnic and cultural groups in the

United States. Using sketches from their first site-specific play, *Radio Mambo: Culture Clash Invades Miami,* and each of the five subsequent plays in the project, they regularly tour the country performing a compilation show also called *Culture Clash in AmeriCCa.*

In a departure from the episodic format of their previous site-specific plays, Culture Clash's most recent research-based play *Chavez Ravine* returns in many ways to the tradition of docudrama in Chicana/o theater. The play had its premier in the summer of 2003 at the Mark Taper Forum in Los Angeles under the direction of Lisa Peterson. *Chavez Ravine* documents the struggle over land rights in a section of Los Angeles known as Chavez Ravine. The ravine once held generations of Mexican American families who were displaced for the purpose of constructing Dodger Stadium. Actress Eileen Galindo joined Richard Montoya, Ric Salinas, and Herbert Sigüenza of Culture Clash to perform the more than fifty characters in the play. The play blends slapstick humor, historical fact, and deliberate fiction as it retells the history of Los Angeles and its people.

Ultimately, Mexican American and Chicana/o drama is a theater of politics, a theater of community, a theater of social justice activism. Its performance venues and writing styles have changed and evolved significantly, from the religious performances begun during the Spanish conquest to El Teatro Campesino's *actos* of the Chicano Movement to professional productions of Chicana/o plays in theaters all over the country. All of these Chicana/o performance traditions are still practiced today, but the art form continues to evolve and diversify with the community. What has not changed, however, is the pervasive activist spirit and community-oriented nature of the work being done in Chicana/o theater.

Further Reading

Huerta, Jorge A. *Chicano Drama: Performance, Society and Myth.* Cambridge: Cambridge UP, 2000.

———. *Chicano Theater: Themes and Forms.* Ypsilanti, MI: Bilingual Press/Editorial Bilingüe, 1982.

Kanellos, Nicolás. *A History of Hispanic Theatre in the United States: Origins to 1940.* Austin: U of Texas P, 1990.

———. *Mexican American Theatre: Legacy and Reality.* Pittsburgh: Latin American Literary Review Press, 1987.

———, ed. *Mexican American Theatre: Then and Now.* Houston: Arte Público Press, 1989.

Ramirez, Elizabeth C. *Chicanas/Latinas in American Theatre: A History of Performance.* Bloomington: Indiana UP, 2000.

Ashley Lucas

MEXICAN AMERICAN GAY LITERATURE Gay Mexican American (Chicano) writing came into its own in the 1980s. While gay Chicanos were certainly writing before this period, they were largely silenced by homophobic Chicano-nationalist and mainstream publishers; and though post-1969 Stonewall gay/lesbian activism led to the founding of small presses that produced and disseminated larger numbers of white gay and lesbian authors, gay literature of color (Chicano especially) continued to receive scant attention.

The renaissance of gay Chicano literature in the 1980s owes much to the activist-intellectual work of lesbian feminsts such as **Cherríe Moraga** and **Gloria Anzaldúa**. The 1981 publication by AuntLute Press of *This Bridge Called My Back,* an anthology edited by Moraga and Anzaldúa, marked an important shift in the publishing of Chicano lesbian literature. Their various creative explorations and explosions of the traditionally straight Chicano vs. Anglo fiction and poetics that defined a 1970s Chicano **canon** helped pave the way for the arrival of the gay Chicano author.

In 1986, the foremost Chicano literary scholar, **Juan Bruce-Novoa**, published the seminal essay, "Homosexuality and the Chicano Novel," wherein he naturalized the union of "gay" with "Chicano." No longer could one read, for example, **John Rechy**'s novels as gay sex-shock narrative; one had to read his work as fundamentally Chicano as well. Moreover, Bruce-Novoa remapped the existing straight Chicano/a literary canon, identifying its implicit homoerotic edge. For Bruce-Novoa, to ignore the gay Chicano voice was to miss the "dynamic and exciting" force at the core of Chicano literature.

Largely the result of such scholarly moves toward inclusion and of the hard work of lesbian and gay activist intellectuals and writers—the establishment of independent publishing venues and the struggle to educate a New York publishing world—gay poets, playwrights, and novelists, began coming into their own.

In the area of poetry, we see a range of different voices, including **Francisco X. Alarcón** (1954–) who blazed new trails with his powerfully gay and indigenous poetic voice as seen in *Ya vas, Carnal* (1984) and *Tattoos* (1984). In both collections, Alarcón uses poetic rhythm and a penetrating, staccato voice to affirm his gay and Chicano **identity** within a racist and homophobic mainstream society. For Alarcón, the black marks on the page were more than just words, they formed images that lashed back at his racist world. In his *Body in Flames* (1991), Alarcón intermixes pre-Columbian myth with his inhabiting of a gay Chicano body in the present; he clears a space for a gay Chicano poetic where mind is no longer forced apart from body. In the mid-1990s yet another important gay Chicano poet arrived on the scene, the late Gil Cuadros. However, rather than unify a mythological past with a gay Chicano present, Cuadros sought to texture his childhood and coming out experience as a teenager in Los Angeles; to capture his feelings of estrangement both from the white gay community that exoticizes his brown body and from his Chicano community that promotes a queer hostile *machismo,* he intermixes poetry and prose in the writing of his memoir, *City of God* (1994)—a powerful testament to his struggle to humanize the gay Chicano experience before his death from an AIDS-related illness.

Gay authors have found solid footing in other genres such as memoir/essay form and drama. For example, one of the first on the drama scene was Los Angeles born and based, **Luis Alfaro**. A self-identifying queer artist-activist, Alfaro's many performances and plays—*Downtown* (1980), *Cuerpo Politizado* (1996), *Straight as a Line* (2000), to name a few—often employ a sharp, biting edge to express the multiform gay Chicano experience. And gay journalist/essayist **Richard Rodriguez** has made a name for himself nationwide. Though his work for the Pacific News Services deals mostly with issues of **race**, his essayistic memoirs bring together issues of being gay and brown in the United States and Mexico; we see this faintly whispered in his best-selling **Hunger of Memory** (1982) and then more boldly in his *Days of Obligation* (1993) and *Brown* (2003). In *Days of Obligation,* for example, he makes public secrets otherwise kept in the closet by his Chicano upbringing: "to grow up homosexual is to live with secrets and within secrets. In no other place are those secrets more closely guarded than within the family home." In *Brown,* he uses his trademark fast-paced and highly stylized journalese to render visible his experiences as queer and Chicano in so-identified post-Protestant/Catholic, postcolonial Americas.

Gay Chicano novelists have carved paths deep and wide into the Chicano and literary canons. We see this especially in the work of John Rechy, **Arturo Islas**, and **Michael Nava**, who have variously used a number of different storytelling techniques and styles—the picaresque, the mystery suspense, stream of consciousness, and mixed media pastiche—to reframe one-dimensional representations of gay Chicanos. We see this, for example, with Rechy's use of the stream of consciousness form to tell the story of Amalia Gómez in his novel, *The Miraculous Day of Amalia Gómez* (1991). Here, Rechy focuses on the psychological transformation of Amalia as she comes to terms with a contemporary racist and violent Los Angeles as well as her son's gay sexuality. And we see in the novels of the late Arturo Islas—*The Rain God* (1984) and *Migrant Souls*—how one can weave with great subtlety the gay voice into the texturing of Chicano family life along the U.S.-Mexico border. Islas complicates his vision of gay Chicano **identity** and experience in his posthumously published novel, *La Mollie and the King of Tears* (1996), where he uses a fast paced first-person voice to tell the story of straight Louie Mendoza, whose discovery of self includes his coming to terms with his own fluid sexuality as well as his brother's gay identity. Author Michael Nava introduced gay Chicano lawyer/detective character, Henry Rios, when he published *The Little Death* in 1986, and he published seven more novels in the series that finally ended in 2001 with *Rag and Bone.* Nava's self-identifying gay and Chicano character, Henry Rios, not only solves grisly murders and crimes but does so while dealing with affairs of thte heart and with a constant sense of lose: friends and love-interests lost to AIDS.

Gay novelists, playwrights, and poets like Nava, Islas, Rechy, Alarcón, Cuadros, Rodriguez, Alfaro, and others have influenced many straight and queer Chicano writers. Their creative visions celebrate the triumph of defying the odds while not losing sight of the goal to foster deep human empathy and understanding.

Further Reading

Aldama, Frederick Luis. *Arturo Islas: The Uncollected Works*. Houston: Arte Público Press, 2003.

Bruce-Novoa, Juan. "Homosexuality and the Chicano Novel." *European Perspectives on Hispanic Literature of the United States*. Ed. Genvieve Fabre. Houston: Arte Público Press, 1988. 98–106. Reprinted from *Confluencia-revista hispanica de cultura y literatura* 2.1 (1986): 69–77.

Foster, David William, ed. *Chicano/Latino Homoerotic Identities*. New York: Garland Publishing, 1999.

Frederick Luis Aldama

MEXICAN AMERICAN LESBIAN LITERATURE   Two radical Chicanas exploded Mexican American literature in the 1980s with their explicit treatment of lesbianism. **Gloria Anzaldúa** and **Cherríe Moraga** hail from different backgrounds and represent different aspects of the Mexican American community, but the anthology that they coedited, *This Bridge Called My Back* (1981), and each woman's first work, Moraga's *Loving in the War Years* (1983) and Anzaldúa's *Borderlands/La Frontera* (1987), changed the face of Chicano literature and culture. Prior to the publications of these works, Chicano literature had briefly seen the treatment of male homosexuality in **John Rechy**'s *City of Night* (1963) and the explicit treatment of female sexuality from the poems of **Bernice Zamora** and those of Alma Villanueva. But Anzaldúa and Moraga introduced not only the frank narration of lesbianism but also a careful consideration of its place in Chicano literature and culture. Anzaldúa's and Moraga's works mix the genres of essay, short story, poetry, and memoir; they are radical in their form as well as their content, suggesting that Chicana lesbian literature not only tells a new story, but also offers a new way of telling stories.

In *This Bridge Called My Back,* Moraga and Anzaldúa present Chicana lesbianism in the context of the radical women of color movement in the United States in the 1980s. Radical feminism, anti**racism**, and challenges to the dominance of heterosexuality fit together, the anthology proclaims. Chicana lesbians belong to a whole movement of women who include Chicana feminists like Norma Alarcón and other radical women of color, from **bell hooks** to Chrystos. These women came together to critique the ways in which patriarchy operates in the guises of **colonialism**, racism, male dominance, and compulsory heterosexuality to deny women access to the full and free exploration and expression of their sexuality and of their personhood. Under the editorial hand of Moraga and Anzladúa, the anthology staked out a space for Chicana feminists and lesbians who had been previously unknown not only in women of color circles, but also in Chicano circles.

Moraga and Anzaldúa's lesbianism is a Chicana more than a Mexican American lesbianism. It is intimately tied to the Chicano/a movement that, beginning in the late 1950s, asserted Chicanos as not immigrants, not hyphenated Americans, but native people of the Southwest, colonized first by Spaniards and then by North Americans. They trace their heritage as *mestizos* (mixed people) to include Aztec, Spanish, and Anglo strands. Moraga and Anzaldúa's Xicanisma (Chicanisma) critiques the male dominance and heterosexual order of the Chicano movement, but from within the movement.

Like the Chicanos, Moraga and Anzaldúa claim their Aztec heritage, although Moraga and Anzaldúa single out La Malinche and La Llorona as their spiritual ancestors. La Malinche was the Aztec woman who supposedly served as Cortez's translator and lover. La Malinche regularly suffers accusations of being a traitor and a whore. But Moraga and Anzaldúa portray her not as the traitor but as the sacrificial lamb to Spanish colonialism, and not as a whore but as the mother of all mestizos. They do not claim La Malinche as a lesbian, but rather as an example of how existing between two supposedly separate identities is a classically Chicana position and also as an example of a Chicana whose sexual life refuses the single two options standard in Chicano culture: virgin (mother) or whore. La Llorona stands as the archetypal bad mother in Chicano folklore, legendary for having killed her own children to wander forever crying and in search of young souls to snatch away. Again, Moraga and Anzaldúa claim not that La Llorona was a lesbian but that she exemplifies the ways in which all Chicana women are expected to become mothers or be forever damned. In La Llorona, they find an ancestor who can be rehabilitated as an emblem of women who stand outside of Chicano sexual and familial mores.

In the essays that make up her memoir-like book, *Loving in the War Years,* Moraga uses an English strongly marked by Spanish, but she also discusses how she was raised monolingually, taught that English was the language of progress. English was also her father's native language, for Moraga is from a half-Chicano, half-Anglo family. For these reasons, Moraga was from a young age acutely ware of concerns about selling out, about losing Chicano culture through an embrace of all things Anglo that, she thought, included lesbianism. Paradoxically, Moraga feels herself to be an outsider both as half-Anglo and as the darkest person in her family. She discusses how skin color as well as sexuality complicate understandings of "the Chicana." For Moraga, a surprising realization was that although male domination serves men, women, and specifically mothers, play a primary role in perpetuating it. She describes how her own mother tried to teach her to be always subservient to her brothers and tried to show her through her own example that an unsatisfactory marriage was preferable to no marriage at all. Moraga refused her mother's lessons in women's oppression just as she refused to believe that lesbianism is by definition foreign and antithetical to Chicano culture. *Loving in the War*

Years represents her effort to stake out a space within Chicano history and culture for Chicana lesbians.

Anzaldúa, in *Borderlands/La Frontera*, shares Moraga's project of rewriting Chicano history to include Chicana lesbians and of considering exactly what it means to be a Chicana lesbian. The language of *Borderlands/La Frontera* combines Spanish and English even more than does *Loving in the War Years* and also discusses the different variations of Chicano "Spanglish." In her discussion of language, Anzaldúa writes not only about how languages like Spanish and English become embattled, but also about how tongues and thus bodies and language about bodies and sexuality are subject to policing from both within and without the borderlands. Anzaldúa writes more explicitly than Moraga of women's sexuality both in terms of the sexual violence that all Chicana women risk and in terms of the sexual pleasure that Chicana lesbians can find with other women. *Borderlands/La Frontera* finds the borderlands that are such an important paradigm in Chicano studies to be also the paradigmatic site for Chicana lesbianism: It is indeed a site of contact between tongues, between cultures, and between people. It is the periphery that is the center of Chicana **identity**. But Anzaldúa also advocates for radical change in Chicano and in Anglo culture, a restitution of what she sees as the repressed Indian part of the *mestizo* identity and an accompanying reconfiguration of the roles of women.

Although they remain the most famous and the most radical, *This Bridge Called My Back*, *Loving in the War Years*, and *Borderlands/La Frontera* are not Moraga's and Anzaldúa's only collaborative or respective works. Moraga has also written a number of plays and short stories and a memoir of her entry into motherhood. Anzaldúa has also edited another radical women of color anthology, *Making Face, Making Soul* (1990), and with Analouise Keating has edited a follow-up to *This Bridge Called My Back*, *This Bridge We Call Home* (2002).

Nor are Anzaldúa and Moraga the only Chicana lesbian authors. **Ana Castillo** is famous not only for her lesbian poems and stories, some of which are collected in *My Father Was a Toltec and Other Poems* (1995) and *Loverboys* (1997), where some, but not all, of the lovers are boys, but also for her novels where lesbianism is less explicit, including *So Far From God* (1993), and *Peel Me Like an Onion* (2000). The first traditional Chicana "coming out story" that traces a girl's discovery and declaration of her lesbianism is **Terri de la Peña**'s *Margins* (1991). De la Peña also writes of lesbianism in *Latin Satins* (1994) and *Faults* (1999). Alicia Gaspar de Alba is a Chicana critic and creative writer whose collection *The Mystery of Survival and Other Stories* (1993) considers the importance of history and of memory as well as the inventive possibilities of collaboration between women across cultures and times. Gaspar de Alba's second book, *Sor Juana's Second Dream* (1999), claims this grande dame of Mexican letters as a foremother to Chicana lesbians. Other Chicana lesbian authors include the poets Emma Pérez and E. D. Hernández. As *This Bridge We*

Call Home indicates, Chicana lesbians may always be pulled between apparently competing loyalties, but they know that they have a right to claim that liminal space as their own and continue to build their community there.

Further Reading

Anzaldúa, Gloria, and Cherríe Moraga, eds. *This Bridge Called My Back: Writings by Radical Women of Color.* New York: Kitchen Table, Women of Color Press, 1983.

Arredondo, Gabriela F., et. al., eds. *Chicana Feminisms: A Critical Reader.* Durham, NC: Duke UP, 2003.

Ramos, Juanita. *Compañeras: Latina Lesbians.* New York: Latina Lesbian History Project, 1987.

Torres, Lourdes, and Inmaculada Pertusa, eds. *Tortilleras: Hispanic and U.S. Latina Lesbian Expressions.* Philadelphia: Temple UP, 2003.

Trujillo, Carla. *Chicana Lesbians: The Girls Our Mothers Warned Us About.* Berkeley: Third Woman Press, 1991.

Keja Lys Valens

MEXICAN AMERICAN POETRY   Often referred to as Chicano or Chicana poetry, this body of work gained national recognition in the late 1960s and early 1970s, against the backdrop of the Chicana/o civil rights movement known as *el movimiento*—meaning the movement. The term Chicana/o refers to people of Mexican ancestry who are either born in the United States or who have resided there for an extended period of time. *Movimiento* activists encouraged its usage as a way of affirming a cultural and political resistance to **assimilation**. This is not to say that Mexican Americans did not produce an extensive amount of work before this time. In Chicana/o literary history, critics have traced a continuity from Spanish colonial times to the present, and literary recovery projects throughout the 1990s have brought to light numerous works written since 1848—the year that the treaty of Guadalupe Hidalgo ended the Mexican American war and in the process, annexed nearly half of Mexican territory, a region we now refer to as the Southwestern United States. By definition, Chicanas and Chicanos are Americans; consequently, their poetry is also American—it is best understood in the context of U.S. history and culture and of how those elements have shaped the experiences of Mexican Americans.

Just as there is no singular Chicana/o experience, it follows then that poetry written by Mexican Americans is as Cordelia Candelaria describes it, "multiplicitous, wide-ranging, and dynamic," made up of "a diversity of voices, styles, idioms, images and personas" (xiv). This diversity accurately reflects Chicana/o cultural *mestizaje,* meaning mixture. Originally applied to the mixture of bloodlines that were the result of the conquest, *mestizaje* is a concept that is used to articulate the cultural mixture between the Mexican and the American that forms the basis of Chicana/o experience. This notion of hybridity makes singular claims of authenticity impossible; indeed, such claims are always limited and misleading.

The Spanish Colonial and Mexican National Periods (1492–1810 and 1810–1848)

Critics have stressed the imperative of including these two periods in the history of Chicano poetry, making a parallel to the inclusion of English colonial writers such as Anne Bradstreet (1613–72) and Cotton Mather (1663–1728) within American literary history. Like their Anglo-American counterparts, these writers chronicled their times and reflected on them in various literary genres, including verse. The colonial expedition led by Juan de Oñate (1598–1608) produced the epic *Historia de la Nuevo Mexico* (1610) written by Gaspar Perez de Villagra (1555–1620), which details the brutalities of conquest. During colonial and national periods, literary culture was deeply influenced by ongoing and intense conflicts, first with Native Americans, and later with Anglo-Americans. Despite their relative distance from Mexico City, Southwest Mexicans stayed in touch with culture and news from Mexico and Spain as they were in constant contact with Mexican traders and government officials. As Anglo-American settlers moved west, interactions between Mexicans and Anglos become the norm, through trade as well as intermarriage. By the 1830s, prior to the annexation of Texas, Mexicans there were outnumbered by Anglos, and by the 1840s the Santa Fe Trail connected St. Louis with New Mexico. This interaction was of course, not always peaceful as evinced in the two-year war between Mexico and the United States, which ended in the treaty of Guadalupe Hidalgo that not only annexed nearly half of Mexican territory, but also made guarantees to Mexican land rights, schooling, language, and religion, most of which were gradually eroded during Anglo-American expansion west.

The Nineteenth Century

In the mid-nineteenth century, a considerable amount of writing was devoted to chronicling the American takeover and its political, material, and cultural implications. Prominent figures dictated their memoirs, and a vast amount of poetry appeared in dozens of Spanish-language newspapers in the Southwest. Often these writers were concerned with the identity of a culture in transition, and they frequently viewed poetry as an instrument of political resistance. This attitude towards the social importance of poetry has shaped Chicana/o poetic production to the present day. Indeed, the literature of *el movimiento* assumes this deep interconnection between poetry and politics.

During the colonial and Mexican national periods, this frontier society lacked the social infrastructure necessary to maintain widespread literacy. In scholarly efforts to reconstruct the literary culture of the period, critics have stressed the need to incorporate oral forms, such as oral histories, folktales and songs, and religious dramas, as well as the *corrido* into literary history. The continuities between literary and oral forms are seen most explicitly in the *corrido,* given the ways that it serves to document the struggles of the common people, commemorate historical events, and monumentalize figures of resistance, such as in the "Corrido of Gregorio Cortez." In 1958 Americo Paredes wrote one of the first sustained studies of Chicana/o literary criticism, *With His Pistol in His Hand: A Border Ballad and Its Hero,* an analysis of this *corrido* and its "development out of actual events and of the folk traditions from which it sprang" (1). Paredes posits that the folk base of Chicano literature is the *corrido,* a position that has deeply influenced the ways that critics have read this tradition. Teresa McKenna explains "that Chicano literature proceeds out of a folk base has been a common assumption of most Chicano critics. That it evolves out of an oral tradition is a widely held corollary to this belief" (29). McKenna elucidates the scholarship on the *corrido* by stressing shared and consensual meaning formed in the relationship between the audience and the *corridista*—that *corridos* are narrated is important. They are socially engaged forms of expression that refer outward into the world. This dynamic between the text, the audience/reader, and the world is important to understanding how literature can embody social protest, as well as engender it.

The Early Twentieth Century (Interaction Period 1910–1942)

According to one of the foremost Chicano literary historians, Francisco Lomeli, this period is characterized by two main factors: "first the adjustment by Chicanos to having to share the Southwest with Anglos; and, secondly an increased influx of Mexican immigrants" (312). Both of these elements are deeply influenced by relationships between the United States and Mexico: primarily the increased need for cheap agricultural labor in the United States following the **Chinese Exclusion Act** of 1882, the Gentleman's Agreement with Japan in 1907–08, and the **Immigration** Acts of 1917, 1921 and 1922, all of which severely limited immigration from other sources (G. Sanchez, 19). Large-scale migrations were made possible by the construction of railroads in Mexico, financed largely by U.S. investments. In the first three decades of the twentieth century, approximately 1.5 million Mexicans migrated to the United States. According to historian George Sanchez, "immigration restrictions directed against Mexicans were at first consistently deferred under pressure by southwestern employers and then, when finally enacted, were mostly ignored by officials at the border. American administrators, in effect, allowed migrants to avoid the head tax or literacy test— instituted in 1917—by maintaining sparsely monitored checkpoints even after the establishment of the border patrol in 1924" (19–20).

Throughout this period, literary activity became centered in the publications of mutual aid societies such as LULAC (the League of United Latin American Citizens) and La Alianza, which worked for the incorporation of Mexicans into American society and worked against racial discrimination. A few collections of poetry and prose have been recovered, such as Felipe

M. Chacon's collection *Poesia y Prosa* in 1924. Jose Ines Garcia published numerous books of poetry in the 1920s and 1930s. Fray Angelico Chavez wrote poetry in a mystical tradition, publishing *Clothed with the Sun* (1939) and *New Mexico Triptych* (1940), among other books. In addition, from 1936 to 1940 The Works Progress Administration in New Mexico collected more than two hundred oral histories, many from Chicana/os.

The Bracero Progam, an agreement between the governments of the United States and Mexico that imported more than 80,000 Mexican migrant workers between 1942 and 1965, is yet another element in Mexican migration to the United States. In this cultural environment of exploitation and discrimination between 1943 and 1964, what Lomeli calls the "Pre-Chicano Period," few Chicana/os made breakthroughs in the publishing world. The Zoot Suit Riots of 1943 have been cited by numerous critics and historians as evidence of widespread discriminatory attitudes of the times. Lomeli cites four major elements in the lack of publication: a negative social stigma that Mexicans could not write, the emphasis given to English at the expense of Spanish, the false illusion of equality after World War II and the Korean War, and perhaps most significant, the "systematic exclusion from any significant educational mobility by a society that needed a ready-made unskilled labor force and labeled [Chicanos] as such" (313).

The Chicano Renaissance (1965–1975)

Coined by Felipe de Ortego y Gasca, this term includes all of the work in every genre of literary and artistic expression that is directly engaged with *el movimiento,* as well as work by other writers addressing the experiences of Chicana/os. Two major influences in this movement were **Luis Valdez** and El Teatro Campesino, which he helped to found in 1965 as an effort to help support the United Farm Workers Union and their organizing efforts. Poetry was one of the major forms of literary and political expression during *el movimiento,* marked by an earnest and prolonged emphasis on self-definition, social justice, and community building. In defining "classic" Chicana/o poetry, that is, a poetry which "evinces a strong narrative or dramatic line," written during and after *el movimiento,* Rafael Perez-Torres lists five major elements: a socioeconomic position of disempowerment, bilingual or interlingual modes of expression, issues of **identity** formation, a variety of vernacular expressions, and an affirmation of indigenous cultural elements (6). During this period, a Chicano cultural nationalism emerged that stressed "barrio themes, a historical uniqueness and [Chicano's] Indian heritage, particularly Aztec" (Lomeli 313). Rodolfo "Corky" Gonzalez's poem "Yo Soy Joaquin" (1967) is a remarkable and historic piece of protest poetry, articulating a Chicano consciousness that was fundamental to *el movimiento,* helping to cement a sense of Chicano identity necessary for social action. Published by the Crusade for Justice in Denver, it was part of a trend of publications and presses that were deeply concerned with the role of literature and publishing within activism. Poetry such as "Yo Soy Joaquin" was frequently read aloud at rallies and distributed in leaflet form. Equally important were the many literary and cultural events such as the Floricanto festivals, which featured the work of writers and artists.

Quinto Sol emerges as a major force in publishing the journal *El Grito*, which showcased such writers as Jose Angel Gutierrez and **Tomás Rivera**. The rise of small presses in Chicano urban communities as well as the rise of presses in Chicano university communities helped to solidify this poetic revolution in print. Poets such as **Lorna Dee Cervantes** and Juan Felipe Herrera started small presses and published the work of their peers, as in Cervantes's *Mango Magazine* and Herrera's broadside *Citybender*. Chicana/o poetry gained national exposure in the early 1970s though the nationwide circulation and printing of early anthologies such as *El Espejo/The Mirror* (1971), *Literatura Chicana: Texto y Contexto* (1972), *We Are Chicanos* (1973) and *Chicano Voices* (1975).

Major figures in *movimiento* poetry include Alurista, Abelardo Delgado, and Jose Montoya. Alurista is perhaps best known for articulating a profoundly indigenous and Chicano worldview. He is widely acknowledged as the author of "El Plan Espiritual de Aztlán" (1969), which references a mythic Aztec homeland as central to Chicano identity (when geographically located, it is almost always in the Mexican territory lost in the Treaty of Guadalupe Hidalgo), and his poetry is deeply invested in questions of indigenous spirituality and its connection to contemporary Chicano barrios, bilingual and interlingual expression, and social justice: We can see all of these elements at play in his first collection *Floricanto En Aztlán* (1971). Abelardo Delgado's *Chicano: 25 Pieces of a Chicano Mind* (1969) takes a different approach, often articulating anger and frustration at **racism** in the United States, as we can see in the poem "Stupid America," where he clearly connects the importance of creativity to survival. Montoya's early poems voice a "new Chicano sensibility, namely its power to dramatize otherness and to bring readers into electrifying contact with social forms wholly different from Anglo American ones" (Saldivar 10). For example, two of his best-known poems, "El Louie" and "La Jefita," both introduce personas particular to Chicana/o culture, the figure of the pachuco and of the long-suffering mother, respectively. Many of Montoya's early works are elegiac and address questions of social justice as well as the place of Chicano poetry within American literature as in "Pobre Viejo Walt Whitman."

Women too were active in creating poetic works of protest and art during *el movimiento*; it is only recently however, that their work has been published and widely anthologized. Along with Lorna Dee Cervantes, Anita Sarah Duarte and Ana Nieto Gomez wrote critiques of machismo in *el movimiento* while affirming the centrality of women's voices and actions. **Bernice Zamora**'s *Restless Serpents* (1975) has received considerable critical attention for the ways she articulates a distinctively Chicana feminist vision that connects the past to the present, while offering a critique of Western male power.

Pinto poetry—that is, poetry shaped by prison conditions and prison culture—is another important element of the Chicano Renaissance. Abelardo Delgado, Ricardo Sanchez, and Raul Salinas write poems that reflect the dehumanizing aspects of imprisonment, and the violence of the border and the fields is institutionalized within the prison. **Jimmy Santiago Baca**, according to Perez-Torres, most clearly writes out of the pinto poetic tradition, in a search for transcendence from violence, using the word as a weapon against oppression (119).

After the height of the Chicano movement in the mid 1970s, publishing shifted to include more women. Marta E. Sanchez's important study, *Contemporary Chicana Poetry* (1985) cites Alma Villanueva, Lorna Dee Cervantes, Lucha Corpi, and Bernice Zamora as authors central to understanding the body of work produced by women during this period. Particularly important is the reinterpretation of mythic female figures, such as *La Malinche,* who goes from traitor to the Mexican nation to a bridge builder and communicator. Since the 1980s many Chicanas, most notably **Pat Mora**, **Naomi Helena Quiñonez**, **Gloria Anzaldúa,** and **Cherríe Moraga,** have explored in their poetry their relationships to female cultural figures, such as the Virgin of Guadalupe, La Malinche, and La Llorona, as well as a host of Aztec goddesses. After the establishment of a Chicana/o literary tradition, Chicana/o poets began to question cultural nationalist models of expression. Previous ways of imagining a Chicana/o identity that centered on a fixed and authentic origin, such as Aztlán, have been reimagined—Aztlán itself has been reconceptualized as a metaphoric and spiritual place of connection rather than a geographical region. Authors such as Anzaldúa and **Guillermo Gomez-Pena** have explored the border and "the borderlands" as an important metaphor for understanding the *mestizaje* of Chicana/o experience and identity. Lorna Dee Cervantes and **Ana Castillo** offer alternative conceptualizations of home that center on their experiences as women and as writers.

The relationship between identity, empowerment, and sexuality is explored extensively in much Chicana/o poetry. Moraga's *Loving in the War Years* (1983) combines poetry and essays to explore questions of racial and sexual identity. Anzaldúa's landmark collection of essays and poems, *Borderlands/La Frontera: The New Mestiza* (1987), articulates the border as the place of belonging for the *mestiza,* and Anzaldúa also theorizes how sexuality, specifically her identity as a *lesbiana,* a Chicana lesbian, has shaped her experience. Numerous collections such as **Sandra Cisneros**'s *My Wicked Wicked Ways* (1987) and *Loose Woman* (1994) and **Francisco X. Alarcón**'s *Body in Flames/Cuerpo en Llamas* (1990) explore the erotic as a potentially empowering site of possibility.

Chicana/o poetry has shaped and been shaped by a distinctly American literary tradition. In Wolfgang Binder's *Partial Autobiographies: Interviews with Twenty Chicano Poets* (1985), many of the poets reflect on the importance of creative writing courses in American universities, such as **Gary Soto**'s connection to his much admired teacher Philip Levine and Sandra Cisneros's experiences at the Iowa Writers' Workshop. We also see the importance of institutionalized support for these writers in grants and fellowships, such as the National Endowment for the Arts creative writing fellowships for Sandra Cisneros, Lucha Corpi, Juan Felipe Herrera, and Gary Soto, and the Frederick Douglas as well as the Ford Foundation fellowship awards for Ricardo Sanchez (xii). This sort of recognition signals not only much needed financial support, but also a clear understanding that these poets are of national importance, and their work reflects not only their experiences as individuals and as Chicana/os, but also their experiences as Americans in a multicultural and multiethnic society. Chicana/o poetry will continue to shape the landscape of American letters precisely because of its affinity with hybridity and cultural interaction and the ways in which it highlights relationships between literature and culture. (*See also* Bilingualism)

Further Reading

Arteaga, Alfred. *Chicano Poetics: Heterotexts and Hybridities* New York: Cambridge UP, 1997.

Candelaria, Cordelia. *Chicano Poetry: A Critical Introduction.* Westport, CT: Greenwood, 1986.

McKenna, Teresa. *Migrant Song: Politics and Process in Contemporary Chicano Literature.* Austin: U of Texas P, 1997.

Lomeli, Francisco. "An Overview of Chicano Letters: From Origins to Resurgence" *Chicano Studies: Survey and Analysis.* Ed. Dennis Bixler-Marquez, et al. Dubuque, IA: Kendall/Hunt, 1992. 309–17.

Ortego y Gasca, Felipe de. "An Introduction to Chicano Poetry" *Modern Chicano Writers: A Collection of Critical Essays.* Ed. Joseph Sommers and Tomas Ybarra Frausto. New Jersey: Prentice Hall, 1979. 108–16.

Paredes, Americo. *With His Pistol in His Hand: A Border Ballad and Its Hero.* Austin: U of Texas P, 1958.

Paredes, Raymund. "Mexican American Literature: An Overview" *Recovering the U.S. Hispanic Literary Heritage.* Ed. Ramon Gutierrez and Genaro Padilla. Houston: Arte Público Press, 1993. 31–52.

Perez-Torres, Rafael. *Movements in Chicano Poetry.* New York: Cambridge UP, 1995.

Saldívar, Jose David. "Towards a Chicano Poetics: The Making of the Chicano Subject: 1962–1982" *Confluencia* 1.2: 10–17.

Sanchez, George. *Becoming Mexican American.* New York: Oxford UP, 1993.

Sanchez, Marta. *Contemporary Chicana Poetry.* Berkeley: U of California P, 1985.

Eliza Rodriguez y Gibson

MEXICAN AMERICAN STEREOTYPES   Between 1836 and the Mexican-American War of 1846 to 1848, the United States wrested control of Mexico's northern half, the vast resource-rich territory stretching from

Texas to California. This formative act of national territorial expansion produced a significant U.S. minority from the Mexican communities of Texas and the Southwest, a minority augmented by continuing mass migration from Mexico since the early years of the twentieth century. Concomitant with the United States's swift evolution as a continental power, the Mexican-origin population became the focus of mass media, popular cultural, and historiographical representations and attitudes that have, since the mid-nineteenth century, functioned as stereotypes about Mexicans in the wider U.S. population.

A contested term, stereotyping generally signifies the production and circulation of clichéd, reductive, and often negative and demeaning ethnic and racial types by which the agents and institutions of a dominant culture claim to identify, represent, and know a particular group or people. The perpetuation of stock Mexican types—for example, the male Latin lover and the female "Mexican spitfire," the lazy greaser, the bandit, the drug runner, the gang member—reflects pervasive and longstanding cultural attitudes in the United States that also affect other U.S. Latinos and, more generally, Latin Americans as a whole. These peoples have been cast variously in the Anglo-American popular imagination as the embodiments of an exotic, dark and sinuous "Latin" sensibility, of irrational and superstitious-cum-magical Catholicism, of heat, spice, emotionality, and musicality, of barely repressed violence, and of potential illegal border-crossing and organized criminality. In the critical literature about such stereotypes, the complex production and circulation of myriad ethnicized "Latin" types in the United States has been called "Latinism" (Berg 4) and "Tropicalization" (Aparicio and Chávez-Silverman). The pervasiveness of "Latin" stereotypes in the United States may also have roots in the Black Legend, an anti-Spanish discourse that emerged in the sixteenth century in Protestant Europe and in England's American colonies. The legend demonized the Spanish as inhumane, rapacious, and cruel and decried the intermixing of Spanish, indigenous, and African peoples throughout the Spanish empire as proof of those peoples' inherent cultural and racial deficiency. The legend implied that the Spanish-speaking inhabitants of the Americas were less civilized than the peoples and cultures derived from non-Catholic northern Europe.

In the Mexican American case, ethnic stereotyping is intimately related to two resilient, and not necessarily mutually exclusive, discourses of otherness. First, Mexican Americans are often said to form a non-"American" or alien sector, and thus a marginal and expendable one. This "alien-izing" discourse has focused on the purportedly foreign signs derived from the "dark" mixed European-indigenous racial history of many Mexicans, as well as the maintenance of the Spanish language. Second, the Mexican American sector is also often treated as a coherent, homogeneous, and readily identifiable constituency, hence the targeting of Mexican Americans, and other Latinos, by the U.S. state as a potentially criminalized and problem sector and by U.S. media and corporate concerns as a lucrative and exploitable consumer market. Both discourses limit the possibility of nuanced representations by ignoring the many complicating factors at work within the diverse Mexican American population: class status, regional location, generational perspective, familial migratory history and lengths of residency, mixed-racial background, gender and sexual differentials, deeply felt commitment to the host society, and bi- or multilinguistic capacities.

For many commentators, the U.S. film industry has been perhaps the most influential perpetrator, both in the United States and beyond, of stock Mexican and Mexican American types. From its earliest days, Hollywood has tended to portray Mexico as a space worthy of U.S. intervention and salvation, as is evident in numerous Westerns that feature Anglo-Americans riding south of the border to rectify injustice and save Mexicans who are unable to look after their own interests. From such films derive a set of globally recognizable Mexican characters: the docile Mexican, propped up against a cactus or saloon wall, sleeping under a highly colored blanket; the dirty, unshaved and vicious *bandito*; the simple and poor *campesino* or rural worker whose heavily accented English provokes audience laughter; the dark untrustworthy temptress; the slick, macho Latin lover. Hollywood film has also generated its own stock types about the Mexican American community itself. This typecasting is evident in the many films made about the border patrol and border policing, which feature unscrupulous Mexican Americans on the wrong side of U.S. law, thus perpetuating the notion that Mexican Americans are more often than not "illegal aliens." A related criminalizing trend animates the more recent genre of inner-city films that focus on Mexican gangs and urban violence. The corporate world, too, has been a rich source of stereotypes about Mexican Americans, a contemporary example being the Taco Bell chain's deployment of a "Mexican" chihuahua in its advertising campaigns. A notable trend in mass media in the 1980s and 1990s was the rise of an erotic-exotic representational gaze, signified by the ubiquitous chili and soundtracks of salsa music, by which Mexican Americans and other Latinos were portrayed as icons of sensuality and libidinal heat.

Since the 1960s, many Chicana/o critics and cultural producers have been concerned to counter prevalent stereotypes either by critiquing them or by answering back with their own representations of Mexican Americanness. This double ambition has driven much Chicana/o film, documentary, theater, literary, visual-art, music and performance work. The self-styled cultural guerilla, Guillermo Gómez-Peña, for example, has consistently mocked stock Mexican types in performances that feature alternative ethnic characters, such as "Mad-Mex" and "El Mexterminator," which are intended to challenge dominant-cultural assumptions and prejudices. This antistereotyping trend has also led to calls for a "Brown out" of the mass media, an attempt to counter the media under-representation of Latinos and to insert more positive and reflective portrayals of Latinos in U.S. popular cultural production, notably film and television. (*See also Born in East L.A.*)

Further Reading

Aparicio, Frances R., and Susana Chávez-Silverman, eds. "Introduction." *Tropicalizations: Transcultural Representations of Latinidad.* Hanover, NH: UP of New England, 1997.

Berg, Charles Ramírez. *Latino Images in Film: Stereotypes, Subversion, and Resistance.* Austin: U of Texas P, 2002.

Dávila, Arlene. *Latinos, Inc.: The Marketing and Making of a People.* Berkeley: U of California P, 2000.

Noriega, Chon A. "*El hilo latino:* Representation, Identity and National Culture." *Jump Cut* 38 (1993): 45–50.

Paul Allatson

MEYERS, BERT [BERTRAND] (1928–1979)   Jewish American poet and educator. Bert Meyers was a member of "the Coastliners," a group of West Coast poets who took their name from *Coastlines* literary magazine. This Los Angeles-based magazine was founded by Gene Frunkin and Mel Weisburd. The name of the journal was intended to invoke the lengthy California coast-line and the dearth of poetic and literary traditions that poets of the mid-twen-tieth century could continue even as they invented new traditions. Calling themselves "the other generation of the 50's" (Weisburd), the Coastliners were brought together in 1956 by Thomas McGrath. In that year, the magazine sponsored what is now an infamous private reading by a then-little-known poet—**Allen Ginsberg**. At this reading, Ginsberg's first in Los Angeles, he was questioned pointedly by a member of the audience. Ginsberg in turn chal-lenged his heckler to a fistfight while removing all of his own clothing.

In distinct contrast to the visibly counterculture lifestyle of the East Coast Beat poets, the Coastliners wished for poetry to reconnect with the main-stream. The Coastliners viewed the Beat's message as more repetitious than unique and poems of social protest as largely ineffective due to their disso-ciative strains. As such, poets like Meyers sought to relay a less starkly drawn sociopolitical reality and to evoke moods that spoke to the undercur-rents or emotional center of events. Meyers relied heavily upon surrealistic imagery, surprising and often random language, and a lyrical sense of the unique environments—urban, small town, and wilderness—that had begun to characterize the West Coast. Like their East Coast counterparts, the Coast-liners also experimented with various drugs—a side note that may explain the evocative tone of Meyers's work.

Born on March 20, 1928, in Los Angeles, Meyers was the son of an insur-ance salesman, Manuel Meyers, and Gertrude Bercovitch Meyers. He mar-ried Odette Miller in 1957. The marriage produced two children, Arat and Daniel. Meyers was self-educated, supporting his family through manual labor, janitorial and warehouse work, house painting, and picture framing. In his mid-thirties, facing declining health, Meyers applied to Claremont

Graduate School. He earned his MA and began doctoral work, then took a teaching position at Pitzer College. His first book of poetry, *Early Rain,* was released by Swallow Press in 1960. It was followed by Meyers's most well-known work—*The Dark Birds* (Doubleday)—in 1968. Between 1973 and 1979, Meyers produced and published three more collections of original poetry, was published in several regional and national poetry journals, and collaboratively translated (with Odette Meyers) *Lord of the Village,* a collection of poetry by Francois Dodat. Though Meyers's works were received well by poets such as Denise Leverton and Marianne Moore, and while Meyers's work has appeared and been reviewed in national literary magazines such as *Hudson Review* and *Harper's,* his work has largely fallen into obscurity. Meyers died of lung cancer, on April 22, 1979, in Claremont, California.

Further Reading

Weisburd, Mel. "The Coastliners." *The Lummox Journal* (May/June 2003). http://home.earthlink.net/lumoxraindog/ (accessed November 2, 2004).

Michelle LaFrance

MEZEY, ROBERT (1935–)   Jewish American poet, translator, and editor. Robert Mezey's poetry, which has received relatively little critical attention, reflects a deep interest in Jewish belief and culture.

Unlike his nearly exact contemporary, **Mark Strand**, Robert Mezey has not acquired a widespread reputation as a major American poet of the late twentieth century. Although Mezey has achieved such distinctions as a Guggenheim fellowship (1977) and a National Endowment for the Arts fellowship (1987), his poetry has not received the sustained attention of a major critic. He has earned the admiration, however, of fellow poets such as **John Hollander** and Kenneth Rexroth.

Born in Philadelphia, Mezey has lived much of his life in California. After taking a BA at the University of Iowa in 1959, he studied at Stanford University, where he came under the influence of the poet and critic Yvor Winters. After a period as assistant professor at Fresno State University (1967–68), Mezey was professor of English and poet-in-residence at Pomona College in Claremont from 1976 until 1999. Mezey does not, however, write frequently about California. His poetry is instead distinguished by its engagement with multiple literary and religious traditions.

His first individual collection, *The Wandering Jew,* was published in 1960; an earlier collaboration with Stephen Berg and Ronald Goodman, titled *Berg Goodman Mezey,* had appeared in 1957. The title work of this first solo collection is a long poem in quatrains that explores the poet's struggles with spirituality and sexuality, tracing the move from boyhood into adulthood. For the young boy, the synagogue offers a sanctuary from the world. As a young man, however, the speaker seeks the company of women instead. The poem's third and final section describes a spiritual restlessness and alludes to the persecution of Jews throughout history. The concluding image is of the poet struggling to live a holy life, seemingly trapped between his convictions and desires, yet hopeful that he will find solace.

Mezey later moved away from the traditional forms used in poems such as "The Wandering Jew." His interest in "open forms" is reflected in the book he edited with Berg; *Naked Poetry: Recent American Poetry in Open Forms* (1969) is an important, if eclectic, anthology of postwar poets, including, among others, Sylvia Plath, **Allen Ginsberg**, Gary Snyder, **Theodore Roethke**, and Rexroth. Later in life, however, Mezey lamented what he perceived as the disastrous impact of free verse on American poetry.

Even as he varied his poetic form, Mezey continued to write about religion in general and Judaism in particular. Although Mezey's poetry ranges widely in its themes and subjects, it demonstrates a recurring interest in his family and the Jewish community to which it belonged. "My Mother," from *White Blossoms* (1965), is primarily written in the form of a letter from mother to son; the speaker notes that his mother is at once a comedian and deadly serious. "One Summer," which appeared in *The Door Standing Open: New and Selected Poems 1965–1969* (1970), remembers the poet's father returning home from work at the factory. More typical, however, is "A Prayer for his Sickness," also from *The Door Standing Open,* in which the poet addresses his Lord and examines the nature of his belief in terms more abstract than those he employs in the domestic "One Summer."

The Wandering Jew was followed immediately by *The Lovemaker* (1960), which won the Lamont Prize. This collection makes evident Mezey's interest in classical literature. "Dream of Departure," for instance, is modeled on Catullus, and "A Bedtime Story" alludes to Sophocles' *Oedipus Rex.* He claims that the first poetry he ever wrote—at age thirteen—was a translation of a passage from Ovid. Mezey has also written variations on poems by various European and several Hebrew poets. He edited *Poems from the Hebrew* (1973), as well as collections of Thomas Hardy and Edwin Arlington Robinson; he has translated the poetry of César Vallejo and Uri Zvi Greenberg.

In addition to his responses to other writers, Mezey has engaged with the literary tradition through his use of varied poetic forms. He has written clerihews, songs, an experiment with puns ("Prose and Cons"), and a thematic sequence ("Couplets"): one of the principal characteristics of Mezey's poetry is its willingness to emphasize the craft of poetry, both within and across languages.

Further Reading

Flinker, Noam. "The Dying of the Light: American Jewish Self-Portrayal in Henry Roth and Robert Mezey." *The Jewish Self-Portrait in European and American Literature.* Ed. Hans Jürgen Schrader, Elliott M. Simon, and Charlotte Wardi. Tübingen, Germany: Niemayer, 1996. 147–57.

Nicholas Bradley

MIDDLE PASSAGE **Charles Johnson**'s *Middle Passage* (1990) is a sea narrative, set in 1830, and follows Rutherford Calhoun, a newly freed slave, escaping personal entanglements by boarding the ship *Republic* in New Orleans, which he later discovers is a slave ship. Calhoun becomes a favorite of the despotic Captain Falcon, which places Calhoun in the middle between developing factions on the ship: the hostile crew versus the rebellious slaves. The cargo for this slave ship consists of members of a legendary African tribe, the Allmuseri, and their mysterious cargo crated in the hold. The slaves revolt, and Calhoun is left to communicate with Captain Falcon, while at the same time trying to preserve his own life with the slaves.

Johnson's narrative is cast as a diary kept by Rutherford Calhoun aboard ship. Calhoun is clever, intelligent, and the most articulate member of the crew. His relationship with Captain Falcon is one of intellectual and verbal dexterity. Johnson details the horrors of prolonged sailing excursions in the nineteenth century and of slave ships in particular, while maintaining a narrative tone both comic and philosophically complex. Johnson challenges the sea narrative genre by mixing elements of picaresque, **slave narrative**, and philosophical novel, while at the same time inverting the conventional narrative locus, a fixed center of truth, represented in *Middle Passage* by the very powerful but unidentifiable "god" in the ship's hold; the force of this indeterminate power creates disorientation and insanity. Johnson, in *Middle Passage*, shifts classical notions of historical authority and narrative authority. Also, Johnson focuses closely on the ship's crew and their own peculiarities and absurdities; their hierarchy is as illogical as the idea of the slaves' revolt, and Johnson uses irony and paradox to question fixed truth and reveal the interdependence of the two sides.

Charles Johnson, Pollock Professor of English at the University of Washington, draws upon Melville (particularly *Moby-Dick* and "Benito Cereno"), Poe, Coleridge, and others in forming his text, but the style is entirely his own. Johnson has published cartoons, literary criticism, fiction, and drama, but *Middle Passage* is his highest achievement thus far, and postmodern critics have noted Johnson's use of language and wordplay to undermine conventional ideas of narrative authority. In 1993 he completed a screenplay for a film version of the novel. *Middle Passage* won the National Book Award for Fiction in 1990; Johnson is the second African American ever to win the award (**Ralph Ellison** was the first in 1953). (*See also* Slavery)

Further Reading

Kawash, Samira. "Haunted Houses, Sinking Ships: Race, Architecture, and Identity in *Beloved* and *Middle Passage*." *New Centennial Review* 1.3 (Winter 2001): 67–86.

Lock, Helen. "The Paradox of Slave Mutiny in Herman Melville, Charles Johnson, and Frederick Douglass." *College Literature* 30.4 (Fall 2003): 54–70.

Steinberg, Marc. "Charles Johnson's *Middle Passage:* Fictionalizing History and Historicizing Fiction." *Texas Studies in Language and Literature* 45.4 (Winter 2003): 375–90.

Bill R. Scalia

MIDDLE PASSAGE, THE   The "middle leg" of the triangular Europe-Africa-America-Europe trading route that traded cheap European goods for Africans whose sale in the Americas bought agricultural goods for Europe. The Middle Passage has come to stand for an increasingly wide array of historical and philosophical elements of the African American experience and literary tradition. These elements range from the inhuman brutality and cultural deracination of the five- to twelve-week voyage whose mortality rate fluctuated around twenty percent, to the emancipative potential of the Middle Passage as a voyage of transformation. Even the most optimistic uses of the Middle Voyage, however, do not deny the savagery of Europeans and their genocidal impact.

The two essential components of the Middle Passage are European injustice and African resilience; the first constitutes the foundation of the African American experience, and the second signifies the ability of Africans to overcome the dehumanization that began with enslavement and continued through **Jim Crow** laws to today's **racism**.

Probably because the horrors of nineteenth century **slavery** needed no supplement, the Middle Passage is largely absent from African American literature before the twentieth century. The main exception is **Olaudah Equiano**'s *The Interesting Narrative of the Life of Olaudah Equiano, or Gustavus Vassa, the African* (1789), whose early account of the Middle Passage both provides details and sets out most of the arguments against racism that African Americans have developed since. Also noteworthy is African-born Ottobah Cuguano's *Thoughts and Sentiments on the Wicked Traffic of Slavery and Commerce of the Human Species* (1787).

It is since the genocide of World War II, however, that the Middle Passage has developed into a prominent theme of African American and Afro-Caribbean literatures. **Robert Hayden**'s poem "Middle Passage" (1944, 1946, 1962), which concludes with the famous "Voyage through death/to life upon these shores," initiates this development. Important uses of the Middle Passage since Hayden's poem include Barbadian writer George Lamming's *In the Castle of My Skin* (1953) and *The Middle Passage: The Caribbean Revisited* (1962), Barbadian Kamau Brathwaite's *The Arrivants: A New World Trilogy* (1973) and *Middle Passages* (1992), **Amiri Baraka**'s "Slave Ship: A Historical Pageant" (1967), **Toni Morrison**'s *Beloved* (1987), **Charles Johnson**'s *Middle Passage* (1990), and Caryl Phillips's *Crossing the River* (1993).

As seen in Johnson's *Middle Passage,* the Middle Passage has progressively become a "place" to understand what it means to be African in **diaspora**. Johnson's novel—like Guadeloupian Maryse Condé's *Hérémakhonon* (1982) and Eddy Harris's *Native Stranger* (1992)—explores both the impossibility of "coming home" to Africa and how much African American and Caribbean cultures are intertwined with European culture. The Middle Passage is and continues to be a space of "wounding" yet potential healing, an in-between space of exile yet also of international (transatlantic) hybridities that work against the binaries of racism and **Afrocentrism**. Scholarly explorations of this evolving idea include Paul Gilroy's *The Black Atlantic* (1993) and Caryl Phillips's *A New World Order* (2001). The Middle Passage looks to become an increasingly important theme during the years ahead.

Further Reading

Diedrich, Maria, Henry Louis Gates Jr., and Carl Pedersen, eds. *Black Imagination and the Middle Passage.* New York: Oxford UP, 1999.

Kevin M. Hickey

MILLER, ARTHUR (1915–2005)   Jewish American dramatist. Along with his contemporary, Tennessee Williams (1911–83), Arthur Miller was one of the two dominant American dramatists of the middle part of the twentieth century. Although creator of more than a dozen plays, Miller is best known for his drama, *Death of a Salesman* (1949), which gave him almost overnight fame and a Pulitzer Prize.

Miller became politically prominent in the 1950s for his refusal to testify against his friends and colleagues during the notorious House Un-American Committee Hearings on left-wing activity and, in later years, for his activities as president of Poets, Essayists, and Novelists (PEN), an international writers organization in which he championed freedom of expression in what was then the Communist-bloc countries that were controlled by the Soviet Union. In the early 1950s he wrote a number of controversial works, including an adaptation of Ibsen's *An Enemy of the People* (1950) and *The Crucible* (1953), about the Salem Witch Trials, both considered to be criticisms of the period of the McCarthy witch-hunts for communists in the United States. Miller had garnered recognition for an earlier drama, *All My Sons* (1947), which received the Drama Critics Circle Award that year, but it was with *Death of a Salesman* that the playwright made his most noted contribution to the American theater. It was his prominence as a result that later gave *The Crucible* its impact as a critique of contemporary American life.

Although the name of the central figure in *Death of a Salesman,* Willy Loman, is not identifiably ethnic, the values that Miller expresses in the course of the last twenty-four hours of this traveling salesman's life are those shared with many Jewish Americans. Willy is "lost" in a world that no longer has any use for him: a traveling salesman who can no longer "sell" and is too worn-out to travel. His one source of pride is his older son, Biff, who becomes estranged from him as a teenager when he discovers that his father has been cheating on his mother. But it is the need to justify himself to Biff that links Willy with a traditional notion of Jewish values that emphasizes the importance of passing on something enduring from one generation to another.

Willy's brother, Ben, embodies the material values of success and wealth that Willy has longed for. But it is Willy's lack of any tradition of ethics that steers him in the direction of his self-destruction when he mistakes these material values for spiritual ones. He complains to his brother, in an imaginary conversation, that he has always felt "temporary about myself" and wishes that his father had not abandoned him when he was little. His lack of traditional ethnic values leads Willy to focus on money as a way of measuring self-worth, even when his son tells him that all he wants is to be out in the countryside, free of the competitive edginess of city life. Even Willy's friend Charley declares at Willy's funeral, "There was more to him in that front stoop than in all the sales he ever made," alluding to Willy's love of building things with his own hands. But his misguided determination to prove his value to Biff ends up in Willy's useless suicide. In fact, he leaves his son nothing but the conviction that his father had "the wrong dreams."

The two most prominent plays in this period, written just a year apart, *After the Fall* (1964) and *Incident at Vichy* (1965), deal with the **Holocaust**. *After the Fall* is a semiauto-biographical work which became

Arthur Miller. *Courtesy of the Library of Congress.*

controversial for an entirely different reason than had Miller's plays in the early 1950s. The latter half of the drama centers on the relationship between Quentin, the central character, and Maggie, his disturbed wife whom many people believed was modeled after Marilyn Monroe. Miller had married her in a highly publicized ceremony in the mid 1950s, and they were divorced just a short while before her death in 1961. But much else in the play is about Quentin's relationship with a new woman in his life, Holga, a German gentile whose family lived through the Nazi period. Miller tries to link the moral responsibility of the Holocaust to the human tendency toward betrayal as Quentin is confronted with betrayals involving history, his own wife, and one of his friends. Although not entirely convincing, the play raises some profound questions about the nature of evil and how people cope with it.

The second of these works is based on an actual incident that took place in Vichy France, which was governed by French collaborators of the Nazis during World War II. In the play, a group of French Jews is rounded up by the Nazis for deportation to the death camps. One of the French Jews, Leduc, confronts a Catholic nobleman, von Berg, with his passive involvement in the Holocaust. In an act of pure altruism, von Berg gives the Jew his pass, enabling him to escape. This recognition of his responsibility for what has happened to the Jews of Europe gives von Berg a heroic status that is as close as Miller comes to presenting an idealized view of human behavior.

Yet another work in which Miller gives some indication of his Jewish background is one of the last that can be considered "classic" among the playwright's dramas: *The Price* (1968). Set in an abandoned apartment house about to be torn down, the play records the conflict between two brothers, Walter and Victor Franz, the former a successful doctor, the latter a policeman on the verge of retirement. Victor confronts Walter with his failure to help their father during the Depression when Victor was forced to give up college in order to support the old man, who had been rendered helpless after he had lost his fortune during the Market Crash of 1929. Each man has paid a "price" for his decision: Walter is wealthy but divorced and estranged from his children; Victor is struggling economically but has a relatively content family life. Although they might well be of Jewish background, it is not the Franzs who inject the specifically Jewish element into the play, but the colorful figure of Gregory Solomon, the eighty-nine-year-old furniture dealer whom Victor had requested come up to evaluate and buy the furniture the family had once owned in more prosperous times.

Solomon, like his biblical namesake, serves as "judge" of the two brothers and their rival claims to justify their lives. Although which of the brothers is "right" is intended to remain ambiguous at the end of the play, it is clear that Solomon comes down in support of the more altruistic Victor who stayed with his father over the more ambitious Walter who abandoned the family to pursue a career in medicine. At the end of the play, Solomon concludes the financial transaction that had been interrupted by Walter's arrival. In sealing the "deal," Solomon affirms Victor's faithfulness toward the bargain he had made with the furniture dealer, Victor's father, and, ultimately, Victor himself.

Throughout Miller's work, however, it is the issue of ethical behavior, more than specifically ethnic values, that dominates his thinking. In his very first play, *They Too Arise* (1936), which was written while he was an undergraduate at the University of Michigan, one of the central figures, Abe Simon, a Jewish clothing manufacturer, objects to the suggestion of his fellow businessmen that they should use strike breakers to defeat a walkout of their employees. He says to them: "I don't know why—but someway it seems to me that this ain't the way an honest man or honest men do business. I can't see that it's the way for Jewish men to act." This ethnically centered notion that ethics is something particularly Jewish is later abandoned in Miller's first successful play, *All My Sons* (1947). In that drama about a gentile manufacturer who sells defective airplane parts during World War II, which results in the death of a number of American pilots, Chris Keller admits that instead of only looking out for his own family business, he recognized that the fliers were all his sons. This recognition leads him to commit suicide.

Therefore, although Miller occasionally used his Jewish American background and sensibility to write about ethical issues from that particular perspective, he had a tendency to universalize his views to include all of humanity, not only Jewish people. In his only novel, *Focus* (1945), Lawrence Newman, who is a Gentile, is mistaken for a Jew when he buys a pair of glasses to correct his failing eyesight. By discovering the underlying anti-Semitism in wartime America, Newman finds himself making common cause with Jews who, until then, he had not realized had ever suffered from prejudice.

Miller did write two later works, however, that centered on the Holocaust: the screenplay for a memoir by a Holocaust survivor, *Playing for Time* (1980), and the drama *Broken Glass* (1994), about a case of hysteria a Jewish American woman suffers as a results of *Kristallnacht,* the night in 1936 in which, throughout Germany, Jewish stores were vandalized and Jews were assaulted and killed as a result of Nazi propaganda. But neither of these made the impact on the American theater that his earlier plays did.

It is difficult to determine whether Miller has had any profound influence on his contemporary or younger dramatists. Although *Death of a Salesman* and *After the Fall* both use rapid shifts in time and place to move along their respective plots, Miller was firmly in the realist-naturalist school of drama that traces itself back to the work of Henrik Ibsen (1828–1906), the great Norwegian dramatist whose craftsmanship and socially conscious drama Miller clearly admired. His adaptation of Ibsen's *Enemy of the People* (1882), which is about a man who refuses to compromise his principles for the economic gain of his community, reveals Miller's own values. One can see the ethical issues Miller raised reflected in the work of such a contemporary dramatist as **Tony Kushner**, whose *Angels in America* (1992) reexplores the McCarthy period that Miller examined in *After the Fall.* But stylistically, Kushner is of a more contemporary school of drama.

Arthur Miller remains one of the towering figures of American drama, more noted for his universal message about the need for brotherhood and humane treatment of all people than he is as a Jewish American playwright. Even in a later play, *The Creation of the World and Other Business* (1973), Miller once again explored the nature of evil through the Fall of Adam and Eve rather than specific Jewish religious issues. In his concern for the need for ethical behavior in a world constantly threatened with materialism and corporate greed, his life was the embodiment of one man's search for a more virtuous society. In his protest against the injustices of the McCarthy period, in his active support for dissidents against Soviet censorship during his tenure as president of PEN, and even in his private life as one of the leaders in a community effort to overturn an unjust verdict against a young man who was falsely convicted of killing his mother, Arthur Miller proved himself to be both creative artist and model citizen, embodying in his own life the convictions he dramatized on the stage.

It is in the nature of Jewish ethics as well as those of Christians to follow the simple teachings embodied in the phrase first spoken by Rabbi Hillel and then rearticulated by Jesus: "Do nothing to others that you would not have them do to you." It is this simple value that is at the heart of Arthur Miller's work, and it is in this universal message that his best plays have their strength and conviction. (*See also* Jewish American Theater)

Further Reading

Bigsby, Christopher, ed. *Cambridge Companion to Arthur Miller.* Cambridge: Cambridge UP, 1997.

Corrigan, Robert W., ed. *Arthur Miller: A Collection of Critical Essays.* Englewood Cliffs, NJ: Prentice-Hall, 1969.

Freedman, Morris. "The Jewishness of Arthur Miller: His Family Epic." *American Drama in Social Context.* Carbondale: Southern Illinois UP, 1971. 43–58.

Huftel, Sheila. *Arthur Miller: The Burning Glass.* New York: Citadel, 1965.

Martin, Robert A., ed. *Arthur Miller: New Perspectives.* Englewood Cliffs, NJ: Prentice-Hall, 1982.

Nelson, Benjamin. *Arthur Miller, Portrait of a Playwright.* New York: McKay, 1970.

Shatzky, Joel. "Arthur Miller's 'Jewish' Salesman." *Studies in American Jewish Literature* 2 (Winter 1976): 1–9.

Joel Shatzky

MILLER, E. ETHELBERT (1950–)   African American poet, literary activist, considered by many to be one of the most influential forces in literature in America currently. Heavily anthologized and acknowledged for his recognition of the quality lent to American society and its culture by its diversity and for his generosity and encouragement to many other poets. Miller was witness to the struggle in a new black consciousness and the **Black Arts Movement** political processes beginning in the 1960s and resonant with the rallying cry of **race** pride and independence in thought and practice. A writer from 1968, he was one of sixty American authors honored by Laura Bush and the White House in 2001 at the First National Book Festival.

Miller lives in Washington, DC, where he is the director of the African American Resource Center at Howard University, his alma mater, and a prominent member of the Washington, DC, arts community. He holds an honorary doctorate of literature from Emory & Henry College, where he is affiliated with associated writing programs. His incisively crafted poems are included in *Our Souls Have Grown Deep Like the Rivers: Black Poets Read Their Work,* a one-of-a-kind CD set gathering of over seventy poems from the **Harlem Renaissance** to hip-hop, from **W. E. B. Du Bois** to Public Enemy. His works also appear on *Jazz Poetry Cafe: The Blackwords Compilation* CD. He is featured in the *Poet and the Poem Collection* from the Library of Congress in a fifty-nine-minute cybercast, and on *The Writing Life* cable TV series in a national prize–winning show (1995) with Henry Taylor and again in 1997 in a show hosted by Michael Collier. A strict reviewer of poetry, he edited *In Search of Color Everywhere: A Collection of African American Poetry* (1994), one of the first anthologies of

African American poetry since 1960. This vibrant and accessible compendium, containing selections from anonymous spirituals to the classics of **Langston Hughes**, was awarded the 1994 PEN Oakland Josephine Miles Award and made a Book-of-the-Month selection. He also wrote *Whispers, Secrets, and Promises* (1998) and *First Light: New and Selected Poems* (1994) and edited *Beyond the Frontier: African American Poetry for the 21st Century* (2002).

Love permeates his works. This is seen in his autobiography, *Fathering Words: The Making of an African-American Writer* (2000). With its punning title, it is poignant, realistic, and, in style, idiosyncratic and akin to the musicality of **jazz**, one of Miller's enthusiasms. Miller has said that when he talks about poetry he often talks about matters of the heart. This renowned writer believes in the integrity of the group and is an advocate for understanding and the openness that diversity makes possible. His own poetry is simple and clean, centered in realism, and of honest reflection on matters American express the sum of this great American poet. (*See also* African American Poetry)

Further Reading

Coleman, Wanda. "Letters to E. Ethelbert Miller." *Callaloo* 22.1 (1999): 99–106.
Galbus, Julia. "Fathering Words and Honoring Family: E. Ethelbert Miller's First Memoir." *Re-Markings* 2.2 (2003): 7–19.

Juliet A. Emanuel

MILLER, MAY (1899–1995) African American playwright, actress, and poet. Considered one of the most important female playwrights of the **Harlem Renaissance**, May Miller wrote and published fifteen plays. Daughter of Kelly Miller, an esteemed sociologist at Howard University, May Miller grew up among Washington, DC's black elite. Her parents frequently entertained well-known black scholars and artists including **Alain Locke, W. E. B. Du Bois**, and Carter Woodson. A prolific writer from an early age, Miller published the poem "Venus" in *School Progress* magazine at the age of fourteen. She attended **Paul Laurence Dunbar** High School in Washington, DC, and benefited greatly from the tutelage of poet **Angelina Weld Grimké** and playwright Mary Burrill, who were both teachers there. Immediately after high school, Miller attended Howard University, became involved with the Howard Drama Club, and entered a robustly productive period of her career as a playwright.

One of Miller's early plays, *The Bog Guide* (1925), was published and awarded a prize by *Opportunity* magazine. Many of her pieces were performed throughout the country in small theaters, and a recent resurgence has brought her work back to the stage. Miller's plays often center around political and racial issues; although some might assume that she participated in supporting the ideology of Negro uplift, Miller also did not shy away from difficult subjects, such as class struggles within the black community. In *Scratches* (1929), first published in *Carolina Magazine*, Miller focuses on intraracial color prejudice. As coeditor and contributor to *Negro*

History in Thirteen Plays, Miller shapes three of her four one-act plays around the lives of women: Harriet Tubman, **Sojourner Truth**, and the rebellious daughter of Haitian King Christophe.

For twenty years, Miller utilized her skills as an inspirational pedagogue to support herself by teaching drama, dance, and speech at **Frederick Douglass** High School in Baltimore. In fact, the four plays she contributed to the *Negro History* collection were originally written to inspire her students. Miller also performed in a number of plays, including sharing the stage with Frank Horne in Georgia Douglas Johnson's *Blue Blood.* Often attending Georgia Douglas Johnson's "S Street Salon" (also known as "the halfway house") in Washington, DC, Miller was friendly with **Langston Hughes**, **Countee Cullen**, **Zora Neale Hurston**, Alain Locke, and many of the leading figures of the Harlem Renaissance who visited the literary coterie.

With the support of her husband, John Sullivan, Miller retired from teaching high school in 1944 and dedicated the remaining fifty-one years of her life to writing stories and essays and composing poetry. During those years she published seven volumes of poetry, including *Into the Clearing* (1959), *Poems* (1962), *Not That Far* (1973), and *Dust of Uncertain Journey* (1975). Miller's poetry, compressed and imagistic, varied in theme from meditations on nature to a response to the bombings on Hiroshima and Nagasaki. Fervently committed to humanism, Miller's work never lingered in the personal but instead moved to the universal condition of mankind. Her deeply layered images gouged through surfaces, laying bare the struggles of being human. In 1986 May Miller won the Mister Brown Award for excellence in drama and poetry. In her later years, Miller remained productive, reading her poetry for luminaries such as former President Jimmy Carter, sitting on literary boards, and coordinating poetry projects for underprivileged youth. May Miller quietly, yet profoundly, smoothed the path for later African American poets and dramatists.

Further Reading

Brawley, Benjamin. *The Negro Genius.* New York: Dodd & Mead, 1937.

Patton, Venetria K., and Maureen Honey. *Double-Take: A Revisionist Harlem Renaissance Anthology.* New Brunswick, NJ: Rutgers UP, 2001.

Roses, Lorraine Elena, and Ruth Elizabeth Randolph, eds. *Harlem's Glory: Black Women Writing 1900–1950.* Cambridge, MA, & London, England: Harvard UP, 1996.

Stetson, Erlene, ed. *Black Sister: Poetry by Black American Women, 1746–1980.* Bloomington: Indiana UP, 1981.

Turner, Darwin T. "The Negro Dramatist's Image of the Universe, 1920–1960." *College Language Association Journal* 5 (1961): 106–20.

Lorna J. Raven Wheeler

MILLICAN, ARTHENIA JACKSON BATES (1920–) African American novelist and short story writer. Arthenia Millican's distinction in African American literature lies in her plausible and humane depiction of rural Southern black folk when many of her contemporaries were exploring themes of urban black militancy in the 1960s. She follows the cultural tradition of **Zora Neale Hurston**, **Richard Wright**, **Ernest Gaines**, and **Alice Walker**, whose fiction interprets the lives of agrarian blacks in Florida, Mississippi, Louisiana, and Georgia, respectively. A native of Sumter, South Carolina, and the daughter and granddaughter of Baptist ministers, Millican locates her stories in actual and fictional sites near Sumter, and she explores such themes as the tensions between good and evil, youth and age, Christianity and Islam, and communal and self-**identity**. Millican's major published works include two short story collections, *Seeds Beneath the Snow* (1969) and *Such Things from the Valley* (1977), and a novel, *The Deity Nodded* (1973).

Published the same year that Arthenia Bates Millican received her PhD from Louisiana State University, *Seeds Beneath the Snow* contains a dozen vignettes that depict the aspirations and strivings of black youth destined to expand their visions. In "Dear Sis," an underaged brother leaves home to join the U.S. Navy; in "Home X and Me," a school girl learns the meaning and use of a lemon squeezer in her home economics class; in "A Ceremony of Innocence," which became the fifty-first chapter in *The Deity Nodded*, a young Muslim convert returns home to visit an elderly poor black Christian woman; and in "Return of the Spouse," a young married father of eight children is lured into adultery only to return to his forgiving wife. Reviewers praise the collection as a witty, absorbing work with realistic portrayals.

In *Such Things from the Valley*, a collection of two short stories, Millican addresses issues that were emerging and prominent concerns of black feminists writing during the 1970s. "Rena" explores the historical and intersecting obstacles of race, gender, and class that have circumscribed black women since slavery. "Where You Belong" illuminates intraracial class prejudice among middle-class black women who deny recognition to a rising newcomer. Together, the two stories offer a fresh perspective of black women's struggles for independence and identity in a provincial community.

The Deity Nodded is a celebration of a black woman's rise from the narrow, rural confines of her Southern Christian environment to her full acceptance into the Northern black Muslim sect. Tisha Dees, the protagonist, is a thinly veiled disguise of Catherine J. Rhodes, Millican's younger sister, a convert to Islam in the 1960s.

Millican's unpublished fiction includes two novellas, *Benny* (1979) and *A Journey to Somewhere* (1985), and two collections of short stories, *The Bottoms and Hills: Virginia Tales* (1975) and *Bayou Twigs* (1979). A meticulous writer, Millican will be remembered for her faithful depiction of poor, but never hopeless, black folk in the rural South.

Further Reading

Dandridge, Rita B. "The Motherhood Myth: Black Women and Christianity in *The Deity Nodded*." *MELUS* 12 (Fall 1985): 13–22.

Owusu, Adimu. "The Development of Black Women: An Interview with Arthenia Bates-Millican." *Nuance* 1.7 (March 1982): 14–16.

Rita B. Dandridge

MILNER, RON (1938–2004)   African American playwright, screenwriter, director, activist, and teacher. For all of Ron Milner's contributions to the **Black Arts Movement** and the community theater tradition, his realistic and provocative plays, which recreate African American life, remain his most important contribution. Refusing to write for a white, Broadway audience, Milner's dynamic, rhythmical dramas encourage the destruction of a racist tradition that conditions African Americans to feel inferior. In its place, Milner urges his audience to validate a tradition that celebrates blackness and liberates the African Americans psychologically, mentally, aesthetically, and physically.

Milner's plays are artistically powerful and musical. He derived the titles and forms for *Who's Got His Own* (1965) and *Jazz-Set* (1979) from the African American musical tradition. Each character is a musical instrument; they play together as an ensemble, and then each person steps forward to take a solo. Each character in *Jazz-Set* represents a member of a **jazz** ensemble: tenor (saxophone), alto (saxophone), pianist, trumpet, drummer, and bassist. In addition, the musical rhythms that run throughout *The Warning: A Theme for Linda* (1968) were derived from the rhythm and **blues** of Motown, particularly Smokey Robinson's love songs and hard, funky blues. Several of Milner's other plays have jazz or Motown playing on a radio or record player in the background.

Although Milner's plays explore the moral complexity and social frustration of African Americans, they are ultimately optimistic. Written during the turbulent 1960s, *Who's Got His Own* portrays an African American family that struggles to find truth and redemption in an angry, racist world. In this intense and highly psychological play, each character symbolizes a moment in African American history. Tim Sr., who represents the past, saw his father lynched by the Ku Klux Klan (KKK), and because he cannot stand up to the white establishment, he takes his frustration out on his family. Tim Jr., who represents the militant attitudes of the present, resents the humiliation he feels for his father, and he beats a white friend nearly to death for failing to understand his pain. Clara, who represents one possible future, rejects her family and her culture, attempts to integrate into the modern, "**race**less" society, and is rebuffed by the **racism** of "liberal" whites. The mother, who seems almost outside of time, plays the religious martyr, and although she is empathetic and loving, her blindness to her family's problems makes her unable to soothe their pain. The play portrays the bitterness African Americans feel in America and how it negatively affects them. However, by exposing the truth, the family becomes closer, and the play ends optimistically, with the African American community committed to unity and militance.

Milner's plays are didactic, if not moralistic. Milner resisted the latter category, but he writes that he did intend his plays to instruct, wanting them to challenge both African Americans and whites to examine themselves. In *What the Wine-Sellers Buy* (1974), Milner illustrates how the community's morals influence young African Americans. The teenaged Steve must choose between the criminal, materialistic teachings of the pimp/hustler Rico and the moral, spiritual teachings of his mother. Steve uses drugs and plans to pimp his girlfriend to earn money after his mother loses her job. His soul is at stake, and in the end he discovers what it means to be a man, choosing not to trade his love or his self-respect for easy money.

Unfortunately, not enough people make the choice Steve makes, and two decades later Milner again explores the financial lure of drugs to struggling African American families in *Urban Transition: Loose Blossoms* (1995). This realistic play shows how a working family moves out of the ghetto and struggles to maintain a middle-class lifestyle when the frustrated husband and father, Earl, is injured and cannot earn a living. It shows how some adults, like E.J.'s mother Cheryl, rationalize the source of the financial help and expensive gifts they receive from their drug-dealing sons. Furthermore, it shows how other adults, like Earl and his friend Bert, value education and honest work over easy money. However, E.J. ignores their moralistic warnings, and he is murdered by his drug-dealing partner and childhood friend, Eric.

Like Milner's other plays, *Checkmates* (1990) is about how African Americans struggle to maintain the familial unit and find their own place in a world controlled by white men and white ideologies. The play explores the contemporary obsession with competition and upward mobility and the tension it creates between married people. Like Milner's other plays, *Checkmates* is intense, thought provoking, and realistic, before ending optimistically. (*See also* African American Drama)

Further Reading

King Jr., Woodie. "Introduction." *What the Wine-Sellers Buy Plus Three: Four Plays by Ron Milner.* Detroit: Wayne State UP, 2001. 11–19.

Smitherman, Geneva. "Ron Milner, People's Playwright." *Black World* 25.6 (1976): 4–19.

Matthew Teorey

MIN, ANCHEE (1957–) A Chinese immigrant writer and artist. With the publication of the best-selling memoir *Red Azalea* (1994), which chronicles her experiences growing up during China's Cultural Revolution, Min emerged as a notable writer in Chinese immigrant literature. In 1984, with the help of the actress Joan Chen, Min fled to the United States, where she started learning English and writing about experiences from her past. Since then, she has published four critically acclaimed novels: *Katherine* (1995), *Becoming Madame Mao* (2000), *Wild Ginger* (2002), and *Empress Orchid* (2004).

With a simple and straightforward writing style, Min, in her memoir *Red Azalea* recounts devastating experiences in the Cultural Revolution that defined her youth. As a witness and survivor, she not only delineates the psychological and sexual perversion of those times but also recounts the physical and emotional difficulties of life as a Chinese woman. Born and raised in Shanghai, China, Min joined the Red Guard, who supported and believed in the Communist leader Mao Zedong's ideas during the Cultural Revolution, in order to escape being beaten and persecuted. At age seventeen, Min was among 100,000 students sent to labor camps near the East China Sea. Under the repressive Communist system, her love affair with a female platoon leader gave her some respite from the harsh physical and emotional conditions surrounding her. Three years later, she was discovered by a talent scout and was recruited and trained to play the protagonists in Madame Mao's propaganda films. But with the death of Chairman Mao in 1976, Madame Mao was arrested and fell from power. Consequently, Min and other supporters of Madame Mao were politically discredited.

In subsequent works, all novels, she celebrates the strength of her female characters during political turmoil. She also creates ambiguous portraits of fascinating but vilified Chinese women. Mixing historical facts and imagination, she re-creates lives of sexually assertive and intellectually ambitious Chinese women who railed against the confines of their culture. For instance, *Becoming Madame Mao* is a powerful reimagination of the life of Madame Mao, who has been reviled as the "white-boned demon." Min has portrayed her life with keen psychological insight and lyrical eroticism, rendering a powerful tale of passion, betrayal, and survival. *Empress Orchid* is another story of a fascinating, strong-willed woman who has been vilified as a grand seductress and murderer. Min draws a vivid portrait of the last empress of the Manchu dynasty, a flawed yet utterly compelling woman. Writing against the official version that castigates the empress as a conniving concubine responsible for the collapse of the Ch'ing Dynasty, Min considers her a shrewd and courageous survivor, political tactician, and respectful leader. She is a figure of indomitable will and passion, but is at the same time a victim of deeply rooted misogyny. In her powerful and brilliantly conceived fictionalized portraits of controversial women intrinsic to Chinese culture, Min has created immensely satisfying tales of love, lust, and revenge set against a backdrop of political upheaval. (*See also* Chinese American Novel)

Further Reading

Somerson, Wendy. "Under the Mosquito Net: Space and Sexuality in *Red Azalea*." *College Literature* 24.1 (February 1998): 98–115.

Xu, Wenying. "Agency via Guilt in Anchee Min's *Red Azalea*." *MELUS* 25 (2000): 203–20.

Su-lin Yu

MIRIKITANI, JANICE (1941–) Japanese American poet, author, choreographer, and political activist. Janice Mirikitani, a Sansei or third-generation Japanese American, is a leader in advocating for human and civil rights, and her poetry and work engage in these movements politically and personally. Her books of poetry include *Awake in the River* (1978), *Shedding Silence* (1987), *We the Dangerous* (1995), and *Love Works* (2002). As executive director of programs at Glide Memorial Church in the turbulent Tenderloin District of San Francisco, Mirikitani's work serves the poor, abused, sick, and homeless. In 2000 Mirikitani was named San Francisco's poet laureate. She has received more than thirty-five awards for her art and community activism.

Her intimate connection with the community and her devotion to empowering women and children are evident in two anthologies she has edited: *I Have Something to Say About This Big Trouble* (1989), children's writings about crack cocaine, and *Watch Out, We're Talking* (1993), adult writings about incest. These two anthologies, along with her other writings, demonstrate Mirikitani's rebellion against silence and her belief in the power of speaking out. Her own poetry speaks out about the Japanese American internment, sexual abuse, **racism**, and poverty. She was an infant when her family was interned in a camp in Arkansas, and Mirikitani's poetry reflects this heritage as it strives to document and resist racism. As a survivor of sexual abuse, Mirikitani speaks and writes candidly about physical and psychological violence, encouraging others to do so as well.

In addition to the powerful poetics of protest and violence, Mirikitani's writings also explore the tender relationship between mothers and daughters, and "Generations of Women," for example, acknowledges matrilineal bonds. In "Why Is Preparing Fish a Political Act?" she invites the audience to share in her memory of her grandmother preparing rock cod for the new year. The narrator cannot duplicate the flavors, but she does follow the legacy of self-respect, just as her grandmother would not respond to *mamasan*. In this case, there is dignity in silence, not conforming to stereotypes, refusing to be polite.

This poem's details of gutting fish, its images of blood, is repeated in another poem about domestic and international violence. Both a woman and a third-world nation are graphically abused in "Assaults and Invasions." Mirikitani's poetry not only speaks out against injustice, but its vivid and violent images call the readers to social activism. After all, "It Isn't Easy" compares writing poetry to disembowelment, the poet's words and body as a testimony, protest, and call to action.

Further Reading

Hong, Grace Kyunwon. "Janice Mirikitani." *Words Matter: Conversations with Asian American Writers.* Ed. King-kok Cheung. Honolulu: U of Hawai'i P, 2002. 123–39.

Lashgari, Deirdre. "Disrupting the Deadly Stillness: Janice Mirikitani's Poetics of Violence." *Violence, Silence, and Anger: Women's Writing as Transgression.* Ed. Deirdre Lashgari. Charlottesville: UP of Virginia, 1995. 291–304.

Usui, Masami. "'No Hiding Place, New Speaking Space': Janice Mirikitani's Poetry of Incest and Abuse." *Chu Shikoku Studies in American Literature* 32 (1996): 56–65.

Karen Li Miller

MITCHELL, LOFTEN (1919–2001)   African American playwright and actor, theater historian and Harlem chronicler, activist, essayist, World War II–U.S. Navy seaman, Guggenheim fellow, Department of Welfare social investigator and administrator of public assistance grants to people of gypsy origin, professor of theater and Afro-American studies at State University of New York at Binghamton, and AUDELCO (Audience Development Committee) Outstanding Theatrical Pioneer award winner. Among Mitchell's most important plays are *The Cellar* (produced in 1952), *Land Beyond the River* (produced in 1957), *Star of the Morning: Scenes in the Life of Bert Williams* (produced in 1965), *Tell Pharaoh* (produced in 1967), and *Bubbling Brown Sugar* (produced in 1975). He also wrote a number of essays, two outstanding books on **African American drama**, *Black Drama* (1967) and *Voices of the Black Theatre* (1975), and a semiautobiographical novel, *The Stubborn Old Lady Who Resisted Change* (1973). Loften Mitchell in his essay "Alligators in the Swamp" holds that an artist must tell the truth, and he therefore considers it his duty to present the black experience truthfully, even at the cost of offending white sensibilities.

The oldest son of Ulysses Sanford and Willia Spaulding Mitchell, Loften Mitchell was born on April 15, 1919 in the rural town of Columbus, North Carolina. He was not even one month old when his parents left south for Harlem, New York. In Harlem, his father worked as a maintenance man, and his mother as a manager of an apartment complex. As a child, Mitchell got the opportunity to watch the vaudeville performances by black artists and thus developed his interest in the theater. On the onset of the Great Depression in 1929, he began to sell newspapers at Harlem theaters to indulge his passion for theatrical entertainment. Mitchell graduated from DeWitt Clinton High School in the Bronx with honors in 1937. He attended Talladega College in Talladega, Alabama, on a scholarship. For his freshman English class term paper, Mitchell chose to do one on the Harlem theater. The instructor, Maurice A. Lee, liked his paper, and it became the basis for his book titled *Black Drama*. At Talladega, Mitchell majored in sociology, and received his BA degree with honors in 1943. After a two-year stint in the U.S. Navy during World War II, he enrolled in the graduate program in playwriting at Columbia University in 1947. He studied playwriting with the famous drama critic and professor John Gassner. In 1948 he accepted a job as a social investigator with the Department of Welfare and continued his studies at Columbia by attending evening classes. In the same year, he married actress Helen Marsh, who bore him two sons, Thomas and Melvin. They were divorced in 1956. He received his master's degree from Columbia University in 1951. He married Gloria Anderson in 1991. Loften Mitchell died on May 14, 2001 after a protracted illness.

Black protest against white **racism** and celebration of black cultural heritage are recurrent themes in Loften Mitchell's writings. His essay "The Negro Writer and His Materials" (1959) is a justification of protest literature. *The Cellar* is the story of a black Blues singer who befriends a fugitive from Southern justice and her fiancé who hounds the fugitive. *Land Beyond the River* dramatizes the historic struggle of Reverend Joseph A. Delaine on behalf of his parishioners' children for equal schools in Clarendon County, South Carolina, and his sufferings at the hands of whites for taking up this cause. The courage, unselfishness, and love for his oppressors shown by Reverend Layne shines through. The play also emphasizes the role of black women as key supporters of education of their children. *Star of the Morning* enacts how Bert Williams and George Walker, meeting for the first time, decide to team up as entertainers; Walker plays the smooth, slick, and well-groomed man, and Williams plays the shuffling, fumbling clown, always getting into trouble. It also dramatizes their awful working conditions and how they parried attacks on their manhood. When Ridge addresses Williams and Walker as "boys," the offended Williams retorts that if Ridge studied human anatomy, he would see a noticeable difference between a boy and a man. Williams refuses to use burnt cork to blacken his face to conform to the stereotypical image of a black entertainer. *Tell Pharaoh* is a tribute to African and African American heritage as well as the African American struggle for equal rights in the wake of 1954 Supreme Court decision in *Brown v. Board of Education*. It traces the history of Harlem through the eras of the Harlem Renaissance, Depression years, McCarthy era, World War II, and the **Civil Rights Movement**. *Bubbling Brown Sugar* gives a guided tour of Harlem of the bygone years for the education and edification of a young black couple, Jim and Ella, and that of the Harvard-educated Charlie, a white young man in his twenties. They travel back in time from the 1970s to the early 1920s. They watch Bert Williams's poker game pantomime, a strolling routine, taste sweet Georgia Brown, meet Bumpy (a numbers racketeer at the Savoy), and listen to a jive at Small's Paradise. This experience completely changes their outlook on life. As for his novel, *The Stubborn Old Lady Who Resisted Change*, it tells the story of an old lady named Madeline Briggs who lived in a dilapidated, ramshackle apartment in Harlem but didn't want to move out because of the associations it had with her gypsy lover, Nicholas Castilo, who died a few days before the wedding date.

Loften Mitchell's two books on the history of black drama are essential studies for proper understanding of the contributions that black artists have made to the theater, as well as the difficulties they faced in their efforts to get rid of their negative stereotypical portraiture, and to be shown as they really are. The chief merit of *Black Drama* lies in its account of the various theatrical groups and moving descriptions of the dramatic artists Mitchell knew and worked with. *Voices of the Black Theatre* is a study of the experiences of seven theatrical pioneers: Eddie Hunter, Regina Andrews, Dick Campbell, Abram Hill, Frederick O'Neal, Vinnette Caroll, and **Ruby Dee**. Based on their taped individual recollections, these artists tell how they got interested in the theater, persons who encouraged them, social conditions under which they worked, and the significant issues they dealt with in their dramatic works. The story of Ruby Dee is really a poignant one: She tells about the battles she had to fight to be accepted as an actress.

Further Reading

Bigsby, C. W. E. "Three Black Playwrights: Loften Mitchell, Ossie Davis, Douglas Turner Ward." *The Black American Writer, Vol. II: Poetry and Drama.* Ed. C. W. E. Bigsby. Baltimore: Penguin, 1969.

Peterson, Bernard L. Jr. *Contemporary Black American Playwrights and Their Plays.* Westport, CT: Greenwood Press, 1988.

Harish Chander

MOHR, NICHOLASA (1935–)   The first and most important literary voice of Puerto Rican American women. Her first novel, the semiautobiographical *Nilda* (1973), offers the story of the girls and women who were left out of **Piri Thomas**'s Puerto Rican American classic, ***Down These Mean Streets*** (1976). Mohr grew up in and describes the same neighborhood as Thomas, but rather than focusing on the violence of the streets, her novels center on the domestic space, the family, and the struggles particular to Puerto Rican American girls.

Perhaps it is the lack of sensational violence perceived to exemplify the Puerto Rican American experience that has kept Mohr's books to a relatively minimal commercial success. Indeed, she reports that the publishers of *Nilda* wanted her to change the story to be more like *Down These Mean Streets,* but she refused. *Nilda* is more like a response to rather than a continuation of Piri Thomas's legacy. Although *Nilda* was selected Best Book of the Year by the School Library Journal and Outstanding Book of the Year by the *New York Times,* marketing worked against Mohr. The lack on violence in her stories as well as their treatment of girlhood allowed publishers to advertise her works for young adults, although they in fact treat incredibly mature subjects such as domestic violence, unwanted pregnancy, the failings of the welfare system, and institutional prejudice. Mohr's books were not a success in the young-adult market because they were inappropriate for that market, but they continue to receive little critical attention outside of the Puerto Rican American community, perhaps because of their young-adult classification.

Like her character Nilda and like Thomas, Mohr was born in New York to Puerto Rican parents. We can read *Nilda* to learn of Mohr's youth. Mohr and Nilda grew up in the 1930s and 1940s in a Puerto Rican American neighborhood in the Bronx. The bilingual daughter of Spanish-speaking parents and the only girl in a family with two brothers, Nilda served as her mother's link to American institutions, translating at visits with the welfare office and for all interactions with her school. Each of the stages in Nilda's girlhood—making friends, going to school, going to camp—is marked by the particularities of being Puerto Rican American as Nilda faces linguistic discrimination, **racism**, and the economic and social realities that limit her family to Spanish Harlem. Nilda must also contend with the discrimination that she faces as a girl: She is not allowed to explore the streets like Piri and, unlike him, is subject to strict concerns about her cleanliness and orderliness as she is constantly reminded of the responsibilities of being a wife and that await her. One of Nilda's brothers follows a path similar to Piri's, becoming involved in gangs and drugs; another enlists in the military and strives to achieve the American Dream. Nilda, and Mohr, on the other hand focuses her energies on school and struggles to be a mediator not only between her family and American bureaucracy but also between her teachers and the Puerto Rican American community. By asserting herself as an intellectual an artistic, Nilda suggests a way to escape and to fight back that are rather different from those proposed by Thomas in *Down These Mean Streets*. Whereas Piri turns to violence, drugs, and finally religion, Nilda repeatedly "escapes" from the harsh reality around her by slipping into a world of imagination. And she fights back against authority figures by succeeding at their game, but on her own terms, countering the misinformation of teachers and welfare workers or appearing to conform to their agenda while actually carrying out her own. Like Thomas in *Down These Mean Streets*, Mohr creates in *Nilda* a literary language that refuses the rules of standard English, but rather than using a highly stylized and slang-laden English intermixed with Spanish, Mohr employs an English that reflects the grammar and accent of Puerto Rican American homes.

Nilda ends in 1945, when Nilda is fifteen. Mohr finished high school and studied painting and printmaking at the Brooklyn Museum of Art School and the Pratt Center for Contemporary Printmaking. She married Irwin Mohr and had two children while painting and working as an art teacher in New York and New Jersey. In addition to *Nilda*, Mohr has written a number of short story collections and several other novels.

Set in the South Bronx between 1945 and 1956, *El Bronx Remembered* (1975) tells the stories of a range of the neighborhood's inhabitants: A housewife feels trapped in her apartment just like her "very special Pet," a chicken named Joncrofo, is trapped in her kitchen; the teenager Alice is about to face a life of deprivation after accidentally becoming pregnant, until she meets her gay neighbor Herman, who offers to set up a household with her. "Herman and Alice," the longest story in the collection, offers a critical appraisal of Puerto Rican American family structures and of the protagonist's failed attempt to find an alternative. Herman and Alice set out to redefine gender and sexual roles in their family, but they soon fall into the set roles of macho husband and servile wife that Alice can only break by turning to the streets and a string of uncaring boyfriends. *El Bronx Remembered* was a finalist for the National Book Award. Even more than *Nilda*, *El Bronx Remembered* mixes Spanish and English to assert the bilingual character to the Puerto Rican American community.

Mohr's next collection, *In Nueva York* (1977) contains a series of short stories organized around the building and the street where "Old Mary" lives. The innovative format of this collection—between short stories and a novel—reflects the connections and disjunctions of the Puerto Rican community in New York. The community is not monolithic; it is composed of people with very different experiences, to the least of which stems from their relationship to the island of Puerto Rico, but their paths cross repeatedly as they negotiate the same streets of the same city.

Felita (1979) is Mohr's only novel truly intended for young-adult readers, telling a story similar to that of *Nilda* but simplified for a younger audience. In *Rituals of Survival: A Woman's Portfolio* (1985) Mohr collects a series of short stories centered on adult Puerto Rican women in New York. Mohr's other works are the novel *Going Home* (1986); the memoir *In My Own Words: Growing Up Inside the Sanctuary of My Imagination* (1994); a biography of Evelyn López Antonetty, *All for the Better: A Story of El Barrio* (1995); the short novel *The Magic Shell* (1995); and two illustrated children's books, *The Song of El Coquí* (1995) and *Old Levita and the Mountain of Sorrows* (1996). Mohr also earned an honorary doctorate of letters from the State University of New York at Albany and has served as a visiting professor at Queens College and as a writer in residence at several institutions including the Smithsonian and the American University in London. (*See also* Bilingualism, Puerto Rican American Novel)

Further Reading

Fernandez Olmos, Margarite. "Growing Up Puerto Riqueña." *Centro* 2.7 (1989–1990): 56–73.

Flores, Juan. "Back Down These Mean Streets." *Revista Chicano-Riqueña* 8.2 (1980): 51–56.

Kevane, Bridget, and Juana Heredia. *Latina Self-Portraits.* Albuquerque: U of New Mexico P, 200.

Luis, William. *Dance Between Two Cultures.* Nashville: Vanderbilt UP, 1997.

Miller, John C. "Nicholasa Mohr." *Revista/Review Interamericana* 9 (1979): 535–54.

Mohr, Eugene V. *The Nuyorican Experience.* Westport, CT: Greenwood Press, 1982.

Sánchez-González, Lisa. *Boricua Literature.* New York: NYU Press, 2001.

Keja Lys Valens

MOMADAY, NAVARRE SCOTT (1934–) Native American poet, Pulitzer Prize–winning novelist, playwright, storyteller, painter, founding trustee of the National Museum of the American Indian, Regents' Professor of the Humanities at the University of Arizona. Momaday has lectured and given readings internationally, and his articles appear in many periodicals. Major works include ***House Made of Dawn*** (1968), ***The Way to Rainy Mountain*** (1969), *Angle of Geese* and other poems (1974), *Owl in the Cedar Tree* (1975), *The Gourd Dancer* (1976), *The Names: A Memoir* (1976), *We Have Been Lovers, You and I.* (1980), *The Ancient Child* (1989), *In the Presence of the Sun: Stories and Poems, 1961–1991* (1992), *Circle of Wonder: A Native American Christmas*

Story (1994), *The Man Made of Words: Essays, Stories, Passages* (1997), and *In the Bear's House* (1999).

Multicultural Experience and the Pulitzer Prize

N. Scott Momaday was born in Kiowa country in Oklahoma. He grew up among the rich oral traditions of the reservations and pueblos of the Southwest and lived among Navajo, Apache, Hispanic, and Anglo children. This tribal history was repeated for his entertainment, but as an adult he recognized the fragile nature of the captivating stories that shape his work. His literary scholarship and painting reflect his desire to preserve this rich cultural experience. Momaday's parents were teachers with artistic interests. His father was a painter and his mother a writer. Like his parents, Momaday's career has integrated writing, painting, and teaching. His credentials reflect interests in political science, law, literature, and language and include a bachelor's degree from the University of New Mexico and an MA and PhD from Stanford.

N. Scott Momaday. *AP/Wide World Photos.*

In the 1960s civil rights and ethnographic studies influenced a new categorization of literary texts. This shift formed a broader concept of literary criticism and increased accessibility of the literary **canon**, opening the way for Momaday's interpretative discourse. Disciplinary viewpoints had previously assigned oral narratives, histories, autobiographies, and similar works to anthropology or labeled them historical documents, but the new canon recognized many of these works as literature, making space for new writers. Benefiting from this shift toward a more inclusive canon, Momaday's Pulitzer Prize–winning first novel, *House Made of Dawn*, received recognition while he was still a relatively unknown writer. Recordings for the Museum of the American Indian, Smithsonian Institute, and National Public Radio, in addition to other national and international events, continue to support and extend Momaday's earlier recognition.

Cultural History, Legend as Art

Through allegory (narratives that dramatize symbolic or abstract ideas), anecdote (short narratives that expose overarching themes), and archetype (recurring cultural symbols, characters, or landscapes), Momaday interweaves history and legend. His art resonates with history, connecting language and the human experience to the natural world, while explicitly translating and celebrating Native American experience. This multicultural approach is recognized by a range of world literature scholars. His gift for storytelling has specifically influenced other Native American writers, including **Joy Harjo** and **Leslie Marmon Silko**. Momaday's reverence for the physical and the metaphysical is demonstrated in the imagery of Rainy Mountain Cemetery and of walking among the stones marking the burial site of family members. This vibrant imagery gives voice to his Kiowa heritage and provides a model for other Native American writers.

Momaday's literary models and paintings are windows into the Kiowa culture, praised by critics for their visual power. Matthias Schubnell calls *The Ancient Child* Momaday's most comprehensive commentary on art—his "most painterly work"—and notes that Momaday, like the German expressionist Emil Nolde, rejects the commercialization of art, preferring to search for the "primal, mythic mentality." This connection of **identity** and artistic genius to "myth, place, and the human unconscious" lifts Momaday's work from its Native American boundaries to establish broader cultural commonalities. His character, Set, searches for primitive identity, reflecting the Expressionists' concern for artistic substance, authenticity, and intrinsic meaning ("Locke Setman" 468).

Critics call Momaday's approach in *The Way to Rainy Mountain* cinematic. Readers view an ancient Kiowa landmark, a knoll rising out of the Wichita Range on the Oklahoma plains. This narrative incorporates concepts of time, place, and self. The descriptions of Oklahoma weather include winter blizzards, spring tornadic winds, and summers that turn the prairie into "an anvil's edge." The images of land, trees, and weather conspire to define time and place. Momaday distinguishes the whole from the isolated elements of this land that nurtures his cultural identity. The land looms large, inhabited by "great green and yellow grasshoppers." The land is lonely, and time crawls. The writer's return to Rainy Mountain provokes an interior monologue, linking the history of the southern Plains Kiowas and his grandmother's Montana forebears. He calls the vast continental interior a "memory in her blood," and he calls his grandmother's inherited reverence for the sun and her later Christian faith images of suffering and hope. Aho's house, once a significant site for feasting and activity and a place for viewing the stars, has become a small place inhabited by funeral silence. A strangely enlarged outline of a cricket against the moon and a warm wind mark the culmination of the writer's pilgrimage.

Voice, Language, and Landscape

These autobiographical descriptions the natural landscapes associated with Momaday's Kiowa heritage are a powerful blend of literary methods and traditions. Momaday's observance of the significance of landscape, or "spirit of place," is an essential element of Native American oral tradition. In *In the Presence of the Sun* Momaday conveys his early fascination with language as a creative link to legend, symbolism, and spiritual, or aesthetic objects. The writer selects narrative and lyric forms, fusing genres, for their capacity to fit his pithy style. He blends the qualities of verse and prose, history and imagination, and personal identity and culture to produce an integrated voice for storytelling. In imaginative prose the writer personalizes his exploration of history and culture to produce what he calls "an act of understanding."

In addition to his blending of verse and prose qualities, Momaday also manipulates characterization to preserve in contemporary English his multicultural experience and Kiowa heritage. In *Ancient Child,* his second novel, the protagonist is an adopted Kiowa-Anglo, and in his collection of poems, prose, and paintings, *In the Bear's House,* the healer (Grey) is Navajo, Kiowa, Mexican, French, Canadian, Scotch, Irish, and English, perhaps reflective of his mother's blended heritage. These works are designed to preserve the traditional sacred elements of a culture that Momaday believes may not be transferring effectively to new generations. In *The Man Made of Words: Essays, Stories, Passages,* a recurrent theme is the threatened loss of the sacred narratives that reflect the culture's oral tradition and explain significant tribal events and beliefs.

Momaday considers his distinctive regional work as also fragments of a universal story. Local geography, customs, and speech, subtly and consciously, influence the regional narratives of his childhood. Memoir becomes a microcosm of layered personal reflection and historical imagery. Momaday uses this blended private and public voice in *The Gourd Dancer* and *The Man Made of Words* to dramatically introduce into American literature people and places that are vital to the understanding of Native American culture. For example, the repeated appearance of the bear is a significant literary and cultural symbol. The writer selects strong cultural imagery and allows the contrasting poetic influences of such writers as Emily Dickinson and Frederick Goddard Tuckerman to work in tandem with themes uncharacteristic of Native American culture, such as the Crucifixion, to tell a more inclusive story.

These contrastive investigations of traditional imagery in Native American and Anglo American culture take Momaday's investigation a step further than some cultural texts go, representing the Native American experience, as Roemer views it, as inherently multiethnic and multicultural. In *House Made of Dawn,* Momaday considers the cultural complexities of young Native Americans who must balance the ancient ways of their ancestors against their own need to survive twentieth-century materialism. In Abel, a young Tano Indian, Momaday represents the experience of individuals caught between cultures. Abel returns from World War II and is plunged into a different kind of war, involving his elders' world of ceremonies, the harsh realities of poverty, and the promised abundance of the urban world. The traditional Native American understanding of the psychic self's origins further complicates these contraries. This experience of self, as mythic and tribal, is inherent in the related concept of the sacredness of the land, with brain, bone, and land being integrally connected. For these individuals, leaving the land is not optional. Self is firmly bound to the land, and going from the land initiates a disintegration of self. Returning to the land is returning to self. This homing pattern, essential to the spherical, cyclical nature of tribal narratives and Native American novels, is especially evident in *The Ancient Child* and *House Made of Dawn*.

Culture's Personal Journey

Like the traditional forms of his culture's storytelling, Momaday's themes are frequently circular in structure, with event incorporated into event and basic subtexts expanding into even more complex themes (see Roberson). Momaday's literary connection of personal narrative and history is simultaneously an overview of the corresponding progression of personal and tribal identity development. In *The Way to Rainy Mountain*, by connecting the migration of the Kiowas and his own journey back to Rainy Mountain, Momaday creates a *whole journey*. This experimentation with sensory, metaphorical, and symbolic language provides a successful vehicle for his literary art and cultural narrative, and the blurring of genre boundaries suggests the indistinct boundaries that frequently redefine self and culture (see Schubnell). Momaday also employs selective omniscience and interior monologue to focus the reader's perception and to capture preverbal sentiments. Momaday's effective documentation of the Kiowa cultural identity through his own personal narrative, myth, and history embraces the literary and cultural objectives of both.

Memories of Rainy Mountain Creek and the culture of childhood clearly shape Momaday's art. The home where his father was born was built in 1913 by Momaday's grandfather, Mammedaty. Momaday remembers first hearing the language of his Kiowa forebears and receiving his Indian name in the arbor beside his grandfather's house. He describes the house and arbor as now in disrepair, inhabited only by the songs and prayers of memory. Momaday has been instrumental in establishing the Buffalo Trust, a cultural archive and center designed to assist young Kiowas. The trust's mission is preserving the Kiowa heritage. The buffalo, representing the sun, is the logo of the association and the sacred symbol of the Kiowa Sun Dance. The Buffalo Trust is a public effort to recover and preserve a vanishing culture. The land of the buffalo has changed, but Momaday's art and the Kiowa concept of time merge the past and present, painting everything that represents either reality as existing side by side, conversing to create mutual understanding. (*See also* Native American Novel)

Further Reading

Fox, Richard Wightman, and James T. Kloppenberg. *A Companion to American Thought.* Cambridge: Blackwell, 1995. 464–66.

Isernhager, Hartwig, ed. *Momaday, Vizenor, Armstrong: Conversations on American Indian Writing.* Norman: U of Oklahoma P, 1998.

Ives, Stephen, director. The West. DVD, VHS. Tampa, FL: Warner Home Video, 2003.

Lincoln, Kenneth. "Old Songs Made New: Momaday." *Sing with the Heart of a Bear: Fusions of Native American Poetry, 1890–1999.* Berkeley: U of California P, 2000. 240–255.

Roberson, Susan L. "Translocations and Transformations: Identity in N. Scott Momaday's *The Ancient Child.*" *American Indian Quarterly* 22.1. (1998): 31–46.

Roemer, Kenneth M. *Approaches to Teaching Momaday's "The Way to Rainy Mountain."* New York: MLA, 1988.

———, ed. *N. Scott Momaday: The Cultural and Literary Background.* Literary Conversations Series. Norman: U of Oklahoma P, 1985.

Schubnell, Matthias. "Locke Setman, Emil Nolde and the Search for Expression in N. Scott Momaday's *The Ancient Child.*" *American Indian Quarterly* 18.4 (1994): 468–81

———. *N. Scott Momaday: The Cultural and Literary Background.* Norman: U of Oklahoma P, 1985.

———, ed. *Conversations with N. Scott Momaday.* Jackson: UP of Mississippi, 1997.

Stella Thompson

MONARDO, ANNA (1956–) Italian American writer and teacher. Anna Monardo's substantial body of work spans a wide range of literary genres: poetry, essays, short stories, erotica, and novels. In addition to writing prolifically, she directs the writer's workshop at the University of Nebraska at Omaha.

The first American-born daughter to Calabrian immigrants, Monardo's motifs arise from her persistent concerns about how love and **identity** are influenced by geography. Her view is that identity is inextricably linked to whichever place is home, an elusive but vibrant life source. Monardo's essay "Ours or the Other Place" (2000) takes us on her journey to locate the geography of her heart. As the first woman in her family to leave her childhood home without the benefit of marriage, Monardo sets off for New York City in search of independence and adventure, where she finds the comfort of home. New York City is the seat of her passion because it reminds her of Italy, an important source of love for Monardo.

In her first novel, *Courtyard of Dreams* (1993), Giulia Di Cuore, the young protagonist, solidifies her identity when she travels to Italy to meet her father's family and spend the summer in their midst. Dual motifs— dreams and courtyards—lead Giulia on her journey toward self-knowledge.

The book opens as Giulia dreams about what her life might have been had she been raised in Italy, spending her days in the safety of the family courtyard, with her cousins, four other Giulias, all named after their grandmother. This prologue evokes an idyllic, sun-filled, joyful, love-saturated Italian tableau. Giulia's dream world is vanquished by her real life in Homefield, Ohio. Surrounded by her loving and devoted Italian microcommunity, Giulia is sheltered from the fearful unknowns of American teenage culture. Only while in Italy—a trip she finally takes when she graduates from high school, after adamantly refusing for years, despite her father's repeated offers—is her sensuously languorous dream revived. At first, reluctant to speak Italian, Giulia makes a startling realization one day while absorbing sunshine on a Calabrian beach: She begins to dream in Italian, proving that Italy resides in her subconscious. The dream motif signals not only times of enjoyment but also helps Giulia to trust her intuition and make important decisions. The courtyard is a structure that protects its inhabitants from that which they fear. It, like the family that brings it life, contains and protects their dreams.

Likewise, in Monardo's second, yet-to-be-published novel, *Pas de Deux,* Italy is the safe place for Mary, the Korean-American dancer and protagonist who is studying African dance in Italy. She gets pregnant and gives birth in Italy, where she feels supported and nurtured by the African women in her dance class. Once she leaves Italy, she has trouble finding the peace again that she found there.

Monardo entices the reader with her lush voice and evocative Mediterranean images, a comforting sense of home that seductively blends Italian and American cultures. (*See also* Italian American Novel)

Further Reading

Romano, Carlin. Review of *Courtyard of Dreams. Philadelphia Inquirer* (September 8, 1993): E1+.

Suzanne Hotte Massa

MONTALVO, JOSÉ (1946–1994) Chicano poet. José Montalvo's work is characterized by the poet's awareness of his personal life taking place within a political context. For Montalvo, writing itself is political. He suggests this in an afterward to his first collection of poems, *Pensamientos Capturados: Poemes de José Montalvo* (1977). He sees his work as opportunity for the white world to look beyond stereotypes into the private thoughts of the Chicano, specifically the Chicano poet as he muses on subjects ranging from the injustice of war fought by conscripted, oppressed peoples to the dedication of a grandson to his Mexican grandmother.

Montalvo was born in Piedras Negras in Northern Mexico and moved to San Antonio in 1959. After an honorable discharge in 1971 from the U.S. Air Force, Montalvo returned to San Antonio with his wife and attended San Antonio College. He completed an AA in 1973 and a BA in 1974 at St Mary's University in San Antonio. Montalvo was deeply involved in San

Antonio as both a poet and a political activist. He gained local notoriety for his powerful public readings in San Antonio and across the country.

Montalvo's work is characterized by rhythmic style and direct language (both Spanish and English). In his third collection, *The Black Hat Poems* (1987), these are exemplified in the poem "What the Sasquash-centennila Means to Me," a cutting yet humorous indictment of a local celebration of the sesquicentennial of the battle of the Alamo. Montalvo recounts the injustices faced by Chicano and native inhabitants of Texas under the control of white Americans.

Montalvo's final collection of poetry, *Welcome to My New World* (1992), was written after Montalvo began using traditional healing methods to treat his terminal cancer. Characterized by introspection, spirituality, and a sense of self-definition based on masculinity, ethnicity, and human mortality, the tone in this work is more subdued and pleading than earlier works. In the poem "Will the Flowers Bloom" he remembers his first child as an infant and wonders about her future in a violent, war-torn world. In "Welcome to My New World," the speaker rejects the violent world offered by a father figure and enters the gentle, peaceful world of the pagan, indigenous mother. In these poems, acceptance and peace subdue the anger of his earlier works.

Montalvo's poetry has received minimal critical attention in spite of his keen observations of both the political and personal aspects of human and Chicano life, and the precise use of language that characterizes his work.

Further Reading

Sanchez, Ricardo. "Earthiness, Honesty, and Rusticity: The Poetry of José
    Montalvo: An Introduction." *!A mí qué!* José Montalvo. San Antonio: Raza
    Cosmica, 1983. 8–10.

Angela M. Williamson

MOODY, ANNE (1940–) African American activist, author, and autobiographer. Moody became aware of America's racial injustices at an early age, and by the time she entered college she was extremely active in national civil rights organizations. In her writing and her public life, Moody has fought for African Americans' human rights, political representation, social equality, and individual freedom from exploitation, discrimination, and violence.

Moody's most famous work, her award-winning autobiography *Coming of Age in Mississippi* (1968), recounts her life as an African American girl who faces **racism** as she develops her self-identity and grows to adulthood in America's Deep South. Moody's autobiography is factual but includes some fictional techniques. The narrative's tone and plot development are novelistic, and she recreates several conversations and events in more detail than she could have remembered. In addition, Moody dramatizes her psychological self-exploration as she struggles against stereotypes and searches for a public voice.

Coming of Age fits into the rich African American tradition of literary autobiographies that began with the narratives of escaped slaves, such as **Frederick Douglass** and **Harriet Jacobs**. A number of famous southern authors and activists, such as **Booker T. Washington**, Mary Church Terrell, **Zora Neale Hurston**, and **Richard Wright**, contributed their own talents to this literary tradition. Moody, like the previous autobiographers, emphasized the value of education and actively resisted the oppressive attitudes and exploitative institutions of white America. After Moody, other political and social activists, such as **Malcolm X** and **Audre Lorde**, published their own autobiographies.

Although Moody wrote fiction, such as *Mr. Death: Four Stories* (1975) and several uncollected short stories, she considered herself first and foremost an activist. *Coming of Age* is more than a literary work; it documents how the lives of typical Southern African Americans intersect with America's racial history and the organizations fighting racism. Born in Mississippi to sharecropping parents, Moody is four when her autobiography begins. She depicts racism from a child's perspective, describing plantation life, segregated schools and movie theaters, and daily verbal and physical abuse against her people.

As Moody grows older, she develops a deeper awareness of the hardships and horrors African Americans face in the South. She despises white people for believing they are racially superior and using their position to acquire unfair social privileges. She also despises the apathy within her own community, wishing more African Americans would actively fight for justice, equality, and personal dignity. Even as a child, Moody disagrees with family members and friends who believed it was not their "place" to protest injustice or even to vote. She becomes angry when her frustrated father runs away from his family instead fighting for social improvements. A teenaged Moody accepts the responsibility of earning money for the family, experiencing bigotry and exploitation first-hand as a maid and tutor.

After high school, Moody enters Tougaloo College, where she succeeds academically and works fearlessly and tirelessly against segregation, discrimination, and lynching in the South. An independent and proud young woman, Moody wants her life to have purpose, so she joins several civil rights organizations: National Association for the Advancement of Colored People (NAACP), Congress of Racial Equality (CORE), and Student Non-Violence Coordinating Committee (SNCC). She speaks out against injustice, registers Southern African Americans to vote, and participates in boycotts, such as the 1963 sit-in to integrate the Woolworth's lunch counter in Jackson, Mississippi. Moody's activism gets her arrested, and several times her life is threatened. She uses her own experiences to teach workshops on self-protection to activists and demonstrators. Finally, Moody expresses both hope and despair for the movement's future as she participates in the 1963 March on Washington, where **Martin Luther King Jr.** gives his famous "I Have a Dream" speech.

Moody's autobiography ends in 1963, when she became disillusioned with the **Civil Rights Movement** and left the South. She had become more militant and no longer believed a grassroots, nonviolent organization could defeat the causes of racism or liberate her people. Moody, however, was not done fighting social problems. In 1964 she moved to Ithaca, New York, to become the civil rights project coordinator at Cornell University. A few years later she moved to New York City to continue writing and serve as counselor for the city's antipoverty program.

Further Reading

McKay, Nellie. "The Girls Who Became the Women: Childhood Memories in the Autobiographies of Harriet Jacobs, Mary Church Terrell, and Anne Moody." *Tradition and the Talents of Women.* Ed. Florence Howe. Urbana: U of Illinois P, 1991. 105–24.

Rishoi, Christy. *From Girl to Woman: American Women's Coming-of-Age Narratives.* Albany: State U of New York P, 2003.

Matthew Teorey

MOORE, OPAL (1953–) African American short story writer, poet, essayist. Moore's noteworthy flair in several genres coupled with her academic leadership and teaching legacy render her a cornerstone of the African American community and internationally as well, as a Fulbright lecturer at Johannes Gutenberg-Universitat in Mainz, Germany, in 1994.

While attending Illinois Wesleyan University's School of Art, she had her first overt experience with **racism**. The shock drove her to write in her journal about the incident, which eventually led to Moore's self-expression through poetry. Alhough she completed her BFA at Wesleyan in 1974, she enrolled in the graduate program at the University of Iowa several years later to focus on writing fiction.

A year after earning her BFA, Moore's classic book on phonics-first instruction, *Why Johnny Can't Learn* (1975), theorized why students were not learning to read. Earning her MA in 1981 and MFA in 1982 from Iowa's Writers' Workshop, she studied the craft of fiction writing with **Paule Marshall** and **James Alan McPherson**. Marshall continued as her mentor, critiquing her treatment of male characters until they were sympathetically drawn yet still flawed characters. Moore has cited **Gwendolyn Brooks** and **Toni Morrison** as influences.

Moore taught creative writing and African American literature at several universities before joining the faculty at Spelman College in Atlanta, Georgia, where she heads the department of English. Her essays on the study and teaching of African American literature advocated transformation.

"A Happy Story" was published in *Callaloo* in 1989 and collected in *Homeplaces: Stories of the South by Women Writers* (1991). Moore's common themes of cynicism and overcoming hardship are reflected in the story, which also delineates the essential difference in worldview between women and men. The narrator tries to reconcile the ideals of happiness and freedom within the limitations placed upon her by race and gender. Her artistically trained eye and observational powers are instantly recognizable in her poems and short stories, as is the rhythmical lyricism of her lyrical style.

Moore's short story "The Fence" was published in *African American Review* in 1995. Its young female narrator rails against the restrictions observed on Sunday and describes gender differences in the adults that she observes. Transformed by a difficult situation in which she is caught atop a fence, she discovers new strength, and in the end her personal philosophy transforms from a gate swinging both ways to a solid, immovable fence.

Three stories—"Eulogy for a Sister," "If I Fly Away: John's Song," and "The Mother's Board"—appeared in *Callaloo* in 1996, and her work was anthologized in *Honey Hush!: An Anthology of African American Women's Humor* (1998). Besides poetry and prose, her writing appears in the *Washington Post.* Moore's book reviews of contemporary fiction and children's literature appears in *Black Issues Book Review, Black Issues in Higher Education,* and *Iowa Journal of Literary Studies.*

Rebecca Tolley-Stokes

MORA, PAT (1942–) Chicana poet, essayist, children's author, and literacy advocate. Mora, a bilingual and bicultural native of El Paso, has been grouped variously with Chicana and Latina writers, women writers, Southwestern writers, and Texas writers. From these perspectives Mora writes eloquently about diverse topics, including the Southwestern landscape; women and their multifaceted roles in the family, the community, and society; and traditional, popular, and modern culture and their intersections, especially along the U.S.–Mexico border. Mora has received fellowships in poetry (from the National Endowment for the Arts) and leadership (from the W. K. Kellogg Foundation); her work appears in numerous anthologies and textbooks; and her books have won the Southwest Book Award, Premio Aztlán Literature Award, and the **Tomás Rivera** Mexican American Children's Book Award, among other honors, awards, and accolades. Before turning to full-time writing, she taught English at the secondary and postsecondary levels and worked in university administration.

Each of Mora's five books of poetry encompasses a singular concept. The feminine and, especially, maternal force of the Southwestern desert underlies the poetry of *Chants* (1984). The poetic voices that speak in *Borders* (1986) tell of crossing, challenging, or uniting the diverse borders that delineate, confront, and separate: borders between women and men, one culture or language and another, the privileged and the disenfranchised, acceptance and rejection. The poetry about women, community, growing up, aging, and healing, among many other topics in *Communion* (1991), culminate in an entire section on the creative process and, the ultimate communion in the last poem, significantly titled *"Dar a luz"* (To give birth).

Allusions to water—sacred or profane, symbolic or ordinary—run through *Agua Santa/Holy Water* (1995). *Aunt Carmen's Book of Practical Saints* (1997) is a poetic sequence in the intimate colloquial voice of Aunt Carmen as she addresses the saints to whom she has prayed over the years. Mora writes in English with a smattering of Spanish, primarily in free verse, but with a keen interest in working with traditional genres and forms. *Aunt Carmen's Book,* for example, contains numerous stanzas and techniques of popular Hispanic origin as well as some set forms, including a Shakespearean sonnet, a pattern poem, a villanelle, and a sestina, genres that also appear in other books. In her most recent poetry, Mora turns to another time-honored genre, the ode; the working title of her forthcoming collection is *Adobe Odes.*

Despite the singular vision of each discrete book, however, Mora interweaves these motifs throughout all her books. Recurring themes include the nurturing qualities of women, nature, cultural traditions, and the positive force of belief systems such as healing and the devotion of saints among Mexican Catholic women. Literal and figurative borders symbolize the multiple hybrid identities and experiences underlying the processes of discovery and affirmation that provide the unifying axis of Mora's poetry. The desert is another foundation of Mora's creative vision, as she explains in the poem "My Word-House," a metaphor for her work that she develops more fully in her nonfiction books *Nepantla: Essays from the Land in the Middle* (1993) and *House of Houses* (1997). The motivation for bringing together the twenty essays of *Nepantla* is Mora's understanding of her "place in the middle" (the meaning of the Nahuatl *nepantla*): the middle woman between her mother and her daughter, the middle of life, and the middle of the United States, having left her native Southwest for the first time to move to the Midwest in 1989. A spirit of belonging pervades the personal, cultural, and critical essays of *Nepantla.* In the course of the collection, Mora explicates many of her poems and uses others to illuminate her ideas, while exploring her world, her words, and the writing life. *House of Houses* is a family memoir of fictionalized encounters with relatives in an invented house—Mora's "word-house," the book she has written based on her family's stories. Memoir, fantasy, folklore, and poetry intermingle in this house with many of the characters readers have met in Mora's poetry.

Since 1992, Mora has published a prolific and highly acclaimed body of children's literature that encompasses a wide range of genres for young readers: poetry and rhyme, biography and memoir, fiction, and folk literature. Many of the books are bilingual or available in Spanish editions, and several adapt or rework topics Mora introduced in her poetry. The bilingual picture book *The Desert Is My Mother/El desierto es mi madre* (1994) began in English in *Chants* as "Mi Madre." Mora retells the poem "The Young Sor Juana" (in *Communion*) as a fictionalized biography in *A Library for Juana: The World of Sor Juana Inés* (2002). The subject of the Mexican folk tale *The Gift of the Poinsettia/El regalo de la flor de Nochebuena* (1995), coauthored with the film scholar

Charles Ramírez Berg, appeared first in "Poinsettia," in *Chants*. Mora also has published *My Own True Name: New and Selected Poems for Young Adults, 1984–1999* (2000), which includes poetry from *Chants, Borders*, and *Communion* along with "Dear Fellow Writer," an original foreword to encourage potential young writers to tell their stories.

Of special note in Mora's oeuvre for children is the picture book *Tomás and the Library Lady* (1997), illustrated by prominent book artist Raúl Colón and the 1998 winner of the Tomás Rivera Mexican American Children's Book Award (Texas State University at San Marcos). *Tomás* tells the heart-warming and inspirational story of a young boy in a family of Texas farm workers who discovers the world of books one summer in a public library in rural Iowa under the guidance of the librarian. The boy grew up to be Tomás Rivera (1935–84), the renowned Chicano author of the novel . . . *y no se lo tragó la tierra* (1971) and chancellor of the University of California at Riverside (1979–84). Mora's children's literature in general and *Tomás and the Library Lady* in particular exemplify her role as a lifelong reader and tireless advocate for children, libraries, and books. In this passionate spirit, Mora helped establish El Día de los Niños/El Día de los Libros (Children's Day/Book Day), celebrated annually since 1997 in the United States on April 30, the culmination of National Poetry Month. Mora explains her views more fully in "Confessions of a Latina Author," an eloquent and well-informed personal manifesto that challenges publishers, editors, and educators to address and promote the reading needs of Latinos and—because Pat Mora's world view is not exclusionary—of all children. ("Confessions," based on a presentation at the annual conference of the American Library Association in San Francisco on June 27, 1997, was published by *The New Advocate* in the fall of 1998.) Mora is a popular speaker on writing, diversity, education, and leadership at conferences for librarians and educators. (*See also* Bilingualism, Border Narratives, Mexican American Children's Literature, Mexican American Poetry)

Further Reading

Almon, Bert. "Pat Mora." *American Writers: A Collection of Literary Biographies.* Ed. Jay Parini. Supplement 13. New York: Scribner's, 2003. 213–32.

Mora, Pat. Interview with Elisabeth Mermann-Jozwiak and Nancy Sullivan. *MELUS* 28.2 (2003): 139–50.

———. Interview with Karin Rosa Ikas. *Chicana Ways: Conversations with Ten Chicana Writers.* Karin Rosa Ikas. Reno: U of Nevada P, 2002. 126–50.

Murphy, Patrick D. "Conserving Natural and Cultural Diversity: The Prose and Poetry of Pat Mora." *MELUS* 21.1 (1996): 59–69.

Senick, Gerard J. "Mora, Pat(ricia) 1942– ." *Something about the Author: Facts and Pictures about Authors and Illustrators of Books for Young People.* Vol. 134. Detroit: Gale, 2003. 110–18.

Catharine E. Wall

MORAGA, CHERRÍE (1952–) Chicana poet, playwright, essayist, teacher, and activist. Currently a resident of Oakland, California, Cherríe

Moraga is one of the most influential and widely cited Chicana writers, and a key figure in the women-of-color feminist movement. Her coedited anthology with Gloria Anzaldúa, *This Bridge Called My Back: Writing by Radical Women of Color* (1983), and her first multigenre work, *Loving in the War Years: Lo que nunca pasó por sus labios* (1983), were groundbreaking works that helped to establish Chicana feminist lesbian visibility in Chicana/Chicano and feminist studies, political activism, and literary production. Moraga's reputation in multiple disciplinary and literary contexts was consolidated by the publication of her prose and poetry collection, *The Last Generation* (1993); her meditation on queer motherhood, *Waiting in the Wings* (1997); and her coediting of several important Chicana and Latina literary anthologies. She has also authored a string of highly successful and politically uncompromising plays, most available in published script form: *Giving Up the Ghost* (1986), *Shadow of a Man* (1992), *Heroes and Saints* (1994), *Heart of the Earth: A Popul Vuh Story* (2000), *The Hungry Woman: A Mexican Medea* (2000), *Watsonville: Some Place Not Here* (2000), *Circle in the Dirt: El Pueblo de East Palo Alto* (2002), and *Waiting for Da God* (2004).

Born in the working-class community of Whittier, California, to a Mexican American mother and an Anglo American father, Moraga was among the first generation of Chicanos or Chicanas to undertake university studies in the wake of the civil rights achievements and struggles of the 1960s. She completed a teaching degree in English literature (1974), and an MA in creative writing (1980) from San Francisco State University. From the early 1970s Moraga was involved in the gay and lesbian rights and feminist movements, and attempting to construct the political and creative spaces in which she could explore and reconcile her multiple identifications as a light-skinned lesbian feminist Chicana.

These **identity** concerns—which had not before been the subject of Chicana writing—animated her editorial involvement with Gloria Anzaldúa in *This Bridge Called My Back,* a now **canon**ical collection of essays, testimonies, and poetry by women from diverse backgrounds that has had enormous influence in ethnic and feminist debates in the United States since its appearance. The equally influential *Loving in the War Years* presented a more sustained textual exploration of Moraga's lesbian feminist Chicana persona and her bicultural borderlands origins. In this experimental work—a combination of poetry, essays, and personal testimonies whose language also slips between English and Spanish—Moraga elaborates on the many discursive, historical, and sociopolitical factors that have prevented Chicana lesbians from coming out in safety. Throughout *Loving in the War Years* Moraga attempts to identify and counteract the assimilatory protocols that led to her loss of Spanish, her years spent passing as Anglo, and her educated distance from her mother's working-class Mexican American habitus. As she says, "I write this book because we are losing ourselves to the gavacho [whiteman]." Similarly, she aims to counter the **racism** of Anglo American **feminism** as well as the misogynistic and

homophobic values of the Chicano family home, working-class community, and political movement. Announcing the self-conscious rejection of
her "**whiteness**" and the rhetorical embrace of "brownness," *Loving in the
War Years* thus stands as a highly personal, complex, and always potentially
contradictory quest for community building and identificatory healing
with other lesbians of color, particularly Chicanas.

The essays and poems grouped in *The Last Generation* continue this multi-
valent quest for identity security. The collection also confirms Moraga's
renewed interest in a viable Chicano nationalism that enables multiple gendered and sexualized identity options and community affiliations. This
ambition is articulated in the essay "Queer Aztlán: The Re-formation of the
Chicano Tribe," which appropriates and "queers" the mythical Aztec name
for the U.S. Southwest popularized by the Chicano Movement of the 1960s
and 1970s. In this essay Moraga argues that before a genuine "queer" Chicano nation can appear, Chicanos need to become involved in the decolonization or de-assimilation of Chicano identities and communities. Moreover,
Moraga's proposed queer Aztlán requires gay Chicanos, like the male
architects of the original movement, to unlearn their dependence on patriarchal structures and discourses. Another essay from *The Last Generation*,
"Art in América con acento," argues that Chicano art practice must relate
Chicano experiences of internal colonization to the United States's imperial
and military interventions in Latin American states.

Moraga's highly respected and widely performed plays have provided her
with another venue in which to elaborate on the political and aesthetic concerns of her prose and poetry. Her debut play, *Giving Up the Ghost,* was the
first Chicano theatrical work to foreground lesbian characters and experiences. As its title implies, the play's protagonists, the Chicanas Marissa and
Corky and the Native American Amalia, confront an array of spectral pres-
ences, experiences, and forces—ambivalent maternal figures, competing languages, fluid gender boundaries and sexualities, dead lovers, sexual abuse
and rape, identity secrets, pre-Columbian spiritual practices—in their struggles to find a voice, a place in representation, and a politicized and supportive community among women of color. Similar elaboration of the need for
queer community building occurs in *Shadow of a Man*, which explores a married gay Chicano character and the impact of his self-repression on his family
and objects of desire. In *Heart of the South* and *The Hungry Woman*, Moraga
draws on Native and Meso American spiritual practices and mythical figures
in order to acknowledge the intimate connections between indigenous and
Chicano struggles in the U.S. context. In other plays, Moraga's interest in
questions of Chicana gender and sexual identity are linked to working-class
resistance to economic exploitation—farm workers in the case of *Heroes and
Saints* and cannery workers in *Watsonville.* Her *Circle in the Dirt* looks at the
possibilities for and limits to pan-ethnic and multiracial community construction in the small working-class and migrant neighborhood of East Palo
Alto. The play proposes a need for pan-ethnic affiliations and consciousness

of shared oppressions in order to overcome institutional and internalized racism, and to heal the antagonisms that have arisen between distinct ethnic groups living in a neighborhood subject to destructive urban renewal programs.

As the complex concerns of her writings attest, since the early 1980s Moraga has sustained her uncompromising refusal to disentangle her political activism from her aesthetic concerns as a cultural worker and producer. The result is one of the most important bodies of work in Chicano writing. To this achievement must be added her tireless support and mentoring of younger Chicana and Chicano writers and cultural workers over many decades. This role is exemplified by her current position as artist in residence at Stanford University's departments of Spanish and Portuguese and drama, where her one-act play, *Waiting for Da God,* was produced in collaboration with a director and actors from the student body. (*See also* Mexican American Drama, Mexican American Lesbian Literature)

Further Reading

Alarcón, Norma. "The Theoretical Subject(s) of *This Bridge Called My Back* and Anglo-American Feminism." *Criticism in the Borderlands: Studies in Chicano Literature, Culture and Ideology.* Ed. Héctor Calderón and José David Saldívar. Durham, NC, and London: Duke UP, 1991. 28–39.

Allatson, Paul. "'I May Create a Monster': Cherríe Moraga's Transcultural Conundrum." *Literature and Racial Ambiguity.* Ed. Teresa Hubel and Neil Brooks. Amsterdam and New York: Rodopi, 2002. 271–96.

Ikas, Karin Rosa. *Chicana Ways: Conversations with Ten Chicana Writers.* Reno: U of Nevada P, 2002.

Yarbro-Bejarano, Yvonne. "Cherríe Moraga." *Dictionary of Literary Biography.* Vol. 82: Chicano Writers First Series. Ed. Francisco A. Lomelí and Carl R. Shirley. Detroit: Gale/Bruccoli Clark Layman, 1989. 165–77.

———. *The Wounded Heart: Writing on Cherríe Moraga.* Austin: U of Texas P, 2001.

Paul Allatson

MORALES, ROSARIO (1930–) Poet, essayist, activist. Morales was born and raised in Spanish Harlem and the Bronx, and her parents were Puerto Rican/Jewish migrants from Naranjito. Her childhood was filled with poverty. She left home to attend college and later married a communist Ukrainian Jew who was from Brooklyn.

One of her most significant contributions to Latina literature is the collection *Getting Home Alive* (1986), which she coauthored with her daughter, **Aurora Levins Morales.** The collection is composed of short stories, poems, essays, prose pieces, and dialogues between the two. Some of the prominent themes include **identity**, especially as a female and a minority, cultural borderlands, class, and familial ties, especially mother-daughter relationships. In the collection, Morales shares with the reader her life experiences, including the painful miscarriage that she writes about in "Birth," her family's poverty in "Destitution," her introduction to Judaism in "Synagogue," her role as a communist in "Bad Communist," her love for her husband, Dick, in "Trees," and her love affair with Puerto Rico in "Nostalgia." She also writes about visiting Puerto Rico in "Puerto Rico Journal." Although she identifies Puerto Rico as "home," she recognizes that she views it from the eyes of a tourist. Ultimately, Morales realizes that she is an outsider in this place that she has fantasized about as a result of the stories that her father shared with her when she was a child. Moralizes comes to understand that this imagined home, in reality, is not her home at all. Although she feels a degree of relief when she returns to the United States, there too she feels oppressed, as well as threatened by violence. Morales realizes that she is "never safe" and mourns the absence of a true homeland in her life. In this collection, she also acknowledges the frustration that she experiences as a result of forced **assimilation**; for example, in "I Recognize You," she conveys the sadness that she feels because learning Standard American English has robbed her of the rhythms of her "home talk" as well as her cultural "wholeness." Similarly, in "Getting Out Alive," she explains that she cried the first time that she heard her tape-recorded voice because it "showed no signs of El Barrio." Also evident is that Morales finds objectionable the role that the United States has as a global power; for example, she writes about all those who have died in "El Salvador." "In Roadkill," she explains that because of our busy lives, we take for granted the significance of the death that surrounds us daily. She also discusses her concern for the environment in "Pollution," and in "I'm on Nature's Side" she criticizes the white man, in his varied roles, for spraying poisons for pest control. She confesses that she identifies with these pests because, to the white man, her people are another form of pest, but she declares, "We will survive!" Overall, however, the collection is a celebration of her unique identity as a Jewish Puerto Rican. In "The Dinner," Morales pays tribute to the earthy qualities of the women in her culture who cook together and eat in the kitchen, not the formal dining room. In "I Am What I Am," Morales rejoices in her role as a United States American and all that it entails: a Puerto Rican girl who attends college and speaks Yiddish, Spanish, and "fine refined college educated English." She proclaims proudly, "Take it or leave me alone."

Another significant contribution to Latina literature is Morales's essay "We're All in the Same Boat," published in the important collection *This Bridge Called My Back: Writings by Radical Women of Color* (1981). In this essay, Morales rejects labels such as white and middle class because, she says, they limit. As well, she reminds us that we are all capable of being racist and sexist, regardless of our color and gender. She proposes that we wage war against the harmful ideas that we have been taught in order to eliminate these destructive attitudes.

Further Reading

Khader, Jamil. "Subaltern Cosmopolitanism: Community and Transnational Mobility in Caribbean Postcolonial Feminist Writings." *Feminist Studies* 29.1 (2003): 63–204.

Rojas, Lourdes. "Latinas at the Crossroads: An Affirmation of Life in Rosario Morales and Aurora Levins Morales's *Getting Home Alive.*" *Breaking Boundaries: Latina Writing and Critical Reading.* Ed. Asunción Horno-Delgado, et al. Amherst: U of Massachusetts P, 1989. 166–77.

Stefanko, Jacqueline. "New Ways of Telling: Latinas' Narratives of Exile and Return." *Frontiers* 17.2 (1996): 50–69.

Diane Todd Bucci

MORI, TOSHIO (1910–1980)   Pioneer Japanese American short-story writer and novelist. Toshio Mori's most famous work is *Yokohama, California* (1949), a collection of short stories largely written before World War II and initially slated for publication in 1942. *Yokohama* only emerged as a text of literary significance some thirty years after, when Mori's works were rediscovered by a new generation of Asian Americans in search of their roots.

Mori's short stories document and explore the essence of humanity through the everyday interaction of the Japanese Americans of San Leandro, California, that he mostly writes about. Encapsulated in each intimate vignette is the timelessness of human lives, the eventfulness of each supposedly ordinary day, and the quiet pleasure of discovering meaning, heroism, and adventure in the mundane lives of each person in the community. For instance, in "The Seventh Street Philosopher," a launderer to a rich old lady is revealed to be a thinker and passionate speech maker. *Yokohama* is filled with stories such as "The Woman Who Makes Swell Doughnuts," contrasting the rich interior life and nondescript exterior existence of the person next door.

Sometimes read as a sentimental, elegiac remembrance of a gentler Asian American world, *Yokohama* could not escape the charged racial environment in postwar America. There was an increased need to explain that Japanese Americans, newly stereotyped as an unreliable threatening race, were essentially Americans too. Modifications made before the 1949 edition went to press added stories such as "Tomorrow Is Coming, Children" and "Slant-Eyed Americans," which introduced a more overt note of racial unsettledness to the collection. Mori is silent on the issue of the atomic bomb, but the collection's renewed emphasis on the universality and the humanity of the Japanese American community it depicts only serves to highlight what might be the concerns of its initial readership.

Although Mori had earlier received the endorsement of **William Saroyan** and *Yokohama* was generally well received by reviewers, such positive feedback did not translate into high sales. The war had disrupted Mori's budding literary career, but he continued to write even as he worked full-time in his nursery cultivating flowers. However, with the rising ethnic awareness of the 1970s, his novel *Woman from Hiroshima* (1978) was published in limited edition. A year later, his second collection of short stories was published as *The Chauvinist and Other Stories* (1979). Here, stories such as "1936" highlight the ephemeral quality of life—the rarity of each moment that once lived will not come by again. Similarly capturing the possibilities encapsulated in a time and space where individuals without any apparent shared interests, people of all nations or ethnicities, might coexist and relate to each other in the best possible way is "The Sweet Potato."

Another collection of Mori's works, *Unfinished Message* (2000), includes the novella "The Brothers Murata" (original title is "Peace, Be Still"), completed in 1944 during Mori's confinement in the Topaz Relocation Camp in Central Utah. Here we have a darker exploration of the American psyche whereby the neighborly community spirit so evident in *Yokohama* is shadowed by the ominous pervasiveness of removal and the divisiveness of broken ties. The politically volatile decision of whether to enlist as American soldiers or to fight for their civil rights and their rightful status as American citizens is played out between the different choices made by two Nisei (second-generation Japanese American) brothers. Defined by the moment and its historical circumstances, the whole issue of what constitutes American democracy is put to test.

Like most Nisei, Mori felt the responsibility to bridge the gap between the Japanese American and white communities by promoting interracial understanding. Hence he was more interested in portraying the here and now of local Japanese American lives than in delving into the history and writing of Japan, a nation he had never seen. By his own admission, Mori's literary influences primarily included Whitman, Thoreau, Emerson, and Sherwood Anderson. Ironically, it was the Asian influences in some of their works that drew him to learn more about Zen and Buddhist beliefs, which infuse his work.

Mori's language is plain yet poetic, infused with the vernacular of his primarily Japanese American subjects who are first and foremost noted for their common human spirit. His corpus of works includes unpublished writings such as the novel "Way of Life" (working title), written in the 1960s, which is about a white community during the Great Depression. (*See also* Internment, Japanese American Novel)

Further Reading

Leong, Russell. "An Interview with Toshio Mori." *Amerasia Journal* 7.1 (Spring 1980): 89–108.

Poh Cheng Khoo

MORRISON, TONI (1931–) African American novelist, editor, and literary critic. The only African American to win a Nobel Prize in literature, Toni Morrison is a visionary writer who celebrates the rich cultural heritage of black life in sharp, vivid prose. One of the most important American novelists and intellectuals of the twentieth century, Morrison has had a profound impact on a generation of young writers of color and on the development of the African American literary **canon**.

The second of four children, Morrison was born Chloe Anthony Wofford in the small, industrial town of Lorain, Ohio. Morrison's father, George, a hardworking shipyard welder, held as many as three jobs at once and believed in the moral superiority of African Americans. Ramah, Morrison's mother, was more optimistic about the possibility of achieving racial harmony, and instilled in her children a firm belief in self-reliance, community, and family. Morrison grew up listening to her parents spin long, enchanting tales of deceased relatives, ghosts, and powerful dreams. Reading was also a favorite childhood activity for the young writer, who was especially fond of Leo Tolstoy, Fyodor Dostoevsky, Jane Austen, and Gustave Flaubert. Morrison attended integrated schools, where she consistently impressed her teachers. Although only one member of her family had attended college, she was determined to continue her education at the university level. In 1949 she enrolled at Howard University, where she studied English literature and the Classics. At Howard, Morrison changed her name to Toni and joined the theatrical group, the Howard University

Toni Morrison, 1977. *Courtesy of the Library of Congress.*

Players. In 1955 Morrison received a master's in English from Cornell University. She wrote her thesis on the theme of suicide in the works of Virginia Woolf and William Faulkner. After working briefly at Texas Southern University, Morrison returned to Howard in 1957 to teach English. The following year she married Harold Morrison, a Jamaican architect with whom she had two sons, Harold Ford and Slade Kevin. Morrison returned to Lorain after her marriage ended in 1964, but soon thereafter she accepted an editorial position with Random House in Syracuse. Alone in New York with her two young children, Morrison began writing as a way to combat her solitude and isolation. In the evenings, she returned to a story she began while teaching at Howard, a brief sketch of a childhood girlfriend who wished for blue eyes. This story would eventually become *The Bluest Eye* (1970), Morrison's first novel.

Although *The Bluest Eye* was not a commercial success, its vibrant prose and courageous exploration of destructive American values attracted critical attention. Exploring the origins and devastating consequences of racial self-hatred, Morrison focused her novel on the most ignored member of society, a poor, black girl who longs for blue eyes. Pecola Breedlove believes herself to be ugly and accepts the beauty and virtue of whiteness. Although Morrison's description of Pecola's descent into insanity offers a pointed critique of white American values, the novel is primarily concerned with the health and responsibilities of the black community.

Morrison was working in New York City when her second novel, *Sula* (1973), was published. Nominated for a National Book Award, *Sula* describes the relationship between childhood friends Sula Peace and Nel Wright. While Nel marries and settles into a conventional life in the Midwestern Bottom community, Sula attends college, travels, and becomes a social rebel. Upon her return to the Bottom, Sula is perceived as evil because she refuses to conform to traditional conventions and patterns of behavior. In this poignant novel of oppositions, Morrison examines the interdependency between good and evil and the complex relationships between black women.

As an editor at Random House, Morrison sought to develop the African American canon by promoting the work of key literary and historical figures. She helped to publish books by **Toni Cade Bambara**, **Gayl Jones**, **Angela Davis**, and Muhammad Ali. She also edited *The Black Book* (1974), an anthology of the history of African Americans. During her research for *The Black Book,* Morrison came across the history of Margaret Garner, a slave woman who killed her daughter rather than give her up to her master. This story would provide the inspiration for Morrison's masterpiece, the novel *Beloved* (1987).

Morrison's third book, ***Song of Solomon*** (1977), received massive critical acclaim. A national bestseller, it won the National Book Critics Award and was the first African American Book of the Month Club selection since ***Native Son*** (1940). In *Song of Solomon,* Milkman Dead undergoes an epic quest for **identity**. The privileged son of a materialistic father and a troubled mother, Milkman embarks on a search for gold that becomes a transformative journey for cultural knowledge and understanding. *Song of Solomon* contains some of Morrison's most memorable characters, including Pilate, Milkman's wise aunt, who was born without a navel and converses with her dead father. Drawing upon **African American folklore** as well as biblical stories, Morrison explores mythic concerns of flight, family, and responsibility while offering a fundamental ethos of hope and love. In 1980 Morrison was named to the National Council of the Arts by former President Jimmy Carter, and a year later was elected to the American Academy and Institute of Arts and Letters.

Following the widely anticipated publication of her fourth novel, *Tar Baby* (1981), Morrison became the first black woman to appear on the cover of *Newsweek. Tar Baby* is set on an imaginary Caribbean Island and involves the love affair between Jadine, an educated black model, and Son, a handsome drifter. They meet at the estate of Valerian Street, a retired white millionaire, who is accompanied by his fragile wife Margaret and their black servants, Sydney and Ondine Childs. Although Jadine is the niece of Sydney and Ondine, she occupies a different social circle due to the patronage she receives from Valerian. Some critics found Morrison's exploration of social hierarchies to be overly didactic, whereas others described her portrayal of white characters as shallow and clichéd. Despite these mixed reviews, *Tar Baby* is marked by Morrison's signature lyrical style and her preoccupation with issues of community and identity.

In 1983 Morrison left Random House and began teaching creative writing at the State University of New York in Albany as the Albert Schweitzer Professor of the Humanities. During this time, she began work on the unpublished play *Dreaming Emmett.* In her only work for the theater, Morrison recreates the murder of Emmett Till and the white men who were acquitted of the crime. Till speaks from the dead to describe his brutal death.

Morrison continued to explore voices beyond the grave in her internationally acclaimed bestseller **Beloved**. Set in Reconstruction-era Ohio, *Beloved* tells the story of Sethe, an escaped slave woman who murders her daughter rather than return to a life of bondage. Morrison describes Sethe's struggle to keep her slave memories from consciousness along with her need to confront the ghosts of her past. Sethe's repression is unsettled by the arrival of Paul D, a man she knew in **slavery**, and Beloved, a troubling stranger who doesn't seem to know who she is. In this powerful novel, Morrison describes the dehumanizing effects of slavery and the complexities of maternal love. Although most critics praised *Beloved* for its soaring prose, innovative narration, and rich characterizations, controversy erupted after it failed to win the National Book Award and the National Book Critics Circle Award. In response, forty-eight prominent African American writers and intellectuals, including **Maya Angelou**, **Alice Walker**, and **John Wideman**, published a letter in the *New York Times* decrying this oversight. Later that year, *Beloved* was awarded the Pulitzer Prize, and it continues to be hailed as a major contribution to American literature.

In 1988 Morrison was named the Robert F. Goheen Professorship of the Humanities at Princeton University, becoming the first black woman to hold an endowed chair at an Ivy League institution. Morrison's appointment was part of a major effort at Princeton to develop its African American studies program. She was joined by such prominent black intellectuals as **Cornel West** and Arnold Rampersand. While teaching creative writing and working with the African American, American, and Women's studies departments, Morrison began work on her sixth novel, *Jazz* (1992). The most technically ambitious of Morrison's books, *Jazz* is narrated by an unnamed and unreliable speaker who demands a collaborative storytelling relationship with the audience. This enigmatic voice describes the violent love triangle between Violet and Joe Trace and a haughty teenager named Dorcas. While recounting the thrilling sense of possibility that New York

City offered blacks following the Great Migration of the 1920s, the narrator describes Joe's love affair with Dorcas and his subsequent murder of the young girl. Although *Jazz* received mixed reviews, it confirmed Morrison's commitment to taking stylistic risks in her work and demonstrated her belief in the dynamic nature of storytelling.

In her only work of literary criticism, *Playing in the Dark: Whiteness and the Literary Imagination* (1992), Morrison examines the **racism** in American literature, arguing that historically readers have been constructed as white. She describes a largely ignored but extremely influential "Africanist presence" in texts by such canonical authors as Edgar Allan Poe, Willa Cather, and Ernest Hemingway. Morrison contends that works by white Americans are haunted by a black presence that acts as a repository for anxieties concerning slavery, **race**, and the tenuous construction of American identity. Morrison continued to expand the scope of her critical gaze in *Justice, En-Gendering Power: Essays on Anita Hill, Clarence Thomas, and the Construction of Social Reality* (1992), a collection of essays she edited on the Supreme Court Justice's controversial appointment. Although many critics disagreed with Morrison's contention that Thomas rejected his black identity in order to succeed in white America, the publication of this book along with her growing popularity as a novelist propelled her into the national spotlight. She became a major public figure, offering strong opinions on issues as diverse as the 1992 Los Angeles riots and the American literary **canon**.

In 1993 Morrison received the Nobel Prize for Literature. Her acceptance speech focused upon the power of language and narrative to create identity and community. Morrison has since become an international celebrity, lecturing widely even as she continues to teach and write. Her books have continued to be bestsellers in part because of the support of Oprah Winfrey and her influential book club. In 1998 *Beloved* was made into a film, starring Winfrey. That same year, Morrison published ***Paradise*** (1998), a novel set in an all-black town in Oklahoma. Exploring issues of exclusion and acceptance, *Paradise* describes the invasion of a local convent by a group of men who believe that the refuge for wandering women has become a threat to their town. Morrison returns to themes of community and the problematic but necessary role of social pariahs in this sweeping novel of a town's rise and fall. Morrison's most recent novel, *Love* (2003), describes the complex relationships of the Cosey family and the decline of their beachfront resort, a once luxurious vacation destination for African Americans. *Love* again highlights the elegance of Morrison's prose and her firm dedication to writing for and about the black community. (*See also* African American Novel)

Further Reading

Conner, Marc C., ed. *The Aesthetics of Toni Morrison: Speaking the Unspeakable.* Jackson: UP of Mississippi, 2000.

Gates, Henry L., and K. A. Appiah, eds. *Toni Morrison: Critical Perspectives Past and Present.* New York: Amistad, 1993.

McKay, Nellie Y. *Critical Essays on Toni Morrison.* Boston: G. K. Hall, 1988.

Page, Philip. *Dangerous Freedom: Fusion and Fragmentation in Toni Morrison's Novels.* Jackson: UP of Mississippi, 1995.

Peach, Linden. *Toni Morrison.* New York: St. Martin's Press, 2000.

Stephanie Li

MOSKOWITZ, FAYE STOLLMAN (1930–) American Jewish essayist, memoirist, short-fiction writer. Faye Moskowitz writes about family life in a Jewish household in middle America, poignantly evoking portraits and situations laced with bittersweet pain and joys. Her work reveals family members in their quirkiness, suffering, estrangement, gratitude, warmth, and restrained happiness—all in a Jewish, although not necessarily religious, environment.

The eldest child and only daughter of a scrap metal business owner and his homemaker wife, Moskowitz spent most of the childhood in Jackson, a non-Jewish Detroit suburb, which shaped her sense of self as an outsider and simultaneously sharpened her skills as an observer. Ten years later, in 1945, the family returned to Detroit and their comforting, familiar Jewish neighborhood. Her senior year in high school, 1948, was pivotal: She met and married her husband Jack, her mother died, her father-in-law died, and the State of Israel was established, all of which find their way into her work. Her essays and stories are saturated with themes based on the Detroit/Jackson years and reflect what she has called "mitzvah training," or values that evolved from her Jewish upbringing.

Before long, she and Jack became active in local politics, translating her liberal idealism into support for the Democratic Party. A move to Washington, DC, in 1962 led to more liberal activism as well as her higher education. She studied creative writing under Louis Schaffer at George Washington University, earned bachelor's and master's degrees, completed courses for her doctorate, and developed as a writer. Her first publications were pieces written for the op-ed pages of the *Washington Post,* the *Chronicle of Higher Education*, the *Jewish Journal,* and articles for *Lilith, Belles Lettres,* and *Modern Maturity.* Her confidence as a memoirist prompted her to send work to the *New York Times* Homes Section, which eventually led to her series of "Hers" columns. A three-month residency at a writers' colony in Vence, France, gave her needed distance to grow, and the *New York Times* articles gave her recognition as a professional writer. She became a commentator on National Public Radio, wrote columns for *Women's Day,* and accepted positions as the director of the middle school at the Edmund Burke School and as an instructor in the George Washington University Adult Education Program, the latter leading to a full-time faculty position and then chair of the university's English department. Moskowitz is the recipient of numerous awards, including the EdPress Special Merit Award, Bread Loaf Scholar, First Prize for Poetry by Arts Project Renaissance, and the PEN Syndicated Fiction Award.

Four of Moskowitz's books are highly artistic, unpretentious autobiographical essays and stories that stem from the intimacies of family life. They bear connection to the tradition of Jewish literary giants through their theme and their oral texture. She explains that she is a slow, careful writer whose ideas evolve into stories that preserve, for the most part, a way of life based on the *shanda* principle: That is, Jewish families conducted their lives in a manner that avoided bringing any shame, or *shanda*, to the immediate family and to the extended Jewish people.

In *A Leak in the Heart: Tales from a Woman's Life* (1985), Moskowitz moves between Jackson, Washington, and Venice. She chronicles vulnerabilities, hers and others', and introduces her readers to resilient immigrants and first-generation Americans who express their love for one another less through language than through normal deeds of caring, unconsciously fulfilling what they perceive to be the right way to behave. *Whoever Finds This, I Love You* (1988) presents stories that portray a child's death, recovery from a mastectomy, the ritual of the bridal shower, and first-person stories of ordinary life from the pen of a writer who finds irony and humor in the painful process of growing up. Memory is the real subject of *And the Bridge Is Love: Life Stories* (1991). She recalls schoolgirl embarrassments and mother–child conversations, both as the child and as the mother. As in her other books, the poverty of the Depression seeps into conversations as unobtrusively as it shapes values. Although published over ten years later, *Peace in the House Tales from a Yiddish Kitchen* (2002) reads like the second part of *Bridge*. Moskowitz, the narrator, juxtaposes Jackson or Detroit with Washington, poignantly connecting recent events with their earlier counterparts. We experience her mother's death from breast cancer from the lens of her own recovery from the same disease. The stories, as is true of her earlier works, are rooted in the home, the shop, the classroom, and even the strange, almost alien European city. In all these recollected tales, Moskowitz's candor, wit, and sensitivity are matched by richness of her style, redolent with the textures of everyday life. She gathered similar stories and poems in her anthology, *Her Face in the Mirror: Jewish Women on Mothers and Daughters* (1994), a unique collection of works that document the complexity, love, frustration, and compassion that characterize Jewish women and their daughters.

Further Reading

Beck, Evelyn Torten. "An Interview with Faye Moskowitz." *Belles Lettres* 1.2 (November/December 1995): 7–8.

Childress, Mark. "Snow White and the Dirty Kids." *New York Times Book Review* (August 12, 1988): 12.

Myrna Goldenberg

MOSLEY, WALTER (1952–) African American mystery, science fiction, and fiction writer, social analyst, and editor. Walter Mosley gained prominence through his popular and critically acclaimed mysteries about reluctant black investigator Easy Rawlins, a series that was publicly endorsed by President Clinton in 1992. However, he delights in breaking through boundaries and refuses to be confined or categorized. Thus, in addition to creating a second detective series, he has written science fiction, a **blues** novel, an existential novel, two short-story collections about a philosophical ex-convict named Socrates, and two nonfiction books analyzing contemporary problems. He has also edited *Best American Short Stories 2003*.

Ezekiel "Easy" Rawlins was partly inspired by Mosley's father, Leroy, an African American school custodian and storyteller who died in 1993. Mosley's mother is a Russian-Jewish schoolteacher. *Gone Fishin'* (1997), the first novel Mosley wrote

Walter Mosley. *AP/Wide World Photos.*

about Rawlins, is a coming-of-age story set in Texas in 1939 with some violence but no mystery. Publishers didn't know what to make of the novel, and it was only published after the Rawlins detective series became successful.

Easy is a working-class hero who undertakes investigations out of economic or social pressures. In *Devil in a Blue Dress* (1990), which shows him becoming a detective in 1948, he agrees to look for a white woman gone missing in a black environment because he needs the cash offered by a white man who became rich by trading favors. Easy too learns to trade favors as a means of surviving. He also discovers his need for friends, even ones like Raymond "Mouse" Alexander, a "bad man" of folkloric proportions like Stagolee. At the end of *Devil in a Blue Dress*, Easy questions his conscience about his decision to conceal murders committed by his bad-man friend while telling the police about a less vicious murderer to save himself. He lets his conscience off easy because a poor black living in a money-driven racist society has limits on his ethics, and he has made the best choices available to him. Easy's ethics are necessarily situational. Other books in the series include *A Red Death* (1991), *White Butterfly* (1992), *Black Betty* (1994), *A Little Yellow Dog* (1996), *Big Bad Brawley Brown* (2002), and *Six Easy Pieces* (2003).

Mosley's second mystery series, including *Fearless Jones* (2001) and *Fear Itself* (2003), focuses on book-loving Paris Minton and his violence-prone friend Fearless Jones. Although Paris figures out most of each mystery, Fearless sometimes outsmarts him because his wisdom is from the heart, whereas Paris's is from the head. Fearless's ethics also outshine Paris's. In *Fear Itself*, Paris seeks to hide and hold onto a priceless book, but Fearless, through trickery, gets it back to its rightful owner.

Mosley's science-fiction novel *Blue Light* (1998) explores the mysteries of human potential and the obstacles in its way. The narrator is named Chance, and the ending is provocatively ambiguous. *Futureland* (2001) speculates about a world in which the gap between rich and poor is immense, and technology does as much to entrap as to enrich humanity, depending upon who is operating it.

Among the finest blues novels ever written, *RL's Dream* (1995) tells the story of ailing black guitarist Soupspoon Wise and Kiki Waters, the white Samaritan who shelters him when he is evicted. Kiki helps Soupspoon tape his knowledge of the blues and play again, and he helps her cope with her own blues.

Mosley expects his novel *The Man in the Basement* (2004) to be compared to Albert Camus's *The Stranger*. Its plot, however, is unique. A white mercenary wishing to atone for racial atrocities pays an amoral black man to imprison him. This leads the black man to a new understanding of himself, his ancestors, and his place in the world.

Mosley's short-story collections *Always Outnumbered, Always Outgunned* (1997) and *Walking the Dog* (1999) center on Socrates Fortlow, who murdered two friends and never ceases to reflect on the violence in him and the world. Life continually tests him and enlarges his understanding—and ours.

Mosley's own enlarged understanding is shown directly in his nonfiction books *Workin' on the Chain Gang: Shaking Off the Dead Hand of History* (2000) and *What Next: A Memoir Toward World Peace* (2003). In whatever form he expresses his vision, Mosley stands tall as a highly talented and individualistic thinker and writer. (*See also* African American Detective Fiction)

Further Reading

Ashley, Mike. *The Mammoth Encyclopedia of Modern Crime Fiction*. New York: Carroll and Graf, 2002.

Priestman, Martin, ed. *The Cambridge Companion to Crime Fiction*. Cambridge: Cambridge UP, 2003.

Steven R. Carter

MOSS, HOWARD (1922–1987) Jewish American poet, critic, and editor, Howard Moss was an important figure in the world of poetry in the mid-twentieth century. A prolific author, Moss published fifteen books of poetry, four books of criticism, five plays, and edited several critical texts as well. His poems, often written in formal verse, explore, among other subjects, themes of nature, art, and the city. Perhaps best known as poetry editor of the *New Yorker* for almost forty years (from 1950 until just before his death), Moss served as an example of new formalism to poets of his generation and, through his position, was able to influence and command this trend. Although his later poetry was less regularly end-rhymed and metered than his earlier, his poems retain a consistent regularity of rhythm and tone.

A native New Yorker, Moss first won *Poetry* magazine's Janet Sewal David Award for his own poetry in 1942. He then published his first book (*The Wound and the Weather*) in 1946. He received numerous awards in his lifetime, including the National Book Award for his *Selected Poems* in 1972, which subsequently received the Lenore Marshall/*Nation* Poetry Prize in 1986, the same year he received a fellowship from the Academy of American Poets. Moss was inducted into the American Academy and Institute of Arts and Letters in 1968.

Moss wrote several books of critical essays, including one on Proust. As a critic he wrote astutely about contemporary poets and in *Minor Monuments: Selected Essay* (1988), he considers the poet's voice, use of the line, and poet's story, writing as both a critic and a practicing poet. In *Instant Lives* (1972), Moss collaborated with illustrator Edward Gorey to present a series of clever literary vignettes that humorously portray various famous artistic figures such as the Brontë sisters, Jane Austen, James Joyce, and John Donne, as well as painters Paul Gauguin and El Greco, and musicians such as Mozart and Bach.

A poet of the city and rhythms of urban life as well as of nature, Moss's keen observations are felt throughout his work, as seen in the poem "Tropical Fish" in which he observes the fish in great detail, or his playfulness in "Einstein's Bathrobe" or the poem "The Refrigerator" in which he dialogues with his household's appliance and assures it that it is appreciated. Moss is also known as a great elegist, with elegies for family members found throughout his oeuvre ("Elegy for My Father" and "Elegy for My Sister"), which chronicle family relationships and shifts of loss. Moss also wrote elegies for seasons, such as "September Elegy" with its description of fleeting light and changing feeling, or to memorialize a sense of things passing, as in "A Dead Leaf" in which he recalls his busy city schedule and the movement of the months with an awareness of the self within this landscape as he writes, "the last late leaf/ Settles on my upturned, aging hand."

Further Reading

Bawer, Bruce. "The Passing of an Elegist." *New Criterion* 6.3 (November 1987): 35–37.

Christensen, Peter G. "Chekhov in the Poetry of Howard Moss and Denise Levertov." *South Atlantic Review* 54.4 (November 1989): 51–62.

Gioia, Dana. "The Difficult Case of Howard Moss." *Antioch Review* 45.1(Winter 1987): 98–109.

Leiter, Robert. "Howard Moss: An Interview." *American Poetry Review* 13.5 (September–October 1984): 27–31.

Saunders, Judith P. Gahan, Brendan M. "Moss's 'Cardinal'." *Explicator* 60.4 (Summer 2002): 224–26.

Smith, Dave. "Castles, Elephants, Buddhas: Some Recent American Poetry." *The American Poetry Review* 10.3 (May–June 1981): 37–42.

St. John, David. "Scripts and Water, Rules and Riches." *Antioch Review* 43.3 (1985): 309–19.

Elline Lipkin

MOSTWIN, DANUTA (1921–) Polish American novelist, short-story writer, and scholar in the field of social psychology. Danuta Mostwin emigrated, via England, to the United States after World War II, because she, her parents, and her husband, all participants in military efforts against the Nazis, feared persecutions in then communist Poland. In 1951 they settled in Baltimore, Maryland, where Mostwin has pursued her academic career while employed as social worker and therapist. In 1971 she earned a PhD degree at Columbia University, with her thesis "The Study of Social Adjustment of the Polish Immigrant Family in the United States after the Second World War." In 1980 the National Association of Social Workers Inc. published her book *Social Dimension of Family Treatment,* and she was nominated to the post of full professor at the Catholic University in Washington, DC. Her major contribution to theory of immigrant adjustment has been the introduction of the concept of "third value," which results from integration of the Native and the American cultural norms and custom.

Parallel to academic research and employment, Mostwin continued to write fiction. Known to Polish readers of émigré magazines as a young new voice among numerous writers in postwar exile, she achieved strong recognition with her debut novel *Dom starej lady* (House of an Old Lady), published in London in 1958. The novel differed from other representations of the émigré predicament in its lightly humorous approach to the tragic situation of former war heroes, now reduced to paupers whose justified claims to respect and restitutions were met with utter indifference in the country of former allies. She perfected the complex motif of reversal of fortune in two subsequent émigré novels, *Ameryko! Ameryko!* (America! America! 1960) and *Ty za wodą, ja za wodą* (I over the Ocean, You over the Ocean, 1972), which were praised by reviewers for nonstereotypical portraits of their diverse characters, including visitors from the communist Poland. Although these three novels were drawn from observation of her own milieu of the uprooted and degraded Polish intelligentsia, in her collections of short stories, *Asteroidy* (Asteroids, 1964), *Słyszę jak śpiewa Ameryka* (I Hear America Singing, 1988), *Odchodzą nasi synowie* (Our Sons Are Departing, 1977), as well as in *Olivia* (1965), the novel whose central character is a young American drifter, Mostwin used the material from her social work and wrought striking images of lives marginalized by poverty, old age, maladjustment, or, long before it became fashionable, stubborn otherness. *Two Novellas of Emigration and Exile,* published by Ohio University Press in 2004, are a small but well-chosen sample of Mostwin's quietly powerful talent.

She has also written a cycle of four novels that carry the often traumatic history of one family in Poland from the beginning of the twentieth century until the aftermath of World War II: *Cień księdza Piotra* (Father Peter's Shadow, 1985), *Szmaragdowa zjawa* (The Emerald Apparition, 1988), *Tajemnica zwyciężonych* (The Secret of the Vanquished, 1992), and *Nie ma domu* (Home No More, 1997). Their realistic scope, honesty in dealing with uncomfortable political matters, and documentary episodes from World War II battlefields are rare in Poland's literature of the postwar era, when writers had been restrained by censorship. For the same reason, only now, after the fall of communist regime, are Danuta Mostwin's collected works being published in her native country. A recipient of many émigré awards, in recent years she has been honored in Poland with the highest orders and distinctions. At the Polish Embassy celebration of fifty years of her achievement as a foot soldier of social work, a scholar, and a creative writer, Maryland's Senator Barbara Mikulski praised Danuta Mostwin as one of the most outstanding citizens in the history of Baltimore—the port of arrival to a homeless exile who in return for its rugged hospitality placed it on the map of contemporary Polish American literature. (*See also* Polish American Novel, Polish Émigré Writers in the United States)

Further Reading

Rostropowicz Clark, Joanna. "Danuta Mostwin's Puzzles of Identity." *Two Novellas of Emigration and Exile.* Athens: Ohio UP, 2004. i–xvi.

Stpie, Marian. *Trzecia wartość. O twórczości Danuty Mostwin.* Wyd. Uniwersytetu Jagiellońskiego, Kraków 2000.

Joanna Rostropowicz Clark

MOTLEY, WILLARD (1909–1965) Novelist, journalist, essayist. Willard Francis Motley, best known for his massive, naturalistic novels of Chicago slum life, was a best-selling writer of "**race**less" fiction, producing four novels, none that features a majority of black characters. Insisting throughout his career that he had no interest in being identified strictly as a black writer, he repeatedly criticized other black writers (including **James Baldwin**, whom he famously called a "professional Negro") who did not share his universalist goals.

According to his biographer, Robert E. Fleming, Motley knew even as a child that he was destined to write socially conscious literature, and he began early to prepare himself for his career, traveling across the country on a bicycle in search of material beyond the narrow confines of the largely white, middle-class Chicago neighborhood in which he had grown up a member of the lone black family. The first novel he produced, *Knock on Any Door* (1947), was written after Motley moved into and exhaustively researched the seedy neighborhood of Chicago's Little Sicily. *Knock on Any Door* tells the story of Nick Romano, an Italian American altar boy who turns to a life of crime after his family suffers a reversal of fortune and is compelled to move to a poor urban neighborhood. Originally a sensitive child, Nick is brutalized by his surroundings, first in Denver and then in Chicago, and becomes hard and violent in response. Although a series of individuals, including a figure who represents Motley himself, attempt to help Nick, he ultimately kills a policeman and is executed after a courtroom drama recalling both *Native Son* and the real-life case of Bernard Sawicki, who also inspired **Nelson Algren**'s *Never Come Morning* (1942). Although the novel was dismissed by Robert Bone as nothing more than "*Native Son* without the racial implications," *Knock on Any Door* was both a critical and a popular success. However, his next book, *We Fished All Night* (1951) was far less well received, and in 1958 he returned to his original setting and some of his original characters, publishing *Let No Man Write My Epitaph* (1958), a sequel to *Knock on Any Door* that told the story of Nick's illegitimate son, born after his execution to a minor character in the first novel. Like its predecessor, it enjoyed excellent sales and was made into a film, despite the fact that it is a far less powerful treatment of similar themes. Motley's final, posthumously published novel, *Let Noon Be Fair* (1966), was set in Mexico, where he had lived with his adopted son since his **immigration** in 1951; like *We Fished All Night,* it was a comparative failure.

Although Willard Motley has enjoyed somewhat more critical attention than many other minor African American writers of the 1950s (most notably in the 1970s when a spate of articles and a full-length treatment of his work suggested a reawakening of interest), his novels are not widely discussed or taught today. He remains a marginal figure whose life and works are generally ignored or misunderstood.

Further Reading

Abbott, Craig S., and Kay Van Mol. "The Willard Motley Papers at Northern Illinois University." *Resources for American Literary Study* 7 (1977): 3–26.

Fleming, Robert E. *Willard Motley*. Boston: Twayne, 1978.

Giles, James R., and Jerome Klinkowitz. "The Emergence of Willard Motley in Black American Literature." *Negro American Literature Forum* 6.2 (1972): 31–34.

Klinkowitz, Jerome, and Clarence Major. *The Diaries of Willard Motley.* Ames: Iowa State UP, 1979.

Stephanie Brown

MOURNING DOVE (HUM-ISHU-MA; CHRISTINE QUINTASKET) (1888–1936) Native American author and activist. Mourning Dove was born in 1888 as Christine Quintasket, a member of the Okanogan tribe, one of the Colville Confederated Tribes in eastern Washington State and part of the Salishan language family. She is the first Native American woman to publish a full-length novel, the 1927 *Cogewea: The Half-Blood.* In addition to the novel, she also published a collection of traditional Salish tales, *Coyote Stories* (1933), and her autobiography, *Mourning Dove: A Salishan Autobiography,* was compiled posthumously from her papers and published in 1990.

Mourning Dove had little formal schooling; she first was sent away to boarding school at age six or seven, and at school was punished for speaking Salish, her native (and at the time, only) language. After only a few months there, she became seriously ill and returned home. She did not resume her schooling until some years later, and although she stayed in school for several years, she was dissatisfied with her progress. At twenty-four, she enrolled at a business school for two years to learn typing and improve her English writing, and here she began to keep a journal and notes that eventually developed into the novel *Cogewea.* The novel, a variation on the classic romantic Western, contains many autobiographical elements; focused on Cogewea, a mixed-blood female protagonist, it describes a woman trying to navigate her way between two cultures, white and Native American. Mourning Dove, too, claimed mixed-blood heritage, maintaining that her father's father was a Scotsman. Census records, however, indicate that Joseph Quintasket was a full-blood, and Mourning Dove's siblings similarly denied that their father was of mixed heritage. Instead, it is likely that Mourning Dove invented this white grandfather to make herself more sympathetic to white readers, and perhaps this imagined heritage serves as a suitable metaphor for her position, as a Native American woman and a successful English author, as a cultural mediator and go-between. The novel's structure, too, shows the influences of both Native American and European traditions, as traditional Okanogan stories play a vital role in the story, although the tale is written in the genre of the Western romance.

Mourning Dove began writing her journals around 1913, but it was not until she met Lucullus McWhorter in 1915 that she received encouragement and assistance with her writing project. McWhorter collaborated closely with Mourning Dove on *Cogewea,* and long passages in the novel (primarily concerned with anthropological and historical detail) can be attributed to him. Although the novel was finished in 1916, Mourning Dove and McWhorter had difficulty finding a publisher, partly because of war-related paper shortages and partly because publishers were unwilling to take the risk of publishing a novel by a Native American woman. When they finally did locate a publisher, Mourning Dove and McWhorter were forced to subsidize the publication costs. Given that Mourning Dove was not well-off, this was an additional hardship for her. She had already been working long hours picking fruits and doing other seasonal work, often writing in the evening after ten hours of physical labor, and now began working longer hours and even briefly opened a lunch stand. Nevertheless, she and McWhorter raised the funds necessary for the novel to be published, eleven years after its completion. On her subsequent book of folk-tales, *Coyote Stories,* Mourning Dove collaborated with editor Heister Dean Guie, a friend of McWhorter's, in reshaping the tales to appeal to a white audience. (It was Guie's suggestion that these tales be written for children rather than for adults.)

In addition to being a well-known—although by no means wealthy— author, Mourning Dove was active in tribal politics and in 1935 became the first woman elected to the Colville council. She was active in promoting Native American land rights as well as in the effort to persuade the Bureau of Indian Affairs to reduce its personnel on the Colville reservation.

Her financial difficulties and the pressure of public life took a toll on Mourning Dove's health, and she was often ill. Her death at the relatively young age of forty-nine speaks to the stresses of the life that she lived; but her writings give testament to what she was able to accomplish in spite of her difficulties. (*See also* Native American Autobiography, Native American Novel)

Further Reading

Miller, Jay, ed. *Mourning Dove: A Salishan Autobiography.* Lincoln: U of Nebraska P, 1990.

Viehmann, Martha L. "'My People . . . My Kind': Mourning Dove's *Cogewea, the Half-Blood* as a Narrative of Mixed Descent." *Early Native American Writing.* Helen Jaskoski, ed. New York: Cambridge UP, 1996. 204–22.

Miriam H. Schacht

MUELLER, LISEL (1924–) German American poet and translator. In 2002 Mueller received the Ruth Lilly Prize by the Poetry Foundation of Chicago for consistent excellence in writing poetry in the past forty years.

Mueller's themes in her poetic writing have remained constant, although the angles and the backdrops may have changed: Her poetry addresses the disturbing feelings and images associated with being forced to leave her home and having to adapt to a new culture and learning to communicate successfully in an incomplete foreign language, her "second" language. Dislocation, homesickness, abandonment, the challenges of acculturation, and loss are recurring motifs. Her early book of verse, *The Private Life* (1976), deals with the issues of maintaining her/our public and private selves. The juxtaposition of terror, magic, and beauty of the *Märchen der Gebrüder Grimm (Grimms' Fairy Tales)*, a text central to her long-lost source culture, dominates her Pulitzer Prize–winning poetry collection, *Alive Together: New and Selected Poems* (1996).

After growing up in an upper-middle-class family in Hamburg, Germany, her first home, she left Germany with her family in 1939 because her father, Fritz C. Neumann—a teacher by profession—was a political dissident. They moved to Evansville, Indiana, her second home. She married Paul E. Mueller on June 15, 1944, and the couple had two daughters. Now she resides in Chicago in a retirement community. Young Lisel quickly acquired the English language in its spoken and written forms; she graduated from the University of Evansville with a BA in sociology in record time in 1944. Furthermore, Ms. Mueller completed some graduate work in comparative literature with a specialization in folklore and mythology at Indiana University.

The death of her mother—who was also a teacher—triggered in Lisel a period of intense introspection that resulted in her first poetry collection,

Dependencies (1965). *The Private Life* (1976), *Voices from the Forest* (1977), and *The Need to Hold Still* (1981)—which received the National Book Award— followed. *Second Language* appeared in 1986; *Waving from Shore*, which received the **Carl Sandburg** Prize, was published in 1989; *Alive Together: New and Selected Poems* (1996), her latest book, was awarded the Pulitzer Prize for poetry in 1997. As a writer, Mueller has continued to translate selected works from German into English.

Mueller's poetry is both experimental and traditional; folkloristic and mythological elements from various cultures, including the Native American, are woven into her texts. Therefore, an unusual blend of physical, metaphysical, personal, and commonly experienced elements is achieved in each of her poetic creations. Winner numerous awards and recognitions for her poetry, she has been a writer-in-residence at Washington University in St. Louis and at the University of Chicago, among others. Although suffering from glaucoma, she is currently on the board of the Poetry Center in Chicago, and she gave a reading in June 2004 at the Printers Row Book Fair in Chicago. Most of her original manuscripts can be found at the Library of Lake Forest College in Lake Forest, Illinois.

Further Reading

"Mueller's Latest Collection." *Poetry* CXXX. 2 (June/July 1977): 61–65.

"'Voices from the Forest': Mueller's Latest." *BOOKFORUM* (Summer 1976): 54–55.

Claudia A. Becker

MUKHERJEE, BHARATI (1940–) Award-winning Indian American novelist, short-story writer, and essayist. Bharati Mukherjee was born on July 27, 1940, in Calcutta, India, to an upper-class Hindu Brahmin family. Influenced in her early years by Western education in England and Switzerland, Mukherjee was a keen and ardent reader and by the age of eight had already read many Western as well as Bengali classics. After receiving her BA and MA degrees in India, Mukherjee came to America to attend a writing workshop in the Iowa Writers Workshop in 1961. She subsequently earned her MFA in creative writing in 1963 and PhD in English and comparative literature in 1969. Mukherjee's writing career began while teaching at McGill University in Montreal. She has taught creative writing at Columbia University, New York University, and Queens College and is currently a distinguished professor at the University of California, Berkeley.

While studying for the writing workshop at Iowa in 1961, she met fellow student Clarke Blaise—a naturalized American citizen of Canadian origin—and fell in love with him. They got married, and Mukherjee moved with Blaise to Canada after completing their studies. Mukherjee could not assimilate her **identity** in the Canadian terms of mosaic culture. After fourteen years of life in Canada, she migrated with her family to United States in 1980 and has vehemently embraced the American multicultural notion of identity. After her naturalization as an American citizen, she has openly declared and celebrated her **assimilation**ist attitude and adoption of an American identity. Her rejection of a hyphenated identity as an Indian American or Asian American writer reveals her demand that she be considered equally at par with the European immigrants who do not feel the need to claim such an identity. She also denounces the labeling of postcolonial writer in relation to her works. Mukherjee insists that she be seen as an American writer following the ideals of the American dream in a heterogeneous, multicultural America.

A predominant theme in Mukherjee's fiction as in other immigrant fiction is the issue of identities that one must learn how to transform in order to survive in contemporary, multicultural America. In the process, sometimes cultures and traditions are deemed to be shed off in favor of new and different ideals that suit such transformation. Mukherjee situates herself in the American tradition and compares herself with writers such as **Bernard Malamud** and **Maxine Hong Kingston**, who also deal with transformation and forging of new identities in their fiction. She denounces the self-conscious exiles replete with nostalgia and diasporic longings as in the works of other writers of Indian origin such as Salman Rushdie, Amitav Ghosh, and **Ved Mehta**. She welcomes the maximalist approach of America's new immigrants who have shed all past lives and languages to assume newer, American identities. In "Immigrant Writing: Give Us Your Maximalists" she explains her authorial stance of an immigrant rather than a diasporic, expatriate writer. Her refusal to relate to the exile sensibility is on account of excessive pain and sense of loss endured therein. This does not mean that she avoids the pain that is very much present in the lives of her fictional characters. She refuses to see her own position as an immigrant in terms of loss. Her affirmation of her self-defined identity precludes the experience of pain. Her characters thus learn to grow out from their painful experiences.

Mukherjee's own denial of an exilic position of expatriation demands that her labeling as a writer of exile or postcolonial writer be truncated and that her fiction be seen as representation of American ideals and beliefs. She believes herself to be an ex-colonial who, in the ethnic and gender-fractured world of contemporary American fiction, is able to enter several lives fictionally. Like a chameleon, she discovers her material from her adapted surroundings and is thus able to Americanize herself instead of getting framed by predefined, ideologically charged notions of a minority identity.

Mukherjee writes about the immigrant group that she feels had not been written about in American fiction. Her stories and novels are full of characters that confront their various identities in different geopolitical spaces. Although her earlier writings, such as *Days and Nights in Calcutta* (1977), record her experiences of being a colonial who writes in a borrowed language (English) in an alien country (Canada), her later writings, especially the ones written after her migration to America are celebrated efforts to forge a new identity for herself as well as other immigrants in her fiction.

Her fiction can be seen as representative of showing the evolution of an immigrant from a diasporic, expatriate sensibility. The three stages identifiable in her fiction are those of expatriation, transition, and **immigration**. In her earlier works she writes as a diasporic writer trying to find her identity in Indian heritage, as in *The Tiger's Daughter* (1971) and *Wife* (1975). Her frustration at the racial intolerance and discrimination faced in her years in Canada is evident in *Darkness* (1985) and *The Sorrow and the Terror* (1987); and finally she claims a status of the American immigrant in works such as *The Middleman and Other Stories* (1988), *Jasmine* (1989), *The Holder of the World* (1993), and *Leave It To Me* (1997). Her recent novel, *Desirable Daughters* (2003), seems to accentuate all of these issues in a very subtle manner. Apart from fiction, Mukherjee has also coauthored two books of nonfiction with her husband, Clark Blaise: *Days and Nights in Calcutta* and *The Sorrow and the Terror*.

Mukherjee drew national attention when she won the prestigious National Book Critics Circle Award for best fiction for her collection titled *The Middleman and Other Stories* in 1988. Truly multicultural, the various stories depict the transformation of America in the light of migration and cross-cultural journeys. Beginning with "The Middleman" and ending with her widely anthologized story "The Management of Grief," the collection reveals the intricacies, complexities, as well as dilemmas faced by the new immigrants in America. Coming from diverse backgrounds and different countries such as Italy, Vietnam, Philippines, Afghanistan, and Trinidad, these immigrants reflect dauntless courage in attaining the American experience and identity and learn to survive challenges brought therein. The title story deals with Alfie Judah, an Iraqi-born immigrant who inadvertently becomes a middleman in illegal arms deals to rebel guerrilla groups in South America. Alfie, like other characters in Mukherjee's fiction, learns to survive in multicultural America that is also imperialistic and violent. Another story "Fathering" deals with clash of identities in the life of an American Vietnam veteran named Jason who has to choose between his peaceful life with wife Sharon or to be a father to his Vietnamese daughter Eng who is suffering from the war. "The Management of Grief" deals with the story of a Hindu woman, Shaila Bhave, whose husband and two sons are killed in a plane explosion. She learns to manage her grief in a cross-cultural manner and rebuild her life anew.

A critical survey of some of her novels likewise reveals a trajectory from pessimism to affirmative optimism that is followed by most of her characters. In *The Tiger's Daughter*, the protagonist Tara, an English-educated expatriate visits India and is unable to connect because of being treated as an outcast in Bengali society because of her marriage to an American. The narrator reflects on the decline of Calcutta amidst communist uprisings. Tara feels alienated from her friends and people around her. Her violent rape by an evil politician is symptomatic of the violation and exploitation of innocent peasants in the name of progress. In the end the old world is abandoned when Tara leaves India to be back with her loving husband in America.

Jasmine deals with a story of a young, naïve Indian widow whose illegal entry to America reveals the hidden dangers faced by immigrant women and how she must shed her past and old selves and learn to transform herself to be able to survive in America. She is through the course of the novel Jyoti Vijh, Jasmine, Jane Ripplemeyer, and Jase. She has lived in Punjab, India, New York, Iowa, and in the end leaves for California. She makes her own destiny and seems to succeed in the end. However, this process of making one's destiny is not an easy one. Her initial plan to come to America and commit the ritual of *sati* after her husband's death by terrorist bombing is abandoned when she is raped on the first night of her arrival in America. Her suicidal plan is replaced with her killing of the rapist instead as Jasmine learns to survive in America. Revealing indomitable courage, she is able to choose her own destiny eventually instead of one of loneliness and widowhood as predicted by an Indian astrologer in the beginning of novel. Her relationships with Taylor, an American professor, and Bud, an Iowan banker, reveal different notions about the American experience. Her choice to leave Bud, who is paralyzed, and go with Taylor in the end signifies the pursuit of American dream that seems to promise fruitful choices to her than in life with Bud as a care-giver.

Leave It To Me is another novel that deals with the theme of transforming identities. The narrator Devi is like Jasmine, a woman with multiple identities. She is first introduced as Debby DiMartino, the adopted daughter of Italian American parents living in Schenectady, New York. She learns from her adopted mother about her birth in India and that her mother was an American hippie of the seventies. Debbie's anxiety about her birth parents progresses the novel ahead and reveals a darker, more violent America. She learns that her father was a Eurasian sex-guru and a serial killer. In search for her biological mother, Debbie changes her name to Devi and like an avenging Goddess incurs violent acts during this pursuit. Her different relations with men end with violent acts as arson and even murder. Through the portrayal of starkly sensational violence, Mukherjee impels the readers to understand how violence, as also was the case in *Jasmine,* becomes instrumental in transforming one's self.

Desirable Daughters deals with the intriguing tale of Tara Bhattacharjee and her two sisters amidst prejudices, ambitions, familial ties and shocking secrets. The narrator, Tara, is divorced from her billionaire husband and is raising her teenaged son and living with a Buddhist boyfriend. Comparable to **Amy Tan**'s famous novel ***The Joy Luck Club*** that also highlights different lives across different generations, *Desirable Daughters* portrays skillfully through the stories of three sisters, Tara, Padma, and Parvati, a complicated portrayal of lives in between cultures in India and America. The novel's beginning depicts Tara's namesake ancestor, who is five years old in 1879 and is married to a tree in a ritual as her husband dies from a snake bite on the wedding night. The narrative moves to Tara's visit with her son to the same forest where her ancestor became a "Tree-Bride." The sudden appearance of a young man who claims kinship to Tara's family unravels the family secrets as Tara is forced to confront her sisters and learn the family's shady past. Chris Dey claims to be the illegitimate son of Padma Mehta and Ron Dey. Amidst secrets, deceptions, and a near-fatal bombing, the novel is a tale of going back to one's roots, past, and history and getting connected with it. Tara learns to accept her past and legacy from which she was separated and reconsiders the choices that she had made in her life in America.

The critical reception to Mukherjee's works has been mixed. Although it has drawn enthusiastic response from Western critics for her celebration of American identity, her rejection of a hyphenated identity and dismal portrayals of India have drawn harsh criticism from some of the Indian critics. Regardless, Mukherjee's contribution to the American literary scene is significant in its changing perceptions about ethnicity in general. (*See also* South Asian American Literature)

Further Reading

Alam, Fakrul. *Bharati Mukherjee.* New York: Twayne Publishers, 1996.

Nelson, Emmanuel, ed. *Critical Perspectives.* New York: Garland, 1993.

Parvinder Mehta

MULATTO   The mulatto or mulatta has been a recurrent figure in African American literature from its inception. In fact, many critics consider it as one of the oldest racial stereotypes. Characterized by a double or mixed heritage and ascendancy—often being the offspring of a white and black liasion—the main problem this figure poses is the dilemma of **identity** while simultaneously personifying the ultimate racial taboo in America, that is, miscegenation.

The history of the mulatto figure can be traced back to **slave narratives**—many slave narrators were mulattoes, for instance, **Frederick Douglass**—but it soon came to be identified with the so-called tragic mulatto figure that was the protagonist of tragic mulatto fiction, a widely popular genre during the nineteenth century. As defined by the classical depiction provided by **Sterling A. Brown**, the tragic mulatto is the victim of a divided inheritance, constantly experiencing an internal conflict between his or her black and white sides. According to Brown, the stereotype presents a black part of his inheritance that corresponds to the baser instincts, mainly indolence, savagery, and sensuality, whereas the white half would encompass his or her intellectual abilities. Brown justifies the profuseness of this stereotype in anti**slavery** fiction as a means to create sympathetic feelings in the white audience to which this fiction was clearly addressed in order to promote the **abolition** of slavery.

Although there has been an unceasing critical debate on opinions such as Brown's, it is nevertheless obvious that the use of the mulatto figure allowed for the representation of what could not be portrayed otherwise, the patent breaking of the prohibition of intimate relationships between both **race**s. In that sense, the mulatto or mulatta protagonist of the nineteenth-century novels embodied both the racial and sexual other. Their whiteness and beauty—and therefore their identification with the white race—were exalted over all to explore the manifold contradictions inherent in the racist ideology upheld by the society of that age. However, their tragic fate was preordained, as they usually committed suicide due to the impossibility to live on either side.

The tragic mulatto tradition is later followed by the so-called passing fiction, especially in the decade of the twenties. In many **Harlem Renaissance** novels the mulatto or mulatta continues to be the main protagonist, who is involved in passing as white to take advantage of the opportunities only available to white people. In this case, their light-skinned bodies are instrumentalized as their passport to obtain what they desire. This passing tradition revises the previous one by focusing on the problematic construction of a satisfying sense of identity out of their schizophrenic lives and also by complicating the motives and symbolism of the characters. Some of the most important writers who make use of this tradition are **James Weldon Johnson**, **Nella Larsen**, and **Jessie Redmon Fauset**. (*See also* Passing)

Further Reading

Sollors, Werner. *Neither Black nor White Yet Both.* Cambridge, MA: Harvard UP, 1997.

Starke, Catherine. *Black Portraiture in American Fiction.* New York: Basic Books, 1971.

Mar Gallego

MULLEN, HARRYETTE (1953–)   African American poet, scholar, and critic. In her poetry and literary scholarship, Harryette Mullen fuses oral, folk, pop, and literary traditions. Currently a professor of literature and writing at the University of California at Los Angeles, Mullen was born in Florence, Alabama, and raised in Fort Worth, Texas.

Mullen once said in an interview, "We are all mongrels" (Bedient 652). This assertion is made palpable in Mullen's *Sleeping with the Dictionary* (2002), which garnered her widest audience to date, along with a National Book Award nomination. *Sleeping with the Dictionary* is an *abecedarian* collection, a festival of words inspired by the *American Heritage Dictionary* and employing surrealist composition techniques, punning, musicality, and an ear not only for the dictionary but also for "saxophone streets and scratchy sidewalks" of American culture.

Mullen, influenced by work from the **Harlem Renaissance** and the **Black Arts Movement**, initially focused on African American **identity** and voice as rooted in orality. Her first book, *Tree Tall Woman* (1981), reflects that focus. Later, she began to question whether an "authentic" African American voice could be rendered in written language. Two subsequent books, *Trimmings* (1991) and *S*PeRM**K*T* (1992), resisted any single identity or voice. *Trimmings*, a book of prose poems, inspired by the work of Gertrude Stein and by the socioeconomic theory of Karl Marx, investigates femininity as it is shaped by consumerism.

S*PeRM**K*T, whose title plays on the word "supermarket," extends Mullen's interest in consumer culture with prose poems that subjectively tour a typical American grocery store. Familiar parts of American life are made strange as associations lead to uncomfortable juxtapositionings of words and images.

As Mullen became more widely known as an avant-garde poet, she began to notice that her audiences were predominantly white compared to those who had come to hear her read from and speak about *Tree Tall Woman*. Her next book, *Muse & Drudge* (1995), was an attempt to bring those audiences together. As the title suggests, this sequence of four-line stanzas, which draws heavily on **blues** themes and phrasing, raises questions about idealized or denigrating representations of women; further, it calls attention to the double marginalization of women of color, alluding at times to the observation, voiced in **Zora Neale Hurston**'s *Their Eyes Were Watching God*, that black women are the "mules of the world."

Mullen's *Blues Baby: Early Poems* (2002), which includes *Tree Tall Woman* and previously uncollected poems from of Mullen's early career, reveals how she has contributed to and been shaped by the Black Arts and feminist movements even as she has moved in multiple artistic directions. (*See also* Black Arts Movement)

Further Reading

Bedient, Calvin. "The Solo Mysterioso Blues: An Interview with Harryette Mullen." *Callaloo* 19.3 (1996): 651–69.

Crown, Kathleen. "'Choice Voice Noise': Soundings in Innovative African-American Poetry." *Assembling Alternatives: Reading Postmodern Poetries Transnationally*. Ed. Romana Huk. Middletown, CT: Wesleyan UP, 2003. 219–45.

Thomas, Lorenzo. *Extraordinary Measures: Afrocentric Modernism and Twentieth-Century American Poetry*. Tuscaloosa: U of Alabama P, 2000.

Ellen McGrath Smith

MULTICULTURALISM   Multiculturalism is the assertion of the value of cultural diversity within Western societies and of the international significance of non-Western cultures. It is a reaction against **Eurocentrism, whiteness,** and patriarchy, especially as those perspectives have served as sources of and have provided measures of cultural value. It is an outgrowth of interrelated cultural phenomena: the postcolonial reconstruction of precolonial cultural traditions; the increasing mobility of populations and the resulting pluralism in most if not all societies; the political, social, and economic activism and the cultural self-assertion of minority populations; and the progressive movements promoting the rights of women and of gays and lesbians. As a movement, multiculturalism profited from the great attention given to ethnic heritage and the formalization of ethnic studies programs in the 1960s and the 1970s.

Interestingly, the term *multiculturalism* was coined in the early 1960s in Canada, which to outsiders might seem to be one of the most racially homogenous nations in the world and therefore an unlikely setting for the initiation of a discussion of how diverse cultures interact. When the Canadian federal government began using the term *bicultural* to describe the nation, it intended to appease the French-Canadian activists in Quebec and to diffuse the separatist movement in that province. However, it created another controversy because spokespersons for Canada's Native Americans and significant Asian minority were soon protesting their apparent exclusion from the national dialogue. Gradually, the Canadian government began to use *multicultural* instead of bicultural, except when addressing issues directly related to French Canada. Yet, as the term *multiculturalism* has become more widely used internationally, its definition has become more elastic, and the Canadian government has begun to substitute the phrase *cultural mosaic*.

In the 1980s, multiculturalism became the catchword for the shift in emphasis within elementary, secondary, and university curricula from the ideas and works of dead white males to those of people of color and other previously marginalized voices. The pedagogical aim was both to broaden the perspectives of those raised on assumptions of cultural privilege and to legitimize the self-expression of those whose cultures had previously been regarded as either inconsequential or inferior. In effect, the promotion of open cultural exchanges among students from diverse cultural backgrounds would also equalize the opportunities for educational achievement for all students, regardless of their cultural heritage. And education is seen as the key to political, economic, and social empowerment.

Proponents of multiculturalism have treated concepts such as **race**, **ethnicity**, and sex as problematic because they presuppose straightforward categories and because they inherently promote preferences and reinforce prejudices. But cultural phenomena such as multiethnic and multiracial ancestries and transgenderism have made the traditional categories seem arbitrary and moot. Thus, proponents of multiculturalism have offered as alternatives the more flexible and adaptable concepts of cultural identity and gender identification.

The United States has long been described as a melting pot, and that cultural conception has been a very important element—if not *the* central mythic element—of the national **identity**. The multicultural concepts of cultural diversity and cultural pluralism would seem compatible with the traditional concept of the melting pot. Critics of multiculturalism—and, in particular, opponents of the emphasis on multiculturalism within education—have argued, however, that the American **assimilation** of cultural variation has not previously meant the celebration of *continuing* cultural differences.

Instead, opponents of multiculturalism have argued that assimilation has traditionally signified the process by which cultural minorities have become largely indistinguishable from the majority and have been absorbed into or subsumed within the mainstream culture. Through this process, even distinctive cultural markers have typically been reduced to rather superficial affirmations of one's cultural heritage—holiday traditions, fashion preferences, and culinary options. Cultural heritage has not remained the primary way to define an assimilated individual's personal or communal identity. Indeed, even those superficial cultural indicators have been mainstreamed in ways analogous to restaurant franchising. Most Americans, regardless of ancestry or geographic location, have fairly ready access to restaurants that offer Italian, Mexican, or Chinese cuisine. Moreover, there is no longer any assumption that the majority of the diners at, say, an Italian restaurant will be Italian Americans or that even the owners of an Italian restaurant will necessarily be Italian Americans. In fact, to extend this line of discussion even a bit farther, much of the menu at an Italian restaurant in an American city is likely to be more American than Italian and would be unavailable at a restaurant in Rome or in another Italian city.

Critics of multiculturalism have complained that its proponents have placed a greater emphasis on continuing cultural difference than on assimilation. These critics have warned of the dangers of cultural balkanization, of the loss of a sense of national identity to the acceptance of increasingly diverse and seemingly competing cultural identities. They have warned against the erosion of the fundamental values on which the national identity and prosperity have seemingly been fashioned. They have complained most vehemently about the general unwillingness of the proponents of multiculturalism to acknowledge the deficiencies of cultures other than the traditional Western culture. And they have frequently expressed dismay at the paradox that within the supposedly "open exchanges" promised by multiculturalists, pejorative labels such as racist, fascist, and chauvinist have frequently been applied to critics of multiculturalism in order to divert their energies, if not to silence them completely.

Proponents of multiculturalism have countered that Eurocentric, white, and patriarchal values may have largely defined American culture but they have never done so exclusively. Proponents have made the case that Western history, and especially American history, has always been defined by the tension between assimilation and pluralism. In fact, this tension has been a largely positive source of much of the energy fueling the most dynamic political, economic, social, and cultural transformations of Western societies. Furthermore, proponents of multiculturalism have argued that the emphasis on cultural hegemony, rather than on cultural pluralism, has permitted the rationalization of many of the worst injustices within Western societies. Within the United States, these injustices have included the dispossession of Native Americans, the enslavement of African Americans, and the exploitation of unskilled immigrant labor. Clearly, the conflicts over multiculturalism have been as much about the historical interpretation of the past as they have been about shaping the futures of Western societies.

Nonetheless, demographic trends suggest that within the next half-century what are now minority cultures in the United States may replace or reconstitute what has been the nation's majority or mainstream Anglo American culture. In his article "America's Increasing Diversity" published in the March/April 2004 issue of *Futurist*, Nat Irvin II presents a broad range of statistics that point to the inevitability of this dramatic transition. By 2025 the non-Hispanic white population of the United States will decrease to 60 percent of the total population, and by 2050 it will constitute just under 50 percent of the total. And there is an international corollary to this decline. In 1997 Caucasians accounted for about 17 percent of the world's population, but by 2010 they will constitute only 9 percent of the total. It is not so much the case that white populations are declining but, instead, that nonwhite populations are increasing at a much greater rate. As Irvin points out, between 2000 and 2050, nonwhites will account for more than 90 percent of the growth in the U.S. population. More specifically, according to the latest census data for the twenty fastest-growing U.S. cities, over the last decade the African American population has increased at almost five times the rate for non-Hispanic whites, and the Asian American and Hispanic populations have increased at about fourteen times the rate for whites.

One might think that these trends would make arguments over multiculturalism moot, but, in fact, they have seemingly caused the arguments to intensify not just within the United States, but in the United Kingdom, Australia, Germany, France, and most nations with large immigrant populations. The critics of multiculturalism have generally adopted one of two basic political strategies: either to mandate broad assertions of the continuing efficacy of the traditionally predominant culture or to legislate against specific practices of other cultures. The first strategy would include such actions as the identification of English as the official language in states such as Florida, Texas, and California, where the acknowledgement of **bilingualism** on official forms and street signs has become a salient issue. The second strategy would include the recent ban in France on female students' wearing traditional Muslim head coverings to class.

The proponents of multiculturalism have advanced their cause in a variety of ways. In some instances, the tactics have seemed somewhat trite. For instance, in 1993 the National Education Association designated the third Monday of October as National Multicultural Diversity Day. The designation is something of a redundant tongue-twister, which only reinforces the sense of skeptics that it is something being forced onto and perhaps foisted onto American mainstream culture. On the other hand, in 1976 proponents of multiculturalism from academia and publishing created the Before Columbus Foundation, which has provided substantial support for projects that have substantively promoted multiculturalism in the arts and education. To provide just one significant illustration of this work, in 1992 the Before Columbus Foundation sponsored W. W. Norton's publication of a pair of anthologies of multicultural fiction and poetry.

Recent anthologies with a multicultural emphasis have included Robert Pack and **Jay Parini**'s *American Identities: Contemporary Multicultural Voices* (1996), **Rita Dove**'s *Multicultural Voices* (1995), Laurie King's *Hear My Voice: A Multicultural Anthology of Literature from the United* States (1993), Alan C. Purves's *Tapestry: A Multicultural Anthology* (1993), and Elizabeth P. Quintero and Mary K. Rummel's *American Voices: Webs of Diversity* (1997). Anthologies restricted to one literary genre have included James R. Payne's *Multicultural Autobiography: American Lives* (1992), Anne Mazer's *America Street: A Multicultural Anthology of Stories* (1993), Ishmael Reed's *From Totems to Hip Hop: A Multi-Cultural Anthology of Poetry Across the Americas, 1900–2002* (2002), and **Maria Mazziotti Gillan** and Jennifer Gillan's *Unsettling America: An Anthology of Contemporary Multicultural Poetry* (1994).

In addition, some multicultural anthologies have had a somewhat more specialized focus. Margaret L. Anderson and Patricia Hill Collins's *Race, Class, and Gender: An Anthology* (2003) has a more pointedly political, economic, and feminist slant. In Mary Frosch's *Coming of Age in America: A Multicultural Anthology* (1995) and in Maria Mazziotti Gillan's *Growing Up Ethnic in America: Contemporary Fiction about Learning to Be American* (1999), the immigrant's adaptation to America culture is juxtaposed with the adolescent's gradual adjustment to maturation. David Landis Barnhill's *At Home on the Earth: Becoming Native to Our Place: A Multicultural Anthology* (1999) concentrates on responses to the natural world and environmental issues. Multicultural anthologies with a special emphasis on gender have included Estelle Disch's *Reconstructing Gender: A Multicultural Anthology* (2002), Amy Kesselman, Lily D. McNair, Lily D McNair, and Nancy Schniedewind's *Women: Images and Realities, A Multicultural Anthology* (2002), Amy Sonnie's *Revolutionary Voices: A Multicultural Queer Youth Anthology* (2000), and Franklin Abbott's *Boyhood, Growing Up Male: A Multicultural Anthology* (1998). Several notable anthologies of multicultural literature have had a more international focus—for instance, Victor J. Ramraj's *Concert of Voices: An Anthology of World Writing in English* (1994) and John McRae's *Now Read On: A Multicultural Anthology of Literature in English* (1999).

Some terms commonly associated with multiculturalism actually predate it, whereas others have developed in its wake. In the late 1940s, Fernando Ortiz coined the term *transculturation* to designate the dramatic increase in exchanges between cultures and the gradual blending of cultures due in large part to rapid advancements in technologies related to communications and transportation. More recently, *interculturalism* has become the standard term for the promotion of tolerance and the vilification of racism and ethnic prejudice within a particular society. It designates the institutional development of programs that promote the recognition of and the acceptance of cultural diversity. The phrase *identity politics* refers to the attempt to exploit cultural identification or issues related to multiculturalism for political gain. Although initially a descriptive label, the phrase has subsequently acquired generally pejorative connotations.

Further Reading

Amoia, Alba, and Bettina L. Knapp. *Multicultural Writers Since 1945: An A-to-Z Guide.* Westport, CT: Greenwood Press, 2004.

Auerbach, Susan, ed. *Encyclopedia of Multiculturalism.* New York: Marshall Cavendish, 1994.

King, Laurie. *Hear My Voice: Bibliography: An Annotated Guide to Multicultural Literature from the United States.* Menlo Park, CA: Addison-Wesley, 1994.

Kutzer, M. Daphne, ed. *Writers of Multicultural Fiction for Young Adults: A Bio-Critical Sourcebook.* Westport, CT: Greenwood Press, 1996.

Lee, A. Robert. *Multicultural American Literature: Comparative Black, Native, Latino/a and Asian American Fictions.* Jackson: UP of Mississippi, 2003.

Long, Robert Emmet. *Multiculturalism.* New York: H. W. Wilson, 1997.

Miller, Suzanne M., and Barbara McCaskill, eds. *Multicultural Literature and Literacies: Making Space for Difference.* Albany: State U of New York P, 1993.

Miller-Lachmann, Lyn. *Global Voices, Global Visions: A Core Collection of Multicultural Books.* New Providence, NJ: R. R. Bowker, 1995.

Singer, Judith Y., and Sally A. Smith. "The Potential of Multicultural Literature: Changing Understanding of Self and Others." *Multicultural Perspectives* 5.2 (2003): 17–23.

Susser, Ida, and Thomas C. Patterson, eds. *Cultural Diversity in the United States: A Critical Reader.* Oxford, UK: Blackwell, 2000.

Martin Kich

MUMBO JUMBO Published in 1972, *Mumbo Jumbo* is **Ishmael Reed**'s third and most experimental novel. Mixing prose with poetry, text with image, and linear narrative with intertextual cross-referencing, the book's vanguard aesthetic locates it in a genealogy of genre-defying black fictions that includes **Jean Toomer**'s modernist *Cane* (1923) and Trey Ellis's post-modern *Platitudes* (1988).

In the 1920s a psychic epidemic called "Jes Grew" sweeps the nation in the form of dance-hall fêtes, sexual liberation, and **jazz**. A life-affirming and spiritually animated religious culture, Jes Grew is pitted against the Wallflower Order, an ancient Judeo-Christian secret society that seeks to wipe out every trace of the Dionysian ethos on the world scene. The novel's fifty-year-old protagonist, Papa LaBas, is the founder of the Mumbo Jumbo Kathedral and a Jes Grew proponent; he embarks on a quest to find the jive movement's sacred Text of origins before the Order's maverick agent, Hinckle Von Vampton, does.

Various subplots disclose what is at stake in the Text is either being recovered by LaBas or falling into the hands of purifying cultural suprema-cists: A former Kathedral assistant, Berbelang, leads the multiethnic *Mu'taf-ikah* terrorist group in liberating artifacts from "Centers of Art Detention" (museums) and returning them to the native cultures from which they were "stolen"; Von Vampton attempts to divert Jes Grew away from Harlem by promoting a "Talking Android" **race** man of letters, first through the black

Woodrow Wilson Jefferson, who must lighten his skin, and then through the white Hubert "Safecracker" Gould, who must appear in blackface; and the Order's leaders instigate a financial crisis in the U.S. economy—what will come to be known as the Great Depression—so as to eliminate Jes Grew's material grounding. In light of these conflicts, LaBas discovers that the Text has been destroyed by a black Muslim, Abdul Sufi Hamid, whose religious beliefs repress organic, affective life as much as the Order's ideologies do. Although the Text is lost forever, LaBas senses that this is not the last the world has seen or heard of Jes Grew.

Critics have been keen to focus on the struggle over civilizational discourse that transpires between Jes Grew and the Wallflower Order. Yet Reed's positing Haiti as a HooDoo "outside" to such discourse emphasizes that culture is a syncretic product of Western and non-Western contact zones of myth, religion, political economy, and the arts. The novel is thus not so much an attack on the West as it is a refiguring of history as precisely hybrid, shifting, and global. Indeed, the mystery behind Jes Grew may be that it continues to perform its "Work" in the most unexpected of places: Harold Bloom has named *Mumbo Jumbo* one of the five hundred most important texts in the Western **canon**. (*See also* African American Novel)

Further Reading

Gates, Henry Louis, Jr. "On 'The Blackness of Blackness': Ishmael Reed and a Critique of the Sign." *The Signifying Monkey: A Theory of Afro-American Literary Criticism.* New York: Oxford UP, 1988. 217–38.

Hogue, W. Lawrence. "Historiographic Metafiction and the Celebration of Differences: Ishmael Reed's *Mumbo Jumbo*." *Productive Postmodernism: Consuming Histories and Cultural Studies.* Ed. John N. Duvall. Albany: State U of New York P, 2002. 93–110.

Mason, Theodore O., Jr. "Performance, History, and Myth: The Problem of Ishmael Reed's *Mumbo Jumbo*." *Modern Fiction Studies* 34.1 (1988): 97–109.

McGee, Patrick. *Ishmael Reed and the Ends of Race.* New York: St. Martin's, 1997.

Kinohi Nishikawa

MUÑOZ, ELÍAS MIGUEL (1954–) Cuban American writer. Born in Cuba, Elías Miguel Muñoz migrated to the United States in 1969 and spent his adolescence in California. He completed an MA (1979) and a PhD (1984) in Spanish at the University of California at Irvine. An accomplished poet, critic, and pedagogue, Muñoz is better known for his English-language novels, in which gay and lesbian themes have been in the foreground, especially intolerance toward homosexuality within Cuban exile culture.

Muñoz began writing poetry in 1979 as part of a literary workshop by Mexican writer José Agustín. He began publishing in anthologies and journals in the early 1980s. His two collections of poetry appeared in 1989: the Spanish-language *No fue posible el sol* (*The Sun Was Not Possible*) and the bilingual *En estas tierras/In This Land.* Muñoz also published two books of literary criticism: *El discurso utópico de la sexualidad en Manuel Puig* (*The Utopian Discourse of Sexuality in Manuel Puig*, 1987), an analysis of four novels by Argentine writer Manuel Puig, and *Desde esta orilla: poesía cubana en el exilio* (*From This Shore: Cuban Exile Poetry*, 1988), a study of exiled Cuban poets.

Muñoz gained more recognition for his fiction. His first novel, *Los viajes de Orlando Cachumbambé* (*The Travels of Orlando Cachumbambé*, 1984), was written in Spanish and deals with a recurring theme in his works: the problems faced by a young Cuban in the United States torn between cultures.

Crazy Love (1988), his first novel in English, centers on the Toledo-Fernández family, which migrates from Cuba to California. The main character is Julián, a young artist whose bisexual relationships symbolize life between cultures. His family includes an indomitable Cuban grandmother, an abusively patriarchal father, and an assimilated Cuban American younger sister. Throughout the exile process, they face class and gender conflicts (including homophobia and domestic violence) whose roots lie on social disparities and patriarchal customs in Cuba.

The Greatest Performance (1991) also establishes a connection between patriarchal domination in Cuban (American) households and political repression on the island. Through the alternating gay and lesbian narrative voices of childhood friends Mario and Rosita, the novel follows them through their coming of age in revolutionary Cuba, separation through exile, and reunion as adults in California, where she becomes his caregiver as he is dying from AIDS. *Brand New Memory* (1998) is another coming-of-age novel where teenage Cuban American Gina Domingo comes to terms with her Cuban roots after an unexpected visit from her grandmother Estela, who supplies past histories of the island suppressed by her refugee parents.

Elías Miguel Muñoz's other writings include the musical theater piece *L.A. Scene* (adapted from *Crazy Love*), staged Off Broadway in 1990, and pedagogical material for U.S. students, most notably a series of novellas—*Viajes Fantásticos, Ladrón de la mente* (*Fantastic Voyages, Mind Thief*, both 1999), and *Isla de la Luz* (*Island of Light*, 2001)—aimed at learners of Spanish. (*See also* Cuban American Novel)

Further Reading

Deaver, William O. "Gender Construction in Elías Miguel Muñoz's *The Greatest Performance*." *RLA* 8 (1996): 439–41.

Prieto Taboada, Antonio. "That's Who We Are!: Cuban-American Literature, Hispanic Discourse and Cultural Emblems in Elías Miguel Muñoz's *Crazy Love*." *Dispositio* 16 (1991): 95–107.

Roberto Carlos Ortiz

MURA, DAVID (1952-) Japanese American poet, creative nonfiction writer, and essayist. As a Sansei, third-generation Japanese American growing up in a primarily Jewish upper-middle-class suburb in the Midwest, David Mura has made significant contributions to the growing field of Asian American poetry. In terms of reinventing and representing physical features of Asian Americans, Mura's poetry shares a resistant stance against stereotypical perceptions with works by other poets such as **Li-Young Lee**, **Cathy Song**, and **Marilyn Chin**. Mura has actively participated in exploring **ethnicity**, **identity**, and cultural relations in multiethnic American society. He has served as the Artistic Director of the Asian American Renaissance, an Asian American arts organization in Minnesota, as well as an Artist Associate at Pangea World Theater.

Mura has published two collections of poetry. His early poems collected in *After We Lost Our Way* (1989) reflect various perspectives of the struggles of the Issei, Nisei, and Sansei (first-, second-, and third-generation Japanese Americans) over identity construction. Driven by the anxiety of being disconnected with history, Mura tries to piece together bits and pieces overheard from his relatives' conversations in the pursuit to strike a balance in his poems between the past and the present, between belonging and not belonging. Writing about his first-generation grandparents and American-born parents, to some extent, is Mura's means of filling in the gaps through research and imagination. In his second book of poetry, *The Colors of Desire* (1995), Mura addresses the complications of rage and reconciliation in a world marked by racial and cultural diversities. The multiple voices of the poems in this volume scrutinize the connection between history, ethnicity, sexuality, and identity. The inseparability between collective history and personal desire suggested in his poems provokes further exploration.

Funded by a U.S./Japan Creative Artist Fellowship in 1984, Mura traveled to Japan for a one-year trip. Based on his experience and reconsideration of his identity as a Sansei writer, Mura published his first memoir—*Turning Japanese: Memoirs of a Sansei* (1991). The work won a 1991 Josephine Miles Book Award from the Oakland PEN and has been listed in the *New York Times* 1991 Notable Books of the year. Starting his trip as a self-identified American, Mura was compelled to rethink his connection with Japan that had been absent since his childhood and was challenged as well to reconsider his ethnic American identity. Such rethinking and realizations profoundly influenced his understanding of being American and provided the impetus to change his self-identification from an American to a Japanese American.

Mura started his discussion on the complicated intersection of ethnicity, sexuality, and identity in his essay "A Male Grief: Notes on Pornography and Addiction" (1985). In his second memoirs—*Where the Body Meets Memory: An Odyssey of Race, Sexuality, and Identity* (1996), he continues the exploration of the uncertainty and struggle over sexuality and **race** in his personal history. With striking honesty, Mura recollects his obsession with pornography during the troubled years of his adolescence and his confused and at times disastrous affairs in young adulthood. This memoir ends with the author's family life with his wife and children.

Mura's recent book—*Song for Uncle Tom, Tonto, and Mr. Moto: Poetry and Identity* (2002)—is a selection of essays and interviews. In these articles, Mura discusses **multiculturalism** in contemporary America and addresses various aspects of literature that have influenced his own writing. From an ethnic American writer's perspective, he examines the development of Asian American poetry. Moreover, viewing the young artists who work in varied art forms and make efforts to break the boundaries between poetry and performance as part of a new wave, Mura predicts the multiethnic and multicultural future of American poetry.

Together with African American writer Alexis Pate, Mura has written, produced, and performed in a short film titled *Slowly This* (1995) for the PBS series "Alive TV." In the show, the two artists discuss ethnicity and interethnic relations.

Further Reading

Slowik, Mary. "Beyond Lot's Wife: The Immigration Poems of Marilyn Chin, Garrett Hongo, Li-Young Lee, and David Mura." *MELUS* 25.3/4 (Autumn–Winter 2000): 221–42.

Taylor, Gordon O. "'The Country I Had Thought Was My Home': David Mura's *Turning Japanese* and Japanese-American Narrative since World War II." *Connotations* 6.3 (1996–1997): 283–309.

Zhou, Xiaojing. "David Mura's Poetics of Identity." *MELUS* 23.3 (Autumn 1998): 145–66.

———. "Race, Sexuality, and Representation in David Mura's *The Colors of Desire*." *Journal of Asian American Studies* 1.3 (October 1998): 245–67.

Lan Dong

MURAYAMA, MILTON (1923–) Japanese American novelist whose writings focus on the history of the Japanese in Hawai'i, from the beginning of the twentieth century through World War II and its aftermath. He has played a fundamental role in revitalizing literature from Hawai'i by representing the complex multiethnic history and constitution of the land, portraying Hawaiian themes realistically and using authentic language to validate these experiences. He captures vividly the language, eclectic cultural practices, and complex political, racial, and social affiliations of the Asian immigrants who live and work there, as well as the difficult cultural and generational clash between the Issei (first-generation Japanese immigrants) and their Nisei children. His portrayal of Hawai'i and its people is devoid of the romantic sheen traditionally associated with literature about the islands, which tends to exoticize the place.

Born in Lahaina, on the island of Maui, Murayama was raised in a plantation village similar to the one portrayed in his novels. He served as an interpreter and translator in India and Taiwan during World War II, from 1944 to 1946. After the war, he earned a BA in English from the University of Hawai'i in 1947 and an MA in Japanese and Chinese from Columbia University in 1952. Murayama's novels all revolve around the Oyama family, revealing the cultural and class problems of Japanese American in Hawai'i through the perspective of its members—the mother, Sawa, and her sons Toshio and Kiyoshi. In this manner, he provides a multilayered and multigenerational portrait of plantation life in the early part of the twentieth century.

His first novel, *All I Asking for Is My Body* (1975) won the American Book Award from the Before Columbus Foundation in 1980, as well as a Hawai'i Award for Literature. The story focuses on the tension between a young Nisei Tosh Oyama and his parents. Narrated by Tosh's younger brother, Kiyoshi, we learn of the debt the family has to pay and how the parents make their children responsible for it, in a cycle of acquired family obligations that the sons reject. Murayama explores the complex dynamic of clashing value systems: the Japanese tradition of filial piety and an American sense of independence, in the context of an exploitative and politically oppressive plantation system. The contrast between the parents and their eldest son is also highlighted by the differences between the two brothers: Tosh is restless and angry, Kiyoshi is quiet and studious and eventually helps resolve the family's debt by gambling. Though Kiyoshi seems to act like the traditional filial son as he solves the family's debt, he is the one who leaves the plantation and opts for his own freedom, while Tosh remains and works for the plantation.

One of the book's important contributions to the development of literature from Hawai'i was its innovative use of pidgin to present a realistic portrait of the time and the people. This culture-specific form of English illustrates the speaker's class and position in that society. In the context of Asian American writing, Murayama's use of this language validates it as a highly expressive literary tool for characterization, heightening the book's cultural authenticity.

Five Years on a Rock (1994) is Murayama's fictionalized biography of his mother, Sawa. Narrating the story of a Japanese "picture bride," this book is a valedictory for the thousands of young Japanese women who were married to strangers and came to live in a strange land. The story begins with the family's decision to send Sawa to Hawai'i to marry the eldest son of the Oyama family, which Sawa agrees to for filial reasons, knowing she is helping her family out of its poverty. She discovers quickly that the reality of her new life differs from her dreams. Sawa recounts matter-of-factly the inner struggles she has with loyalty, her exhaustion and the painful births of her children, the debts the family incurs, their oppressive poverty. Her determination and strength, as well as her decision to submit, are what help her survive.

In Hawai'i, Sawa sees herself moving farther and farther away from her dream of returning to Japan. Constantly aware of cultural differences, she also sees her children grow up alien to traditional Japanese ways. The fact that they are not filial in the way she and her husband were raised to be is most evident in Toshio, a stubborn and impulsive child who makes loud judgments on his father's defects, to his mother's consternation. The novel ends with the promise of more hardship, of Sawa's anguish of having to deny her sons an education because they need the boys to help them make ends meet.

Murayama's third novel, *Plantation Boy* (1998), opens before the bombing of Pearl Harbor in 1941. Narrated by Toshio, it focuses on his process of overcoming prejudice in order to fulfill his dream of becoming an architect. When the United States declares war against Japan, Toshio is rejected by the military because of a broken eardrum and has to stay behind as his friends leave and their parents are interned in relocation camps. Toshio is presented as ambitious and frustrated at the treatment of the Japanese in the United States: He describes the irony of watching Japanese parents led to relocation camps while their sons are dying in action at war. He also finds himself caught in a double bind of culture: His obligations to his parents clash with his dreams. But Toshio is also survivor, although his dream of being an architect is finally realized many years after the war.

By focusing on the experiences of one family, Murayama provides a coherent portrait of an evolving culture in a complex time in a place that itself has been subject to continual **immigration** and intercultural contact. The author's use of pidgin as an expressive language, his concern with the gender and generational struggles, issues of prejudice and **racism**, make his work fundamental to a clear perspective on the history and culture of Asian immigrants in Hawai'i. (*See also* Hawai'i Literature, Internment, Japanese American Novel)

Further Reading

Sumida, Stephen H. "*All I Asking for Is My Body*, Milton Murayama." *A Resource Guide to Asian American Literature.* Ed. Sau-ling Cynthia Wong and Stephen H. Sumida. New York: MLA, 2001.130–39.

Luangphinith, Seri. "Milton Murayama (1923–)." *Asian American Novelists: A Bio-Bibliographical Critical Sourcebook.* Ed. Emmanuel S. Nelson. Westport, CT: Greenwood Press, 2000. 251–56.

Rocío G. Davis

MURRAY, ALBERT (1916–) African American essayist, novelist, cultural, and music critic. In his life and work Albert Murray embodies the qualities of an Omni-American, the title he gave to one of his works of cultural criticism. At a time when black militancy was in vogue and ethnic association was being promoted, Murray advanced a concept of national **identity** that challenged prevailing norms. By Murray's estimation, African Americans are no less and no more American than others of different ethnic descent. The combined folklores of white supremacy and black pathology, he asserted, disguise the fact that all Americans are multicolored. Murray has sustained this opinion throughout his prolific and long career and never retreated from the belief that just as the products of African American creativity belong to and describe a uniquely American idiom, so too are all the artifacts of Western culture available to the black artist.

Murray was born in Nokomis, Alabama, and graduated from Tuskegee Institute in 1939. He joined the U.S. Air Force in 1943 and retired as major in 1962. During his service, Murray attended New York University and received an MA in 1948. For several years he taught literature and composition to civilians and soldiers in the United States and abroad. Following *The Omni-Americans* (1970), Murray published *South to a Very Old Place* (1971) that extends his argument in a series of memoirs, interviews, and reports that document the positive aspects of black life in the South. *The Hero and the Blues* (1973), which derived from a series of lectures given at the University of Missouri, is where Murray developed his concept of literature in the **blues** idiom. The blues, Murray asserted, represents an entire set of cultural tools for living, an expansive range of styles and attitudes and possibilities for creating meaningful art, and a strategy for survival and triumph over **racism.**

Murray performed in prose this blues idiom in his first novel, *Train Whistle Guitar* (1974), where the protagonist receives from his family and neighbors in the segregated South the cultural tools necessary for leading a successful life. Semiautobiographical, the hero of the novel possesses a sense of fundamental individual self-worth combined with community responsibility similar to the relationship between **jazz** musicians who trade eights on a head tune, each soloing for a time but always returning to the communal sound. The ideas set forth in his essays and fiction reached their fullest expression in *Stomping the Blues* (1976), where Murray's swinging articulation of the blues ethic demonstrated not just his command of the idiom's meaning but his ability to perform it as well.

In 1985 Murray collaborated with Count Basie on his autobiography *Good Morning Blues*, and in 1991 he published *The Spyglass Tree*, a sequel to his first novel. Long associated with novelist **Ralph Ellison** (with whom Murray spoke every day until Ellison's death) and artist Romare Bearden, together they represent an exemplary trinity of African American aesthetics in music, word, and image, as each drew from the genre of the other to create a holistic vision of African American cultural contributions to society. Murray honored Bearden when he wrote a catalog essay on his paintings, "Romare Bearden: Finding the Rhythm" (1991), which extends his promotion of jazz traits to visual arts. And he has been instrumental in assisting the Ellison estate as it continues to bring out work by the author. *The Blue Devils of NADA* (1996) is a further meditation on blues and jazz greats. *The Seven League Boots* (1996) completed his fiction trilogy.

When not writing, Murray acts as an inspiration and creative consultant for the Lincoln Center Jazz Orchestra, conducted by Wynton Marsalis, Murray's godson. Marsalis has adopted and tried to institutionalize through the orchestra Murray's conception of African American music, ensuring that jazz is understood and received by the American public as its greatest contribution to world culture. For jazz, Murray believes, extends, elaborates, and refines the great principles of all enduring classical art and does so with a uniquely American inflection that constitutes its genius. The blues, from which jazz originates, Murray identifies as life-affirming, as a means of making the best out of a bad situation by its ability to articulate and express the conditions of that circumstance while also providing a strategy for living with and triumphing over those conditions with dignity, grace, and elegance. Murray's life and art performs the same trick and affirms the enduring spirit of humanity.

Further Reading

Carson, Warren. "Albert Murray: Literary Reconstruction of the Vernacular Community." *African American Review* 27.3 (1993): 287–95.

Gnenari, John. "Jazz Criticism: Its Development and Ideologies." *Black American Literature Forum* 23.3 (Fall 1991): 449–523.

Kimberly Rae Connor

MURRAY, PAULI (1910–1985)   African American lawyer, professor, poet, women's rights advocate, historian, biographer, and Episcopal priest. Pauli Murray was born November 20, 1910, in Baltimore, Maryland. Her parents were Agnes Georgianna Fitzgerald Murray and William Henry Murray. When Murray was three years old, her mother died, which caused her and her five siblings to be placed in the homes of different relatives. Murray was taken to the home of her maternal grandparents in Durham, North Carolina, while the other five children were placed in the home of another relative in Baltimore. Three years after the death of their mother, the children experienced another loss when their father became mentally ill and was institutionalized. He remained in Crownsville State Hospital until his death in 1923.

Murray's Fitzgerald relatives instilled in her a yearning for and an appreciation of education. One of her earliest teachers was Pauline Fitzgerald, Murray's aunt who was living in the home with Murray, along with her grandparents. Pauline Fitzgerald was a schoolteacher and was the relative most responsible for Murray's care and upbringing. Her influence inspired Murray to learn to read before she reached school age.

When Murray was awarded a bachelor of arts degree in English from Hunter College in 1933, that degree would be the first in a long line of academic degrees. In 1944 she received a law degree from Howard University; in 1945 she received a master of laws degree from the University of California at Berkeley. Enrolling in law school at Yale University in 1961, Murray received a doctoral degree in juridical science in 1965. Eight years later she enrolled in the General Theological Seminary, and in 1973 was awarded a master of divinity degree.

Murray's training in law, theology, letters, and history, which was her minor at Hunter College, led to her success as a lawyer, professor, writer, women's right's advocate, civil rights advocate, and clergywoman. Murray was, in fact, the first African American woman to be ordained by the Episcopal Church, a historic moment that occurred in 1977.

As a lawyer Murray brought lawsuits against universities for failing to admit women to their graduate programs. She herself had been denied admission to Harvard University's law school because she was a woman. She had also been denied admission to the law school of the University of North Carolina, Chapel Hill, located just ten miles from Durham, the city in which Murray was raised. Her advocacy for women resulted in her becoming one of the founders of the National Organization for Women, more commonly known as NOW. Murray taught at various American universities, including Yale and Brandeis. While teaching in Accra, Ghana, she coauthored with Leslie Rubin *The Constitution and Government in Africa* (1961).

Murray's best-known publication is *Proud Shoes: The Story of an American Family* (1956), an account of the lives of her Fitzgerald relatives. Her other publications include *Dark Testament and Other Poems* (1970) and

Pauli Murray. *Courtesy of the Library of Congress.*

her posthumously published autobiography, *Songs in a Weary Throat: An American Pilgrimage* (1987). The autobiography maps her personal development and political evolution; simultaneously, it reveals her quest for spiritual enlightenment meaning in her life.

On July 1, 1985, Murray's pilgrimage ended when she died of throat cancer. Her funeral was held July 5 in Washington, DC, at the National Cathedral where she had been ordained.

Further Reading

Hine, Darlene Clark, Elsa Barkley Brown, and Rosalyn Terborg-Penn. *Black Women in America: An Historical Encyclopedia.* Vol.2. Bloomington: Indiana UP, 1993. 825–26.

Humez, Jean M. "Pauli Murray's Histories of Loyalty and Revolt." *Black American Literature Forum* 24.2 (Summer 1990): 315–335.

Kerber, Linda K. *No Constitutional Right to Be Ladies: Women and the Obligations of Citizenship.* New York: Hill and Wang, 1998. 185–99.

Vick, Marsha C. "Pauli Murray." *Notable Black Women.* Ed. Jessie Carney Smith. Detroit: Gale, 1992. 783–88.

Joyce Russell-Robinson

MYERS, WALTER DEAN (1937–)   African American author of numerous works of fiction, nonfiction and poetry written in multiple genres: historical fiction, science fiction, biography, autobiography, fairy tales, and more. Although he has published numerous articles and short stories in various journals, most notably the *Liberator* and *Black World,* he is highly regarded for his literature for children and young adults. He has dedicated himself to providing literature for children about African American experiences that resonate with young readers. While growing up in Harlem, Myers was an avid reader and writer. Because of a speech impediment, one of his teachers encouraged him to express himself via poetry. Myers would read and write voraciously throughout his youth, although he dropped out of school twice, at age fifteen and sixteen. At seventeen, he dropped out a final time and enlisted in the army. However, he later earned a BA degree from Empire State College.

It was not until after he had served time in the army and worked at several jobs, including postal work, that he began to work hard at becoming a published author. In his memoir, *Bad Boy: A Memoir,* Myers describes the impact **James Baldwin**'s "Sonny's Blues" had on him, as an aspiring writer. For the first time, Myers saw the black urban experience validated in literature. Myers maintains that reading Baldwin's work permitted him to write about his own experiences of growing up black and male in a major urban center. Myers sought out other black writers, **John O. Killens**, Chuck Stone, and even Baldwin, himself, in order to be a part of a network of black male writers. Later, he became a member of the Harlem Writer's Guild. Although Myers had published a number of poems, articles and short stories, it was not until 1968 when he entered a contest for black writers sponsored by the Council on Interracial Books for Children, and actually won, that he became a children's book author. His first children's book, *Where Does the Day Go?* illustrated by Leo Carty, was published in 1969. His first novel for teens, *Fast Sam, Cool Clyde, and Stuff,* which actually began as a short story and is set on 116th Street in New York, soon followed. The youths in the novel attempt to make sense of their lives and the adversities that plague them. Myers's books seem to be influenced largely by his own experiences and interests. *Fallen Angels* and *Patrol,* for example, are two books that focus on soldiers involved in combat. Other obvious features of Myers's work that reflect his experiences include the Harlem setting of many of his books as well as the focus on black males coming of age.

Many of Myers's novels contain images of black males that are self-affirming and encouraging. For example, *Handbook for Boys* (2002) features two young boys who have been given the opportunity to avoid a jail sentence in exchange for working with a neighborhood barber. The boys encounter a community of black men from which they learn how to become respectable members of the community. Similarly, *The Beast* (2003) gives readers a glimpse at an inner-city youth who is determined to do well in an elite Connecticut prep school and go on to college, although he is struggling to understand what has happened to his girlfriend who is on drugs. Critics are already praising his latest book, *Shooter* (2004). Through interviews, reports, and journal entries, readers learn the story behind what motivated Len Gray to kill a high school classmate before committing suicide.

Myers has also contributed short stories for youth to a number of notable collections, including Michael Cart's *Necessary Noise: Stories About Our Families as They Really Are* (2003). His contribution, "Visit," focuses on a young black male who has committed a heinous crime. As he awaits conviction, he receives a visit from his estranged father.

Myers has won numerous honors for his work. He received the first Michael L. Printz award for young adult literature ever awarded for *Monster* (1999). The novel was also named a National Book Award finalist, a Coretta Scott King Author Honor Book, and a Boston Globe-Horn Book. He has also received the American Library Association Margaret A. Edwards Award for his contribution to young adult literature and the New York Council on Interracial Books for Children Award. His son, Christopher Myers, has illustrated several of his award-winning picture books, including *Harlem: A Poem,* a Caldecott Honor Book. (*See also* African American Young Adult Literature)

Further Reading

Bishop, Rudine Sims. *Presenting Walter Dean Myers.* Boston: Twayne Publishers, 1990.

Myers, Walter Dean. *Bad Boy: A Memoir.* New York: HarperCollins Publishers, 2001.

KaaVonia Hinton-Johnson